Managing NONPROFIT ORGANIZATIONS in a Policy World

To Burton and Reagan
S.V.

To Dave and Maya, who suffered through this project far more gracefully than I
S.A.

Managing NONPROFIT ORGANIZATIONS in a Policy World

SHANNON K. VAUGHAN
Western Kentucky University

SHELLY ARSNEAULT
California State University, Fullerton

Los Angeles | London | New Delhi
Singapore | Washington DC

Los Angeles | London | New Delhi
Singapore | Washington DC

FOR INFORMATION:

CQ Press
An Imprint of SAGE Publications, Inc.
2455 Teller Road
Thousand Oaks, California 91320
E-mail: order@sagepub.com

SAGE Publications Ltd.
1 Oliver's Yard
55 City Road
London, EC1Y 1SP
United Kingdom

SAGE Publications India Pvt. Ltd.
B 1/I 1 Mohan Cooperative Industrial Area
Mathura Road, New Delhi 110 044
India

SAGE Publications Asia-Pacific Pte. Ltd.
3 Church Street
#10-04 Samsung Hub
Singapore 049483

Acquisitions Editor: Charisse Kiino
Development Editor: Nancy Matuszak
Production Editor: Libby Larson
Copy Editor: Kate Macomber Stern
Typesetter: Hurix Systems Pvt. Ltd.
Proofreader: Dennis W. Webb
Indexer: Wendy Allex
Cover Designer: Michael Dubowe
Marketing Manager: Jonathan Mason
Permissions Editor: Adele Hutchinson

Printed in the United States of America

A catalog record of this book is available from the Library of Congress.

978-1-4522-4005-3

This book is printed on acid-free paper.

SFI label applies to text stock

13 14 15 16 17 10 9 8 7 6 5 4 3 2 1

Brief Contents

Detailed Contents

PART II. STRATEGIES OF NOT-FOR-PROFIT ORGANIZATIONS

Preface

The idea for *Managing Nonprofit Organizations in a Policy World* was born from our agreement that we cannot understand nonprofit organizations without understanding public policy, and that we cannot fully understand policy change without considering nonprofits. Through our work teaching MPA students (many of whom were currently in or planning a career with nonprofit organizations), serving on nonprofit boards and as an executive director, writing grant proposals and teaching workshops on how to write them, as well as reading countless books, articles, and web posts, we have developed an even stronger appreciation for the connections between nonprofits and public policy. We view this relationship—in which nonprofits make policy, are affected by policy, influence policy, and are subject to policy—as interconnected as the pieces of a puzzle. These four facets of the nonprofit-policy relationship form the framework for *Managing Nonprofit Organizations in a Policy World;* we assert throughout the book that all aspects of nonprofit management encompass one or more of these ways in which nonprofits interact with public policy.

This book was written primarily with students in Master of Public Administration (MPA) or Master of Public Policy (MPP) programs in mind because these are the students and programs we know best. However, because we strongly believe that the interconnected relationship between nonprofits and public policy is crucial to understanding the nonprofit sector and its management, this text is valuable for all graduate students and upper-division undergraduate students studying the nonprofit sector in fields such as business administration, social work, political science, and public health. It is designed as a foundational text for courses specifically on the nonprofit sector but is also appropriate as a supplemental text for public policy courses.

ORGANIZATION OF THIS BOOK

The book is organized into four parts. Part I, "Fundamentals and Environment of the Voluntary Sector," is an overview of the nonprofit sector as a whole, as well as the policy environment in which nonprofits operate. Chapters in this section define and identify the different types of not-for-profit organizations, including philanthropic foundations. Because the American system of government offers many points of interaction for nonprofits in the policy process, Part I also includes discussion of federalism and the intersectoral nature of public service provision. The theoretical basis for the existence of the nonprofit sector is established and the multiple aspects of the relationship between not-for-profit organizations and public policy are examined. Finally, because not-for-profit organizations operate within the constraints of federal, state, and local regulation, the impact of regulatory policies on the management and operation of organizations in the nonprofit sector is explored.

Part II, "Strategies of Not-for-Profit Organizations," addresses the major skills and strategies necessary for nonprofits to advance themselves and their causes, which often involves the implementation of public policies. It is important for those working in and funding nonprofit organizations to understand and be able to articulate the organization's mission because a strong sense of mission is critical for nonprofits. Tools such as strategic planning enhance commitment to a well-defined mission, enabling nonprofits to better operate under existing public policies as well as influence future ones. Lobbying and advocacy are viewed as distinctly different activities in the nonprofit sector; thus, we explain the importance of these differences and explore the explicit means of encouraging government officials to change public policy. We also address the issues of ethics and accountability, with particular emphasis on the self-policing strategies used by nonprofits as well as the recent wave of state and federal policy actions to strengthen accountability. Finally, because not-for-profit organizations with solid brand recognition are more likely to be chosen as implementation partners, we discuss the importance of marketing in the voluntary sector. Marketing involves the strategic positioning of the nonprofit organization to appeal to donors, clients, and policymakers, and is therefore a crucial factor to the success of any nonprofit organization in terms of its ability to raise both money and awareness of public problems.

Part III, "Management Issues," emphasizes the nuts and bolts issues of operating a not-for-profit organization. Nonprofits exist to pursue the public good, often with public funds; therefore, it is in the public interest for these organizations to be managed effectively. Aspects of nonprofit management, such as budgeting and human resource management, affect public policy indirectly through their impact on the general operations of nonprofits as they pursue their missions. Other issues, such as resource development and evaluation, have more direct public policy implications. Importantly, all these management issues are affected by public policy in the form of local, state, and federal legislation. We discuss issues of resource development, particularly grants, highlighting the policy and mission implications of pursuing diverse sources of revenue. Issues of good governance by the board and executive director, as well as effective human resources management, are crucial to successful pursuit of mission, as well as implementation of public policy. Because nonprofits are increasingly asked by government and private funders to conduct program evaluations in order to maintain or acquire additional funding and contracts, we discuss both internal and external uses of evaluation for nonprofit organizations.

Part IV, "The Future of the Nonprofit Sector," contains a concluding chapter that explores emerging sector trends of importance to nonprofits. In it we discuss the policy implications of the blurring of the lines between the three sectors, as well as the political, social, and economic trends which create even more complexity in these relationships. We discuss the impact of new funding arrangements and intersectoral partnerships that have created pressure for more professionalized management and evaluation of nonprofit activity.

The chapters begin with a list of policy implications—ways in which the policy-nonprofit relationship is illustrated in each chapter—and conclude with questions for review and an assignment that requires additional research to complete. Suggested readings and a list of web resources are also included, so faculty and students can cover selected topics in greater detail at their discretion. While these lists are far from exhaustive, they represent readings and resources that fit well with our goal of connecting nonprofit management and public policy.

FEATURES

Four feature boxes complement the main narrative, all designed to emphasize how each topic relates to issues of public policy and good organizational management. **Case Studies** explore nonprofit organizations and management concerns in depth, such as AARP's (formerly, the American Association of Retired Persons) advocacy and influence on health care reform and financial mismanagement at the Central Asia Institute. Each case study highlights the interconnected relationship nonprofits have with policy and includes questions that encourage critical thinking and discussion.

An international focus on nonprofits is featured in our **Going Global** feature boxes, which look at how nonprofits operate on an international scale, from Médecins Sans Frontières putting volunteers and staff on the front lines in pursuit of the organization's mission to assessing the accountability of nonprofit efforts overseas. In some instances, the Case Study and Going Global boxes naturally combine to allow an examination of a relevant issue in nonprofit management with a global scope. These are identified as **Going Global Case Studies**.

For Example boxes illustrate specific chapter themes through situations drawn from a variety of nonprofits, such as how the Blue Ridge Conservancy's operations serve to mitigate competition between economic and environmental interests and how the Girl Scouts use program evaluation to assess and improve their operations. In addition, **For More Information** boxes guide students and faculty to additional resources on specific topics, including advocacy and lobbying tips, provisions of the Sarbanes-Oxley Act relevant to nonprofit organizations, and where to access a variety of online grants databases.

ACKNOWLEDGMENTS

We would like to thank all of those who reviewed our book proposal and draft manuscript and provided invaluable feedback, helping us to craft the final result, among them Naim Kapucu, University of Central Florida; Kelly LeRoux, University of Illinois at Chicago; Darlene Xiomara Rodriguez, Salem College; Jessica Sowa, University of Colorado–Denver; and Max Stephenson, Virginia Tech University. Our thanks also go to Ruth DeHoog and Dorothy Norris-Tirrell for their comments on early drafts and their support of our efforts.

We were fortunate to have the assistance of stellar graduate students throughout this process and want to thank Tanya Jordan, for her comments on our original proposal, and Mike Dickerson and Jessica Deakyne, who read the first draft of the manuscript and gave valuable feedback from the MPA student perspective. This project is indebted to the nonprofit practitioners who helped us along the way by granting us interviews, offering advice and providing contacts for more information. They include Dr. Susan Silberman, formerly with AARP; Dr. Kevin Meehan, former Executive Director of Orange County Youth and Family Services; Lynelle Bilsey, from Shelter Network; Cari Hart, of Hart Community Homes/Monkey Business Café; Kristin Tierney, from the Girl Scouts of Greater Los Angeles; Nancy Chandler and Benjamin Murray, formerly with National Children's Alliance; Dolly Farrell and Robert Dziewulski, formerly with Watauga County Habitat for Humanity; and Sandy Ostdiek, who introduced us to Old Bill's Fun Run.

Our heartfelt appreciation to Charisse Kiino, CQ Press college publisher, whose support and guidance made this project possible, and our profound thanks to CQ Press development editor Nancy Matuszak, whose skill at seeing the big picture made this project far better than it otherwise would have been. We also want to thank our production editor, Libby Larson, and our copy editor, Kate Macomber Stern, for their interest in our topic and great attention to detail.

Our overwhelming gratitude goes to our family, friends, and colleagues, who provided the support and encouragement that sustained us on this journey. Shannon wants to especially thank her husband, Burton, for his unwavering love, confidence, and wise counsel, and for helping her to understand the private sector perspective. She also expresses her love and appreciation to their daughter, Reagan, for all the joy she adds to life and for understanding, as well as a toddler could, when Mommy had to "work on stuff." Shelly wants to extend special thanks to Kathleen Costello of the Gianneschi Center for Nonprofit Research at CSUF for her generosity and friendship, Sarah Hill for always offering an ear and some dark chocolate, and Jarret Lovell for being her cheerleader and advocate.

About the Authors

Shannon K. Vaughan is assistant professor in the Department of Political Science at Western Kentucky University, where she teaches primarily in the MPA program. Her research interests include the impact of nonprofits on public policy, nonprofit funding issues, and ethics. Among her published works are articles in *Public Integrity*, *Review of Policy Research*, and the *Journal of Health and Human Services Administration.* Her teaching experience includes courses in public policy analysis, not-for-profit organizations, grants, and budgeting. Shannon served as executive director of a small nonprofit and as grants specialist for two regional planning and economic development agencies. She is a member of the Association for Research on Nonprofit Organizations and Voluntary Action (ARNOVA) and the American Society for Public Administration.

Shelly Arsneault is a professor in the division of Politics, Administration and Justice at California State University, Fullerton, and serves as the Coordinator/Advisor for the Master of Public Administration program. Her research focuses primarily on social welfare policies in the arenas of poverty, welfare, and health policy. Among her published work are articles in *State and Local Government Review, American Review of Public Administration, The Social Policy Journal,* and *Review of Policy Research.* Her emphasis on policy led naturally to her interest in nonprofit organizations as direct service providers and policy advocates. Shelly recently co-authored a report on the nonprofit sector in Orange County, California. She is a member of the American Society for Public Administration, the American Political Science Association, and the National Association of Schools of Public Affairs and Administration (NASPAA) Section on Nonprofit Management.

1 What Is the Nonprofit Sector?

Our sacred promise to improve lives has been—and must continue to be—our ultimate purpose for existing. . . . Americans have high expectations for us: We are the primary outlet for their humanitarian impulses, their conduits of goodwill and generosity. We are the way individuals give back, so that we as a society can move forward.

Diana Aviv, President and CEO, Independent Sector

Imagine that it is 1980 and a second-grade teacher learns that one of her 7-year-old students has been abused by a trusted family member. Once the teacher completes her mandatory call to police, the child is taken from her home by uniformed officers and subjected to a thorough examination in a sterile room at the hospital. Following a series of tests and questions, she is then taken to the police station and asked even more confusing questions before being handed over to a child protective services employee, who sits on a cold bench with her as she waits to be retrieved by her grandparents. As frightening and bewildering as all of this must be for her, the ordeal is far from over for this young victim. In the months that follow, she is taken to the police station several more times, is assessed by various counselors, and questioned by prosecutors and other court staff; in essence, she continues to be traumatized.

Throughout her ordeal, this young victim has interacted with professionals in government (the police officers, child protective services employee, and the state prosecutors), the private sector (the physician), and the nonprofit sector (since the hospital in which she was examined is likely a not-for-profit entity). Various public policies affect the process she endured, from the legal requirement that teachers notify law enforcement of possible abuse to the specific statutes which classify the type of abuse and the penalties associated with conviction. Aside from these legal requirements, however, in 1980 there were no public policies or programs designed to reduce the trauma of navigating the legal and health care systems imposed on victimized children. As is often the case, this problem took years to recognize and years more to address; as is also often the case, those involved pursued a nonprofit option to solve this systemic problem. The nonprofit National Children's Alliance and hundreds of children's advocacy

POLICY IMPLICATIONS OF NONPROFIT ORGANIZATIONS

- Nonprofits are inextricably linked to public policy.
- Our history as a British colony facilitates our understanding of the origins of the U.S. nonprofit sector, e.g. through the impact of the Statute of Charitable Uses and the Revolutionary spirit which defined the Constitution and also informs the proclivity for both voluntary and government action.
- The nonprofit sector has grown dramatically in size in recent years and represents a diversity of interests. This leads to competition for resources and for attention from policymakers.
- U.S. tax policy is also relevant for the growth and diversity of the sector, particularly with regard to the incentives for the development of philanthropic foundations and their ability to direct resources.

centers have been developed nationwide to provide that systemic solution through provision of child-centered services; most of these centers are nonprofits and are discussed further below.

NONPROFITS AND PUBLIC PROBLEMS

As will be discussed throughout this book, nonprofit organizations in the United States address public problems and are imbued with public policy. It is impossible to understand the formation, operation, and management of nonprofits without a commensurate understanding of the public policy context they inhabit. Not-for-profit organizations both act and are acted upon with regard to public policy; in order to pursue their missions, they often advocate for government support and must comply with government mandates. The nonprofit sector has a symbiotic relationship with public policy—each is influenced to varying degrees by the other; this is the central theme of our book. Nonprofits are inextricably linked to public policy, and understanding the relationship between the two is a significant factor in successful nonprofit management.

For example, let us return to the issue of child abuse. Although there is now nearly universal recognition of child abuse as a public problem in the U.S., that was not always the case. In fact, the first case of child abuse was prosecuted in 1874 under an animal cruelty statute because at the time there was no law aimed specifically at the protection of children. As a result of this case the first child protective services agency, the nonprofit New York Society for the Prevention of Cruelty to Children (NYSPCC), was formed in 1875 by Henry Bergh and Elbridge Gerry.[1] By 1908, similar societies were in existence in 44 states, as well as Great Britain and most other European countries plus India, South Africa, Australia, and South America.[2] By the mid-1940s, city, county, and state government agencies had taken over most of the primary tasks of the nonprofit Societies for the Prevention of Cruelty to Children (SPCC), which from that time forward have served in partnership with government in the protection of children.[3]

This is one of many examples in which nonprofit action helped define as well as address a public problem. SPCC agencies were on the leading edge of delivery of services to abused children—receiving complaints, conducting investigations, and taking cases to trial—prior to adoption of legislation stipulating specific protections for children; most subsequent child abuse legislation can be traced back to their advocacy efforts.[4] These organizations were in effect changing public policy by taking responsibility for a public problem in the 1870s. More than a century later, Bud Cramer, then district attorney for Madison County, Alabama, and his colleagues organized a new nonprofit response to child abuse—namely the alleviation of the trauma of prosecution inflicted on child victims of sexual abuse, such as the little girl described in the opening vignette. Through Cramer's leadership and the efforts of many volunteers, the National Children's Advocacy Center (NCAC) was established in Huntsville, Alabama, in 1985.

NCAC has become a model for centers throughout the United States and other countries[5], and led to the creation of National Children's Alliance (NCA), which provides information "and technical assistance to promote the development and operation of children's advocacy centers (CACs) across the United States."[6] Children's advocacy centers provide an alternative and collaborative approach to standard criminal justice procedures in the handling of child abuse cases. A children's advocacy center is a centralized, child-friendly facility in which law enforcement, social services, legal, medical, victims' advocate, and counseling professionals come together as a team to interview, examine, and provide support services to child victims. Importantly, as noted earlier, most children's advocacy centers are nonprofit organizations.

While many think of nonprofits and their involvement in public policy as relatively new phenomena, not-for-profit organizations have taken on public roles and purposes for generations. Indeed, by 1835, Alexis de Tocqueville had observed that Americans were constantly forming civil associations: "If it is proposed to inculcate some truth or to foster some feeling by the encouragement of a great example, they form a society."[7] By the time of Tocqueville's writing, public work was already being facilitated through the efforts of nonprofit organizations including churches, museums, colleges, and universities. As Hammack explains, there was little government opposition to nonprofit organizations in the early decades of the nineteenth century. Most courts and legislatures by this time "had accepted the view that nongovernment, nonprofit organizations provided essential services, reinforced religious education in ways important to civil peace, reduced the need for tax-supported government action, permitted variety and flexibility in the provision of services."[8]

Examples of the varied influence of the nonprofit sector in the realm of public policy, therefore, abound in American history. The American Red Cross delivered direct services to victims of forest fires as early as 1881, and in 1958 the policy advocacy efforts of the Child Welfare League of America facilitated federal legislation requiring states to hire full-time child welfare caseworkers. An example of nonprofit influence on public policy through the court system comes from the Police Foundation's research on the use of deadly force. Their findings were extensively cited in the 1985 U.S. Supreme Court decision *Tennessee v. Garner*, which modernized police policy by reserving the use of deadly force by officers to cases in which a life is threatened. Each of these examples illustrates the ways in which public policy has been encouraged, informed, tested, or delivered by nonprofit entities.

Since all nonprofits operate within the public policy arena, it is critical for those working in not-for-profit organizations as well as in government entities to understand the very important role that nonprofits play. Similarly, it is important to recognize that public policy influences nonprofit organizations and their management. From their tax status, to the federal policies that affect their personnel practices, to the mandates required by government contracts, not-for-profit organizations are both guided and limited by public policies as they pursue their missions; they affect and are affected by public policy.

It is the aim of this book to set the work of nonprofit organizations firmly within the milieu of public policy and to highlight the fact that effective nonprofit management requires a keen understanding of the complex relationship between the nonprofit sector and the policy world. In order to meet the broader needs of society it is essential that not-for-profit organizations and the public agencies that work with them are able to successfully navigate this complexity.

WHAT IS A NONPROFIT?

Nonprofit organizations are generally understood to provide goods or services but are neither private businesses nor government operated. The term "nonprofit," however, is a misnomer. These organizations can and often do have revenues that exceed expenditures—that is, they make a profit—but the distinction between nonprofits and private business is that nonprofits must retain excess revenues for the benefit of the organization; excess revenues in private business are distributed to owners/shareholders. Not-for-profit is therefore a more precise descriptor, but the two are used interchangeably throughout this text. While "nonprofit" is the more dominant term throughout the general literature, other terms sometimes used include "charitable," "voluntary," or "philanthropic organizations." All refer to the same type of tax-exempt organizations, and exemption from taxes is the primary characteristic that affects legal designation of nonprofits and the rules and regulations pertaining to them.

As will be discussed in greater detail in Chapter 4, a determination letter from the Internal Revenue Service (IRS) is considered the primary document needed for legal recognition as a tax-exempt organization. According to the IRS, however, nonprofit status is actually a concept of state law; registration within a certain state grants the organization certain benefits with regard to exemption from state taxes. Exemption from federal income tax requires separate action and compliance with additional requirements. Exemption from local, state, and federal income taxes are significant incentives for the development of not-for-profit organizations, but first and foremost, nonprofits exist to address a public problem or need that, for whatever reason, is not adequately served through government or the private market. Theories on the reasons why nonprofits are more attractive options than governments and markets are the focus of Chapter 3.

Public Charities

At this point it is important to distinguish among the different types of nonprofits, since it is their classification according to the Internal Revenue Code (IRC) that gives most nonprofits their legal recognition. Public charities are those organizations recognized under section 501(c)(3) of the IRC whose purposes generally fall into the categories of religious, charitable, scientific, literary, or educational endeavors. At 63.7 percent of all tax-exempt organizations in 2009, public charities represent by far the largest category of not-for-profit organizations (see Figure 1.1 on page 15). As such, most practitioners and researchers in the nonprofit sector focus their efforts upon organizations classified as public charities. This is not surprising as charitable purposes are the foundation for the nonprofit sector dating back as early as 1601 when Queen Elizabeth I accepted the Statute of Charitable Uses:

> . . . some for relief of aged, impotent, and poor people, some for maintenance of sick and maimed soldiers and mariners, schools of learning, free schools, and scholars in universities, some for repair of bridges, ports, havens, causeways, churches, seabanks, and highways, some for education and preferment of orphans, some for or towards relief stock or maintenance for houses of correction, some for marriages of poor maids, some for support, aid and help of young tradesmen, handicraftsmen, and persons decayed, and others for relief or redemption of prisoners or captives, and for aid or ease of any poor inhabitant concerning payment of Fifteens [a tax], setting out of soldiers and other taxes. . . .[9]

The statute was adopted in order to delineate the relationship between church and state since churches were the primary vehicle through which charitable endeavors were accomplished. Following English law, early American churches remained the dominant providers of charity in the colonies and later within independent states. Accordingly, the Statute of Charitable Uses was instrumental in establishing the boundaries of tax-exempt activity by enumerating what would generally be considered public purposes and benefits provided by charities and it continues to affect the legal perspective of what is and is not acceptable activity by charitable organizations today.[10] See Going Global 1.1 for further discussion of British and other international influences on the origins of the U.S. nonprofit sector.

GOING GLOBAL 1.1

International Influences on Early U.S. Nonprofits

While efforts of U.S. nonprofits overseas will be highlighted throughout the text, it is useful initially to consider the influence of international policies on voluntary organizations in colonial and post-Revolutionary America.

The Statute of Charitable Uses—while quaint in its language—was British policy adopted in the seventeenth century that continues to have a lasting influence on how nonprofit organizations are organized and viewed by government in the U.S. The enumeration of what were considered "legitimate objects of charity" had a profound and lasting impact on what U.S. legislative and judicial authorities would consider to be tax-exempt activities.

The power of the Catholic Church in areas of the New World controlled by Spain and France coupled with the dominance of the Anglican Church throughout the British Empire led to the formal policy, and commonly held public opinion throughout the British colonies that there should be one religion and that the church should be supported by taxes. This resulted in the church essentially operating as an arm of the government, providing education and human services in addition to religious services to citizens. With religious diversity already established in many parts of colonial America, by the early eighteenth century even those who continued to believe that there should be a single religion established by government were unable to agree as to which should be the one official church. Subsequently, religious and political leaders such as Cotton Mather and Benjamin Franklin became effective advocates for voluntary societies. Mather's *Essays to Do Good*—which are believed to be the inspiration for Franklin's collection of Silence Dogood letters—is believed to be the first American tutorial on the benefits of establishing voluntary societies. Because Cotton Mather wanted the Puritan church to be the official religion, which was not possible given the British policy regarding the sole authority of the Anglican Church, he sought the only avenue he saw open for Puritan social influence by promoting collective action outside of government or religion.

After gaining independence from Great Britain (and the Church of England), citizens of the new United States had galvanized their preference for limited government; the First Amendment to the Constitution reflects the correspondingly prevalent sentiment in opposition to an established religion. The voluntary associations promoted and established in the early to mid-1700s were thus an attractive conduit through which to provide collective goods and services; this penchant for voluntary action has deep historical roots grown from international seeds.

International seeds continued to take root, for example, in the case of the ASPCA. Established in 1824, England's Royal Society for the Prevention of Cruelty to Animals (RSPCA) spawned the establishment of New York's SPCA when Henry Bergh (also responsible for NYSPCC, discussed previously) met with the Earl of Harrowby—then president of the RSPCA—on a visit to London in the mid-1860s. Bergh's mortification at witnessing bullfighting on a visit to Spain, the inhumane treatment of animals he saw while a diplomat to Russia, and the notes he gleaned from the success of England's RSPCA all culminated in 1866 when the New York legislature passed a charter incorporating the nonprofit ASPCA on April 10; nine days later it adopted the nation's first anti-cruelty law.

For more information on the history of the U.S. nonprofit sector, see *Making the Nonprofit Sector in the United States,* edited and annotated by David Hammack. Additional information on the history of RSPCA and ASPCA can be found at www.spcai.org and www.apsca.org.

Today, the terms "charitable organization" and "public charity" are applied to organizations which provide a large and diverse array of public goods and services. The terms are loosely applied and routinely thought to encompass all organizations exempt from tax under section 501(c)(3) of the Internal Revenue Code. However, private foundations—which are not public charities—are also most often classified as 501(c)(3) organizations but are regulated much differently from charities. The growth in the number of these organizations is also reflected in Figure 1.1, and they are discussed further below. This muddied distinction can be linked to the Statute of Charitable Uses, as it is the specific listing of what constitutes a tax deductible contribution that results in most 501(c)(3) organizations being referred to as charities. Section 170 of the IRC (which creates the tax deduction) defines charitable contributions using the same language as in section 501(c)(3) to identify eligible organizations[11]. Accordingly, what distinguishes a public charity from other 501(c)(3) nonprofits is not clear in the regulations, leading to a general misconception that only public charities are organized under section 501(c)(3) of the IRC.[12]

Other 501(c) Nonprofits

Today, of course, the voluntary sector includes more than public charities. Not-for-profit organizations encompass a broad spectrum of activities. The second largest category of tax-exempt organizations are those incorporated under IRC section 501(c)(4)—civic leagues, social welfare organizations, and local associations of employees such as AARP, the NAACP, and Rotary Clubs. Unlike 501(c)(3) organizations, those organized under section 501(c)(4) are allowed greater latitude with regard to lobbying and political activity. However, only certain volunteer fire departments and veterans' organizations described in section 501(c)(4) are eligible to receive tax-deductible contributions, whereas most charities described in section 501(c)(3) are eligible to receive tax-deductible contributions.[13] A list of the major categories of tax-exempt organizations other than those organized under section 501(c)(3) is included in Table 1.1.

TABLE 1.1 Other 501(c) Nonprofit Organizations, 1999 and 2009

		1999		2009	
	IRC Section	Number of Orgs	% of All Orgs	Number of Orgs	% of All Orgs
Civic leagues, social welfare orgs, etc.	501(c)(4)	124,774	10.4%	111,849	7.1%
Fraternal beneficiary societies	501(c)(8)	103,725	8.6%	77,811	4.9%
Business leagues, chambers of commerce, etc.	501(c)(6)	70,718	5.9%	72,801	4.6%
Labor, agricultural, horticultural orgs	501(c)(5)	60,530	5.0%	56,292	3.6%
Social and recreational clubs	501(c)(7)	56,429	4.7%	57,255	3.6%
Posts or organizations of war veterans	501(c)(19)	34,608	2.9%	34,593	2.2%
All other 501(c) nonprofits		41,909	3.5%	43,223	2.7%
Total Other 501(c) Nonprofits		492,693	41.0%	453,824	28.7%
Total 501(c)(3) Public Charities		631,902	52.5%	1,006,670	63.7%
Total 501(c)(3) Private Foundations		77,978	6.5%	120,617	7.6%

Source: National Center for Charitable Statistics, Retrieved from http://nccsdataweb.urban.org/PubApps/profile1.php?state=US

Foundations

As mentioned previously, most foundations are classified as 501(c)(3) organizations but are differentiated from public charities by the IRS; they are subject to more stringent regulations, as discussed in Chapter 4. In 2009, private foundations comprised 7.6 percent of all nonprofits, and 10.7 percent of organizations classified as tax-exempt under section 501(c)(3). The nonprofit Foundation Center is the leading authority and resource for and about foundations in the United States (see Box 1.2). While the IRS distinguishes primarily between operating and grantmaking foundations (see Table 1.2), the Foundation Center

Table 1.2 Foundation Types at a Glance

Type of Foundation	Source of Funds to Establish	Method of Dispersal of Funds
Independent (family) foundation	Individual or family gifts or bequests	Grants
Operating (private) foundation	Individual or family gifts or bequests	Operate own programs
Corporate foundation	Assets from a publicly held company	Grants
Corporate operating foundation	Assets from a publicly held company	Operate own programs
Public foundation	Government grants, individuals, foundations	Grants

uses the terms "private foundation" in lieu of "operating foundation" and "public foundation" instead of "grantmaking" in order to distinguish between the various sources of funding. Private foundations derive their funds from "an individual, a family, a corporation, or some combination of related parties"[14]; these foundations may grant funds to other organizations or may use funds to operate their own programs. Public foundations, however, have grantmaking as their primary purpose. Funding generally comes from multiple sources including government grants, individuals, and private foundations.[15]

The Foundation Center identifies four types of private foundations: 1) independent foundations; 2) operating foundations; 3) corporate foundations; and 4) corporate operating foundations. Independent foundations (also referred to as family foundations) comprise nearly 89 percent of the foundations in the Foundation Center database. These foundations are established by individuals or families through large gifts or bequests of funds, stocks, and properties, and are varied in size, scope, and types of interests. Most independent foundations do not employ staff; the donor and/or family members manage resources and distribute funds.[16] Prominent family foundations include the John D. and Catherine T. MacArthur Foundation, the Robert Wood Johnson Foundation, and the W.K. Kellogg Foundation, each of which has had major policy influence through the projects it funds. The Robert Wood Johnson Foundation, for example, now partners with the nonprofit Alliance for a Healthier Generation in its mission to change school policy regarding food and beverage options in order to alleviate the problem of childhood obesity; these efforts are highlighted in Chapter 2.

Box 1.2

FOR MORE INFORMATION

THE FOUNDATION CENTER

The Foundation Center was recognized as a 501(c)(3) tax-exempt organization in 1957 and today is the leading authority on philanthropy in the U.S. Its primary resource is information, maintaining the most comprehensive database on grantmakers and their grants in the U.S. Research, education, and training programs are directly provided by the Center. There are five regional library/learning centers–Atlanta, Cleveland, New York, San Francisco, and Washington, D.C.—along with a network of more than 400 "funding information centers" located in public libraries, educational institutions, and community foundations across the nation.

The mission of the Foundation Center is "to strengthen the nonprofit sector by advancing knowledge about U.S. philanthropy." This is done primarily through their website and five regional centers. The Center conducts its own research, as well as facilitates the research of others on U.S. philanthropy. Through its information database, the Foundation Center provides access to IRS Form 990 information as well as information on numerous funding sources. In addition, free online tutorials and webinars are available on preparing grant proposals, while additional publications and workshops are available for a fee.

Educational resources available through the Foundation Center aid nonprofit managers by providing practical assistance in identifying and pursuing grant funding. Data on the nonprofit sector, particularly through its searchable database of Form 990 information, enhances knowledge of the field and provides researchers and policymakers with valuable information. In addition, the Center launched a $15-million, 50th Anniversary campaign in 2006 to raise funds for capacity-building activities. Capacity-building is an important issue within the field, since provision of funds specifically to professionalize the operations of nonprofits will likely have a long-term policy impact by strengthening the sector as a whole.

To learn more about the Foundation Center resources and services, go to http://foundationcenter.org.

Source: The Foundation Center, http://foundationcenter.org/about/.

Operating foundations—such as the J. Paul Getty Trust—are also established with assets given by individuals or a small group of donors, but unlike other family foundations they use their resources to operate their own programs rather than or in addition to distributing funds to other organizations. Family foundations that move toward direct charitable activities and away from grantmaking would likely benefit from reclassification by the IRS to be private operating foundations.[17] IRS restrictions and requirements for private operating foundations are less strict; for example, greater deductibility of new donations is allowed and they have a different payout requirement.[18] More information on the regulations and restrictions that apply to foundations is included in Chapter 4.

Corporate foundations[19] are established with assets received from a publicly held company, although they are a separate legal entity. These foundations—including the Alcoa

Foundation and Enterprise Rent-A-Car Foundation—are typically established as means to target giving in the geographic locations where the company operates, to support children of employees through scholarships, and/or encourage charitable giving and volunteer efforts of company employees. Like family operating foundations, corporate operating foundations run their own programs rather than distribute funds to other organizations. Most foundations of this type have been established by pharmaceutical companies for the direct distribution of medications such as the Bristol-Myers Squibb Patient Assistance Foundation and the Lilly Cares Foundation.

Like the nonprofit sector in general, foundation growth has been dramatic in the past 20 years. Foundations held an estimated total of $583.4 billion in assets in 2009, up from $448.6 billion in 1999, but down from the decade high of $682.2 billion in 2007. While the number of foundations has increased each year in the last three decades, the rate of growth from 2007 to 2008 was the smallest, most likely because of the economic crisis. Approximately 32,300 foundations held assets of at least $1 million or distributed funds in excess of $100,000 in 2007; 63.6 percent of them were established between 1990 and 2008. Table 1.3 includes the timeline of establishment for these foundations, as well as total number of active private and community foundations by decade. The Foundation Center estimates a termination rate of 1.5 percent in 2006, when 1,080 foundations that had been active in 2005 ceased operation.[20]

TABLE 1.3 Growth in Number of Active Foundations

Dates	Number of Foundations[21] Established	Percent of Those Foundations Active in 2005–2006	Total Private and Community Foundations
Before 1940	596	2%	N/A
1940–1949	807	3%	N/A
1950–1959	1,959	7%	N/A
1960–1969	2,025	7%	N/A
1970–1979	1,274	4%	22,088
1980–1989	4,816	16%	32,401
1990–1999	11,274	38%	56,582
2000–2006	6,709	23%	72,477

Source: Steven Lawrence and Reina Mukai, *Foundation Growth and Giving Estimates*, The Foundation Center, 2008, p. 4. Establishment data not available for 3,164 foundations; data incomplete for 2000–2006.

Classification of Nonprofits

While the Internal Revenue Code includes almost 30 sections delineating different eligibility requirements for tax-exemption, until the 1980s organizations were not uniformly classified by type. Because the not-for-profit sector is so diverse, a classification system was deemed necessary to yield meaningful information by grouping organizations by purpose, type, or major function. As such, the National Taxonomy of Exempt Entities (NTEE) was designed by the National Center for Charitable Statistics (NCCS) in cooperation with major nonprofit organizations. The value of the NTEE lies in its ability to:

- facilitate the collection, tabulation, presentation, and analysis of data by the types of organizations and their activities;
- promote uniformity and comparability in the presentation of statistical and other data collected by various public and private agencies; and
- provide better quality information as the basis for public policy debate and decision-making for the nonprofit sector and for society at large. [22]

New National Taxonomy of Exempt Entities—Core Codes (NTEE-CC) include about 400 categories. Codes are organized with consistent hierarchical logic that affords ease of use. A discussion of the major groups and divisions, as well as the impact of NTEE on research and public policy, is included in Box 1.3.

While the data in Figure 1.1 and Table 1.1 are helpful in illustrating the size of the voluntary sector according to different types of tax-exempt status, the diversity of functions among these organizations makes understanding of the scope of the sector less clear. Examination by NTEE categories, however, affords a more illuminating view of the sector because NTEE classification includes all nonprofits in all sections of tax-exemption. The diversity within the sector highlights the many and varied public policy ramifications of nonprofit efforts.

Table 1.4 reflects change in the number of registered not-for-profit organizations by major purpose or activity between 2000 and 2010. As you can see, while the sector as a whole grew, the proportion of certain types of nonprofits fluctuated. Public and societal benefit nonprofits decreased as a percentage of total nonprofits while the relative share of religious organizations increased; mutual/membership benefit organizations showed a decline in numbers as well as proportion. Decline in the number of mutual/membership benefit organizations most likely reflects trends identified in recent scholarship on the decrease in civic engagement in the United States (see Robert Putnam's *Bowling Alone*, for example). Regardless, it is clear to see that the NTEE enables a better understanding of the work being done by nonprofits and specifically how the voluntary sector is changing. Since 1999, for example, nonprofits have increased their presence in the area of human services by 25 percent, indicating greater involvement in policy areas such as child protection, social welfare, and job training.

Box 1.3

FOR MORE INFORMATION

NATIONAL TAXONOMY OF EXEMPT ENTITIES

NTEE is comprised of 26 major groups (labeled A through Z) and seven common codes. Whereas the 26 major groups are organized under ten broad categories (listed in Table 1.4), the common codes are used within each major group to delineate activities of organizations. Common codes also allow use of a fourth digit to provide more detail about a kind of organization within a group. For example, National Children's Alliance is an affiliate organization coded as I037, where the I indicates the major group Crime & Legal-Related, which falls under the broad category of Human Services, and 03 refers to the common code Professional Societies and Associations. The fourth digit was taken from the decile level of the NTEE-CC, which in this case is I70 Protection Against Abuse. Use of the 7 as the fourth digit indicates that NCA is not only a professional association within the field of criminal justice, but that the organization specializes in protection against abuse.

IRS determination specialists use the information from applications for tax-exempt status to classify organizations according to the NTEE-CC. This classification makes data collection and dissemination by the National Center for Charitable Statistics more useful, thus enhancing our understanding of the nonprofit sector. In addition, the Foundation Center also uses a slightly more detailed version of the system to classify grants and those who receive them.

While the NTEE codes have proven immensely valuable, due to the availability of digitized data from Part III of the Form 990 through the NCCS/Guidestar database, the National Center for Charitable Statistics has developed the Nonprofit Program Classification (NPC) System. Whereas the NTEE classifies nonprofits according to their organizational purpose, the NPC codes reflect the nonprofits' actual activities. It is expected that these enhanced data will be not only more useful for researchers but also for potential donors and volunteers for nonprofits, as it facilitates a greater understanding of their activities. In addition, policymakers at all levels of government who are interested in the role of the voluntary sector will be better served through the availability of more complete and detailed information regarding the activities and impact of nonprofit organizations.

A complete list of the NTEE-CC and further discussion of the NPC are available at nccsdataweb.urban.org.

SCOPE AND FUNCTION OF THE NONPROFIT SECTOR

The nonprofit sector is also known as the voluntary sector, the independent sector, or the third sector, in contrast to the public sector (government) and the for-profit (private business) sector. When nongovernmental organizations that are active in other countries are included in the discussion, reference is generally made to Nongovernmental Organizations or NGOs. Since this text focuses primarily on nonprofit activity in the U.S., the terms nonprofit, not-for-profit, or voluntary sector will be used interchangeably throughout. References to NGOs should be construed as denoting an international emphasis.

TABLE 1.4 Change in Registered Nonprofit Organizations by NTEE Category, 1999 and 2010

	Dec. 1999[a]		Nov. 2010[b]		
NTEE Category	**# of Orgs**	**%**	**# of Orgs**	**%**	**Change**
Arts, Culture, and Humanities	91,275	7.6	124,965	7.7	33,690
Education	159,896	13.3	216,443	13.4	56,547
Environment[23]	35,732	3.0	59,174	3.7	23,442
Health[24]	75,885	6.4	100,517	6.3	24,632
Human Services[25]	296,081	24.7	413,359	25.7	117,278
International, Foreign Affairs, and National Security	12,781	1.1	20,838	1.3	8,057
Public and Societal Benefit[26]	302,591	25.2	357,345	22.1	54,754
Religion Related, Spiritual Development	138,996	11.6	253,054	14.5	114,058
Mutual/Membership Benefit Organizations	85,057	7.1	78,106	4.8	(6,951)
Unknown	4,979	0.4	11,502	0.7	6,523
Total	1,203,273	100.00	1,617,303	100.00	

Source: National Center for Charitable Statistics, Registered Nonprofit Organizations by Major Purpose or Activity (NTEE Code), 1999.

a Data extracted from: http://nccsdataweb.urban.org/NCCS/V1Pub/index.php; 2010.

b Data extracted from: http://nccsdataweb.urban.org/NCCS/V1Pub/index.php.

Growth of the Nonprofit Sector

The number of tax-exempt organizations that comprise the nonprofit sector continues to grow in the United States. According to statistics from the Internal Revenue Service (IRS) and published by the Urban Institute's National Center for Charitable Statistics (NCCS), the number of nonprofit organizations grew by 31.5 percent between 1999 and 2009 (See Figure 1.1.) While data on the number of organizations that cease operations are limited, the Urban Institute has studied the survival rates of small public charities—specified as those that meet the filing threshold but have revenues, expenses, and assets of less than $100,000 per year. Of the original group of 63,493 small nonprofits that filed the Form 990[27] in 1997, Boris and Roeger[28] estimate that about 16.7 percent were inactive or defunct by 2007, and almost

21 percent saw their revenues decline to below the requirement for filing. Conversely, 28.5 percent of the small organizations saw their revenues, expenses, and assets increase to more than $100,000 per year over the decade studied.

As shown in Figure 1.1, public charities continue to increase as a proportion of total nonprofits, as well as in real numbers. In 2009, almost two-thirds of all organizations recognized as tax-exempt under section 501(c) of the Internal Revenue Code (IRC) were public charities, up from just over half ten years earlier. It is important to note that this reflects only the number of reporting public charities, and the definition of reporting public charity changed in 2008. Prior to 2008, a reporting public charity was one with more than $25,000 in gross annual receipts that was therefore required to file a Form 990; since 2008, only organizations with more than $50,000 in gross annual receipts are required to file a Form 990.

Since prior to 2008 organizations making less than $5,000 in annual revenues were not required to either register or report to the IRS, and those with between $5,000 and $25,000 were not required to file the Form 990, data on these nonprofits are limited. Boris and Roeger[29] estimate that about 63 percent of 501(c)(3) organizations did not meet the requirements to file with the IRS in 2007, suggesting the sector is far larger and more complex than the data on reporting charities indicate. While information on very small nonprofits is likely to improve in subsequent years because all public charities (excluding churches[30]) must now file the Form 990-N, commonly called the e-postcard, those data are not yet sufficiently available. Throughout this book we, like most in the field of nonprofit scholarship, focus primarily on organizations large enough to be Form 990 filers because of the data available

FIGURE 1.1 Number of U.S. Nonprofits Registered with the IRS, 1999 and 2009

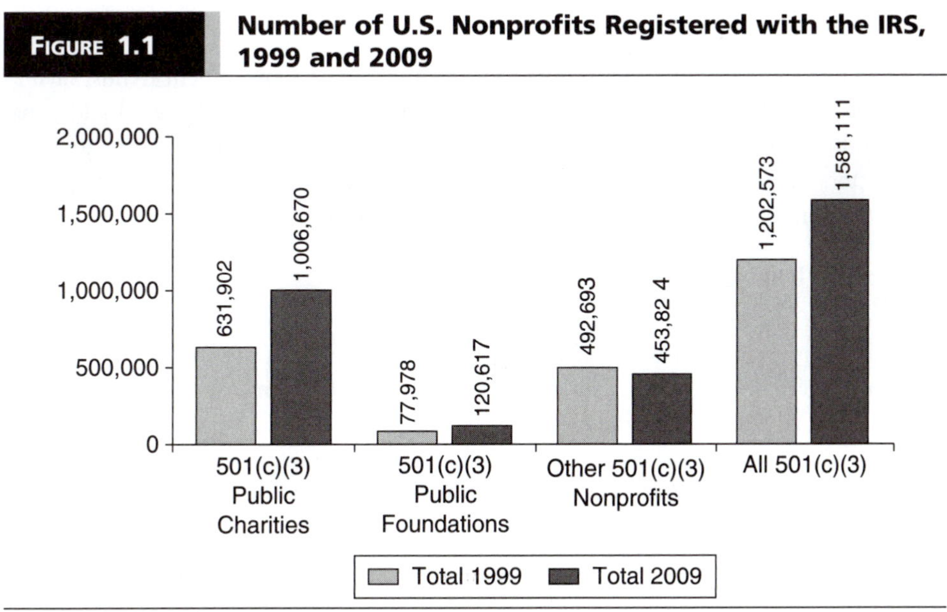

Source: National Center for Charitable Statistics, http://nccsdataweb.urban.org/PubApps/profile1.php?state=US.

pertaining to them. These data give credence to the claims of numerous nonprofit scholars that the sector as a whole is experiencing tremendous growth.

This growth had its beginnings in the post-World War II era and has been attributed to several factors, including greater affluence among Americans and changing government policy priorities. Increasing American affluence has allowed people to simultaneously contribute more to the nonprofit sector and to purchase the services that nonprofits provide, especially education services.[31] In addition, extreme wealth allows individuals to form philanthropic foundations; for example, in 2000, billionaire and Microsoft co-founder Bill Gates and his wife formed the nation's largest grantmaking foundation, the Bill & Melinda Gates Foundation.

Government policies have also facilitated the growth of the voluntary sector. During the 1960s, President Lyndon Johnson's Great Society created social programs to address health needs, legal aid, urban renewal, and an expansion of social welfare services. The Johnson administration was the first to offer a major infusion of federal funding to nonprofit organizations to help government provide these services.[32] More recently, creation of AmeriCorps in 2003, and its subsequent expansion in 2009 through the Serve America Act have infused the nonprofit sector with a cadre of young and eager volunteers.

Furthermore, the civil rights movement in the 1950s and 1960s added substantially to the growth of the nonprofit sector. The efforts of African American and women's rights groups during those years paved the way for many of today's nonprofit associations, including those representing both sides of the abortion issue, environmental conservation efforts, and gay rights. Finally, increased government use of privatization—hiring contractors from the nonprofit and private sectors—has also increased the number of not-for-profit organizations operating in the United States.

Given the long history of not-for-profit involvement in public policy, the growth of the sector will undoubtedly offer nonprofits continued influence. Government trends, such as continued federal devolution of policy responsibility to the states, will afford additional opportunities for nonprofit involvement in addressing public problems. Taken together, these factors demonstrate the need for academics, policymakers, and the public to pay far more attention to the role of nonprofits in the policy process.

Economic Impact of Nonprofits

Growth in the number of organizations is only one factor in the scope of the nonprofit sector and its importance in both academic and practical terms. Data from the Bureau of Economic Analysis (BEA) reflect that in 2011 nonprofit institutions constituted 5.5 percent of the U.S. Gross Domestic Product (GDP). This represents an increase from 4.85 percent in 1999 but a decrease from the decade-high of 5.73 percent in 2009.[33] Between 1999 and 2009, U.S. GDP grew by approximately 47 percent[34]; during this same time, revenues and assets of reporting nonprofits grew by 33.9 and 38.7 percent, respectively. In 2009 (the latest year for which complete data are available), reporting nonprofits received $1.87 trillion in revenue and held $4.3 trillion in assets.[35] These statistics illustrate that not-for-profit organizations produce a significant and increasing impact on the U.S. economy. In addition, with revenues and assets that have grown at a rate dramatically greater than growth in GDP, the nonprofit sector is positioned to be an even larger force for public policy influence because of greater resources for service provision, research, and advocacy.

According to the Urban Institute, the nonprofit sector accounted for nine percent of wages and more than 10 percent of jobs in the 2009 economy[36]; this marks a continued increase (from 4.4 percent in 1994 and 5.9 percent in 2007) in nonprofit employees as a percent of all workers. Studies indicate that workers in nonprofits are compensated at similar levels to their counterparts in other sectors—slightly more than for-profit employees but somewhat less than workers in state and local government. In 2007, the average hourly wage for nonprofit workers was $21.68 compared to $21.08 for employees at for-profits, and $23.77 for state and $25.26 for local government workers, respectively. It is important to note, however, that these data reflect wages for all workers in each sector; when examining wages for management occupations only, private sector average hourly earnings are highest at $41.38 and nonprofit sector earnings are lowest at an average of $34.24 per hour.[37] In addition to the economic impact of paid employees, volunteers make significant contributions via the nonprofit sector. In 2009, volunteers contributed 14,963,262 hours, equivalent to 8,802,000 full-time employees. The value of their time is estimated at $278,615,940, further illustrating the growing importance of nonprofits on the U.S. economy and labor market.[38]

PHILANTHROPY AND POLICY SOLUTIONS

As discussed above, foundations and the programs that they fund and operate have been vital to advancing social goals in the United States since the turn of the twentieth century. Among America's first modern philanthropists, Andrew Carnegie and John D. Rockefeller both pronounced very public goals for their respective foundations: Carnegie to facilitate "the advancement and diffusion of knowledge and understanding,"[39] and Rockefeller "to promote the well-being of mankind throughout the world."[40] Established during the Progressive Period in American History (1880–1920), these were the pioneering foundations—a new means of organized philanthropy to facilitate social change by influencing collective political action. According to Sheila Slaughter and Edward T. Silva, resource holders such as Carnegie, Rockefeller, and Russell Sage put their wealth to use to influence the "process of ideology formation—[defined as] the production, dissemination, and consumption of ideas" because it was believed that such ideologies "supplied the social cement for collective political action."[41]

Thus, the Progressive movement ushered in a new era in which nonprofit organizations affected how public problems were perceived and how policy solutions were derived.[42] For example, the Council on Foreign Relations (CFR), a nonpartisan nonprofit, has been instrumental in U.S. foreign policy since 1921 when it was founded by grants from the Rockefeller and Carnegie Foundations. The CFR designed important parts of the charter that created the United Nations, helped to craft the Marshall Plan for post-World War II recovery in Europe, and advocated for nuclear nonproliferation agreements throughout the 1970s and 1980s; its journal, *Foreign Affairs,* has long been considered one of the most influential publications covering U.S. foreign policy issues.[43]

In addition to these public policy-shaping activities, philanthropic foundations have for decades engaged in civic strengthening activities, which are undertaken to facilitate the democratic process by encouraging transparency in governance, improved public leadership, and increased civic participation.[44] Work in these areas, often part of community foundation efforts, includes voter registration, get-out-the-vote campaigns, leadership programs, and collaborations with governments and community organizations to pursue governance and electoral reforms.

PUBLIC PROBLEMS AND THE POLICY PROCESS

The work of the early foundations to bolster collective political action builds upon a long history in which government entities and not-for-profit organizations have worked together to provide public goods and services to American citizens. Public goods, also called collective goods, are those that fulfill a need or demand where the benefit cannot be restricted to those with the ability to pay for them. For example, clean air is a collective good. All members of a community benefit from clean air, but access to the air cannot be restricted to those who do not introduce pollution. Because access to collective goods cannot be restricted to those who pay for them, strong incentives exist for people to become "free riders"—that is, those who consume collective goods and services without paying their share of the cost. Public goods, therefore, are typically not provided via the private market—which restricts provision of goods and services to activities which generate profits—but rather through the public sector. This often leads to what are known as collective action problems.[45]

Collective action problems involve those situations in which individual self-interests conflict with social interests—that is, private benefits result in social costs. The classic example is the tragedy of the commons, in which it is in each individual's self-interest to use as much of a common resource as possible; however, if that happens, the resource will be depleted. Therefore, it is in the collective interest for each person to use less, thereby managing the resource together.[46] For example, the collision between economic development and environmental protection often results in competition between the two sides over problem definitions and appropriate policy solutions.[47] Nonprofit organizations are often involved in developing and managing solutions to such collective action dilemmas. One example of a nonprofit mitigating the competition between economic and environmental interests comes from the Blue Ridge Conservancy, highlighted in Box 1.4.

Collective action dilemmas and other public problems are often addressed through the creation of public policy, which is traditionally considered to be government's response to perceived problems. Indeed, government action is routinely viewed as a way to validate claims about public needs, those "that a community recognizes as legitimate and tries to satisfy as a community."[48] Of course all members of a community will not agree on society's problems nor will all agree on appropriate solutions. Thus, public policy requires that a political deal be struck offering an acceptable balance of benefits and costs across society.[49]

Box 1.4

FOR EXAMPLE

THE BLUE RIDGE CONSERVANCY: MITIGATING COMPETING INTERESTS

Founded in 1997, the nonprofit Blue Ridge Rural Land Trust (BRRLT) served a seven-county area of Western North Carolina with a mission of "neighbors helping neighbors work to preserve rural communities and culture in northwestern North Carolina through the protection of the land resource upon which they depend." Begun with the support of the local Resource Conservation and Development Council—a nonprofit organization sponsored by the U.S. Department of Agriculture—the BRRLT had protected over 5,500 acres through conservation easements by the end of 2005. Another 5,750 acres had easements pending in Spring 2006. BRRLT helped protect the commons by preserving the landscape—that is, the view everyone shares when looking out over a rural mountain vista. The land may be individually owned, but the view is a common resource.

In 2010, BRRLT merged with another nonprofit, the High Country Conservancy, to form the Blue Ridge Conservancy. Both nonprofits were formed as land trusts and their merger combined a history of protecting over 15,000 acres in the northwestern region of North Carolina. Each organization promoted the strong tradition of private property rights; landowners retain ownership and specific use of their property (e.g. for farming), but the development rights are conveyed to the land trust in perpetuity. The land can be sold or transferred through inheritance but must be conserved and protected from development by subsequent owners. Such reduction in development potential results in significant tax savings to property owners; North Carolina led the states in providing state income tax credits for land or easements donated for conservation purposes. However, since the lands remain private property, they continue to generate property tax revenue for local government. This is an important example in which nonprofit organizations collaborated to make policy and resolve the collective action problem of land preservation.

Additional information is available at blueridgeconservancy.org.

For example, Lowi's classic policy typology addresses these varying perspectives on public problems and solutions by distinguishing between distributive policies, redistributive policies, and regulatory policies.[50] Distributive policies tend to be noncontroversial because they offer targeted benefits but distribute costs so widely as to go unnoticed by most people—for example, university research grants. Redistributive policies, on the other hand, are more controversial, as they are seen as offering benefits to one group, such as welfare recipients, via direct cost to another group—for example, taxpayers. Finally, regulatory policies target individual or industry behavior, thus typically offering widespread benefits, such as cleaner air, with narrow costs to a certain industry or consumer group.

The proliferation of the nonprofit sector has helped to expand the size, scope, and function of organizations prepared to meet public needs and influence citizens' lives beyond what government can or is able to do. In his discussion of public policy, B. Guy Peters recognized the important role that nongovernmental actors—government's agents via contract—play in the policy process. Therefore, his definition of public policy is particularly useful when studying nonprofit organizations. Peters wrote that "public policy is the sum of government activities, whether pursued directly or through agents, as those activities have an influence on the lives of citizens."[51] Accordingly, based on our academic and professional experience, and the characterizations of numerous scholars in the field,[52] we define public policy as: the actions taken by governments, not limited to statutes and regulations, but including programs and direct service delivery by government agents and nonprofit organizations that seek to address public needs. This definition both informs and guides the discussion of nonprofits and public policy throughout this book.

Stages of the Policy Process

Public policies and programs are typically the result of a long and complex process—sometimes decades in the making. As noted above, the policy process typically begins with identifying a problem and deciding whether it is inherently a public problem necessitating a public solution. Although the classic model of the policy process is a simplification, it continues to offer a useful framework for studying public policy in the United States. This model includes several stages, generally proceeding in the following manner: problem recognition, agenda-setting, policy formulation, adoption of the policy, policy implementation, and finally, evaluation.

First, is the problem recognition phase during which a failure in the social, economic, or political system is identified. The problem can be identified by a citizen or group of citizens, a politician, a bureaucrat, an interest group, or a nonprofit organization, much like the New York Society for the Prevention of Cruelty to Children identified the problem of child abuse in 1875. Often a coalition of these actors recognizes a problem and comes together to seek a government solution. Vital to attracting government attention and action is the problem's policy image—the perception and framing of the issue. Policy image is formed, and can be manipulated, through a combination of the emotional appeal, symbolism, and factual evidence surrounding the problem.[53]

In the agenda-setting stage, the issue attracts a wider audience, including policymakers and politicians. Oftentimes a policy entrepreneur brings the problem to government's attention, as in the case of Bud Cramer, who as a district attorney led the effort to establish the first children's advocacy center (CAC). Later, as a U.S. Congressman, Cramer placed this new facet of the problem of child abuse on the federal agenda, advocating legislation and funding for the CAC model.

With enough attention from those inside government, and with their agreement that the problem warrants public action, the issue can move to the policy formulation phase. During this third phase, a possible solution to the problem is sought; a variety of alternative solutions can and will be considered by policymakers.[54] Often in the policy formulation phase, lawmakers solicit information and ideas from stakeholder groups, including nonprofits, as they pursue a policy solution. Policy advocacy by groups such as National Children's Alliance, for instance, is often critical to policy formulation. A final policy is agreed upon by lawmakers during the phase known as policy adoption.

Fundamental to the process following policy adoption is the implementation stage, during which the mandate of the policy is carried out by those in government or their agents in the nonprofit or private sector. An example of policy implementation is the actual delivery of services for abused and neglected children offered by children's advocacy centers. Next, is the evaluation phase, in which the outcomes of programs and policies are measured and stakeholder feedback is processed by the agencies carrying out the policy. National Children's Alliance monitors the performance of the children's advocacy centers they accredit to ensure standards of operation; while not the only evaluation of center outcomes, this is another example of the role nonprofits play throughout the policy process. The evaluation and feedback stage often leads to policy reform, as the limitations, unintended consequences, or failings of the policy as implemented become clear. Policy reform is considered a regular part of the policy process; as Charles Lindblom explained, "Policy is not made once and for all; it is made and re-made endlessly."[55]

Collaboration

Particularly useful for a discussion of nonprofits in the policy process is research on the scope and impact of collaboration by various actors. Scholars have varyingly referred to these collaborations as policy networks, subsystems, subgovernments, issue networks, policy communities, or advocacy coalitions. What all have in common is the understanding that policy problems, solutions, advocacy, and analysis are influenced by a variety of actors, often working in concert to advance specific goals.[56]

The basic concept of the issue network was introduced by Hugh Heclo in 1978 to explain how long-dominant iron triangles lost control over certain policy issues. An iron triangle is a closed policymaking group, traditionally consisting of three relevant parts: a government agency, congressional committees, and interest groups, who share interest in an issue and seek to control access to the policymaking process in order to facilitate a mutually beneficial policy outcome. Heclo's concept of the issue network better illustrated the diversity of actors and complexity of the policymaking process in most policy areas, and later scholars expanded on this idea, further capturing the nature of the relationships between actors involved in the policy process. For example, the Advocacy Coalition Framework describes in greater detail the system of actors "from a variety of public and private organizations who are actively concerned with a policy problem or issue."[57] The Advocacy Coalition Framework incorporates the idea of policy-oriented learning[58] facilitated by coalition members such as policymakers and other public officials, university faculty, think tanks, and nonprofit organizations including foundations and those delivering public services. Many of these actors work together on a specific policy area over long periods of time. For example, not-for-profit organizations like the Society for the Prevention of Cruelty to Children and National Children's Alliance have been active members of coalitions that have influenced the policies surrounding child abuse in the U.S. for decades. The various collaborative models offer a useful way to examine the ongoing role that nonprofits play at each point in the policy process.

As this discussion shows, there are many points at which foundations and other nonprofit organizations have an impact on public policy. Those in the nonprofit sector can act as policy entrepreneurs, identifying public problems and bringing them to the government's agenda. Foundations and other nonprofit organizations are often vital in the policy formulation phase. During this process, nonprofits may be asked to participate in hearings, provide data, or submit position papers to assist policymakers in crafting a policy that will eventually win adoption. Once adopted, the complex process of policy implementation begins, often involving the division of responsibilities between governments at the local, state, and federal level, and the use of outside service contractors. Increasingly, nonprofit organizations are engaged in direct implementation of public programs and policy as they deliver public services. The sector also has an important role to play in the policy evaluation and feedback process, particularly when the clientele of nonprofit organizations are affected, or when services have been delivered by a not-for-profit organization.

Further, not-for-profit organizations exist independently of government institutions, engage in public activity, and make public policy decisions every day—for example, deciding the content and location of recreational programs for senior citizens; choosing how and where to feed the homeless; and determining which concert, play, or art exhibit is most appropriate for their communities. On the other hand, they also operate within the constraints of tax policy, employment law, and policies that prescribe accountability over their finances and governance. In the course of addressing collective action dilemmas, meeting public needs, and defining public problems, not-for-profit organizations continually affect and are affected by public policy. This, of course, has far-reaching implications for the management of organizations in the nonprofit sector. Society's best interests are at risk if a not-for-profit organization is given tax-exempt status, receives federal or foundation grants, is tasked with direct service delivery, and encouraged to participate in the policy formulation and implementation processes when that organization is ill-equipped for these responsibilities. While issues of nonprofit management are addressed more specifically in Chapters 11 to 14, it is important to keep in mind that due to the symbiotic nature of the nonprofit sector and public policy, good management techniques are important beyond their impact on any single organization.

At this point it should be clear that the nonprofit sector is integral to the policy process, is often limited by policy mandates, and is frequently responsible for public policy action. Accordingly, it is inadvisable to work in or study the nonprofit sector without a basic understanding of its relationship to public policy and the policymaking process. Likewise, we argue that given the frequency with which not-for-profit organizations deliver services that were once delivered by government, policymakers and public sector employees must also understand the workings of the nonprofit sector. Facilitating understanding of the interrelatedness and often interdependence of not-for-profit organizations and public policy is the aim of this book.

OUR APPROACH

The book is comprised of three parts: Fundamentals and Environment of the Voluntary Sector, Strategies of Not-for-Profit Organizations, and Management Issues. Each section focuses on the important relationship between public policy and the nonprofit sector; accordingly, each chapter begins by highlighting the policy implications of the nonprofit issues discussed therein.

In some instances nonprofits are policy actors and in others nonprofits are affected by public policy decisions; in all cases, nonprofits are inextricably linked to the world of public policy. (See Figure 1.2.) Throughout the text we argue that nonprofits and public policy interact in four primary ways:

1. nonprofits make policy, for example, by opening their doors and providing services to the public to implement solutions to public problems;
2. nonprofits influence policy through efforts such as advocacy and lobbying;
3. nonprofits are affected by public policy, such as laws which encourage use of nonprofit service providers; and
4. nonprofits are subject to public policy, such as state and federal regulations regarding the handling of donor funds.

These categories illustrate the interlocking relationship between nonprofits and public policy; thus, they are depicted in Figure 1.2 as pieces of a puzzle.

We view the relationship between nonprofits and public policy as symbiotic, a union marked by reciprocity and overlap. Understanding the nature and impact of this

FIGURE 1.2 Nonprofits in a Policy World

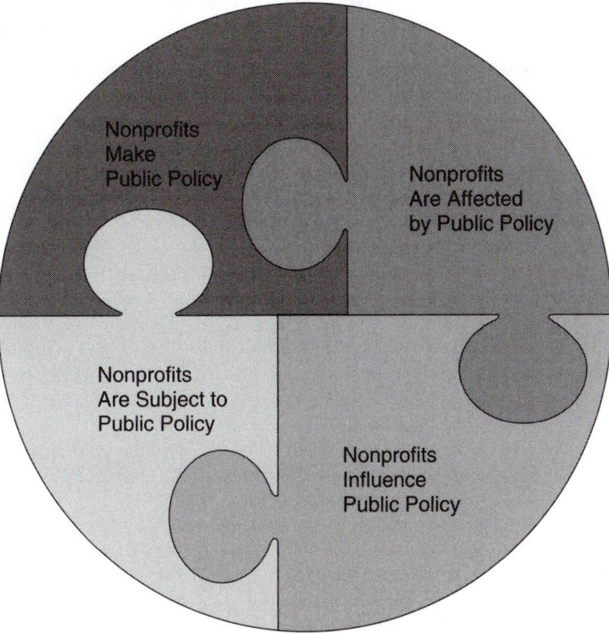

interrelatedness is the focus of this book. At the same time, we highlight the skills and strategies with which nonprofit organizations must be equipped in order to pursue their missions and get the most from their relationships with the public and for-profit sectors.

Part I, Fundamentals and Environment of the Voluntary Sector, is an overview of the nonprofit sector as a whole. Chapters in this section are designed to define and identify the different types of not-for-profit organizations and provide the theoretical basis for the existence of the nonprofit sector, as well as its relationship to public policy and government at the federal, state, and local levels. Part II, Strategies of Not-for-Profit Organizations, focuses primarily on the role of nonprofits as actors within the policy process—that is, how their operations influence public policy and the alleviation of public problems. The chapters throughout Part II address the major strategic planning topics for nonprofits, including developing and adhering to mission, vision, and organizational goals, lobbying and policy advocacy, and issues of organizational ethics and accountability. In addition, the relevance of marketing for nonprofits and the growing trend to brand one's organization and product are discussed.

Finally, Part III, Management Issues, emphasizes the nuts and bolts issues of operating a not-for-profit organization. Throughout the chapters in this section, public policy is highlighted with regard to how local, state, and federal legislation affects the day-to-day activities and management of nonprofits—that is, ways in which nonprofits are acted upon by public policies. It is important for nonprofit organizations to address capacity and long-term viability; thus, general issues of administration such as budgeting, management, funding, and evaluation are the focus of this section. Finally, because some personnel issues in the not-for-profit sector are unique, this section delves into the role of volunteers and creating effective relationships between executive directors and boards of directors; their decisions and the work that they do have a significant impact on the lives of individual citizens and society at large.

We believe that all not-for-profit organizations are affected by public policy and that many affect policy as well. Some nonprofits are founded specifically to pursue policy change while others influence policy inadvertently. Regardless of intent, voluntary sector organizations have an important role to play in the arena of public policy; therefore, throughout this book nonprofit management is discussed with an emphasis on the public consequences of not-for-profit action. In the end, our goal is to equip managers in both the nonprofit and public sectors with the information they need to navigate the complexities of managing nonprofit organizations in a policy world.

Questions For Review

1. The nonprofit sector has been an important part of U.S. society since its beginnings; why have we only recently begun to recognize its importance?
2. The nonprofit sector has grown dramatically in recent decades. What does this growth mean for the provision of public goods and services by the public (government) sector?
3. Identify examples of collective action problems other than those being addressed by the Blue Ridge Conservancy. Discuss how and why not-for-profit organizations address problems such as these.
4. Discuss how foundations are in a unique position to influence public policy. Give an example of how foundations work in cooperation with public charities to identify and address public problems.

Assignment

Because the Statute of Charitable Uses has had such a long-lasting impact on the legal framework and policy orientation of nonprofits, access the article "The Political Use of Private Benevolence: The Statute of Charitable Uses," by James J. Fishman, at http://digitalcommons.pace.edu/lawfaculty/487. Read pp. 28–43 and pp. 49–61 and compose an essay that addresses the following questions:

1. Why was the Statute of Charitable Uses (1601) deemed necessary by both the public and the government? What public problems/needs was the law designed to address?
2. How does the history of the statute inform your understanding of the scope and function of the nonprofit sector in the United States? Consider which activities were deemed charitable and which were not, the role of local governments as well as the national government, and issues of accountability.

Suggested Readings

Fishman, James J. "The Political Use of Private Benevolence: The Statute of Charitable Uses" (2008). *Pace Law Faculty Publications.* Paper 487, http://digitalcommons.pace.edu/lawfaculty/487.

Foundation Center. *Foundation Fundamentals,* 8th ed. Washington, D.C.: Foundation Center, 2008.

Hammack, David C., ed. *Making the Nonprofit Sector in the United States.* Bloomington: Indiana University Press, 1998.

Hardin, Garrett. "The Tragedy of the Commons." *Science* 162 (December 1968): 1243–1248.

Prewitt, Kenneth, Mattei Dogan, Steven Heydemann, and Stefan Toepler, eds. *The Legitimacy of Philanthropic Foundations.* New York: Russell Sage Foundation, 2006.

Sabatier, Paul A., ed. *Theories of the Policy Process.* 2nd ed. Boulder, CO: Westview Press, 2007.

Stone, Deborah. *Policy Paradox: The Art of Political Decision Making.* Rev. ed. W.W. Norton & Company: New York, New York, 2002.

Web Resources

Association for Research on Nonprofit Organizations and Voluntary Action, www.arnova.org
The Foundation Center, www.foundationcenter.org
Independent Sector, www.independentsector.org
Internal Revenue Service, www.irs.gov/charities
National Center for Charitable Statistics, nccsdataweb.urban.org
Urban Institute, www.urban.org

2 Federalism and the Relationships between the Public, Nonprofit, and For-Profit Sectors

I embrace the view that a trilateral conception of the institutions of the Prince, the Merchant and the Citizen encompasses the essential elements of the organizational map of the polis—the domain of both policy and action.

Adil Najam

Suppose that you and your two children have fallen on hard times and find yourselves in need of welfare services in the state of California. Under the rules of the 1996 federal Personal Responsibility and Work Opportunity Reconciliation Act (PRWORA, otherwise known as welfare reform), your family is eligible to receive cash assistance for up to five years[1] as long as you maintain eligibility and are compliant with program rules. In keeping with America's system of federalism, California follows federal guidelines and requires that you find work within two years of initial admission to the program.[2]

To aid you in that effort, the California Work Opportunity and Responsibility to Kids Program (CalWORKS) includes a Welfare-to-Work component which provides job training and readiness, remedial and/or vocational education, and job search services. CalWORKS rules require that you spend 32 hours per week in welfare-to-work activity. Because county governments administer this state program, you are assigned a county caseworker for an initial eligibility determination and are then directed to the Bay County Jobs Partnership (BCJP). The partnership provides job training and placement services for welfare recipients and is a consortium of

POLICY IMPLICATIONS OF FEDERALISM

- The nature of the American system has always encouraged the formation of nonprofit organizations.
- Federalism allows nonprofits to influence policy at the federal, state, and local levels by identifying and framing public problems, advocating policy solutions, funding pilot projects, and engaging in direct service delivery.
- Government programs since the 1960s, especially the 1996 welfare reform, created many opportunities for nonprofits to influence and make policy as government contractors.
- The increase in collaborations between nonprofit, public, and for-profit organizations increases opportunities for nonprofits to be involved as policy actors and to be subject to government policy regulations.

for-profit and nonprofit sector organizations. Thus, aside from the initial program determination, you will have relatively little interaction with public sector employees at the county, state, or federal level; rather, services for this public program will be delivered by government contractors from the nonprofit and for-profit sectors.

This scenario is quite common and, while complex, the system is seamless to the point that citizens are often unaware that public sector employees are not delivering their services. It is to this complex system that we turn in this chapter, briefly discussing the history of federalism and the complex relationship between organizations in the nonprofit, public, and for-profit sectors. The extensive network linking federal, state, and local governments with the not-for-profit sector has been referred to as nonprofit federalism and is key in the implementation of policies and delivery of services. Increasingly, collaborations between organizations in all three sectors affect public policy; thus, it is important to understand how American federalism and intersectoral relationships influence the work of nonprofit organizations.

THE U.S. FEDERAL SYSTEM AND ITS RELATIONSHIP WITH NONPROFIT ORGANIZATIONS

Federalism, the division of authority and responsibility between the national and subnational governments, is the cornerstone of the American system. Unique in 1789, the U.S. Constitution outlines a system which combines a national level of government with certain, limited responsibilities over a group of state governments, each with its own limited responsibilities. The evolution of federalism over time has led to a much more intergovernmental system of joint funding, delivery, and regulation of many public policies, as exemplified by the chapter's opening vignette. The nonprofit sector continues to be a critical element in this intergovernmental policy system, as (1) nonprofits have framed public problems and pursued policy change; (2) foundations have funded policy research and pilot projects; and (3) nonprofits have delivered public policy at each level of government.

Importantly, the role of associations and societies—"the multiplicity of interests"—was encouraged in *The Federalist Papers,* which were written in 1787 and 1788 to convince wary Americans to adopt the Constitution. Arguably the most well-known of the eighty-five papers are Federalist No. 10 and No. 51; both discuss the problem of factions in a democracy, particularly majority factions which can trample the liberties of the minority. Federalist No. 10 and No. 51 make it clear that in order to control the ills of faction in a free society, the Constitution must respect the pursuit of individual and group interests; each group will serve as a check on the power of another. As Federalist No. 51 explains, "Whilst all authority in [government] will be derived from and dependent on the society, the society itself will be broken into so many parts, interests, and classes of citizens, that the rights of individuals, or of the minority, will be in little danger from interested combinations of the majority." Thus, Americans have long been encouraged to join associations and societies to enjoy solidarity with like-minded peers and to advance their policy interests.

While American federalism has remained in place for over two centuries, it has not evolved without conflict—the Civil War serves as our prime example. The Civil War also exemplifies that nonprofit organizations have a long history of influence on policymaking and politics in the United States. In 1833, decades before the war that would finally bring an end to slavery, the American Anti-Slavery Society (AAS) was founded as the first national advocacy group for the abolition of slavery. By the 1830s, state level abolitionist groups and the AAS were exercising their right to organize and petition federal and state governments against slavery. AAS was among the first membership organizations in the country, and in 1850, there were an estimated 250,000 members in over 1,300 AAS auxiliaries. Members represented nearly 2 percent of the nation's population at the time.[3] In addition to questioning the morality of slavery, its members played a pivotal role in moving the abolition of slavery to the national political agenda, where the economic interests of plantation farmers conflicted with the societal and religious interests of those in the anti-slavery movement. Ultimately the AAS policy goals were two-fold: first, emancipation of slaves, and second, legal protections for the rights of freed slaves and all African Americans. The Emancipation Proclamation of 1863 met the first goal, and since ratification of the Fifteenth Amendment granting African Americans the right to vote seemed to fulfill the second, the AAS dissolved in 1870.[4] Of course, it would take another century and several generations of organizers to reach the goal of full legal protection for African Americans.

The issue of slavery highlights the classic questions of American federalism: Which level of government is in charge; which level of government can and should take responsibility for different public policy problems? In the first decades following ratification of the Constitution, state governments retained much power, and each level of government operated within distinct spheres with minimal overlapping responsibilities. During the early years of federalism, the United States was relatively small and largely agrarian; thus, neither level of government was involved in broad policy activities.[5] In addition, ratification of the

Constitution did not occur without a fight from those who supported the high degree of autonomy enjoyed by states under the former Articles of Confederation; the Tenth Amendment, which reserved some powers to the states, was one concession granted to these "Anti-Federalists" in order to achieve ratification. Maintaining the union of the United States under the Constitution was an ongoing and difficult struggle in the early years of the republic, as George Washington and others sought to carve out the role of the national government in relation to what had traditionally been the purview of the states; this resulted in what has been characterized as dual federalism or the layer cake model of governing.

Social services, as they existed in these early years, followed the structure for provision laid out by the Statute of Charitable Uses in 1601, in which churches and charities took care of the ill and elderly, orphans and the poor, rehabilitation of criminals, and other such activities. These types of social services were commonly understood to be the responsibility of the church and community and were not performed by governments or for-profit organizations. The scope of nonprofit involvement in the delivery of social services is extensive and dates from the end of the eighteenth century in the United States. In 1797, for example, Isabella Graham founded one of the first female-controlled charities, The Society for the Relief of Poor Widows with Small Children, in New York City. Even at this time many organizations devoted to the care of the destitute worked in partnership with government.[6] For example, Lester M. Salamon notes that by the 1890s, half of New York City's public expenditures for the poor went to the voluntary organizations that provided services.[7] These groups "provided needed services for cash-starved and overburdened governments. In effect, they subsidized the state by cutting social service costs through their contributions of money and time."[8]

Societal changes during the twentieth century, particularly following the Great Depression and Franklin Delano Roosevelt's New Deal, moved the country from small and agrarian to large and industrial. With state governments struggling to meet their budget obligations and the national unemployment rate hovering at 25 percent, the federal government stepped in to create new programs and take on new policy responsibilities to address the urgent needs of the nation. These new responsibilities included aid to pensioners and the unemployed, creation of job programs, and provision of welfare support to poor children. While not without political controversy, these policy changes reflected strong popular support for an increased role by government in the provision of services. This resulted in a quadrupling of federal spending as a percentage of Gross National Product between 1929 and 1939, in what Thomas J. Anton describes as "the first great watershed" of modern federalism.[9]

At the same time, the movement toward more professionalized government gained a footing in social service-related fields, including education and social work. The policies of the New Deal added to the numbers of government employees hired and programs administered directly through public agencies. Thus, after the 1940s, American federalism changed again with the growth of state and local governments, including the employment of hundreds of thousands of new public sector employees to administer programs in public education, health, and planning. It was during this era that Morton Grodzins coined the phrase "marble-cake federalism" to describe the increasingly sophisticated system of intergovernmental relations, which includes not only national and state governments, but also cities, counties, special districts, and quasi-governmental entities such as regional development organizations.[10]

With this growth of government, the role of charities, churches, and other philanthropic organizations waned, until federal policies of the 1960s encouraged the growth of partnerships between public and nonprofit organizations. Between 1962 and 1974, for example, the federal government amended the Social Security Act a number of times, encouraging state agencies to employ nonprofit entities in service delivery.[11] The Great Society programs of Lyndon Johnson and Richard Nixon's New Federalism ushered in an era of increased public attention to social and economic problems. Thus, Anton describes the period between 1965 and 1975 as modern federalism's "third great watershed."

Johnson's administration saw passage of the Civil Rights Act, Medicare, Medicaid, and the creation of Head Start, each a significant expansion of the role of the government. Since that time contracting with nonprofits for delivery of social services has increased to the point that Salamon suggests the nonprofit sector is responsible for direct delivery of more health and social services than is government.[12] Further, President Richard Nixon's introduction of general revenue sharing changed the funding relationship between levels of government and increased the amount of federal funding to states and local governments. The establishment of the Environmental Protection Agency (EPA) under the Nixon administration represented an expansion of government activity in this policy area, leading to the subsequent creation of a large number of environmental nonprofits. Of particular note, administration and service delivery of health, social service, and environmental policies involve all three levels of government as well as organizations in both the not-for-profit and for-profit sectors.

Nonprofit Federalism

This extensive network linking federal, state, and local governments with the not-for-profit sector has been called nonprofit federalism by Salamon, who argues that the complex set of partnerships provides innovative solutions to many social problems. For example, Salamon contends that because nonprofits are closer to the target population, easier to mobilize, and generally less bureaucratic, direct provision of services often begins at the local nonprofit level.[13] This helps to illustrate the functional theory of federalism, which describes the situation in which services are provided at the level deemed most appropriate—in many cases, the level of the local nonprofit.[14] The demand for services and/or funding can eventually exceed local nonprofit resources, at which point nonprofits may turn to the government for financial or policy assistance.

During periods of public support for smaller government or less direct government intervention, nonprofit federalism offers political rewards to elected officials who support and subsidize nonprofit service delivery rather than services delivered by public entities, in line with what Peterson terms the legislative theory of federalism.[15] This notion of political reward for using nonprofit organizations and the long reliance on partnerships between the nonprofit and public sectors in the U.S. is not surprising when one remembers that individual sovereignty is a guiding principle of the American system. Vincent Ostrom explains the logic: "If individual citizens can be presumed to exercise the basic authority specifying the terms and conditions of government and to know what it means to govern, they can exercise the basic responsibility for governing their own affairs. . . . In democratic societies, people acting individually and voluntarily with others govern their own affairs without being subject to the ever-present tutelage of government."[16]

The underlying belief in citizen authority over the state is key to what Seymour Martin Lipset calls the American Creed, characterized by "liberty, egalitarianism, individualism, populism, and laissez-faire,"[17] and subsequently a significant factor in the growth of the nonprofit sector and the relationship between nonprofits and public policy. As a result of the American Creed, individual Americans tend to be more generous philanthropists in terms of their time and money than those in other countries,[18] and correspondingly tend to support *less* direct government action on many public problems when compared with other developed nations. Rather than seek assistance from government, Americans have often called upon and created nonprofit organizations to fill perceived gaps in social policy. One such example is Second Harvest Food Bank, a member of the larger nonprofit Feeding America, which heads a network of food banks across the nation to secure donations from local and national food manufacturers to be distributed in 200 communities nationwide. Although a variety of federal food programs exist, nearly 50 million Americans faced food insecurity in 2010.[19] These gaps between government policy and human need often facilitate the creation of nonprofit organizations; theories of nonprofit sector creation are addressed in greater detail in Chapter 3.

THE THREE SECTORS

Three distinct institutional sectors exist in the United States: (1) private business and commerce—known as the for-profit sector; (2) national, state, and federal government—known collectively as the public sector; and (3) charities, volunteer organizations, and associations—known as the nonprofit sector. Therefore, examination of federalism in practice—that is, intergovernmental relations—must include not simply the relationships between federal, state, and local governments but all three sectors of the economy as well.

In characterizing the three sectors, we especially like Nerfin's[20] and Najam's[21] metaphors of the Prince, the Merchant, and the Citizen, in which each sector represents an important component of society: (1) the Prince represents political society; (2) the Merchant represents market society; and (3) the Citizen represents civil society. As Najam explains, these " . . . are powerful images for conceptualizing the three-legged organizational stool balanced on the *state,* the *market,* and the *voluntary association* sectors. . . . [T]hese images provide us with a canvas broad enough to holistically understand the three sectors, not merely as residuals of the others but as the integrated, and interacting, social mesh that they have always been—each, in its own way, trying to define the public interest."[22]

The three sectors often operate in conjunction with one another because of the increasingly complex tenor of society and governance. Goldsmith and Eggers explain that this governing by network operates through intersectoral partnerships, which rely "less on public employees in traditional roles and more on a web of partnerships, contracts, and alliances to do the public's work."[23] Given the current dynamic environment in which ideas, resources, and responsibilities are shared among the three sectors, government agencies and nonprofits have sought relationships not only with one another but have also sought ways to incorporate the for-profit sector in pursuing the public interest through the provision of public goods and services.[24]

Organizations in the not-for-profit sector hold a unique position: They are not public organizations, but they often seek to enhance the public welfare; they are not profit-making, but they often need to attract private resources. As the vignette at the start of the chapter indicates, government increasingly relies on both the nonprofit and for-profit sectors to provide welfare services, such as job training and placement. The collaborative efforts of the public, nonprofit, and for-profit sectors in the delivery of welfare, education, health care, and other services highlight the overlapping nature of the three sectors. Because of this overlap, those working in and with nonprofit organizations must be aware of the differences between the three, as they have important consequences for the activities and administration of not-for-profit organizations.

Characteristics of the Three Sectors

Not-for-profit organizations can vary dramatically, but all have three characteristics in common: (1) unlike government, they are voluntary—that is, they cannot coerce participation; (2) while they may earn income, unlike businesses, they do not distribute profits to stakeholders; and (3) unlike both government and business, they operate without any clear lines of accountability or ownership.[25] In addition, most nonprofits, particularly those classified under Section 501(c)(3) of the Internal Revenue Code, enjoy a unique tax status whereby they are exempt from corporate taxes, local property taxes on land and buildings, and, as long as direct political activity does not constitute a significant amount of organizational resources, donors are eligible to deduct contributions from their income taxes. Thus, while the nonprofit sector shares some characteristics with the for-profit sector and the public sector, it is distinctly different from each.

Burton A. Weisbrod has done extensive research on the nonprofit sector and its relationship with the public and for-profit sectors.[26] He argues that the key distinctions between the three lie in the different constraints and goals under which each sector operates. For example, the tax exemptions that nonprofits enjoy are justified on the grounds that their services are of a public nature. These unique tax benefits, however, can create disparate levels of competitiveness with for-profit firms operating in the same industry. At the same time, those in the nonprofit sector are under more political constraints than are those in the for-profit sector, where lobbying activity is far less circumscribed. The public sector, through regulatory policy, has a great deal of influence over the activities of both for-profit and nonprofit organizations.

Other ways in which the three sectors differ involve their labor forces and the behavior and structure of their organizations. These differences have a clear impact on how organizations in the three sectors are managed. For example, as Weisbrod explains, nonprofit organizations receive vast amounts of voluntary labor, which means that they have lower overall labor costs. Only in the public school system does the public sector even come close to the nonprofit sector in the amount of labor volunteered; in for-profit organizations, voluntary labor is extremely rare.[27] This leads to a difference in organizational goals and outcomes, as nonprofits are often better suited to labor-intensive work than comparable for-profit organizations. Furthermore, organizations in fields such as social services, education, and health care have, until recently, found profits relatively difficult to attain. The reliance on voluntary labor, of course, results in unique challenges for human resource managers in nonprofit organizations.

Differences in organizational behavior are also driven by the distinct ways in which each sector governs its resources. The for-profit sector, because it is dependent upon sales for financial resources, will only produce what it can sell at a profit. Further, for-profits can be expected to minimize production costs and to provide goods or services only to those capable of paying for them. In the public sector, which is dependent upon taxes for its resources, provision of goods and services will be determined via political processes; this provision can be expected to be offered at little or no direct cost to citizens. For the nonprofit sector, dependent on gifts, donations, and grants for its revenue, goods and services can be distributed as the nonprofit organization sees fit.

However, there are typically constraints on nonprofit organizations, as funders often attach conditions or restrictions on the use of their gifts and grants. Obviously, nonprofit boards and executive directors seek to minimize the conditions imposed because they have more discretion over the use of organizational income when there are fewer strings attached. When not-for-profit organizations face extensive restrictions on the use of their resources, or when they receive grants and gifts for specific uses, they may find themselves subject to co-optation or mission drift, in which the organization loses touch with its stated mission and takes on new priorities to fit grantor or donor wishes. This problem highlights the crucial nature of the mission for nonprofit organizations and their wise use of resources; the centrality of mission for nonprofits is the focus of Chapter 5.

Finally, the three sectors differ with regard to organizational structure. The level of interaction with the public, the degree to which formal oversight exists, and how oversight is conducted vary between entities in the nonprofit, for-profit, and public sectors.[28] For example, organizations in the public sector are widely recognized to be the most hierarchical because of the high levels of constraint and authority that legislative bodies and members of the public exercise over government agencies. In the for-profit sector, organizations are under the constraint and authority of shareholders, a board of directors, and/or the owner of the firm, while politics and the general public have little direct influence on organizational behavior. The nonprofit sector lies somewhere in between these two. Because of their public purposes, nonprofits must be attentive to the political sensitivities of the communities they serve, but boards of directors often take a very hands-off approach.[29] Not-for-profit organizations typically have flatter and more informal structures than organizations in the other sectors.[30] Table 2.1 gives an overview of the different characteristics generally associated with organizations in each of the three sectors.

TABLE 2.1 Basic Differences between the Nonprofit, Public, and Private Sectors of the Economy

Characteristics	Nonprofit Sector	Public Sector	Private Sector
Social model	Civil society	Political society	Market society
Public participation	Voluntary	Required	Voluntary
Type of goods provided	Public/quasi-public goods	Public/collective goods	Private goods
What is valued?	Achievement of social purposes and satisfaction of donors	Achievement of politically mandated mission	Financial returns delivered to shareholders
Goal specificity	General, mission driven	General, politically determined	Specific, profit driven
Source of financial resources	Grants, gifts, donations, fees	Taxes, fees	Sales
Earns profit?	Yes; profits must be directed back into the organization	No	Yes; profit-seeking
Provides goods/ services via what mechanism?	Organizational mission; donor/ grantor direction	Political processes	Market forces; profit maximization
Source of authority	Board of directors	Citizens; government institutions (executives, legislatures, judiciary)	Board of directors; shareholders; corporate executive or owner
Organizational structure	Less formal	Hierarchical/ bureaucratic	Hierarchical
Labor	Typically "at will"; large percent of volunteers	Often civil service/ union protections; rarely volunteer	Typically "at will"; occasional union protections; very rarely volunteers

Intersectorality and Welfare Policy

The nonprofit, for-profit, and public sectors intersect in many ways and on many policy problems, and nowhere is that more evident than in the area of welfare policy. While social services have long been provided by the public and nonprofit sectors acting together and independently, the 1996 reform of the welfare program Aid to Families with Dependent Children (AFDC) brought the for-profit sector into this policy area in new and important ways. The events leading up to this reform exemplify nonprofit federalism and the intersection of the public, for-profit, and nonprofit sectors.

As a presidential candidate in 1992, Bill Clinton vowed "to put an end to welfare as we know it" if elected president. This was not Clinton's first foray into the world of welfare reform; in 1988 as Governor of Arkansas and chair of the National Governors Association, Clinton had secured broad support from the nation's governors to pass the first freestanding welfare reform bill in 26 years, the federal Family Support Act.[31] Thus, when President Clinton signed the Personal Responsibility and Work Opportunity Reconciliation Act (PRWORA) in 1996, it is not surprising that it gave more discretion to the states over their welfare programs.

The change in authority over the welfare program occurred through what is known as devolution, a process by which the federal government passes program responsibility and funding to the states.[32] PRWORA, better known simply as "welfare reform," changed the entitlement status of the former AFDC program and replaced it with a time-limited, work-oriented program, Temporary Assistance to Needy Families (TANF). These changes to the nation's largest safety net program for children and their parents gained the attention of many groups—both among governments and among the nonprofit and for-profit sectors—that influenced the direction of the final welfare reform. These groups included the National Governors Association, the National League of Cities, and the U.S. Conference of Mayors. [33] In addition, there was strong opposition to a number of proposed reform provisions, voiced most notably by nonprofit advocates of the poor such as the Center for Law and Social Policy, Catholic Charities USA, and the Children's Defense Fund.[34]

As the opening vignette illustrates, the reformed program requires that adult welfare recipients obtain jobs within two years, and much of the program is administered at the local level, through what is known as second order devolution. At the local level, delivery of services to clients is often completed by nonprofit and for-profit sector contractors. The reasons for the increased use of contractors in welfare provision are fairly clear. As Winston, Burwick, McConnell, and Roper explain, "Welfare reform provided an impetus to privatization in several ways. Its work requirements spurred states and localities to find new ways to deliver employment services. By dropping the requirement that eligibility for cash assistance be determined by public employees, it encouraged contracting out of a broader set of services. And the change to funding through block grants gave new incentives for privatization."[35]

Add to these incentives the most common reasons that governments use contractors—purported cost savings and ease of program start-up—and welfare assistance became a policy area ripe for service delivery by organizations outside of the public sector. A study by the U.S. General Accounting Office (GAO) found that state and local governments in forty-nine states and the District of Columbia had used contractors for TANF-related services by 2001; of the one billion dollars spent on federal and state TANF contracts that year, approximately 87 percent went to nonprofit organizations.[36]

The complexity of these intersectoral relationships is illustrated in an Urban Institute report on contracting between the nonprofit and public sectors, which found nearly 33,000 nonprofit organizations implementing 200,000 government contracts for human service programs in 2009. Over three-quarters of these nonprofits have more than one government contract and similar numbers of organizations have contracts with local, state, and federal agencies. While these nonprofits influence clients and policy by their direct service delivery, the vast majority are also subject to policy regulations as a condition of their grant receipt. For example, over 60 percent of organizations reported that their government contracts explicitly limit administrative spending, 54 percent require matching grants or cost sharing, and 89 percent are required to submit reports on the results and outcomes of their programs.[37]

Faith-Based Organizations

Adding even more complexity to social service delivery, the 1996 welfare reform act included a provision known as Charitable Choice, which encouraged states and counties:

> . . . to increase the participation of nonprofit organizations in the provision of federally funded welfare programs, with specific mention of faith-based organizations; establish eligibility for faith-based organizations as contractors for services on the same basis as other organizations; protect the religious character and employment exemption status of participating faith-based organizations; and safeguard the religious freedom of participants.[38]

Although it was included in the 1996 welfare reform, the Charitable Choice provision did not receive much attention until 2001, when President George W. Bush institutionalized it with the formation of his Office of Faith-Based Initiatives. Three assumptions led to creation of the office: (1) that faith-based organizations (FBOs) are discriminated against in the awarding of public funds; (2) a large number of FBOs would like to partner with government to serve the most needy but are an untapped resource; and (3) FBOs are more effective than secular providers at transforming the lives of those in need. Bush's Office of Faith-Based Initiatives fueled the controversy over Charitable Choice because it represented a shift from merely allowing faith-based organizations to compete in limited ways for government grants and contracts to specifically encouraging their participation and affording explicit protection for religious practices.[39]

Concerns about the use of FBOs in social service delivery have come from people of various points of view, including: (1) those concerned about the perceived conflict with First

Amendment protections from state-sponsored religious activity;[40] (2) those concerned about the lack of capacity that small religious organizations have to compete for public contracts;[41] (3) those concerned that Charitable Choice may not actually offer choice to clients but rather lock them into seeking services from FBOs;[42] and (4) social work professionals who believe that "the driving force behind social change should remain the responsibility of the state."[43] What the research suggests is that concern over Charitable Choice and FBOs was largely unfounded.[44]

First, there is little evidence to support the contention of discrimination against FBOs. Catholic Charities USA and the Salvation Army, for example, have long partnered with government in the provision of social services. In addition, approximately 70 percent of soup kitchens and food pantries are run by religiously-affiliated organizations, and many receive federal commodities.[45] Second, despite efforts by state agencies to recruit FBOs, it appears that few submit applications for federal funding.[46] Rather, faith-based social service coalitions continue to be primarily funded by individuals and congregations; government grants are their third most common revenue source.[47] In 2004, the most recent year for which data are available, less than 13 percent of federal social service grants went to FBOs.[48] Finally, the research indicates that there are few differences in effectiveness between faith-based and secular providers of welfare services; most differences are small and seemingly represent disparate strengths rather than inherent weaknesses.[49] Accordingly, the fears of those who were concerned about Charitable Choice should be somewhat allayed.

Not-for-Profit Organizations as Government Contractors

The concern that small FBOs and other neighborhood nonprofits lack the capacity to administer government grants and contracts, on the other hand, likely has merit.[50] The costs of monitoring program progress, reporting, and auditing often exceed the capacity of small nonprofits. It is important, therefore, that nonprofit organizations consider these costs as well as the possible benefits before seeking public contracts.

Benefits. First, in their public policy role, not-for-profit organizations are often eager to contract with governments to meet the needs of citizens in their communities. Their level of experience and expertise in specific policy areas and their first-hand knowledge of the communities they serve often make nonprofits indispensable allies in the provision of public goods and services. In fact, Salamon notes that nonprofit organizations "frequently find themselves in the fortuitous position of needing the federal government less than the federal government needs them."[51] Second, nonprofits can gain much needed financial resources from government contracting. Those contracts can add legitimacy to individual organizations, which enhances their reputations and, in turn, leads to greater access to other government grants and sources of funding.[52] In addition, competition with for-profit firms for government grants and contracts can foster innovation and improve performance in nonprofit organizations.[53]

Costs. The disadvantages for nonprofits include the fact that government funding is often insufficient to meet citizen needs for services and that governments often have accounting and reporting requirements that may be difficult for small nonprofits to meet.[54] Small organizations may feel pressure to employ a more professional staff to meet these requirements.[55] Most importantly, the services for which the organization has been contracted may not coincide with the historic mission of the nonprofit organization. Indeed, a common concern in managing nonprofits is that chasing either government or foundation money will lead the organization away from its primary mission and take it into policy areas, communities, or services that have little to do with the original purpose of the organization. This is an important problem known as mission drift and will be revisited in both Chapters 5 and 9.

INTERSECTORAL COMPETITION

Several factors, including the drive toward public sector privatization, have facilitated competition between organizations in the three sectors. While the public and nonprofit sectors have long been partners in service delivery, the entry of for-profit organizations into new markets like welfare assistance and job training came as a bit of a shock, especially to nonprofit organizations with long histories in these policy arenas. In some cases public policies have created incentives for profit-making firms to enter areas previously dominated by nonprofits. In health policy, for example, the federal HMO (Health Maintenance Organization) Act of 1973 encouraged employers to offer a choice of health insurance options to employees and opened the market to for-profit firms that saw the potential for growth.

Thus, as Salamon reports, nonprofits have lost market share particularly quickly to for-profit organizations in the health care field.[56] Gray and Schlesinger explain that "Publicly traded, investor-owned companies that own multiple facilities have become typical in all domains within health care, including hospitals, nursing homes, HMOs, dialysis centers, and even hospices."[57] In this environment, it is increasingly difficult and yet often more important for nonprofit organizations to maintain a political voice as advocates for themselves and the clients and communities they serve. Lobbyists hired by for-profit health organizations generally have greater access to elected officials and can more easily pursue public policies favorable to their clients. For example, for-profit lobbyists have sought to change the state and local tax-exempt status of nonprofit hospitals and have fought against rules restricting the conversion of nonprofit hospitals to for-profit status.[58]

Government grants and contracts have encouraged intersectoral competition in other ways. For example, few could have imagined that in the wake of welfare reform nonprofit organizations would have to compete against a defense contractor for social welfare contracts. That is exactly what happened in 1996 when Lockheed-Martin created its Welfare Reform Services Division and won eleven welfare contracts in three states.[59] Such competition, particularly for small, community-based organizations, has had a notable impact on nonprofits as they compete with profit-making firms in delivery of social welfare services.[60]

The structure of most government contracts for welfare assistance relies on performance-based measures that reward quick job placement for clients. These policies provide an example of the ways in which nonprofits are subject to public policy, as they have had immediate effects on nonprofit providers of welfare services. For example, most of these contracts provide payment on a per-client basis and only after job placement has been secured; for the nonprofit organization without vast resources with which to sustain itself, these policies can have devastating consequences. The incentives in this system can lead providers to eschew more costly support services and to engage in creaming, which involves serving the easiest-to-place clients first, leaving the most vulnerable, those with significant or multiple barriers to employment, without sufficient assistance. Sanger summarizes the dilemma: "Valuable and worthy nonprofits are becoming more businesslike; some have even formed for-profit subsidiaries. However, they also show signs of 'losing their souls' in their capitulation to market imperatives. Still others risk extinction."[61] This dilemma represents a significant struggle for nonprofits as they seek to improve efficiency in the management of resources while maintaining effectiveness in the pursuit of mission, topics discussed in depth in later chapters.

In addition, there are simple market forces that have led to increased intersectoral competition, particularly between the for-profit and nonprofit sectors.[62] The growing financial needs of nonprofit organizations have led them to compete with for-profit firms through commercial ventures. These activities—for example, the Girl Scouts' cookie sales, insurance packages through AARP—may or may not negatively affect the core mission of the organization but are increasingly important as a potential source of organizational revenues.

Many scholars and practitioners have expressed concerns about for-profit ventures and values creeping into the world of nonprofits, including market rivalries between nonprofit and for-profit organizations which have often resulted in complaints of unfair competition from both sides.[63] How does one justify the tax-exempt status of a nonprofit day-care center, for example, when a for-profit center receives no such tax benefit? Further, critics have asked, if nonprofits perform the same functions as organizations in the for-profit sector—nursing homes, hospitals, job training centers—are they not simply "for-profits in disguise"?

Evidence indicates that the answer to this question is no; most studies show that nonprofits behave differently from for-profits even in the same industry.[64] Nonprofit hospitals, for example, are more likely to locate in poor, underserved areas while for-profits are more likely to locate in communities where people can afford to pay for their services.[65] In provision of services to welfare clients, nonprofit providers have continued to demonstrate their commitment to helping long-term recipients overcome the many barriers to employment that they face while for-profit firms have been found to avoid this clientele because they are more expensive to serve.[66] Most nonprofits take their role as representatives of civil society very seriously and use their organizational missions to guide their activities. This results in different organizational behavior even when serving the same clientele as their for-profit competitors.

Those in the nonprofit sector are often concerned that in the competitive marketplace nonprofits are at a disadvantage; however, research indicates that nonprofit organizations do not have to lose to for-profit firms in the competitive market.[67] Their advantage lies in what has been called the "distinctiveness imperative," the ability of nonprofits to maintain their positions because of attributes such as trustworthiness and their ability to serve social purposes without concern about profit.[68]

Relying on examples of community development corporations and technology assistance providers, Marwell and McInerney describe three possible outcomes for nonprofit agencies in the competitive marketplace: displaced markets, stratified markets, and defended markets.[69] Their research suggests that nonprofits are only at risk of being displaced when many consumers find themselves with the means to purchase a service and for-profit providers find the market to be profitable, as has been the experience for some health care providers. In the stratified market, both for-profit and nonprofit organizations find their own niche by serving distinct groups of citizens (for example, low-income versus upper-income families). In defended markets, organizations in the nonprofit sector continue to be highly valued as providers based on their ability to address societal needs; thus, for-profits generally lack an incentive to compete and do not enter these markets.

Nonprofit managers must understand that they will have to work harder than ever to succeed in this increasingly competitive environment. For example, it is important for nonprofits to improve their management capacity in order to compete successfully, even in policy areas that have traditionally been within their purview.[70] In addition, not-for-profit sector managers must recognize their strengths and weaknesses in this new, competitive environment using their perceived trustworthiness to their advantage and understanding that labor-intensive, complex, and highly visible policies are well-suited to implementation by their organizations. O'Regan and Oster explain, "Nonprofits perform well in the provision of complex, hard-to-evaluate goods and services, and when the ability to sharply reward managers is less important than the ability of those managers to keep focused on matters of long-term reputation and goals and to balance the interests of various constituents who have a stake in the operation."[71]

INTERSECTORAL COLLABORATION

While intersectoral competition is an important trend, nonprofits also find opportunities to work in collaboration with those in the for-profit and public sectors as well as with other nonprofits. Partnerships between multiple nonprofits are often formed to share needed resources—physical space, information technology, payroll services, or fundraising capacity—especially for small organizations.[72] A nonprofit sometimes forms a partnership with multiple organizations from all three sectors; this happens often in welfare policy delivery. One example of this type of collaborative effort is the Detroit area Downriver Community Conference Partnership (DCC), which works in the area of welfare-to-work policy. (See Box 2.1.)

Box 2.1

FOR EXAMPLE

THE DOWNRIVER COMMUNITY CONFERENCE PARTNERSHIP: COLLABORATING ACROSS SECTORS

Highlighting the concepts of nonprofit federalism and intersectorality is the nonprofit Downriver Community Conference Partnership (DCC) in the suburbs south of Detroit, Michigan. DCC members include 19 cities, the nonprofit Arab Community Center for Economic and Social Services, the Southeast Michigan Council of Governments, the Southern Wayne Regional Chamber of Commerce, and the for-profit firms Ross Innovative Employment Solutions and Employment & Training Designs, Inc. Both state and federal grants allow the DCC to provide employment services to welfare clients through the Michigan Jobs, Education and Training (JET) program. The state Department of Human Services refers clients to the DCC, which operates seven Employment Service Centers in the region. These centers provide job search assistance, offer information on resume writing, provide access to occupation guides and career exploration tools, and link employees with employers. As a registered 501(c)(3) organization, DCC accepts cash donations and operates the Chrysalis Boutique, which takes donations of gently used work clothing and offers it free to low-income men and women for job interviews and the workplace.

For information on the Downriver Community Conference Partnership: www.dccwf.org/index.php.

Collaborations between the nonprofit and public sectors are extensive—from public policy research and development to project planning—and operate in a wide variety of policy areas, from the environment to social welfare to education. While there is no definitive research to indicate how many of these collaborative arrangements exist, they are clearly considered a growing trend. In one of the only studies to empirically examine these collaborations, Beth Gazeley and Jeffrey L. Brudney surveyed hundreds of nonprofit and local public sector organizations in Georgia, finding that intersectoral partnerships were extensive; over half of the respondents reported that they were involved in at least one cross-sector collaboration.[73]

Essential to the success of these partnerships was mission compatibility, a motivation to partner, and sufficient staff resources to manage the collaborative project. Importantly for public sector managers, local governments reported more benefits from partnership than did those in the nonprofit sector, including improved service delivery and higher levels of citizen satisfaction and trust in government.[74] The Gazeley and Brudney study confirms that the motivations for collaboration differ by sector; for nonprofit organizations the desire to increase revenues motivates partnership, while the public sector seeks partnerships to access expertise.

As noted earlier, public sector privatization has opened the doors to a variety of collaborative arrangements between the three sectors. For example, Salamon[75] and Sanger[76] each note that nonprofit organizations have become subcontractors, hired by for-profit organizations to deliver welfare services paid for by public grants. In other cases, nonprofits have become the prime contractors. For example, O'Regan and Oster[77] note that nonprofit sector organizations have subcontracted to for-profit firms when tasks lend themselves to a businesslike emphasis on cost, such as human resource management, particularly when labor negotiations are involved.

There are also examples where the nonprofit and for-profit sectors have formed equal partnerships to provide government contract work. In Wisconsin's welfare program, Wisconsin Works (W-2), the YWCA of Greater Milwaukee has partnered with two for-profit firms, the Kaiser Group and CNR Health, to manage and provide welfare services in the Milwaukee area by forming YW-Works, organized as a limited liability for-profit company. The fact that YW-Works is a profit-making venture with profits shared among its three partners allows the YWCA to reinvest its portion of the profits back into the organization, while the for-profit partners can redistribute profits to shareholders.[78]

An important trend in collaborations involves for-profit organizational donations that help nonprofits operate their programs and projects. For-profit firms have donated goods such as groceries to food pantries and computers to job-training sites. While the public sector motivation for partnership with nonprofits is typically to make use of nonprofit expertise, and the nonprofit motivation for partnership with either the public or private sector is usually to gain resources, firms in the for-profit sector are typically motivated to collaborate with nonprofits in the name of creating goodwill in the community.[79]

For example, we see many efforts by major corporations across the United States, including American Express, Coca-Cola, and Eddie Bauer, to partner with nonprofit organizations. Minneapolis-based retailer Target Corporation annually donates 5 percent of its income to community grants and projects and has done so since 1946.[80] In addition, Target has teamed with Proctor & Gamble once a year since 1999 to donate a portion of the purchase price of Proctor & Gamble products to St. Jude's Children's Hospital in Memphis, Tennessee. Together, this partnership had raised nearly $7 million for the hospital by 2009.[81] We discuss the pros and cons of these partnerships in Chapter 9.

In many cases such partnerships simply provide revenue for nonprofits engaged in meeting public needs, as in the case of St. Jude's, while in other cases, collaborative efforts are at the forefront of public policymaking. An example comes from efforts to remake the languishing city of Detroit through the New Economy Initiative, a complex collaborative effort involving nonprofits making important public policy decisions concerning transportation, land use, and industrial development strategies in collaboration with city government and for-profit firms. Among the initiatives being undertaken are investments in education, reviving a culture of entrepreneurship, industrial property reuse, and creation of a light-rail system. The Ford Foundation is the primary funder of the light-rail project and will pay the costs of land use planning and acquisition of property for stops along the rail line. To address the problem of an over-abundance of vacant land in the city, the Kresge Foundation has hired a nonprofit consultant, Initiative for a Competitive Inner City (ICIC), to develop an industrial development strategy. The ICIC has hired a for-profit urban planning firm to assist in assessment and planning for industrial reuse throughout Detroit. For its part, city government has sought to open additional land parcels to new uses and eliminate blighted neighborhoods by encouraging residents in sparsely populated parts of the city to relocate to nine districts that have been deemed more viable. The city's policy strategy has included removing federal housing subsidies and reducing city services such as trash removal in blighted areas; it will use federal funding to rebuild and renovate homes in the nine viable districts as an incentive for residents in the city and suburbs to relocate.[82]

There are policy implications for government when the public sector is a partner in such extensive collaborations. For example, might a city lose control over land use planning when a private foundation is funding the project, or might a public agency be left picking up the pieces after a failed collaboration? What is the appropriate level of government oversight and regulation under these circumstances? Collaborations of such magnitude are new enough that they lead us to more questions than conclusions.

Occasionally, partnerships between nonprofits and for-profits can create or change public policy without government involvement. One such example is the Alliance for a Healthier Generation, which has changed food and beverage policies in thousands of public schools across the nation without government policymaking. (See Case Study 2.2.) These partnerships showcase the goodwill of for-profit firms, which enhances their reputations, while at the same time helping their nonprofit partners make a positive impact on society. As Salamon explains, "The most successful of these efforts deliver benefits to both the corporation and the nonprofit."[83]

These intersectoral collaborative efforts have been facilitated by groups such as the Independent Sector's Three Sector Initiative. A collaboration of seven groups from the public, nonprofit, and for-profit sectors, the Three Sector Initiative has been examining the changing relationships between the sectors since 2000.[84] These changes have led some to argue that the blurring of the sectors places us at the threshold of a new type of organizational unit: the for-benefit organization which will lie somewhere outside of the traditional three economic sectors, with a common interest in pursuing social purposes through business activity.[85]

In an interesting example of how nonprofits are affected by public policy that is not directly related to them, several states have recently facilitated this sector blurring by passing Benefit Corporation (B Corp) legislation. Beginning in April 2010, Maryland became the first state in the nation to allow incorporation under B Corp status, creating a new type of for-profit corporation that is required to: (1) create a positive social or environmental impact, (2) consider non-financial interests as part of expanded fiduciary responsibilities, and (3) report its social and environmental performance as assessed by a third party. Because B Corps allow organizations to pursue a socially responsible mission while also distributing profits to owners and shareholders, some policy entrepreneurs will likely choose this route rather than start a nonprofit endeavor.

The nonprofit organization B Lab is the leader in advocacy for and certification of B Corps. It argues that B Corp status allows company boards and officers the ability to pursue both social mission and financial profits, while ensuring greater transparency to investors

CASE STUDY 2.2

The Alliance for a Healthier Generation Partners with For-Profits to Make Public Policy

In May 2005, two nonprofits, the American Heart Association and the William J. Clinton Foundation, joined forces to create the Alliance for a Healthier Generation, which seeks to "reduce the nationwide prevalence of childhood obesity by 2015." Working with for-profit partners in the food and beverage industries, the Alliance has made important strides in a short time. For example, together with the American Beverage Association (ABA)—the trade association of non-alcoholic beverage companies—the Alliance created a set of School Beverage Guidelines in 2006 with a memorandum of understanding that ABA bottlers and distributors would amend their contracts with public schools and districts to include more low-calorie and high-nutrient beverage choices in the public school system.

By 2010, the ABA's final progress report indicated that 98.8 percent of schools—both those with compliance contracts *and without*—were in compliance with the School Beverage Guidelines. In addition, the ABA reported that the amount of full-calorie carbonated soft-drinks shipped to the nation's schools had decreased by 95 percent from 2004 and the percent of calories in school beverages had been cut by 88 percent.

These extraordinary results affect some 135,000 schools and over 53 million students in the U.S. The Alliance's corporate partners in this effort included the three major U.S. soft-drink manufacturers, Coca-Cola, PepsiCo, and the Dr Pepper Snapple Group. The creation and implementation of the School Beverage Guidelines was accomplished without government involvement; in effect, public policy in tens of thousands of school districts across the country was changed by a partnership of organizations in the nonprofit and for-profit sectors.

Building upon this success, the Alliance for a Healthier Generation created a set of Competitive Foods Guidelines to help schools make healthier choices outside of their standard meal programs—for example, in food offered in vending machines, a la carte during meal times, and in school stores. As with the original beverage partnership, participating companies included the biggest names in the food industry, including Kraft Foods, Dole Food Company, and Mott's, as well as smaller, regional companies such as Anderson Erickson Dairy, Farmland Dairies, and Shamrock Farms.

At the same time, the Alliance started the Healthy Schools Program, which includes more than 13,000 participating schools and encourages physical activity and healthier eating. Healthy Schools provides a variety of resources, including free on-line tools such as the Healthy Schools Product Navigator; web tips to encourage healthier school parties and fundraisers; and resources for parents, community members, and schools interested in learning more and/or joining the Healthy Schools Program. The Alliance annually recognizes schools that have successfully created healthier campuses through designations of bronze, silver, gold, or platinum, and designates ten individuals as Healthy Schools Program Champions. These awards are presented at the Alliance's annual Healthy Schools Program Forum. There is no cost to schools to join the Healthy Schools Program.

More recently, in 2011, the Alliance announced a voluntary agreement with major food industry companies such as McCain Foods USA, Rich Products Corporation, and Schwan's Food Service, to provide healthier food options to U.S. schools at competitive prices. Participating food companies have pledged to increase the sales of compliant products by at least 50 percent within five years. Further, the agreement streamlines the ordering process and makes it easier for schools to identify healthier food options, including those high in protein, low in fat, and cooked without trans fats.

The efforts of the Alliance have been recognized nationally, as it was ranked in 2010 by Philanthropedia as tenth out of 100 nonprofits in the category of Nonprofit in Childhood Nutrition/Health. The Alliance for a Healthier Generation continues to affect policy in food, nutrition, and exercise in U.S. schools without aid of legislation, executive orders, or judicial settlements. Public policy has been advocated, made, and implemented by voluntary agreements between the nonprofit and for-profit sectors and the support of public schools and school districts across the nation.

QUESTIONS TO CONSIDER:

1. What motivated for-profit food and beverage companies to amend their sales contracts with public schools to meet voluntary standards such as the School Beverage Guidelines?
2. Why did beverage sales patterns change in schools ***without*** contracts or memorandums of understanding?
3. What does this case suggest about making public policy without formal passage of legislation?
4. Is this example unique? If so, in what ways? If not, in what other policy areas might voluntary agreements between the nonprofit and for-profit sectors be successful in making public policy?

Additional information is available at www.healthiergeneration.org and www.schoolbeverages.com.

and other stakeholders. This can be particularly important when a for-profit company faces a liquidity scenario, as in the example of Ben & Jerry's, the ice cream company well known for its socially responsible business practices. In 2000, when Unilever offered to buy the company for $326 million, founders Ben Cohen and Jerry Greenfield were concerned that their social responsibility goals would be ignored. The legal advice given to the board of directors, however, indicated the sale should go forward: the board was advised that their primary concern was the financial best interests of their shareholders.[86] Today, the Vermont-based Ben and Jerry's could have sought incorporation as a B Corp to ensure both their socially responsible vision and their fiduciary responsibilities to shareholders, since Vermont is one

GOING GLOBAL 2.3

Cafédirect Works across the Sectors, Creating De Facto Policy

Cafédirect offers an interesting example of sector blurring and international cooperation in the area of fairly traded coffee, tea, and cocoa. The story of its creation begins with the International Coffee Organization (ICO), an intergovernmental organization that brings together exporting and importing governments to address the challenges of coffee production and sales through international cooperation. Since 1963, the ICO has brokered seven International Coffee Agreements. Cafédirect was founded in 1991 after the collapse of the 1989 International Coffee Agreement dramatically decreased market prices and threatened coffee growers in developing nations. This partnership between the public, for-profit, and nonprofit sectors led to the first company to market coffee under the Fairtrade label in the United Kingdom.

Cafédirect provides a link between grower and consumer communities, works with over 39 grower organizations in 13 developing countries, and benefits more than a quarter million farmers around the world through its three core commitments: (1) Grower Focused in All We Do; (2) Integrated Environmental Action; and (3) An Inspirational & Accountable Business. Its Fairtrade obligation requires reinvestment of 30 percent of Cafédirect's profits, although it has actually reinvested over 50 percent of profits in its 20 years in business. Reinvestment funds have helped to develop growers' businesses and the communities in which they farm and live. Since 2009, its development projects have been managed by the Cafédirect Producers' Foundation (CPF), a nonprofit organization formed by Cafédirect and led by growers. The nonprofit status of CPF allows it to raise additional funding to support growers and provide them access to training, education, and other services needed to improve their operations.

Given the nature of intersectoral collaborations and the longevity of Cafédirect, it is not surprising that the original partnership has undergone changes beyond the creation of CPF in 2009. For example, three of its original partners, Traidcraft, Twin Trading, and Equal Exchange, sold their shares in 2010[87] and in 2011.[88] Cafédirect partnered with Oikocredit Ecumenical Development Society U.A., a worldwide microfinance cooperative that shares resources through socially responsible investing, as a way to further its commitment to global justice. Oxfam, an international nonprofit whose mission is "a global movement of people working with others to overcome poverty and suffering" has retained its role as a founding partner and continues to sell Cafédirect products on its website.

The nature of the international community means that there can be no global policymaking in the way that policy is made in the United States. On the other hand, nongovernmental organizations (NGOs) such as Cafédirect exist to address the very real needs of communities around the globe. The collaboration that created Cafédirect is an example of people in the public, for-profit, and nonprofit sectors joining forces to mitigate the dramatic consequences of the breakdown of the 1989 International Coffee Agreement. They pursued collective action on a global scale, making de facto policy while operating outside of any formal policymaking sphere to better the working and living conditions of coffee growers in developing countries.

For more information:

Cafédirect, http://cafedirect.co.uk

Oikocredit Ecumenical Development Society U.A., www.oikocredit.org/en/home

Oxfam, www.oxfam.org/

of eleven states to have passed B Corp legislation. The other states with legislation include California, Hawaii, Illinois, Virginia, Maryland, Massachusetts, Louisiana, New Jersey, New York, and South Carolina; legislation is pending in Colorado, Pennsylvania, and Washington, D.C. The subsequent impact on the nonprofit sector from this change in public policy is an worthy topic for future study.

An interesting international example of the for-benefit concept comes from Cafédirect, a Fair Trade beverage company based in the United Kingdom that purchases coffee, tea, and cocoa directly from small growers in Africa, Latin America, and Asia. (See Going Global 2.3.) This unique partnership was created by four organizations: (1) Equal Exchange, a worker cooperative; (2) the international nonprofit; (3) foundation-owned Traidcraft; and (4) the government-created agency Twin Trading.[89] Whether or not sector blurring will truly result in a new form of organization remains to be seen, but it is certainly true that the relationships between the public, for-profit, and nonprofit sectors are increasingly complex.[90]

CONCLUSION

In this chapter we have covered a great deal of ground: from the founding of the United States and the creation of its federal system, to nonprofit federalism, which describes the current complex relationship between nonprofits and federal, state, and local governments. In the past several decades, the entry of for-profit organizations has added to the complexity of delivering services and implementing policy in the public interest. At every point in U.S. history, voluntary associations have played an important part through their role as Citizen, representing civil society in the push and pull between the public, nonprofit, and for-profit sectors. For example, this push and pull was seen clearly in the fight over slavery in the mid-nineteenth century. The economic interests of plantation farmers, the public interests of the states and federal government, and the civil and religious interests represented by anti-slavery societies created a volatile period in U.S. history, and the influence that nonprofits had over the politics and policy of the issue are exemplified by the Emancipation Proclamation and the Fifteenth Amendment. Today, the relationships between the three sectors can be conflictual or cooperative, depending on the issue.

Although each of the three sectors in the U.S. economy has its own distinct motives, goals, and organizational structure, the three sectors are intertwined, particularly in the arena of public policies and programs. Whether through direct service delivery, program funding, advocacy, collaboration, or contracting, the intersectorality of the system is apparent. As was discussed, this is especially true in the social welfare policy arena where federal welfare reform in 1996 gave state governments increasing responsibility for welfare provision and reform. Many states looked to local governments to deliver services, and all three levels of government increased their reliance on contractors—both nonprofit and for-profit—for delivery of welfare services.

These contracting relationships create opportunities for nonprofits to influence the direction of public policies and programs. First, contracting offers access to a fairly consistent stream of revenue. Government grants can also affect nonprofit involvement in public policy by inviting new organizations to participate in public programs, as the Social Security Act amendments did in the 1960s and the Charitable Choice provisions of welfare reform did for faith-based organizations. However, acting as public sector agents can also be problematic, especially for small organizations that may lack the capacity to effectively compete for government grants. Other times, grants may subject nonprofit agencies to requirements that cause them to deviate from their stated missions to win a contract, or to spend precious resources monitoring and measuring their performance to satisfy government auditors.

The U.S. system, characterized by both nonprofit federalism and intersectorality, is incredibly complex, and it is becoming more and more difficult for the average citizen to know where government ends and the nonprofit and for-profit sectors begin. Competition and collaboration between organizations in the three sectors have opened opportunities for each sector and at the same time shed light on the weaknesses of each. To be successful, it is imperative for those managing not-for-profit agencies to remember their fundamental missions and the distinctiveness of their organizations in the broader system. In addition to good management practices, nonprofit managers must remember that they have several advantages over the Merchant and the Prince: their perceived trustworthiness, their ability to act as advocates for the citizens and communities that they serve, and their expertise in addressing the complex, hard-to-evaluate problems of individuals in modern society.

Questions For Review

1. How do the increasing use of nonprofit federalism and the role of public sector contracts and grants affect nonprofit organizations, for better and for worse? Give specific examples from the reading and/or your own experience.
2. Describe the differences between the public, nonprofit, and private sectors in the United States. Are the differences as described in this chapter real and meaningful, or have the three sectors increasingly become indistinguishable from one another?

3. The three sectors are engaged in both collaboration and competition. In what ways are the public and private sectors helpful to the nonprofit sector and in what ways are they harmful to the nonprofit sector?

Assignment

For this web-based assignment, you will need to think of a specific policy or service area in which all three sectors, nonprofit, public, and for-profit, operate. The examples abound: from arts and entertainment to daycare centers and education, the intersectorality of the American economy is difficult to miss. Once you have determined a specific area of inquiry, search the web to find examples of organizations in each sector that deliver the same basic goods or services. Note the similarities and differences between the three in terms of web design and style, their references to the people they serve, and the people who manage and run the organizations, their sources of income, their organizational missions, vision statements, goals, and so on. Can you easily tell which organizations are in which sector, or are the distinctions between the three sectors blurred?

Suggested Readings

Boris, Elizabeth T., and C. Eugene Steuerle. *Nonprofits and Government, Collaboration and Conflict.* Washington, DC: Urban Institute Press, 2006.

Lipset, Seymour Martin. *American Exceptionalism: A Double-Edged Sword.* New York: W.W. Norton & Company, 1996.

McCarthy, Kathleen D. *American Creed: Philanthropy and the Rise of Civil Society, 1700–1865.* Chicago: University of Chicago Press, 2003.

Salamon, Lester M. *Partners in Public Service.* Baltimore: Johns Hopkins University Press, 1995.

Weisbrod, Burton A., editor. *To Profit or Not to Profit: The Commercial Transformation of the Nonprofit Sector.* New York: Cambridge University Press, 1998.

Weaver, R. Kent. *Ending Welfare as We Know It.* Washington, DC: Brookings Institution Press, 2000.

Web Resources

B Corporation, www.bcorporation.net/

Census Bureau Federal Audit Clearinghouse, "Data Collection Form for Reporting on Audits of States, Local Governments and Non-Profit Organizations," http://harvester.census.gov/fac/

Fourth Sector Network, www.fourthsector.net

Three Sector Initiative of the Independent Sector, www.independentsector.org/programs/leadership/3Sector_Overview.html

3 Theories of the Nonprofit Sector and Policy Change

Nonprofit organizations in the United States—educational, charitable, civic, and religious institutions of every size and mission—represent the most widespread organized expression of Americans' dedication to the common good . . . Individuals have continued to use their First Amendment freedoms of speech and association to create and energize organizations that define common needs, rally popular support, and pursue innovative approaches to public problems.[1]

Panel on the Nonprofit Sector

If you have ever driven a car on a foggy night up (or down) a mountain, you have likely given thanks for the white-painted line that delineates the travel lane from the shoulder of the road. Our gratitude should be directed primarily at the Dorr Foundation and the efforts of its founders, John and Nell Dorr. John Dorr was a chemical engineer who worked with Thomas Edison and founded a company that made him wealthy enough to establish the Dorr Foundation in 1940. In the early 1950s, his wife, Nell, called attention to the propensity of drivers, when facing oncoming headlights or bad weather, to either hug the center line or swerve dangerously toward the shoulder. Dorr addressed this problem by speculating that a white-painted line along the shoulder would serve to guide drivers into the center of the travel lane and increase traffic safety.

Initially unable to convince the Connecticut Highway Commission to paint lines on the Merritt Parkway, the Dorrs used their Foundation to fund demonstration projects to test the lines' effectiveness. The test of the lines on New York's Hutchinson River Parkway led to a 55 percent decrease in traffic accidents over seven months. Within a decade, due to the investment by the Dorr Foundation and the lobbying actions of John Dorr, the white lines had gained nearly universal acceptance on the nation's highways.[2]

POLICY IMPLICATIONS OF NONPROFIT SECTOR THEORIES

- Demand-side theories focus on the development of nonprofit organizations to fulfill the demand for public goods; supply-side theories focus on the interests of the donors, staff, and volunteers of nonprofits as the reason nonprofits come into being.
- Nonprofits are most likely to be favored with public policy action and government support when they are focused on a public need or when public opinion favors limited government action.
- Policy entrepreneurs, policy image, and policy venue are important elements in defining and raising awareness of public problems and initiating policy change. Stages of the policy process, as well as different levels of government represent numerous potential venues for nonprofits to affect public policy.

THEORIES OF THE NONPROFIT SECTOR

The example above and our earlier discussion in Chapter 1 show that nonprofit organizations have long been used as a mechanism for resolving collective action problems, as well as a way for individuals to make manifest their own interests and goals for a better society. Meeting public needs and passion for public purposes are critical concepts in the understanding of why nonprofit organizations are developed, and they serve as the basic rationales for the existence of the nonprofit sector. Not-for-profit organizations serve as instruments of service delivery to meet needs—often referred to as the instrumental rationale for a nonprofit's existence. Likewise, nonprofits also facilitate the expression of individual values in order to enhance the public welfare—often referred to as the expressive rationale for why nonprofits exist. Accordingly, we use instrumental and expressive rationales as organizing principles throughout this chapter to highlight the distinct, complementary, and sometimes controversial theoretical underpinnings of the sector. In addition, because nonprofits exist within the parameters of public policy and often must create or change policy in order to pursue their missions, theories of policy change are also pertinent to the discussion within this chapter.

Incorporating the facets of instrumental and expressive rationales, scholars tend to group theories of the nonprofit sector along two primary dimensions—demand-side and supply-side. Demand-side theories are those that focus on the instrumental role of nonprofits in providing services to meet societal needs. Supply-side theories suggest that nonprofits exist for expressive purposes—that is, to allow individuals to express their own values and pursue their preferences regarding the public interest. Nonprofits should not be viewed as strictly instrumental or expressive, however, because organizations usually contain elements of each, and a balance of each perspective is needed for a successful voluntary sector.[3]

Demand-Side Theories: Nonprofits Form to Respond to Unmet Needs

The collection of theories encompassed under the rubric of demand-side explanations of nonprofit formation basically argue that nonprofits are formed in response to an unmet need.

A large (or vocal) group demands certain goods and services that neither the government nor the market provides in sufficient quantities or appropriate applications, so a nonprofit is formed to meet those demands. Food pantries and free clinics are examples of nonprofits formed to address urgent public needs. How public demands are translated into nonprofit action is explained through four primary theories discussed in this section: (1) government-market failure; (2) contract failure; (3) nonprofit federalism; and (4) resource dependency. Research in these four areas describes the demand-side approach with regard to government-nonprofit relations. Each of these embodies an argument as to why nonprofit organizations are formed and why the sector has experienced significant growth in recent years.

Government-Market Failure. The market is typically understood as the first venue of organized interaction in society; for example, people bartered for goods and services before there was currency and before there was a government to regulate activity. Markets provide goods and services when: (1) access to those goods and services can be restricted to those with the ability to pay and (2) when those who want the goods and services are willing to pay an amount that will generate a profit for the business that provides them. When these conditions are not met, markets generally elect not to provide the goods or services, or do so at a level or in a manner that is insufficient for public demand.

With regard to public goods and services, the government often steps in when the market fails to provide in order to ensure the goods and services are made available in accordance with the wishes of the majority of its constituency. Clean air is a classic example of a public good that markets will not provide. Access to the air we breathe cannot be restricted only to those with an ability to pay, so companies have little incentive to incur costs to limit air pollution caused by manufacturing unless required to do so by government. Goods or services desired by only a minority of the population, however, will not be provided by either government or the market, and thereby fall victim to what Burton Weisbrod terms government-market failure. At this point, the voluntary sector will be mobilized, in that not-for-profit organizations will be formed to fill the gaps left by government and the market in meeting the demand for collective goods.[4]

Contract Failure. The theory of contract failure explains the existence of nonprofit organizations as resulting not from the unwillingness of the market or government to provide certain public goods and services, but because of public perceptions that they do not provide them well. Hansmann, for example, explains that nonprofit delivery of goods and services results from a loss of trust by consumers in the goods provided by the for-profit sector.[5] Because not-for-profit organizations do not distribute profits to benefit private parties, their mission is viewed more favorably and gives consumers more confidence that quality is not sacrificed for efficiency in the goods and services produced. In addition, Coase argues that large bureaucracies are often considered inefficient because as an organization gets bigger the administrative costs of adding new transactions (services) rise.[6] At a certain point it becomes cheaper to contract out an activity rather than perform it internally. Because public bureaucracies frequently suffer from complaints about this type of inefficiency, contracting out provides an attractive option for government agencies.

Accordingly, governments seek to contract out the provision of public goods or services when the administrative costs associated with providing them directly become prohibitive. Since nonprofits have different incentives from for-profit organizations and are considered more trustworthy, monitoring and contract enforcement costs are expected to be lower with not-for-profit organizations.[7] When a program has a heterogeneous target population, for example, the costs associated with gathering and applying information about potential recipients can be extensive; contracting with a local organization that already delivers services to the intended constituency and has established that knowledge base is therefore a more efficient use of resources.

As an alternative to direct government action to meet public demands and as a preferred option to the private market, nonprofits influence public policy. Likewise, nonprofits are affected by public policy when those contracting decisions provide them with additional resources and program responsibilities. It can also be politically advantageous to contract with nonprofits. When support for smaller government prevails, contracting with nonprofit organizations is a politically acceptable means of reducing the size and scope of government. Volunteerism is a concept steeped in American tradition, and nonprofit service delivery engenders the spirit of voluntary action in ways that direct government intervention does not. Furthermore, nonprofit service providers are generally more attractive not just because they are more trustworthy than for-profit firms, but because they are more voluntary than is government.

Voluntary Failure and Nonprofit Federalism. Voluntary failure occurs when not-for-profit organizations are unable to provide the necessary levels of public goods or desired services on their own and must seek assistance from government in order to pursue their missions (see, for example, the case of children's advocacy centers discussed in Box 3.1). Lester A. Salamon argues that neither the government-market failure nor the contract failure model adequately portrays the relationship between government and the voluntary sector. As history shows, rather than government, it is often the voluntary organizations that are first on the scene when the market fails. Volunteers are comparatively easier to mobilize and quicker to action than government entities because of the inherent slowness to change built into the U.S. system of government. The relationships between governments and nonprofits develop, therefore, due to voluntary failure; Salamon refers to these relationships as nonprofit federalism.[8]

As discussed in Chapter 2, functional and legislative theories of federalism are also relevant to the discussion of nonprofit federalism.[9] As the functional theory of federalism dictates, government is better able to finance service delivery in some areas, but because nonprofits are closer to the target population, easier to mobilize, and generally less bureaucratic, actual provision of services is initiated by not-for-profit entities. During periods of public support for smaller government and less direct government intervention, nonprofit federalism also follows the tenets of legislative theory wherein elected officials find it politically rewarding to support and subsidize the efforts of nonprofits. In this sense, nonprofits make policy through the direct provision of public goods and services and also influence policy by seeking government action and assistance.

Resource Dependency Theories. Acquisition of resources is key to the survival of most nonprofits.[10] Pursuit of those resources, however, can often take organizations in directions they prefer not to go. Government funding, for example, is generally viewed as a very stable funding resource[11] and, as discussed previously, nonprofits often turn to government for financial assistance. However, dependence solely on government for the financial resources necessary for operations leaves nonprofits vulnerable. Issues of revenue volatility and goal displacement, discussed below, are seen as generally less invasive with government funding, but compliance with funding requirements exacts a toll. Excessive rules and regulations pertaining to reporting, monitoring, and other issues are examples of how nonprofits are subject to policy and may weaken the nonprofit's control over its own organizational structure and operations. In this case, goal displacement can occur when the means of service provision become the dominant focus of the organization; adherence to proper procedures in order to maintain funding displaces the goal of reaching program outcomes.[12]

While there are many funding options open to nonprofits, it is important to remain mindful of the strengths and weaknesses of each as well as the negatives associated with overdependence on any one source. Revenue diversification is often touted as the antidote for resource dependence; having a budget that relies on multiple revenue streams decreases the problems associated with any one type.[13] The nature of the goods and services that the organization provides, however, can restrict the ability of the organization to diversify revenues and their proportion to one another. For example, nonprofits that provide mostly public goods, such as programs to reduce the recidivism rates of recently released offenders, rely heavily on government funding; nonprofits that provide mostly private goods, such as the symphony, rely heavily on private contributions and commercial revenues from ticket sales.[14]

Supply-Side Approach: Personal Interests and Resources Drive the Development of Nonprofits

The example of a symphony lends itself well to understanding the supply-side approach to studying the origin and growth of the nonprofit sector. A central tenet of supply-side theories is that the genesis of all nonprofits is not found simply in meeting demand; some nonprofit organizations are developed and maintained because of the specific interests of the donors, volunteers, and staff associated with them, as in the case of a symphony. This rationale suggests that resources drive the tasks as much as a specific demand for the activity. Returning to the example of the Dorr Foundation and traffic safety, it is important to note that it was the specific interests of John and Nell Dorr and their willingness to contribute their own financial resources that led to the white lines on the highway. An iteration of the white lines may eventually have been implemented as awareness of need increased with traffic accidents, but the efforts of the Dorrs supplied the remedy prior to a public outcry.

Although donor-dictated philanthropy is often criticized when it does not meet the most urgent public needs, as the symphony and Dorr examples illustrate, the supply-side orientation can be advocated on normative grounds. In order to meet needs it is important to encourage a sector that protects and promotes those who make the decision whether to donate their funds, time, or talents. Supply-side theories also incorporate the concepts of policy entrepreneurship in which innovative individuals use the nonprofit sector to give expression to their values or faith, and social entrepreneurship whereby commercial venues are used to foster charitable goals.[15] In this sense, nonprofits make policy and influence policy but are not reacting to the lack of public policy, as was noted with discussion of the demand-side theories.

Demand and Supply: Instrumental vs. Expressive Rationales

Economic theories addressing the existence of nonprofit organizations established a general belief that these organizations "were really gap-filling entities that historically have arisen when public needs were sufficiently strong."[16] This demand-side approach gave rise to a normative argument that the purpose of nonprofit organizations should be to meet the demands of those who are the neediest—the disadvantaged and disenfranchised of society. However, according to Peter Frumkin, nonprofits seek to fulfill this mission not only by providing the direct delivery of services (instrumental rationale), but also by fostering civic and political engagement as a means to allow individuals to express their values and beliefs (expressive rationale).[17]

Tensions exist between government and nonprofits, even when the not-for-profit organizations seek to fill demands not met by government or the market. Contracted service delivery raises issues of codependence and loss of autonomy by the nonprofits. As they become increasingly reliant on government contracts to survive, nonprofits are perceived as simply an implementation arm of government rather than an independent group in pursuit of a well-defined mission. Such a heavy focus on the instrumental role threatens the ability of these organizations to provide for the expression of values by their members, donors, volunteers, and staff.[18]

Tensions between governments and nonprofits are also palpable in the supply-side theories. Because social entrepreneurs seek to combine commercial ventures with charitable goals, they often come dangerously close to the line between for-profit and not-for-profit ventures. The privileged tax-exempt status enjoyed by nonprofits causes tensions with business regarding unfair competition and leads government to question why they are forgoing tax revenue to encourage commercial activities, especially in tough economic times. State and local governments such as California may also scrutinize the work of nonprofits to see whether the benefit to the state or locality is enough to offset the tax expenditures. This can be particularly pertinent for nonprofits that operate overseas, as discussed in the Going Global 3.1 case involving the Bill & Melinda Gates Foundation.

GOING GLOBAL 3.1

Donor Interests and International Causes

With an asset trust of $33.5 billion, the Bill & Melinda Gates Foundation is the largest U.S. foundation based both on asset size and total giving ($3.055 billion in 2009). Since 1994, the Gates Foundation has granted a total of more than $26 billion, 72 percent of which ($18.884 billion) was granted in the program areas of global health and global development. The foundation supports work through grants in more than one hundred countries and each of the fifty U.S. states. The first of their original fifteen guiding principles for the foundation explicitly states that the work of the foundation is driven by the "interests and passions of the Gates family," a decidedly supply-side rationale for establishing the foundation and determining what projects to fund.

The work of private foundations, particularly one with assets in the billions of dollars, has the potential for tremendous impact on public policy, especially in countries with scarce resources, overwhelming problems, and poor infrastructure. In his annual letters, Bill Gates outlines the foundation's program area funding priorities for each upcoming year. His 2012 letter reflects a continued commitment to global initiatives—namely innovations in agriculture (primarily through better seed development) and global health improvement. Global health initiatives reflect ongoing concerns, but issues specifically mentioned as 2012 priorities are: (1) providing vaccines to children in poor countries, continuing their work to make this the "decade of vaccines"; (2) preventing, treating, and finding a cure for AIDS; and (3) enhancing family planning services, particularly access to contraceptives, for poor women in developing countries.

Once the world's wealthiest individuals, Bill Gates, along with his wife Melinda and his father, Bill Gates Sr., chair the foundation and share its guiding philosophy that "every life has equal value."[19] Through their global initiatives, the specific interests of the Gates family influence and make public policy in other countries, as their funding helps define public problems and devise solutions to them. For example, the foundation's 2005 annual report highlighted funding for phase I trials for a new vaccine for meningitis; in 2010, the vaccine was introduced in three African countries severely affected by the disease. As CEO Jeff Raikes stated in his letter in the 2010 Annual Report, developing and implementing the new vaccine was the result of a public-private partnership that involved the Gates Foundation, private pharmaceutical companies, the U.S. government, and African governments. Such partnerships reflect the potential of private foundations to influence public policy on a global scale.

For more information on the Bill & Melinda Gates Foundation and to read the annual letter, go to www.gatesfoundation.org.

Even the expressive dimension of the supply-side orientation causes difficulties, particularly when the expression of values and faith are core elements of nonprofits engaged in direct service delivery under government contracts. Religious faith is often central to the mission of nonprofits that receive service contracts from government. For organizations such as Catholic Charities USA, reconciling the tenets of that faith with government requirements is often a source of tension.[20] For example, the Catholic Church has always opposed abortion and the use of contraception as key tenets of its religious faith; in November 2011, the U.S. Conference of Catholic Bishops (USCCB) lost federal funding for its program to assist victims of human trafficking after eight years of support by the Department of Health and Human Services (DHHS). USCCB had made clear since its first application for funds through the Trafficking Victims Protection Act (TVPA) that it would not use the grant funds nor allow its subcontractors to use the funds for the provision of abortion or contraceptive services, conditions of the contract to which DHHS agreed.[21]

In 2009, the American Civil Liberties Union (ACLU) filed suit against DHHS claiming that the government violated the Establishment Clause of the Constitution by allowing USCCB "to impose a religious-based restriction on the use of taxpayer funds."[22] In 2011, DHHS chose not to award a new contract to USCCB and instead divided the TVPA funds among three other organizations; it is not clear from the official record whether that decision was based on the issues identified in the ACLU lawsuit or was related to another factor. In March 2012, U.S. District Judge Richard G. Stearns issued a summary judgment on behalf of the ACLU and determined that DHHS had violated the Establishment Clause of the Constitution. USCCB received over $69 million in federal grants and contracts in fiscal year 2010,[23] and as an expression of faith has included the provision regarding abortion and contraception in numerous other contract agreements. As such, this judgment should have interesting implications for the future contracting relationship between the government and Catholic agencies.[24]

Subsequently, what is the motivation for development of the not-for-profit sector? Economists argue that nonprofits exist for the same reason that governments exist—failure of the private sector market to provide collective goods. Supply-side rationale and Salamon's theory of nonprofit federalism, however, cannot be ignored. Hence we ask, why a nonprofit instead of government? We would argue that both supply- and demand-side arguments explain the existence of the nonprofit sector. In the example of children's advocacy centers (see Case Study 3.2), significant policy change such as the adoption of legislation is not a necessary condition for center operation, but professional interest and policy entrepreneurship are. Centers exist not simply because there is a need for the enhanced services they provide. They exist because they also serve the interests of the donors, staff, and volunteers associated with them, as is reflected in the activists' passion for and involvement with center development. Although taking the necessary steps to structure a 501(c)(3) organization and getting IRS approval for that level of tax-exempt status is not difficult, actually establishing a children's advocacy center (CAC) involves a great deal of time and effort to get the necessary professionals committed to its development and operation. Centers represent a venue other than government through which public services can be delivered and are a good example of the relationship between governments, nonprofits, and public policy.

CASE STUDY 3.2

Children's Advocacy Centers (CACs) Established as a Nonprofit Venue

Children's advocacy centers (CAC) were introduced in Chapter 1 as predominately nonprofit venues that provide an alternative approach to standard criminal justice procedures in the handling of child abuse cases. A children's advocacy center is a child-friendly facility, usually operated by a not-for-profit organization, which provides a centralized location for law enforcement, social services, legal, medical, victims' advocate, and counseling professionals to come together as a team in order to interview, examine, and provide support services to child victims. The concept of CACs is revisited here because the centers provide a useful illustration of nonprofit influence on policy change.

Even after child abuse was recognized as a public problem to be addressed via the criminal justice system, the child victims who were rescued from their immediate abuse situation were often subjected to additional trauma during the process of taking their cases through trial. In order to build these cases, law enforcement and prosecution officials set about gathering evidence in a manner similar to other criminal cases, which resulted in physical examination and repeated interviewing of the child victim, often by professionals who were not trained specifically to question children. It is important to note that children typically have a limited vocabulary and even without having experienced a trauma often seek to provide answers they think adults want to hear. As such, especially in the past, cases of child sexual abuse in particular began to break down at trial or on appeal when conflicts emerged in victims' recollections of events. One notable example was the McMartin Preschool trial in California; this was one of the longest and most expensive criminal cases in history, which ultimately resulted in acquittal of the two defendants on 52 counts of alleged sexual abuse of children. It was determined that the alleged victims were likely interviewed repeatedly by different officials and in such a way as to lead them to provide certain types of responses, casting doubts on the credibility of their claims.

As one of many prosecutors throughout the country who saw the trauma inflicted on child victims and who faced the difficulties involved with prosecuting cases with questionable evidence and testimony, Bud Cramer and a group of colleagues in Huntsville, Alabama, sought a nonprofit solution to what they saw as a growing public problem. The National Children's Advocacy Center (NCAC) was established in 1985 and became a model for other centers throughout the United States and in other countries, an example of policy diffusion discussed in this chapter. Central to the CAC model is the multidisciplinary team approach, which is designed to minimize the number of times a child victim must tell the story of abuse and submit to other traumatic activities associated with preparing a case for trial. This strengthens the case for prosecution by enhancing the evidence gathered, but more importantly provides assistance to the children to facilitate recovery.

The NCAC began operations in 1985, and the first state legislation pertaining to children's advocacy centers was adopted in 1986; Hawaii passed the first statutes—one regarding multidisciplinary teams and the other to establish a statewide support organization, commonly referred to as a state chapter. According to data obtained from a survey we conducted in 2004, at least five states had a CAC in operation in 1987; by 1997, more than 140 centers provided services in at least ten states. As the number of states with centers increased, formal public policy change in the form of legislation also diffused among the states, but in various ways. For example, California had one of the first CACs, established in 1985, but as of 2004 their legislature had not adopted a single CAC statute, which, according to responses to our survey and discussion with CAC activists from California, was despite their repeated efforts to encourage adoption of at least some type of legislation. Texas, on the other hand, had at least one center in 1990 and, by 1997, all seven types of legislation were in effect in the state; at the time of our survey, Texas and Utah were the only two states that had adopted all seven types. According to the Western Regional CAC, since 2007 every state has had at least one center in operation and 25 states have adopted some form of CAC legislation.

The seven types of legislation sought by activists within the CAC movement are as follows:

1. Requires that investigation and processing of child abuse cases be handled by multidisciplinary teams (MDT) with participation of CAC staff
2. Creates a state-level organization to coordinate activities of CACs in the state
3. Provides for direct funding or competitive grant programs for centers throughout the state; does not include one-time appropriations
4. Mandates that centers within the state must meet minimum standards for operation
5. Requires that CAC staff have access to and maintain confidentiality of child abuse case records
6. Provides some degree of liability protection for CACs within the state
7. Stipulates the size and disciplines/organizations/individuals to be represented on the CAC boards of directors within the state

Our survey data indicate that not all CAC activists pursue formal policy change through adoption of statutes; some pursue a few types but not all seven, and some have actively pursued legislation for years, to no avail. Data indicate that states do not adopt the types of legislation in any particular order—that is, there is no one type of statute that precedes all others. In addition, our subsequent research has shown a strong positive correlation between development of children's advocacy centers, media coverage of the centers, and adoption of state statutes. Our findings support the tenets of Punctuated-Equilibrium Theory (PET), that a change in policy image (measured by the media coverage) coupled with a change in policy venue (measured by the increase in the number of nonprofit children's advocacy centers) contributes to a change in formal public policy (measured by the adoption of state legislation).

While formal policy change—that is, the adoption of legislation specific to children's advocacy centers—is not a necessary condition for center operation, professional interest and policy entrepreneurship are. The efforts of policy entrepreneurs across the country have been instrumental in the growing movement toward development of children's advocacy centers and, subsequently, in the promotion of CAC legislation. Policy entrepreneurs are significant factors in several theories of policy change, particularly PET and the policy innovation and diffusion theories mentioned here. Centers exist not simply because there is a need for the enhanced services they provide, but because these organizations also serve the interests of the donors, staff, and volunteers associated with them. As such, the supply-side rationale of theories of nonprofit development is exhibited by the role of activists as policy entrepreneurs in facilitating center development.

Additional information is available at www.nationalchildrensalliance.org.

QUESTIONS TO CONSIDER:

1. Discuss how the operation of a children's advocacy center embodies a change in public policy. What types of operational changes and challenges likely exist because the multidisciplinary teams include members who are representatives from public, private, and nonprofit organizations?
2. Since center operation alone causes a change in ways that child abuse cases are handled (a policy change), why would CAC activists seek policy change in the form of state legislation? Likewise, why would some choose not to pursue adoption of state statutes?
3. Discuss the importance of policy entrepreneurs to the development and expansion of the CAC model. What are the most likely ways entrepreneurs have facilitated diffusion of the concept throughout the states?
4. Is the development of children's advocacy centers a unique example of policy change by nonprofits? If so, in what ways? If not, discuss other examples and how the theories of policy change and nonprofit development help you to understand the relationship between nonprofits and policy.

NONPROFITS AND PUBLIC POLICY: FUNCTIONAL AND LEGISLATIVE THEORIES OF FEDERALISM

Central to our argument throughout this text is that not-for-profit organizations are an important venue with regard to public policy since nonprofits both make policy through direct service delivery, and influence formal policy through advocacy efforts. As such, discussion of the functional and legislative theories of federalism is relevant to understanding nonprofits as venues for public policy change. According to functional theory, government will expand operations within its area of competence but will be limited or not operate at all in those areas where it is less competent—that is, will provide more goods and services when such expansion is deemed to be efficient and effective. In the case of a local police department, for example, analysis of crime scene evidence such as fingerprints is performed in-house but DNA evidence is sent to the state bureau of investigation.

Legislative theory, on the other hand, contends that the political needs of legislators will drive them to distribute government services in order to maximize their ability to claim credit, or to shift burdens so as to minimize their blame. For example, funding to restore the childhood sod home of the late entertainer Lawrence Welk can be safely argued on functional grounds to be a local matter; however, because the members of Congress from North

Dakota, where the home is located, sought to benefit their district with an additional tourism opportunity, a line-item appropriation for this restoration project was included in the federal budget.[25] Therefore, functional theory represents a more efficient (this is how it should be done) distribution of government resources, whereas legislative theory embraces the more politically feasible (this is how it really gets done) model.

Similarly, if the theory of nonprofit federalism holds, the particular needs of not-for-profit organizations drive the demand for policy change. For example, legislation will follow creation of the CACs when there is a critical mass of service delivery through these venues and a need by them for government assistance in order to continue providing the desired level of service.[26] The functional theory of federalism follows this argument; because nonprofit organizations are closer to their target audiences, they will be better able to serve them. Government should get involved only to the extent that funding and/or technical assistance is needed to further the nonprofit service delivery. Legislative theory holds that legislators will adopt policies consistent with their re-election strategies; therefore, to the extent that service provision through not-for-profit venues is preferred by voters, legislatures will create policy change that furthers those efforts.

THEORIES OF POLICY CHANGE

Policy reform or change is considered a normal part of the policy process and nonprofits play a significant role. Just as there are various explanations for the existence of the nonprofit sector, there are a variety of theories of policy change. Punctuated-Equilibrium Theory seeks to explain instances in which public policy experiences a dramatic shift or leap rather than incremental change.[27] Multiple Streams theory argues that policy change is facilitated by having the right person, in the right place, at the right time, to address a public problem by raising sufficient awareness.[28] These and other concepts are pertinent to understanding policy change as it relates to nonprofits.

Punctuated-Equilibrium Theory: Explaining Non-Incremental Policy Change

According to the theory of punctuated equilibrium, politics in the United States does not reach equilibrium;[29] rather, stability exists as a result of a " . . . complex system of mutually non-interfering policy monopolies buttressed by powerful supporting images."[30] Stability exists, therefore, because of the way political institutions are structured and the way in which those institutions define policy issues. Change is usually incremental, but in those instances when the image of the policy is redefined and the institutional venue changes, significant policy change can occur quickly. These policy leaps are referred to as punctuations in the political equilibrium, and interest group activity such as nonprofit advocacy is often an integral part of this process.[31]

Policy Image. Policy image is defined as "how a policy is understood and discussed."[32] How a problem is defined, or rather which definition of the problem is accepted by decisionmakers, is critically important to the formulation of public policy. Framing a problem in a certain way, or seeking to redefine what actually is the problem, is usually the first strategic action of a nonprofit pursuing policy change. Through the use of symbols, metaphors, and presentation of causal factors, it is possible to influence perception of problems by making certain considerations seem more important than others.[33] Studies have found that public opinion is formed based upon the weight people attach to the information with which they are presented.[34] People accept a definition of a problem (or change their minds to accept a re-definition of the problem) because they shift the weight attached to relevant factors presented in an argument. Framing is important, therefore, for its ability to advance one belief over another.

For example, in a study of policy image change in the issue areas of child abuse and mental illness, we examined the impact of nonprofits on public problem definitions. We conducted a multi-year content analysis of newspaper coverage of National Children's Alliance (NCA) and the National Alliance on Mental Illness (NAMI). During the period studied, these nonprofits each sought a specific change in policy image in their respective issue areas. We found that the growth in affiliates of these two national nonprofits corresponded with an increase in newspaper coverage, as well as increases in public policy change through legislative action. Like many students of nonprofits before us, we were unable to isolate the causal nature of a relationship we perceive to be symbiotic. However, our findings suggest that nonprofits are effective at changing the way public problems are defined and support the tenets of punctuated-equilibrium theory in that a change in policy image corresponded with policy change.[35]

Changing the policy image can be a successful strategy for smaller or less resource-rich organizations. The California Wellness Foundation—a private, independent foundation formed in 1992—assisted in the promotion of local gun control measures by bringing about a redefinition of gun violence from a public safety problem to an issue of public health. (See Box 3.3.) Through grants to gun control interests and by financing a public opinion poll, the foundation worked to re-frame the issue. Gun violence was framed as a disease with handguns as the primary agent of infection, thus moving the focus from crime prevention to an issue of public health.[36]

One of the factors involved in the change of policy image and ultimate success in changing policy with regard to gun control initiatives was widening the scope of conflict. Any time a third party enters a conflict between two groups, the outcome is altered regardless of the nature of the third party's action.[37] Conflict expansion in most cases requires that a policy entrepreneur be present to put forth a new definition of the problem.[38]

Policy Entrepreneurs. Policy entrepreneurs are basically change agents. These individuals see problems from new perspectives and develop innovative approaches to solve them; they are able to effectively mobilize and lead others in support of their proposed solution.[39] Why they expend the energy and resources necessary to accomplish this is arguably because of an attempt to express their individual values, beliefs, or political views in pursuit of policy goals. Policy entrepreneurs often choose the nonprofit sector to

Box 3.3

FOR EXAMPLE

THE CALIFORNIA WELLNESS FOUNDATION: CHANGING POLICY IMAGE

The California Wellness Foundation (TCWF) was founded in 1992 when Health Net converted from a nonprofit organization to for-profit status. By order of the California Department of Corporations, approval of the conversion to for-profit status required Health Net to create TCWF by transferring $300 million and 80 percent equity in Health Net's parent holding company (equivalent to the state's valuation of Health Net at the time of conversion). With these funds, TCWF pursues a mission "to improve the health of the people of California by making grants for health promotion, wellness education and disease prevention." Grants average $50 million per year; since 1992, the foundation has awarded 6,213 grants totaling more than $780 million.[40]

TCWF grants have funded research and public education programs that contributed to the passage of ordinances in more than 300 cities to restrict access to handguns, as well as state legislation to ban the sale of so-called "junk guns." Although TCWF cannot be isolated as the sole cause of these policy changes, the foundation is widely recognized as a leader in the movement to treat gun violence as a public health issue. Gun-related deaths and injuries have declined significantly in the almost twenty years since TCWF launched their funding program; for individuals 12 to 24, firearm deaths dropped 42 percent and injuries from firearms decreased 52 percent.[41]

Gary L. Yates, president and CEO of TCWF, testified before the Little Hoover Commission on Youth Crime and Violence Prevention in September 2000. His comments make clear how the foundation frames the issue of violence with regard to public policy:

> The Foundation recognizes that violence is a public health issue, and that preventing violence is not just a public safety matter but a public health mandate. Violence results in premature death, serious injury and disability, especially among our youth. The Foundation's Violence Prevention Initiative is grounded in a public health approach, which takes into account not only the individual but also the physical and social environments that foster or inhibit violence and the agents of violence, such as guns.[42]

Additional information is available at www.calwellness.org.

facilitate their efforts because nonprofits are more accommodating of the expressive dimension inherent in entrepreneurship.[43]

Candy Lightner, the founder of Mothers Against Drunk Driving (MADD), is an example of such a policy entrepreneur, using a nonprofit venue to influence public policy. When her young daughter was killed by a drunk driver, she became increasingly frustrated by trying to get government to pay attention to the problem of drunk driving and take action to protect other families from the suffering she experienced. At the time young Cari Lightner was killed, drunk driving was not seen as a public problem: "[D]rinking and driving was how people got home. It was normal behavior."[44] Changing the perception of the problem was the first step in the way Candy Lightner as policy entrepreneur brought about a nationwide movement and public policy response to the problem of drunk driving. (See Box 3.4.)

Box 3.4

FOR EXAMPLE

MOTHERS AGAINST DRUNK DRIVING: POLICY ENTREPRENEUR DEMANDING ACTION

Following the 1980 death of her 13-year-old daughter when she was struck by a drunk driver, Candy Lightner and a friend started Mothers Against Drunk Drivers (MADD) because they were frustrated with the lack of response from public officials. Traffic safety advocates within government at the time were also frustrated with the lack of public attention to a growing problem. According to Jim Fell, national board member for MADD and official with the National Highway Traffic Safety Administration (NHTSA) in 1980:

> Congress had put $35 million into Alcohol Safety Action Programs around the country, but nothing was happening. Judges were treating it with a wink and a nod. . . . Alcohol was involved in nearly 60 percent of fatal crashes and we were banging our heads against the wall. Then, all of a sudden, a woman named Candy Lightner came along, kicking and screaming about her daughter who had been killed.[45]

Results came fairly quickly for the fledgling nonprofit. Almost immediately, other victims came forward with their stories, sending in donations and forming MADD chapters across the nation. In 1982, President Ronald Reagan formed the Presidential Commission on Drunk Driving, and that same year, Congress passed a federal highway bill which gave funds to states with anti-drunk driving efforts. By 1983, a total of 129 new anti-drunk driving laws had been passed in more than half of the states. One of the biggest early victories for MADD was when President Reagan signed the Uniform Drinking Age Act in 1984; this effectively raised the legal drinking age to 21 nationwide.

MADD continues its efforts to change behavior and change policy. While drunk driving fatalities decreased 24 percent between 2006 and 2010, MADD has a goal to help reduce the number of fatalities due to drunk driving below 10,000 by the end of 2012. Their goals also include reducing the number of underage consumers of alcohol by 5 percent and to increase the number of victims served by MADD to more than 65,000 by the end of 2012. Since MADD cites 2010 data as the most recent regarding drunk driving fatalities, it will be some time before they can assess achievement of the first goal. However, the organization has promising data regarding their success in reducing the number of underage consumers of alcohol. Among 8th, 10th, and 12th graders, alcohol consumption decreased by 8 percent, 4 percent, and 3 percent, respectively, between 2008 and 2011. MADD more than doubled the number of victims served between 2004 and 2011, to more than 63,000 victims and survivors of drunk or drug-related crashes. With regard to public policy, MADD cites that in 2011, more than 36,000 e-mail messages regarding underage drinking or drunk driving were sent to legislators; the organization also partners with the National Highway Traffic Safety Administration on the "Drive Sober or Get Pulled Over" campaign to stop drunk driving.[46]

Additional information is available at www.madd.org.

Multiple Streams Theory: Coupling Problems, Policies, and Politics for Change

MADD, under the leadership of Candy Lightner, was able to raise public awareness of the problems associated with drunk driving and compel policymakers to act. The work of Candy Lightner and MADD provide a good example of multiple streams theory and the way policy decisions are made under complex conditions. In these situations, several definitions of a problem exist simultaneously with various ideas for potential solutions. Accordingly, a policy entrepreneur such as Candy Lightner is key to the coupling of the problems, policies, and politics streams necessary for policymaking under conditions of ambiguity. Successful coupling of at least two, but generally all three, of the multiple streams is necessary to bring about policy change. Coupling is the process of joining a problem definition to an appropriate policy solution at a time when the public will be generally supportive. It falls to the policy entrepreneur to know when and how to bring about the coupling of the streams, usually by sensing the public mood and identifying critical moments in time known as windows of opportunity.[47]

Venue. A policy window presents the opportunity to shift public attention to new perspectives on a problem. How, when, and where the window of opportunity opens, as well as the current state of the public mood, affect the number and types of possible venues through which policy entrepreneurs can attempt to promote policy change. In their leading work on agenda-setting, Baumgartner and Jones use the term 'policy venue' to refer primarily to government institutions—for example, legislative bodies, committees, and executive branch agencies; however, their definition is broad enough to encompass nongovernmental entities, such as nonprofit organizations, as well. With the increasing prevalence of the provision of public services by not-for-profit organizations, these agencies are likewise demonstrating their "authority to make decisions concerning [an] issue."[48]

Policy advocates increasingly find that it is possible to effectively change public policy through direct service provision without appealing to a government institution first. Consider again the example of the Dorr Foundation in the opening vignette. Although the Dorrs initially appealed to the state of Connecticut to test their idea about the white lines, when they were unable to obtain government support, they implemented the project with their own funds. It is important to note that implementation required the tacit support of government because the roads on which the lines were painted were public roads; however, because public roads are maintained by city, county, and state transportation agencies, the foundation had multiple jurisdictional venues through which to pursue government approval.

Both inherent organizational factors and resource availability determine the options of venues to target. Groups with a sizable and active membership but limited finances may have little access to some institutional venues. For organizations with few members but with significant financial resources and associated political clout, institutional venues such as the legislative body are much more feasible.[49] Using the courts, for example, requires substantial financial resources, commitment of time, and, unless the group's composition includes legal professionals, at least a partial abdication of control to someone outside the group.[50] It is wise, therefore, for nonprofits to be politically savvy and understand which institutional or jurisdictional venue will be most amenable to their desires for policy change.

Because of the potential limits on possible venues open to a nonprofit, agenda entrance requires successful linkage of policy image with a receptive venue. Multiple venues of political action mean that multiple policy images can exist simultaneously. There is no one objective definition of a policy problem because problem definition is itself a political process.[51] Political actors view a problem from several different perspectives and are capable of constructing causal stories that assign responsibility for a problem in various ways.

Gaining acceptance of a problem definition involves targeting the relevant audience to promote a preferred solution. People disagree over whether or not something is a problem, what the cause of the problem is, and whether or not there can or should be a public policy solution. Therefore, in order to facilitate policy change, proponents must target the appropriate audience—such as the general public, the mass media, and legislative decision makers—with an acceptable causal story. Success in bringing about a policy change depends on which policy image becomes the dominant one. A change in venue can facilitate a change in the dominant rhetoric, which can thereby lead to policy change. Policy subsystems can be created or destroyed through the interaction of policy image and venues, and nonprofits are often among the organizations pursuing the change in both.

STAGES OF THE PROCESS AS VENUES FOR POLICY CHANGE

The stages of the policy process—problem definition, agenda-setting, policy formulation, policy adoption, implementation, and evaluation—offer multiple venues for action. The implementation stage has been shown to provide a venue for policy change—for example, in the case of Habitat Conservation Plans developed pursuant to the Endangered Species Act (ESA). Habitat Conservation Plans are developed through the U.S. Fish & Wildlife Service under the Endangered Species Act and are designed to mitigate tensions caused when the interests of property developers conflict with the provisions of the law. Property developers who found it more difficult to influence policy at the problem definition or formulation stages of policymaking found success during the implementation phase of the ESA. In this instance, implementation served as a venue whereby property developers were able to avoid the more burdensome requirements of ESA by taking actions such as appealing to those administering the provisions of the act to design regulations favorable to their interests. Because developers engaged during the implementation stage to pursue policy outcomes favorable to them, advocates for environmental interests were forced to engage in the implementation arena as well, in order to combat what they perceived to be the negative influence of developers. Although environmentalists had succeeded in the policy adoption stage through passage of the ESA, their ultimate impact on the policy was dependent on success during implementation, as well.[52]

Venue is an important element in the policymaking process. While much of our argument is based on the role of nonprofits as a policy venue, the stages of the policy process are also relevant for discussion, since they represent multiple access points at which nonprofits can engage with government to pursue policy change. Nonprofits often make policy, for example, through direct service delivery, and by virtue of doing the work, they engage in agenda-setting by raising awareness of a public problem. In the policy formulation stage, nonprofits influence policy by being actively engaged in devising solutions to public problems. In the implementation stage, nonprofits that contract with government to provide services are subject to policy when they must meet the stipulations for receipt of funds. In the evaluation stage, nonprofits can be affected by policy when the most efficient and effective means of addressing public problems are evaluated; the results can serve to expand or diminish the role of nonprofits in meeting public needs.

POLICY CHANGE IN THE STATES

U.S. federalism ensures that some government activities are left to the purview of the states. Implementation within a federal system of government, therefore, offers even more challenges and opportunities for venue shopping as federalism affords multiple potential access points through various levels of government. The gun policy fight illustrated in the example of the California Wellness Foundation emphasizes this point since it included controversy over the appropriate level—that is, jurisdictional venue—for government action. Whereas gun rights organizations favored state government action, gun control groups focused on local government entities to press for tighter restrictions.[53] As discussed in Chapter 2, devolution as a policy choice by the national government has placed even more activities at state discretion in recent years. Because legislation related to nonprofit organizations more often falls within the realm of state authority, it is relevant to examine the differences among the states in policy change.

In our federal system of government, states are considered laboratories of innovation, engaging in policy experiments and learning from the successes and failures of their fellow states' agencies. States have traditionally differed in the policies they adopt, both temporally and substantively. Many states utilize federal pass-through dollars as well as state funds to subsidize nonprofit service delivery through the process of second-order devolution. As states move away from direct service delivery and rely instead on not-for-profit organizations, state policies change as a result. Nonprofit service providers have become increasingly important actors in the policy process, and their preferences are reflected in the policy choices made by state governments. Differences in state policy choices have spawned a significant body of research, centering primarily on (1) the internal determinants of variations in state policy adoptions and (2) the diffusion of policies among the states. It is important to note that while research has tended to focus on either internal determinants or diffusion, the reality is that internal factors cannot be assumed to affect state policies exclusive of any action by other states, nor can diffusion occur without some impact from internal determinants.[54]

Policy Diffusion among the States. Diffusion is defined as "the patterns by which organizations adopt a particular innovation across both space and time."[55] Geographic proximity is one factor in diffusion; successes or failures of neighboring states are used as heuristics by states seeking a policy solution.[56] Diffusion also has a temporal dimension; innovativeness has been found to be both issue and time specific.[57] Risk-averse elected state officials tend to wait for sufficient time to pass to evaluate the success of a policy in other states before making a decision to adopt it themselves. Therefore, diffusion follows a temporal pattern of adoption by a few adventurous states, a period of evaluation by the remaining states, and then increased frequency of adoption as the benefits of the policy become apparent.[58]

Internal Determinants of State Policy Adoptions. Politics, resources, and demands are all forces that affect the decisions of the states to adopt particular policies.[59] The impact of these forces on a state's decision to approve legislation favorable to nonprofits varies according to the competitive climate within the state as well as the type of policy being addressed. Not-for-profit organizations, therefore, need to understand each force within their state—the political climate, level of and competition for resources, and the severity of the problem they seek to address—in order to be successful at shaping policy within their field of interest.

CONCLUSION

Theories of the nonprofit sector and how policy change occurs are relevant to practitioners as well as scholars. The chicken-or-the-egg conundrum evident in the demand-side theories highlights the importance of examining the extent to which not-for-profit organizations determine public policy or are at the mercy of it. Nonprofit federalism is important to the study of nonprofits because if nonprofit organizations are first responders in the provision of public goods or certain types of services, it is reasonable to expect that their service delivery successes affect state adoption of legislation to further their activities.

The supply-side theories of the nonprofit sector are also relevant to discussions not only of why the sector exists, but also how nonprofits facilitate adoption of policy relevant to them. Policy entrepreneurs embody the supply-side concept by promoting a new way of looking at a public problem and new ways to address it. These policy entrepreneurs are critical actors in policy change by facilitating changes in policy image and finding new venues through which to pursue policy action. Not-for-profit organizations—alone and through partnerships with governments and the private sector—are increasingly the venue of choice for innovation in delivery of public goods and services. Understanding where they originated and how they affect public policy are therefore important to working for or with any not-for-profit organization.

Questions For Review

1. Why is it important to understand the origins of the nonprofit sector? Include discussion—description, strengths, weaknesses, etc.—of one of the theories of the nonprofit sector.
2. List and discuss three ways in which not-for-profit organizations have an impact on policy change.
3. Discuss the concept of policy venue. How are nonprofit organizations used as a venue through which to pursue policy change?

Assignment

After reading Box 3.4, access www.madd.org for more information on the work of the nonprofit MADD (Mothers Against Drunk Driving) and respond to the following questions:

1. Which of the theories of the nonprofit sector discussed in the chapter best explains the creation of the MADD organization? Why?
2. List two formal public policy changes—that is, specific legislation—pursued by MADD. What was the general strategy used by the organization in pursuing formal policy change? Discuss the extent to which the organization has been successful.
3. How do the theories of policy change discussed in the chapter facilitate your understanding of the influence of organizations such as MADD on public policy? Discuss, for example, the role of policy entrepreneurs, policy image, and venue.

Suggested Readings

Baumgartner, Frank R., and Bryan D. Jones. *Agendas and Instability in American Politics.* Chicago: University of Chicago Press, 1993.

Boris, Elizabeth T. "Nonprofit Organizations in a Democracy: Varied Roles and Responsibilities." In Boris, Elizabeth T. and Eugene Steuerle, eds. *Nonprofits and Government: Collaboration and Conflict,* 3–29. Washington, DC: Urban Institute Press, 1999.

Salamon, Lester M. *Partners in Public Service.* Baltimore: Johns Hopkins University Press, 1995.

Stone, Deborah. *Policy Paradox: The Art of Political Decision Making.* New York: W.W. Norton, 2002.

Web Resources

Center on Philanthropy, www.philanthropy.iupui.edu

Hauser Center for Nonprofit Organizations, www.hks.harvard.edu/hauser

Johns Hopkins Center for Civil Society Studies, www.ccss.jhu.edu

The Urban Institute, Center on Nonprofits and Philanthropy, www.urban.org/center/cnp

4 Regulating Not-for-Profit Organizations

The fact that the tax laws drive the regulation of charities today is less surprising than the transformation of those laws and the way in which they are administered that has taken place since the enactment of the income tax in the early twentieth century.

Marion R. Fremont-Smith

Staff and Board members of the Central Asia Institute (CAI), a nonprofit organization recognized as a tax-exempt public charity under Section 501(c)(3) of the Internal Revenue Code, found themselves thrust into a media frenzy following a CBS *60 Minutes* exposé of Greg Mortenson, author of the best-selling *Three Cups of Tea* and founding Executive Director of CAI. The *60 Minutes* report, as well as a 75-page article by Jon Krakauer (a former supporter of Mortenson), alleged that Mortenson lied in his books about key points including how he was introduced to the community where he built his first school, misled supporters regarding the actual number of schools that had been built through CAI, and misused charitable donations to finance lavish travel while on tour to sell his book.[2] Subsequently, two disgruntled donors initiated a class action lawsuit against CAI, and the attorney general for the state of Montana (where CAI is headquartered) launched an investigation.[3] Attorney General Steve Bullock released the results of his investigation in April 2012, and announced a settlement agreement with Greg Mortenson that included restitution of funds and monitoring by the attorney general's office for a period of three years.[4] CAI was subsequently dropped from the class action suit when plaintiffs agreed that the attorney general's office was the only entity that could take legal action.[5] This example illustrates some of the ways in which nonprofit organizations are subject to regulation: from policies enforced by state attorneys general and the courts, to oversight by donors and the media.

POLICY IMPLICATIONS OF REGULATING NONPROFITS

- Regulation represents the most significant way in which not-for-profit organizations are subject to and affected by public policy.
- Congressional oversight has led to regulatory policy changes, such as the Sarbanes-Oxley Act and the Pension Protection Act, with direct impact on nonprofits.
- The Internal Revenue Service is the primary regulator of U.S. nonprofits; states' attorneys general are major enforcers of nonprofit regulatory policy.
- Court decisions and government contract compliance requirements are indirect regulation; accreditation and ratings systems are examples of nonprofit self-regulation.

REGULATORY POLICY INCREASINGLY AFFECTS NONPROFITS

Most of the earliest nonprofit organizations in the United States were established under the authority of an organized religion, which was commonly referred to as "the church." Regulators continue to use the term "church" to denote a body of religious believers of any faith as a means to differentiate religious congregations from other types of nonprofits. The distinction is particularly relevant with regard to regulatory policy because "churches"—which includes mosques, temples, synagogues and all other places of worship as well as conventions and associations of churches—are regulated in a way that is substantially different from other nonprofits.

Because of government's historic reluctance to intrude on activities believed to be within the purview of the church, policymakers have traditionally taken a more lenient approach to the regulation of all nonprofit activity. Recent proliferation of nonprofit organizations, questionable political activity by some nonprofits, and even scandals in the for-profit realm, however, have caused Congress, the Internal Revenue Service (IRS), and some state legislatures to tighten regulations regarding not-for-profit organizations. We are therefore led to ask: How are not-for-profit organizations regulated? To what extent do federal and state laws and administrative rules restrict the behavior of these organizations? How, also, does the sector govern itself? Government regulations as well as self-regulatory measures of nonprofit organizations are the focus of Chapter 4.

Policy scholars[6] have long differentiated between types of public policies, including regulatory and self-regulatory ones. Regulatory policies are categorized as those which restrict behavior of some and protect others. Self-regulatory policies are those whereby government cedes its right of regulation to those individuals and organizations being regulated; these are generally viewed as advantageous to the entities being regulated.

Government rules and regulations have generally been regarded as enforceable against businesses but are becoming increasingly relevant with regard to the nonprofit sector, especially considering the recent growth in the sector. As the nonprofit sector continues to grow in both size and scope, accountability issues become increasingly important. Because nonprofits operate within an environment in which they are significantly affected by and subject to regulatory and self-regulatory policies, understanding regulation from all levels of government is particularly relevant for nonprofit managers.

NONPROFITS SUBJECT TO FEDERAL GOVERNMENT REGULATION

The development of the regulation of charity has been delineated into three general phases: (1) development of broad parameters for regulatory activity and a general reliance on self-policing; (2) establishment of borders between exempt and non-exempt activity of nonprofits through passage of the Unrelated Business Income Tax (UBIT) and clarification of lobbying restrictions; and (3) regulatory expansions regarding foundation management and excess benefits limitations.[7] While Congress did not envision the Internal Revenue Service as the regulator of the voluntary sector when it granted tax-exempt status to public charities following enactment of the income tax, the IRS has proven quite effective in this role. In addition to supervision by the IRS, Congress engages in direct regulation of nonprofits through both passage of legislation and oversight activity.

Rules and Regulations of the Internal Revenue Service

As indicated above, regulation of nonprofits by the IRS is basically an unintended consequence, albeit a positive one, of federal policy regarding the income tax and establishing the parameters for exemption from it. Examination of information available through the IRS website provides a clear indication that the agency views its regulatory role as an important responsibility. The sections below outline the criteria for awarding tax-exempt status, as well as discussion of the rules and regulations promulgated by the IRS with regard to annual reporting, taxes on unrelated business income, and lobbying activity.

Tax-Exempt Status. First and foremost, the IRS has authority over nonprofit organizations because it is the IRS which determines whether or not and under what conditions an organization is recognized as tax-exempt. Tax-exemption is a significant financial resource for an organization because it reduces operational expenses. To date, the Internal Revenue Service has established almost 30 categories of tax-exempt organizations (see Chapter 1), but it is section 501(c)(3) of the Internal Revenue Code (IRC) that is generally the most relevant category in the study of nonprofits. This is so not only because these organizations comprise more than 60 percent of all tax-exempt organizations, but also because these nonprofits are accorded additional privileged status. Not only are 501(c)(3) organizations exempt from paying taxes, contributions to these organizations are tax deductible, which grants them a substantial advantage in soliciting donations. As a result, greater restrictions have been placed on their activities.

Most organizations seeking recognition as tax-exempt public charities are required to submit Form 1023, *Application for Exemption Under Section 501(c)(3) of the Internal*

Revenue Code. As a result of the Tax Reform Act of 1969 (discussed further below), Sections 509(a)(1) through (4) were adopted into the Internal Revenue Code (IRC) in order to distinguish between private foundations and other 501(c)(3) organizations commonly referred to as public charities. This distinction is necessary because of the additional restrictions placed on foundations in order to achieve and maintain their tax-exempt status. Definition of what constitutes a private foundation and the additional restrictions imposed are the focus of Box 4.1.

Box 4.1

FOR MORE INFORMATION

PRIVATE FOUNDATIONS' TAX-EXEMPT STATUS

Section 509(a)(1) to (4) define a private foundation by specifying which 501(c)(3) organizations are not private foundations, namely:

Section 509(a)(1): traditional public charities—for example, churches (and their auxiliaries), educational organizations, hospitals and medical research entities, and certain nonprofits that support charitable organizations, as determined by an income test.

Section 509(a)(2): organizations such as museums and orchestras that charge admission and receive more than one-third of revenue from contributions, grants, fees, and "gross receipts" from tickets and other sales that are related to the exempt purposes of the organization; no more than one-third of revenue can be from sources such as investment income or unrelated business income.

Section 509(a)(3): supporting organizations—that is, nonprofits that do not themselves receive public support but provide support to one or more 501(c)(3) organizations through a formal relationship whereby they are operated, controlled, or supervised by or in conjunction with the supported organization (for example, a parent–subsidiary relationship or a subsidiary–subsidiary with a joint parent relationship).

Section 509(a)(4): a special category of organizations that test for public safety.

Private foundations are subject to more onerous requirements than public charities (that is, the other 501(c)(3) organizations), namely:

Section 4940: required to pay a two-percent excise tax on net investment income

Section 4941: prohibited from self-dealing—that is, cannot engage in specified transactions with a disqualified person. "Disqualified person" is defined in detail and generally refers to an individual with a close relationship to the foundation. Five basic categories of prohibited transactions generally involve: 1) sale of property; 2) loans; 3) provision of goods and services other than in the same manner as to the general public; 4) financial compensation; and 5) transfer of income or assets.

Section 4942: payout requirement of 5 percent of net investment assets (administrative and fundraising expenses can be included in the 5 percent).

Section 4943: cannot maintain "excess business holdings" in any business enterprise; designed to eliminate the use of foundations primarily as tax shelters rather than for charitable purposes.

Section 4944: subject to tax on investments considered to be risky

Section 4945: subject to tax on political and other activities Congress deems improper.

Source: Nicholas Cafardi and Jaclyn Fabean Cherry, *Understanding Nonprofit and Tax-Exempt Organizations* (Newark, N.J.: LexisNexis, 2006).

Organizations other than private foundations with gross annual receipts that are normally less than $5,000 as well as all churches are automatically exempt from taxes so long as they meet the requirements of section 501(c)(3). To qualify for recognition as a 501(c)(3) tax-exempt organization, the nonprofit must demonstrate on its Form 1023 that each of the following is true:

1. The organization is organized exclusively for, and will be operated exclusively for, one or more of the purposes (charitable, religious, and so on) specified.
2. No part of the organization's net earnings will accrue to the benefit of private shareholders or individuals.
3. The organization will not, as a substantial part of its activities, attempt to influence legislation (unless it elects to come under the provisions allowing certain lobbying expenditures) or participate to any extent in a political campaign for or against any candidate for public office.[8]

The First Amendment to the U.S. Constitution as well as history and tradition afford churches the greatest freedom from regulation of all not-for-profit organizations. Congress, state legislatures, and the Internal Revenue Service all grant significant leeway to religious organizations in their activities. According to the IRS, the term church includes all places of worship such as temples, mosques, and synagogues, as well as conventions and associations of churches. All churches are automatically exempt from taxes regardless of budget size, and, as will be discussed later, are not subject to the requirements to file the Form 990.

However, ministries are still subject to oversight and certain restrictions imposed by government, particularly with regard to direct endorsement of political candidates. For example, the Church at Pierce Creek, located in Binghamton, NY, lost its tax-exempt status when it took out a full-page ad in two national newspapers urging Christians to oppose Bill Clinton's 1992 bid for the presidency due to his positions on specific moral issues; the ad contained a "sponsored by The Church at Pierce Creek" tag line and a request for tax-deductible donations to defray the expense of the ads, in blatant disregard of the IRS ban on electioneering.[9] Similarly, the Christian Coalition—prominent in the mid-1990s for their support of policies and candidates of the conservative right—lost its 10-year effort to attain tax-exempt status as a 501(c)(4) social welfare organization.[10]

Form 990. Because tax-exempt organizations are not required to pay federal income taxes, they do not file annual tax returns. Instead, they file the Form 990, which is an informational return designed to increase accountability of nonprofit organizations. In 2010, the IRS changed the basic Form 990 subsequent to the 2008 changes in the revenue threshold requirements.[11] Since 2008, all tax-exempt organizations (excluding churches) with annual gross revenues in excess of $50,000 are required to file the Form 990.[12] The Form 990 now includes a core form consisting of eleven parts that must be completed, and up to 16 individual schedules which organizations complete when applicable. Part IV of the core form is a checklist for nonprofits to use to determine which schedules must be submitted. Most organizations need to fill out five or fewer schedules.

New to the redesigned form is Part VI, which is the governance section. In this section, among other things, organizations are asked to provide information pertaining to (1) members of the board of directors; (2) conflict of interest policies; and (3) procedures for documenting meetings. Provision of this information is not required by law, but the IRS added this section in an effort to improve compliance with the information that is required. Because this section provides the opportunity and space to explain in detail responses to questions elsewhere on the form, organizations can address potentially troublesome issues. Nonprofits are encouraged to use the new Form 990 to their advantage, especially the governance section, which can be used as a type of annual report.[13] Governance issues related to ethics and accountability, including conflicts of interest, are discussed further in Chapter 7.

Organizations with gross receipts of less than $200,000 and total assets that do not exceed $500,000 can file the simpler Form 990-EZ, which consists of a four-page core form and up to seven schedules. Nonprofits (again, excluding churches) whose gross receipts do not typically exceed $50,000 are exempt from filing a Form 990, but since 2008 have been required to submit a Form 990-N, also known as the e-postcard because it is filed electronically. The annual electronic notice requires the provision of eight basic pieces of information, including employer identification number (EIN), tax year, legal name and mailing address, any other names used, the name and address of a principal officer, website address if applicable, confirmation that gross receipts are less than $50,000, and notification if the nonprofit has or is about to terminate.

The most recent Form 990 filed by a nonprofit can usually be accessed online, either through the organization's own website or via sites such as www.FoundationCenter.org or www.GuideStar.org. In addition, the National Center for Charitable Statistics makes aggregate data from the Form 990 available through data files and reports on its website, www.nccs.urban.org; access to some databases requires registration and/or payment of a fee. While all Form 990 data provide valuable information and insight regarding the voluntary sector, the addition of the 990-N is a particular boon for nonprofit research. As discussed in detail in Chapter 1, prior to 2008 it was difficult for scholars and researchers to measure the actual size and scope of the voluntary sector because there was no reliable measure of the number of very small nonprofits. Since the e-postcard also collects information on nonprofits that have ceased operations, tracking the real growth in the number of nonprofits should be more accurate. Better information on the size and scope of the voluntary sector assists policymakers as they develop and revise regulations for the sector and as they seek to further incorporate the work of nonprofits into policy related to the delivery of public services.

Unrelated Business Income Tax (UBIT). In 1950, Congress instituted the UBIT in response to concerns that nonprofit organizations had an unfair competitive advantage over businesses. Prior to 1950, nonprofits were exempt from paying taxes on any income received based on a "destination of income test"—meaning that when the income was used by a tax-exempt organization, it was exempt from taxes. After 1950, income was assessed for exemption based on the degree to which it was generated in accordance with the achievement of the purposes for which the organization was granted tax-exempt status.[14]

According to the IRS, "unrelated business income is income from a trade or business, regularly carried on, that is not substantially related to the charitable, educational, or other purpose that is the basis for the organization's exemption."[15] Determining relatedness, however, is not straightforward under the law—for example, gift shop sales. When the Museum of Modern Art (MoMA) sells reproductions of its artwork in the museum gift shop, the income is related to the organization's tax-exempt purpose–facilitating appreciation of the arts. However, income from the sale of t-shirts and coffee mugs celebrating the city of New York are not related to art appreciation and are subject to the UBIT.[16]

The UBIT was designed to address issues of unfair competition when nonprofits engage in operations dominated by the private market. Competition associated with business that is related to the purposes of the exempt organization and therefore exempt from the UBIT is increasingly an issue raised by for-profits, however. Since more for-profit businesses are entering fields of activity traditionally within the purview of nonprofits—for example, hospitals and day care centers—[17] new arguments regarding competitive disadvantage arise. Tax-exemption provides a significant economic advantage to nonprofits, as does the advantage of reputation. When nonprofits and for-profits provide the same goods or services, consumers will tend to patronize nonprofits because their mission is viewed more favorably and consumers have a higher degree of trust in them than in their for-profit counterparts.[18]

When an exempt organization has more than $1,000 in annual unrelated business income, it must file Form 990-T and is subject to tax on that income. UBIT receipts in 2008 totaled $336 million. While 501(c)(3) organizations accounted for just over 25 percent of the Form 990-T's that were filed, almost half of the total tax receipts ($167 million) came from public charities.[19] Approximately 3.5 percent of 501(c)(3) public charities *report* having earned sufficient unrelated business income to be subject to the tax.[20]

The emphasis added to the word "report" is relevant. The figures cited above seem to indicate that for-profit businesses have little to fear from competition with the nonprofit sector, except for the fact that these figures are self-reported. Since the likelihood of an audit is low due to scarce resources at the IRS, it is difficult to know the extent to which self-reporting and reality converge in terms of the scope of unrelated business income.[21] Accordingly, participants at the 1999 Seminar on Emerging Issues in Philanthropy concluded that the "UBIT has, in effect, become a voluntary tax and has served as an 'intermediate sanction' short of the loss of tax exemption."[22] Changes included in the Pension Protection Act of 2006, discussed in detail below, are designed to increase transparency with regard to the UBIT.

Lobbying: IRS and Supreme Court Action Regarding Nonprofits' Political Activity

Lobbying, which along with advocacy is the focus of Chapter 6, represents a way in which nonprofits seek to influence public policy through support or opposition to specific legislation. The Supreme Court determined, in *Buckley v. Valeo,* that Congress may regulate express advocacy (lobbying); the extent to which Congress can regulate the discussion of policy issues is still unclear.[23] For example, 501(c)(3) organizations are prohibited from any type of electioneering, and while they are allowed to legally engage in lobbying activity, Congress and the IRS have imposed a number of restrictions on their political activity. There are certain 501(c)(4) social welfare organizations, however, that can legally engage in activities to promote candidates for public office, and political organizations can seek tax-exempt status under Section 527 of the IRC.

Between 1996 and 1999, the IRS issued several private letter rulings interpreting section 527 of the Internal Revenue Code. Organizations recognized under Section 527 are political organizations such as parties, political action committees (PACs), associations, or funds that exist to receive contributions and make expenditures for what the IRS terms an exempt function; this type of tax-exempt organization is commonly referred to as a 527. For purposes of Section 527, an exempt function "is influencing or attempting to influence the selection, nomination, election, or appointment of an individual to a federal, state, or local public office or office in a political organization"; an exempt function also includes the election of members of the Electoral College, as well as activities that directly or indirectly support one of the specified exempt functions.[24]

The 1996–1999 rulings were controversial because they allowed 527 organizations to engage in substantial electioneering without restriction. As long as the 527 focused on issues rather than candidates and did not act in coordination with a candidate, these independent expenditures were deemed exempt from disclosure requirements. In response to criticism that these rulings resulted in the creation of stealth PACs, since the organizations were not required to disclose the identities of their donors, in mid-2000, Congress sought to close the 527 loophole. Amendments to the IRC required all tax-exempt organizations making over $25,000[25] annually—whether they advocated for candidates, issues, or both—to register with the IRS (Form 8871), file annual information returns (Form 990), and disclose donor names (Form 8872). Opponents argued that this placed an undue reporting burden on many political organizations already subject to state election board disclosure requirements, and the constitutionality of the law was called into question.[26] The 2010 Supreme Court ruling in *Citizens United v. Federal Elections Commission*—discussed further in Chapter 6—has added to the ability of tax-exempt organizations to engage in political activity, and the questions regarding disclosure of donor identities raised after the 2010 and 2012 elections have added to the controversy surrounding the activity of political nonprofits.[27]

Although electioneering by 501(c)(3) organizations is forbidden or strictly regulated, and they are barred from using federal grant or contract funds for lobbying activity, Congress and the IRS generally support advocacy activities, including lobbying with private funds, by nonprofits. The Tax Reform Act of 1976 clarified and expanded the scope of lobbying activity permissible by 501(c)(3) organizations, specifically by narrowing the legal definition of lobbying subject to restriction. Lobbying is differentiated from other advocacy activity because it is said to occur only when there is an expenditure of funds by the tax-exempt organization in conducting activities aimed at influencing specific legislation. Advocacy involves providing information in an effort to educate about and promote an issue or overall policy response.[28] The rules regarding nonprofit lobbying are discussed in more detail in Chapter 6.

Congressional Oversight and Legislation Directly Affect Nonprofit Action

Congress has engaged in oversight of the voluntary sector through its directives to the IRS, as well as through legislation and oversight hearings. Although nonprofit organizations had long been an integral part of U.S. society, the Revenue Act of 1913 officially defined them and permanently established their tax-exemption to facilitate administration of the new federal income tax. Subsequent revisions to the Act refined the role of nonprofits as follows:

1. In 1934, Congress included the "no substantial part" rule regarding lobbying activity (see Chapter 6).
2. In 1936, charitable contributions by corporations became tax-deductible.
3. The Revenue Act of 1938 explicitly stated the rationale for tax-exemption as justified because the loss of government revenue is offset by the relief from appropriating public funds in the provision of public goods and services provided by nonprofits.
4. The 1950 imposition of the Unrelated Business Income Tax, as discussed above.
5. In 1954, the Internal Revenue Code underwent a significant restructuring whereby the sections were revised to incorporate the renumbering still in place today, including Section 501(c)(3) and the almost 30 categories of other tax-exempt organizations; the prohibition regarding electioneering by 501(c)(3) organizations was also a part of this restructuring.[29]

House and Senate hearings typically accompany legislation, and reports commissioned by the Senate Finance Committee have often foreshadowed legislative activity pertaining to nonprofits. The Commission on Industrial Relations, referred to as the Walsh Commission because it was chaired by Senator Frank Walsh, was established in 1912 at the request of President Taft because of his concerns regarding the degree to which foundations were accountable to the public. No legislation derived from the Walsh Commission, but many of its issues resurfaced in subsequent investigations in the House of Representatives—the 1952 Cox Committee and the 1953 Reece Committee—which focused on potential subversive or lobbying activity.[30]

Interestingly, over the course of congressional hearings, critics from each end of the political spectrum denounced foundations as instruments of cultural manipulation. In 1912, critics attacked foundations as instruments of "capitalist manipulation."[31] Critics during the 1950s argued that foundations were undemocratic, elitist, and sought to use their power to shape the future according to their own values,[32] by "encouraging 'empiricism,' 'moral relativity,' and 'collectivist' political opinions in education and the social sciences."[33] These proved to be simply the opening act for later investigations led by Congressman Wright Patman, which culminated in the Tax Reform Act of 1969.

Tax Reform Act of 1969. Scholars identify the Tax Reform Act of 1969 as one of the great watershed events in the history of American philanthropy.[34] While the act affected all charitable organizations in some way, the overwhelming majority of changes were aimed specifically at private foundations, which were defined clearly for the first time and subjected to significant regulation. Among the most significant changes brought by the 1969 Tax Reform Act were the imposition of a tax on investment income and the imposition of a minimum payout requirement, discussed further below.

Representative Wright Patman of Texas has been referred to as "the strongest Congressional critic in the history of foundations."[35] His investigation of foundations began in 1961 and spanned more than a decade. Through extensive questioning of foundation officials and examination of the scarce public information available about them, Patman identified what he considered to be the five primary areas of concern regarding foundations:[36]

1. As their assets were rapidly increasing, so was their economic power;
2. Foundations were being used by some as tax shelters and means to funnel money to friends and family;
3. Oversight of foundations by the IRS was insufficient;
4. Foundations focused too much of their funding efforts overseas; and
5. Businesses, particularly small businesses, were placed at a competitive disadvantage to those that were owned or controlled by foundations because of the tax advantages the foundations enjoyed.

As a result of the Patman hearings and the subsequent IRS investigation at his request, several recommendations were made to address the problems identified; many, although not all, of the recommendations were codified in the Tax Reform Act of 1969. Among the most significant changes brought about by the Act was the imposition of a 4 percent (later reduced to 2 percent) excise tax on investment income, and the minimum payout requirement. Under the minimum payout requirement of the Act, foundations must distribute in grants an amount equal to all of their investment income for the year or 6 percent (later reduced to 5 percent) of the value of their assets, whichever is greater.

In addition, foundations were restricted in their ability to own or control businesses; since many foundations were endowed with stock from the donors' companies, this was a particularly onerous requirement for many. These stipulations were included to address concerns over the rapid accumulation of wealth by foundations and their use primarily as tax shelters by some; they were designed to force use of foundation funds for the public interest in order to justify the tax-exemption granted to the donors. Other changes of note included restrictions on grants to individuals, a prohibition against self-dealing, and the delineation between foundations and public charities. While both are classified as tax-exempt under Section 501(c)(3), only foundations are subject to the more stringent requirements, including the excise tax, payout minimum, and greater limitations on lobbying and advocacy activity. The payout minimum in particular had a significant impact on the sector as it mandated that foundations grant at least a specified portion of their wealth to charitable work. Limitations on lobbying and advocacy were designed to minimize the strategic advantage of the significant resources of foundations in influencing public policy.

Sarbanes-Oxley Act. Commonly referred to as SOX, the Sarbanes-Oxley Act was passed in 2002 in response to major corporate scandals involving companies such as Enron. Although enacted primarily to deter fraud in publicly traded companies, two provisions of SOX apply to all organizations, including nonprofits. Title III, Section 806, and Title XI, Section 1107, provide whistleblower protection to employees by making it "a federal crime for any entity to retaliate against employees who report suspected fraudulent financial activities."[37] The second provision, regarding document management, is found in Title VIII, Section 802, and Title XI, Section 1102. These sections make it "a federal crime to alter or destroy documents in order to prevent their use in an official proceeding."[38] SOX thereby increased the regulatory authority of the federal government over nonprofit organizations.

SOX has also contributed to the increase in state regulatory authority over not-for-profit organizations. Several states have enacted or are considering their own legislation to extend many of the provisions of the Sarbanes-Oxley Act specifically to nonprofit organizations. California's Nonprofit Integrity Act (see Chapter 7) requires the state's nonprofits to comply with some of the best practices provisions of SOX, including auditing committees.[39]

According to the Urban Institute's National Survey of Nonprofit Governance, the implications of extending the SOX provisions to nonprofits are varied. Most nonprofits already comply with some of the provisions, but some would require many nonprofits to change their behavior. For example, more than half of nonprofits surveyed indicated it would be somewhat or very difficult to comply with provisions requiring an audit committee, and over 60 percent indicated it would be difficult to comply with a requirement to rotate the audit firm and/or lead auditor every five years. This is significant because if more than half of nonprofits expect difficulty in complying, the audit requirements are likely to be particularly onerous for small nonprofits. Indeed, among nonprofits with annual budgets under $100,000, 28 percent said it would be very difficult to comply with the audit committee requirements.[40]

In contrast, half of the nonprofits surveyed already have a conflict of interest policy in place for their board members. However, once again the difference between small and large organizations is compelling: 23 percent of small nonprofits have a conflict of interest policy compared with 95 percent of large nonprofits.[41] While this demonstrates that there is already significant compliance with SOX best practices within the nonprofit sector, it also suggests that disparity in the size of nonprofits will likely determine the capacity for overall compliance should these provisions be made mandatory.

Of the 1,007,384 public charities registered with the IRS in 2009, only 362,926 were reporting public charities. This means that just over 36 percent of 501(c)(3) organizations met the reporting threshold of having annual gross receipts over $50,000, thereby requiring them to file Form 990. Of those reporting, 74.4 percent had annual expenses of less than $500,000.[42] This indicates that much of the nonprofit sector is comprised of relatively small organizations[43] that likely have limited organizational capacity. Therefore, additional regulatory demands will likely have a significant impact on the sector as a whole. SOX and its impact on nonprofit ethics and accountability are discussed further in Chapter 7.

Pension Protection Act of 2006. Charles Grassley (R-IA) was first elected to the U.S. Senate in 1980; since then, he has devoted a significant portion of his efforts to government oversight, with particular emphasis on tax issues related to the nonprofit sector. In October 2004, Grassley and Senator Max Baucus (D-MT), as Chair and Ranking Member, respectively, of the Senate Finance Committee, encouraged Independent Sector to convene a Panel on the Nonprofit Sector and submit a report with recommendations to Congress. The original report was submitted in June 2005, with a supplement published in April 2006.

Many of the recommendations of the panel were codified in the Pension Protection Act of 2006 (PPA). Although the legislation deals primarily with issues regarding employer-provided pension plans, Title XII includes Provisions Relating to Exempt Organizations.[44] The key provisions represent significant regulatory changes for 501(c)(3) organizations:

- As referenced in the discussion of the IRS Form 990, since 2008 all tax-exempt organizations (excluding churches) have been required to file an annual information return—whether Form 990, Form 990-N, Form 990-EZ, or Form 990-PF. Failure to file for three consecutive years results in automatic revocation of tax-exempt status; on June 8, 2011, the IRS released its first list of automatic revocations, which included approximately 275,000 nonprofits;

- Organizations that file returns for unrelated business income tax (Form 990-T) must now allow public inspection of them;
- Donor-Advised Funds (DAF) were clearly defined by law for the first time and subjected to more stringent regulation; rules imposed on private foundations regarding restrictions on excess business holdings and disqualified persons were applied to DAF. Substantiation requirements as well as IRS disclosure and reporting requirements were significantly increased for DAF;
- New requirements were imposed upon supporting organizations, controlling organizations, and credit counseling organizations;
- Excise taxes and the excess benefits penalty doubled; and
- Numerous provisions dealing with charitable giving, including new standards for deductibility of the value of donated used household goods and clothing were included; many of these allowances and restrictions on deductibility had sunset provisions attached.[45]

Work by the Panel on the Nonprofit Sector continues. In October 2007, the Panel released *Principles for Good Governance and Ethical Practice,* which includes analysis of more than 50 self-regulation and best practices systems.[46] The key provisions of the Pension Protection

GOING GLOBAL

Regulatory Impact of International Activities by Nonprofits

Of the 362,926 reporting public charities in 2009, approximately two percent (7,218) were classified as international and foreign affairs nonprofits.[47] One of the rationales for allowing a tax exemption for nonprofit organizations flows from what is termed public benefit theory—because nonprofits provide a public benefit that government does not have to provide at taxpayer expense, nonprofits should receive commensurate relief from paying taxes. Through rules based on a 1944 ballot initiative, the State of California has been increasingly moving from the broad "public purpose test" toward a more narrow "community benefit test" that is geographically specific.[48] Tougher economic times have caused state and local government officials to look more closely for ways to increase revenues and, as such, California's Board of Equalization has recently increased its scrutiny of whether the activities of the state's nonprofits, including those which provide charitable work overseas, benefit Californians enough to justify a property tax exemption.

The controversy involved with the stricter standards imposed by the Board of Equalization comes largely from the difficulty in implementation. While the Board of Equalization collects taxes and certifies eligibility for exemption, each county's tax assessor is responsible for determining whether use of the property by a nonprofit provides a "primary benefit" to the state. Defining primary benefit has proven elusive and difficult to quantify,[49] resulting in disparity among how assessors determine eligibility for the exemption. For example, World Vision International near Los Angeles and Direct Relief International in Santa Barbara each do a great deal of work overseas and do not pay property taxes. However, the International Community Foundation, which supports nonprofits in Mexico and Latin America was denied a property tax exemption by the San Diego County assessor on the seven acres it owned approximately nine miles from the Mexican border. The Foundation subsequently donated the property to a nonprofit it established that meets the community benefit test and now leases one of their buildings, thus continuing to avoid property tax. Nonprofits in California have been cautioned to carefully consider the potential for losing their property tax exemption if they cannot demonstrate that the nonprofit confers "meaningful," "important," or "significant" benefits to people in California.[50]

Federal action has also had a regulatory impact on the international activities of U.S.-based nonprofits. Following the attacks of September 11, 2001, President George W. Bush signed Executive Order 13224, which prohibits donations or other transactions with individuals or entities (including charitable organizations) that support terrorists or terrorist activities. The Department of the Treasury was charged with maintaining a list of suspected terrorists/organizations subject to the Executive Order. Unlike other executive orders that remain in effect until revoked, Executive Order 13224 is subject to the National Emergencies Act, which means it must be renewed annually; it has been renewed each year since enacted, across both the Bush and Obama administrations. Likewise, individuals/organizations have been added to the list periodically each year through 2012. As of February 23, 2012, the list of Specially Designated Global Terrorist Entities published by the Treasury Department was nearly 100 pages in length.[51]

The length of the list and the periodic addition of names to it are relevant for nonprofits, especially foundations and other grantmaking entities that must ensure the nonprofits to which they grant funds are not suspected of terrorist activity. To that end, the Treasury Department has compiled a set of Anti-Terrorist Financing Guidelines: Voluntary Best Practices for U.S.-Based Charities, which Treasury indicates should "provide valuable recommendations for the charitable sector to consider in adopting practices that better protect it from the risk of abuse or exploitation by terrorist organizations."[52] Compliance with the recommended best practices is not mandatory, and the Treasury Department specifically stipulates that adherence to the guidelines does not constitute a legal defense against either civil or criminal liability.

Nonprofits that engage in international activities often feel the need to be particularly vigilant and therefore expend the necessary resources to ensure compliance with the Treasury Department guidelines. For example, the International Community Foundation explicitly states on its website that it regularly checks the names of nonprofit staff and directors of its grantee organizations against the list of prohibited persons. International Community Foundation also makes direct reference to its adherence to the recommended best practices in its procedures from the initial grant through administration.[53]

Act applicable to tax-exempt organizations serve to increase transparency and enhance accountability within the sector. Opening the Form 990-T to public inspection, for example, allows for a better understanding of the commercial activities of tax-exempt organizations and the extent to which they compete with private sector organizations. Tightening the regulation on donor-advised funds brings administration of this type of philanthropy more in line with the restrictions imposed on foundations. DAF can operate somewhat like mini-foundations, and tighter restrictions are designed to prevent problems previously seen with foundations when donors received a tax deduction for contributing funds but maintained control over their disbursal.

State Regulation: Offices of the Secretary of State and Attorney General

While most states require nonprofits to register for incorporation with the secretary of state, state regulation is enforced by states' attorneys general. Attorneys general oversee: (1) board members' duties of obedience, loyalty, and care; (2) donor-imposed restrictions on gifts; and (3) solicitations of charitable contributions.[54] In all states, attorneys general have either statutory, case law, or implied authority to oversee charitable organizations.[55] Even though attorneys general theoretically have significant authority to regulate nonprofits, in most states they are not actively involved in regulation primarily because of limited resources.[56]

Board Members and the Duty of Care

Members of the board of directors of a public charity are accorded duties of obedience, loyalty, and care. It is assumed that, since 501(c)(3) organizations are prohibited from distributing excess revenues outside of the organization, board members have no incentive other than to act in the best interest of the nonprofit. Great trust, therefore, is placed in those who oversee the operations of not-for-profit organizations. However, the IRS and state regulators do provide oversight, particularly with regard to potential *self-dealing* activities—that is, those benefiting someone with a significant interest in the organization such as a manager, director, or significant contributor. Form 990, annual filing of which is required by all nonprofits with more than $50,000 in annual gross receipts, contains information regarding self-dealing activities. On the new Form 990 these activities are addressed in Schedule L. While in many instances these transactions were completed to the benefit of the filer, for those instances in which self-dealing did occur, evasive answers in this section can be a red flag to the IRS and state regulators.[57] Self-dealing and boards of directors are discussed further in Chapter 12.

Donor-Imposed Restrictions on Gifts

Donor-Advised Funds (DAF), in which donors retain some control over fund distribution, have increased in popularity in recent years, coinciding with the growth in the number of community foundations[58]—737 in 2009 up from 208 in 1981—as reported by the Foundation Center.[59] With this growth has come increased regulation, namely under the Pension Protection Act of 2006. While more donors are now seeking to maintain control over their charitable contributions without establishing their own foundation, attempts at donor control are not new phenomena. There is a long history of donors placing restrictions on their largesse and a corresponding history of the involvement of attorneys general in litigation as a result.[60]

Foundations and charitable trusts established by donors with a fairly broad mission—for example, alleviating the suffering of the poor, facilitating environmental conservation—place minimal restrictions on directors in managing the trust and disbursing funds. Donors can be too specific, however, resulting in trusts and foundations whose narrowly defined missions can be impossible or at best impractical to accomplish, or even illegal to implement. In addition, some donors stipulate missions that are accomplished without depletion of funds, which creates its own set of challenges. As highlighted in the opening vignette, attorneys general often get involved to protect the donor's wishes by launching investigations. In the case of the Buck Trust outlined in Case Study 4.3, the attorney general for the State of California engaged in a lengthy lawsuit in order to protect donor intent in the case of a narrowly-defined charitable trust. While the donor's intent prevailed, this case raised serious questions about the appropriateness of donor's wishes with regard to pursuit of the public interest.

CASE STUDY 4.3

The Buck Trust and the Regulatory Impact of Donor Intent

In 1975, Beryl Buck died without direct heirs and bequeathed approximately 70,000 shares of Belridge Oil Company stock to the San Francisco Foundation (SFF) for the specific purpose of caring for the needy or addressing other charitable, religious, or educational purposes in Marin County, California. While the allowable activities to be undertaken with the funds were quite broad, the geographic focus was narrow and problematic—Marin County is one of the wealthiest counties in the state. In addition, at the time of the bequest, the shares of stock had an estimated worth of $7 to $10 million. Under the requirements of the Tax Reform Act of 1969, foundations were restricted in their ability to own businesses, causing many to divest themselves of most of the shares of stock with which they were initially endowed by their founder(s). Accordingly, the SFF sold the majority of the Buck Trust's shares in Belridge Oil Company stock in 1979, for a reported $264 million gain in assets. By 1984, the trust was worth over $400 million, with an annual investment income of approximately $30 million.[63]

The San Francisco Foundation serves not only Marin County but also four other counties in the Bay Area—San Francisco, Alameda, Contra Costa, and San Mateo. Shortly after receiving the Buck Trust, the directors began to feel the pressure of managing funds which had nearly tripled the size of the Foundation and brought with them a great deal of controversy. Nonprofits in the other four counties of their service area complained at the disparity in grants given to Marin County. In 1982, the public interest law firm Public Advocates filed suit against SFF claiming it had violated its charter by granting a disparate proportion of its funds in Marin County compared to the other counties in its service area. The suit alleged that approximately 70 percent of grant applications from Marin County were approved compared to less than 20 percent of applications from the other four counties. The disparity was further evident in the per grantee distribution of funds—$88,000 on average for each Marin County grant versus $18,000 for all other grantees.[64] While it seems obvious why nonprofits in the other parts of the SFF service area would oppose the geographic restrictions of the Buck Trust, it is important to note that Marin County residents were not united in support of the arrangement. Although many nonprofits and elected officials felt the Trust should be dedicated to Marin County as Mrs. Buck intended, others felt the magnitude of beneficence would have detrimental effects on levels of volunteerism and charitable contributions by the residents of Marin County. There was a sentiment among many that the Buck Trust funds would come to be viewed as the only game in town, leading individual donations and the willingness of many to volunteer their time to decline amidst a pervasive attitude that the Buck Trust would pay for what was needed.

The situation reached a climax in 1986 when the San Francisco Foundation petitioned the court to alter the terms of the trust under the cy pres doctrine, arguing that Mrs. Buck could not have foreseen that her bequest would multiply to the extent it had and that it was *impractical* to expend the funds solely on an area as wealthy as Marin County. The court disagreed; impractical was not considered the same as illegal or impossible, standards used in other cases involving cy pres. While the level of need in Marin County was less than in other counties, the area was by no means devoid of people who needed assistance, leading the court to conclude that the donor's intent could and should be carried out as stipulated in the provisions of the trust.[65]

As a result of losing their petition and as a condition of resolution of the case, control of the Buck Trust was transferred from the San Francisco Foundation to the newly created Marin Community Foundation (MCF). Despite the creation of MCF, the San Francisco Foundation did not change its service area, which includes all five counties in the Bay area and therefore continues to serve Marin County and to grant funds to organizations within Marin County; net assets for the San Francisco Foundation exceeded $956 million in 2010.[66] While the Buck Trust funds were the impetus for establishment of the Marin Community Foundation and the Trust continues to be the largest fund it manages, MCF also administers 390 family and community funds, has ten supporting organizations, and continues to solicit donations on behalf of philanthropic causes in Marin County; net assets for MCF exceeded $244 million in 2010.[67]

As of 2010, the assets of the Buck Trust were valued at $695 million. Under the minimum payout requirements enacted under the Tax Reform Act of 1969 (and since amended), foundations are required to distribute a minimum of 5 percent of their assets each year. While 4 percent of the assets of the Buck Trust are contributed each year to organizations in Marin County, the remaining 1 percent goes to support three projects that, while located in Marin County, have a much broader geographic impact: (1) Buck Institute for Age Research; (2) Buck Institute for Education; and (3) the Marin Institute, which is focused on reducing alcohol abuse.[68] In 2010,

MCF itself received from the Buck Trust $3.2 million in contribution revenue to complete their five-year strategic plan, as well as $7.2 million in administrative fees.[69]

In fiscal year 2010, the Marin Community Foundation distributed $23.2 million in grants on behalf of the Buck Trust.[70] According to its 2010 Master List of Grants, MCF granted an additional $29.7 million through its other funds, plus $4.34 million granted by MCF supporting organizations. In 2010, MCF granted funds from the Buck Trust as well as its other funds under thirteen initiatives identified in the 2010–2014 strategic plan. Among the initiatives were

1. Closing the Educational Achievement Gap—$2.37 million to 18 nonprofits, including $900,000 to the organization 10,000 Degrees to support their College for All program;
2. Ending the Cycle of Poverty—$1.477 million to 13 nonprofits, including $54,000 to Adopt a Family of Marin to prevent homelessness among low-income families with children;
3. Integration of Immigrants—$750,000 to 19 nonprofits, including $183,333 to Legal Aid of Marin to establish the Opportunity Center, which provides ESL classes among other services; and
4. Arts in the Community—$670,000 to 21 nonprofits, including $54,000 to Bread and Roses to support arts opportunities for institutionalized residents of Marin County.

In each case mentioned above, the Buck Trust grants to the nonprofits were combined with grants from other funds managed by MCF. Grants through the other MCF funds and its supporting organizations encompass a wide geographic area that includes Marin County nonprofits as well as others in the Bay Area, throughout California, and across the country.[71]

QUESTIONS TO CONSIDER:

1. How was the concept of donor intent used to regulate the activities of the San Francisco Foundation with regard to management of the Buck Trust funds?
2. What difficulties were present in trying to stay true to the donor's intent while abiding by federal law regarding minimum payout of funds?
3. Consider the financial information presented above regarding assets and grantmaking of the San Francisco Foundation and the Marin Community Foundation. Does it appear that the court's interpretation of cy pres was appropriate for the disbursal of the Buck Trust funds, or were the fears of critics that spending the funds only in Marin County would have devastating consequences realized? Explain your interpretation.
4. Consider the four relationships that describe nonprofit interaction with public policy (make policy, affected by policy, influence policy, subject to policy) and discuss the ways in which formation and management of the Buck Trust reflect any or all of these relationships between nonprofits and public policy.
5. Is the Buck Trust a unique example of regulation of a nonprofit? How does this case inform your understanding of the challenges faced in regulating not-for-profit organizations?

More information on the Marin Community Foundation is available at www.marincf.org. Additional information on the nonprofit sector in Marin County can be found in the *Marin County Nonprofit Landscape Study, 2008,* available from the Center for Volunteer and Nonprofit Leadership of Marin, www.cvnl.org.

In cases where the donor's intent is either illegal—for example, funds to establish a school exclusively for white male orphans—or impossible—for example, a bequest of insufficient funds to carry out the specified purpose—trustees or directors may ask the court to invoke the cy pres doctrine to modify the terms of the trust. Cy pres is an old French law term meaning "so close."[61] Under cy pres, a court can allow use of the donor's funds for other than the explicitly stated purpose, so long as the use of the funds is as close as practicable to the donor's intent. Charities have long been viewed as friends of the court, and courts are subsequently loathe to divert funds intended for charitable purposes back to potential heirs—hence, use of cy pres. However, the courts are equally hesitant to override the legally stated intent of donors. The result is what scholars refer to as the influence of the dead hand in American philanthropy.[62]

Regulation of Charitable Solicitations by the States

As of 2010, 39 states require nonprofits that solicit donations within their borders to register with the designated state charity official. Most (34) also require annual financial reports to be filed with the state. Of the states that require registration, only three—Colorado, Florida, and Oklahoma—have not yet adopted the Unified Registration Statement (URS) promoted by the National Association of State Charity Officials (NASCO) and the National Association of State Attorneys General.[72] The URS was developed by NASCO and the attorneys general in order to streamline compliance with state regulations by providing uniformity in reporting requirements.[73]

Recent research indicates that the nonprofit sector as a whole might benefit from fewer rules and regulation.[74] Since the offices of state charity officials reportedly spend about two-thirds of their resources tracking registration and reporting, the ability to engage in oversight and enforcement of abuse is limited. Six states without registration or reporting requirements do not report significantly higher incidences of fraud and abuse.[75] Likewise, even states that require registration and annual reporting most often rely on citizen complaints to initiate investigations of wrongdoing; as stated earlier, limited resources hamper regulatory efforts in most state offices.

INDIRECT REGULATION: COURTS AND CONTRACTS

The Tenth Amendment to the Constitution reserves certain powers to the states. Accordingly, the federal government has often used stipulations attached to the receipt of grant funds as a means to encourage behavior that it could not compel the states to undertake. Likewise, compliance requirements attached to receipt of government grants serve as an indirect means to regulate nonprofits, as do the conditions placed on nonprofits with government contracts. Court cases also serve as an indirect means of regulation. For example, the ACLU lawsuit against the Department of Health and Human Services (DHHS), discussed in Chapter 3, illustrates indirect regulation of nonprofit grantees; the ACLU sought to change the conditions for DHHS funding in order to either change the services provided by Catholic Charities or have them removed as a DHHS grantee.

Government Grants and Contract Compliance

In 2008, 8 percent of total revenues for reporting public charities came from federal, state, and local government grants; an additional 24.3 percent of revenue derived from fees for goods and services from government.[76] Making receipt of funds conditional on compliance with activities such as historic preservation and maintenance of a drug-free workplace enable the federal government to expand regulatory authority through enticement (a carrot rather than a stick). Such requirements are neither unique to nor targeted toward regulation of the nonprofit sector, but the pursuit of government grants and contracts to deliver public services has direct implications for operations within the nonprofit sector.

While most public charities are not required to submit to specific auditing procedures, federal grant recipients are. Federal grant recipients are also required to provide specific information such as budget data and program details, and are subject to site visits and records review of all grant program activity. In addition, too heavy a reliance on government funds for operational support can lead to vendorism, whereby the nonprofit exists simply to implement the government grant or contract.[77] Mission is of paramount importance to the voluntary sector; it is what defines and directs nonprofit activity. When the focus on mission is compromised by increased attention to government regulation, the sector as a whole is weakened. This is not to imply that nonprofits should forgo the pursuit of government grants. As has often been stated, government and nonprofits have long enjoyed a mutually beneficial partnership in the provision of goods and services. However, it is important for nonprofits to remain mindful of the compliance costs associated with government grants and contracts, as well as the program and service delivery benefits of receiving them.

Regulation through the Courts

As noted in the opening vignette, individuals are not likely to prevail in a lawsuit against a nonprofit organization, usually because of the tenets pertinent to trust law. In order to be valid, private trusts must have an identifiable beneficiary with the capability of overseeing the trust. In contrast, charitable trusts (and foundations) have no individual beneficiaries.[78] Accordingly, the courts have usually held that only the state—through the attorney general—has legal standing with regard to enforcement authority.[79] For example, Oregon law clearly states that "no court shall have jurisdiction to modify or terminate any trust of property for charitable purposes unless the Attorney General is a party to the proceedings."[80] Thus, cases brought by disgruntled donors such as those described in the opening vignette are generally dismissed by the courts, and complaints are referred to the office of the relevant state's attorney general.

In some cases, directors and officers of a nonprofit may initiate a suit in state court to enforce charitable duties, and in rare instances, individuals have been given limited standing in state courts such as Wisconsin and California.[81] However, in general individuals do not have standing to sue nonprofits, and they are specifically prevented from suing in U.S. Tax Court. Alleged abuses by charities have led some in the field to suggest that Congress extend standing to sue in Tax Court to private individuals. The Panel on the Nonprofit Sector (PNS) addressed this in their supplemental report of 2006 with a recommendation that Congress not take action. Their investigation concluded that principles of current state and common law are sufficient to enforce the fiduciary duties of charitable organizations. Any additional benefit derived from broadening the pool of those with enforcement capabilities would be overridden by the harm brought from increased potential for nuisance lawsuits that might deter volunteers from serving on boards and would divert charitable funds to legal defense fees.[82]

SELF-REGULATION IN THE VOLUNTARY SECTOR

In response to passage of the Tax Reform Act of 1969, leaders in the philanthropic community took it upon themselves to organize the Commission on Private Philanthropy and Public Needs. Commonly known as the Filer Commission, this effort sought to provide a comprehensive examination of the voluntary sector in order to explain and advance the role of nonprofits in American society. Led by John Filer, then CEO of Aetna Life and Casualty Company, the Commission was instrumental in promoting research on the nonprofit sector as well as in coordinating and enhancing the work of nonprofits in addressing public problems. Institutional infrastructure developments facilitated by the Filer Commission include: (1) the establishment of the first academic center for not-for-profit research at Yale University; (2) merger of the National Council on Philanthropy and the Coalition of National Voluntary Organizations to form a new organization, Independent Sector; and (3) groundwork which paved the way for the National Center for Charitable Statistics.[83]

In the first phase of charity regulation cited above, self-policing was the norm, primarily because there were no other mechanisms in place.[84] Even with the developments in external regulation discussed here, the nonprofit sector continues to regulate itself in a variety of ways. Evaluation by watchdog groups such as the American Institute of Philanthropy and www.Ministrywatch.com, promotion of the adoption of Codes of Ethics by Independent Sector, Internet dissemination of Form 990 financial disclosures via GuideStar, and accreditation procedures are just a few of the venues by which the voluntary sector seeks to promote and maintain accountability.

Watchdog Groups as Sector Regulators

A number of systems have been created to rate or rank nonprofits as a means of providing donors and the public with a reliable way to compare organizations. In 2005, the National Council of Nonprofit Associations and the National Human Services Assembly (NCNA-NHSA) formed a joint task force to evaluate the rating and ranking systems of several of these nonprofit watchdog organizations. This project was undertaken out of concern that the potential exists for donors and the media to be misled or misinformed by the rating and ranking systems currently put in place by a myriad of watchdog groups. The task force examined materials from nine entities.[85]

In the first group, rating systems of four not-for-profit organizations—American Institute of Philanthropy (AIP), Better Business Bureau Wise Giving Alliance (BBB-WGA), Charity Navigator, and Standards for Excellence Institute (SFXI)—and one government entity, the Combined Federal Campaign, were compared. For the second group, four for-profit publications—*Chronicle of Philanthropy, Forbes, Nonprofit Times,* and *Smart Money*—that rate or rank charitable nonprofit organizations were compared. Each entity was examined based on (1) organization and structure; (2) method of rating or ranking; and (3) evaluation standards/criteria.[86] Results indicate that there is the greatest consistency among the ranking systems of the four for-profit publications. Of particular note, none of the publications used program delivery or effectiveness in their rating/ranking systems. More information on the nonprofit evaluators in the NCNA-NHSA study is found in Box 4.4.

Because of variability in the criteria used to evaluate charities, it is advisable for donors to be well-informed about the watchdog group itself before employing its ratings or rankings in evaluating charities. NCNA-NHSA advises that there is sufficient variation among the systems currently employed to cause confusion and even misinterpretation, leading to denial of contributions to worthy charities. They recommend use of a set of criteria to evaluate the raters that includes among other things (1) ensuring the rating organization makes its methodology and criteria for evaluation readily available and understandable; (2) applies the same evaluation standards to itself; and (3) offers its findings free-of-charge to donors and those charities that are evaluated. Lastly, the NCNA-NHSA task force argues that while financial measures such as fundraising and overhead cost ratios are important measures, they are insufficient indicators of nonprofit strength and worthiness. Rating/rankings should include measures of program effectiveness and service delivery in order to depict the true capabilities of the charities evaluated.

Using Accreditation to Enforce Standards and Best Practices

Numerous nonprofit organizations exist for the purpose of accrediting other nonprofit organizations—that is, to establish, maintain, and enforce best practices and standards of behavior within a particular field of expertise. While accreditation is most readily associated with institutions of higher education and health care facilities, other organizations within the nonprofit sector also seek to regulate themselves in this manner.

For example, as discussed in previous chapters, National Children's Alliance (NCA) is a national-level not-for-profit organization that was established through a federal grant to provide technical support and financial assistance to develop children's advocacy centers (CAC) nationwide. In 1991, NCA recognized its first full member centers, those CACs that met all of the best practices standards set forth in the model. CACs submitted to an

Box 4.4

FOR MORE INFORMATION

NCNA-NHSA RATE THE RATERS

In 2005, the National Council of Nonprofit Associations (NCNA) and the National Human Services Assembly (NHSA) published the results of their study on prominent evaluators of nonprofit organizations. A brief synopsis of three of the watchdog groups they studied follows:

- American Institute of Philanthropy (AIP)—the mission of AIP, as stated on their website, www.charitywatch.org, is "to maximize the effectiveness of every dollar contributed to charity by providing donors with the information they need to make more informed giving decisions." The ratings system employed is a grade scale—A+ to F—with additional information on assets, fundraising costs, and program expenditures. Ratings are published tri-annually in AIP's *Charity Rating Guide.* More than 500 organizations have been evaluated through in-depth analysis of public information as well as information submitted by AIP, including audits, tax forms, and annual reports. Program effectiveness, while not provided for every organization evaluated, may be available through articles published in the *Charity Rating Guide,* on the website, or in media/donor communications.
- Better Business Bureau Wise Giving Alliance (the Alliance)—according to their website, www.bbb.org/us/Wise-Giving, the Alliance "helps donors make informed giving decisions and advances high standards of conduct among organizations that solicit contributions from the public." The Alliance specifies that it does not rate or rank charities but does apply a pass/fail grade to each in terms of its Standards for Charitable Accountability. Information submitted by the nonprofit organization is the basis for the evaluation. Nationally soliciting nonprofits are chosen for evaluation based on the volume of inquiries the Alliance receives; the *Wise Giving Guide* is published four times per year. Reports on thousands of organizations have been prepared over the years, but only recent reports (less than two–years old) are distributed. The Alliance places responsibility for program effectiveness assessment on the nonprofit's board; it requires the nonprofit's board to mandate a biennial performance evaluation with a written report of results.
- Charity Navigator—the mission of Charity Navigator is to work to "guide intelligent giving," as stated on their website, www.charitynavigator.org. This watchdog uses financial ratios to evaluate organizational efficiency and capacity; ratings are assigned on a scale of 0 to 4. More than 3,000 nonprofits have been rated based on public information, including Form 990 data, website information, and the organization's brochures. Currently, the ratings are based solely on Form 990 data; providing program effectiveness ratings is a goal for the future. Ratings are available through the searchable database on their website.

Source: NCNA-NHSA, *Rating the Raters: An Assessment of Organizations and Publications that Rate/Rank Charitable Nonprofit Organizations, 2005.*

application and site review process of evaluation to achieve full member status.[87] After 2002, NCA moved beyond recognition of associate and full members to become an accrediting body of children's advocacy centers nationwide. Accreditation brings with it an assurance of quality and continued monitoring that center activities will meet the stringent standards of best practices in handling cases of child sexual abuse. Because the delivery of services by nonprofits is often a means by which they make policy, improving service delivery through accreditation and establishing best practices standards enhances the impact of nonprofits on public policy.

CONCLUSION

The nonprofit sector is subject to a great deal of government regulation and engages in a significant amount of self-regulatory behavior. However, the size, scope, and diversity of not-for-profit organizations pose substantial challenges to effective regulation of the sector as a whole. As the number of nonprofits increases, the competition for scarce resources also increases. More and more nonprofits are exploring commercial ventures to diversify and stabilize their funding streams, leading to greater relevance of the UBIT. Also, as nonprofit activity increases as a portion of GDP, the impact on local, state, and federal tax bases becomes a greater concern.

Most public charities do not lobby, so regulatory activity which focuses heavily on lobbying as currently defined has little effect on the majority of 501(c)(3) organizations. Most nonprofit organizations, however, do advocate for their causes and constituencies. Regulatory activity aimed at diminishing the voice of nonprofits regarding public policy, therefore, will continue to meet stiff resistance. Independent Sector is one of the leading voices for the voluntary sector and has been quite successful in its advocacy efforts.[88]

Despite the fact that only two of its provisions apply specifically to nonprofit organizations, the Sarbanes-Oxley Act does have an impact on the nonprofit sector. Many in the field look upon the provisions of SOX as best practices for nonprofits, behaviors that would be in the best interest of individual nonprofits and the sector as a whole. State regulation of nonprofit organizations includes best practices legislation, either based on SOX provisions or at the request of the organizations it would govern.

Implementation is also an important factor. Enacting stricter government regulations and strengthening the sector's commitment to governing itself are not enough. Without adequate resources to enforce regulations, they will not have the desired effect. To this end, the Panel on the Nonprofit Sector identified federal and state enforcement as its number one recommendation in its report to Congress on strengthening nonprofit governance. They recommend that additional funding be provided to the IRS as well as state charity oversight agencies, plus provision of greater access to IRS information by state attorneys general.

Regulation—by government entities and through self-regulation—represents the most significant way in which the voluntary sector is affected by and subject to public policy. While the scope of regulatory action applicable to the sector has increased, the data indicate that the voluntary sector is not opposed to more stringent oversight per se. Not-for-profit organizations in general recognize the need for greater accountability and standards of behavior. However, the implications of regulatory activity are significant for the nonprofit sector. Diversity of organizations dictates the relevance of certain types of regulations as well as nonprofits' capacity to comply with them. As with most policies, there is rarely a "one size fits all" approach.

Questions For Review

1. What must an organization demonstrate to the Internal Revenue Service (IRS) in order to be recognized as tax-exempt under section 501(c)(3)? Explain the rationale for each requirement.
2. Describe the Unrelated Business Income Tax (UBIT) and explain why it was instituted. Has this proven to be an effective way to regulate nonprofit activity? Why or why not?
3. How do the Title XII provisions of the Pension Protection Act of 2006 extend or expand on the earlier requirements of the Tax Reform Act? Explain how the changes are both welcomed and opposed by the philanthropic sector.
4. Identify and explain three ways in which nonprofits are subject to either indirect or self-regulation. What are the merits and limitations of these approaches to monitor the voluntary sector?

Assignment

Go to the IRS Stay Exempt website at www.stayexempt.irs.gov/VirtualWorkshop.aspx to access the Virtual Workshop on Tax-Exempt Status (Training Topics 1 of 5). Complete the virtual workshop, which should take approximately 30 minutes. You will need to listen to the audio commentary and be prepared to type and submit responses to scenarios provided throughout. Upon completion of the Virtual Workshop, summarize the main points and evaluate the effectiveness of the workshop in improving your knowledge and capability to advise a nonprofit on the requirements for maintaining tax-exempt status.

Suggested Readings

Brody, Evelyn, and Joseph J. Cordes. "Tax Treatment of Nonprofit Organizations: A Two-Edged Sword?" In *Nonprofits and Government: Collaboration and Conflict,* 2nd ed. Edited by Elizabeth T. Boris and C. Eugene Steurele, 141–180. Washington, DC: The Urban Institute Press, 2006.

Cafardi, Nicholas and Jaclyn Fabean Cherry. *Understanding Nonprofit and Tax-Exempt Organizations.* Newark, NJ: LexisNexis, 2006.

Fremont-Smith, Marion R. *Governing Nonprofit Organizations: Federal and State Law and Regulation.* Cambridge, MA: Belknap Press of Harvard University Press, 2004.

Friedman, Lawrence M. "Charitable Gifts and Foundations." Chapter 8 in *Dead Hands: A Social History of Wills, Trusts, and Inheritance Law.* Stanford, CA: Stanford Law Books of Stanford University Press, 2009.

Irvin, Renee A. "State Regulation of Nonprofit Organizations: Accountability Regardless of Outcome." *Nonprofit and Voluntary Sector Quarterly,* 34, 2 (2005): 161–78.

Web Resources

IRS Stay Exempt Tax Basics for Exempt Organizations, www.stayexempt.irs.gov
List of State Offices that Regulate Charities, www.nasconet.org/agencies
National Association of State Charity Officials, www.nasconet.org
Panel on the Nonprofit Sector, www.nonprofitpanel.org
Unified Registration Statement and Multi-State Filing Project, www.multistatefiling.org

5 The Role of Mission and Strategic Management

Non-profit institutions exist for the sake of their mission. The first task of the leader is to make sure that everybody sees the mission, hears it, lives it.

Peter F. Drucker[1]

Imagine that you were raised in New York City surrounded by all of its arts and cultural amenities. You saw plays on Broadway with your family, visited the Metropolitan Museum of Art on school field trips, listened to the orchestra in Van Cortland Park on summer afternoons, and played the lead in your high school musical. All of these experiences infused in you a love of the arts and appreciation for the uplifting effects that art, theatre, and music have on people's lives. As an adult, your career has taken you far from New York City and to your dismay children in your community have little access to the arts. Budget cuts have meant that the public schools no longer have a commitment to bringing arts and culture to students. There is no money for school field trips, and funding for visual arts, theatre, and music programs was cut years ago. As a strong proponent of all forms of artistic expression, you find this situation untenable and decide to do something about it: You decide to bring children's theatre productions and opportunities to the community through creation of a Youth Community Theatre Project. Your long-term vision is to partner with the local school district to bring art back into the schools, but for now, armed with an idea, your passion, and a list of potential donors, you are ready to make this happen.

THE MISSION: CRITICAL FOR NONPROFIT SUCCESS

Mission can be described as the reason for being, the driving force, or the guiding purpose of an organization. In the nonprofit sector, mission is what

POLICY IMPLICATIONS OF MISSION AND STRATEGIC MANAGEMENT

- Nonprofits are mission-driven organizations; the missions and values that drive them to pursue their public purposes are, therefore, key to the types of policies they seek to pursue and influence.
- Nonprofit leaders, especially founding leaders, have a distinct influence on the missions of their organizations and the programs, activities, and policies the nonprofit pursues.
- The mission can be affected by public policy in a variety of ways:
    - Budgets can be cut, leading nonprofits to act;
    - Government priorities can change, allowing nonprofits to step in to create policy, or subjecting nonprofits to policies that change the ways in which they pursue their missions;
    - Governments can decide to provide a service, or to stop providing a service, which changes the work of nonprofit organizations;
    - New public grants or subsidies can be created that nonprofits decide to pursue.
- Formal mission statements and strategic plans are techniques of good management that keep nonprofits focused on their missions, so their work meets public needs.

guides organizations as they address public needs. Whether through direct program delivery or policy advocacy, mission has always been the critical driver of organizations in the not-for-profit sector. Those who found, fund, and work in nonprofit organizations do so because of their commitment to the purpose of the organization. As Charles T. Goodsell explains in *Mission Mystique*, "more than any other quality, a strong sense of mission is indispensible to morale, image and success."[2]

Nonprofits such as the hypothetical Youth Community Theatre Project (YCTP) in the opening vignette are founded by policy entrepreneurs who see the chance to make a difference. In the case of YCTP, a perceived government failure—the lack of public commitment to the arts—has opened a window of opportunity for a committed individual to bring theatre to children who would not otherwise enjoy or participate in the performing arts. Its mission will guide the decisions that YCTP makes, the programs it pursues, and the impact it will have on policy.

We also discuss nonprofit missions from a practical perspective, with a number of key concepts framing our discussion of articulating and pursuing the nonprofit mission. These concepts include clarification of organizational values and the creation of a *mission statement* that is guided by those values; articulation of a longer-term *vision statement;* use of the tools of strategic management and planning; and the setting of organizational goals. All of these will help the not-for-profit move from its guiding mission through identification and achievement of objectives that can be celebrated and publicized to important organizational stakeholders.

Finally, there are important legal ramifications of the nonprofit mission that must be understood. Herrington J. Bryce describes five characteristics that must be present in order for nonprofits to maintain their legal status as tax-exempt organizations. The nonprofit mission must be: (1) a social contract, or promise between the organization, its members, and society that it will serve the purposes for which it has been granted tax exempt status; (2) permanent, in that the mission is voted upon by the board members and not subject to dramatic changes, especially those changes that may threaten the tax-exempt status of the organization; (3) clear, in that it articulates an approved tax-exempt organizational purpose with clarity; (4) approved, by the board, the state, and the IRS; and (5) demonstrable, the nonprofit must be able to show how and from where it received its income and resources, and for what purposes those resources were used.[3]

Whether seeking grant funding from government or foundations, seeking donations of time and money from the public, engaging in policy advocacy on behalf of clients, or delivering services to the community, a strong mission gives the organization its sense of direction. As funders increasingly seek measurable outcomes from the organizations that they support, a strong mission and vision tied to organizational values and goals offer the nonprofit a clear way to demonstrate its success. When considering collaborations with other organizations across sectors, the mission of the nonprofit is critical to finding like-minded entities that will partner in policy advocacy, funding, and implementation.

ORGANIZATIONAL VALUES AND THE ROLE OF STAKEHOLDERS

A nonprofit organization is created to *do something.* In our opening vignette the founder seeks to fill in a gap left by school budget cuts and bring children's theatre opportunities to the community through creation of the Youth Community Theatre Project. The values of the founder are the principles that will guide the project and help the organization to find its niche in the broader environment. As Lakey, Lakey, Napier, and Robinson note, "Values are the bedrock of all organizational policies. They form the foundation for the vision, mission, and goals of the group."[4] Let us assume that the founder of YCTP values access, education, and bringing high-quality theatre productions to children in a community with few opportunities to enjoy the performing arts. Founding board members will be selected because they feel similarly passionate about these issues, and together they will take these values and infuse them into the work of the organization.

Values are inextricably linked to mission in the not-for-profit sector, and both a clearly articulated mission and strong values are vital for nonprofit success. For example, organizational values and mission are important in communication with stakeholders. Clientele, grantors, staff, volunteers, policymakers, and others must have a solid understanding of why the organization exists, the values it seeks to uphold, and the approach it takes to fulfill its purpose.

Mission and values are also important for differentiating organizations because they become part of each nonprofit's unique organizational culture. The culture of an organization has been described as its personality—the unique and intangible qualities that describe "how we do things around here." The concept includes the norms, values, rituals, and symbols of the organization, including logos, mottos, and celebrations. The uniforms worn by Girl and Boy Scouts and the ceremony surrounding earning patches and merit badges are obvious examples of their organizational cultures, which value community service, personal responsibility, and celebrating success. These cultural attributes are widely recognized by those directly involved in scouting as well as by the general public; such recognition is important in attracting and maintaining the support of external stakeholders. With large nonprofits such as the Scouts, well-known missions and values foster ongoing relationships with participants, donors, and other partners that help them to address the public needs for which the organizations were created.

THE ROLE OF LEADERSHIP IN PLANNING AND MEETING NEEDS

Many authors have noted the importance of the organization's leadership for advancing the nonprofit mission. In their study of nonprofit leadership, Barry Dym and Harry Hutson found that effective nonprofit leaders align themselves with the values, mission, strategies, and culture of their organizations. They write, "The leader's raison d'être is to guide her organization toward the fulfillment of its mission by clarifying objectives and developing strategies, requiring others to design and implement tactics, and to hold them accountable for their efforts."[5] A clear example of this comes in the Case Study of the National Foundation for Infantile Paralysis, in Case Study 5.2. The foundation, whose original mission was to create a vaccine to eradicate the polio virus, was able to use the high profile of its co-founder to develop strategies for fundraising, medical research, and clinical vaccine trials that dwarfed even federal involvement in polio eradication. Its strategies and reach are legendary and have led to decades of valuable research and policy that have improved health outcomes for infants and children worldwide.

Bringing together the concepts of leadership and organizational culture, Edgar Schein has written, "it can be argued that the only thing of real importance that leaders do is to create and manage culture." [6] In particular, the role of the founding leader has been especially important to shaping the mission and culture of nonprofit organizations. It is the founding leader's enthusiasm and passion that is the starting point for organizational action. This is probably best exemplified by the legacy of John Muir, founding president of the Sierra Club. His unwavering love of nature and wish to protect and experience it has guided the Sierra Club since its founding in 1892. The motto displayed on the club's website, "explore, enjoy, and protect the planet," is a continuing reflection of Muir's vision (see Box 5.1).

ox 5.1

FOR EXAMPLE

JOHN MUIR AND THE SIERRA CLUB: A FOUNDING LEADER'S PASSION AND ORGANIZATIONAL ACTION

Described as the spiritual leader of the Progressive Era conservation movement, John Muir arrived in the Yosemite Valley in 1868 and never stopped fighting for the protection of America's western wilderness. A prolific writer, Muir published books and newspaper and magazine articles on Alaska, the Sierras, the Yosemite Valley, Hetch-Hetchy, and the early National Park System. His work described in great detail the natural beauty of these areas and the need for government protection of them. For example, in 1890, he described at length the proposed Yosemite National Park in *Century* magazine, urging swift passage of proposed legislation for the federal protection of Yosemite from the devastating effects of commercial endeavors such as logging and ranching.

In 1892, Muir and several colleagues created the Sierra Club "'to explore, enjoy, and render accessible the mountain regions of the Pacific Coast; to publish authentic information concerning them,' and 'to enlist the support and cooperation of the people and government in preserving the forests and other natural features of the Sierra Nevada.'"[7] Muir served as Sierra Club president until his death in 1914. Over 120 years later, the Club's mission statement remains true to the original:

> To explore, enjoy, and protect the wild places of the earth; To practice and promote the responsible use of the earth's ecosystems and resources; To educate and enlist humanity to protect and restore the quality of the natural and human environment; and to use all lawful means to carry out these objectives.

The Sierra Club's influence on public policy has continued unabated over the decades. For example, shortly after founding the club, in 1897, Muir published a piece in the *Atlantic Monthly,* lauding the management of forest areas in France, Switzerland, and Japan, and arguing that in the United States "a change from robbery and ruin to a permanent rational policy is urgently needed."[8] The activism of Muir and the Sierra Club led directly to the protection and federal acquisition of Yosemite National Park in 1906 and the eventual creation of a nationwide system of federal parks and their attendants, the National Park Service.[9] Today, there are 397 national parks, the most recent of which is New Jersey's Paterson Great Falls National Historical Park. For their contributions, Muir and the Sierra Club were highlighted in the 2009 Ken Burns documentary series, *The National Parks: America's Best Idea.*

Muir's continuing influence on the mission of the Sierra Club and its success in changing public policy is made clear through the admiration of Yvon Chouinard, the founder of the outdoor clothing company, Patagonia. In an interview with the club's *Sierra Magazine,* Chouinard said

> If you think about all the gains our society has made, from independence to now, it wasn't government. It was activism. People think, 'Oh, Teddy Roosevelt established Yosemite National Park, what a great president.' BS. It was John Muir

who invited Roosevelt out and then convinced him to ditch his security and go camping. It was Muir, an activist, a single person.

Muir's history and passion are embraced by the Sierra Club and its members; the club's website, for example, contains an entire subsection entitled the John Muir Exhibit, which documents the life and accomplishments of its founder. Muir's guiding principles continue to guide the activities and policies that the club pursues, as exemplified in its mission statement. John Muir's Sierra Club stands as an example of the enduring power of one person's vision and commitment to harness the power of organized action and affect the public good.

For additional information, www.sierraclub.org and www.sierraclub.org/john_muir_exhibit/

Note: Daniel Duane, "The Revolution Starts at the Bottom," *Sierra Magazine,* March/April 2004, *http://www.sierraclub.org/sierra/200403/interview.asp*.

In addition to leadership from the executive, the leadership of the board of directors is vital to advancing the nonprofit's mission; many argue that one of the first and foremost responsibilities of the nonprofit board is the determination and maintenance of the organizational mission.[10] Moreover, the board should be willing and able to clearly articulate that mission to others. Ingram recommends that each board member have an "elevator speech"—a compelling synopsis of the organizational mission that can be explained in a minute or less.[11] Further, as will be discussed below, organizational leaders are responsible for periodic assessment of the nonprofit mission, its accomplishment of organizational goals, and the strategic planning that moves it closer to reaching those goals.

MANAGING THE MISSION

In the world of philanthropic foundations, the mission often includes an intention to pursue rather lofty goals, as in the case of the Carnegie Corporation of New York. Begun by Andrew Carnegie in 1911, the Carnegie Corporation is one of the oldest foundations in the United States. Its original charter with the state of New York indicated that its purpose was "to promote the advancement and diffusion of knowledge and understanding among the people of the United States" and "to do real and permanent good in this world."[12] Foundations with social change goals such as Carnegie's almost always pursue their missions with a policy focus because, as Emmett D. Carson writes, "Change-oriented mission statements—by necessity—require a foundation to pursue public policy efforts that attempt to fundamentally change how the system operates."[13]

The Carnegie Corporation has continued to exhibit a desire for social change, as it evolved over the past century from primarily being a grantmaking foundation to serving as a hub of policy activity and analysis.[14] The results of corporation activity are widely recognized: from the Carnegie libraries, to the Teachers Insurance and Annuity Association of America (now TIAA-CREF), to the Children's Television Workshop (now Sesame Workshop), the work of the corporation has touched the lives of virtually all Americans. The boards of trustees and staff that have carried out the mission of the corporation since Carnegie's death in 1919 have moved the foundation along this social change trajectory, while following the same general mission set forth in the original 1911 charter of promoting knowledge and understanding and doing "real and permanent good in this world."[15]

A broad organizational mission such as the Carnegie Corporation's allows the nonprofit to adjust its activity to match a changing external environment. Likewise, a flexible mission allows the organization to find efficient ways to use its resources.[16] A similar idea is *mission stickiness*—the concept that organizations do themselves a disservice if they stay too committed to their original missions when their environment demands change.[17]

On the other hand, resource dependence—a nonprofit's reliance on revenues from outside sources—can lead the organization away from its mission, a problem known as mission drift or mission creep. According to Burton A. Weisbrod, "aggressive commercialism is causing nonprofits to sacrifice subtle elements of their social, collective-good mission—for which the subsidies and tax-exemptions are given—in the interest of generating revenue."[18] Others have argued that the essential mission of a nonprofit organization can be threatened by factors beyond commercial endeavors, including attempts to meet the priorities of external funders, having too large an endowment, and pressures to operate more like a business.[19] Peter C. Brinckerhoff admonishes nonprofit managers that when faced with the challenges of market pressures, "you need to use your mission, your values, and your personal ethical compass to guide you and set appropriate limits."[20] Ultimately, it is the responsibility of the leadership of each nonprofit to understand its mission and determine which opportunities it should seek out and which will lead it too far from its primary purpose.

The Nonprofit Mission and Change

One responsibility of nonprofit leaders is the periodic review of their organization's mission as times and the organization change, potentially resulting in a change to the mission or administration of the organization.[21] Karl N. Stauber, for example, details the change in mission undertaken by the Northwest Area Foundation in 1998. The foundation covers the eight northern states of Washington, Oregon, Idaho, Montana, North Dakota, South Dakota, Minnesota, and Iowa. An independent foundation, for its first 50 years the Northwest Area Foundation, behaved as a traditional grantmaker, awarding grants to organizations in 39 different categories.[22]

In 1996, foundation leaders began to see a new environment for philanthropic organizations as the federal government reduced its level of public policy involvement. This federal policy change affected the role of the foundation and led its leaders to reexamine its mission. As Stauber explains, the social change model of philanthropy in which "foundations promote change by legitimizing issues, funding the creation of new types of institutions, and then garnering government support for the issue and the institutions," was no longer viable due to the retrenchment of federal policy activism.[23] Therefore, after 50 years of operating under a broad mission of social change, the foundation narrowed and revamped its mission to address a single problem, persistent poverty, through direct funding of community organizations. Today, its mission is to "support efforts by the people, organizations and communities of our eight-state region to reduce poverty and achieve sustainable prosperity."[24] The Northwest Area Foundation adapted its mission and strategies to better fit a changing policy environment and, therefore, better serve the communities in its service region.

There are certainly lessons here for savvy nonprofit leaders: First, they must have a clear understanding of the nature of their organization and its mission, and they must also recognize the fact that the organization and its environment *will* change. Consider again the case of Candy Lightner, founder of MADD, which was highlighted in Box 3.4. By all accounts, MADD is a highly successful nonprofit organization with chapters in all 50 U.S. states, 10 Canadian provinces, and affiliates internationally. It has dramatically changed public perceptions and the laws regarding drunk driving in a very short period of time. However, just 8 years after founding MADD, Lightner quit, insisting that other leaders were moving the organization too far in a prohibitionist direction and arguing that "'zero tolerance' is counterproductive, impractical and a waste of limited resources."[25] In this example, change came from the nonprofit's leadership but against the wishes of the founder. In keeping true to her original values, vision, and mission, Lightner left MADD when the organization changed direction in a way that she could not accept.

As in the examples of the Northwest Area Foundation and MADD, organizational change typically comes from the top. In order to change operations with the least opposition, leaders must speak with a unified voice and solicit the input of staff and stakeholders.[26] When change occurs, it naturally causes discomfort to those within the nonprofit and the clientele that the organization serves, pointing again to the importance of open communication and participatory decision-making. The role of the board and the executive director is critical: they must remain unified, reiterate the changes to the mission and administration of the organization, and hold training and information sessions with staff and volunteers as an important way to help everyone in the organization ease into its new phase.

Finally, an organization will occasionally completely fulfill its mission. Drucker suggests that when this happens, nonprofit leaders should take the opportunity to expand or change the original mission.[27] Given the nature of most nonprofit activity—feed the hungry, cure disease, alleviate the effects of poverty—complete fulfillment of the organizational mission is rare. Famously, it happened with the National Foundation for Infantile Paralysis (NFIP), established by President Franklin D. Roosevelt and his former law partner, Basil O'Connor, to eradicate the polio virus. See Case Study 5.2 for more information on how the foundation's mission evolved from development of a rehabilitation facility, to eradication of the polio virus, to prevention of infant mortality and other birth defects by what is now called the March of Dimes. FDR's efforts with the NFIP were memorialized in 1946 when his profile was placed on the U.S. dime.

CASE STUDY 5.2

The National Foundation for Infantile Paralysis Achieves Its Mission

In the late summer of 1921, Franklin Delano Roosevelt and his family vacationed at their island home near the coast of Maine. The previous 12 months had been exhausting, as Roosevelt first made an unsuccessful bid for the vice presidency in 1920 and then spent most of the summer of 1921 defending himself in a Naval scandal. A vacation with his wife and children, far from the public eye, seemed to be the perfect reprieve. Instead, soon after his arrival, Roosevelt fell very ill and was diagnosed with the polio virus. Although polio typically afflicted children, hence the name infantile paralysis, FDR was 39 years old when he contracted the virus. While his health eventually improved, he would never again walk unassisted.

Seeking relief from the disease, Roosevelt spent time at the Meriwether Inn in Warm Springs, Georgia, taking advantage of its soothing spring waters. Convinced of the waters' ability to provide relief to polio sufferers, in the mid-1920s, Roosevelt purchased the Meriwether Inn and its surrounding property for $200,000. Roosevelt and his law partner, Basil O'Conner, agreed to found the nonprofit Georgia Warm Springs Foundation as a means to raise money for the renovation and operation of the resort as a rehabilitation facility for those crippled by the effects of polio. FDR envisioned the facility partially as a commercial venture—income from healthy vacationers and charitable contributions would offset the reduced fees charged to those afflicted with polio who sought treatment in the soothing waters of the resort's warm springs. Unfortunately, fear of the virus led healthy vacationers to abandon the resort and, after the stock market crash of 1929, contributions to Warm Springs nearly dried up; alternate funding was needed to keep the facility open. Thus, following FDR's presidential election in 1932, the Warm Springs Foundation used Roosevelt's birthday as the occasion to host 6,000 Presidential Birthday Balls across the country, raising over $1 million. These became annual events and were promoted as a way to raise funds for Warm Springs with the slogan, "Dance so that others may walk."[28] By 1935, the Warm Springs facility was financially secure, and the foundation announced that 70 percent of funds raised at the annual dances would remain in their home communities to address the needs of local polio victims.

In addition to the Birthday Balls, a particularly noteworthy fundraiser was the annual Mother's March, in which mothers walked up and down their neighborhoods collecting donations. Amid concerns that the title might be perceived as exclusionary, the name was changed to the March of Dimes, as a play on words related to the *March of Time* newsreels played in movie theaters. People offered handfuls of dimes for collection tins and even taped dimes to postcards and mailed them to the White House. Building on the theme, a promoter calculated that 90,000 dimes laid end to end would fill one mile. In a series of radio ads based on the

Mile O' Dimes concept, supporters were encouraged to start a dime line down their sidewalk to raise $9,000 a mile.[29]

Over the next few years, however, the link between FDR and the Georgia Warm Springs Foundation led many of his political opponents to refuse to support the charity; the mission of Warm Springs, providing rehabilitation to those with polio, was threatened by politics. It was at that point that the larger National Foundation for Infantile Paralysis (NFIP) was created by presidential proclamation on September 23, 1937. The new NFIP kept the Warm Springs facility as a center for research, but broadened its organizational mission to support research nationwide to facilitate treatment of those afflicted with polio and to explore the potential for a vaccine to prevent it.[30] David M. Oshinsky notes that NFIP "became the gold standard for private charities, the largest voluntary health organization of all time," whose success at fundraising, public relations, care of patients, and funding of medical research would be the role model for future health-related philanthropy.[31]

The National Foundation is described as being so focused on the mission of curing polio that it actually lobbied against federal research funding. An official with the National Institutes of Health (NIH) told Congress in 1953 that the scale and scope of NFIP support for polio research was so immense that it freed the NIH to focus on other diseases that did not benefit from similarly strong financial support.[32] By 1954, funds raised through the NFIP's March of Dimes had helped Dr. Jonas Salk develop a successful polio vaccine. The subsequent public trials of Salk's vaccine were funded and administered largely by the National Foundation, in cooperation with public schools and health departments in 211 counties across the country.[33] Over the next four years, over 450 million doses were administered around the globe. Largely eradicated in the United States by the early 1980s, the Centers for Disease Control last reported a case of polio in an unvaccinated Minnesota child in 2005.

In 1958, with its mission of finding a cure for polio accomplished, the National Foundation turned its attention to the prevention of birth defects and infant mortality. At a press conference at the Waldorf-Astoria in New York City, Basil O'Conner, still heading the foundation, announced that its future lay in being a "flexible force" in public health. In 1979, the NFIP changed its name to the March of Dimes, and in the early 1990s, its official mission statement became, "Our mission is to improve the health of babies by preventing birth defects and infant mortality." The motto, "Saving babies, together" was introduced in 1997.

The March of Dimes has had much success over the past five decades in the research and advocacy of prenatal and perinatal health care. Its activities have included funding research on fetal alcohol syndrome, premature births, and tests and treatment to eliminate several causes of mental retardation. The organization has actively influenced the policy arena as well, leading the way for a system of Neonatal Intensive Care Units across the United States which have had a positive effect on the health outcomes of premature and low birth weight babies; further, the organization helped to secure mandatory insurance coverage of tests and treatment for 30 serious infant disorders in all 50 states.[34] In the early 1990s, March of Dimes launched the national Folic Acid Campaign to educate women about the benefits of folic acid on developing fetuses. Influenced by the March of Dimes' effort, within two years the federal Food and Drug Administration approved folic acid fortification of the U.S. grain supply. In 1997, March of Dimes volunteers advocated for congressional approval of the State Children's Health Insurance Program (S-CHIP), which expanded medical coverage for children of the working poor.

Today the march continues; its biggest fundraiser, WalkAmerica, is a pledge-walk that involves more than 400,000 participants and raises over $90 million annually. From the original Georgia Warm Springs Foundation's mission of creating a rehabilitation facility for polio sufferers, to the broadened mission of seeking a cure for polio as the National Foundation for Infantile Paralysis, to the current mission of preventing birth defects and infant mortality, the March of Dimes has been an important actor in health care and policy for over seven decades.

For additional information, see the Centers for Disease Control at www.cdc.gov/vaccines/vpd-vac/polio/dis-faqs.htm; the March of Dimes at www.marchofdimes.com/789_24332.asp; and Post-Polio Health International www.post-polio.org.

QUESTIONS TO CONSIDER:

1. What motivated the change in mission from Warm Springs to the National Foundation for Infantile Paralysis to the March of Dimes?
2. When a cure for polio was found, why didn't the National Foundation for Infantile Paralysis simply enjoy its success and close its doors?
3. Contrary to most charities seeking eradication of disease, the National Foundation for Infantile Paralysis (NFIP) sought to limit federal funding of research on polio. Why did the NFIP take that policy stance? Would you have urged the foundation to act differently? Why or why not?
4. Consider the four relationships that describe nonprofit interaction with public policy (make policy, affected by policy, influence policy, subject to policy) and discuss in which way(s) the National Foundation for Infantile Paralysis, and later the March of Dimes, interacted with public policy.
5. Is the National Foundation for Infantile Paralysis/March of Dimes a unique example of the relationship between nonprofit mission and public policy? What does this case suggest about successful organizations and their missions?

The Importance of the Mission Statement

In nonprofit organizations a well-crafted, concise, and distinct mission statement serves multiple purposes. First and foremost it should be an accurate reflection of the mission and purpose of the organization. Research has found that a strong and clearly articulated mission is an important component in the success of a nonprofit organization and has been found to be a critical factor in making organizational improvements and motivating innovation.[35] The mission statement also provides a basic framework to help evaluate the nonprofit's effectiveness, offering credibility to clients, donors, and grantmaking institutions. Furthermore, the mission statement acts as a motivator for boards, staff, volunteers, and donors.[36] For example, research has found that employee attachment to the organization's mission is positively related to satisfaction and retention in nonprofit organizations.[37]

The critical nature of a strong mission statement has led scholars to suggest a fairly consistent set of characteristics for its development. First, there is general agreement that a good mission statement is clear, concise, and to the point. According to Holland and Ritvo, it should be "memorable and easy to explain."[38] Second, the nonprofit mission statement should express the societal need that the organization fills. It should also be distinct enough for people to distinguish this nonprofit from another organization. Because the mission statement becomes the foundation for setting the organization's priorities and long-term goals, it must demonstrate the organization's commitment to its underlying values. "Experience has shown that neglecting to create a solid foundation for planning by achieving consensus on the basics of mission, vision and values will likely lead to a breakdown in planning at some later stage."[39] While a specific and operational mission statement is more easily put into action by a nonprofit's staff, translating a mission statement into a concrete program can be difficult, especially if community circumstances, funding sources, or public policies change operating conditions for the nonprofit organization.[40] It is important to remain mindful of the fact that a mission statement serves both to enable and constrain the organization.[41]

Let us return to our opening vignette for a practical example. As the Youth Community Theatre Project prepares to write its own mission statement, it has collected statements from several children's theatre programs around the country: STOP-GAP in Costa Mesa, California; All Children's Theatre (ACT) in Providence, Rhode Island; and Nashville Children's Theatre (NCT) in Nashville, Tennessee.

- *STOP-GAP* is a non-profit organization whose purpose is to use theatre as a therapeutic and educational tool to make a positive difference in individual lives. (www.stopgap.org/html/home.htm)
- *All Children's Theatre* is committed to the enrichment, entertainment, and education of young people in a theatre arts environment that promotes empowerment of all children. (www.actinri.org/index.php)
- *Nashville Children's Theatre* is an ensemble of professional artists who bring unique vision and compelling voice to the creation of meaningful theatre for Nashville and Middle Tennessee audiences. We strive to make the imaginative celebration of our hopes, struggles, and joys a vital part of the shared experience for young people, families, and our community. (www.nashvillechildrenstheatre.org/index.htm)

Each of these three has a long history in the communities that they serve. The youngest, ACT, has been in Providence since 1987, while NCT is the oldest children's theatre in the United States, having been founded in 1931. Although each of these nonprofit theatre groups has a general mission of enriching children's lives through theatre, there are differences among the three that are made clear through their mission statements.

For example, STOP-GAP uses theatre as a means of education and therapy. One gets the sense from their mission statement that they emphasize the value of theatre for special needs populations; in fact, they take their interactive theatre productions and workshops to hospitals and shelters in addition to schools and education centers. STOP-GAP emphasizes interactive methods that allow audience members to participate in exploring themes of safety, substance abuse prevention, and alternatives to violence, for children and other populations in need.

The mission of All Children's Theatre implies that its actors are young people and it values providing a participative environment for children. Again, the impression one gets from the mission statement is on target: ACT offers acting classes for children between the ages of 4 and 18, puts on multiple theatre productions each year, and conducts an outreach program to schools, after-school centers, and daycare facilities.

Finally, the mission statement from Nashville's long-running NCT suggests that it values theatre productions designed specifically for children and families. Again, this impression is correct: NCT performs approximately 200 shows a year for school groups and families. While NCT offers a series of teaching workshops and camps for children, its focus has been on performance of child and family-oriented theatre productions since 1931.

The organizational mission statements for these not-for-profit children's theatre groups convey the distinct character of each organization and the values which each finds most important; this is a key function of a good mission statement. For the founding leadership team of YCTP, this exercise would be quite valuable. They would now be in a position to take their values, identified earlier as access, education, and bringing high quality theatre productions to the community, and craft a mission statement that reflects these values and can serve as a tool to convey the mission and values of YCTP to community stakeholders.

Organizational Vision

In conjunction with the mission statement is the organizational vision, a look forward that is sometimes written as a formal vision statement, and at other times incorporated into the language of the mission. A vision statement describes the hopes for the organization and becomes an important touch point for organizational growth and guiding leaders into the future. Werther and Berman write that the "vision statement is an ennobling, articulated statement of what an organization is and what it is striving to become. It answers the questions of what the world would be like if the mission were attained."[42]

An example comes from All Children's Theatre in Providence, Rhode Island, whose vision statement is:

> The All Children's Theatre (ACT) seeks to be a model for excellence in theatre arts education for all young people. ACT endeavors to include all young people in its ACTing Company, educational and community outreach programs. We strive to empower our participants by offering a 'total theatre' experience including acting, directing, playwriting, design and technical theatre as well as arts administration (http://www.actinri.org/about.php).

Several of the phrases used in this vision statement—"seeks to be" and "we strive to"—are good examples of what a vision statement should do: Offer a sense of the future for the organization and guide its leaders as they make decisions about which opportunities they should seek, clientele they should serve, and policies they should pursue.

Because the organizational vision incorporates more than just the work of a single nonprofit—how the world would be changed if the mission were achieved—one nonprofit's vision likely connects with that of other groups and often involves collaborative efforts. In the case of the Sierra Club, John Muir's vision to protect the wilderness of the Pacific Northwest and promote a U.S. National Park Service crossed the border into Canada to help inspire creation of Canada's National Park System. The cross-border efforts of the Sierra Club and Sierra Club Canada are discussed further in Going Global 5.3.

GOING GLOBAL 5.3

Sierra Club's Vision and Mission Extends to Canada

As discussed in Box 5.1, the Sierra Club was founded in the United States in 1892 with a mission to protect America's wilderness. Yet while the northern U.S. territory ends at the Canadian Border, many of the most beautiful natural features of the North American Continent are shared by the two countries, including the Great Lakes, the Waterton-Glacier International Park, and both the Appalachian and Rocky Mountain ranges. Not surprisingly, then, the work of the Sierra Club and founder John Muir have long had an influence on Canadian conservation efforts. Muir's philosophy and writings on the Canadian wilderness, for example, are said to have heavily influenced the work of James Bernard Harding, named the first Commissioner of the National Parks of Canada in 1911.[43] In a clear example of the effect of a policy entrepreneur's vision and a nonprofit's mission on policy across international borders, Harding is credited as the founding father of Canada's National Park system.

The Sierra Club added its first Canadian chapter in 1963 and in 1989 opened a national office in Ottawa. In 1972, the Sierra Club Canada Foundation (SCCF) was created as a registered charitable foundation with the Canadian Revenue Agency. SCCF generates funding from individuals and foundations to provide resources for environmental protection projects, education, and research. Canadian regulations on tax-deductible donations are stricter than in the United States, allowing tax deductions only for registered charities. Organizations cannot register as charities unless their work falls into one of four charitable categories: poverty relief, advancement of education, advancement of religion, or other purposes deemed appropriate by the Canadian courts. Charities are allowed a limited amount of nonpartisan political activity, so long as it is "connected and subordinate" to the organization's charitable purpose *and* "substantially all" of the organization's resources are devoted to charitable activities. The SCCF is a registered charitable organization and does not engage in political action; therefore, its donations are tax-deductible.

In 1992, the Canadian chapters separated from the U.S. organization and formed Sierra Club Canada, which was incorporated as an agent of SCCF and is a nonprofit organization engaged in political advocacy. While Sierra Club Canada and SCCF are governed by separate and autonomous boards of directors, they work together in pursuit of mutual goals. The primary work of Sierra Club Canada involves advocacy and action in four areas: (1) environmental and health policies, (2) biodiversity protection, (3) atmosphere and energy policies, and (4) moving toward a sustainable economy. The Canadian government does not allow tax deductions for nonprofit organizations (only for registered charities); therefore, donations to Sierra Club Canada are not tax-deductible.

Sierra Club Canada's mission is to "empower people to protect, restore and enjoy a healthy and safe planet!" This statement echoes the Sierra Club's "explore, enjoy, and protect the planet," and reflects the visions of both Muir and Harding.[44] Sierra Club and Sierra Club Canada occasionally work together; for example, in 2005 they presented a joint resolution to oppose a mega-quarry in Digby Neck and Islands, Nova Scotia, and in 2011 the two joined forces in a campaign against tar sands oil production. In most efforts to influence public policy, however, Sierra Club Canada's five national chapters focus on distinctly Canadian environmental issues, such as Nuclear-Free Canada and a major campaign to save the grizzly bears of Alberta.

For additional information:

Sierra Club Canada, www.sierraclub.ca/en

Sierra Club Canada Foundation, www.sierraclub.ca/foundation

Canada Revenue Agency, www.cra.gc.ca

STRATEGIC PLANNING AND MANAGEMENT

The organization's mission and vision statements answer the Why and Who questions; the strategic plan helps address the questions of What, Where, When, and How. Once a nonprofit has developed a clear mission statement and vision, it can begin *strategic planning*—a systematic process involving goal identification and determination of logical action steps designed to fulfill the organizational mission. Cohen and Eimicke explain that the greatest value in strategic planning "is in helping align an organization's mission, goals, and means for achieving them with its available resources."[45] A strategic plan should ultimately provide evaluation and feedback that can lead to organizational learning and improvement (see Table 5.1). Planning and goal setting are considered essential tools for good management in any organization and can be used by nonprofits to enhance their ability to affect public policy either through implementation of existing programs or by pursuing policy change.

Again, the role of leadership is vital in this process. Determination of the direction of the organization and creation of the strategic plan should be undertaken by the nonprofit board and the executive director with input from the management staff. Ingram suggests that effective strategic planning involves staying "focused on The Big Picture—the high-order levels of policy and strategy—not the details."[46] Rather, the details will be carried out by the nonprofit staff and volunteers. It is the responsibility of the organization's leaders to communicate about why and how the new strategies will be pursued and then train and

Table 5.1 Steps in the Strategic Planning Process

Steps
1. Determination of Nonprofit Values, Mission, Vision
2. Setting of Organizational Goals to Accomplish Mission
3. Organizational Accounting via SWOT Analysis or Other Analytical Tool
4. Systematic Planning of Strategies to Meet Organizational Goals
5. Measure Outcomes/Evaluate Performance in Meeting Goals
6. Learning from Evaluation: Midcourse Corrections/New Strategies

Source: Adapted from Steven Cohen and William Eimicke, *Tools for Innovators* (San Francisco: Jossey-Bass Publishers, 1998).

develop staff members, providing them with specific performance guidelines so everyone involved with the organization acts in accordance with the mission of the nonprofit.

Organizational Goals

Strategic planning first identifies objectives or *organizational goals.* Nonprofits should be prepared for a great deal of discussion at this stage of the process, as different stakeholders may disagree on the organization's order of priorities. Once agreement has been reached, the planning process involves identifying the means to meet those goals.[47] For nonprofit organizations, the mission statement will drive the objectives that are pursued and thus can both facilitate and constrain organizational activity. Organizational goals are specific outcomes that are used to indicate the organization is fulfilling its mission.

Consider again the opening vignette's YCTP. With its mission of enriching the cultural life of the community's children by providing them an introduction to and education in the performing arts, the board of directors must determine the goals that will help to accomplish this mission. A specific goal associated with YCTP's mission might be "to share with children the excitement of the theatre through creation of interactive programming."

Organizational Accounting

After developing a clear sense of mission and specific organizational goals, it is important for the nonprofit to take an honest accounting of itself both internally and externally in order to determine specific strategies that can be used to fulfill those goals. Importantly, an assessment of financial capacity—over time—is vital to an attainable strategic plan; good plans without the financial resources to carry them out are useless.[48]

Organizational accounting can be done more or less formally through an analysis of the strengths, weaknesses, opportunities, and threats (SWOT) that the nonprofit faces. Kevin P. Kearns suggests that the most useful SWOT analysis will be part of an iterative process of matching, "in which the objective is to identify salient links between internal strengths and weaknesses and external opportunities and threats."[49]

The organization must be honest about its internal strengths and weaknesses in terms of its available resources and capacity and be aware of the external threats and opportunities that it faces. It is important to remember that not everyone within the organization will view the same conditions in the same way; thus, a good SWOT analysis will involve multiple stakeholders. Gathering good and varied information may involve using surveys, focus groups, and interviews. Using the nonprofit's leadership to host focus groups and conduct interviews can be a valuable way to engage board members in the process and indicate to stakeholders the high level of commitment the board has to the organization and its future.[50] It is important that those involved in the SWOT analysis be committed to it; otherwise, it can become little more than an exercise in making lists, and its results are simply ignored.[51]

Kearns recommends that decisions on strategic planning be facilitated through creation of a two-by-two matrix of external opportunities and threats and internal strengths and weaknesses. Each cell in the matrix offers a generic strategic option for decision-makers. The four decision categories are Comparative Advantage, Investment/Disinvestment, Mobilization, and Damage Control. (See Figure 5.1.)

When performing the SWOT analysis, the nonprofit's internal constituents include its leadership, staff, volunteers, clients, participants, and members. Their perspectives must be considered as the organization evaluates its strengths and weaknesses. Perhaps it has particularly devoted volunteers, or board members who are politically well-connected. On the other hand, it may lack certain resources that keep it from fully meeting its mission; perhaps no one on staff is adept at writing successful grant applications, or the organization lacks adequate computer technology to handle an increase in demand.

FIGURE 5.1 SWOT Matrix Linkages and Strategic Options

		External	
		Opportunities	***Threats***
Internal	***Strengths***	Comparative Advantage: The nonprofit is in a position to leverage its strengths and capitalize on opportunities	Mobilization: The nonprofit needs to mobilize its strengths to avert threats or turn threats into opportunities
	Weaknesses	Investment/Disinvestment: The nonprofit must decide whether or not to invest scarce resources in potential opportunities or cut its losses	Damage Control: The nonprofit is in a vulnerable position and must decide how best to control or minimize its threats

Source: Adapted from Kevin P. Kearns, "From Comparative Advantage to Damage Control: Clarifying Strategic Issues Using SWOT Analysis," *Nonprofit Management and Leadership* 3 (1992): 3–22.

Externally, the organization must take into account the perspectives of stakeholders such as donors, policymakers, politicians, the general public, the media—any group that is important to the organization and the pursuit of its mission. Some will be obvious allies, others will be obvious opponents, and some may be either one, depending on the circumstances. Consider the situation of a church which allows a local not-for-profit to operate an evening soup kitchen out of its parish hall. An important strength of the soup kitchen has been the support it receives from church congregants and leadership because it meets an important need in the community and helps to fulfill the outreach mission of the church. However, this support could quickly wane if soup kitchen guests begin sleeping on or defacing church property.

The organization must also be aware of external threats such as other organizations in the area whose missions are similar, and who become competitors for clientele, fees, and grants. These groups may be in the nonprofit, public, or for-profit sector, reminding us again about the importance of operating with a distinct organizational mission that differentiates one nonprofit from other, similar organizations; differentiation is discussed in more detail in Chapter 8.

On the other hand, organizations within the same general service industry may offer opportunities for collaboration in service delivery, fundraising, policy advocacy, and even management, such as sharing bookkeeping expertise or physical space for particularly small organizations. Other opportunities may come in the form of sympathetic city council members or public policies that support the mission, both in terms of finances and through encouraging the kind of services the agency provides. New public policies and new sources of grant funding from governments or foundations are important opportunities about which the leadership of a nonprofit must be always aware.

As we note throughout this book, it is vital that not-for-profit organizations are mindful of the political process, the policies that will affect them, and the policies that they can affect. For example, the American Recovery and Reinvestment Act (ARRA) of 2009 offered $50 million in one-time federal grants to state arts agencies and regional arts organizations for the preservation of jobs in the arts community during the economic recession. Nonprofits were eligible to apply directly to the federal government or through their state governments for access to stimulus funds. Savvy nonprofits in the arts community, like the Nashville Children's Theatre discussed earlier, applied to their state arts agencies for financial help in preserving jobs; the NCT was awarded a $25,000 grant on July 8, 2009.[52] The one-time nature of these federal and state grants underscores the importance of watching closely for policy and grant opportunities to arise and always being ready to put together a successful grant application.

Systematic Planning

Once a thorough accounting of the organization's situation has been completed, strategies can be created to help meet organizational goals. The strategic plan can be considered a road map: the nonprofit has its mission and objectives (where it wants to go and what stops to make along the way), and the strategies are the directions that will help it reach its final destination. Strategic planning should also include targets in the same way that travelers use estimated times of arrival. Of course, there will be multiple routes that the organization can take and a variety of means to get to the destination, but ultimately, the mission must be the driving force for all strategic decisions made by the nonprofit leaders.

Consider again the example of YCTP's goal "to share with children the excitement of the theatre through creation of interactive programming." Achieving this goal would likely involve outreach to parents, grandparents, teachers, and community members who are patrons of the arts. It might involve accessing space to deliver on-site programs and activities or bringing amateur theatre productions to the community. Exposing children to theatre in this manner could involve hands-on activities involving costume design, set decoration, and special effects. All of these strategies for meeting the goal may be used or some may be beyond the current capacity or resources of the organization; some may become long-term goals for which additional resources can be sought. Because the organization's resources, potential partners, and strengths and weaknesses have been evaluated before beginning this journey, the road map for meeting organizational goals—the strategic plan—will be much easier to follow.

Measuring and Evaluating Outcomes

Finally, it is increasingly important to consider the performance of the organization in meeting its goals. For the nonprofit whose mission is vague and outcomes are unclear or long-term in nature, this can be difficult. As Frumkin and Andre-Clark note, nonprofits are unique in that they

> . . . face a far more complex test of relevance that is related to their mission. For a nonprofit to thrive, it must fulfill a mission that is valued by the community, staff, board, and funders. Nonprofits must create value within operational and environmental constraints that are at once more complex than those faced by corporations and more opaque than those confronted by government.[53]

For this reason it is suggested that nonprofits use multiple methods and measures of the outcomes of their service activity and that both direct and indirect value are assessed when determining targets and measuring outcomes.

For YCTP, we have set a goal of sharing with children the excitement of the theatre using a strategy that involves creation of interactive programming. How well we have shared that history may not lend itself to easy measures; however, we can easily track the number of children who have been engaged in our activities, their ages, and the types of programming that garnered the highest levels of participation. Although tracking numbers served is an example of measuring *outputs* (or "units of service") rather than measuring *outcomes* (the benefit to participants), it offers an objective target and allows us something tangible to report to donors, the public, the government, and our volunteers.[54] Further, because it offers us goals and tells us whether or not we are meeting them, measuring outputs allows for comparison from year to year—a measure of the growth of our program. We can assess how well our programs meet our less-tangible goals by the fact that children continue to seek out our programs and by taking surveys of children, parents, and program contributors. These more qualitative measures of success will then become important components of the

YCTP's year-end report and marketing materials. For example, quotes from parents praising the quality of our programs and activities are invaluable in marketing the nonprofit to other families, donors, and the public and will make the job of fundraising much easier.

Learning from Evaluation

The strategic planning process is of most value when it is cyclical; therefore, evaluation of performance and measurement of goals are vital to making use of strategic planning. When the organization evaluates itself and finds that it has met its goals, it may wish to set new goals. If it finds that it has fallen short, it can use the results of evaluation to refine its strategies, seek new resources or new approaches, or reevaluate its original goals. To go through the steps of strategic planning and ignore the important feedback gathered through evaluation is a waste of precious resources; the strategic plan should be a process of systematic planning and learning for the future.

Finally, a word about *business plans* for nonprofit organizations, which are fundamentally different from strategic plans. The Alliance for Nonprofit Management is a key source of information about when and why a nonprofit should create a business plan (see Box 5.4). While a strategic plan is recommended for all nonprofits, a business plan borrows more

Box 5.4

FOR MORE INFORMATION

THE ALLIANCE FOR NONPROFIT MANAGEMENT

The Alliance for Nonprofit Management, located in Washington, D.C., is an umbrella organization for Management Services Organizations (MSOs) and others that offer support services to nonprofits; its members seek to improve the management capacity for all nonprofit organizations. The Alliance mission is "To increase the effectiveness of individuals and organizations that help nonprofits build their power and impact." Its guiding principles are:

Quality—promoting increasingly higher standards throughout the practice of nonprofit capacity building;

Collaboration—building on mutually beneficial working relationships with an array of community, business, and government partners and stakeholders; and

Inclusiveness—fully including the diverse mosaic of society's cultures in its membership, leadership, and staff.

The alliance brings together members with similar interests via affinity groups, grants annual Best Practices awards, holds conferences, and disseminates reports to members. Its website offers guidance on topics of interest to nonprofit managers, including ethics, financial management, and strategic planning. Funding for the Alliance comes from major foundations including the New York Community Trust, the Annie E. Casey Foundation, and the American Express Foundation.

To learn more about the Alliance for Nonprofit Management resources and services, go to www.allianceonline.org/.

heavily from the for-profit sector; it is focused on strategies for generating income and improving the marketability of the organization. The concepts important in business planning for nonprofits include market analysis, revenue projections, and marketing plans. They require quantifiable outcomes as measures of success, and they focus on specific products and services because they are typically written for potential investors and lenders. A solid business plan helps a nonprofit send the message that there will be a return on investments and loans will be repaid.[55] Rouson suggests that the best candidates for using business plans are large nonprofits with a wide range of programs, so business planning helps the organization "to determine how much to invest in each activity."[56] Nonprofits that rely heavily on fees-for-service or commercial ventures would likely benefit from development of a business plan in addition to a strategic plan, as a way to better understand the market for their goods and services and attract the capital that they require to serve the needs of their organization.

CONCLUSION

The values, mission, and vision of the nonprofit play a vital role in creating the sense of purpose that drives the organization. Whether communicating internally or externally, seeking funding or a change in policy, delivering services or creating programs, nonprofits must keep their missions in the forefront of all organizational activity; not to do so would break the social contract between the nonprofit and society and could ultimately lead to the loss of tax-exempt status.[57] For philanthropic foundations, mission guides how they spend their money—that is, which projects and public policies will be pursued and therefore which nonprofits are awarded grants. Importantly, strategic planning techniques help organizations to identify and more fully understand their purpose and execute their mission and vision statements. While we recognize that this is not always easy, especially for resource-poor nonprofits and those with particularly difficult-to-measure goals, using these tools to systematically assess the organization's capacity and opportunities followed by iterative planning is essential to good nonprofit management. Good management, of course, is essential to meeting the organization's mission.

Although this chapter describes the nuts-and-bolts concepts of articulating mission and vision statements and doing strategic planning, it is clear that doing these things well is a bridge to implementing and affecting public policy. When the tools and strategies discussed here are applied in well-managed not-for-profit organizations, they are used with an eye toward the public purposes of the nonprofit and the policy implications of their activity. Whether one considers the Carnegie Corporation's role in the establishment of public libraries; the public service campaign of the March of Dimes, which led the Food and Drug Administration to approve folic acid enrichment in the U.S. grain supply; or the advocacy efforts of the Sierra Club, leading to creation of the National Park System, we see the major impact that nonprofits have had on public policies and programs. Even when we consider the missions of smaller organizations such as children's theatre projects, the public role these organizations play is clear: through the outreach and services they offer in communities, the educational value they offer to schools and other institutions, and the public funding they often receive, the missions of nonprofit organizations embody public policy in many ways.

Questions For Review

1. We have made the argument that a strong mission and vision and a solid strategic plan will help to strengthen the role of nonprofit agencies and philanthropic foundations in the public policy process. Trace the logic of this argument.
2. A key point of this chapter has been the importance of having a well structured and solid mission statement. If they are so important, how can we explain why nonprofit mission statements are often lacking in substance or are occasionally not even developed?
3. Consider the process of strategic planning in large versus small nonprofit organizations: Are there ways in which the process differs depending on organizational size? Does the need for strategic planning vary according to organizational size?

Assignment

For this web-based assignment, you will collect and analyze the mission statements of at least three nonprofit organizations that operate in the same general area of nonprofit activity, such as the children's theatre example in the chapter. Begin by looking only at the organizations' formal mission statements; what sense of each organization do you get? Consider what the chapter indicates a mission statement should do and determine whether or not these mission statements meet those goals. Then, do a more thorough analysis of each organization from other information offered on the website: Did the mission statement do an adequate job of conveying the distinct characteristics and the actual mission of each organization or not?

Suggested Readings

Allison, Michael, and Jude Kaye. *Strategic Planning for Nonprofit Organizations.* (San Francisco: Jossey-Bass, 2005).

Brinckerhoff, Peter C. *Mission Based Marketing: Positioning Your Not-for-Profit in an Increasingly Competitive World,* 2nd ed. Hoboken, NJ: John Wiley & Sons, 2003.

Kearns, Kevin P. "From Comparative Advantage to Damage Control: Clarifying Strategic Issues Using SWOT Analysis," *Nonprofit Management and Leadership* 3,1 (1992): 3–22.

Kluger, Jeffrey. *Splendid Solution: Jonas Salk and the Conquest of Polio.* New York: G.P. Putnam's Sons, 2004.

Lagemann, Ellen Condliffe. 1989. *The Politics of Knowledge: The Carnegie Corporation, Philanthropy, and Public Policy.* Middletown, CT: Wesleyan University Press, 1989.

Oshinsky, David M. *Polio: An American Story.* (New York: Oxford University Press, 2005).

Weisbrod, Burton A., editor. *To Profit or Not to Profit: The Commercial Transformation of the Nonprofit Sector.* New York: Cambridge University Press, 1998.

Web Resources

Alliance for Nonprofit Management, http://www.allianceonline.org

Foundation Center (Establishing a Nonprofit Organization; mission statement), http://foundationcenter.org/getstarted/tutorials/establish/statements.html

6 Lobbying and Advocacy

Politics, Policy, and Possibilities[1]

Politically active nonprofits contribute to democratic governance by representing *civic concerns in policymaking, by enlarging opportunities for citizen* participation *in public decisions, and by creating* accountability *between government and citizens.*

Elizabeth J. Reid[2]

The executive director (ED) of a medium-sized nonprofit in a major U.S. city is in a quandary. Her organization delivers welfare-to-work services for recipients of the Temporary Assistance to Needy Families (TANF) program, including remedial reading and math education, GED preparation, and daycare services for program participants while they are engaged in training, job readiness, and job search activities. Since 1998, the organization has had a relatively high level of success in helping clients to get and keep jobs and leave the welfare system.

Unfortunately for this executive director and her clients, Congress is considering legislation that would change the funding formula for programs such as hers. These changes would have a detrimental effect on the number of clients she could serve and may eliminate her ability to provide the daycare services that many of her clients find invaluable. The implications of this legislation are worrying nonprofit leaders all over the country, and a national organization of which her nonprofit is a member has suggested that executive directors and board members meet with their congressional representatives and voice their objections to the proposed legislation. The national organization has even suggested asking program clients to contact their representatives and senators on behalf of their programs. Although she is concerned about her program and its participants, our executive director worries that political activity might further endanger her government funding; furthermore, she thinks that these suggestions sound a lot like *lobbying* and as a 501(c)(3), her agency cannot lobby members of Congress. Or can it?

POLICY IMPLICATIONS OF LOBBYING AND ADVOCACY

- Advocacy and lobbying are legal for nonprofit organizations and are frequently undertaken by them with the explicit goal of influencing public policy.
- Lobbying involves direct attempts to influence legislation; advocacy involves attempts to shape public opinion via media, research, outreach, and community events.
- Internal Revenue Service (IRS) regulations, the Internal Revenue Code (IRC), other federal regulations, and congressional inquiries into nonprofit activity affect the way nonprofits operate.
- Many large nonprofits have sophisticated advocacy operations and have created 501(c)(4) affiliates for the specific purpose of legislative lobbying.
- Philanthropic foundations are subject to more restrictive IRS regulations on lobbying; however, they *can* legally fund nonprofit advocacy efforts.

ARTICULATING THE NONPROFIT VOICE WITHIN GOVERNMENTAL CONSTRAINTS

Even more than for-profit organizations, nonprofits like the one described above have an important stake in the policy process. Unlike their profit-making peers, however, the Internal Revenue Service (IRS) imposes limits on the level of lobbying activity in which nonprofit and philanthropic organizations can engage. As noted in Chapter 4, there is a clear legal distinction between lobbying and advocacy. According to the IRS (which is the entity that matters for nonprofits with regard to retaining tax-exempt status), lobbying occurs only when there is an *expenditure of funds* on activities designed to influence specific pieces of legislation. Advocacy is said to encompass all other efforts to educate and promote an issue or policy response. As Geller and Salamon explain, "so long as they are not supporting particular candidates for elected office or particular legislative enactments, nonprofits can engage in other forms of policy work without limit."[3] Restricting lobbying activity is one of the ways in which the federal and state governments regulate the nonprofit sector.

Because lobbying and advocacy are distinct activities, they will be discussed separately in this chapter. However, we begin with the most important point: Both policy advocacy and legislative lobbying are legal activities for organizations in the nonprofit sector. In addition, while private philanthropic foundations are subject to different regulations, they too can legally use advocacy and lobbying in important ways to influence public policy and the policy process. Chapter 6 begins by looking at nonprofit organizations in the legislative arena; issues specific to foundations will be discussed at the end of the chapter.

Lobbying and advocacy are important concepts, and delineation between the two is quite important for tax-exempt organizations, particularly those organized under section 501(c)(3). These public charities can lose their tax-exempt status if attempts to influence legislation constitute a substantial part of their activities; organizational fines, taxes on expenditures, and even individual fines on staff and board members can also result from such activity. Conversely, nonprofits can legally engage in legislative lobbying, and policy advocacy is often done by not-for-profit organizations with great success. The issues and processes, however, are complex, and nonprofits often operate in fear of IRS investigations or suggestions that they have broken the law if they are seen as being overly involved in lobbying activity. Further, as the example of the executive director in our opening vignette illustrates, those in organizations heavily dependent on government resources may worry that political activity will reduce their ability to win future grants or access other government funds.[4]

In addition, several congressional actions against nonprofit lobbying in the 1960s left an indelible impression on many nonprofit organizations that they could not engage in lobbying activity. First, in 1966 came the revocation of the 501(c)(3) status of the Sierra Club after its efforts to stop dam building on the Colorado River. Three years later, Congress enacted the 1969 Tax Reform Act, the provisions of which had a chilling effect on advocacy by philanthropic organizations.

For the Sierra Club, the trouble stemmed from their response to a congressional proposal to build two dams on the Colorado River, the result of which would have been to turn part of the Grand Canyon into a 500-foot deep lake.[5] The club's response was to run full-page ads in major newspapers condemning the idea and, just before a House subcommittee vote, the ads included a form that readers could clip and send directly to Wayne Aspinall (D-Colorado), the subcommittee chair.[6] Likely at the behest of Aspinall, the IRS had a notice of investigation hand-delivered to the Sierra Club the next day; its tax-deductible status was suspended during the investigation and eventually revoked.[7]

The club's response illustrates the complexity of options available to nonprofit organizations. First, they reactivated the existing 501(c)(3) Sierra Club Foundation, which had tax-exempt status and was eligible to receive tax-deductible donations. Next, they re-classified the Sierra Club as a 501(c)(4) social welfare organization, which means that it can engage in unlimited lobbying; under this status, while the organization itself is tax-exempt, it cannot receive tax-deductible contributions.[8] In addition, the Sierra Club created the Sierra Club Political Committee which, as a traditional political action committee, is regulated by the Federal Election Commission. The Sierra Club Political Committee receives no tax-exemption, and its donors' contributions are not tax deductible. The public response to Sierra Club following the incident was quite favorable, and both membership and donations increased in the aftermath; the impact of the revocation of their tax-deductible status, however, had a far more negative effect on lobbying activity throughout the nonprofit sector.[9]

In 1969, the Tax Reform Act had a significant impact on the sector by limiting the amount of lobbying in which foundations could engage or fund. As discussed in Chapter 4, the 1969 Act was passed following a series of dramatic congressional hearings on purported foundation abuses. The hearings spanned the 1950s and 1960s, culminating in a memorable investigation of the Ford Foundation.

Members of Congress were troubled by several Ford Foundation projects which funded registration of African American voters in the south and desegregation of schools in the north. The last straw, however, came after the 1968 assassination of presidential candidate Bobby Kennedy, when the Ford Foundation provided generous fellowships to eight former Kennedy staffers; many members of Congress viewed these as grants for political purposes.

Described as dramatic and explosive, the congressional hearings resulted in changes to the tax laws that imposed more federal control over foundation behavior.[10] Among the changes brought by the 1969 Tax Reform Act were the imposition of a tax on investment income, the addition of payout minimums that required foundations to distribute a certain percentage of their assets annually, the creation of new conflict of interest rules, and restrictions on foundation funding of voter registration. As Bass et al. explain, "Foundations were shell-shocked by the new law, and it has had a lasting impact."[11] Subsequently, since the late 1960s many nonprofit leaders have been trained to fear congressional hearings, the IRS, and additional restrictions on policy activity. It is no surprise that many nonprofits eschew political activity altogether.

Recently, however, there has been a concerted effort to encourage nonprofits and foundations to engage in and fund lobbying and advocacy. Beginning around 2000, groups such as the Center for Lobbying in the Public Interest, the Strengthening Nonprofit Advocacy Project, Grantmakers for Effective Organizations, the National Committee for Responsive Philanthropy, and Independent Sector have encouraged increased advocacy and lobbying throughout the nonprofit sector. As Bob Smucker, founder of the Center for Lobbying in the Public Interest (CLPI), writes on the CLPI homepage: "Nonprofit lobbying is the right thing to do. It is about empowering individuals to make their collective voices heard on a wide range of human concerns."[12]

NONPROFIT ADVOCACY CAN SHAPE THE POLICY ENVIRONMENT

Regardless of whether or not one's organization decides to engage specifically in lobbying, the limits of which we discuss in more depth later, advocacy efforts are vital. Arons, Levine, and Simone define public policy advocacy as including "a wide range of activities designed to shape decisions and uses of resources that affect people, causes, and communities."[13] Advocacy, therefore, does not have to be focused on legislation but rather can include efforts to change public opinion or behavior using media campaigns, research findings, educational outreach, and by hosting community events. Advocacy can be directed at government officials, but it need not be; individual businesses or entire industries may be the targets of nonprofit advocacy campaigns.[14] Further, citizen groups can bring initiatives directly to voters in states that allow direct democracy such as California, Oregon, and Washington.[15]

In 1995, Lester Salamon forecasted that the advocacy role of nonprofits would decline as organizations became more involved in the competitive marketplace and managers lost the time and incentive for competing in the political realm. This prediction has clearly not come to fruition. On the contrary, what has been more notable is the success of the nonprofit sector in the policy realm, especially considering its relative dearth of resources when compared with the for-profit sector. Advocacy efforts are often quite successful and organizations increasingly work toward these ends: the IRS reports that over 1,000 nonprofits are in the category of organizations that work to change public opinion and policy; of these, over 75 percent have been created since 1970.[16]

Less than a decade after making his original prediction, Salamon reversed himself, attributing the increased political clout of the nonprofit sector to "changes in public attitudes and in political circumstances" and "the capacity and effectiveness of the citizen organizations themselves."[17] As such, the influence of nonprofit advocacy has increased even though profit-making interest groups continue to outspend nonprofits by wide margins.[18] Among the reasons for this success is the fact that "nonprofit advocacy has become highly professionalized, with complex organizations mobilizing hundreds of thousands of members, conducting expert research, and using sophisticated public relations techniques."[19]

Most nonprofits have also made good use of the Internet as a tool to enhance public relations and mobilize supporters. A Web presence offers an organization an easy way to maintain contact with clients, members, politicians, and other stakeholders and has been instrumental in keeping lines of communication open while facilitating fundraising and advocacy efforts.[20] The national Parent Teacher Association (PTA), for example, keeps in touch with stakeholders via PTA Action Updates and PTA Action Alerts sent directly to millions of e-mail addresses by the PTA Office of Programs and Public Policy. Similarly, savvy nonprofits are making increased use of social networking media by seeking fans on Facebook and inviting stakeholders to "follow us on Twitter."

Another trend increasing the advocacy capacity of the nonprofit sector is the growing participation in associations and coalitions of nonprofit organizations, as in the nonprofit example in our opening vignette. In a survey of 311 nonprofits, Salamon and Geller found that 89 percent belong to at least one membership or coalition organization, and 87 percent of those organizations are involved in some type of lobbying or policy advocacy efforts.[21] Similar to the discussion of advocacy coalitions in Chapter 1, a key benefit of these coalitions and associations is that most are field-or issue-specific, offering members the ability to work together over time and pool information and resources. Often, the associations offer training and encourage members to engage in policy activity. In other cases, the associations focus on advocacy and lobbying, allowing the individual member organizations to focus on their primary organizational missions.[22]

The Importance of Advocacy in Pursuit of Mission

Increased ability and effort regarding policy advocacy are vital as the stake in the political arena has grown for nonprofits in direct relation to government reliance on them. As discussed in Chapter 2, in the past several decades federal, state, and local governments have increasingly sought a subcontracting relationship with nonprofits to administer government social service programs. For even longer, since Lyndon Johnson's Great Society, the federal government has sought to take advantage of the capacity of nonprofits—their grassroots orientation, flexibility, and ability to raise private funds.[23] Because of their relationship with government it is imperative that nonprofit organizations, both large and small, find and use their voices in policy advocacy and the legislative process.

For some nonprofit and philanthropic organizations, such as those whose mission is to pursue broad, societal goals such as civil rights protection or environmental conservation, advocating public policy and social change is their primary focus. More often, nonprofits play an advocacy role only occasionally, as an incidental part of their broader service delivery functions.[24] When nonprofits act, they address policy problems in a variety of ways in relation to diverse public interests, such as recreation and cultural programs as well as alleviating homelessness. Advocacy, including structuring problems and solutions with regard to means and methods of service delivery, is embedded in their service delivery choices.

The role of not-for-profit advocacy is to build leverage in the system. Rather than simply changing "the world one client at a time, advocacy efforts focus on broad changes in systems and policy."[25] Frumkin identifies three key ways in which nonprofits create this leverage. First, nonprofits can bring neglected issues to the attention of the media and the wider public. Second, because they exist outside of the formal government structure, they can introduce policymakers to new ideas and unique solutions to social problems, expanding the range of policy options. Finally, changes that nonprofit organizations effectuate at the local level can reverberate throughout the system, shaping and reshaping decisions and priorities at the state, national, and even international levels.[26] For examples of the work that nonprofits do to effect change in problems in the international arena, see Going Global 6.1.

GOING GLOBAL 6.1

Nongovernmental Organizations and Issues of International Concern

Although there is no way to make policy on a global scale, the nature of globalization and improved technology have meant that many issues garner international attention and draw advocates who seek redress of problems that affect people around the world. These advocates, or policy entrepreneurs, often take it upon themselves to develop nongovernmental organizations (NGOs) to address global problems, including human rights violations, the environment, and diseases such as HIV/AIDS and malaria that affect the global community. The most recent data on NGOs indicate that in 2005 there were more than 20,000 such organizations operating around the world to effect change in these and other issue areas.[27]

Since NGOs have no global policymaking body to lobby, they seek change via appeals to international organizations such as the United Nations (UN), by encouraging policy in individual nations, and through advocacy regarding international treaties and conventions. For example, following World War II the UN General Assembly created the Geneva Conventions, the core guidelines of international humanitarian law. Among the Additional Protocols of the Geneva Conventions was the 1950 creation of the office of the UN High Commissioner for Refugees (UNHCR), the United Nations Refugee Agency. The agency's mission is maintenance of legal protections and provision of humanitarian aid to refugees; when a nation signs on to the Geneva Conventions, it has agreed to follow these protocols.

Many NGOs, therefore, assist refugees and other displaced persons, providing shelter, medical care, and food aid in addition to ensuring that the human rights of these populations are protected and that nations are abiding by the Geneva Conventions. Again, since there is no global entity to make or enforce international policy, NGOs often focus their policy advocacy efforts on raising awareness of public problems; to do so, they tend to rely on individuals who already have the public's attention to help them. One such organization is USA for UNHCR, which has benefitted since 2001 from its association with actor Angelina Jolie. In her role as Goodwill Ambassador, Jolie has traveled extensively to war-torn countries, spoken on behalf of refugees before UN meetings, and donated an estimated $5 million to aid the humanitarian efforts of USA for UNHCR.

The extent to which NGO's utilize celebrity to enhance their advocacy efforts varies and often reflects the interest and commitment of the individuals involved. For example, actor Ted Danson co-founded the nonprofit American Oceans Campaign in 1987; in 2001, it merged with Oceana, an international advocacy organization created to protect the world's oceans. Among its international policy victories, Oceana counts the end of shrimp trawling in Belize, bans on the use of driftnets in Morocco and Turkey, and bans on shark finning in Chile and the United States.[28] In his capacity as an Oceana board member, Danson has testified before Congress a number of times, urging "visionary changes to the way we manage oceans" and arguing that the "oceans should be governed for the public trust."[29]

The Elton John AIDS Foundation (EJAF), founded by singer/songwriter Sir Elton John in 1992, is another example of the celebrity of an individual being put to use to raise awareness and bring about change on a global scale. Over its two decades in operation, EJAF has raised over $225 million to fund HIV/AIDS education and prevention programs implemented in 55 countries across the globe. John has testified before Congress on occasion, urging additional U.S. funding for global HIV/AIDS relief.

Policy advocacy is clearly an important part of the work of many NGOs, and their efforts have influenced policy and legislation in various countries, as the examples from Oceana and the Elton John AIDS Foundation illustrate. NGOs are also involved in direct policymaking, as these organizations make important decisions about how best to use funds for programs at the local level.[30] Raising global awareness of previously unknown problems and raising the resources to combat them are also crucial to global NGO involvement and is made easier by the public attention that follows a celebrity advocate. In all of these ways, NGOs are important actors in problem recognition, advocacy efforts, and policy implementation of international programs.

For additional information:

Elton John AIDS Foundation, http://ejaf.org/

Oceana, http://oceana.org

USA for UNHCR, The UN Refugee Agency, www.unrefugees.org

Policy advocacy is an important part of what nonprofits do, and when asked about specific activities, researchers have found that most have engaged in some sort of advocacy efforts. For example, in a 2000 study of 1,173 nonprofits conducted by the Strengthening Nonprofit Advocacy Project (SNAP), about 75 percent reported having engaged in some type of effort to influence public policy at least once. Similarly, Salamon and Geller found that 73 percent of the 311 nonprofits they studied had engaged in policy advocacy or lobbying in the previous year (62 percent in policy advocacy and 59 percent in lobbying). Furthermore, 61 percent of those organizations reported engaging in advocacy or lobbying efforts once a month or more.[31]

While their involvement can be described as wide, it is not particularly deep; the form of advocacy employed by organizations in the study varied, and tended to be of the least demanding type. While 57 percent reported signing correspondence to a government official, only 35 percent engaged in grassroots lobbying, encouraging the public to communicate with officials. Further, while 55 percent had responded to a request for information from a public official, only 29 percent had organized a public event and only 24 percent had released a research report. As Salamon and Geller conclude, "lobbying and advocacy, while widespread and varied, tend to involve relatively limited-commitment activities for most organizations most of the time."[32]

Of those not-for-profit organizations that engage in lobbying and policy advocacy, the motivation is clear. Nearly 90 percent in the SNAP study "said that the key reason for their advocacy was to carry out their nonprofit missions."[33] Research suggests that groups are most likely to engage in advocacy (1) to raise awareness about important issues; (2) when they perceive government to be threatening their ability to deliver services; or (3) because of the relevance of legislation to their programs and the people they serve.[34]

An example of the involvement of not-for-profit organizations in policy advocacy comes from a general overview of the policy issues important to the National Alliance on Mental Illness (NAMI) and its Public Policy Platform. It is clear that NAMI casts a wide net with its policy advocacy efforts, from service delivery, to health insurance coverage, to mental health financing. NAMI also includes a wide variety of stakeholders in its efforts, including patients and their families, researchers, and policymakers at the local, state, and federal levels. The creation of a set of public policy priorities is consistent with the trend by nonprofits to advocate for important policy change on behalf of their constituents, engaging both policymakers and the public. More information on NAMI is included in Box 6.2.

Importantly, research indicates that not-for-profit organizations have been quite successful in their advocacy efforts: While public charities are a small percentage of the interest group organizations in Washington, D.C., they are a major force in congressional testimony and press coverage on issues and are far more likely to get legislation passed regarding their issues than are private business interests.[35] Fundamental to this success is the fact that knowledge is power; because nonprofit organizations have a wealth of information about social problems and programs to address them, their policy recommendations carry significant weight with legislators at the federal and state levels. An example comes from a Minnesota consortium of nonprofits, which fought off $200 million in state cuts to social

Box 6.2

FOR EXAMPLE

THE NATIONAL ALLIANCE ON MENTAL ILLNESS: CREATING PUBLIC POLICY PRIORITIES

Nonprofit organizations often set public policy priorities. The following is an example from the Public Policy Platform of the National Alliance on Mental Illness.[36]

> NAMI advocates for research and services in response to major illnesses that affect the brain, including schizophrenia, schizoaffective disorder, bipolar disorder, major depressive disorder, obsessive-compulsive disorder, panic and other severe anxiety disorders, borderline personality disorder, post traumatic stress disorder (PTSD), autism and pervasive developmental disorders, and attention deficit/hyperactivity disorder.

The Public Policy Platform includes policy statements on issues such as access to treatment, Medicare, legal rights of the mentally ill, and criminal justice policies. To advance its public policy efforts, NAMI's webpage includes a Legislative Action Center with pages devoted to State Advocacy and an Advocacy Action Center. Each of these provides resources to help mental health advocates drive national and state policy debates on reform and investment in the nation's system of mental health care and financing. Among NAMI's most important policy successes to date is the federal mental health parity law, signed in 2008, which guarantees insurance coverage for substance abuse and mental health disorders equal to that provided for treatment of any other chronic health condition.

The NAMI Legislative Action Center includes legislative alerts and updates (which advocates can receive via email), tools to find federal and state elected officials, daily House and Senate floor activity and committee hearing schedules, and information on the issues and legislation important for policies related to mental health. Advocates can access media relations materials, including templates for press releases and advocacy training tools, through NAMI online and are encouraged to share legislative alerts on relevant legislation using Facebook and Twitter.

For additional information: www.nami.org

services in 2002. The director of the consortium explains: "We found that if you weren't at the table you were on the table when it came to welfare reform. Decisions will be made with or without our information. Which do you prefer?"[37]

Regardless of whether the organization exists to provide goods and services to clientele or has its primary purpose in advocacy, it would be difficult to overestimate the influence of nonprofit organizations on law, policy, and regulation in the United States. From women's suffrage to civil rights for African Americans to consumer protection, advocacy efforts of nonprofit organizations have changed American society and its laws for decades.[38] For an in-depth example of the power of nonprofit advocacy, see Case Study 6.3 on the work of AARP in health care reform.

CASE STUDY 6.3

AARP's Advocacy and Influence on Health Care Reform

In February of 2007 the nonprofit, nonpartisan, 501(c)4 membership organization AARP (formerly known as American Association of Retired Persons) sent teams of staffers to the early presidential primary and caucus states of New Hampshire, Iowa, North Carolina, Florida, and Nevada for one purpose: to ensure that health care was a major policy issue on the agenda of every presidential candidate during the early campaign season. As a key member of the effort known as Divided We Fail, AARP collaborated with the Business Roundtable, the Service Employees International Union (SEIU), and the National Federation of Independent Business (NFIB) in an effort to find

> bi-partisan solutions to ensure affordable, quality health care and long-term financial security—for all of us. The need for health and financial security is something we all share, not just for ourselves, but for future generations. It is the promise of America.[39]

To tout its bipartisan status, Divided We Fail created a mascot, the elephonkey, which is a fictional animal with the head and trunk of an elephant and the ears and tail end of a donkey. Further, its health policy reform efforts were supported by over 100 other organizations—mostly nonprofits—including 100 Black Men, the American Academy of Family Physicians, the March of Dimes, the Girl Scouts of the USA, and B'nai B'rith International.

In Iowa, during the build-up to the presidential caucuses in January 2008, advocacy by AARP included holding nonpartisan town hall meetings and candidate forums, co-sponsoring candidate debates, and engaging in a media campaign aimed at putting health care reform on the policy agenda and making it a priority for candidates and the public alike. Donning red shirts that featured the DividedWeFail.Org logo and elephonkey on the front and the words "AARP Demand action, answers, and accountability on health and financial security," members of AARP were everywhere that candidates and voters gathered. Candidates often commented on the familiar red shirts while on the campaign trail, and AARP's efforts did not end with the campaign season. This level of effort on the part of AARP and its Divided We Fail partners clearly illustrates their level of commitment to making health care reform a priority for the incoming presidential administration.

In July of 2009, President Obama held a tele-town hall meeting on health care reform with AARP members from across the country, at which he acknowledged AARP's role in health policy reform:

> We're now closer to health care reform than we ever have been before, and that's due in no small part to the outstanding team that you have here at AARP, because you've been doing what you do best, which is organize and mobilize and inform and educate people all across the country about the choices that are out there, pushing members of Congress to put aside politics and partisanship, and finding solutions to our health care challenges.[40]

While the Divided We Fail partners were unified in seeking health care reform, the coalition experienced divisions when it came to the specific details of policy as it was drafted in Congress during 2009. For-profit partners wanted the reform to rely on private health insurance with minimal employer requirements, while labor unions and other progressive partners sought universal health coverage and public insurance competition with for-profit insurers. Thus, after spending two years and $20 million to put health care reform on the national policy agenda, the coalition became divided over the outcomes of reform—not uncommon when such coalitions face the reality of public policymaking.[41]

Although obviously influential, the actual impact of AARP and Divided We Fail cannot be measured; however, it is important to note that health care reform was the highest domestic policy priority of the first year of the Obama administration. Major reform legislation, the Affordable Care Act, was signed into law in early 2010.

AARP's involvement with enactment of the reform, however, was not without negative consequences for the organization: in mid-2009, it lost an estimated 60,000 members as a result of its apparent support of President Obama's plan; that represents about 1.5 percent of its approximately four million members.[42] More importantly, members of Congress also expressed concern. In early 2011, Republican members of the House Ways and Means Committee announced an investigation into AARP's financial holdings and tax status, arguing that it appeared to be operating as a for-profit health insurance company rather than a tax-exempt nonprofit organization. They claimed that the organization had strayed from its traditional mission of helping seniors.[43] Further, they argued that AARP's insurance company stood to gain $1 billion over the next 10 years from the health care reforms it had advocated.[44] AARP and its supporters argued that its tax-exempt status was solid: it does not hold stock or pay dividends, and all profits are invested back into services for its members. As with many congressional investigations into nonprofit lobbying activity, this investigation did not result in any action.

AARP is among the largest membership nonprofits in the country. Because AARP was one of its partners, the advocacy efforts of Divided We Fail were far larger in scope than most organizations can undertake; however, their tactics, such as hosting forums, gaining media attention, and creating public spectacle, can be replicated by nonprofit advocates of all sizes. The potential to meet the needs of one's clients through advocacy and lobbying make it essential that nonprofits engage in these efforts to influence public policy.

QUESTIONS TO CONSIDER:

1. What motivated the AARP, Business Roundtable, the SEIU, and the NFIB to form a coalition to seek dramatic change in U.S. health care policy?
2. This case study suggests that coalitions of groups seeking policy change often break down when the details of that policy are being developed. Why would that be the case?
3. The AARP is a 501(c)(4) organization, which can engage in unlimited direct lobbying activity. Its efforts to seek health care reform with Divided We Fail, however, were enough to pique the interest of members of the House Ways and Means Committee, some of whom questioned AARP's tax-exempt status. What, if any, evidence is there in this case that AARP should lose its tax status?
4. Consider the four relationships that describe nonprofit interaction with public policy (make policy, affected by policy, influence policy, subject to policy) and discuss the ways in which AARP's health care reform activities reflect these relationships.
5. Is the AARP/Divided We Fail example unique? If so, in what ways? If not, in what other policy areas might coalitions form to influence public policy?

For additional information, see AARP, Divided We Fail, www.aarp.org/issues/dividedwefail/

WHAT IS "LOBBYING"?

Earlier we defined lobbying as occurring only when there is an expenditure of funds on activities designed to influence specific pieces of legislation. There are many nuances to the Internal Revenue Code (IRC) regarding nonprofit lobbying, but the most important factor for public charities is that utilizing a substantial part of their expenditures for either direct or grassroots lobbying is cause for denial or revocation of tax-exempt status. The primary difference between *direct* and *grassroots* lobbying has to do with the target of influence. Direct lobbying involves correspondence and conference with legislators and their staffs or publication of materials intended to influence legislative activity, when reference is made to *specific legislation* and the group's view on that legislation. Note, however, that when such actions are undertaken at the request of the legislative body, in testimony before the legislature, for example, the nonprofit has not engaged in lobbying.

Grassroots lobbying involves expenditure of funds to appeal to the general public to take action in support of or opposition to specific legislation.[45] Thus, when an organization simply informs the general public and its own membership of its position on pending legislation, it has not engaged in lobbying. If, however, that information includes a call for action by the general public, the organization has engaged in grassroots lobbying; similarly, a call to action aimed specifically at an organization's own members is considered direct lobbying.

Although Congress has generally been supportive of the rights of nonprofits to lobby, studies find that few organizations do so.[46] The key barrier to nonprofit lobbying activity appears to be a lack of resources: time, staff, and funding.[47] Other important barriers include the tax laws and IRS regulations, the skill levels of staff and volunteers, the fact that the organization receives government funding,[48] and negative attitudes toward lobbying from their boards, staff, and the public. Further, Salamon and Geller find that foundation resource dependence may pose a barrier to lobbying; in their research, nonprofits that rely heavily on foundation grants are *less likely* to engage in policy advocacy or lobbying.[49]

Myths about Nonprofits and Lobbying

The myth that 501(c)(3) organizations cannot lobby has been promulgated because of the Sierra Club incident and the 1969 Tax Reform Act discussed earlier, as well as several attempts to restrict lobbying that have been introduced and defeated more recently. For example, during the Reagan administration, revisions to Office of Management and Budget Circular A-122 sought to broaden restrictions on advocacy activity by nonprofit organizations, as did the Istook Amendment in the 1990s. These proposed limitations, while ultimately unsuccessful, were designed to increase the administrative burden on nonprofits by forcing them to isolate lobbying funds from all other operational funds. This furthered the misperception among not-for-profit organizations that they cannot legally engage in lobbying activity.

In addition, the myth that nonprofits cannot lobby persists because they often misunderstand their rights under the law, as exemplified in the opening vignette. In his research, Jeffery Berry found that nearly half of the respondents he surveyed gave incorrect answers to a series of questions testing knowledge of their organization's rights in advocating a legislative position before Congress; only 61 percent knew they were allowed to publicly state a general policy position.[50] Similarly, confusion over lobbying laws was identified as one of the most common barriers to effective lobbying in the 2000 study by the Strengthening Nonprofit Advocacy Project.[51] Further, Salamon and Geller found that 31 percent of their survey respondents mistakenly believed their organizations were prohibited from lobbying. In truth, of course, all nonprofits can legally lobby; the confusion lies in the determination of *allowable* lobbying activity.[52]

Lobbying Allowable under the Law

Lobbying is only of concern to the IRS when an organization expends funds to influence legislation; thus, if there is no expenditure of funds (i.e., mailings, travel, staff time, etc.), there is no lobbying. Under federal tax laws, legislation is defined as an "action by Congress, a state legislature, a local council or similar governing body, and the general public in a referendum, an initiative, a constitutional amendment, or a similar procedure."[53] It includes attempts to influence members of the Senate during confirmation of judges to the federal courts and proposals for laws in other countries. For tips on engaging in advocacy and lobbying, see Box 6.4.

It is equally important to note that for nonprofit organizations, lobbying members of the executive branch, including mayors, governors, presidents, and agency directors, is perfectly acceptable under the law. Likewise, filing a suit or amicus curiae brief in court is not considered lobbying; thus, nonprofits are free to do both. Self-defense activity, in which the nonprofit organization lobbies to protect its own existence, powers, or tax-exempt status, is also allowed without restrictions.

Even the laws that prohibit legislative lobbying are more flexible than they may seem on the surface. First, nonprofits face no restrictions on communication with legislators if they are asked for advice or to testify before a legislative body. Furthermore, public charities can conduct nonpartisan policy analysis, as well as publish and disseminate the results, without the costs accruing as lobbying expenses—even if legislative action is needed to implement the results—as long as the organization does not call for specific legislative adoption or action.[54]

Finally, communication with legislators designed solely to educate or inform about an issue in general is not considered lobbying and is therefore permissible. It is important to keep in mind that such education efforts are undertaken with relative frequency, making the relationships between elected officials and nonprofit organizations reciprocal: while nonprofits often have a vested interest in legislative outcomes and policy, policymakers often rely upon the help and expertise of those in nonprofit organizations as they make important policy decisions. The differences between "education and advocacy" and "advocacy and lobbying" might appear to be subjective. Indeed, Jeffery Berry has concluded: "the difference between educating legislators and lobbying legislators has no real meaning outside of the tax code. It is the same thing."[55] For those working in the nonprofit sector, however, the tax code is the meaning that matters.

Box 6.4

FOR MORE INFORMATION

ADVOCACY AND LOBBYING TIPS

Make an Appointment: If you are a constituent, be sure that the person who schedules your appointment knows that you live in the legislator's district. If you have to meet with a staff member, remember that senior staff can wield a lot of power and are often able to give you more time than the legislator.

Be Reliable: Be on time for your appointments. If you tell a legislator that you will send them additional information, *do so promptly.*

Introduce Yourself: If you are not a district voter, introduce your organization and explain its importance to the legislator's district.

Be Prepared: Provide organized, useful, clear, concise, and accurate information. When you are lobbying about specific legislation, know the bill number, bill author, proponents/opponents, where the bill (or budget issue) is in the legislative process, and have responses to the opposition's arguments.

Do not hesitate to say: "I don't know, but I will try to get that information for you."

Do not guess or make up an answer.

Do not waste their time or yours: Be succinct! Avoid getting sidetracked and stay on message.

Give anecdotes and specific examples pertinent to your organization or its clientele. Legislators need to hear the "real world impact" of issues; give them a personal story that will stick with them.

Anticipate tough questions such as, "If we don't cut this funding, then where should we cut?" It's your task to advocate for your issue and clients, not to provide solutions to all social problems.

Beware of overkill. Recognize when you've gotten what you came for, or as much as you'll get.

Be specific about the action you would like the legislator to take.

Be Respectful and Polite: If you disagree with the legislator's position, say so, but focus your arguments on the facts and your reasons for disagreeing. If a legislator is not supportive on the issue, accept that fact but continue lobbying through letters, district, or capital office visits. Remember, today's unsupportive legislator could be your ally on the next issue.

If You Are in a Group, Select a Spokesperson and Assign Roles: Appoint one person to begin the conversation (make sure all present introduce themselves). Plan what each member of the group will discuss, and role-play prior to your meeting. Give *everyone* in the group an opportunity to speak. Be sure that each person in your group takes notes for later debriefing.

Leave Something Tangible: Leave a fact sheet, informational brochure, business card, or a copy of a bill—anything tangible that will visually remind the legislator of your visit and your issue.

Debrief and Follow-Up: Immediately following your meeting, you (and group members) should review your meeting notes and evaluate the meeting to identify strengths and weaknesses for next time. Be sure to follow through with any promises made in a *timely manner.*

Thank You Letter: Send a thank you letter that (1) expresses your appreciation for the meeting; (2) summarizes the purpose of the meeting; and (3) reiterates the action you want taken by the legislator. *No* form letters!

Keep Them Accountable: Follow your legislators—their votes, statements on issues, and the bills they sponsor. Send a letter, email, or make a telephone call to let them know that you approve or disapprove of their actions.

Source: Adapted from the Government Relations Office, California Faculty Association, "Do's and Don'ts of Lobbying," and from the Center for Lobbying in the Public Interest, "Personal Visits with a Legislator."

Limits on Lobbying: The "Substantial Part Test" and 501(h)

The federal government instituted tax deductions for charitable contributions in 1917 as a way to facilitate charitable giving by taxpayers. By 1930, however, a federal appeals court held that organizations receiving tax exempt donations could not engage in "agitating for the repeal of laws"[56] because the tax exemption could be considered a government subsidy. In the 1934 Revenue Act, Congress instituted the substantial part test, disallowing tax-exempt status for organizations that engage in legislative lobbying as a substantial part of their activities.[57] The substantial part test derives from the provision of Internal Revenue Code (IRC) section 501(c)(3) which regulates nonprofit expenditures such that " . . . no substantial part of the activities of which is carrying on propaganda, or otherwise attempting, to influence legislation . . ." For better or worse, however, what constitutes a substantial amount of an organization's time or money has not been consistently defined.

Thus, while lobbying is a legal activity for 501(c)(3) organizations, many of them are still reluctant, uninterested, or financially unable to engage. Until April 2003, the IRS routinely conducted targeted audits on a sample of public charities that reported lobbying activity.[58] The fear of audit and the possible loss of tax-exempt status if lobbying activity were deemed excessive under the ambiguous substantial part rule have caused many nonprofits to eschew any legislative lobbying activities.

Fortunately for public charities, the substantial part rule can be avoided if the organization simply chooses the 501(h) election, which was created in the Tax Reform Act of 1976 to provide clearer guidelines for nonprofits engaging in lobbying activities. Although public charities must actively elect to fall under the expenditure test of the H election by filing Form 5768, choosing this set of rules affords greater predictability and protection regarding permitted lobbying activity. Nonprofits that do not choose the H election will, by default, fall under the substantial part rule governing lobbying. The determination of what amount of lobbying constitutes a substantial part of organizational activity is then left to subjective interpretation (see Table 6.2).

The H election sets specific ceiling amounts on nonprofit lobbying expenditures, as noted in Table 6.1. These limits are set based on a sliding scale of exempt-purpose expenditures, which include all expenses for organizational programs but do not include expenses related to managing investments, unrelated businesses, and certain fundraising. Total lobbying expenditure limits include the amounts that can be spent for either direct or grassroots lobbying.[59] Many experts recommend that nonprofits, particularly those engaged in lobbying, choose the H election because the substantial part test leaves them vulnerable to a subjective interpretation by authorities with no consistent rules regarding penalties.[60] Opponents of the lobbying limitations have called for, at a minimum, the repeal of the distinction between direct and grassroots lobbying[61] and a clarification of IRS regulations governing nonpartisan voter activities.[62] For a comparison of the differences between the substantial part rules and section 501(h), see Table 6.2.

TABLE 6.1 Limits to Lobbying under Section 501(h) Election of 1976

Total Exempt-Purpose Expenditures	Direct Lobbying Expenditure Limits	Grassroots Lobbying Expenditure Limits
Up to $500,000	20% of exempt-purpose expenditures	One-quarter
$500,000–$1 million	$100,000 + 15% of excess over $500,000	$25,000 + 3.75% of excess over $500,000
$1 million–$1.5 million	$175,000 + 10% of excess over $1 million	$43,750 + 2.5% of excess over $1 million
$1.5 million–$17 million	$225,000 + 5% of excess over $1.5 million	$56,250 + 1.25% of excess over $1.5 million
Over $17 million	$1 million	$250,000

Source: Adapted from Bob Smucker, *The Nonprofit Lobbying Guide*, 2nd ed. (Independent Sector: Washington, D.C., 1999) and CLPI (Center for Lobbying in the Public Interest), *Make a Difference for your Cause.* Washington, DC: Center for Lobbying in the Public Interest, 2006.

Far fewer organizations have chosen to take the H election than proponents of the legislation anticipated. This could be attributed to the recordkeeping burden of complying with section 501(h), but it is more likely that most charities do not engage in a great deal of lobbying and expenditures by those that do lobby generally constitute less than ten percent of their funds.[63] Because data are not available regarding taxes collected on violations of the lobbying limitations, it is difficult to assess the full impact of the H election on the nonprofit sector.[64]

Other Options: 501(c)(4) Affiliation and Professional Lobbyists

The 1983 Supreme Court decision *Regan v. Taxation with Representation of Washington*, affirmed the government's right to limit lobbying activity by citing precedent that tax-exemption is a privileged status and that limiting lobbying activity by public charities is not a restriction on free speech but rather a restriction on the subsidy received. The court did, however, expand the ability of 501(c)(3) organizations to lobby indirectly by allowing them to create or affiliate with 501(c)(4) organizations.[65] Organizations that are tax-exempt under section 501(c)(4) of the IRC are not restricted in their ability to lobby; however, it is important to remember that contributions to 501(c)(4) organizations are *not* tax deductible.

The *Regan* decision makes it clear that public charities can control the activities of their affiliated 501(c)(4) organizations, and that the two organizations may share the same legislative priorities, boards of directors, office space, facilities, and staff. There are some restrictions on 501(c)(4) organizations: they must be incorporated as a separate legal entity, must

TABLE 6.2 The "Substantial Part" Test vs. 501(h) Election Rules

	Nonprofits under the Substantial Part Rules	Nonprofit 501 (h) Electors
What is "Lobbying" activity?	No clear definitions; organization must keep careful accounting of public policy activity	Clear definitions; many activities are not considered lobbying and are not subject to limits
What are the spending limits?	Lobbying activity cannot be "substantial part" of nonprofit efforts, but "substantial" is undefined	Clearly defined (see Table 6.1)
What counts?	Money spent and volunteer time	Only money spent, not volunteer hours, for example
How involved is the record-keeping and accounting?	All lobbying activities and expenses must be recorded. Detailed descriptions of activities and a classified schedule of expenses reported on annual information return Form 990 Schedule C filed with IRS	All lobbying expenses must be recorded; expenses are reported on annual information return Form 990 Schedule C filed with IRS
What are the penalties for exceeding limits?	If revocation of tax-exempt status occurs, nonprofit is assessed a 5 percent excise tax on all funds spent on lobbying. Directors/officers can be personally taxed if found to have willfully authorized the substantial lobbying	Organization assessed a 25 percent excise tax on spending over allowable limits; no penalties for directors/officers
When does revocation of tax-exempt status occur?	Unclear; a nonprofit could lose its status in a given year	If lobbying exceeds 150% of allowable limits for four or more years

Source: Adapted from Bob Smucker, *The Nonprofit Lobbying Guide,* 2nd ed. (Independent Sector: Washington, D.C., 1999) and CLPI (Center for Lobbying in the Public Interest), *Make a Difference for your Cause.* Washington, D.C.: Center for Lobbying in the Public Interest, 2006.

fund their activity solely using non-tax-deductible funds, and must keep adequate records to show that all costs are properly divided between the 501(c)(3) and the 501(c)(4) organizations for such expenses as rents and leases, salaries, equipment, and so on.

Recently, the 2010 Supreme Court decision *Citizens United v. Federal Elections Commission* added to the ability of a host of organizations including 501(c)(4) social welfare organizations, 501(c)(5) labor unions, and 501(c)(6) trade associations, to engage in "electioneering communications" and make "independent expenditures" in federal and state elections.[66] The *Citizens United* decision means that these organizations may now refer to a specific candidate in television communications—including cable or satellite—within 30–60 days of an election.[67] Further, they are now allowed to spend money expressly to elect or defeat a particular candidate, as long as they are not acting in coordination with any political party or candidate for office and have complied with all applicable federal election and tax laws.

Occasionally, a nonprofit organization will seek professional assistance in advancing its legislative agenda and hire a lobbyist. While this may be anathema to many nonprofits, it is possible that a specialist in the legislative process might be needed if the organization faces a legislative crisis or there are other indicators that a legislative professional is needed.[68] In particular, organizations would benefit from a professional lobbyist if they (1) are missing key votes or are unaware of the committee and subcommittee changes being made to their legislative priorities; (2) have difficulty meeting with legislators or their staff; or (3) simply do not understand the legislative process.[69]

PUBLIC POLICY ADVOCACY AND FOUNDATIONS

Perhaps even more than the average 501(c)(3) organization, foundations are often leery about engaging in public policy advocacy for fear of running afoul of IRS rules. As discussed earlier, the Tax Reform Act of 1969 imposed strict legal limits on types of foundation grantmaking as well as requiring greater transparency in IRS reporting. These factors have certainly curbed the public policy activity of philanthropic foundations.[70] The rules for private foundations—those deriving their funds from an individual, family, or corporation—are particularly restrictive: while they can make grants to nonprofits that engage in policy advocacy and legislative lobbying, they cannot support specific lobbying activity, nor can they support partisan get-out-the-vote or voter registration drives.[71] Private foundations may only engage in lobbying to protect their own interests.[72] On the other hand, community (or public) foundations—those deriving funds from government, or individual and private foundation sources—fall under the same rules as charity nonprofits and therefore can engage in the same public policy activities. In addition, community foundations are allowed to make grants to nonprofits for legislative lobbying. A good source of information on advocacy and lobbying by philanthropic foundations is the Alliance for Justice (see Box 6.5).

Unfortunately for those who think that philanthropic foundations should be more politically active, they rarely make use of the full range of these options. In 2010, for example, the Foundation Center reported that only 12.3 percent of foundation giving fell under the category of public affairs/society benefit, which includes civil rights, social action and advocacy, community improvement and development, and public affairs, including consumer protection and multidisciplinary public policy research.[73] Fear is the key explanation for foundation reluctance to fund political efforts—fear of violating IRS regulations; fear of appearing to wield too much power; boards of directors' fears of alienating the public; or fear of harming a family name by advocating on controversial issues.[74]

Box 6.5

FOR MORE INFORMATION

ALLIANCE FOR JUSTICE

The Alliance for Justice (AFJ) is an association of over 90 organizations nationwide that is "dedicated to advancing justice and democracy." To that end, AFJ has fought for environmental, consumer, and civil rights for over 30 years. Their efforts are based on the belief that "all Americans have the right to secure justice in the courts and to have our voice heard when government makes decisions that affect our lives."

In 2004, AFJ published *Investing in Change,* a guide for grantmakers interested in funding advocacy efforts. The activities that AFJ considers advocacy include policy research and analysis, public education campaigns, non-partisan voter education and get-out-the-vote drives, and lobbying efforts. Their comprehensive guide includes an in-depth review of the laws surrounding lobbying and how they affect philanthropic foundations, as well as tools for evaluating the success of advocacy efforts.

AFJ has written other publications on nonprofit and foundation lobbying and advocacy, including resources on lobbying and election laws in the 50 states. In addition, they hold regular web-based workshops on a variety of issues related to policy advocacy and legislative lobbying in the not-for-profit sector.

To learn more about the Alliance for Justice and its resources, go to www.AFJ.org.

Beginning in 2007, discussion and research on the importance of philanthropically funded policy advocacy began to grow, and many groups, such as the National Committee for Responsive Philanthropy and the Alliance for Justice, have subsequently encouraged foundations to get more politically involved.[75] For example, Emmett D. Carson, president and CEO of the Silicon Valley Community Foundation, wrote that "change oriented" foundations—those whose mission statements say they are oriented toward social change—should be fully involved in public policy efforts and act as catalysts to that change. Carson argued: "Only public policy engagement can affect the laws that determine how people will be treated, what services will be provided, what behaviors are acceptable, and the incentives and disincentives to compel compliance."[76]

Shaping Policy, Strengthening Community

As discussed in Chapter 1, Arons has identified two forms of policy involvement that foundations often take: (1) public policy shaping activities, including influencing agenda-setting, policy formulation, and implementation of laws, programs and regulations and (2) civic strengthening activities, which facilitate the democratic process by encouraging transparency in governance, improved public leadership, and increased civic participation.[77] Foundations are increasingly involved in both policy arenas, and with significant success.[78] Important examples come from the National Committee for Responsive Philanthropy (NCRP). In 2008, NCRP began publishing the results of a study that examined the impact of philanthropic foundation grants on advocacy, organizing, and civic engagement in New Mexico, North Carolina, Minnesota, and Los Angeles. The study examined the work of nonprofits in each jurisdiction over a five-year period, encompassing a host of policy areas including civil rights, poverty, workers' rights, transportation, and immigration.

NCRP reports that foundation grantmaking had significant impacts on shaping policy and strengthening civil society in these diverse regions of the United States. In North Carolina, for example, an investment of $20.4 million in 13 nonprofits led to $1.8 billion in benefits to the communities and constituents of those nonprofits; importantly, foundations provided 86 percent ($17.5 million) of the $20.4 million invested. Tangible policy outcomes in North Carolina included passage of a Patient's Bill of Rights that included a provision securing hospital visitation rights to same-sex couples, and an increase in the state's minimum wage from $5.15 to $6.15 an hour. Civic strength was improved through coalition building and mobilization of those in affected communities. These efforts resulted in over 125,000 people becoming members of community organizations, more than 76,000 attending public events or meetings to voice their policy concerns, and over 31,000 constituent communications with government officials. [79]

Similar results were found in the other three regions. In New Mexico, the investment in nonprofits resulted in more than $2.6 billion in benefits; in Minnesota, where foundations provided 70 percent of the $16.5 million investment, the benefit accrued was more than $2.28 billion; and in Los Angeles, where foundations provided 77 percent of the $ 75.5 million in funding for advocacy and civic organizing, the community benefit was $6.88 billion. These dollar amounts do not include the nonmonetary benefits accrued to the people and communities studied, nor do they include the multiplier effect of these efforts. For example, the minimum wage increase in North Carolina affected 139,000 workers whose higher incomes allowed them to re-circulate that money in the local economy, thus making the value of the advocacy efforts even greater than the amount that could be quantified (for more details on the NCRP study, see www.ncrp.org/publications).

CONCLUSION

Entering the realm of policy advocacy and lobbying is certainly complex for nonprofit organizations. The rules and regulations, spending limits, potential consequences for violators, and the negative connotations of lobbying are enough to dissuade any 501(c)(3) from stepping into the fray of legislative activity. On the other hand, advocacy and lobbying are vital to most nonprofits and can be quite rewarding; they are also legal activities. While numerous attempts have been made to increase the stringency of lobbying regulations, Congress has been consistent in its reluctance to significantly curtail nonprofit policy efforts. With the 1976 lobbying law, Congress made it even easier for nonprofits to engage in lobbying.

Educating, informing, and persuading politicians and the public about preferred policy outcomes is a key function of nonprofit organizations and is increasingly important due to the growth of the nonprofit sector, especially in the health and social service policy arenas.

Nonprofits that represent and serve needy and marginalized populations do their clientele a significant disservice if they are not engaged in legislative advocacy, as these citizens often have no one else to speak for them in the policy arena. As David Cohen, long-time public interest lobbyist, has written, "being a public interest lobbyist is a career you can write home about," adding that, "[m]ost important, a public interest lobbyist helps create what social analysts call the 'civic balance,' allowing the public interest to be incorporated into public policy."[80] The influences of this activity are great and can range from local grassroots impact to international change.

The increasing number of nonprofit organizations and growing governmental reliance on nonprofits make it important for those in the not-for-profit sector to familiarize themselves with the lobby laws and make good use of their ability to speak for and on behalf of their clients and constituents. Fortunately for organizations in the nonprofit sector, the past decade has been one of increased capacity for advocacy, allowing many not-for-profit groups to become quite adept at maneuvering through the political landscape and achieving their policy goals.

Questions For Review

1. In what ways do lobbying and advocacy for nonprofit organizations differ? Are these meaningful differences?
2. What is the difference between grassroots lobbying and direct lobbying? Under what circumstances may a nonprofit engage in each, and what are the constraints on each?
3. What is the proper role of nonprofit organizations in advocacy and policymaking? Does it depend upon the type of organization?
4. If you were consulting with a nonprofit organization, what factors would you take into consideration in making the determination to choose between the "substantial part" and the H election for tax purposes?

Assignment

For this assignment, reread the opening vignette and answer the following questions: first, if the executive director meets with members of Congress on behalf of her organization and clients, is that considered lobbying or advocacy? If she meets with them, does she risk jeopardizing the tax-exempt status of the organization? What about asking program participants to contact their representatives and senators—is that lobbying, and does it threaten the organization? What are the limits on political activity for this organization, and what would you recommend that the executive director do in this situation?

Suggested Readings

Arons, David F., ed. *Power in Policy, A Funder's Guide to Advocacy and Civic Participation.* Fieldstone Alliance: Saint Paul, MN, 2007.

Bass, Gary D., David F. Arons, Kay Guinane, and Matthew F. Carter. *Seen but not Heard: Strengthening Nonprofit Advocacy.* Washington, DC: Aspen Institute, 2007.

Berry, Jeffrey M. *A Voice for Nonprofits.* With David F. Arons. Washington, DC: Brookings Institution Press, 2003.

Libby, Pat. *The Lobbying Strategy Handbook.* Thousand Oaks, CA: Sage Publications, 2012.

Pidgeon, Walter P., Jr. *The Legislative Labyrinth.* New York: John Wiley & Sons, 2001.

Smucker, Bob. *The Nonprofit Lobbying Guide,* 2nd ed. Washington, DC: Independent Sector, 1999.

Web Resources

The Center for Civil Society Studies at Johns Hopkins University, www.jhu.edu/ccss

Center for Lobbying in the Public Interest, www.clpi.org

The Center for Philanthropy and Public Policy at the University of Southern California, www.cppp.usc.edu

Foundation Center, www.foundationcenter.org

IRS Charities & Nonprofits, www.irs.gov/charities/index.html

National Committee for Responsive Philanthropy, www.ncrp.org

National Council of Nonprofits, www.councilofnonprofits.org

7 Ethics and Accountability

True ethical behavior must be internally driven. External agents can only force compliance, not encourage choice, and ultimately, virtuous behavior is a choice.

Ronald R. Sims[1]

Having recently retired and relocated to a new city, Bill is interested in getting more involved in his new community. In early February, he saw a flyer at the library about a local nonprofit organization that will be hosting a week-long day camp for kids in early June. The program includes nature walks, crafts, clean-up day at the park, canoeing at the lake, as well as reading time at the senior center; with so much activity, the organization needs volunteers to assist. After 30 years as a middle-school teacher and track coach, Bill is sure he has the experience and the capabilities to make a useful contribution. Since he's relatively new to the area, Bill asks a few friends for their impressions of the nonprofit. While none had worked directly with the organization, none had heard anything negative about it, either. He searches the group's website and decides to send a message volunteering to help with the day camp.

Since he worked with kids for so many years, he knows how difficult it can be to recruit volunteers and organize kids' programs, so he expects a reply to his offer that is a mixture of relief and gratitude that someone signed up without being cajoled. He was a bit surprised, then, when he received a prompt and courteous e-mail reply from the day camp committee chair, thanking him for his offer, but rather than simply telling him what his volunteer duties would be, gave him information about an orientation session for potential volunteers. At the orientation session, he would be given information about the organization and the day camp programs, as well as afforded the opportunity to ask questions. If he still wanted to volunteer, he would be asked to complete an application that included information about his prior professional and volunteer experience, and to provide written consent to submit to a criminal background check. All volunteers who cleared the screening process would then be required to attend two training sessions prior to the camp and would be given a packet of

POLICY IMPLICATIONS OF ETHICS AND ACCOUNTABILITY

- Ethics encompass a sense of public service and desire to meet public needs through service delivery and policy advocacy. For nonprofit administrators, duty is key to ethical behavior.
- A strong ethical culture and system of accountability are important attributes for a nonprofit to be able to fulfill its public service mission, as it facilitates public confidence in the organization's ability to meet public needs.
- Transparency relates to openness in providing information and is viewed as a component of good policy.
- Accountability relates to taking responsibility for one's actions and is especially pertinent with regard to nonprofit finances; nonprofits have a diverse array of stakeholders to hold them accountable.
- Public policies such as the Sarbanes-Oxley Act and the IRS Form 990 are external means of compelling ethical behavior by nonprofits; codes of ethics and conflict of interest policies are internal means by which nonprofits foster an ethical culture. Public perception that a nonprofit consistently acts in an ethical manner and is held accountable for its actions is necessary for the organization to garner the support needed to deliver services and advance its positions on public policy.

information that included contact information for the staff and members of the board, as well as copies of the nonprofit's code of ethics and policies on confidentiality, whistle-blowing, and so on. Upon reading all this, Bill does not know whether to be overwhelmed or impressed; he is definitely intrigued enough to sign up for the orientation session.

DEVELOPING ORGANIZATIONAL COMMITMENT TO ETHICS AND ACCOUNTABILITY

All organizations—from informal groups of students working on an assignment to well-established nonprofits employing hundreds of people—develop a distinctive culture in which there are norms of behavior that become accepted and types of behavior that are shunned. Embedded within an organizational culture is its ethical culture—that is, the degree to which those within the organization value doing what is right, just, and fair. As many scholars have argued, a strong culture of ethics does not happen without deliberate effort within an organization and it cannot simply be imposed from the outside.[2] In this chapter, we discuss the elements of a strong culture of ethics and the means by which to facilitate its development within an organization. External constraints such as the Sarbanes-Oxley Act (SOX) and internal measures such as codes of ethics, as well as other policies designed to encourage accountability, are also addressed. Additionally, the benefits associated with public perception of a strong ethical culture are discussed; organizations with a commitment to ethics are viewed not only as more trustworthy for service delivery but also more worthy of support for their policy positions on issues.

Defining Ethics

Philosophers have discussed and debated the nature of ethics for centuries, but for our purposes, a useful definition of ethics must evoke practical application in an administrative setting. Transcending law and regulations, ethics connote what Lord John Fletcher Moulton called "obedience to the unenforceable," something he likened to old-fashioned manners; Moulton argued that manners encompass both duty and morals but go beyond both. Exhibiting manners involves complying with social expectations of acceptable behavior that cannot be enforced, which is basically doing the right thing even when there are no external means to compel you to do so.[3]

A model for administrative ethics based on the concept of duty was developed by ethics scholar James Svara. Acknowledging the narrow scope of duty in the broader scheme of ethics, Svara argues that duty lies at the core of ethical behavior by public and nonprofit administrators and is therefore a central tenet in terms of understanding the ethical culture of public and nonprofit organizations. Duty is the aspect of ethics based on public service and one of the four components—along with virtues, principles, and benefits to society—that comprise the standards of right and wrong with regard to human behavior. He defines administrative ethics, accordingly, as

> . . . well-based standards of right and wrong that prescribe what public administrators ought to do, in terms of duty to public service, principles, virtues, and benefits to society.[4]

Furthermore, most persons in public service, including those in the nonprofit sector, have already internalized a similar working definition of administrative ethics. People who work in the public service are drawn to such work because they are motivated by the opportunity to meet public needs.[5] Nonprofit employees are more likely to place a high value on public service and are likewise more responsive to intrinsic motivators than external rewards for performance. The challenge for nonprofits is to formalize and expound upon this individual conceptualization of ethics to foster a culture of ethics throughout each organization and sector-wide.

Transparency Combats Corruption, Inhibits Compromise, and Affects Policy

Transparency is also a key component of an ethical culture; since the 1990s, the term has been associated with issues of good governance within nonprofit organizations. Initially discussed as a means to counter corruption, use of the term has evolved to include "a means to encourage open decision-making and public disclosure, to increase accountability, and as a value to incorporate in policies and by which to evaluate policies."[6] Transparency relates to the level of perceived openness in the provision of information, which contributes to the level of trust accorded to the provider of the information.

It is important to note there is a downside to transparency. While openness in conveying information can lead to greater trust in the content of the information, increased openness during discussions can inhibit frankness in communications that is often vital to successful negotiations, such as when compromise is necessary to adopt or implement public policy. In addition, for nonprofit practitioners transparency was initially linked to issues of regulation and subsequently carries negative connotations—for example, the increased costs associated with compliance. Conversely, for those engaged in policymaking and research, transparency is also seen as a solution to problems caused by limited access to information, and therefore is believed to make a positive contribution to each stage of the policy process.[7] As nonprofits are increasingly involved in the policy process, these differing perspectives on transparency have important implications.

Three metaphors associated with transparency have been developed.[8] In the first one, transparency is an indirect metaphor for good governance; transparency counteracts corruption because trust is engendered through open decision-making. Secondly, transparency is a direct metaphor for open decision-making; transparency is used to connote the degree to which it is easy to obtain and use information as well as to determine when confidentiality and restriction of access are appropriate. In the final case, transparency relates to issues of policy—that is, "the inputs, outputs, and outcomes of decisions."[9]

Policy scholars view transparency as an inherent attribute of public policy; policies fall along a continuum from transparent to opaque, with more transparent policies being preferred. Transparent policies have accountability measures built into them; these accountability measures represent a facet of policy inputs in that they affect the manner in which information is generated and made available. Likewise, the information that is disseminated as a result of transparent policies is a policy output and is designed to aid program participants in choosing program services. When the information is actually used by the public in making decisions, the provisions regarding transparency facilitate better outcomes. Accordingly, transparency is seen as a necessary component of good policy, and nonprofits that provide greater access to information about the work that they do will tend to be more attractive to donors and policymakers.

For example, the Community Development Block Grant program administered by the U.S. Department of Housing and Urban Development contains a requirement for public hearings—a transparency provision in the policy—to determine the community projects to be proposed. When area residents attend the hearings to receive information on potential projects and then act on that information to choose which project would be most beneficial to their community, the transparency provisions are directly related to the policy outcomes. Transparency is therefore "an attribute as complex as measuring effectiveness and efficiency and equally as important as accountability."[10]

A commitment to transparency is important for nonprofits seeking to develop an organizational commitment to ethical behavior. Open access to financial and program information limits the possibilities for corrupt practices and facilitates informed decisions by donors, volunteers, and program participants. However, it is important to remain aware of the constraints that open decision-making can place on the frank and honest exchange of ideas when disparate perspectives exist as to the nature of a public problem and/or the best way to address it. In general, public policy goals are facilitated through a commitment to transparency; open meetings and public participation in decision-making can help nonprofit managers better understand the needs of their constituencies and enhance the culture of ethics within the organization.

Transparency may be particularly important for organizations that do their work at significant distance from donors and government regulators. In the case of U.S.-based nonprofits that provide services internationally, donors and government regulators must rely to a greater degree on the information provided by the nonprofit since site visits are rarely an option. Going Global Case Study 7.1 contains a case study that compares the work of two U.S.-based nonprofits which provide services in Africa. These examples illustrate divergent perspectives on organizational transparency and accountability.

GOING GLOBAL CASE STUDY 7.1

Assessing the Accountability of Nonprofit Efforts Overseas

Africa is the poorest of the world's continents, and people within its 54 countries face numerous challenges to improve their lives. Two of the primary obstacles to overcome involve access to clean water and universal education for children. U.S. and international efforts to assist include government research and funding through the U.S. Agency for International Development (USAID) as well as projects and advocacy by numerous nongovernmental organizations (NGOs), including the United Nations Educational, Scientific and Cultural Organization (UNESCO). With so many NGOs actively working to address these and other problems through direct service delivery and attempts at policy change, it is difficult for donors (or potential donors) to monitor nonprofit efforts. As you read the following case, keep in mind that nonprofits differ with regard to their ethical cultures and commitments to transparency and accountability. This diversity is illustrated by two U.S.-based nonprofits with projects in Africa—water.org and Raising Malawi.

In July 2009, Matt Damon, co-founder of Africa H20, and Gary White, founder of Water Partners, merged the two organizations to establish water.org, a nonprofit focused on assisting communities in Africa, South Asia, and Central America with providing clean water and sanitation services. A brief scan of the homepage at www.water.org yields much information about the nature of the problems addressed by the organization, proposed solutions, and its two decades of experience in the water sector. Basic water facts are depicted graphically throughout the website to highlight the problems, such as (1) 3.575 million people die each year from a water-related illness; (2) approximately 1 in 8 people (884 million) lack access to safe water supplies; and (3) women around the world spend 200 million hours per day collecting water. References for the water facts are cited (with links when available), and include sources such as the United Nations, UNICEF, and the World Health Organization. Information on projects by country is also available.

In addition to information on the organization's activities, financials for the organization are also posted, including 10 years of audited financial statements, 10 years of IRS Form 990s, and copies of each annual report since 1998. It is also noted that water.org holds a four-star rating from Charity Navigator as well as the "Best in America" seal of excellence from Independent Charities of America. Further, the ten members on the Board of Directors, as well as each staff member—25 in the U.S., 6 in Africa, and 6 in Asia—are identified on the website by name and photo with an accompanying narrative of each person's relevant experience. Also included under the About Us tab is a page designated Donor Care, with contact information—e-mail, phone, and mailing address—for the organization as well as information regarding their donor privacy policy. The Media tab includes links to recent coverage of the work of water.org by news outlets such as ABC News, USA Today, and the Huffington Post, as well as links to press releases by water.org and its philanthropic partners.

While media reports on water.org have been overwhelmingly positive, news stories about Raising Malawi have focused largely on scandals related to allegations of poor management and financial improprieties. Raising Malawi was formed in 2006 by the entertainer Madonna to address issues of extreme poverty and hardship faced by orphans and vulnerable children in the landlocked East African country of Malawi. The website includes information about the five issue areas on which the organization focuses, including (1) HIV/AIDS; (2) poverty; (3) orphans; (4) children's mental health; and (5) education. While some statistics are offered to illustrate the nature of the problems in each issue area, the sources for the data are identified simply as UNAIDS, UNICEF, or USAID, without specific references or links to reports which would allow for independent confirmation. For example, one statistic listed on the home page—namely that the average life expectancy in Malawi has dropped to 36 years old—does not include a source reference; this statistic conflicts with reports from the U.S. State Department and the Central Intelligence Agency that the average life expectancy in Malawi is 52 years. Likewise, the nonprofit International Medical Corps (IMC) is listed as one of the partner organizations for Raising Malawi; however, Malawi is not included in the list of countries where it works on the IMC website.

Other than repeated references to the involvement of Madonna with the organization, there is no information available on the website regarding the staff or members of the board of directors. A blog post dated April 20, 2011, indicates that the board of directors for Raising Malawi retained Global Philanthropy Group, Inc. to design a new strategy for the organization, make major management changes, and take the appropriate steps to re-structure Raising Malawi as an independent nonprofit; it was originally established as a supporting organization for the religious Kaballah Centre in Los Angeles, which was the focus of investigations by the IRS and Federal Bureau of Investigation (FBI) in early 2011. Raising Malawi was also embroiled in scandal when reports surfaced in March 2011 that $3.8 million had been spent with no demonstrable progress toward construction of a $15 million academy designed to educate approximately 400 girls. The April 20, 2011, blog post indicated the new strategy for Raising Malawi would be announced in upcoming weeks, and on January 20, 2012, the nonprofit announced it would spend $300,000 through a partner organization, buildOn.org, to build 10 schools that would educate approximately 1000 children, half of whom would be girls.

Raising Malawi partners are listed by name on the website, some with links to their organizations' websites, but there is no information as to the nature of each partnership. Information on the Our Impact page of the Raising Malawi website is quite general; the only specific project information listed relates to the project with buildOn.org to construct ten schools. Financial information is not provided on the website. IRS Form 990 data are available through GuideStar at www.guidestar.org. Raising Malawi has not yet been rated by Charity Navigator.

While monitoring the activity of any nonprofit that is not in your hometown can be difficult, those involved with activities overseas present even greater challenges. Donors and potential donors must rely on limited information sources—the nonprofit's own website, press reports, information from partner organizations, and ratings groups such as Charity Navigator. Assessing the relevance and quality of the available information can be an additional impediment.

QUESTIONS TO CONSIDER:

1. As a potential donor, would you be more likely to donate to water.org, Raising Malawi, or neither organization? Why? Which specific types of information presented above are most important to you in making the decision to donate? Which types of information are irrelevant to your decision?
2. Based on the limited information presented above, what is your initial impression of the ethical culture of each nonprofit? Explain.
3. Suggest ways in which each organization could enhance its level of accountability to supporters.
4. Consider the four relationships that describe nonprofit interaction with public policy (nonprofits make policy, are affected by policy, influence policy, are subject to policy) and discuss the ways in which the accountability issues discussed with regard to water.org and Raising Malawi reflect these relationships.
5. Is either the water.org or Raising Malawi example unique with regard to nonprofit accountability? If so, explain how and discuss the ways in which public policy has facilitated the level of accountability for the organization(s).

The Importance of Accountability

Accountability refers to the willingness of individuals or groups to take responsibility for their actions, either because of their internal determination of responsibility or because they are held accountable by an external authority that has an interest in the impact of the individual or group action. For example, for-profit organizations are accountable to their shareholders, public organizations are accountable to their citizens, and nonprofits are accountable to their stakeholders. Nonprofits that reflect a commitment to accountability demonstrate that they value the public interest more than their own self-interest. It is important to note that issues of accountability in the not-for-profit sector are generally more complex than in business or government because nonprofit stakeholders are often more diverse, which makes reconciling their competing demands on the organization more difficult. The nonprofit in the opening vignette illustrates an organizational commitment to accountability through its requirements for staff and volunteers with regard to preparing for the day camp. As discussed, the organization's commitment to transparency and its method of establishing accountability (for example, through background checks and training sessions) may not be seen as desirable by all its stakeholders. Qualified volunteers such as Bill may choose to take their talents elsewhere rather than spend time on training they see as unnecessary, or potential donors may see the training requirements or background checks as too expensive and prefer their funds be used for more direct programming.

Nonprofits have traditionally enjoyed a good reputation as a choice for service delivery because they are typically viewed as more voluntary than government and more trustworthy than business. They are seen as more directly accountable for the work that they do because potential donors and volunteers have the option of withdrawing support if the work of the organization deviates from the acceptable. However, recent scandals within the sector have tarnished its image somewhat, and consequently, as lines continue to blur among the three sectors, the higher levels of ethical behavior within nonprofits have begun to slip.[11] According to the Ethics Resource Center's (ERC) National Nonprofit Ethics Survey,[12] nonprofit organizations experienced higher levels of financial fraud in 2007 than either business or government; also, nonprofits experienced violations of law or organization standards at levels comparable to both for-profit and public organizations. For the first time since the survey began in 2000, more than 50 percent of nonprofit employees reported having witnessed at least one type of misconduct; conflicts of interest, lying to employees, abusive behavior, and misreporting of hours worked were the most common types of misconduct observed.[13]

On a more positive note, almost one-third of nonprofit employees report working in an organization that has a well-implemented ethics and compliance program, and eleven percent of nonprofit organizations are reported as having a strong ethical culture. Well-implemented ethics programs and strong ethical cultures continue to be more widespread in the voluntary sector than in business or government. Furthermore, the presence of each has been shown to reduce ethics risk, as levels of misconduct and the pressure to compromise ethical standards are lower in nonprofits with well-established ethics programs and strong ethical cultures.[14]

Fostering a Strong Ethical Culture

While understanding the concepts of ethics, transparency, and accountability are important, placing these concepts within a framework helps illustrate how an ethical culture can be developed in nonprofit organizations. Maslow's theory of human motivation[15] provides the framework for a hierarchy of ethical values in a nonprofit setting developed by Strickland and Vaughan. Similar to Maslow's assertion that lower level physical needs must be met before higher level social needs can be fulfilled, nonprofits must first satisfy basic levels of accountability before developing a strong ethical culture. The five levels include: (1) Financial Competence, which includes wise asset management; (2) Accountability, which involves transparency and honesty; (3) Reciprocity—similar to Maslow's affiliation needs—refers to the mutually beneficial relationship that should be established with donors; (4) Respect for all stakeholders, which involves responsiveness to their differing perspectives; and (5) Integrity, which is comparable to self-actualization in that the nonprofit has "an internalized moral code, is able to engage in creative problem-solving, and pursues its mission to the fullest extent possible."[16]

As stated earlier, a strong ethical culture cannot be imposed on an organization by external forces. While laws and regulations can compel a nonprofit to comply with basic standards of financial competence and accountability and to address certain aspects of the nonprofit's relationship with donors and clients, achieving reciprocity, respect, and integrity can only be accomplished through internal efforts. For example, as a potential volunteer, Bill from the opening vignette would like to donate his time and expertise to the nonprofit's provision of day camp services. In order to ensure a mutually beneficial reciprocal relationship and out of respect for the perspectives of the children who will attend the camp as well as their parents, camp sponsors, and the other volunteers, the organization screens all potential volunteers. This helps match the needs of the organization with the capabilities of the volunteers; because the nonprofit's clients in this instance are children, the screening process also helps to ensure the safety and security of participants. While the nonprofit is not required by law to conduct background checks or provide extensive training for volunteers, the board and day camp committee have decided to expend resources for these purposes. Providing for the safety of the children as well as a positive experience for volunteers are both sufficiently valued by the nonprofit to warrant the additional costs of screening and training.

While the National Nonprofit Ethics Survey (Figure 7.1) indicates that more nonprofits have strong ethical cultures when compared to business or government, the number of nonprofits with weak or weak-leaning ethical cultures has increased from 38 percent in 2000 to 42 percent in 2007.[17] Fifty-eight percent of employees in the nonprofits surveyed reported that their organization has a strong or strong-leaning ethical culture, a decrease from the 63 percent reported in each of the three previous surveys. According to the Ethics Resource Center, strong ethical cultures are found in nonprofits "where top management leads with integrity, supervisors reinforce ethical conduct, peers display a commitment to ethics, and the values of the organization are embedded with decision-making."[18]

FIGURE 7.1 **Measuring Ethical Culture in Nonprofit Organizations**

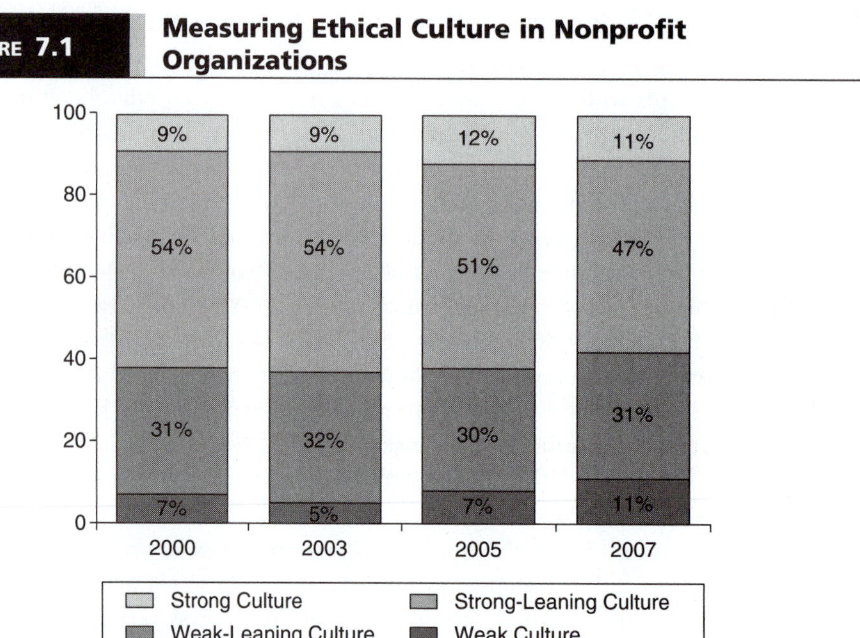

Source: Ethics Resource Center, *National Nonprofit Ethics Survey: An Inside View of Nonprofit Sector Ethics,* 2007, 5, www.ethics.org/files/u5/ERC_s_National_Nonprofit_Ethics_Survey.pdf. Reproduced by permission of Ethics Resource Center.

Leadership, therefore, is a crucial factor with regard to organizational ethics. Nonprofit organizations are better able to address their ethics risk, defined as how often misconduct occurs and how often it is reported, when their leaders are instrumental in establishing and maintaining a strong ethical culture.[19] The link between leadership and accountability has also been supported by empirical research; the presence of transformational leadership in nonprofits was found to have a strong, positive relationship with the level of accountability demonstrated by nonprofits.[20]

Likewise, leadership figures prominently in the five most important components to achieving a strong ethical culture organization (SECO), which are: (1) the focus of leaders' attention; (2) leaders' responses to crises; (3) leaders' overall behavior; (4) allocation of rewards by leaders; and (5) handling of personnel issues such as hiring and firing by the nonprofit leadership.[21] Leaders set the tone for ethical behavior by constantly communicating the value to the organization of acting in an ethical manner.[22] When the public perception is that a nonprofit is acting in the public interest rather than its own, the organization is in a better position to deliver public services and successfully advocate for its public policy issues. As discussed earlier, ethics must be internalized as an organizational value in order to promote an ethical culture. Codes of conduct—discussed further below—are useful tools by which to communicate the value of ethical behavior to stakeholders, but they must be disseminated throughout the organization and incorporated into employee training in order to successfully encourage stakeholders to internalize the commitment to ethics.

SYSTEM OF ACCOUNTABILITY: INFLUENCES ON NONPROFIT BEHAVIOR

As stated earlier, nonprofits are accountable to their stakeholders. Since there is often a great diversity of stakeholders for a nonprofit, four spheres of accountability have been delineated. First, nonprofits are accountable to the government through its role in regulating behavior through laws and regulations. The voluntary sector as a whole provides the second sphere of accountability through its role in providing peer review and self-regulation. Direct constituents of a nonprofit—clients, staff, members, donors, funders—who seek to control the organization's mission and ensure the effectiveness of programs and services represent the third sphere. Finally, the general public, as taxpayers, are entitled to information and reassurance about the social value of the work of the tax-exempt organization.[23]

It follows, therefore, that nonprofit accountability has four basic goals: (1) adherence to the highest ideals and principles with regard to financial management; (2) pursuit of best practices and good governance; (3) responsiveness to donors' wishes and faithfulness to the nonprofit's mission; and (4) effectiveness in providing for the public good and protecting the public trust.[24] Achieving these goals requires a system of accountability that combines external constraints and internal measures, while taking into account how important it is that the public has a positive perception of the organization's commitment to ethics and accountability.

External Constraints on Nonprofits

Laws and regulations represent external constraints on nonprofit behavior. Nonprofits must comply with the provisions or face sanctions ranging from financial penalty to loss of tax-exemption. As discussed in Chapter 4, many of the legal restrictions on nonprofits were enacted in response to perceived abuses and were designed specifically to reduce certain behaviors. Scandals such as the fundraising improprieties of the Red Cross following the tragedies of 9/11 and allegations of fraud surrounding voter registration by the now-defunct ACORN organization increased scrutiny of the nonprofit sector. Somewhat predictably, scandal has spread along with the proliferation of fundraising via social media; more than 2,000 of the Internet sites soliciting donations to provide relief following Hurricane Katrina were found to be fraudulent, according to the FBI,[25] calling attention to what is sure to be a growing concern among those who seek to protect donors.

Public perception of nonprofits embroiled in scandal affects their ability to weather the storm. For example, the American Red Cross has a long-standing reputation for providing crucial services following disasters. Despite severe criticism of how the organization solicited and handled donations in the wake of the events of September 11, 2001, the nonprofit took steps to mitigate the scandal and because of its reputation for trustworthiness, has continued to enjoy the benefits of a strong nonprofit brand and currently enjoys a four-star rating from Charity Navigator. Conversely, the community-organizing nonprofit known as ACORN was unable to survive allegations of fraud in its efforts to register voters. The organization came under investigation in several states, and the scandal was increasingly seen as a partisan issue by both supporters and opponents of the nonprofit. Ultimately, Congress ceased federal funding of the organization, which contributed to its demise. Increased scrutiny of nonprofits in the wake of scandal has resulted in cries for greater regulation and the passage of legal requirements and restrictions, such as those discussed below.[26]

Sarbanes-Oxley Act. Commonly referred to as SOX, this law was enacted in 2002 in direct response to the corrupt corporate practices of Enron, WorldCom, and Arthur Andersen. It is relevant to the discussion of nonprofit ethics because the two provisions that apply universally to organizations, including nonprofits, caused quite a stir in the sector. As a result of the passage of SOX nonprofits are required to preserve certain documents, including financials, for five years and must institutionalize the protection of whistle-blowers and prohibit retaliation against informants. Most organizations choose to comply with these requirements through the adoption of document retention policies and whistle-blower protection policies.

Upon passage of SOX and the realization that these two provisions would apply equally to nonprofits, there was a sense of general concern about the level of burden that compliance would place on the sector, particularly on small nonprofits. Nezhina and Brudney found that in addition to the two mandatory provisions identified above, SOX contains 17 requirements that are deemed by experts in the field to be relevant, although not mandatory, for nonprofits.[27] Box 7.2 contains the list of relevant provisions.

Because of the concern regarding the impact on nonprofits of the SOX provisions, Nezhina and Brudney sought to determine the degree to which nonprofits have complied with the act. Through their survey of approximately 300 nonprofits, they discovered that all but 2 had adopted at least one SOX-like provision prior to the passage of the act, and that the majority of SOX-like practices existed within the sector prior to 2002. For example, prior to SOX, 92 percent of respondents conducted a regular external audit and almost 72 percent had a conflict of interest policy. The findings of this study suggest that SOX has likely not posed an undue burden, at least on larger nonprofits since such a high percentage already had similar provisions in place. Likewise, research that indicates low levels of adoption of SOX-like practices by nonprofits may be misleading;[28] the low levels may be a function of previous adoption rather than a resistance to incorporating SOX-practices by nonprofits.

Form 990. As discussed briefly in Chapter 4, the redesigned Form 990 includes a new section on governance issues, which includes questions about such things as conflict of interest policies and meeting documentation. Filers are not required to include this information but are encouraged to do so in the interest of greater transparency and accountability. Part VI of the new Form 990 also asks questions regarding whistle-blower protections and document retention policies, pursuant to the mandatory provisions of SOX. Organizations are asked to

Box 7.2

FOR MORE INFORMATION

PROVISIONS OF THE SARBANES-OXLEY ACT RELEVANT FOR NONPROFIT ORGANIZATIONS

Provisions of the Sarbanes-Oxley Act that affect nonprofit organizations are summarized as follows:[29]

- Auditors prohibited from performing certain non-audit services
- Audit firm must be rotated every five years
- An audit firm cannot perform an audit for an organization whose executive was employed by the audit firm within the previous year
- Board of directors must establish an audit committee
- Board of directors must ensure the audit committee operates independently
- Audit committee must be given the authority to select, compensate, oversee, and discharge the auditor
- CEO and CFO must certify the accuracy of financial reports
- CEO must be given responsibility for the evaluation of internal controls
- Personnel must be prohibited from exercising undue influence on the auditor
- All off-balance-sheet transactions must be disclosed
- Personal loans to executives and directors must be prohibited
- Electronic filing of all public disclosures must be instituted
- Internal control reports must be incorporated into annual reports
- Must disclose whether a code of ethics has been adopted for senior executives
- Must disclose whether at least one member of the audit committee is financially qualified
- Personnel are subject to criminal penalties for knowingly destroying, altering, concealing, or falsifying records in order to obstruct a federal investigation
- Federal income tax returns must be signed by the CEO

disclose information about the composition of their boards of directors and to discuss their procedures for managing conflicts of interest when they occur. While there is no enforcement mechanism tied to provision of information in the governance section, the IRS asserts that because voluntary compliance promotes good governance, it is in the best interest of the individual nonprofit as well as the sector as a whole.[30]

Benzing, Leach, and McGee studied the readiness of arts and culture nonprofits in the greater Philadelphia area to comply with the provisions of the new Form 990 as well as SOX. Approximately half of the organizations surveyed have written ethics and whistle-blower protection policies, and slightly more than half require board members to complete a conflict of interest form. Similar to the findings of Nezhina and Brudney,[31] Benzing et al. found that the overwhelming majority of the nonprofits studied have an annual external audit and almost half have an audit committee. As with other studies, Benzing and colleagues found that size and age are directly related to SOX compliance; older and larger arts and culture nonprofits are more likely to adhere to SOX-related best practices. Of particular note with regard to their findings is that a large percentage of the nonprofit executives who responded to the survey believe that compliance with the provisions of SOX does promote transparency and improves financial management at little cost to the organization.[32]

California's Nonprofit Integrity Act. Whereas SOX was spawned from corrupt corporate practices, the Nonprofit Integrity Act was a response to scandal in the nonprofit sector. See Box 7.3 for more information on the fraudulent fundraising practices that led California's attorney general and a state senator to shepherd these reforms into law in 2004. The act is basically an extension of the relevant SOX requirements to nonprofits operating in the state of California but was viewed by many in the sector as the harbinger of things to come for nonprofits nationwide. According to the National Council of Nonprofits, which regularly monitors state legislation, that has not been the case. Seven years following adoption in California, no other states have followed suit.[33] This seems to confirm the prospect raised in Chapter 4 that increased state regulation of nonprofits imposes a burden that is not commensurate with anticipated increases in accountability.

Decades of regulatory efforts by the states have resulted in what Reneé Irvin calls a "50-state mix of fees, registration, auditing, and financial reporting requirements."[34] While these regulations were initially intended to enhance nonprofit accountability and public trust, there are also other motivations for increased regulation—namely, the political benefits to elected compliance officials such as states' attorneys general who benefit from an image of fighting charitable fraud and abuse, as well as the revenue generated from registration and compliance fees. Regulations are also designed to protect the interests of donors as well as to safeguard those who benefit from charitable goods and services.

The resulting hodge-podge of state regulations has spawned a system that actually discourages compliance by many nonprofit organizations, which find the rules to be too complex or costly. Those organizations that do comply with the myriad reporting requirements contribute to the drain on resources of compliance officials. State charity officials devote a significant amount of their budgets to the monitoring of registration and reporting requirements, leaving few resources for investigation of fraud and abuse. From her comparison of states with and without registration and reporting requirements, Irvin concludes that even among states with strict regulations, consumer complaints are the primary means of identifying fraudulent activity. There is little evidence to indicate that state reporting requirements are effective at reducing instances of fraud.[35]

These legal and regulatory constraints promote ethical behavior by imposing penalties for failure to comply. While effective at increasing the availability of information about nonprofit organizations and providing a basis for the investigation of fraud and abuse, these measures have limited ability to advance a culture of ethics within the nonprofit sector. Rather, ethical behavior must be internalized by the organization.

Box 7.3

FOR EXAMPLE

CALIFORNIA'S NONPROFIT INTEGRITY ACT: COMBATING CORRUPTION, PROMOTING ACCOUNTABILITY

Signed into law on September 29, 2004, by Governor Arnold Schwarzenegger, California's Nonprofit Integrity Act took effect on January 1, 2005. Whereas the Sarbanes-Oxley Act of 2002 was designed in response to scandal in the for-profit sector, California's legislation was designed specifically to apply to the nonprofit sector. According to the state's attorney general at the time of adoption, Bill Lockyer, the reform measures he proposed that were introduced as SB 1262 by State Senator Byron Sher were prompted by two specific scandals, each of which involved fraudulent fundraising practices.[36] Both involved suits brought by the state's attorney general, but one also involved a contentious lawsuit between two not-for-profit organizations.

In mid-2003, PipeVine, an organization formed by and closely linked with the United Way of the Bay Area (UWBA), closed its doors amid allegations that it did not deliver almost $20 million in donations that it had collected on behalf of various charities. The organization processed donations received from workplace campaigns and online fundraisers such as Network for Good and then routed those funds to charitable nonprofits for a fee. Following months of investigation and contentious negotiations, the United Way of the Bay Area agreed to pay a $13 million settlement to resolve the case.[37] Subsequently, Network for Good sued the United Way of the Bay Area for donations lost as a result of the collapse of PipeVine, arguing that even though PipeVine was spun off from its founder, UWBA, the two organizations remained intertwined. In 2007, the court ruled that while UWBA had not committed fraud, it had engaged in misconduct, specifically the manipulation of financial records in an attempt to conceal its role in the downfall of PipeVine. On an interesting note, the attorney for Network for Good, Sharon Mayo, praised the ruling, commenting that it demonstrated nonprofits are held to the same standards as for-profits.[38]

Nine of the thirteen key provisions of the act pertain to fundraising. A summary of the key provisions is available from the California Registry of Charitable Trusts at: http://caag.state.ca.us/charities/publications/nonprofit_integrity_act_nov04.pdf. Although no other states followed its lead, California's reaction to the PipeVine case is an example of both nonprofit action leading to policy creation, and state government subjecting the sector to increased regulation.

Internal Measures Exercised by Nonprofits

As discussed in Chapter 4, the nonprofit sector was long believed to be capable of policing itself. The altruistic nature of nonprofit missions and the requirement that excess revenues be retained by the organization rather than distributed to shareholders were believed to be sufficient to ensure that nonprofits would act in the public interest. As the size and scope of the voluntary sector has grown and nonprofits have repeatedly demonstrated that they are not immune to scandal, scholars, practitioners, and policymakers have increased their attention to nonprofit ethics. Internal actions such as the development of codes of ethics, as well as policies regarding confidentiality and donor privacy, significantly enhance the ethical culture of a not-for-profit organization.

Codes of Ethics. Independent Sector recommends that all charitable organizations have a formally adopted, written code of ethics that reflects the values and best practices agreed upon by staff, board, and volunteers. All directors, staff, and volunteers should be familiar with the code and agree to abide by its principles. The code should include expectations of how the staff, board, and volunteers should conduct themselves—for example, with regard to confidentiality and in showing respect for clients and others within the organization.[39]

Codes of ethics are increasingly needed by nonprofits that have a more diverse group of stakeholders. When members, staff, board, and clientele do not have a shared moral philosophy, a code of ethics is a useful vehicle through which to identify common values that are important to the organization.[40] Through his content analysis of 150 codes of ethics of tax-exempt membership organizations, Gary Grobman concluded that there are significant differences among codes according to their primary constituency—public, for-profit, or nonprofit. His results indicate a difference in values across sectors. For example, more than half of nonprofit codes mentioned issues of proficiency or competence, compared to 28 percent of government codes. Although not one government or for-profit code mentioned sexual misconduct, nearly 25 percent of nonprofit codes mentioned it. Nonprofits were also substantially more likely to address issues of client dignity and pluralism in their codes when compared with public and for-profit organizations. Interestingly, only one-third of all the codes mention quality of services, and only 38 percent have codes that identify enforcement mechanisms by which to address noncompliance.[41]

Codes of ethics have three basic purposes: (1) to constrain behavior by stipulating the types of conduct to be avoided; (2) to guide those within the organization by specifying obligations or preferred actions; and (3) to inspire by establishing broad goals of desirable conduct that should be emulated throughout the organization.[42] The low number of enforcement provisions seems to indicate that by design, most codes of ethics tend to be inspirational rather than regulatory.[43] Independent Sector provides information and resources on core concepts as well as legal and compliance issues related to developing a code of ethics.[44]

Policies on Conflicts of Interest and Confidentiality. In their Principles for Good Governance and Ethical Practices, the Panel on the Nonprofit Sector makes a recommendation, in Principle 3, as follows:

> A charitable organization should adopt and implement policies and procedures to ensure that all conflicts of interest, or the appearance thereof, within the organization and the board are appropriately managed through disclosure, recusal, or other means.[45]

It is important to note that not all conflicts of interest are bad for the nonprofit. Some members of the board might have personal or financial interests in the work of the nonprofit that would result in an illegal or unethical transaction, but in other cases transactions might be in the best interest of the organization. For example, suppose that a board member of a grantmaking foundation also serves on the board of a nonprofit that has applied to it for funding. Since the board member is in a leadership position with both organizations and can therefore influence decisions, there is a potential conflict of interest. However, because this foundation encourages its staff and board members to be actively engaged with charities that they might fund, it is neither illegal nor unethical for the board member to be involved with both organizations. It is imperative, however, that he or she disclose the potential conflict and would not receive a material gain from any transaction between the two. Nonprofits often mitigate conflicts of interest through the use of conflict of interest forms; sample forms are available through the National Council of Nonprofits. Box 7.4 contains more information on resources available from the council.

Many social service nonprofits collect personal data on clients through the course of providing services. All nonprofits that receive contributions from individuals collect at least minimal data on donors. Treating clients and donors with respect and preserving their trust in the organization require a commitment to maintaining the confidentiality of data to the full extent of the law. Adopting a policy of confidentiality and donor privacy is embodied in the Panel on the Nonprofit Sector's Principle 33.[46] As discussed in Box 7.4, a sample confidentiality policy is also available through the National Council on Nonprofits.[47]

The internal measures and external constraints discussed above are intended to facilitate the development and maintenance of a strong ethical culture. They also serve as documentation of the organization's commitment to ethics and accountability, thereby contributing to a positive public perception of the nonprofit's ability to deliver services and promote sound public policy. In order for a nonprofit to determine the merits of its actions regarding organizational ethics, the National Council of Nonprofits recommends the organization undertake a comprehensive ethics audit every 3 to 5 years.[48]

Box 7.4

FOR MORE INFORMATION

NATIONAL COUNCIL ON NONPROFITS

Initially founded in 1989 to provide a venue for collaboration among state associations of nonprofits, the National Council of Nonprofit Associations changed its name in 2008 to reflect a new federated membership model. By allowing local community-based nonprofits to join the National Council via membership in their state associations, the National Council of Nonprofits now provides resources and a policy voice for 37 state association members and more than 24,000 community-based nonprofits.

In addition to direct member support activities, the National Council publishes the e-newsletters *Nonprofit Advocacy Matters* and *Nonprofit Knowledge Matters* and conducts research and analysis on issues and challenges relevant to nonprofits. The council is also actively involved in public policy, identifying trends in state and federal policies and advocating on behalf of its nonprofit members.

The National Council has developed a series of resources related to promoting nonprofit ethics and regulatory compliance:

- **Ethics and Accountability in the Nonprofit Sector.** General information on ethics and accountability, including definition of a code of ethics as well as discussion of the importance of ethical leadership are included in this part of the resources section of the website. Laws and regulations regarding nonprofit ethics plus information on self-regulation via charity watchdog organizations is included as well. www.councilofnonprofits.org/resources/resources-topic/ethics-accountability

- **Conflict of Interest.** General information on conflicts of interest as well as sample conflict of interest policies are available at www.councilofnonprofits.org/conflict-of-interest.

- **Conducting an Ethics Audit at Your Nonprofit.** A two-page "road map" designed to help nonprofits assess compliance with external constraints and internal measures designed to facilitate ethical behavior in the organization is available at www.councilofnonprofits.org/sites/default/files/Conducting%20an%20Ethics%20Audit.pdf.

CONCLUSION

Despite numerous efforts by Congress and state legislatures, many of which have been successful at improving reporting and compliance efforts of nonprofits, the ethical character of organizations is still largely determined by internal forces. Basic financial competence and accountability measures can be mandated by law and regulation and most organizations will comply out of fear of negative consequences associated with non-compliance. However, in order to promote Moulton's obedience to the unenforceable, the leaders within the organization have to set an ethical tone.

As Bill in our opening hypothetical situation discovered, an organization with a strong ethical culture puts the needs of its clientele first, expending extra resources when necessary to promote safety and security for program participants as well as ensure competence and build confidence among the volunteers and staff delivering its program services. Informing participants about their rights, especially with regard to privacy and confidentiality of information, reflects respect for the individual. Developing and disseminating a code of ethics, especially one that specifically addresses consequences for violations, serves to inspire as well as compel all those involved with the organization to be accountable for their actions in the public interest. Basically, ethics means striving to do the right thing—particularly when it is difficult to do so and when no one is looking.

Fostering a strong ethical culture and maintaining a system of accountability are crucial elements for nonprofits, since these organizations rely on public trust and confidence for their survival. To reiterate, nonprofits have a long history of trustworthiness and public confidence in their altruism. However, as the size, scope, and diversity within the nonprofit sector, as well as the size of assets under its control have grown significantly in recent years, scandals have also proliferated and somewhat diminished the automatic assumption of trustworthiness. In order for nonprofits to effectively deliver public services and be successful policy advocates, the public must have confidence that the organizations are acting in the public interest and not for their own purposes. Nonprofits, therefore, must pay greater attention not only to building strong ethics and accountability within their organizations, but to making sure the public is aware of their efforts.

Questions For Review

1. Define ethical behavior as it pertains to nonprofit organizations. Are organizational ethics different from personal ethics? Discuss the extent to which the two concepts are related to or divergent from one another.

2. Is deliberate cultivation of an ethical culture needed in nonprofit organizations? Why, or why not? How is development of an ethical culture different for nonprofits as opposed to public or for-profit entities?

3. To what extent are external constraints imposed by state and federal policymakers useful to building a culture of ethics within nonprofit organizations? Do you agree or disagree with the assertion that external constraints are not sufficient to facilitate a strong ethical culture within an organization? Explain.

4. To what extent are internal measures to promote transparency and accountability useful in fostering an ethical culture in nonprofits? Discuss the strengths and weaknesses of specific measures that nonprofits can undertake voluntarily to enhance their commitment to ethics.

5. Why is public perception of a nonprofit's commitment to ethics and accountability important? How does a nonprofit's reputation for trustworthiness affect its ability to deliver public services and engage in policy advocacy?

Assignment

Choose a large nonprofit organization of particular interest to you and for which you can obtain information to assess the strength of its ethical culture. Use websites such as charitynavigator.org, guidestar.org, or charitywatch.org to rate the organization on external compliance factors such as financial competence and transparency. To assess the extent to which the nonprofit has internalized a strong ethical culture, explore its website, annual reports, and Part VI of the Form 990 (completed since 2008 when the form was revised) for information. Does the organization have policies regarding conflict of interest and confidentiality? Does the organization voluntarily comply with the relevant provisions of SOX? What other information did you find useful in assessing whether the nonprofit has a strong ethical culture? What are your conclusions regarding the organization's commitment to ethics?

Suggested Readings

Ball, Carolyn. "What is Transparency?" *Public Integrity* 11,4 (2009): 293–307.

Independent Sector. *Obedience to the Unenforceable: Ethics and the Nation's Voluntary and Philanthropic Community.* http://www.independentsector.org/uploads/Accountability_Documents/obedience_to_unenforceable.pdf (2002).

Irvin, Renée A. "State Regulation of Nonprofit Organizations: Accountability Regardless of Outcome." *Nonprofit and Voluntary Sector Quarterly* 34, 2 (2005): 161–178.

Svara, James H. *The Ethics Primer for Public Administrators in Government and Nonprofit Organizations.* Sudbury, MA: Jones and Bartlett, 2007.

Web Resources

California's Nonprofit Integrity Act, http://caag.state.ca.us/charities/publications/nonprofit_integrity_act_nov04.pdf

Independent Sector Principle 2: Code of Ethics, www.independentsector.org/code_ethics_principle_2

IRS Public Disclosure Requirements, www.irs.gov/charities/article/0,,id=96430,00.html

Required Disclosures Tutorial, www.stayexempt.irs.gov/VirtualWorkshop/RequiredDisclosures.aspx

8 Marketing the Nonprofit Organization

The choice facing those who manage [nonprofit] organizations is not whether to market or not to market, for no organization can avoid marketing. The choice is whether to do it well or poorly . . .

Philip Kotler and Sidney J. Levy[1]

Donna has recently joined the board of directors of End Littering, a small, local nonprofit established to address the environmental and aesthetic problems created by persistent discarding of trash along roads and in parks throughout the county. At the first board meeting following completion of a new strategic plan—which includes a revised and broadened mission statement—the board is ready to launch a new program in a larger service area. While the county in which End Littering is located mandates recycling and offers curbside collection, the surrounding five counties do not. In these largely rural areas, curbside recycling is not available and collection sites are few, sporadically located, and operated by disparate groups.

One of the objectives identified in the new strategic plan is to locate recycling containers at multiple and consistently-located sites throughout the new service region. The board hopes to partner with the county governments to locate reclamation sites at rural trash collection facilities and also to partner with local businesses—for example, grocery and big box stores—to have receptacles located in their parking lots. Ease and consistency of access to recycling centers is expected to decrease the trash going into landfills and reduce the amount of trash being tossed on the side of the road.

Being relatively new to the board, Donna has been looking for an opportunity to make a unique contribution, so she is excited to be able to offer her experience in corporate communications to help create a marketing plan. Following her offer, a fellow board member looked at her in confusion and remarked, "But, we're a nonprofit. We're not selling anything. Why would we need marketing?" Looking around the table, Donna sees nods of agreement by some and puzzled looks from others, and realizes that in this

POLICY IMPLICATIONS OF NONPROFIT MARKETING

- Marketing is a process through which a nonprofit better understands how to pursue its mission and how to communicate its mission to its target audience; marketing has an important but mostly indirect relationship with public policy.
- By identifying and segmenting their target audiences, nonprofits are able to tailor their marketing techniques and communications strategies to deliver services and advocate for policy change.
- Differentiation is the process by which a nonprofit sets itself apart from others; by establishing its position vis-à-vis competing organizations, a nonprofit gains an advantage in recruiting volunteers, obtaining resources, or attracting clients.
- Establishing a brand identity for integrity, effective service delivery, and valuable policy priorities assists the nonprofit in more efficiently communicating its worth to stakeholders.
- Corporate partnerships can be mutually beneficial relationships, contributing needed revenues to the nonprofits and enhancing the reputation of the business through the alliance; these relationships indirectly affect public policy in that the revenues generated increase nonprofits' ability to deliver services and engage in policy advocacy. The partnerships also have potential policy risks if either partner engages in an activity or promotion that is counter to the policy positions of the other.

case, marketing begins at home. Her first task is to sell the rest of the board on what marketing can do for their nonprofit organization.

MARKETING BASICS

Marketing has two basic conceptualizations: a negative one that is predominant and a positive one that is rapidly gaining acceptance.[2] In the negative view, marketing is perceived to be the process by which organizations trick consumers into buying things they do not need or into believing things that are not true. What many in the field of marketing argue, however, is that deliberately misleading marketing techniques are used only at the fringes of current business practices, mainly because of recognition that such misinformation is ultimately detrimental to the company's bottom line.[3]

The more positive view of marketing embodies "sensitively *serving and satisfying human needs*."[4] According to the American Marketing Association (AMA), "Marketing is an organizational function and a set of processes for creating, communicating, and delivering value to customers and for managing customer relationships in ways that benefit the organization and its stakeholders."[5]

This definition (updated in 2004) reflects significant changes in the conceptualization of marketing—namely, that marketing: (1) is not just within the purview of marketers because everyone associated with the organization has a duty to participate; (2) is designed to produce revenue, so it should give all stakeholders an adequate return on investment (ROI); and

(3) is not about generating "irrelevant goods and services"—the dark side of marketing—but is about meeting specific wants and needs of consumers.[6]

General Marketing Principles and Techniques

Marketing in general is most readily associated with principles and techniques designed to sell goods and services—what is commonly referred to as commercial sector marketing. In order to give consumers what they want and need, organizations devise a marketing plan that identifies the techniques most suitable for "creating, communicating, and delivering value to customers" as the AMA definition cited above indicates. At the core of this definition is the focus on customers as the target audience for all marketing endeavors.

A marketing plan is similar to a strategic plan in that it is a document derived through a process of organizational assessment, identifying goals and objectives that are codified in a formal written document which is used for implementation and evaluation of the marketing efforts. It is easier to identify and implement suitable marketing techniques and communication strategies such as direct mailings, radio ads, and Facebook pages when they are derived from program objectives. Therefore, undertaking activities such as revising and updating the organization's website while the board is in the midst of the strategic planning process is not a good idea.

One of the central aspects of a marketing plan is the way in which the organization devises its marketing mix—that is, how the organization plans to utilize the marketing tools known as the 4P's—product, price, place, and promotion—to influence its potential customers. Price, place, and promotion are tools used primarily to position the product itself relative to its competitors.

Mere mention of the golden arches evokes a mental picture of a logo and a wealth of information associated with the fast-food giant McDonald's. This happens because of what the AMA refers to as branding, in which "brand recognition and other reactions are created by the accumulation of experiences with the specific product or service, both directly relating to its use, and through the influence of advertising, design, and media commentary."[7] Branding results when an organization is able to successfully position its product relative to the competition. This is accomplished through differentiation, where product attributes are highlighted in order to demonstrate how they are distinct from and better than competing goods and services. All of the aforementioned are principles and techniques most readily associated with commercial marketing but that are also applicable to what is termed social marketing, discussed further below. Each is also relevant for nonprofit marketing.

Marketing in a Nonprofit Environment

Philip Kotler and Sidney Levy are credited with the seminal article applying the principles of marketing to nonbusiness organizations and for broadening the definition of marketing to encompass nonprofits:

> Marketing is that function of the organization that can keep in constant touch with the organization's consumers, read their needs, develop "products" that meet these needs and build a program of communications to express the organization's purposes.[8]

Somewhat ironically, marketing has traditionally suffered from an image problem, particularly among nonprofits. As our hypothetical board in the opening vignette illustrates, many in the nonprofit sector have been resistant to the concept of marketing, perceiving it to be tainted by the negative attributes of commercial business. In his study of public services marketing in the United Kingdom, Angus Laing states that a more positive view of the marketing of public services is warranted. He argues that the philosophical perspective that marketing weakens the public sector ethos is misguided; rather, it can be stated that "marketing concepts are in fact entirely consistent with democratic values in that they reiterate the primacy of the citizen in [public] services."[9]

Whether you embrace the positive view of marketing or continue to relegate it to the dark side of organizational management, the reality is that nonprofit marketing is no longer an obscure concept. Indeed, there are currently three academic peer-reviewed journals devoted specifically to nonprofit marketing—the *Journal of Nonprofit & Public Sector Marketing,* published since 1993; the *International Journal of Nonprofit and Voluntary Sector Marketing,* published since 1996; and the *International Review on Public and Nonprofit Marketing,* published since 2004.[10] More than 30 textbooks have been published specifically on nonprofit marketing, most since the mid-1990s, and blogs devoted to the concept proliferate. As Kotler and Levy suggest, the debate is not whether nonprofits engage in marketing, it is whether they do it well or not. A well-constructed marketing plan enhances nonprofit effectiveness, as Donna in the opening vignette is well aware. Accordingly, the marketing plan is the subject of the following sections.

THE IMPORTANCE OF A MARKETING PLAN

As discussed above, a marketing plan contains the goals and objectives for the marketing efforts of an organization; the plan is developed through a process similar to an overall strategic planning process. A marketing plan should include identification of target audiences or markets and the barriers to reaching them, as well as the goals and objectives that specify the actions the nonprofit is encouraging target audiences to take. It also sets out a positioning statement that outlines how the organization wants the target audience to perceive its goods, services, and mission with regard to other nonprofits; this also reflects the nonprofit's brand identity. It is also important that a marketing plan include procedures for implementation and evaluation of the marketing efforts identified.[11]

Not-for-profit organizations generally have two primary goals in developing their marketing plans: to increase visibility of the organization and its programs, and to generate resources. Sarah Durham coined the term "brandraising" to describe the process by which a nonprofit establishes its unique identity and develops a system of organizational communication that facilitates achievement of visibility and fundraising goals, as well as promotion of the overall mission. Just as communities came together to assist their neighbors in building—or raising—their barns, brandraising embodies the concept that it takes everyone in a nonprofit to effectively construct and implement a marketing plan. Marketing plans are best developed after the organization's vision and mission are fully articulated—that is, after the strategic planning process has been completed.[12] Key elements in the marketing plan are the nonprofit's target audience/stakeholders, differentiation of the nonprofit through positioning, and the nonprofit's brand identity, each of which is discussed further in the sections that follow.

Identifying the Nonprofit's Target Audience

Target publics are variously identified as (1) those who will be served by the nonprofit;[13] (2) internal stakeholders such as employees as compared with external publics;[14] (3) fundraising, program, and advocacy audiences;[15] and (4) multiple market stakeholders.[16] Defining a target public as those who will be served by the nonprofit might appear to be the most comprehensive and straightforward definition, but it is surprisingly complex. Consider the example of End Littering, the hypothetical nonprofit from the opening vignette. Who is actually served by the nonprofit? Is it everyone in the six-county geographic region? If so, is everyone served equally?

Commercial sector marketing focuses on the selling of goods and services and is generally associated with private business; since many nonprofits also offer goods and services, often at a price to consumers, the strategies associated with commercial sector marketing can also apply to nonprofit marketing. However, since selling a product is not usually a nonprofit's mission, the simple transactional relationship that predominates in private business does not always translate well to the voluntary sector. In those instances, the term more appropriately applied would be social marketing. Marketing professor Philip Kotler and colleagues differentiate social marketing because (1) it seeks to change behavior—for instance, ending addiction—rather than sell a product; and (2) the primary beneficiary of the marketing efforts is society in general rather than a corporate shareholder (or the nonprofit's revenues).

Social marketing experts argue that its most fundamental principle is to view the target audience as customers, in order to identify potential barriers to changing their behavior.[17] A customer orientation is seen as a positive focus on the individuals targeted for service by the nonprofit; it is not viewed as a commercial exchange relationship. However, this universal concept of the customer is not shared by all nonprofit scholars. Indeed, referring to those served by a nonprofit as customers has evoked quite heated debate. For example, while those who purchase tickets for a nonprofit symphony's performance are readily acknowledged as customers, to identify either college undergraduates or individuals in a court-ordered substance abuse program as customers instead of students or clients, respectively, significantly alters the perception of the relationship. Students and clients recognize that they will be held accountable for finishing specified tasks in order to successfully complete the program or course of study in which they are enrolled; customers expect that paying the required fee is sufficient to ensure they will receive their desired outcome.

The problem is not simply that nonprofits have a different relationship with those they serve; it is that there are multiple relationships because nonprofits serve multiple groups.

Some correlation can be drawn with private businesses that also serve the interests of their owner(s) or shareholders, but nonprofits have more diverse and a greater number of stakeholders to whom they are accountable. For example, according to Sarah Durham's[18] model of audience-centric communication strategies, a nonprofit should design communication and marketing strategies to inform and influence three specific audiences: (1) resources; (2) program; and (3) advocacy. Fundraising goals are one of the primary goals and objectives included in a marketing plan, so the first audience to target involves those with resources to assist the nonprofit in accomplishing its mission. The second, or program audience, includes current and potential clients of the programs and services provided by the organization. Policymakers and the interested public—those members of the general public who are or who are likely to become interested in the work of the nonprofit—comprise the third audience; this is the advocacy audience and includes the individuals likely to help the nonprofit achieve its public policy goals through legislative action and heightened public awareness.

Segmenting the Target Audience. Viewing the nonprofit's target audience in three parts such as those identified by Sarah Durham involves segmentation. Through segmentation, those devising a nonprofit's marketing plan seek to identify the segments of target publics most likely to respond to the organization's offers of services or requests for assistance. Segmentation as a marketing strategy is even more relevant for a nonprofit that must maximize the use of limited resources; identifying the portion of a target audience that is most likely to respond favorably allows a nonprofit to tailor its communication efforts in a way that is more cost-efficient as well as effective.

Social media are a prime example of potential venues for segmented communications. Facebook and Twitter presences flourish among nonprofit organizations, representing a quicker and less expensive communication medium than mass mailings. However, social media as well as websites and even basic e-mail require an investment of personnel resources to establish, update, track, and respond in a timely manner in order to maintain effectiveness as a marketing strategy. In addition, nonprofits should keep in mind that social media experts speculate that Facebook may be reaching its market saturation point,[19] and that only 0.02 percent of people who "like" a Fan page ever return to it.[20] The point for nonprofits to take from the low incidence of return is that getting someone to "like" their Facebook page is only a first-step marketing strategy; once "friends" have been recruited, the organization must tailor its offerings to continually market the work of the nonprofit to them. In addition, although use of social networks has increased substantially since 2008, less than half of the adults surveyed through the Pew Internet and American Life Project report using social network tools such as Facebook, Twitter, LinkedIn, and others.[21] However, as the Going Global Case Study 8.1 demonstrates, social media represent a powerful marketing tool with significant impact and consequences for the nonprofits that use them.

GOING GLOBAL CASE STUDY 8.1

Kony 2012, A Cautionary Tale about Social Media

Social media can be a powerful marketing tool, as the young filmmakers and policy advocates of the nonprofit Invisible Children discovered when their film Kony 2012 went viral and became the most rapidly distributed video in Internet history. While the nonprofit had utilized film as its primary marketing tool since its formation in 2005, distribution generally involved showings on college campuses and in high schools to raise awareness and generate funds. As you read this case study, consider the impact of the immediacy of the Internet as a means of communicating a nonprofit's message and the degree to which social media can heighten awareness and bring pressure to bear on policymakers.

In the late 1980s, Ugandan forces led by Yoweri Museveni overthrew the regime of Tito Okello. When President Museveni sought to impose his rule over the Acholi people, closely aligned with Okello, Museveni's government was met by an array of resistance groups. Within a few years Museveni's forces were able to defeat all but the Lord's Resistance Army (LRA), led by Joseph Kony. Over the next two decades, the northern Acholi region of Uganda was embroiled in war with atrocities on both sides. Early in the 2000s, the world became aware of LRA abductions and use of child soldiers, and in 2005, the International Criminal Court (ICC) issued its first arrest warrants. Joseph Kony was at the top of the list.[22]

At about this same time, three young men, Bobby Bailey (21), Laren Poole (19), and Jason Russell (24) traveled to Africa to make a film; their subject became clear one evening when they found themselves stuck in the Ugandan city of Gulu where thousands of children came each night to sleep on the streets, in bus depots, and in hospital hallways to avoid being abducted from their homes by LRA rebels.[23] Appalled by a conflict and conditions that were previously unknown to them, in 2005 they formed the nonprofit Invisible Children (IC), located in San Diego, California, with the following mission: "Invisible Children uses film, creativity, and social action to end the use of child soldiers in Joseph Kony's rebel war and restore LRA-affected communities in Central Africa to peace and prosperity."[24]

While never a large group, the LRA has been powerful: it is estimated to have killed tens of thousands, abducted tens of thousands of children for use as soldiers and wives, and displaced more than 1.5 million people.[25] For these reasons, the LRA has been a popular subject of international NGOs in addition to Invisible Children, including Resolve, the Enough Project, and Human Rights Watch. The strategy used by IC included road shows to high schools and colleges across the country, at which they screened their films to generate support for the cause. By 2008, the LRA and Kony were one of the most well-known international issues among students in the United States.[26]

Also in 2008, President George W. Bush sent 20 special-operations advisors to the region of northern Uganda, southern Sudan, the Democratic Republic of Congo, and the Central African

Republic, where LRA forces had spread. In May 2010, President Obama signed the Lord's Resistance Army Disarmament and Northern Uganda Recovery Act, and in October 2011 he announced that he would be sending 100 "combat-equipped troops" to go after Kony.[27] After the bill's passage, a dozen members of the House of Representatives publicly praised IC for its advocacy on the LRA legislation.[28]

Shortly thereafter, IC made Internet history with the March 2012 release of a 29-minute film, Kony 2012. As the film declares, IC's intent was to make Joseph Kony more famous than George Clooney: to raise awareness of his crimes and his status at the top of the ICC list of war criminals, as well as to keep pressure on governments, particularly the U.S. government, to help bring Kony to justice. In the film IC identified two lists, one of the top 20 culturemakers and one of the top 12 policymakers, whom it believed were essential for viewers to contact with the message that U.S. withdrawal of support for finding Kony would have dire consequences. The film urged viewers to directly contact these 32 influential people via Facebook, Twitter, or e-mail, to forward the message to friends and family, and to get involved in making Kony (in)famous in order to bring him to justice. This effort was to culminate in worldwide "cover the night" activities that would include posters, t-shirts, wall art, and other ways to convey the message of Kony 2012. Using classic language of policymaking, they noted that there was a "window of opportunity" to find Kony, and that it would not be open for long.

The use of film and social media has always been a tool in IC's strategy to advance their cause. For example, in 2010 IC was the recipient of a Chase [Bank] Community Giving contest in which it won $1 million by collecting votes on Facebook.[29] The Kony 2012 video, however, was something different; it quickly went viral, receiving more than 100 million views in less than a week to become the most rapidly distributed Internet video in history. It is at this point that the controversy began in earnest, which ultimately led IC's "cover the night" activities to fizzle.[30]

The Kony 2012 film has been criticized as simplistic in that it gives essentially no background into the history of the Ugandan conflict; odd and manipulative in its scenes of Jason Russell's five-year-old son; bigoted in its suggestion that African problems need Western solutions; and even harmful to the cause as it risks creating compassion fatigue among a public that cannot sustain the momentum and effort that it would take to bring change to this complex, war-torn region.[31] IC's finances and management have been questioned as has the fact that only 37 percent of expenses go for programs on the ground in Central Africa.[32] Ironically, for an organization run by savvy young people expert in the use of social media, the exposure and notoriety of Kony 2012 took an immense toll on Russell, IC's filmmaker and one of its founders. He was arrested for public exposure and hospitalized just two weeks after the release of the film for what was described as "brief reactive psychosis," a condition thought to have been brought on by the intense mental and emotional strain of the public attention garnered by the release of Kony 2012.[33]

To counter its critics, IC presented a follow-up video one month after the original to clarify its mission and goals. It should also be noted that IC has a 3-star rating from Charity Navigator (which awards a maximum of 4 stars), including 4 stars in the financial category, and the chief prosecutor for the International Criminal Court announced his support and appreciation for the work of IC shortly after the first film went viral.[34] Further, if making Kony widely known was its goal, IC surely succeeded.[35] Among the culturemakers who Tweeted about the film were Taylor

Swift, Oprah Winfrey, Justin Beiber, and Alec Baldwin.[36] Finally, there is no question that Kony is a warlord who cut a path of kidnap, rape, torture, and murder across Central Africa for more than two decades.

In the end, the "cover the night" activities, set for April 20, 2012, did not result in the desired blanketing of the landscape with the Kony 2012 message. It may be that the criticism of the Kony 2012 campaign was too much to maintain momentum among supporters. Conversely, it could be that this type of Internet "click-and-send-your-money approach"—called "clicktivism" or "slacktivism" by detractors—is simply too passive to result in take-to-the-streets style mass activism.[37] IC was definitely caught off guard by the intense interest and subsequent criticism of its tactics and message.

Again, it is important to point out that in the realm of international problems there is no single policymaking body. Indeed, the United States has not even ratified the statute of the International Criminal Court, so Kony's status as an indicted war criminal there may carry little weight in the United States. Still, advocacy pressure from IC and others affected the passage of the Lord's Resistance Army Disarmament and Northern Uganda Recovery Act and placement of 100 troops in the region to help the Ugandan Army find Joseph Kony. Shortly after the release of the first video, the African Union offered to send 5,000 troops to assist in the efforts.[38] In June 2012, the United Nations Security Council endorsed a plan to end the threat from Kony and the LRA, and the U.S. State Department expanded its program to reward those who track down Kony and his supporters with up to $25 million.[39] Whether or not this is enough to bring a warlord to justice, is, as of this publication, yet to be seen. Regardless of the outcome or the wisdom of using the Kony 2012 film as its medium, Invisible Children will forever hold a place in nonprofit history as an amazing use of social media to market a nonprofit's mission.

The story of Kony 2012 is, of course, a cautionary tale for nonprofit organizations. They must prepare for marketing efforts that are *too* successful as well as criticism of their efforts. The old adage "all press is good press" is certainly not true for organizations in the nonprofit sector.

QUESTIONS TO CONSIDER:

1. What motivated the heavy use of social media and the release of Kony 2012 by Invisible Children?
2. In a survey just two weeks after the release of Kony 2012, the Pew Research Foundation found that those in the 18–29 age group were twice as likely to have heard "a lot" about the video and nearly twice as likely to have watched it. What might nonprofit organizations take from those findings?[40]
3. Consider the mission of Invisible Children. Does their mission have any bearing on the use of social media and, in particular, the Kony 2012 film? Why or why not?
4. Consider the four relationships that describe nonprofit interaction with public policy (make policy, affected by policy, influence policy, subject to policy) and discuss in which way(s) Invisible Children has interacted with public policy. How does its status as an NGO affect those interactions?
5. In what way(s) is Invisible Children and Kony 2012 a unique example of a nonprofit organization? What does this case suggest about successful use of social media by nonprofits?

The main point in this regard is to know your multiple audiences; if your organization has the resources, engage in market research to determine the different target segments of your audience and discover how each prefers to be contacted. At a minimum, once you have engaged a client, donor, or volunteer, ask how he or she prefers to be contacted by the nonprofit and how frequently. Tailoring communications has long-term benefits in addition to cost savings: clients, donors, and volunteers feel more valued and are more likely to remain engaged with the organization.

As you can see, nonprofits need to direct their communications to meet the different information needs of each segment of their target audience. Consider again the hypothetical case of End Littering. In order to market their new program to increase recycling in the surrounding counties, the board has determined that it needs to develop "audience-centric" communication strategies. Durham suggests that "instead of telling [your audiences] why your organization is so great, start by understanding who they are and how they'll benefit from supporting your work."[41] For example, End Littering hopes to locate recycling containers in the parking lots of big box stores throughout the surrounding counties, as well as at county-maintained rural trash collection sites. In order to facilitate the needed collaboration with private and public sector entities, the End Littering marketing efforts should include information about how the proposed partnership would benefit each through the potential for increased consumer traffic at the businesses and lower fees for the county government for solid waste disposal. It is also important for the nonprofit to ensure that its efforts comply with local ordinances and other policies, that it will not pose an additional burden on either the county or host businesses, and if it will, for the organization to delineate how it will mitigate the negative effects.

In the case of those for whom nonprofit organizations seek to provide services, communication strategies may also need to address individuals who do not want or may even actively resist receiving services. Convincing an alcoholic in denial to accept treatment requires a different approach than informing homebound seniors about the new meals-on-wheels program, for example. As has been highlighted throughout this book, nonprofit service-delivery is imbued with policy implications. Accordingly, the marketing plan should also incorporate ways to meet the information needs of policymakers and to heighten public awareness not only of the needs being met but the overall importance of the public problems and issues involved.

Consider the case of the American Cancer Society (see Box 8.2). While they cast the widest possible net with their tagline "The Official Sponsor of Birthdays," they target their information and varied appeals to address different audiences. All nonprofits have multiple target publics and stakeholders who seek different types of information and respond in different ways to their missions and means of pursuing them. Therefore, through marketing, nonprofits seek to differentiate themselves with stakeholders in order to increase their likelihood of success.

Box 8.2

FOR EXAMPLE

AMERICAN CANCER SOCIETY: MARKETING MORE BIRTHDAYS

In 1913, the American Society for the Control of Cancer (ASCC) was established and was subsequently reorganized in 1945 to form the American Cancer Society (the Society). With 300 million volunteers and more than $900 million in public support revenues in 2010, the society is the largest investor in cancer research in the United States, outside of government. Founded by a small but committed group of physicians and business leaders who sought to end the social stigma attached to a cancer diagnosis, this nonprofit has continued to raise public awareness and dispel myths regarding the disease, as well as advance research toward its prevention and cure. In the United States alone, more than 13 million people are cancer survivors, largely because of the efforts of the American Cancer Society; in their words, "we've helped create more than 300 birthdays each and every day just since the early 1990's."

The familiar white Sword of Hope logo—a sword to represent a crusading spirit with the handle formed by caduceus, the twin-serpent representing science and medicine—was chosen in 1928 through a nationwide poster contest. In April 2009, the society launched a new "Official Sponsor of Birthdays" brand campaign, with the new trademarked slogan situated adjacent to the iconic logo. Based on the fact that birthdays are something everyone has in common, the society seeks to engage its target audiences through a common theme of the importance of celebrating another year. More than 50 music artists including Justin Bieber, Celine Dion, Rihanna, Darius Rucker, and the Village People have recorded music videos of the song *Happy Birthday,* some of which are used in the national ad campaign and all of which are available as downloads with a donation to the society through the website morebirthdays.com.

In addition to the Official Sponsor of Birthdays tagline, the society weaves the "more birthdays" theme throughout its website and in press release materials. The society identifies its four target audiences through an abbreviated version of its mission statement used in headings throughout its website (cancer.org): "Saving lives by helping people stay well, get well, find cures, and fight back." The "stay well" message targets individuals without cancer by providing information on prevention; the society spent almost $150 million in 2010 for prevention activities. Those who have been diagnosed with cancer and their loved ones comprise the "get well" target audience; the society spent in excess of $270 million in 2010 on patient support (its largest program expenditure category), and an additional $112 million on detection and treatment. "Find cures" refers to the efforts of the American Cancer Society to research new treatments and pursue a cure; $148.6 million was spent in 2010 on research. Finally, the society asserts that they "save lives by . . . fighting back through public policy"; in cooperation with their nonpartisan advocacy affiliate the American Cancer Society Cancer Action Network, they advocate for public policies to "create a world with less cancer and more birthdays."

The American Cancer Society provides an excellent example of nonprofit use of a vast array of marketing techniques. Through their familiar logo, repeated references to being the "Official

Sponsor of Birthdays," consistent application of logo, tagline, and color scheme in both the web and print media, use of celebrity sponsors with diverse appeal, and audience segmentation, the society has created a successful marketing campaign. The extent to which they are able to fund prevention, patient support, and research efforts is testament to their success.

For additional information, see www.cancer.org and www.morebirthdays.com.

Differentiating the Nonprofit through Positioning

A mission statement allows a nonprofit to frame the issues with which it is involved and suggest solutions to address public problems. For example, the American Cancer Society mission statement not only identifies its four target audiences but frames its issue involvement as saving lives, as well as its proposed solutions of helping to prevent cancer, survive cancer, cure cancer, and advance public policy related to cancer. Communicating the issue frames and proposed solutions is one of the key elements of nonprofit marketing, and its primary purpose is to express how the nonprofit is unique from other organizations in its approach. Referred to as differentiation, it is the process through which an organization identifies how it is different from others and why it warrants the resources needed to accomplish its goals. Organizations target their communications to relevant stakeholders and accomplish differentiation through a process called positioning, designed to enhance the brand strength and brand equity of the organization.

Positioning through the Marketing Mix. In the language of marketing, organizations differentiate themselves through positioning, which basically involves influencing how stakeholders perceive the reputation of one nonprofit relative to others. Nonprofits achieve a desired position by devising a marketing plan that includes a mix of the 4 P's also used in commercial sector marketing: product, place, price, and promotion. For nonprofits, *product* refers to the goods or services offered in pursuit of its mission or the behavior change it wishes to facilitate; in the case of End Littering the product would be a cleaner, more beautiful county. *Place* refers to the service area of the organization, and *price* relates to the value of the programming offered (even when no fee is charged). *Promotion* is how the nonprofit communicates its purpose, activities, and accomplishments.

Each of the 4 P's represents an opportunity to set the organization apart from others. For example, the local YMCA could market its fitness facility and programs as having greater value to potential clients when compared to a for-profit gym because the fees are significantly lower, but the quality of equipment and classes is comparable. Even nonprofits that usually do not face direct competition in providing services—such as a halfway house for released offenders—do compete with a pool of other nonprofits seeking funds from similar sources. Likewise, the halfway house can market itself as having greater value to potential donors than other social service nonprofits because of the number of clients served and outcomes achieved; by providing information on how the community as a whole is improved by the work it does—that is, through promotion, the nonprofit sets itself apart from other nonprofits competing for the same pool of resources.

Promotion is defined as comprising the methods by which a nonprofit communicates with its target audiences, and

> . . . promotion refers to any activity of an organization that intends to inform, persuade, or remind its target publics about the organization or its offers, when and where they are or will be available, and other pertinent information the target market may need in order to change its feelings, beliefs, or behavior.[42]

Communication strategies identified as useful in promoting nonprofits include public service announcements (PSA's), paid advertising, and publicity/public relations. For example, following the devastating earthquake in Haiti in 2010, former presidents Bill Clinton and George W. Bush were featured in radio and television PSA's produced by the Ad Council (www.adcouncil.org), in which they asked viewers and listeners to donate to the Clinton Bush Haiti Fund. While public service announcements are more readily associated with the work of nonprofits than paid advertising, the television commercials run by the American Cancer Society (see Box 8.2) and the United Methodist Church (see Box 8.4), as well as the Salvation Army ads that run around the holidays are notable examples of paid advertising by nonprofits. With regard to positioning through publicity and public relations, a common tactic is to engage a celebrity spokesperson; the relationship between celebrity and charity is explored further in Box 8.3.

Developing the Nonprofit's Brand Identity

The overall goal of the marketing plan is to establish a brand for the organization. A brand is "the collection of perceptions in the minds of [a nonprofit's] target publics that is based on how they value and relate to the organization's mission, offers, and reputation."[43] No longer the sole purview of commercial products such as Coca-Cola or Kleenex, many nonprofits such as the Red Cross and the American Cancer Society are now considered to be nationally recognized brands.

Brands are considered "important vehicles for differentiating among services, people, ideas, and organizations."[44] Because of the mental connection with cattle ranching, brands are often thought of as logos or symbols that represent a product or organization (e.g., the curved Coke bottle or Mickey Mouse's ears). While these elements are important, branding also includes names, taglines (or slogans), and color scheme, as well as typeface and fonts used in printing.[45] Table 8.1 lists the taglines of several of the nonprofits highlighted throughout this book, along with their website addresses, to facilitate examination of their logos and color schemes. These symbolic elements are designed and intended to evoke a positive emotional response to the organization and its mission.

Box 8.3

FOR EXAMPLE

THE CELEBRITY SPOKESPERSON: PROMOTING A CHARITABLE CAUSE

On September 4, 2011—for the first time since 1966 when he began the show to raise funds for the Muscular Dystrophy Association (MDA)—Jerry Lewis did not host the annual Labor Day telethon. He was abruptly dropped as host and dismissed as the national spokesman for MDA in early August 2011, despite an almost 60-year tenure with the nonprofit. In the 45 years that Mr. Lewis served as host, the telethons raised approximately $2.5 billion dollars. Neither MDA nor Mr. Lewis commented on why the decision was made with such short notice.[46] For those of us who grew up watching what was a major television event and made our first forays into philanthropy with a donation for "Jerry's Kids," it was the end of an era. For those who saw the telethon as a fundraising relic and the image of "Jerry's Kids" as out-of-touch with the reality of life with muscular dystrophy, it was a new beginning for the national nonprofit.

Nonprofits frequently seek affiliation with a celebrity spokesperson to increase attention to their organization, its mission, and policy efforts. U2 lead singer Bono, for example, has built a solid reputation for charitable activism for the people of Africa, particularly those suffering from HIV/AIDS. In 2002, he co-founded the nonprofit DATA—an acronym for debt, AIDS, trade, Africa—to raise public awareness and influence public policy on those issues; he has been an effective advocate, meeting with U.S. presidents and members of Congress, as well as other world leaders, and calling attention through his celebrity to crises affecting the continent (see, for example, his December 9, 2005, interview on PBS's *Frontline* at http://www.pbs.org/wgbh/pages/frontline/aids/interviews/bono.html).

Likewise, the late Paul Newman set the charitable gold standard for nonprofit commercial ventures, primarily by using his name and likeness on specialty food products sold to benefit his Newman's Own Foundation. Since 1982, the foundation has given more than $300 million to thousands of charities, through grants to support projects worldwide, including funds to support children with serious health concerns and to facilitate solutions to issues of hunger and poor nutrition, as well as for his Hole in the Wall camps for seriously ill children (www.newmansown.org).

Because by definition celebrities are accorded attention wherever they go and whatever they do, nonprofits seek their affiliation and support to share in that limelight. Relationships between celebrities and charities, however, run the gamut between successful and less-than-stellar. Finding the right match between the mission and policy priorities of a nonprofit and the interests and reputation of the celebrity is key to a mutually beneficial relationship.

For additional information on the generally positive effects of celebrity charity work and how to promote a good relationship between a nonprofit and its celebrity benefactor, see the article by Mark Harris entitled "How to Train Your Celebrity: Five Hollywood Charity Myths," www.fastcompany.com/magazine/157/how-to-train-your-celebrity.

TABLE 8.1 Examples of Nonprofit Slogans and Taglines

Nonprofit	Tagline	Website
Alliance for Justice	Fighting for a Fair America	www.afj.org
American Humane Association	The nation's voice for the protection of children and animals	www.americanhumane.org
ASPCA	WE ARE THEIR VOICE	www.aspca.org
Blue Ridge Conservancy	Saving the Places You Love	www.blueridgeconservancy.org
Carnegie Corporation of NY	"To do real and permanent good in this world"	www.carnegie.org
Columbus Association for the Performing Arts	LIVE ENTERTAINMENT IN COLUMBUS	www.capa.com
Foundation Center	Knowledge to Build On	www.foundationcenter.org
Governmental Accounting Standards Board	Communicating Values in Financial Reporting	www.gasb.org
March of Dimes	working together for stronger, healthier babies	www.marchofdimes.com
Milton Hershey School	Opening new doors for children in need	www.mhs-pa.org
National Alliance on Mental Illness	Find Help. Find Hope.	www.nami.org
National Children's Alliance	Empowering local communities to serve child victims of abuse	www.nationalchildrensalliance.org
Police Foundation	Supporting innovation and improvement in policing since 1970	www.policefoundation.org
Sierra Club	Explore, Enjoy, Protect the Planet	www.sierraclub.org

It has been empirically demonstrated that individuals exhibit an emotional response to nonprofits and their work by ascribing to them human traits and characteristics. This is conceptualized by marketers as a brand personality, sometimes referred to as brand image.[47] Brand personality may be particularly relevant with regard to soliciting contributions because donors tend to react more favorably to brands that reflect their own values—whether their actual values, or those to which they aspire.[48] Stakeholders ascribe personality traits to nonprofits along four primary dimensions—integrity, sophistication, ruggedness, and nurturance. Charity brand personalities differ from commercial brands in that most traits attributed to nonprofits are not unique to one organization but are likewise shared with similar charities. Differentiation thus becomes more challenging as nonprofit brands must maximize their distinctiveness, as well as overcome traits that were not deliberately developed by their organization.

Framing. As stated earlier, brands are generally associated with symbols and logos but encompass much more. When considered as a collection of perceptions that affect how an individual responds to an organization's mission, branding embodies what public policy scholars refer to as issue framing. Consider again the example of local gun control policies in California discussed in Chapter 3, in which proponents sought to reframe the issue of gun violence as a public health rather than criminal justice issue. While changing the predominant school of thought on an issue or public problem is difficult, it is obviously not impossible in view of the many examples discussed throughout this book. Framing is generally not sufficient to cause individuals to change what they believe, but it can change how and what they think about in response to issue frames.[49] Issue frames are embedded in a marketing plan and are important for nonprofits, not only to promote the organization but to highlight the predominance of how it perceives public problems and solutions relevant to its work.

The Impact of Brand Strength and Equity. The relevance of a brand to a nonprofit's target audiences and the extent to which it serves to differentiate the organization and its services from its counterparts is termed brand strength. Brand equity refers to the value-added aspect of marketing activities—that is, the extent to which certain marketing strategies increase the brand relative to similar nonprofits and their services. In measuring brand equity, several marketing research models use dimensions such as loyalty, esteem, quality, and relevance.[50] Respondents to a 2005 survey by the American Marketing Association identified the following three characteristics as the most important when deciding whether or not to give to a charity: (1) "Trust in the Organization"; (2) "Personal Belief in the Organization's Goals"; and (3) "Reputation of the Organization."[51] Each of the three is generally considered to be an attribute of a brand. See Box 8.4 for a discussion of the United Methodist Church and its "Open Hearts, Open Minds, Open Doors" brand campaign.

As a theoretical construct, brand equity as the value-added dimension of marketing is relatively easy to grasp. In practice, measuring a nonprofit's brand equity is quite difficult, usually because the intangible elements such as perceptions and feelings about public problems and nonprofit missions defy consistent quantification. Many nonprofits address this by establishing marketing benchmarks, which involves identifying similar organizations and tracking relative changes in their marketing activities and stakeholders' responses over time.[52] Colleges and universities routinely engage in benchmarking on issues such as faculty salaries, student retention, and alumni services; tracking the marketing strategies of similar institutions assists the organization in staying current and competitive in their service delivery venues.

It is important for nonprofits to be aware of their position in the sector relative to other nonprofits, as well as their position relative to for-profit and public sector entities. As the lines continue to blur between the three sectors, and the number of nonprofits continues to rise at fairly rapid rates, branding becomes increasingly important for charities competing for volunteers, limited funding, and the attention of policymakers. An increasingly common tactic is for nonprofit and for-profit organizations to seek to differentiate themselves through cooperative ventures, generally referred to as corporate social responsibility (CSR).

Box 8.4

FOR EXAMPLE

THE UNITED METHODIST CHURCH: COMMUNICATING THE BRAND

In 2001, the United Methodist Church (UMC) launched a welcoming and advertising campaign centered around the slogan "Open Hearts. Open Minds. Open Doors." You may have seen the television ads or read the slogan in print, next to the church's cross and flame logo and above the phrase, "The people of the United Methodist Church." Since its inception, the campaign has moved through the Igniting Ministry phase, beginning its Rethink Church focus in early 2009. Each of the quadrennial evolutions within the brand campaign maintains ties to the original focus of "Open Hearts. Open Minds. Open Doors." As United Methodist communications general secretary Larry Hollon states

> the brand promise is that you will be received with open hearts, open minds and open doors if you engage with the people of the United Methodist Church. That brand is rooted in the Wesleyan tradition of serving people who are not a part of the established church, but who are seeking spiritual meaning. Rethink Church takes the promise as well as the invitation, and makes it more active.[53]

The campaign is generally viewed as a success with regard to the slogan, its ease of remembrance, and its effect on raising awareness of the UMC. While Mr. Hollon's statement succinctly links the campaign and brand to the deep roots of the church's mission, others have questioned its overall effectiveness in communicating what the church values and promotes. Just as the funniest and most cutting-edge commercial is only useful if you remember the product as well as the punch line, a good slogan is only useful insofar as it communicates accurately the desired brand attributes of the nonprofit. Andrew Thompson[54] contends that to many the slogan conveys an "anything goes" approach, illustrated through comments from church members that the United Methodist Church is a church "where you can believe anything you want." This, he argues, is neither true nor an attribute intended by the marketing plan.

The United Methodist Church has a long-term, demonstrated commitment to marketing as an effective tool to pursue its mission to "Make Disciples." The United Methodist Communications website even has a section to assist churches in creating their own marketing plans (www.umcom.org/churchmarketingplan). Through United Methodist Communications and its partnerships with advertising firms such as BOHAN and the Buntin Group, the church seeks to engage members and seekers through multiple venues; for example, the Rethink Church campaign focus includes social media as well as traditional television and print outlets, and emphasizes service and mission opportunities as means to connect with its target audiences.

For additional information, see www.umc.org, www.umcom.org, www.rethinkchurch.org, and bohanideas.com/case-studies/rethinking-church.

CORPORATE SOCIAL RESPONSIBILITY AS A SOURCE OF NONPROFIT SUPPORT

Just as nonprofits and governments enjoy mutually beneficial relationships in the provision of public goods and services, nonprofits and businesses have incentives to form alliances in the public interest. Corporate social responsibility (CSR) refers to the response by for-profit corporations to the growing opinion among consumers that business has an obligation to contribute to the social good. Historically, a few forward-thinking businesses engaged in CSR, but usually through basic philanthropy rather than as a form of marketing. As many economists, lawyers, and management scholars argue, the primary duty of corporations is to their shareholders, which requires the maximization of profits; altruism is not a sufficient reason for business to assist public charities.[55] With growing awareness by companies that they are likely to reap bottom-line benefits from social responsibility initiatives, more are now engaging in activities related to CSR—and the nonprofits involved with those initiatives benefit as well.

Corporate social responsibility embodies various forms of brand alliances between for-profit and not-for-profit organizations, including corporate sponsorship of events such as food drives at concerts to benefit local food pantries, licensing and endorsement of products by nonprofits, as well as donations to foundations from the proceeds of sales. Walk down an aisle of your local grocery store or check your pantry, and you are likely to find at least one product that reflects a CSR endeavor. A box of Cheerios is a good example: in addition to the ubiquitous Box Tops for Education campaign, which provides funding for elementary schools, the Spring 2012 version of the packaging included a certification by the American Heart Association (www.heartcheckmark.org), and the back of the box and a side panel were devoted to the partnership between General Mills and the nonprofit First Book (www.firstbook.org) to provide books to children who lack access to them. According to General Mills, since 2002, the company has donated more than $3.5 million to First Book, has included over 50 million books in boxes of Cheerios, and, in conjunction with Simon and Schuster Children's Publishing (their logo is also on the box), sponsored their fourth annual New Author Contest. The packaging includes notification to consumers that they are helping to provide books to children who need them through the purchase of each box of cereal and can help more with a donation through First Book's website.

Nonprofit Fundraising Events and Corporate Sponsorship

It is unlikely an overstatement to assert that everyone reading this has participated or sponsored a participant in a walk, ride, bike, swim, drive, or golf event for a charitable organization; every one of those events likely involved multiple corporate or business sponsors. Charity event sponsorship, in which a for-profit organization contributes money, volunteers, and/or in-kind donations such as food or t-shirts, is mutually beneficial for the nonprofit and its corporate sponsors. The nonprofit is able to host an event with few overhead costs and gains donors, volunteers, and publicity for its cause, while the for-profit organization increases its visibility, attracting good press, new customers, and conveying a sense of community involvement.

Ted Gup, chair of the journalism department at Emerson College, has an interesting perspective on such events:

> Those who oversee such fund-raising spectacles argue that there is more to these events than meets the eyes—mine included. These walks and runs are incubators for future volunteers and donors. They constitute a public proclamation that others matter. They make the invisible visible. More to the point, it is easier to get relatives, friends and colleagues to open their pocketbooks than it is to win over the largess of strangers. . . . In the end, getting others to give is as much art as science, and if traversing great distances is what it takes to discover that charity begins at home, then so be it. These events have become so deeply rooted in our cities and culture that their eccentricities and irrationalities escape our notice, lost in the blur of matching T-shirts, sponsors' logos and banners.[56]

As Gup so aptly puts it, and as is discussed further in Chapter 9, these types of special events defy logic as fundraisers; the corporate sponsorship of such events is usually the critical factor in ensuring the endeavor generates revenue in excess of the expenses required to stage it.[57] What these events are most successful at accomplishing is a sense of community and shared experience; they allow nonprofits to enhance civic engagement while raising a little revenue and hopefully signing up a few volunteers. The reason these events are attractive to sponsors is because just as it is easier to get friends to open their pocketbooks to donate to charity, it is likewise easier to get "friends"—acquired through shared service to a nonprofit—to open their pocketbooks to buy your products. As such, event sponsorship is a mutually beneficial relationship for nonprofits and their corporate partners. These relationships are often long-term in nature, allowing the nonprofit a steady source of funding to host annual events, and both share in the benefits of marketing the event to participants, volunteers, donors, and the media. Importantly, the community benefits through greater awareness of the public problems addressed by the nonprofit, as well as more resources to resolve them.

Benefits and Risks of Product Endorsements and Licensing Agreements

By endorsing a product or service, a nonprofit organization extends its brand to the for-profit entity that produces it. In the case of the American Heart Association, allowing a company to use its heart checkmark logo with the tagline "certified by the American Heart Association" extends the positive image and reputation of the nonprofit to the product. Therefore, if Cheerios are certified by the American Heart Association, they must be good for your heart. Likewise, the Arthritis Foundation endorses products through its Ease of Use Commendation program. After passing rigorous testing, products that pass are deemed user-friendly for people who suffer from arthritis; the company can then market the product as commended by the Arthritis Foundation.[58] Endorsement of a product by a nonprofit is a statement to the consumer that the organization has tested the product and approves its use as being relevant to accomplishing the mission of the nonprofit. Cheerios help promote heart health, which is part of the mission of the American Heart Association; thus, the nonprofit endorses consumption of the cereal.

While these are examples of explicit endorsements of a product by a nonprofit that are intended to imply a seal of approval, some CSR initiatives stop short of a nonprofit endorsing a company's product. Licensing agreements, for example, allow a business to use a nonprofit's logo in marketing a product but there is no endorsement of the product by the nonprofit. For example, Sesame Workshop, the producer of *Sesame Street*, has a licensing agreement with Earth's Best Organic Foods, which is a sponsor of the television show and uses the *Sesame Street* characters on its packaging and in promotional materials. Sesame Workshop uses the proceeds from the licensing agreement to fund production of the show and other children's activities around the world. Licensing agreements are a mutually beneficial arrangement; the nonprofit receives revenues from the sales of the products, and the for-profit likely generates more sales as consumers are motivated to purchase by the opportunity to assist a nonprofit.

However, there is growing concern among researchers that consumers are likely to infer that every CSR initiative constitutes more than a simple charitable donation. The American Cancer Society, for example, has within its policies regarding CSR that it does not endorse the products or services of its corporate partners. In 1996, after the FDA approved nicotine replacement therapies to help people quit smoking, the American Cancer Society entered into a licensing agreement with SmithKlineBeecham that allowed their logo to be used in advertising for Nicoderm patches and Nicorette gum. Two years later, the attorneys general of 12 states entered into a settlement agreement with SmithKlineBeecham regarding allegations of misleading advertising. The attorneys general contended that the use of the American Cancer Society logo in advertising for the smoking cessation products implied endorsement of those products by the nonprofit, especially when used in ads comparing the products to those of a competitor. The American Cancer Society cooperated fully with the investigation and subsequently altered its CSR policies to provide even greater protection from the inappropriate use of its logo.[59]

Subsequent research by Bower and Grau suggests that the attorneys general in the SmithKlineBeecham case were right: CSR initiatives are likely to generate a perception among consumers of an endorsement by the nonprofit of the company's product. Consumers tend to interpret a licensing agreement or cause-related marketing campaign as a seal of approval by the nonprofit, inferring that the products have been tested and found worthy to support the goals of the nonprofit. Absent an explicit statement of monetary contribution, consumers are more likely to view CSR initiatives as endorsements rather than funding relationships. This is particularly relevant for nonprofits because they can suffer negative consequences from implied endorsements; they could be held legally liable for misleading claims—or consumer fraud—and at a minimum would suffer loss of reputation and diminished brand image, which would certainly hinder their ability to provide public services and effectively advocate for policy changes.

Cause-Related Marketing

The mutually beneficial relationship of cause-related marketing entails an appeal to consumers to purchase a particular product in order to facilitate a donation from the manufacturer of the product to the nonprofit organization. American Express is widely credited with initiating the practice with its support of the restoration of the Statue of Liberty in 1983.[60] In terms of strength and numbers of corporate partners, Susan G. Komen for the Cure

Foundation is the leading pioneer of cause-related marketing. Box 8.5 illustrates their success and commitment to this approach to generating resources for breast cancer research, treatment, and prevention.

Cause Marketing Forum reports that in 1990, spending for cause-related marketing was $120 million;[61] by 2011, CRM spending had grown to $1.68 billion. CRM has been found to benefit corporations in a number of ways. For example, it has been shown to assist companies to "do well by doing good,"[62] may assist in attracting and retaining employees,[63] and generally results in positive outcomes for relevant stakeholders.[64] However, not all companies or nonprofits are well-suited to each other or even to engaging in CRM.

Runté et al. in their qualitative analysis of CRM from a nonprofit's perspective identified a series of goals that nonprofits expect to achieve through partnerships with business entities. Through empirical testing of these goals, the authors differentiate between first order benefits—those primarily related to obtaining operational resources—and second order benefits—those which provide recognition and nonfinancial advantage to the organization. They conclude that through CRM, nonprofits primarily hope to obtain

> event support as well as opportunities for networking and increasing public awareness. . . . Seeking other funding from the business and seeking public donations are moderately important. Using the business as a resource does not appear to be a strong goal or outcome of the CRM alliance.[65]

The authors also stress that while CRM may be a desired strategy, it may not be a realistic one for some organizations. Nonprofits with negative or controversial public images may not be able to attract corporate partners; likewise, corporations that produce and market controversial products, or that have been embroiled in a scandal, may find it more difficult to attract nonprofits willing to accept a brand alliance.[66]

Empirical studies of CRM indicate that structural issues such as how the cause-related marketing campaign is framed are important to the success of these partnerships. In general, promotions are perceived more favorably by consumers if they involve specification by the corporate sponsor of the dollar amount to be donated, both per purchase and in total if the donation is capped. Consumers are also more likely to purchase a cause-related product if it is considered a frivolous or luxury good; this is most likely because the associated charitable donation eases the guilt associated with the purchase.[67] For the most part, consumers view CRM efforts in a positive light; however, companies must be careful when using CRM as part of their overall corporate social responsibility efforts. Providing details about the campaign—what is expected of the customer, what will be donated to the nonprofit, and the overall contributions made once the campaign is complete—has been shown to increase consumer confidence. However, too much marketing of the effort may serve to spotlight the company's gain from the venture and lessen consumer affinity for the nonprofit organization being benefited.[68]

Box 8.5

FOR EXAMPLE

SUSAN G. KOMEN FOR THE CURE: PIONEERING CAUSE-RELATED MARKETING

Nancy Brinker established the Susan G. Komen Foundation (now Susan G. Komen for the Cure) in 1982 in order to fulfill a promise she made to her sister Suzy who was dying from breast cancer; the promise was to do all in her power to end breast cancer forever. While Brinker has long been respected as an influential and knowledgeable member of the cancer community, she and Komen were embroiled in controversy in early 2012 regarding grants to Planned Parenthood. In August 2012, Brinker announced that she would step down as CEO but would assume a different role within the organization she founded. Although it remains to be seen what impact the recent controversy and the change in leadership will have, Komen's impact on the cause of breast cancer can hardly be overstated. Since 1982, Komen has invested more than $1.9 billion in research, education, and community programs to prevent, treat, and ultimately cure breast cancer.

Not only a pioneer in the cause-related marketing movement, Komen for the Cure has demonstrated how successful nonprofit-corporate partnerships can be with regard to raising money and awareness for a cause. Subsequently, the Komen pink ribbon logo has become ubiquitous on products ranging from yogurt to potted dahlias, and consumers know that their purchase will result in a donation by the corporate partner to the fight against breast cancer. Today, Komen lists more than 150 such partners—30 of which have given at least $1 million to the cause. In addition, the Komen Race for the Cure, first run in Dallas in 1983, is among the most successful series of 1k/5k walks and runs for charity in the United States. Race for the Cure relies on national event sponsorship from companies such as American Airlines, Ford Motor Company, and New Balance. Komen's marketing success is demonstrated through widespread recognition of their brand, the ever-present pink ribbon, and the nearly $2 billion it has raised in its thirty years.

Additional information can be found at www.komen.org.

CONCLUSION

Marketing is not something that nonprofits can ignore, except at their own peril. Besides, whether they use the term or not, all nonprofits engage in marketing, even if it is not formally structured as a campaign. Any time the Executive Director writes a grant proposal or a member of the board solicits a donation, information is communicated about the organization in an effort to enhance its image. Research is increasingly demonstrating that nonprofits can benefit from marketing in many ways other than increased financial resources, and getting started with a marketing plan is not the daunting task it may appear to be.

Once the organization has articulated its mission, goals, and objectives, putting together a marketing plan is the next step to help focus efforts on achieving them. It is important to identify the nonprofit's target audiences and determine their preferred means of receiving communication from the organization. Nonprofits should also develop strategies to provide relevant information that appeals to potential clients, donors, volunteers, and policymakers.

Establishing a unique position relative to other nonprofits, whether in the same field or the same geographic area, allows the organization to facilitate a positive brand image. One way to differentiate the organization and share positive brand attributes is through corporate social responsibility, which has been shown to enhance a company's image but also raises awareness and increases financial and human resources for the nonprofit. It is important that a nonprofit chooses its business partners carefully; CSR initiatives with closely related partners may increase the likelihood of implied endorsements when the nonprofit allows the use of its name and logo through licensing agreements.

Finally, cause-related marketing represents the most common CSR initiative and probably the most lucrative. This represents another blurring of the lines between the nonprofit and for-profit sectors, with associated policy implications. Corporate sponsorship has the potential to provide great benefit to the nonprofit's pursuit of mission by expanding the resources available for service delivery. However, corporate partnerships can also be detrimental to the pursuit of mission by causing the nonprofit to commit attention and resources away from its primary goals. Corporate alliances through funding are discussed further in Chapter 9.

Questions For Review

1. Identify the likely target audiences for the hypothetical nonprofit End Littering, introduced in the opening vignette. Discuss strategies the organization could employ to successfully market its new program to the different audiences. What challenges is it likely to face?
2. Compare and contrast the terms differentiation, positioning, and segmentation and discuss how each relates to the marketing efforts of the American Cancer Society.
3. Discuss the benefits of cause-related marketing for both the business and the nonprofit. What challenges are faced by each?
4. In what ways do the marketing efforts of nonprofits incorporate and facilitate their public policy priorities and advocacy efforts?

Assignment[69]

For each of the five issue areas listed, name the first nonprofit organization that comes to mind:

1. disaster relief
2. animal welfare and rescue
3. the visual arts
4. needs of the homeless
5. literacy promotion

Think about the reasons why you chose each and make a list of five adjectives to describe each nonprofit. (If you have difficulty, try thinking in terms of "If this nonprofit were a person, how would I describe him or her.") If you cannot name a nonprofit for one or more of the categories, think about why—did several come to mind, but one does not stand out, or are you simply unfamiliar with the issue area(s). In either event, conduct a search of the Web to select a relevant nonprofit to complete your list of five.

Once you have the list of five nonprofits with associated adjectives, describe the relative strength of each nonprofit's brand with regard to other major nonprofits in that issue area. For the one with the weakest brand, what marketing tools or techniques would you recommend for the nonprofit to employ to better position itself through differentiation?

As an alternative assignment name five local nonprofits that operate in different issue/service areas from one another. Identify five adjectives to describe each of them, and assess the strength of each one's brand within the local community. Because local nonprofits tend to compete with disparate nonprofits, rather than those within the same issue area, for local resources such as corporate giving or volunteers, what particular challenges do these organizations face in differentiating themselves? For the nonprofit with the greatest challenges, what marketing tools and techniques would you recommend for the nonprofit to employ to better position itself through differentiation?

Suggested Readings

Burnett, John J. *Nonprofit Marketing Best Practices.* Hoboken, NJ: John Wiley & Sons, 2007.

Kotler, Philip, and Nancy Lee. *Social Marketing: Influencing Behaviors for Good,* 3rd ed. Thousand Oaks, CA: SAGE, 2008.

Kotler, Philip, and Sidney J. Levy. "Broadening the Concept of Marketing." *Journal of Marketing* 39 (1969): 10–15.

Wymer, Walter, Jr., Patricia Knowles, and Roger Gomes. *Nonprofit Marketing: Marketing Management for Charitable and Nongovernmental Organizations.* Thousand Oaks, CA: SAGE, 2006.

Web Resources

Beth's Blog, www.bethkanter.org

Cause Marketing Forum, www.causemarketingforum.com

Charity Channel, www.charitychannel.com

The Chronicle of Philanthropy Blogs, http://philanthropy.com/section/Blogs/208/

Cone/Duke Report on CRM, www.coneinc.com/content1188

Nonprofit Marketing Guide, www.nonprofitmarketingguide.com

9 Resource Development

Capacity, Campaigns, and Commercial Ventures

People do not give time and money to organizations because organizations have needs; *they give because organizations* meet needs*. . . . [A] gift to an organization is really a gift* through *the organization: It is an investment in the community.*[1]

Imagine you are someone like Tom. He views his life as an opportunity to make a contribution. Over the years he has worked hard—founded a successful company, promoted the well-being of his family, volunteered in his community. Retirement time is approaching and he wants to give more, about $1 million more. The problem is, how can he donate his money so it will be used the most effectively? Having a million dollars to give away is a nice problem to have, but deciding how to give it away is not as easy as it might seem.

Over the years Tom has volunteered for several nonprofits—cooking meals at the Salvation Army shelter, handing out programs for the local theatre group, building houses with a team for Habitat for Humanity, and serving on the board of the state's children's museum. He has given money as well as time to these organizations over the years, so he could simply divide the $1 million among them, but would that have the impact he wants? The nonprofits are different sizes, serve different needs, and vary in fiscal health, so how much does each deserve?

Also to be considered is his alma mater, or rather four alma maters, since he has degrees from three universities and his high school still calls from time to time. His heart and team support lean heavily toward one of the institutions of higher learning, which also happens to be in the midst of a

POLICY IMPLICATIONS OF CAPACITY, CAMPAIGNS, AND COMMERCIAL VENTURES

- All revenue generated by a nonprofit supports the pursuit of the organization's mission, enabling it to influence and make policy through its service delivery and advocacy efforts. The potential risk associated with the pursuit of resources is that it could lead to mission drift.
- Generating earned income—for example, commercial ventures and fees-for-service—is growing in popularity within the sector and serves as a relatively stable source of revenue with fewer restrictions on how it can be used. Corporate philanthropy is a win-win situation: Nonprofits get needed revenues to pursue their missions, and corporate partners get good press along with the tax deduction. When the product offerings of the corporation mesh with the mission of the organization, the potential for policy influence is even greater.
- Individual contributions allow donors to influence policy through the type of nonprofit activity they support; earmarking funds for a specific purpose within an organization further enhances the impact.
- Endowments provide a stable source of revenue through investment income; endowments involve a policy tradeoff between using funds to invest for future needs rather than using them to serve current needs.

major campaign to increase scholarship funding. How nice it would be to endow a scholarship in the name of his parents, who were so instrumental to his achieving the financial success that enables him to donate the $1 million. Scholarships could be awarded to students pursuing a degree in their chosen field of study. Think of the impact those generations of college graduates could have. Is that the best way to give? There are a lot of options for a budding philanthropist, so what should he do?

Deciding how and where to give money may be a dilemma for some potential philanthropists, but obtaining sources of funding is an issue of concern for nearly all nonprofits. Many nonprofits struggle with maintaining the basic organizational capacity to operate their programs to pursue their mission. Fundraising campaigns consume resources as well as generate them, so they must be chosen and executed wisely. Commercial ventures are growing in popularity but raise important public policy issues, as they serve to further blur the lines between the nonprofit and for-profit sectors. These and other aspects of resource development for nonprofits are the focus of Chapter 9.

FISCAL HEALTH AND CAPACITY

For more than 50 years, *Giving USA* has collected data and reported on annual changes in philanthropy and charitable giving. According to their analyses, charitable giving was an estimated $298.42 billion in 2011, which represents an increase of 4.0 percent from 2010, and reflects the modest economic recovery. The revised contributions data for 2009, however, indicated that giving decreased by 6.2 percent (adjusted for inflation) between 2008 and 2009, the steepest decline in real dollars since *Giving USA* began annual reports in 1956. This decline exceeded the 5.5 percent plunge of 1974, the midpoint of the recession of 1973–1975. On a more positive note, charitable giving was 1.8 percent of Gross Domestic Product (GDP) in 1974; by 2010, it was 2.0 percent of GDP.[2]

Nonprofit Sustainability

According to the U.S. Small Business Administration (SBA), approximately half of all new small businesses fail within their first five years and only about 25 percent survive 15 years or more.[3] Comparable data on the voluntary sector are much more limited, but a study by the Urban Institute suggests that not-for-profit organizations fare better, with approximately 70 percent surviving more than 10 years.[4] Even small nonprofits are more likely to survive than small businesses. Elizabeth T. Boris and Katie L. Roeger analyzed 1997–2007 data for 63,495 small public charities[5] and found that 37.6 percent either got smaller (fell below the $25,000 reporting threshold) or dissolved.[6]

Prior to 2008, only those organizations with more than $5,000 in annual revenues were required to register or report to the Internal Revenue Service (IRS), and only those making more than $25,000 had to file the Form 990.[7] As a result, a very small nonprofit that did not meet the reporting threshold could cease operations but have no corresponding paperwork to reflect its change in status, making it even more difficult to ascertain the long-term viability of these organizations. However, because of changes brought about under the Pension Protection Act, as of 2008, all tax-exempt organizations (other than churches) must file an e-postcard; failure to submit the required information for three years in a row results in automatic revocation of tax-exemption. Data from the e-postcard and the automatic revocation provision are expected to make it easier to track long-term sustainability within the sector.

In their oft-cited work on resource dependency theory,[8] Pfeffer and Salancik state that "the key to organizational survival is the ability to acquire and maintain resources."[9] While seemingly obvious, this simple prescription is often difficult for nonprofits to achieve. As shown in Table 9.1, there is great disparity in resources among nonprofits based on size. Small nonprofits include about 30 percent of all reporting public charities but represent less than one percent of total revenues, expenses, and assets.

In 2007, the average reporting charity had about $4 million in revenues, in stark contrast to the average small nonprofit that had approximately $45,000 in revenues,[10] which is hardly enough to sustain one full-time staff person. This is particularly important considering that presence of a paid staff person has been found to be a key attribute of organizational capacity, leading to successful fulfillment of a nonprofit's mission.[11] Paul Light's survey of nonprofit employees found that more than 40 percent believed their organizations rarely or only

Table 9.1 Resource Disparities by Size of Nonprofit

Year	Organization Size	Average Revenue	Percent of All Organizations	Percent of Total Spending*
2007	Small	$45,000	30%	Less than 1%
	Average	$4,000,000		
2009	Budget Less than $500,000		74.4%	2.1%
	Budget $10 Million or Larger		3.9%	85.3%

Source: 2007 data from: Elizabeth T. Boris and Katie L. Roeger, "Grassroots Civil Society: The Scope and Dimensions of Small Public Charities," *Charting Civil Society: A Series by the Center on Nonprofits and Philanthropy* (Washington, DC: The Urban Institute, 2010); 2009 data from: Katie L. Roeger, Amy Blackwood, and Sarah L. Pettijohn, *The Nonprofit Sector in Brief: Public Charities, Giving, and Volunteering, 2011* (Washington, DC: The Urban Institute, 2011).
* Includes spending by all reporting public charities.

sometimes provided enough employees to do the job well, and 70 percent agreed that there was always too much work to do.[12]

The Nonprofit Finance Fund (NFF) conducts an annual survey on the fiscal health of the nonprofit sector. Results of the 2010 survey indicate that of the 1,315 nonprofits responding (more than two-thirds of which had 2009 expenses of $2 million or less), most were struggling in the midst of very difficult economic conditions:

- Only 18 percent of respondents expected to operate without a deficit for the year;
- 89 percent expected 2010 to be at least as difficult financially as 2009;[13]
- almost 60 percent of respondents expected government funding to decrease;
- 55 percent expected funding from foundation and United Way sources to decrease;
- 26 percent of respondents said they received federal government stimulus funding in 2009, but only 32 percent expected to be able to replace those funds when depleted;[14]
- 61 percent of respondents have cash reserves to cover less than three months of expenses; 12 percent of them have no cash reserves.[15]

The responses regarding cash-on-hand are particularly troubling when considering that small nonprofits often struggle with obtaining adequate funding for basic operating expenses. However, the results of the 2012 survey (4,607 respondents, 65 percent of whom had 2011 expenses of $2 million or less) indicate signs of recovery and even growth for nonprofits as economic conditions improve:

- While 82 percent of respondents to the 2010 survey indicated they expected to operate with a deficit for 2010, only 34 percent of respondents to the 2012 survey actually ended 2010 with a deficit; the percent of 2012 respondents who experienced a year-end deficit declined for each of the previous three years, from 36 percent in 2009 to 31 percent in 2011.
- In 2011, 45 percent of respondents received federal government funding or contracts; 57 percent received state and/or local government funding or contracts.[16]
- The situation regarding cash-on-hand has improved each year since 2009; while 14 percent had no cash reserves in 2009, only 9 percent reported no cash-on-hand for 2012. Additionally, respondents with cash reserves to last 3 months or less decreased from 62 percent in 2009 to 57 percent in 2012.[17]

While funding issues are always important for nonprofits, in times of economic crisis the ability to establish and maintain a stable revenue stream is more challenging and the risks regarding organizational survival are much higher.

RESOURCE DEPENDENCE AND REVENUE DIVERSIFICATION

As has been discussed throughout this book, nonprofit organizations make their mission-related, service delivery decisions within the dynamic context of the environment they inhabit. For example, media coverage of natural disasters such as Hurricanes Katrina and Sandy highlighted the work of animal welfare nonprofits in the rescue and sheltering of homeless pets, resulting in more donations at a time of increased demand for service. Conversely, the recent economic downturn has significantly augmented the demand for housing services provided by emergency shelters, without a corresponding influx of financial resources. Nonprofits often compete with one another for available resources, such as government funding, foundation grants, and individual contributions. Public policy changes such as tax laws affecting deductibility of charitable donations as well as stock market declines that reduce the size of endowments are external factors with far-reaching consequences for the sector as a whole. Revenue diversification is a strategy long advocated for nonprofits as a means of spreading the risk of vulnerability in times of economic crisis.[18]

However, there are those who contend that diversification has negative implications for nonprofits. Multiple revenue streams have been shown to create inefficiencies for nonprofits—for example, the impact of non-uniform administrative and reporting requirements.[19] Commercial ventures—a growing source of income for the sector and increasingly popular method of diversifying resources—have critics who argue these activities move the organization's focus from its mission, weaken the public nature of services, and may even call into question the justification for tax-exemption.[20]

Empirical research supports revenue diversification based on benefits theory, "which postulates that revenue streams derive from the nature of the services offered by nonprofit organizations."[21] Nonprofits tend to have a mix of revenue sources that reflects the nature of the goods and services provided by them; therefore, revenue diversification is actually a reflection of what they do. Organizations providing services of a public nature will rely more heavily on public sources of revenue; those providing private goods will have a corresponding degree of revenue from earned income. Because programming determines to a great extent the type of revenue sources most likely to be successfully pursued, nonprofits should integrate program planning with resource development.[22]

Sources of Revenue and Their Relation to Mission

Nonprofit scholars and practitioners categorize revenue sources in diverse ways. For example, public sources of funding generally refer to any government allocation—federal, state, or local—whether in the form of a grant, contract, or line-item appropriation; private sources are, therefore, all non-governmental revenues, including private donations, foundation grants, and proceeds from commercial ventures. Earned income includes the proceeds from commercial ventures such as a thrift shop, but also encompasses fees-for-service, sometimes generated through government contracts. Philanthropic gifts include individual donations, foundation grants, and corporate sponsorship of fundraising events; licensing agreements with corporate sponsors, however, would be an example of earned income. Clearly, attempts to classify the diverse types of nonprofits present challenges due to the potential for overlap, even within the six basic sources of nonprofit revenues we identify and discuss: (1) government grants and contracts; (2) foundation grants; (3) corporate giving or sponsorship; (4) individual contributions and fundraising events; (5) earned income and commercial ventures; and (6) endowments or other investment income.

While Form 990 data yield some information about the degree to which nonprofits rely on each of these sources, the available data are limited and may not adequately reflect how the majority of nonprofits obtain resources. For example, in 2009, 8.9 percent of revenues for reporting public charities came from government grants, with an additional 23.2 percent of total revenue coming from government sources in the form of fees for goods and services, including Medicare/Medicaid. Fees for goods and services from private sources (including tuition and admission tickets) constituted 52.4 percent of total revenue. Private contributions comprised 13.6 percent, with all other sources including investment income constituting the remaining 2.1 percent of total revenue.

These data paint a somewhat distorted picture of the sector, however. When the figures from Table 9.1 are taken into account, the fiscal disparity among different-sized nonprofits becomes clearer. Most reporting charities are relatively small and constitute a very small percentage of total spending. Conversely, the few very large organizations are responsible for the overwhelming majority of total spending. Since about 85 percent of the financial data reflect the revenue sources of only about four percent of the number of organizations, it would be unwise to conclude that very large charities (for example, hospitals and universities) have the same potential types of funding as small ones (for example, homeless shelters).

This illustrates one way in which the nature of the mission as well as size of the nonprofit are relevant to sources of funding. For example, because of their missions hospitals and universities are better able and much more likely to rely on fee-for-service income, whereas human services organizations cannot easily attach a price to their services; more importantly, they often seek to serve a clientele precisely because the individuals *cannot* afford to pay a fee. Hospitals and primary care facilities comprised 2.1 percent of reporting public charities in 2009 yet received 51.2 percent of revenues; human services nonprofits comprised 33.7 percent of charities yet took in only 13.3 percent of total revenues.[23] Although not-for-profit organizations have become quite creative in pursuing commercial ventures, many work in fields that do not lend themselves to generating earned income.

Since resource development is not a one-size-fits-all activity for nonprofits, the most important factor for them to consider is the relationship between resource development and their mission. Mission should always drive the pursuit of revenue sources and determine the revenue strategies selected; as discussed in Chapter 5, altering the nonprofit's mission in order to attract funding is a seductive but dangerous activity. Commercial ventures and other sources of earned income, as well as corporate giving, fundraising, and endowments, are each identified and discussed with regard to its relationship with nonprofit mission in the remaining sections of this chapter. Government grants and foundation funding are the focus of Chapter 10.

EARNED INCOME AS A STABLE SOURCE OF REVENUE

Earned income refers to various types of commercial activity in which a nonprofit is able to sell a product or service or charge a fee in order to generate revenue. Examples include Girl Scout cookie sales, tickets to a local symphony performance, and tuition for a nonprofit preschool. Raising revenues through earned income is attractive for nonprofits because the funds come with few if any restrictions on their use. Because the revenues are obtained through an exchange relationship in which the buyer was probably going to buy a similar good or service anyway, both parties gain something from the transaction. While not a new source of revenue for nonprofits—examples of nonprofit commercial activity date to the early 1900s—its popularity has been growing, due in part to the stability it offers.[24]

A positive finding of the 2010 Nonprofit Finance Fund survey was that approximately one-third of respondents expected funding from earned income sources to increase from 2009 levels.[25] Unfortunately, the question regarding earned income was not included in the 2011 Survey of the Sector to determine whether these expectations were met, but what the 2010 results illustrate is that earned income was viewed as the most stable revenue source by a majority of the more than 1,300 respondents to the survey. More than half of respondents expected government and foundation funding to decrease in 2010, and 44 percent of respondents expected corporate giving and sponsorships to decrease. In contrast, only 23 percent of respondents expected earned income levels to decrease, the same percentage who anticipated drops in individual and board giving.[26]

Commercial Ventures: Bake Sales to Thrift Shops

To make up for revenues lost from other sources is the primary justification cited by nonprofits as they undertake commercial ventures.[27] Whether the venture involves opening a thrift shop, launching a line of designer neckties based on fine works of art, or the ubiquitous bake sale—raised to national proportions with Share Our Strength's Great American Bake Sale (gabs.strength.org)—selling something is increasingly attractive if not necessary for today's nonprofits. Most scholars and practitioners in the field would agree that commercialism is a positive trend for the sector so long as the mission goals of the nonprofit remain paramount in the types of activities undertaken.

Government, nonprofit, and for-profit entities are increasingly engaged in partnerships, shared provision of services, and even competition with one another. With regard to commercial ventures, four primary areas of "blurred boundaries"[28] exist: (1) cross-subsidization of service delivery that does not generate revenue with activities that do produce net earned income, such as thrift shops and gift shops; (2) establishment of for-profit subsidiaries or affiliates, such as professional licensing exams administered by Prometric, a for-profit subsidiary of Educational Testing Services; (3) direct competition between for-profit and nonprofit organizations, such as child care centers; and (4) conversions, such as a nonprofit hospital which converts to for-profit status. Cross-subsidization is quite common and is growing in popularity, as reflected in the survey results regarding earned income discussed above. Conversions are still rare but are gaining momentum in the areas of education and health care, as the ability to charge fees and the need for greater capital expenditures are increasing.[29]

The Unrelated Business Income Tax (UBIT) discussed in Chapter 4 is of particular relevance in a nonprofit's decision to establish a for-profit partner. Although the IRS rules are vague, as a rule of thumb once 15 percent or more of a nonprofit's revenues are derived from unrelated sources, it is time to set up a for-profit subsidiary.[30] As discussed in earlier chapters, nonprofits enjoy a privileged status under the law that often affords them a financial advantage in business operations. Having a for-profit affiliate carry out the unrelated business activities alleviates some of the criticisms regarding unfair competition. Making sure that commercial ventures are closely tied to the organization's mission also helps allay concerns regarding appropriateness of the competition.[31]

Commercial ventures offer opportunity for a stable and unrestricted revenue source, but there are risks involved and no guarantee of success. With thrift shops, for example, nonprofits are increasingly competing not only with each other for donations of quality used goods, but with for-profit consignment shops which have grown in popularity during the recent economic downturn. Also, the greater the reliance on volunteer labor to make the venture succeed, the more challenges the nonprofit will face in recruiting and maintaining an adequate workforce.

Social Enterprises: Market Principles for Social Aims

Tying the commercial endeavor to a larger public service mission carries the benefits even further, as in the case of the Habitat for Humanity (Habitat) ReStore outlets. While ReStore outlets mirror the well-known thrift shop concept, they promote an additional mission of environmentalism and social responsibility. Donations include surplus building materials as well as items removed during home renovations that normally would be discarded in a landfill. ReStore outlets serve to reduce the volume of waste entering landfills by promoting reuse and recycling; many outlets even list the tonnage of waste diverted from landfills on their websites. The first Habitat for Humanity ReStore outlet opened in Austin, Texas, in 1992. By early 2012, the number of ReStores had grown to 825 outlets in 48 states.[32]

While the number of ReStore outlets has not yet reached 50 percent of total Habitat Affiliates, it likely will exceed that percentage in the near future because they are commercial ventures that embody a social purpose. This concept of social enterprise—loosely defined as ventures in which business methods are used to generate revenue to achieve social goals[33]—is growing in popularity. According to enp (enterprising non-profits), social enterprises are "businesses operated by non-profits with the dual purpose of generating income by selling a product or service in the marketplace and creating a social, environmental or cultural value."[34]

Social enterprises are started for reasons that range from strictly financial—to generate revenue for the parent nonprofit—to completely mission-focused, but usually fall somewhere in between. The Social Enterprise Lancashire Network (Selnet) requires demonstration of three primary characteristics before recognizing an organization as a social enterprise: (1) social aims; (2) direct involvement in business activity; and (3) ownership and governance by stakeholder groups with profits distributed among stakeholders or for the benefit of the community.[35] Ownership structure seems to be a point of contention among those debating an acceptable definition: some argue social enterprises must have collective ownership and/or nonprofit status, while others contend the definition should be broad enough to encompass private, for-profit organizations that embody the requisite social goals.[36] It is important to note that social enterprises, like other commercial ventures, involve risks. The for-profit market generally avoids an activity that does not generate revenue. Since social enterprises are by definition trying to make money while filling a social need that the market does not, there is inherent risk but also the opportunity to demonstrate that social aims can be achieved using market principles.

A compelling example involves Hart Community Homes (HCH), a Fullerton, California, nonprofit serving at-risk youth. Since 2005, HCH has operated the Monkey Business Café as a social enterprise. The Café meets the criteria of multiple definitions of social enterprise in that it: (1) uses a business model (food service) to generate revenue; (2) fills a social need that the market will not (job training for young men who have aged-out of the foster care system); and (3) reinvests profits to advance the organization's mission (the revenues generated support the job training efforts and further the mission of HCH to assist former foster children in their transition to adulthood). See Box 9.1 for more information on HCH and the Monkey Business Café.

Box 9.1

FOR EXAMPLE

MONKEY BUSINESS CAFÉ: BUILDING A SOCIAL ENTERPRISE

In 1996, Hart Community Homes (HCH) opened its doors as a residential facility to house foster care youth in Orange, California, paid for via state government contracts. With a mission "to heal, educate and empower at-risk youth to become healthy, productive and self-sufficient adults in the community," HCH serves the most difficult-to-place foster children: 13–18 year old boys. At age 18, California's foster youth are emancipated regardless of the fact that, according to the Children's Advocacy Institute at the University of San Diego School of Law, 65 percent of them age out with nowhere to live.[37] As HCH's executive director looked for better alternatives for the boys formerly in her care, it became clear that California had no services or programs to help emancipated youth make the transition to adulthood. At this point she and her board got creative and decided to launch a social enterprise that would serve her former residents in a way that state policy did not.

HCH was able to lease a large building for a reasonable price and in 2004, opened a thrift store where they could both raise money for HCH and employ boys who had aged out of the foster care system. Competition and a narrow profit margin in the thrift business caused HCH to rethink their commercial venture options, leading to closure of the thrift shop and opening of Monkey Business Café in late 2005. The café, which serves breakfast, lunch, and dinner, also provides a training ground for these at-risk youth to learn about workplace expectations, interaction with the public, and meaningful food service skills including cooking, baking, and catering. Originally a 90-day employment program, Monkey Business now has a minimum 6 month commitment with its employees, in the hope that the work experience and paychecks will lead to self-sufficiency for young men leaving foster care but lacking a familial support system.

While the state of California has subsequently made grants available to some counties to help emancipated foster children with transitional housing, there are still no government job training/workforce development programs targeted to this high-risk population. Thus, Monkey Business must rely on traditional state Workforce Development Grants, private donations, and income from the café to provide the employment opportunities, training, and job readiness services needed by their clients. One thing that sets this social enterprise apart from many others is that both sides, HCH and Monkey Business Café, are under the same organizational structure, and both serve the same populations: young men in need and without family support. The proceeds from the café (as of 2012 there was still no financial profit) are funneled back into the salaries, job programs, and mentoring services that are the organization's mission.

In some ways the café is at a disadvantage in relation to private sector competitors because it cannot follow the standard business model. For example, managers of traditional restaurants staff a minimal number of employees and if business is slow, employees are sent home to maximize profits. At Monkey Business, however, without steady income the young men would never attain self-sufficiency; in order to fulfill its mission a full workforce is used at all times.

On the other hand, as the executive director explains, the social enterprise side of HCH/ Monkey Business Café "gives you the freedom to do what you need to do." Rather than be restricted by state or county policies on who can be served and in what capacity, the fact that Monkey Business earns its own income allows it to fulfill its vision, "To provide the necessary continuum of care to youth in and emancipating out of the foster care system in order to eliminate homeless at-risk youth and adults in the community."

For more information see: www.hartcommunityhomes.org/index.html

THE ROLE OF CORPORATE GIVING AND SPONSORSHIP

As a business owner, our fictitious friend Tom from the opening vignette was well acquainted with requests from local nonprofits for donations. Early in his company's history he established a budget for charitable giving and delineated the specific organizations to be supported. Corporate giving programs, also referred to as corporate philanthropy, generally involve cash or in-kind contributions to not-for-profit organizations and increasingly include support of volunteer efforts by employees.

These giving programs are separate from corporate foundations (discussed further in Chapter 10); they are generally administered by corporate staff using operating budget funds. As such, corporate giving programs usually do not have a separate endowment, and disbursal of funds tends to fluctuate with company profits.[38] The Committee to Encourage Corporate Philanthropy (CECP), in their annual *Giving in Numbers* survey, found that 67 percent of corporate respondents reported decreased profits from 2007 to 2008, and 60 percent reported decreased giving in 2009. However, regression analysis on survey data from a four-year matched set of 95 companies failed to establish a statistical link between annual profits and giving. These results should be interpreted with caution, however. A four-year matched set of data provides for relevant comparisons over time, but the small number of companies included in the set raises concerns about the ability to generalize the findings.[39] From a research standpoint, further study is required to empirically establish this relationship; from a practical standpoint, nonprofits should expect lower levels of corporate giving when corporate profits are in decline.

Why Corporations Give

Started in 1999, CECP is a nonprofit based in New York dedicated to improving corporate philanthropy by focusing on leaders within the business community. Membership in the organization includes more than 170 CEOs and chairpersons of companies that comprise more than 40 percent of all corporate giving in the United States. In 2008, CECP released a report based largely on research by McKinsey & Company, which included in-depth interviews with 24 CEO's and executives as well as a global survey of more than 700 business executives regarding their companies' philanthropic efforts. Among the findings were that

84 percent of international respondents believe society expects businesses to be more actively involved in addressing social, political, and environmental issues than in the past; 75 percent of respondents identified corporate philanthropy as an effective means to accomplish that.[40]

CECP's *Giving in Numbers: 2010 Edition* was based on corporate giving information provided by 170 companies, including 61 of the *Fortune* top 100 publicly traded companies in the United States. According to these data, the median total giving by all 170 companies was $19.26 million; the median for the *Fortune* 100 companies was $56.03 million. Aggregate giving to match employee charitable contributions represented a median of 13.38 percent of total cash giving by the 170 companies; these companies gave a median total of $556 per employee.[41]

Christina Gold, CEO of Western Union Company, in an interview with *The Chronicle of Philanthropy,* noted that corporate philanthropy has moved beyond the traditional method of simply presenting an oversized check to a worthwhile cause, and that there is a growing interest in partnerships to address issues of mutual concern. In the case of Western Union, she stated

> We engage in philanthropy because it is the right thing to do and are not looking for a business return in the traditional sense. However, we have aligned our corporate citizenship with our brand and identity as a corporation. As a business, we create tremendous economic opportunity.[42]

Aligning corporate citizenship refers to the tendency among corporations to channel their philanthropy dollars to causes and issues that are related in some degree to their business interests. In the case of Federal Express, for example, the company focuses its corporate giving in three main areas: (1) emergency and disaster relief (requests for free shipping are granted almost exclusively in this area); (2) child pedestrian safety; and (3) environmental sustainability, primarily in the area of transportation solutions.[43]

The Influence of Corporate Philanthropy

The 2010 edition of CECP's annual *Giving in Numbers* includes data for 95 companies that completed surveys in 2008 and 2009; major findings from analysis of the matched-set data include

- A majority of companies gave less in 2009 than the previous year; however, aggregate giving increased by 7 percent in 2009, due primarily to substantial increases in donations of medicine by pharmaceutical companies.
- A majority of companies decreased funding for international recipients, but the typical manufacturing company gave approximately 25 percent of its philanthropy budget to international causes.
- Almost half of all companies increased their matching-gifts programs between 2008 and 2009.

- More than half of the companies reduced the administrative costs associated with their giving program, most of them by at least ten percent.
- In 2007, 46 percent of respondent's companies offered paid-release time for employees to volunteer; by 2009, 64 percent of the companies offered paid-release volunteer time programs.

The McKinsey & Company analysis found that the most effective corporate philanthropy programs had three primary things in common. They are ones in which the CEO provides active leadership, the giving program is structured in conjunction with the overall business strategy, and where corporate philanthropy is viewed as an investment in the business of the company.[44] In the case of FedEx cited above, more than 75,000 company vehicles are on the road every day; enhancing pedestrian safety and awareness, particularly among children, has direct bearing on the daily operations of the company.[45] Corporations are increasingly aware of the dangers of paying too little attention to social responsibility. Not only can their choice of causes as well as giving levels affect market share, but there is some evidence to suggest that corporate philanthropy has an impact on the ability to recruit and retain employees, as well.[46]

Corporate philanthropy is generally considered a win-win situation for the corporate partners and the nonprofits that receive funding from them. Whether it involves enough ice cream sandwiches to feed 150 kids at the annual farm safety day camp or $15,000 in matching funds to buy playground equipment, nonprofits rely on corporate partners in a myriad of ways. When the mission of the nonprofit organization meshes with the company's product or services, the nonprofit's ability to influence policy is enhanced beyond just the ability to deliver more services with greater resources. In the case of FedEx, for example, the company partners with SafeKids Worldwide, a global nonprofit focused on preventing unintentional childhood injury.[47] FedEx is the sponsor of the nonprofit's Safe Kids Walk This Way program; through grants to establish task forces in local communities, FedEx and Safe Kids Worldwide provide funding to community leaders to determine what projects would best facilitate a safer, more walkable community, especially for children.

INDIVIDUAL CONTRIBUTIONS AND FUNDRAISING

Individual contributions can take the form of cash placed in the Salvation Army kettle or a check mailed to the World Wildlife Fund, but can also encompass donations of used clothing to Goodwill, canned goods to a food bank, and pledges raised for the annual bike-a-thon. While often the first type of revenue that comes to mind with regard to nonprofits, private contributions accounted for just over 10 percent of total nonprofit revenue in 2008, as reported to the IRS. It is important to note that IRS data exclude churches, which are not required to file the IRS Form 990. According to the 2011 edition of *Giving USA* (which does collect data on donations to churches), for 55 years religion has received the lion's share of charitable contributions—33 percent of total giving in 2009. While churches rely almost exclusively on individual contributions, it is likely that small nonprofits also rely on private donations to a disproportionately greater degree than larger ones. According to the Nonprofit Research Collaborative (NRC) February 2011 survey of more than 1,600 nonprofits, 36 percent of the smallest organizations received 75 percent or more of their contributions from individual donors.[48] Changes in giving patterns by individuals, therefore, are more likely to have serious consequences for small as compared to larger organizations. Since 96 percent of NRC respondents indicated they relied on individual contributions to some extent for their budget, how and why donors choose to contribute is an important topic for almost all nonprofits.

Individuals, either through direct contributions or bequests, gave over $242 billion dollars to nonprofits in 2011; this represents 81 percent of total charitable giving for that year.[49] The idea that individuals are more likely to donate when they have a stake in an organization[50] is supported by the NRC study which found that 87 percent of nonprofits reported contributions by board members, as compared with only 18 percent receiving contributions as the result of telephone solicitations. Other major sources of donations received were special events (80 percent of respondents), major gifts (77 percent), and online (74 percent). Among those who used telephone solicitation, only 25 percent reported an increase in donations for 2010; 58 percent of those who used online applications to receive donations reported an increase.[51]

Individual contributions are obviously important to nonprofits, particularly small organizations. As can be seen from the NRC study results above, people contribute to nonprofits primarily because they have established some sort of relationship with the organization. The nature of the relationship can be a long association as with board members or a new affiliation because someone asked them to attend a special event fundraiser. Major gifts—whether through a sizable donation for a specific project or as a bequest in a will—are usually the result of active cultivation of a relationship with the prospective donor.

The process of fundraising, also known as fund development, has its risks as well as rewards. Risks with major gifts may arise when the donor seeks too much control over the funds donated or when the donor stipulates a use of the donation that is contrary to the mission of the organization. In that case, it is in the best interest of the organization to decline the contribution, which can be quite a delicate matter to handle.[52] There are the risks that the process of raising the money will incur expenses that exceed the revenues generated, as noted in the discussion below of special events fundraising. The most serious risk to a nonprofit, though, is the same as with other types of revenue—the risk of mission drift. When a nonprofit receives an influx of individual contributions earmarked for a specific purpose, as in the case of the Red Cross following the events of September 11, 2001 (discussed further below), disbursing the funds for the purpose specified can be a particular challenge and the organization risks loss of credibility if the funds are not utilized as intended.

Using Electronic Media to Solicit Contributions

Idealware is a 501(c)(3) organization established to provide "thoroughly researched, impartial and accessible resources" to assist nonprofits in making decisions about software (www

.idealware.org/about). In November 2009, Idealware conducted a survey of 459 staff members at nonprofits that were currently using some form of social media—Facebook, Twitter, MySpace, LinkedIn, video-sharing, photo-sharing, or blogs. Results indicate that while almost three-fourths of respondents felt social media were effective at enhancing relations with people who already knew their organization, only 26 percent felt social media tools were effective at raising money.[53]

Likewise, the Nonprofit Social Benchmark survey results indicate that less than three percent of the more than 11,000 respondent organizations raised more than $10,000 via Facebook in 2010. In contrast, however, 27 nonprofits reported Facebook contributions in excess of $100,000; 30 percent of those nonprofits had annual budgets of $1 to $5 million.[54] The trend appears to be toward increased online giving. GuideStar reports that in 1999, the largest U.S. charities received total online donations of $7 million, approximately 1 percent of their total contributions. By 2005, the amount had grown to $4.53 billion and represented 10 to 15 percent of total fundraising.[55] According to a survey by *The Chronicle of Philanthropy*, 140 of the top large nonprofits (ranked by funds raised from private sources) generated a total of $1.2 billion in online contributions in 2010, up from $887 million in 2009.[56]

Organizations seeking to increase contributions through electronic media sources need to carefully assess whether the anticipated increase in revenue will be sufficient to exceed the cost of operations. For example, Network for Good (www.networkforgood.org)—a nonprofit organized to assist other nonprofits in recruiting donors and volunteers online—charges fees for their services that as of mid-2012 included (1) a one-time account set-up fee of $199; (2) monthly fees of $49.95 to $99.00; and (3) 3 percent of each donation collected.[57] Similarly, nonprofits considering soliciting donations via text messaging—that is, mobile giving—should be aware that (1) their organization must have annual revenues in excess of $500,000 in order to qualify for mobile giving; (2) monthly fees range from $100 to $500 but can usually be arranged on a month-to-month rather than annual basis, meaning they can be activated for short campaigns if necessary; and (3) maximum donation amounts are generally $5 to $10, depending on the mobile carrier, so organizations need a substantial volume of donors to recoup the operational costs.[58]

The Gift of Giving

In a related vein are situations in which individuals are foregoing gifts to celebrate milestone occasions, soliciting contributions for nonprofits instead. For example, the for-profit tech company Causes (www.causes.com) makes charity gift cards available in some grocery stores in California for those who want to give the gift of giving. In addition, their Birthday Wishes campaign has generated over $11 million for nonprofits; through the campaign, individuals are invited to donate their birthday by asking friends and family members to make a contribution to their specified charity instead of giving them a gift.[59] Probably the most high-profile example in 2011 of donations in lieu of gifts is The Prince William & Miss Catherine Middleton Charitable Gift Fund. For the first time, a royal couple requested that those who wished to give them a wedding gift do so in the form of a donation to their fund to support one of the 26 charities active in the five issue areas identified as important to them.[60] Donations were accepted via the website between March 16th and May 31st; more than £550,000 was donated to the fund by wedding guests and members of the public.[61] While this type of giving has increased in popularity, it is not likely to be a stable source of revenue for nonprofits because they are not actively involved in generating it.

Special Events Fundraising

Social media outlets are not the only fundraising tools for which organizations need to look closely at operational costs. As anyone who has organized a bake sale or golf tournament knows, special events provide great marketing as well as fundraising opportunities, but they usually require a significant amount of human and financial resources to accomplish successfully. As Charity Navigator's 2007 Special Events Study indicates, the cost of conducting special events often outweighs the funds generated by them.

On May 1, 2007, Charity Navigator published the results of its study of those organizations within its database that accurately reported contributions from special events on their 2006 Form 990. They found that: (1) 49 percent of the charities studied use special events fundraising; (2) approximately 15 percent of total contributions were generated by special events; and (3) special events are almost always an inefficient means of raising funds. On average, for every dollar earned in special events contributions, the charities spent $1.33. Religious organizations, who are the least likely to use special events fundraising, are the most efficient, whereas health and arts organizations, which are the most likely to conduct special events fundraisers, are the least efficient. Complicating the analysis, however, is the finding that 46 percent of charities are clearly reporting their special events financial information incorrectly.[62]

In deciding whether, as a nonprofit to conduct a special event, or as a donor to participate in one rather than make a direct contribution, it is important to also consider the intangible benefits of special events. A gala Fur Ball event can be as much a way of rewarding animal welfare supporters and recognizing shelter volunteers as raising funds. A sand sculpting competition has significant expenses associated with it, but it is also likely to receive good press coverage for the not-for-profit organization. Some events, like the American Cancer Society's Relay for Life are successful at raising money as well as generating intangible benefits. In 2006, Relay for Life was the highest grossing special event in the Charity Navigator study, generating $352,193,452; this was also an efficient fundraiser, costing only $0.11 for every $1 raised.[63] Relay for Life raises awareness about cancer and offers emotional support to survivors, their friends and families, as well as to those who have lost loved ones to the disease. As discussed in Chapter 8, special events can also be successful marketing tools for nonprofits.

An innovative way to overcome the costliness of special event fundraising is to generate economies of scale by hosting an event to benefit nonprofits community-wide. In 1997, the Community Foundation of Jackson Hole's Old Bill's Fun Run for Charities was the first event of its kind in the United States. That first year, Old Bill's Fun Run generated more than

$1.8 million; the 2011 total was $7.75 million. Each annual Fun Run has generated more funds than the previous year, and more than $82.5 million has been raised for local nonprofits in its first 15 years.[64]

Events such as Old Bill's Fun Run are a way to address donors' concerns about efficiency—specifically whether a direct contribution would be a more efficient way to donate than by participating in a special event—because they use contributions as matching funds to leverage additional donations. Old Bill's Fun Run was initiated by an anonymous couple (known to the community as Mr. and Mrs. Old Bill), who proposed the idea when they gave their first matching gift. Each year Mr. and Mrs. Old Bill donate the first $500,000 and then co-challengers are recruited to enhance the pool of matching funds; the Community Foundation of Jackson Hole then challenges the community to give. Area nonprofits solicit individual donations to be matched by the challenge funds, leading up to the events of Fun Run Day, which include 2K, 5K, and 10K races as well as information booths provided by participating nonprofits. Matching funds are distributed based on a formula which depends on the total amount of challenge funds raised as well as the funds generated by the participating nonprofits. In 2011, the challenge funds totaled $2,264,887 and the designated contributions from 2,790 donors totaled $5,485,225. This resulted in a 54 percent matching grant to each of the 200 participating nonprofit organizations.[65] More information on Old Bill's Fun Run and the Community Foundation of Jackson Hole may be found at www.cfjacksonhole.org.

Old Bill's Fun Run is not only an example of a consistently successful nonprofit fundraising event, it is a model for how the local nonprofit community can share the expense of fundraising and minimize the negative effects of competing for revenues from a common pool of donors. Too many fundraising events run the risk of inducing fatigue in a community. Potential donors can easily grow weary of being asked to buy yet another item through silent auction, and new nonprofits often scramble to choose a unique event to compete with the 5K's and Fur Ball galas of the long-established organizations. While nonprofits are still likely to host individual fundraisers that reflect in some way on the mission of the organization, community-wide fundraising events such as Old Bill's Fun Run have great potential for the nonprofit community overall.

ENDOWMENTS PROMOTE LONG-TERM VIABILITY

Endowments provide income to nonprofits through the proceeds of their long-term investment and are the final source of revenue to be discussed in this chapter. Nonprofit organizations benefit from having an endowment due to the security of the stable revenue stream that it provides. Revenues are not guaranteed, of course; they are subject to the rate of risk inherent in the investment strategies chosen. When properly established and maintained, endowments can be a valuable tool to ensure the long-term viability of the programs offered by the organization, as well as providing for ongoing maintenance of buildings and materials pertinent to the nonprofit's mission. Endowments can be established with funds for a single donor, as a result of a fundraising campaign aimed at multiple donors, or can be compiled from excess revenues generated by the nonprofit's operations.

Legal Restrictions on Endowments

While commonly understood to be funds invested to provide ongoing income for a nonprofit, endowments are defined in a legal sense based primarily on whether use of the funds are restricted by the donor at the time of endowment. Under the Uniform Management of Institutional Funds Act (UMIFA) of 1972, endowment "refers to a restricted fund whose specifications at the time of the original gift require that the funds are not wholly expendable on a current basis."[66] In this sense, endowments are restricted funds designated by their donor to be invested and a portion of the proceeds disbursed over time for a specified charitable purpose. The Uniform Prudent Management of Institutional Funds Act (UPMIFA) is a revised and updated version of UMIFA that provides guidance and restrictions to nonprofit boards on issues such as investment of funds and expenditures of earnings.[67] As of June 2011, all 50 states had enacted UPMIFA.[68]

One of the primary differences between UMIFA and UPMIFA is the restriction regarding the amount of funds which can be expended from the endowment each year. Under UMIFA, boards had to protect the "historic dollar value" (HDV) of the endowment—that is, the dollar value of the original and subsequent donations to the specified purpose. While initially considered prudent guidance, in severe economic times the provision proved a serious hurdle. The stock market declines in 2001–2002 and 2008–2009 placed many endowments underwater—the term used to describe a situation in which the current value of investments is below the value of the original donation(s)—and the charities that relied upon them were unable to draw from their fund at a time of corresponding budget crisis. UPMIFA addresses this situation by removing the HDV requirement and giving boards the ability to expend "in good faith" as much of the endowment funds as they deem prudent.[69] Some states have adopted an optional provision that prevents expenditure of more than 7 percent of an endowment in one year or requires notification of the attorney general if the charity plans spending that would reduce the endowment below its HDV.[70]

The UPMIFA only applies to endowments as specifically defined in the act—that is, funds restricted by the donor. Funds that are combined from various sources and designated by board members to serve as an endowment are referred to as quasi-endowments and are not subject to the same legal restrictions.[71] For example, if Tom from the opening vignette donated $50,000 to endow a scholarship to benefit a student studying engineering, the university would be subject to the provisions of UPMIFA in administering the endowment. In contrast, if one of the ReStore outlets discussed above had a particularly good year and sales revenue exceeded current operating expenses, the Habitat board could place the excess revenues in its building fund endowment; these funds would be considered unrestricted and not subject to UPMIFA, which means they could be withdrawn and spent completely at the board's discretion.

Nonprofits are not required by law to report the size of their endowments, so data are difficult to obtain. However, on June 2, 2011, *The Chronicle of Philanthropy* published the

Box 9.2

FOR EXAMPLE

THE MILTON HERSHEY SCHOOL TRUST: ENDOWING A BETTER FUTURE

The Hershey Chocolate Company began operations in 1894; in 1909, Milton and Catherine Hershey established a boarding school for orphan boys and established the Milton Hershey School Trust to provide funding. Initially, the Hersheys endowed the Trust with farmland and related accoutrements of the Homestead, Milton Hershey's birthplace. Following the death of his wife in 1915, Hershey transferred most of his wealth—$60 million in Hershey's Chocolate Company stock as well as other assets—to the School Trust in what has been referred to as one of the largest philanthropic gestures of the century.

The School Trust has grown tremendously over the last 100 years. By mid-2011, Hershey's endowment had grown in value to over $8 billion. According to their 2008 Form 990, the Milton Hershey School Trust held 32.2 percent of the total outstanding Common Stock and Class B Common Stock in Hershey's Chocolate Company; this in effect means that the School Trust controls 80 percent of the voting power, thereby making the trust the company's largest shareholder. In addition to chocolate company stock, the trust has 100 percent ownership in the Hershey Entertainment & Resorts Company (HERCO). As these for-profit entities prosper, the Milton Hershey School Trust and the school's students do likewise.

From an initial size of 486 acres and enrollment of 10 boys, the Milton Hershey School has grown to encompass a 2,640-acre campus and enrollment of more than 1,800 underprivileged boys and girls (the original Deed of Trust was modified during the 1970s to allow admission of female and minority students). According to the explanation of mission on Schedule O of the 2008 Form 990, the mission of the Milton Hershey School is to provide "children in financial and social need with an education, housing, food, clothing, medical and psychological health care, and recreational opportunities." Neither the children nor their families are charged tuition or fees, and all students come from families living at or below the federal poverty line. Children as young as four years old are accepted at the School, which educates students from pre-K through 12th grade. The more than 140 student homes are each staffed with full-time, live-in house parents and accommodate 8 to 12 students each. In addition to a free pre-K to 12 education, students are also given the opportunity to earn scholarship credits toward college expenses based on annual academic performance and certain other conditions. In 2008, the trust made college tuition payments in excess of $5 million dollars for 458 students; an additional 862 students accrued more than $2.77 million in tuition credits for future college expenses.

More information on Catherine and Milton Hershey, the Milton Hershey School, and the Hershey School Trust can be found by accessing (1) the school website at www.mhs-pa.org/about; (2) the Hershey's Chocolate Company website at www.hersheys.com and click on *A History of Happiness;* and (3) the website for the Hershey Trust Company at www.hersheytrust.com and click on *Cornerstones—About Hershey Trust Company* and *the Hershey Heritage.*

results of its eighth annual survey of nonprofits and foundations with the largest endowments; 213 organizations provided data for the survey. The 2010 market value of the endowments held by all respondents totaled $340.2 billion; the Bill & Melinda Gates Foundation had the largest endowment, at $36.7 billion. Among respondents, the median rate of return on investments in 2010 was 9.4 percent; the United Way of Greater Rochester (NY) had the highest rate of return at 37.5 percent, while the United Way of Central Maryland (Baltimore) had the lowest at –7.1 percent. While most respondents represented private foundations, some notable examples of charitable endowments include the American Heart Association ($39.7 million), the Houston Ballet ($56.36 million), the Nashville Symphony ($72.24 million), the New York Public Library ($678 million), and Princeton University ($14.4 billion).[72]

For organizations such as the Milton Hershey School, endowments not only provide funds for establishment and basic maintenance but can generate revenue to serve clients beyond the donor's expectations. The $60 million that Milton Hershey donated to the School Trust in 1915, for example, is part of an endowment that exceeded $8 billion in 2011; the trust and the school it supports are discussed further in Box 9.2. Endowments are not without their detractors, however. Some scholars and practitioners argue that endowment funds should be spent to benefit the current generation rather than accumulated by foundations and not-for-profit organizations for future needs.[73] While the overwhelming majority of foundations indicate plans to exist in perpetuity, attention has focused recently on what some believe is a growing trend toward limited life foundations.[74] Issues of perpetuity and payout are discussed further in Chapter 10.

THE POLICY IMPLICATIONS OF CHARITABLE GIVING

Every charitable contribution has at least passive public policy implications; a dollar given to one nonprofit is a dollar denied to the pursuit of another one's mission. Given the growing number of nonprofit organizations and proliferation of donation options, the policy implications of nonprofit funding are increasingly important. Nonprofits strapped for cash may choose funding options that strain their pursuit of mission. Conversely, nonprofits that suddenly find themselves flush with cash from the benevolence of a large gift may struggle with how best to enhance their public interest mission with the new largesse. For example, Ruth Lilly (the pharmaceutical heiress) gave $175 million to the Modern Poetry Association in 2002. At the time the gift was announced, the annual budget of association was $600,000 and its primary activity was publication of *Poetry Magazine.* Obviously, the gift altered the operations of the nonprofit as well as its defined mission, but it also led some to question the public benefit of the gift and whether the funds would be better spent elsewhere.[75] In this case, a favorite line from a movie comes to mind, "More isn't always better . . . sometimes it's just more."[76]

More is not always better even with regard to disaster relief. In the case of the devastating earthquake and tsunami that hit Japan in early 2011, for example, the nonprofit charity watchdog GiveWell.org advised prospective donors to wait before deciding to give, based in part on a belief that even terrible disasters can be over-funded. Unlike the South Asian

GOING GLOBAL 9.3

More Donations Aren't Always Better when Responding to Natural Disasters

When disaster strikes, the public's generosity is magnified. The advent of cable news further enhanced this tendency as we are provided with almost immediate and overwhelming images of devastation and suffering brought about by natural disasters. Recent earthquakes and tsunamis that wreaked havoc half a world away from the United States illustrate the tendency of people to open their hearts and their wallets to help those in need, whether at home or abroad. However, it is not always possible to make things better with a charitable donation. Unlike the dire need in Haiti following the earthquake that leveled much of that impoverished nation, more donations were not likely to significantly affect disaster relief in Japan following the tsunami of early 2011 because the country already had significant resources to commit to recovery efforts.

In contrast with Haiti, whose government announced an appeal for $562 million in assistance three days after the earthquake devastated the tiny island, no official appeal for assistance was released by the Japanese government within the first four days after the massive tsunami engulfed the country in March 2011. The lack of government request for assistance coupled with the Japanese Red Cross statement that they were not seeking external assistance led GiveWell.org to issue a recommendation not to donate to charities soliciting donations for the tsunami relief effort because those donations would likely be used for other purposes. Specifically, the position of GiveWell was that "the people and government of Japan are extraordinarily well-prepared, as well as competent and well-resourced, and do not need significant external assistance . . . [t]herefore, you as a donor do not have the power to improve the relief and recovery effort in Japan." For those who still wanted to make a donation, Doctors without Borders was the recommended option, because they were not soliciting donations specifically for tsunami relief and were explicit that donations to them would be used for their general international relief efforts.[77]

All giving has policy implications, and in this case, the likelihood that donations solicited for one purpose would be used for another led a charity watchdog organization to encourage potential donors to redirect their largesse. For victims of the Japanese tsunami, more funding from donors probably would not have improved the disaster relief efforts. The desire to help, however, makes people susceptible to unscrupulous fundraisers; when the disaster is thousands of miles away, it is even more difficult for donors to ensure their contributions are used as intended. Organizations such as GiveWell.org therefore provide useful counsel for potential contributors.

For more information, go to www.givewell.org.

tsunami of 2004 or the earthquake that struck Haiti in 2010, the Japanese earthquake and tsunami disaster affected one of the world's wealthiest countries with better infrastructure and fewer logistical challenges. While the impact on victims was just as devastating, the Japanese government and philanthropists were in a much better position to handle the situation themselves, as discussed further in Going Global 9.3.[78]

Overfunding in the immediate wake of disaster was a lesson learned by Americans post-9/11. Immediately following the tragedies of September 11, 2001, several well-meaning celebrities rushed to organize a telethon to raise money for the victims and their families. Americans responded with typical generosity, some celebrities gave their own six-figure gifts, and much money was raised for a very good cause. The problems came with regard to disbursal of the funds. Because the funds were raised for a cause and not for a specific organization, the nonprofit infrastructure to disseminate the largesse was lacking. Even the well-established Red Cross experienced difficulties when faced with record amounts of blood donations and more funds designated for 9/11 relief than could be appropriately spent. When the Red Cross tried to use some of the funds generated through the solicitation of donations for 9/11 relief efforts for other purposes, a scandal erupted that ultimately led to the resignation of the CEO, Dr. Bernadine Healy.

As stated earlier, how we as individuals give affects public policy, often in ways we do not realize if the organizations are not properly researched before we write the check. For example, the devastating effects of Hurricane Katrina on New Orleans and parts of the Gulf Coast heightened awareness of the impact of natural disasters on pets. Many were moved by the images of dogs and cats that were abandoned when their owners were forced to evacuate without them. Several nonprofits solicited donations in order to rescue and care for those homeless pets. As with most nonprofits, contributions to animal-related causes have policy implications; Case Study 9.3 illustrates how four different animal-related nonprofits have different public policy orientations.

CASE STUDY 9.3

The Policy Implications of Donations in Support of Animal Causes

All charitable contributions have at least basic policy implications because a dollar donated to one organization is a dollar that is not contributed to any other organization; because nonprofits use their dollars to support a myriad of activities, the direct and indirect impact on public policy varies. For example, within the area of animal care and protection, dollars donated to seemingly similar nonprofits result in at least passive support for quite different policies. Before you write a check to a nonprofit to improve animal well-being (or for any cause, for that matter), it is important to make sure you agree with the philosophical orientation of the organization because your dollars will likely facilitate advocacy activities.

Animal-related nonprofits such as the American Society for the Prevention of Cruelty to Animals (ASPCA), the American Humane Association (AHA), the Humane Society of the U.S. (HSUS), and People for the Ethical Treatment of Animals (PETA) oppose cruelty to animals. Specifics as to what constitutes cruelty and how best to protect the well-being of animals vary among them, however. Organizations with an *animal welfare* perspective oppose cruelty to animals and view pets as private property whose owners have a duty to care for them with compassion. Individuals active in organizations with an *animal rights* perspective distinguish non-human animals as having legal and social rights on par with human animals and advocate guardianship rather than ownership of pets.[79] Variations in the policy stances of the four organizations are illustrated below using two issues: (1) mandatory spay/neuter ordinances and (2) use of animal actors.

Mandatory spay/neuter (MSN) laws are typically local government ordinances aimed at reducing the overpopulation of dogs and cats by requiring pet owners to sterilize their animals or pay a fine. Professional or hobby breeders—that is, individuals who breed and train dogs to be companion or working animals—are generally opposed to these ordinances because of the fines they face in order to continue to breed their dogs and the risk that an animal might be sterilized without their consent if it was lost and taken to an animal shelter. The ASPCA and the AHA support voluntary spay/neuter programs, but neither supports legislation that mandates sterilization of all dogs and cats.[80] HSUS supports mandatory spay/neuter laws.[81] PETA opposes the breeding of dogs and cats, particularly purebred dogs, and advocates for universal spaying/neutering.[82]

Animal actors are those trained to perform for public audiences, primarily in movies, television shows, and commercials. PETA opposes the use of live animals in film, considering all animal actors to be subjects of abuse by their trainers;[83] the Humane Society of the U.S. opposes the use of "captive wild animals" in film and television.[84] The ASPCA is not categorically opposed to animal actors so long as the animals are treated humanely.[85] Their manager of Shelter Behavior and Training, Victoria Wells, has trained animals for commercials and music videos as well as television, and is known for her work on the Animal Planet series *Animal Precinct*.[86] Finally, AHA is the group sanctioned by the Screen Actors Guild to protect animal actors. Through their regulations and on-site monitoring efforts, AHA is responsible for the presence (or notable absence) of the "no animals were harmed . . ." end credit in films.[87]

As these examples make clear, before donating to a cause it is important to review the philosophy and stance on policy issues of any nonprofit organization. In addition to reading information on mission and advocacy activities from each nonprofit's website, it is a good idea to check their ratings and financial information, as well as the reviews posted by previous donors available from watchdog groups such as Charity Navigator (www.charitynavigator.org) and GuideStar (www.guidestar.org). As of April 2012, the Charity Navigator star ratings (4 stars maximum) and overall scores (70 points maximum) for each organization were as follows: HSUS—4 stars, 60.73; AHA—3 stars, 59.31; ASPCA—3 stars, 59.09; and PETA—2 stars, 44.32.[88] Charity Navigator calculates the overall score using a complex formula that takes into account the nonprofit's financial health as well as its level of accountability and transparency. The formula is not simply a sum of the two component scores but rather takes into account the distance of each from a perfect score in order to ensure that a charity performs well on each component in order to receive a high overall score. Stars awarded relate to the overall score: nonprofits with an overall score of 60 or higher earn 4 stars, between 50 and 60 earn 3 stars, and so on.[89]

QUESTIONS TO CONSIDER:

1. Have you made a contribution to any of the organizations discussed above? Were you aware of the policy stances of the organization at the time you made the contribution? To what extent did the policy positions of the organization affect your decision to contribute or the amount of the contribution? If you have not contributed in the past, to which organization would you be the most likely to contribute? To what extent did the policy positions of the organization outlined above affect your choice of organization and/or the amount you would contribute?
2. For each of the four organizations discussed, identify the most likely and least likely sources of funding—including online contributions, special events, commercial ventures, corporate funding/sponsorship, or endowments. Explain.
3. Discuss how the amounts and sources of funding for animal rights vs. animal welfare nonprofits affect or have the potential to affect public policy related to animals, such as pets, service animals, farm animals, and others.
4. Consider the four relationships that describe nonprofit interaction with public policy (make policy, affected by policy, influence policy, subject to policy) and discuss the ways in which these relationships are reflected in the examples of the four animal-related organizations discussed above.
5. Is the situation of competing perspectives such as animal rights versus animal welfare unique among nonprofits active in the same policy issue area? Explain how competing perspectives could either facilitate or hinder public policy development.

CONCLUSION

While charitable giving has declined and endowments have suffered losses as a result of the recent recession, charitable giving represents more than 2 percent of GDP and people continue to respond with financial support in the face of economic and natural disasters. Giving is easier than ever with the advent of donations via text message and the ubiquitous Donate Now button throughout the web. As commercial ventures gain in popularity, nonprofits are faced with increased pressure to market profitable goods as well as charitable services. Corporations seek to enhance their image of social responsibility beyond writing checks for good causes; corporate giving and sponsorship of events involve increasing expectations of partnership rather than passive funding. While a financial benefit, types and sources of funding are important to more than just the bottom line for nonprofits.

As reflected throughout the chapter, resource development is about more than just paying the bills. Policy connotations pervade not just where the money goes, but from where it comes, as well. Commercial nonprofit ventures blur the lines with for-profit competitors; should government subsidize them with tax-exempt status? Endowments provide current tax deductions for donors but the benefits of the foregone tax revenue will not be felt by the public until sometime in the future. As stated in the opening, there are many options available to a budding philanthropist. Tom's $1 million dollar charitable donation is actually an investment—in current programs or for future needs. What would you advise?

Questions For Review

1. Discuss the importance of revenue diversification with regard to nonprofit capacity. Do you think greater diversity is a positive or a negative for nonprofits? Why? Does it depend on the type of nonprofit organization?
2. Discuss the pros and cons of relying on each of the six basic sources of revenue.
3. Choose a type of nonprofit—human services, arts, health, or other—and predict the preferred mix of funding sources—for example, 20 percent earned income, 60 percent foundation grants—and explain why revenues from those sources would be advantageous, and others would not be, for pursuit of the organization's mission.
4. If you were in the position of Tom in the opening vignette, what would you do with your $1 million? Explain how you would donate the funds, why you chose as you did, and discuss the policy implications of your philanthropy.

Assignment

Access the ReStore directory at www.habitat.org/restores and choose an outlet in close proximity or of other interest to you. Using www.guidestar.org, access the Forms 990 for the Habitat for Humanity affiliate associated with your chosen ReStore outlet. Determine how the revenues from the ReStore have changed over the years for which Form 990 data are available. How does the revenue from the ReStore compare to total revenue for the affiliate? How does the ReStore revenue compare to other sources of revenue for the organization?

Suggested Readings

Grace, Kay Sprinkel. *Beyond Fundraising: New Strategies for Nonprofit Innovation and Investment,* 2nd ed. Hoboken, NJ: John Wiley & Sons, 2005.

Kanter, Beth, and Allison H. Fine. *The Networked Nonprofit: Connecting with Social Media to Drive Change.* Hoboken, NJ: John Wiley & Sons, 2010.

Still, Julie M. *The Accidental Fundraiser.* Medford, NJ: Information Today, 2007.

Weisbrod, Burton A., ed. *To Profit or Not to Profit: The Commercial Transformation of the Nonprofit Sector.* Cambridge, UK: Cambridge University Press, 1998.

Web Resources

Beth's Blog, www.bethkanter.org

Committee Encouraging Corporate Philanthropy, www.corporatephilanthropy.org

Federal Audit Clearinghouse, harvester.census.gov/fac

The Foundation Center, www.foundationcenter.org

The Foundation Center offers a free training course entitled Introduction to Corporate Giving, available via eLearning or recorded webinar at: http://grantspace.org/Classroom/Training-Courses/Introduction-to-Corporate-Giving

Idealware, www.idealware.org/reports/fundraising

Nonprofit Finance Fund, www.nonprofitfinancefund.org

USA Spending, www.usaspending.gov

10 Resource Development

Grants

[W]e believe you need to take a step back and look at who you are, when and why you should look for grants, *and* from whom you should look for grants, *before you decide to invest the time and energy it takes to develop or redesign your program and write a winning proposal.*[1]

Jane really likes her new job as executive director (ED) of a small nonprofit focused on health education and safety promotion, except for one point—the organization recently came to the end of its initial three-year start-up grant and the funder has promised only two more years of grant funds to cover basic operations, including Jane's salary. The organization is in year two of a three-year grant from a separate funder, but that grant is for a pilot project and additional funding is not an option; a health education specialist is employed using those grant funds. Fortunately, a larger nonprofit that provides different services to a similar clientele provides office space and utilities rent-free.

While the founding executive director did a good job of organizing programs, materials, and stakeholders, the small annual fundraisers she initiated serve at best only to supplement program activities. Revenues generated through individual contributions and fundraising do not approach the level needed to cover compensation for the part-time secretary, much less salaries for Jane and the health education specialist. Therefore, if she is not able to find a significant revenue source soon, Jane and her colleagues will find themselves without a job. In what should have been a forewarning of things to come, one of the board members casually told Jane not to worry: "You just need to write a grant." Nonetheless, Jane is worried because among the many things she learned in her MPA program was that you do not write a grant; you write a proposal to obtain a grant, and she is pretty sure that obtaining a grant of the size needed is no small feat. It's a good thing she honed her research skills.

POLICY IMPLICATIONS OF GRANTS

- Grants represent one means by which nonprofits are able to make policy and influence policy, as well as means by which they are influenced by policy and subject to policy.
- Governments at all levels and private foundations grant substantial resources to nonprofits every year, and the choices they make regarding what projects and which organizations to fund have an impact on public policy.
- Types of grants offered by funders also have policy connotations—for example, operating grants reflect support for building overall capacity of the nonprofits to facilitate pursuit of their mission and grants of seed money encourage innovative policy development and implementation.
- Government grants and contracts represent a carrot and stick approach to public policy implementation. Governments use the enticement of grant funds to encourage nonprofit provision of a prescribed set of public goods and services; likewise, governments attach requirements to the receipt of the funds to enforce compliance with a broad range of requirements.
- Early foundations were involved in directly shaping public policy by initiating programs and activities, such as the public library system, that were eventually turned over to governments; regulatory efforts such as the Tax Reform Act and the Pension Protection Act limit the ability of foundations to directly influence government action today, but the funding choices foundations make continue to have far-reaching implications for public policy.

THE ROLE OF GRANTS IN THE NONPROFIT SECTOR

Grants are generally defined as payments from one entity to another based on a set of established criteria, and they represent a significant revenue source for nonprofits. Nonprofits utilize grant funds in numerous ways, including to support programs and basic operations as well as to facilitate major capital projects. Government entities grant funds in order to encourage provision of public programs and activities without directly operating them; grantmaking foundations provide grants in pursuit of their mission as well as to comply with federal regulations, as discussed in Chapter 4. For the most part, grants provide a mutually beneficial relationship between funder and nonprofit to pursue policy goals. It is important to note that grants take various forms and have varying requirements associated with them; further, there can be problems when nonprofits pursue grants that do not tightly align with their mission, as will be discussed in detail below.

TYPES OF GRANTS

Under the Constitution, Congress is empowered to provide for the general welfare. Spending for that purpose quite often takes the form of grants-in-aid, commonly referred to as grants.

While grants are generally thought of as given by the federal government to states or localities, grants originate in all sectors and at all levels of government. Government entities have given grants to nonprofits, but governments have also been the recipients of private foundation or corporate grants as well. Government grants totaling $124.6 billion comprised almost 9 percent of total revenues for reporting public charities in 2009.[2] In addition, foundations gave in excess of $45.7 billion in grants that same year.[3] Additional government spending for nonprofits involves fees for goods and services, which comprised 23.2 percent of revenues for reporting public charities in 2009; this type of government revenue is usually administered through contracts (also offered to for-profit sector organizations), which are discussed further below.

While grants are typically monetary awards, some grantors provide goods such as food or computer equipment, or services such as free shipping, as in the example of Federal Express, discussed in Chapter 9. Most government grants are made pursuant to a Notice of Funding Availability (NOFA), which sets forth the guidelines and eligibility criteria for receipt of funds. Foundations usually identify general areas of interest for funding and review proposals on a set schedule—for example, monthly, quarterly, or annually. When seeking grant funding it is important to understand the basic types of grants generally awarded by funders: project grants, operating grants, seed money, and matching grants.

Project or Program Grants

Most foundation grants are in the area of program support, ranging from 43.9 percent of all grant dollars in 1998 to 52.9 percent in 2010.[4] These tend to be the favored types of grants awarded because funders like to support specific projects with recognizable goals and objectives, which their support can help achieve. While project grants are generally the most attractive to funders, they pose challenges for small nonprofits with limited capacity. Paying the rent for office space and salaries for the executive director and secretary are rarely considered eligible expenses under a project grant, although some grantors do allow a percentage of these costs to be allocated to a project. Project grants often require a promise by the organization to continue the programs and services after the grant period ends, which commits the nonprofit to future expenditures without grant funds.

"Bricks and mortar" is the common term used when referring to grants for capital projects, which are awarded in fewer numbers than grants for programming. Some funders refuse to consider funding capital projects; some only fund capital projects. When grants are awarded for construction, renovation, or a major purchase of equipment, the resulting building, hospital wing, or playground is often named for the funder. For example, the Peter J. King Family Foundation in Minneapolis, Minnesota, is an example of a foundation that focuses almost exclusively on the provision of grants for bricks and mortar projects to fulfill their mission of "improvement in children's health, education, and welfare and the family environment."[5] Several of the facilities constructed with grant funds bear the foundation name, such as the Peter J. King Family Health Center and the Salvation Army King Family Foundation Corps Community Center.

Operating Grants

What many small nonprofits need most, including Jane's from our opening vignette, are basic operating funds. Operating grants are largely unrestricted funds that nonprofits can use for overhead expenses such as management salaries, building rent or maintenance, and office supplies. Unfortunately, funders are not as enamored of awarding operating grants as nonprofits are of receiving them. An Urban Institute survey in 2003 of 850 staffed, private foundations found that more than one-third never or rarely gave grants for operating support.[6]

Fortunately, in 2004, Independent Sector (IS) highlighted this issue when it endorsed guidelines drafted by the Building Value Together initiative regarding funding for nonprofits.[7] A primary statement within the guidelines reflects a preference for general operating support, specifically

> Funders can often achieve their strategic goals through core support[8] for organizations whose goals are substantially aligned with their own. Where appropriate and feasible, funders should prefer multi-year, reliable core support to project support.[9]

Unfortunately, while foundation funding for general operating support (expressed as a percentage of total grant dollars awarded) rose steadily from a low of 13.7 percent in 1998, it has not increased significantly since the IS recommendation and seems to have plateaued at around 20 percent, as seen in Figure 10.1.

Despite efforts of the Building Value Together initiative, there does not as yet seem to be a major shift toward increased funding for operating support. However, some scholars contend there is a trend among donors who are establishing new foundations to choose a limited term of operation over having the foundation exist in perpetuity. According to the Urban Institute survey, only 16 percent of limited life foundations rarely or never award general operating support grants compared to 33 percent of perpetual foundations, which report they rarely or never award such grants.[10] If there truly is a trend toward establishing limited life foundations, their increased propensity to fund core support would be a positive development for many nonprofits.

The Building Value Together initiative also heralds the importance of foundation grants to build endowments in order to assist nonprofits in achieving their missions.[11] As discussed in Chapter 9, endowments provide income from the long-term investment of the funds and can consist of restricted and/or unrestricted funds. Unrestricted funds can be used for any purpose the board deems necessary, including operating support; likewise, endowment funds may also be restricted to general operating support. Income from endowments can be used to bolster operating budgets during lean economic times; however, as with core support, there does not as yet seem to be a trend towards increased foundation funding for that purpose. Between 1998 and 2010, foundations granted a total of $7.5 million to nonprofits for endowments; this represents an average of $580,767 per year. As shown in Figure 10.1 the percentage of grant dollars that foundations awarded for endowments averaged 3.85 percent, with a high of 5.6 percent in 2001 and a low of 2.0 percent in 2003; the percentage for 2010 was up slightly from the previous year to 2.9. Because endowments provide a stable revenue

FIGURE 10.1 Types of Support by Foundations

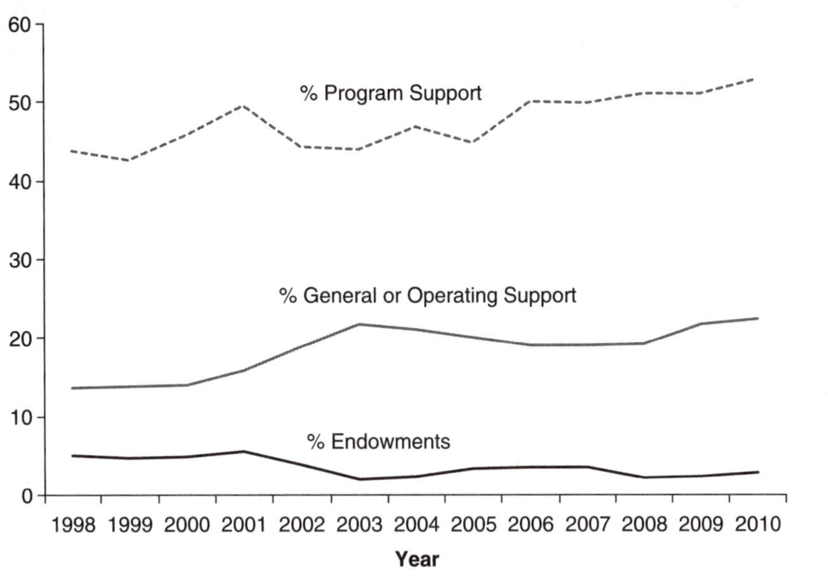

Source: The Foundation Center's Statistical Information Service, 1995–2012. www.foundationcenter.org/find-funders/statistics/

source for nonprofits, foundation funding to establish and build endowments can do much to enhance the organizational capacity of nonprofits. However, because they represent such a small percentage of the grant funds disbursed by foundations, the overall impact on the sector of these types of grant support is not as significant as it could be.

Seed Money

Grants for the start-up of new organizations or pilot programs are commonly referred to as seed money. As mentioned at the start of the chapter, Jane's colleague—the health education specialist—was hired under a grant for a pilot project. The funder awarded $75,000 per year for three years to provide dance instruction and programming for children in the surrounding rural areas, in order to explore the effects of dance as exercise to reduce childhood obesity. (Yes, it is a bit of a stretch for the organization's mission; more on that later.) Grants for start-up projects generally involve programs and activities that might raise an eyebrow or two, precisely because demonstration projects are excellent venues to try unproven strategies for addressing issues of public concern.

Foundations especially, but also government entities, use grants of seed money to fund innovative approaches to solving public problems, often with quite positive results. One prominent example involves the Community Oriented Policing Services (COPS) program implemented through the Department of Justice (DOJ) during the Clinton Administration.[12]

The Police Foundation, which was established in 1970 by the Ford Foundation, was instrumental in research and development of the community-oriented policing model. COPS has been adapted and utilized by police departments nationwide, having a significant impact on law enforcement policy development and implementation. Additional information on the Police Foundation and its role in shaping policing policy is included in Case Study 10.1.

Challenge/Matching Grants

The Foundation Center defines challenge or matching grants as those that, once awarded, "will be paid only if the donee organization is able to raise additional funds from another source(s). Challenge grants are often used to stimulate giving from other donors."[13] Old Bill's Fun Run described in Chapter 9 is a good example of the ability of grant funds to leverage additional donations.

Government grants often use matching requirements as a way to maximize funding impact and facilitate greater commitment from recipient organizations. For example, it has been demonstrated that local governments with greater financial capacity to provide matching funds receive an increased number of federal grants and higher numbers of grants per capita.[14] Matching grants generally receive mixed reviews in the nonprofit community. Grantmakers tend to like them because they enable limited grant funds to be stretched further for greater impact and also ensure significant buy-in for the project from local stakeholders. Nonprofit recipients like them in the sense that they are an approved source of funds for a project but usually harbor misgivings and some degree of apprehension over the resources needed to generate the required matching funds.[15] In the case of Old Bill's Fun Run, challenge grants add another level of funding to a special event; the Community Foundation of Jackson Hole is not dependent on the challenge grants in order to conduct or generate revenue from the event. In other instances, such as government grant programs that require a match, disbursement of any grant funds is contingent upon the nonprofit first demonstrating its ability to provide the required matching funds, which can be difficult for small, cash-strapped social services nonprofits.

GOVERNMENT GRANTS AND FEE-FOR-SERVICE CONTRACTS

As mentioned above, government funding of nonprofits through grants and fees for goods and services comprised more than 32 percent of the nonprofit revenue of reporting public charities in 2009, making government a significant source of revenue for the nonprofit sector. It is important to note the long history of government funds as a source of nonprofit revenue. Government has encouraged and subsidized nonprofit service delivery since the inception of Harvard University, the Metropolitan Museum of Art, and numerous early health care institutions.[16] In the 1960s, when the federal government began to provide substantial sums for the provision of social services, nonprofits were a big part of grant programs. Amendments in 1962 and 1967 to the Social Security Act provided for state agencies to employ nonprofit entities in service delivery. Since then, grant awards and contracting out to nonprofits for delivery of social services has been on the rise.[17]

CASE STUDY 10.1

The Police Foundation: Improving Law Enforcement through Research and Innovation

In 1970, in response to rising crime rates, increased violence, and growing community tensions, the Ford Foundation gave $30 million to establish the Police Foundation, intended to fund policing research and demonstration projects for a five-year period. Success in those early years led to a 23-year funding partnership that culminated in a generous grant from the Ford Foundation to the Police Foundation's endowment to ensure permanence of the institution and its work. The Police Foundation also receives contributions from individuals, corporations, and other foundations; government grants and contracts have also supported specific projects and research.[18]

Probably the most well-known and influential of the Police Foundation's efforts regarding policing policy involves the concept of community-oriented policing, also known as problem-oriented policing. Research in Kansas City, Houston, and Newark funded by the Police Foundation during the 1970s provided the seeds from which the concept of community policing grew. Wilson & Kelling's 1982 "broken windows" theory of crime prevention derived from a Police Foundation research project on police foot patrols in Newark, New Jersey. Community policing and the broken windows theory both center on prevention of crime, with the idea that attention to minor crimes is a means of preventing more serious crime. Research has shown that rather than random patrols being a deterrent to crime, foot patrols and an active presence of the police in a community—such as identifying broken windows and other instances of vandalism and encouraging property owners to fix them—lowers crime rates and contributes to a greater perception of safety among citizens.

This new approach to policing policy took hold in departments across the nation and was raised to national prominence during the early years of the Clinton Administration with the formation of the office of Community Oriented Policing Services (COPS) within the U.S. Department of Justice (DOJ). In 1995, the first round of federal government grants to advance the concept of community oriented policing were awarded. Since then, more than $13 billion in grants have been awarded through the COPS program to over 13,000 state, local, and tribal law enforcement agencies for them to hire or redeploy approximately 120,000 police officers to implement the COPS model. These figures include FY2011 awards of $243.4 million in grants for 1,021 officers at 238 law enforcement agencies. It is important to note that for that funding cycle, DOJ had received applications from over 2,700 agencies with requests for more than $2 billion to hire almost 9,000 officers, reflecting the significant demand in excess of grant resources for the program.[19]

For more than 40 years, the Police Foundation has been "a catalyst for change" in the field of policing. In addition to their COPS research and development efforts, the foundation has funded research on the status of women in policing, collection of data and analysis of the use of excessive force by police officers, and the effects of different shift-lengths on police officer performance. In addition, the foundation has collaborated with government and nonprofit agencies, including the FBI, the American Bar Association, and the Urban Institute to promote policy change and other efforts to improve policing. From their initial research funded by the Ford Foundation, through their work with the federal government's office of Community Oriented Policing Services, and the efforts funded from their own endowment and contributions from supporters, the Police Foundation has had a continuing and significant impact on public policy related to policing. Law enforcement agencies in areas throughout the country have participated in studies funded by the foundation and have benefitted from grants related to policies resulting from that research. As such, the Police Foundation represents a compelling example of the role of grants in public policy.

QUESTIONS TO CONSIDER:

1. The Police Foundation was formed by the Ford Foundation to "foster improvement and innovation in American policing." Does this represent a large-scale effort by a private foundation to tackle a major social ill? Explain.
2. What are the policy implications of the disparity between the number of applications received and the number of grants awarded through the COPS program? What recommendations would you make regarding future allocations for the program?
3. Discuss the benefits of the collaboration between the Police Foundation and DOJ's office of Community Oriented Policing Services. What are the policy implications of the use of both private foundation and government funds to advance public policy pertaining to policing?
4. Consider the four relationships that describe nonprofit interaction with public policy (make policy, affected by policy, influence policy, subject to policy) and discuss the ways in which these relationships are reflected in the example of the Police Foundation and the office of Community Oriented Policing Services.

Nonprofits experience both benefits and costs from government funding. For example, nonprofits should be wary of accepting grants or contracts to provide services that do not coincide with the organization's mission. Indeed, a common concern in managing nonprofits is that chasing public sector funding will lead to mission drift, pulling the organization into policy areas, communities, or services that have little to do with the original purpose of the organization. A related concern is that governments may gain too much control over nonprofit behavior through the rules and regulations that accompany contracts and grants administration, and that this could result in less oversight by nonprofit governing boards.[20] Delayed government payments—a problem for which the public sector is notorious[21]—is another source of concern since these can lead to cash-flow problems for nonprofits.[22]

Further, nonprofits that are entirely dependent on government resources are vulnerable to the whims of public finance and policy priorities.

On the other hand, nonprofits gain substantial financial resources from government sources and have a long history of successful partnership in the provision of public goods and services. The influx of funds and a heightened role in public policy implementation which accompanies receipt of government funds can enhance a nonprofit's reputation and improve access to other government grants and contracts.[23] In addition, preparing the required documents in response to a Request for Proposals (RFP) assists nonprofits in planning and goal clarification. The competition with other nonprofits or for-profit firms also fosters innovation and improves performance sector-wide.[24] All of this helps organizations to succeed in public policy development and implementation. Maximizing the advantages and minimizing the disadvantages of government grants and contracts requires adequate resources and appropriate oversight by both the nonprofits and the government agencies.

Distribution of Government Grants

Grants from governments to nonprofits are either direct—that is, given directly by the government agency to the not-for-profit organization that provides the actual service delivery—or indirect. Indirect grants reach nonprofits via a pass-through agency, usually a department of a state or local government. Most grant dollars for social services nonprofits are distributed as indirect grants.[25] In addition, governments grant funds in four general ways: (1) in a block designed to address a general policy area; (2) according to a set formula; (3) for a specific project or category of activity; and 4) as a line-item budget appropriation.

The Community Development Block Grant (CDBG) program administered by the U.S. Department of Housing and Urban Development (HUD) incorporates three of the ways governments grant funds and therefore serves as an illustrative example of each.

Block Grants. As the name implies, the CDBG represents funds awarded in a block to state and local governments to fund activities within the general area of community development; while the funds are granted to state and local governments, nonprofits are often the recipients of pass-through funds or are the beneficiaries of projects such as building construction or renovation completed by the government agency on their behalf. Block grants are attractive methods of funding for policymakers, administrators, and the general public. While basic threshold requirements are fixed and non-negotiable, such as the CDBG requirement that funds be used to serve primarily low to moderate income residents, recipients are given flexibility to determine how best to use the funds. In the case of CDBG funds, each designated state agency sets the parameters within the CDBG criteria for the specific types of community development activities that would best suit the needs within their state.

Formula Grants. One part of the CDBG is the Entitlement Communities program, in which grants are awarded based on an eligibility formula. Formula grants are the least competitive of the four ways funds are granted since all organizations that meet the criteria are awarded funds, with the amount of the grant determined according to an allocation formula. In the case of the CDBG, cities with a population over 50,000 automatically receive an allocation of the grant, which the cities can then use for their choice of activities so long as they meet the general criteria of the block grant program.

Project Grants. As discussed above, project grants are for specific purposes and are usually the most competitive way in which governments disburse grants. State funds for the CDBG–Small Cities program are usually awarded as project grants on a competitive basis; local governments submit applications and state officials decide which projects will receive funding. For example, the State of Tennessee Department of Economic & Community Development encourages CDBG applications for the purchase of fire trucks or for expansion of fire stations under the HUD-approved criterion of community livability. In contrast, the Commonwealth of Kentucky Department for Local Government rarely, if ever, funds rural fire protection, focusing instead on senior centers, crisis centers, and health departments.[26] Although all applicants must be a local government entity, cities or counties can make application on behalf of a nonprofit organization. Examples include a Tennessee county that applied for funds to renovate an old school building to serve as a community center with programming provided by a local nonprofit and a Kentucky city that applied for funds to renovate four historic structures to be administered as a museum by the local nonprofit historical society.

Line-item Appropriations. Of all the ways governments distribute grants, line-item appropriations are the most political. Sometimes referred to as pork-barrel spending, these funds are often subject to the application process and administrative guidelines of other grant programs, but there is a guarantee of funding so long as the grantee complies with the rules and regulations. As a source of revenue for nonprofits, line-item appropriations are not necessarily less competitive than project grants, since organizations must vie with other nonprofits as well as other government entities for support needed to include the appropriation in the government budget. Likewise, appropriations are not always a sure thing; once the organization gains the necessary support to have the appropriation included in the budget, it still must overcome numerous hurdles, including adoption of the final budget and potential cuts in spending due to revenue shortfalls, before the funds are actually disbursed. Once the funds are disbursed, the nonprofit will still be accountable to the same administrative regulations as other government grant recipients.

Keep in mind that so-called pork-barrel projects are not inherently bad, especially to the recipient organizations. Such projects are usually controversial because they are narrowly focused; whether a state or the federal government (or another source) is the appropriate venue for provision of the project funding is frequently debated. Appropriations aided significantly in the construction of the nonprofit Center for Rural Development in Somerset, Kentucky, for example. The facility serves a 42-county area in eastern and southern Kentucky, including economically distressed Appalachian counties, and focuses on technological, cultural, and economic development for the region (www.centertech.com).

Public Goods and Services via Government Contracts

Not-for-profit organizations are often eager to use their experience to implement public policy in their communities, and governments are typically in need of the expertise and first-hand knowledge of the community that nonprofits possess. This mutually beneficial relationship is often codified by contracting, in which the government agency agrees to pay an agreed-upon fee for the provision of specified goods or services. Contracts differ from grants in that grants typically involve disbursement of a pre-set amount of funds to the grantee, who agrees to engage in a range of activities specified in the grant proposal. For example, a government grant may provide $200,000 for a pilot project to demonstrate the best way to encourage rural women to access and make use of information on health promotion. Contracts usually involve an agreement to pay a set fee for each service provided to the designated clientele during the duration of the contract. For example, a government agency might contract with a nonprofit to provide job training and agree to pay a fee for each client who successfully completes the program.

Generally described as a fairly linear process, contracting begins when the public agency creates parameters and issues an RFP. This is followed by the review of proposals from qualified contract bidders, then the awarding of the contract and determination of final contract details. Following delivery of services, contractors submit to monitoring and evaluation of the execution of the service contract, and the government agency makes a determination regarding whether to renew or terminate the relationship.[27]

Delivery of Services. The process of submitting the response to the RFP and negotiating the contract should provide nonprofits with sufficient information regarding the requirements to fulfill the contract obligations. However, successful delivery of the contracted goods and services depends on several factors: appropriate facilities, adequate financial and technical resources, staff training, specific and consistent program goals that have been agreed upon by both parties, and clientele who can access needed services. Sometimes a nonprofit may lack these attributes, making successful implementation of policy difficult.[28] In some instances, the contracting agency may step in to offer assistance to help improve programs, in order to meet government objectives.[29] Of course, the public sector funding for program implementation may be inadequate to meet citizen needs for services.[30] Each of these represent challenges and opportunities for nonprofits when providing goods and services via government contracts. As repeatedly emphasized throughout this text, nonprofits can most successfully mitigate the challenges they face, including with contracted services, when their program goals are closely aligned with the organization's mission; when fee-for-service contracts reflect what a nonprofit currently does in pursuit of its mission, the organization more likely possesses the expertise and basic infrastructure needed to overcome obstacles to service provision.

Government Monitoring. Effective government monitoring is absolutely vital to successful service delivery; thus, public agencies have increasingly used performance-based contracts to help monitor nonprofit service providers.[31] The ability of governments to monitor contracts, however, has come into question in much of the contracting literature.[32] In keeping with the theories of contract failure discussed in Chapter 3, whereby nonprofits are deemed more trustworthy than business as well as more voluntary than government, there is evidence of *less* monitoring of nonprofit contractors than monitoring of either for-profit or in-house service providers.[33] Constraints on the administrative capacity of government contracting agencies mean that public sector managers are not able to engage in monitoring of the organizations with which they contract to the extent they would like;[34] nonprofits have an edge with regard to trustworthiness, which may be the reason they experience less contract monitoring.[35]

Contract Termination or Renewal. Finally, at the end of the specified contract, the question for the public agency is whether to continue the program through renewal of the contract or to terminate the relationship. The perspective of the public manager is instrumental in determining whether a contractor is deemed to be more or less successful. Public administrators with a management focus will be more interested in the efficiency of the nonprofit, those with a professional orientation will be more interested in agency effectiveness, and politicos will be focused on the political attention (or lack thereof) garnered by the contractor or the program itself.[36]

It is a general rule that more experienced nonprofit contractors will be more effective at winning service contracts. This is likely related to resource availability and the relationships that grow between the contract agency and nonprofit provider. For example, it has been demonstrated that when public managers trusted their nonprofit contractors, they offered them assistance in writing other proposals such as ways to navigate the bureaucracy, tips on reviewers' preferences, insight regarding what programs the legislature might fund in the future, and ways the nonprofit could leverage additional contract funding.[37]

Government Influence and the Risk to Nonprofits. As noted earlier, risks come with the rewards of funding through government contracts and often greater expenses for the recipient nonprofit. Public agencies often impose accounting and reporting requirements that may be difficult for small nonprofits to meet, and they may feel pressure to employ a more professional staff to meet these requirements.[38] Nonprofits must also be concerned with the *crowding out* effect of government funds, in which funds from other sources can decrease when nonprofits receive government contracts.[39] The resulting resource dependency can be particularly problematic for nonprofits when economic conditions cause governments to cut spending on social service contracts.[40] As with other forms of resource dependency discussed previously, the best approach is resource diversification, which may involve less contracting by the nonprofit or negotiation of long-term safeguards within the contract.

Government contracts, therefore, comprise an important funding source for nonprofits, but as will be discussed more in Chapter 11, they can also facilitate or compromise pursuit of stated mission with subsequent policy implications. Nonprofits that rely too heavily on government contracts run the risk of cooptation—that is, the contracting agency exercises more control over nonprofit activity through procedural rules and regulations, resulting in less active oversight by the board of directors.[41] As with the pursuit of foundation or government grant funding, nonprofits should focus on their mission as the deciding factor in whether to seek or accept government contracts to provide public services.

FOUNDATION FUNDING

As discussed in Chapter 4, foundations are defined by the IRS primarily by specifying what they do not do in comparison to other 501(c)(3) tax-exempt entities. Foundations are commonly understood to encompass those nonprofits that have been endowed with funds by one or more primary donors for the purpose of making grants to other nonprofits, in order to facilitate the provision of public goods and services. Not all foundations make grants; however, the more than 76,000 grantmaking foundations in the U.S. distributed in excess of $45 billion in grants in 2009. The bulk of those funds (71 percent) were granted by independent foundations, which include philanthropic giants such as the Bill & Melinda Gates Foundation, Carnegie Corporation, and the Ford Foundation.

It was Andrew Carnegie, John D. Rockefeller, and other titans of the Progressive Era who initiated the growth and development of philanthropic foundations in the U.S. in the early years of the twentieth century, when the scope of the federal government was markedly smaller. For example, the Carnegie Corporation of New York (a private foundation) was established in 1911 with an endowment of $135 million. The 5 percent annual payout requirement for that amount would have been $6.75 million, which contrasts significantly with the 1911 annual budget for the federal Bureau of Education at just under $5 million.[42]

Foundation dollars had a much greater impact during that time due to the correspondingly low levels of government activity. Although the Bill & Melinda Gates Foundation was established with a much larger endowment ($16 billion in 2000) than Carnegie, it equals a very small fraction of current government spending. For example, the 5 percent minimum payout on $16 billion would be $800 million; the corresponding FY 2000 budget for the Department of Education was $3.63 billion.[43] Because of this, the overall policy impact of the Gates Foundation may be somewhat smaller when compared to the work of the early foundations such as Carnegie that successfully undertook the ambitious goal of creating the public library system.[44] However, the Gates family, in conjunction with Warren Buffett, chooses their projects carefully, focusing on a few issues in order to have a greater impact. As Bill and Melinda Gates state in a letter about their foundation, " . . . we think an essential role of philanthropy is to make bets on promising solutions that governments and businesses can't afford to make."[45] Between 1994 and September 2011, the foundation disbursed almost $26.2 billion in grant funds for projects primarily in the areas of global health and education.[46]

Types of Foundations

The Bill & Melinda Gates Foundation is an example of a private, family, grantmaking foundation. As tax-exempt organizations, the IRS classifies foundations primarily into two categories—private grantmaking foundations and private operating foundations. Grantmaking foundations, as the name implies, exist primarily to distribute their funds in the form of grants to other organizations. Included within each category of private foundations are family, corporate, and independent foundations. It is important to note that while community foundations constitute another category of private foundations, as discussed in Chapter 6, they are usually classified by the IRS as public charities rather than foundations. Also, since the IRS recognizes only two categories of foundations for legal purposes, please keep in mind that the other descriptive terms are not official identifiers but serve merely to illustrate the source and guiding influence of the philanthropy. Likewise, they are not mutually exclusive. For example, as indicated in Table 10.1, the majority of U.S. foundations are described as family foundations, which is actually classified as a subset of independent foundations. Additionally, since many corporations are family owned and operated, their associated corporate foundations may reflect the personal giving interests of the family, as in the case of the fifth largest corporate foundation, the Dennis and Phyllis Washington Foundation.[47] An overview of U.S. foundation by type is included in Table 10.1, and discussion of each type is included in the sections that follow.

Family foundations. Actually a subset of independent foundations, family foundations represent the largest number of all foundation types and include those in which the original benefactor(s) and/or members of the family are actively involved in disbursing and administering the philanthropic funds. In the case of Bill and Melinda Gates, each serves as co-chair

TABLE 10.1 Overview of U.S. Foundations, by Type, 2009

Foundation Type	Number of Foundations	Assets (Dollars in Thousands)	Total Giving (Dollars in Thousands)
Family	37,804	$258,017,926	$20,406,369
Independent	30,704	224,936,136	12,346,238
Corporate	2,745	20,335,165	4,570,362
Community	709	49,622,739	4,492,032
Operating	4,762	38,967,585	3,900,269
Total		**$564,950,926**	**$46,781,305**

Source: The Foundation Center, FC Stats, 2011. Aggregate Fiscal Data By Foundation Type, 2009; Aggregate Financial Data for Family Foundations, 2009.

of the foundation, along with William H. Gates Sr. In his annual letter, Bill Gates outlines the funding priorities and strategies for the foundation for the upcoming year; these priorities are shaped and approved by him and his wife, Melinda, with guidance from his father. The work of the Gates Foundation, as with all family foundations, reflects the personal philanthropic interests of the members of the family. It is also not unusual to see a family foundation setting priorities that reflect geographic focus, such as where the family lives or vacations each year. For example, the Prince Charitable Trusts, established from the bequests of Frederick and Abbie Prince, concentrated their grantmaking in Chicago, Washington, D.C., and Newport, Rhode Island.[48]

Independent foundations. These include family foundations, as mentioned above, but also encompass all other grantmaking foundations without a significant community, corporate, or family influence on either the source of the funds or their disbursement. More than half of all independent foundations are classified as family foundations, and many of the remaining independent foundations, such as the W.K. Kellogg Foundation, began as family foundations, but over time the active participation and influence of family members ceased. Some such as the Robert Wood Johnson Foundation strive to continue the philanthropic priorities of their founders; others, such as the Ford Foundation, have been critiqued for moving their mission in a direction distinctly opposed to their founders' philosophies.

Corporate foundations. This type of grantmaking foundation is established with funds from and in conjunction with a for-profit corporation. According to the Foundation Center, the largest corporate foundation based on asset size is Alcoa Foundation.[49] With total assets of approximately $446 million in 2011, the Foundation contributed almost $28 million in 2011 to nonprofit organizations worldwide. Since 1952, Alcoa Foundation has disbursed over $550 million for projects in the areas of the environment, education, and sustainability.[50] Other top corporate foundations by asset size include General Motors Foundation ($157.7 million), Coca-Cola Foundation ($119.1 million), and the Google Foundation ($82.8 million).[51] Corporate foundations generally choose to support projects and issues that relate to their business issues as well as to support the communities in which their employees work and live.

Community foundations. While not typically considered foundations in the legal sense prescribed by the IRS, these organizations operate in ways similar to grantmaking foundations in that they make grants, usually, for the benefit of a geographically defined community. Because they receive broad public support from diverse sources, they are generally recognized by the IRS as public charities rather than foundations. In 2009 there were 737 community foundations nationwide, and their total giving exceeded $4.1 million. Just over half of all community foundations reported holding at least $10 million in assets, and 45 percent reported giving $1 million or more during 2009.[52]

Since they are usually classified as public charities, community foundations have historically been subject to fewer government restrictions than private foundations. However, certain provisions of the Pension Protection Act of 2006 extended some of the regulations imposed on private foundations to donor-advised funds (DAF), a mainstay of community foundations. For the first time, DAFs were legally defined as

> a separately identified fund or account that is maintained and operated by a section 501(c)(3) organization, which is called a *sponsoring organization*. Each account is composed of contributions made by individual donors. Once the donor makes the contribution, the organization has legal control over it. However, the donor, or the donor's representative, retains advisory privileges with respect to the distribution of funds and the investment of assets in the account.[53]

Donor-advised funds have become increasingly popular among philanthropists who wish to organize and direct their giving without establishing the formal structure of a foundation. The new rules regarding DAFs are designed to prevent their misuse as tax shelters—through provisions regarding disqualified persons and the potential for excise taxes as well as rules regarding excess business holdings—in ways similar to how the Tax Reform Act of 1969 restricted private foundations.[54] The Foundation for the Carolinas (FFTC), for example, is one of the largest community foundations in the Southeast (www.fftc.org), ranking eighth among all community foundations in total giving in 2009.[55] Their Center for Personal and Family Philanthropy provides guidance in establishing and maintaining donor-advised funds. In 2011, FFTC had total assets (owned and represented) of $941.3 million and distributed $37.1 million in grants.

Operating foundations. The J. Paul Getty Trust is an example of an operating foundation—that is, a foundation that uses its resources to fund its own programs and activities. Grants may be given for projects and activities of non-affiliated nonprofits, but they would form only a small portion of the funds expended. Because operating foundations face fewer restrictions from the IRS than grantmaking foundations, it is generally advantageous to be recognized by the IRS as an operating foundation. In order to be classified as a private operating foundation, the organization must meet specific IRS requirements regarding the use of foundation income and assets for exempt purposes.[56]

Government and foundation grants of all types represent an important but limited revenue source for nonprofits. As such, successfully pursuing grants is usually a highly competitive process. Government agencies generally announce their grants programs through publication of a NOFA. Foundations publish guidelines for their grants programs on their websites or in relevant publications such as *The Chronicle of Philanthropy* and the Foundation Directory. Finding grant opportunities that align with a nonprofit's mission and constructing proposals that comply with the guidelines and articulate how the nonprofit's mission and expertise fit with the potential funder's goals requires knowledge and skill. Accordingly, identifying appropriate grant opportunities and preparing a successful grant proposal are the focus of the following sections.

PREPARING A GRANT PROPOSAL

The basics of writing a grant proposal can be summed up in one succinct sentence: "Read the guidelines and do exactly what they say to do."[57] In order to accomplish that, however, a little guidance in finding grant opportunities and navigating the process is quite helpful. Throughout the following sections we focus on identifying appropriate grant opportunities, compiling a budget and project narrative, and assembling the final package for submission.[58]

Getting Started

Before ever looking at funding opportunities, it is best for the person preparing the proposal as well as the leadership of the organization to first determine how much money is needed and just what the funds would accomplish. Jane from our opening vignette needs operating funds, preferably through a multi-year grant, in order to give the organization time to explore building an endowment or other possibilities to stabilize a revenue stream for salaries. Beyond thinking in terms of operating vs. programming funds, it is important for Jane to think about the values and mission of her organization in order to determine what type of funder would be the best match. Remember, all grantmaking organizations—government and foundations alike—want to give their money away; they just want to make sure that they give it to the organizations that will be in the best position to use it to accomplish the goals they want to achieve. Identifying grant opportunities is easier than ever before thanks to electronic resources. See Box 10.2 on grants databases.

If a nonprofit wants to start a new project or expand an existing one, renovate a historic structure, or strengthen its organizational capacity, it is important for the person responsible for finding the resources to think through the project before looking for funding opportunities. Taking a shotgun approach to funding searches—identifying available opportunities and sending each a generic proposal—wastes everyone's time and effort. It also increases the likelihood of mission drift through goal displacement; the goal becomes obtaining grant funding—any funding—instead of accomplishing the organization's mission. Stretching and shifting the mission of an organization to fit what the RFP stipulates is not in the best interests of the funder or the grant recipient. Remember Jane's health education specialist and the dance program? The grant brought needed funds into the organization, and while a dance-as-exercise program fit under their broad mission statement, it was not one of the stated goals and objectives within their strategic plan. Jane wants to make sure that the next grant is more closely aligned with their mission.

Budget and Project Narratives

The application guidelines will provide specific instructions for how to construct a project budget, but basically, a budget is a forecast of sources and amounts of revenues and expen-

Box 10.2

FOR MORE INFORMATION

GRANTS DATABASES

Enter the term "grant opportunities" in any of the top Internet search engines, and you'll get anywhere from 70 to 135 million hits—quick and easy to find, time-intensive and laborious to sift through. Fortunately for grants seekers, there are several searchable databases specifically for grants opportunities to make finding the appropriate funding sources more practical. While grants.gov is a free searchable database, many others require a paid subscription to access. If your organization does not have the resources to subscribe, check with your nearest university, public library, local government, or your nonprofit consortium to inquire about shared access.

Examples of several databases with grant opportunities include

- *Grants.gov* (www.grants.gov) is the gateway website for all discretionary grant opportunities offered through 26 federal grantmaking agencies.
- *eCivis* (www.ecivis.com) provides research and guidance as well as a searchable database geared primarily to local government agencies.
- *Community of Science* (pivot.cos.com)—in addition to their searchable database, COS facilitates collaboration and shared expertise among scientists and researchers by encouraging them to post profiles and share their results.
- *Sponsored Programs Information Network,* also known as SPIN (www.infoed.org) has the SPIN Matching and Research Transmittal Service (known as SMARTS), which is an automated e-mail system that alerts subscribers as relevant funding opportunities arise.

ditures as well as the time frame for use of the grant funds requested. Items usually included in the budget are salaries, fringe benefits, travel, equipment, supplies, and indirect costs (overhead expenses such as rent, utilities, etc.). Some grants will not fund certain expenditures; for example, foundations generally do not fund indirect costs, and federal grants prohibit use of government funds for lobbying.

Revenues projected in the budget may, and are sometimes required to, include sources in addition to the grant funds requested. If the grant guidelines specifically require matching funds, be sure to address how those funds will be contributed. Many funders require cash matches but some allow for the match to be provided via in-kind contributions, such as volunteer hours worked. When researching funding opportunities, one must always consider the matching requirements, especially if the nonprofit has limited ability to leverage other revenue sources. If, for example, grant funds are sought for a children's theatre group, and it is expected that tickets will be sold for a performance, the expected revenue from ticket sales should be included in the budget and might meet the funder's requirement for matching funds.

The grant guidelines will stipulate whether funds are available for single- or multi-year grants, which will also determine the time frame for which the budget should be projected. Preparing a detailed budget is a crucial aspect of preparing a grant proposal because it provides the basis for developing the project and assists in determining whether or not it is realistic and achievable. When searching for appropriate grant opportunities, always check the minimum and maximum awards for the grant program, and keep in mind that it is not always the maximum amount that is most important. A number of large foundations only fund large projects; if $10,000 is needed for playground equipment and the foundation did not make a grant under $100,000 in the last five years, chances are the project is not a good match.

It is important to put together a detailed budget for the proposal prior to writing the budget and project narratives. Gathering and documenting cost estimates as well as projecting potential revenues and their sources enable the nonprofit to determine what can be accomplished and what should probably not be undertaken in the project. Some funders require a budget narrative in addition to a project narrative; usually, the budget narrative simply describes the items in the budget and how the estimates were derived. Description of the objectives of the program as well as how they will be achieved is the focus of the project narrative.

In addition to a description of goals and objectives, funders are also looking in the narrative for assurance that the organization has the capacity to carry out the project. To this end, proposal guidelines will often request that applications include a brief history of the organization and information about past success with using grant funds to accomplish program goals. Management and staff expertise as well as the commitment of the board of directors can be used to illustrate organizational capacity. Collaborations are also popular with many funders; the ability to demonstrate the support of the community and civic leaders, as well as cooperative efforts with other nonprofits, is often a requested or even required component of the proposal. Increasingly, grantors are including evaluation as a requirement for all funded projects; they want the proposal to include discussion of how outcomes will be measured and performance will be assessed.

Submitting the Proposal

Grant proposals are often submitted electronically, but some agencies continue to accept printed copies. Check the application guidelines and follow the funder's instructions regarding method of submission and deadline for receipt of the application. Deadlines are generally for the date and time when the proposal must be received by the funder; postmarks are usually not sufficient to meet funders' deadlines.

When pulling together all of the elements for submission of the proposal, it really cannot be stressed enough how important it is to follow the instructions provided by funders. They require certain elements to be presented in a certain manner for a reason; it does not matter what their reason is because they have the money and they set the rules for giving it away. For example, if they ask for a list of the board of directors with contact information, provide it. If they specify that applicants should not include brochures, DVDs, or photographs, do not send them. Do the necessary homework before submitting the proposal and make sure to provide the type and quantity of information funders want so that they can evaluate how well the proposal matches their goals.

It is also important to keep in mind that receipt of a grant will not solve all of a nonprofit organization's resource problems and being denied a grant is not the end of the world. Grants are denied for a variety of reasons; even good projects articulated in well-prepared proposals are sometimes not successful. Funders have a limited amount of resources and sometimes the money runs out before all of the good projects get funded. Sometimes the project was just not a good match for a particular funder but would be perfect for a different one, and sometimes the person preparing the proposal did not put in the level of effort needed to properly research and write it. In either case, the important lesson is to try again; building the experience necessary to successfully pursue grants for a nonprofit takes time, patience, and a constant eye on the organization's mission.

PUBLIC POLICY CONSEQUENCES OF GRANTS AND CONTRACTS

Just as revenues from private donations imply public policy choices, government and foundation grants as well as government contracts embody policy priorities and perspectives. In offering grants for certain activities instead of others, governments and private foundations are promoting their definitions of public problems and soliciting solutions within a prescribed set of parameters. Accordingly, this makes it even more important for nonprofits to make sure that their mission and organizational goals match the funder's perception of the nature of the public problem to be addressed and the most appropriate way in which to address it. As discussed in Chapter 9, individual donors who do not do their research can inadvertently support an organization with distinctly different policy goals. Likewise, a grant or contract relationship can result in problems for either party if the policy priorities are found to be in opposition to one another. It is important, therefore, for grantors and grantees to each consider the risks and rewards of entering into a funding relationship.

Government Funding of Policy Priorities

Grants have long been considered the metaphorical carrot in intergovernmental relations—that is, an incentive to entice states to engage in activities that the national government has no authority to compel them to undertake. Passage of the Morrill Act in 1862 represents one early example. Under the Morrill Act, states that were not "in a condition of rebellion or insurrection against the government of the United States"[59] were entitled to sizable grants of land to be retained or sold to finance the construction of institutions of higher education. As with most federal grant programs, the Morrill Act provided incentives to engage in certain activities—in this case to build colleges and universities. It also discouraged certain behavior; for example, a state in rebellion against the Union was not eligible for funds. This provision was relevant because at the time the act took effect, several states had seceded and the nation was embroiled in the Civil War. It has become increasingly common that grant programs have both carrot and stick elements to them.

Project (also known as categorical) grants are funds given for a specific purpose according to criteria set by the granting agency. Members of Congress tend to prefer categorical grants as a tool to heighten the scope and influence of the national government and have often expressed preference for grants to nonprofit service providers. By establishing the specific project goals and setting the criteria by which those goals should be met, categorical grants allow the national government the greatest power over what public policy issues are to be addressed as well as the manner in which they will be tackled.

Whereas categorical grants allow the national government the greatest influence in targeting funding to specific policy issues and service delivery methods, public problems are not necessarily the same in all states. Because the states are different—geographically, culturally, economically, politically, and in other ways—the policy problems they face are often different. As such, federal funds targeted to specific projects may not match the needs in all states. Community development, for example, means something different in a coal mining town in Pennsylvania than it does in a retirement community in Florida. Categorical grants may be best at targeting funds to meet national priorities in local communities, but discretionary funding such as general revenue sharing[60] is better at giving communities the flexibility to handle their own unique problems; however, that flexibility may also allow communities to ignore the bigger picture if they choose. As the example of the CDBG program discussed above illustrates, block grants fall midway on the spectrum of restrictiveness with regard to program criteria. Block grants continue to be a popular format for grant programs, as they are well equipped to unite the best elements of other grant types and often facilitate collaboration between nonprofits and government entities.

Grants embody public policy in yet another respect—compliance requirements. Often referred to as the stick element of federal grants, compliance requirements are mandates that must be met before grant funds are awarded. These often take the form of cross-cutting requirements, meaning that organizations that receive grant funds must adhere to the requirements throughout the entire organization, not simply with the project for which the grant funds are awarded. For example, organizations that receive CDBG funds must provide assurance that the organization will comply with the Equal Opportunity Act and the Drug-Free Workplace Act throughout the entire time that the organization receives grant funds. The stipulations in these acts pervade all aspects of an organization, not simply the project activities. Box 10.3 contains a list of common assurances required for federal grant programs.

As with grants, government contracts involve a great many conditions. For example, nonprofits will not be able to use contract funds for anything other than what is specified in the contract, and the clients served may be required to meet certain eligibility standards, such as low-income status. In some cases, nonprofits are required to match government funds with their own funds or other resources to win the contract. Finally, other regulations and restrictions, including monitoring and evaluation requirements, are likely to be imposed on the nonprofit contractor.

Consider the example of the federal Charitable Choice provision in welfare reform, which allowed religious and faith-based organizations (FBOs) to pursue social service contracts

Box 10.3

CDBG COMPLIANCE REQUIREMENTS

CDBG application must contain assurances that the grantee will comply with each of the following:

- Equal Employment Opportunity Act
- Fair Housing Law (by completing a Fair Housing Plan)
- National Environmental Protection Act (by conducting an Environmental Review)
- Section 504 of the Rehabilitation Act of 1973 regarding non-discrimination for disabilities
- Americans with Disabilities Act
- Wage Rates established under the Davis-Bacon Act
- Lead-Based Paint Poisoning Prevention Act
- Historic Preservation regulations listed in 24 CFR 570.483(c)(2)

"on an equal basis with secular service providers."[61] States could not discriminate against them in awarding social services contracts and had to allow FBOs to maintain the religious character of their programs—for example, display their religious artifacts and symbols of faith in service delivery.[62] However, the FBOs had to operate under a number of federal regulations in order to maintain contract compliance. Restrictions on faith-based government contractors include the requirement that they submit to open financial audits of government funds, a prohibition on the use of government funds for sectarian worship or instruction, and requirements that faith-based contractors must serve all eligible clients regardless of their religion, religious practices or beliefs, or refusal to participate in any religious activity.[63]

As we have discussed, there has been a tremendous increase in the number of government grants as well as the amount of contract work that the nonprofit sector has done for government in recent decades, especially in social services. When utilizing government funds for their operations, nonprofit organizations play a particularly important role with respect to policy implementation. The purposes for which government funds are given to nonprofits, either through grants or contracts, have important policy connotations, as both funder and recipient seek to maintain control over the execution of policy priorities and mission.

Foundation Funding to Influence Policy

Foundations routinely have an impact on public policy with the research and projects they fund, although the scope of that impact has changed over time and varies across organizations. The early foundations played a substantial role in shaping public policy, serving as precursors to government programs and activities, even agencies. For example, the Carnegie

Corporation was instrumental in establishing what is now an extensive network of public libraries owned and operated by local governments. The Dorr Foundation instituted a major traffic safety innovation with the white-painted lines on the shoulders of roads, which continues to be implemented by transportation officials at all levels of government. Finally, the Rockefeller Foundation's fellowship training program for scientists served as the program model for the federal government's National Science Foundation.[64] Growth of the federal government and passage of regulations such as the Tax Reform Act of 1969 and the Pension Protection Act of 2006 limit the ability of today's foundations to have the same large-scale impact on public policy as the philanthropic titans of the Progressive Era. Nonetheless, foundations retain significant influence over how public problems are defined, which problems reach the attention of public policymakers, and how potential solutions are implemented.

Foundations are not without their critics when it comes to policy influence, however. Since establishment of the minimum payout requirement under the Tax Reform Act of 1969, foundation critics and proponents have continued to debate the merits of accumulation and distribution of philanthropic assets.[65] Debate focuses largely on whether tax-exempt assets are best used for current or future generations. Accordingly, policymakers' concerns about philanthropy center largely upon issues of longevity, as well as size and control.[66] The minimum payout requirements adopted in 1969 were designed to address issues of size by requiring a minimal level of asset disbursal each year; issues of control were addressed somewhat through the excess business holding rules. What failed to make it into the legislative mandates were proposals that specifically addressed the debate over benefits to current or future generations; those proposals not adopted would have required payout of all assets and termination of the foundation after 40 years (a limited-life requirement), and would have limited donor control of foundations to 25 years or less (the requirement that all family foundations eventually convert to independent foundations). Thus, the debate continues regarding whether foundations that exist in perpetuity or those with only a limited life span best serve the public interest.

Proponents of limited life foundations argue that foundations should not exist in perpetuity and that the minimum payout should be increased because the tax revenue foregone through tax-deductibility of donations should be recouped via philanthropy that serves the needs of the current generation rather than saved for later ones. In-perpetuity proponents argue that higher minimum payouts would present unnecessary risks to the endowment principal during economic downturns when investment income declines; failure to protect the ability of the endowment to generate future income endangers the pursuit of long-term solutions to public problems as well as the longevity of the organizations supported through foundation grants.[67] The overwhelming majority of those who establish foundations choose the perpetual model. There are some notable exceptions, however, such as the Mary Flagler Cary Trust, which was established with $72.5 million in assets and operated from 1968 to 2009, and the Prince Charitable Trusts, which had $128.3 million in assets in 2009 and concluded its grantmaking operations in 2012. Each argument has merits, and the debate will likely continue. Survey evidence suggests that 8 to 10 percent of foundations are structured with a limited lifespan, but it is not clear whether this represents a trend.[68]

In addition to debating whether current or future generations should benefit from the policy implementation facilitated by foundation funding, some suggest that foundations are not as effective at influencing public policy as they should be. Waldemar A. Nielsen in particular took issue with the effectiveness of the largest foundations in addressing the large-scale issues of the 1980s:

> That the United States is so well endowed with such an array of institutions to analyze its difficulties, devise and test new solutions, and help adapt the social, political, and economic apparatus to the requirements of changing circumstances should be deeply reassuring. But the gap between the potentiality and the actuality is regrettably very great.[69]

Nielsen concluded that while a few of the major foundations did live up to their potential to address the big problems in big ways, the majority focused too narrowly on what he described as "lesser, even parochial matters."[70] He criticized those foundations that were primarily reactive, in that they sought to address problems others brought to them and did useful but not really inspiring work. With regard to public policy, foundations have the potential and the duty, Nielsen contends, to tackle the major social ills in a comprehensive and proactive manner.[71]

Many foundations continue to tackle such ills, even if not with the obvious impact of the early works of the Carnegie Corporation and others. As by far the largest grantmaking foundation, the Bill & Melinda Gates Foundation is an example of a foundation that addresses social ills on a global scale, putting its vast resources to work on comprehensive solutions to health and education problems in some of the world's neediest areas. In his annual letter, Bill Gates explains the vision of the foundation and specifies its strategic approach to solving the large-scale problems that an institution with its resources is uniquely positioned to address.

CONCLUSION

As Jane already knew, grants are an important resource for the nonprofit sector, but relying on them as the sole or even primary source of revenue is problematic. As discussed in Chapter 5, mission creep is a very real danger for nonprofits. Resource dependency exacerbates the problem as cash-strapped public charities find the potential for receiving any grant funds too enticing to resist. Board members as well as staff can become quite adept at finding justifications for moving just beyond the fringe of the mission statement because of the need for additional resources. Many argue that a diversified revenue base, as discussed in Chapters 10 and 11, is more likely to provide a stable revenue stream that enhances pursuit of mission rather than distracts from it.

That said, however, grants have an important place in the funding stream for nonprofits. Likewise, they have important implications for the implementation of public policy. Government grants allow state and national policy goals to be implemented in a way that is tailored to the specific needs of a community because nonprofit organizations have a more intimate knowledge of the local clientele. Foundation grants allow for innovation and experimentation in addressing major social problems without the political difficulties associated with government use of taxpayer dollars. While grants may pose the threats of mission drift and cooptation by the funder, grant funding also has the potential to free a nonprofit from the burden of seemingly endless fundraising. Less time spent on raising funds allows staff to concentrate more on delivering needed services.

Questions For Review

1. Compare and contrast the different types of grants with regard to their attractiveness for funders and for grant recipients. Discuss how the different grant types embody different policy connotations.
2. From a donor's perspective, discuss the pros and cons of establishing a private family foundation, an operating foundation, or a donor-advised fund with a community foundation. Which would you prefer? Why?
3. Discuss the challenges and policy implications of accepting government grants and contracts for nonprofit organizations. Under what circumstances would you suggest an organization become a contractor?

Assignment

Choose a nonprofit organization—either the one at which you work, one for which you have volunteered, or one you choose at random in your community—and develop an idea or project for which it would be suitable to apply for grant funding. Identify four potential sources of grant funding for the project and determine

- name of the funder
- funding range for grants awarded
- application deadlines
- eligibility criteria
- funder's areas of interest
- why you think this would be a good source

Your university library and office of sponsored programs are good potential sources of assistance in accessing available databases for the funding search.

Suggested Readings

Karsh, Ellen, and Arlen Sue Fox. *The Only Grant-Writing Book You'll Ever Need,* 2nd ed. . New York: Carroll & Graf, 2006.

Nielsen, Waldemar A. *Golden Donors: A New Anatomy of the Great Foundations.* New Brunswick, NJ: Transaction Publishers, 2002.

The Foundation Center Proposal Writing Short Course, which can be accessed at: http://fdncenter.org/learn/shortcourse/prop1.html.

Web Resources

Code of Federal Regulations, www.gpoaccess.gov/cfr/
Federal Audit Clearinghouse, harvester.census.gov/fac
Federal Government Grants, www.grants.gov
Federal Register, www.gpoaccess.gov/fr/index.html
The Foundation Center, www.foundationcenter.org
The Grantsmanship Center, www.tgci.com/funding.shtml
USA Spending, www.usaspending.gov

Administration and Management

Great nonprofits know that they must continually close the gap between their outward-looking vision—their constant desire for greater impact—and their need to invest in themselves.

Leslie R. Crutchfield and Heather McLeod Grant[1]

One of the largest nonprofits in the country is in trouble. In operation for over 75 years, its size and stature have made it an important source of food aid for families living in poverty and a formidable force in the policy arena. Unfortunately, mismanagement of both money and mission has rocked its core. The reputation of the institution has been tarnished, donations are down, foundations are considering withdrawal of funding, and the number of volunteer hours committed has dropped by over 25 percent from one year ago.

Fortunately, at this point most of the original accounting and management problems have been resolved and a dozen top officials, including the chief executive officer, have left the organization. The search is on for a new leader, and among the top contenders is the former president of a Fortune 500 Internet firm with an MBA from Harvard and a very high profile. Some are excited about the reputation and management team that this woman would bring to the organization; others are skeptical that she can apply her profit-making skills in the nonprofit sector. Many are asking the question, "What does she know about managing a nonprofit organization?"

MANAGING NONPROFIT ORGANIZATIONS

We all know that good management is essential to the success of any organization, but what does "good management" really mean? Particularly in the nonprofit sector, questions about management practices persist. How do we know when nonprofit organizations are successful? As Peter Drucker asked: What is the bottom line when there is no "bottom line"?[2] Does program success equal organizational success? Would more efficient nonprofit management create savings that could fund more and better programs: what Bradley, Jansen, and Silverman called the "$100 billion opportunity"?[3]

POLICY IMPLICATIONS OF ADMINISTRATION AND MANAGEMENT

- Nonprofit management is shaped by internal and external factors that affect the policies and programs they pursue and can affect the ways in which they pursue them.
- Management differs by sector, and the public purposes of nonprofits require them to be accountable to the public, particularly in terms of financial management.
- To pursue their missions, nonprofit organizations must be well-managed, using consistent communication with stakeholders and evaluating their program outcomes to determine their impacts on society.
- Good management is necessary for nonprofits to reach their goals; they are increasingly building management capacity through training of boards and employees, engaging in strategic planning, and professionalizing their management techniques.
- Nonprofits derive a substantial amount of revenue from grants, contracts, and donations, which causes them to face more legal constraints on the use of revenues than their for-profit counterparts.

Management at all levels—from first-level supervisors to mid-level managers to directors and governance boards—is vital to building and maintaining effective nonprofit organizations and retaining committed employees.[4] While issues relating specifically to executive directors and boards are the topic of Chapter 12, the current chapter focuses on strategies and concerns in the day-to-day management of nonprofits, including issues of efficiency and effectiveness, building organizational capacity, and well-managed budgets and finances. All of these are important for meeting organizational missions and goals. We discuss these issues while offering a review of current practices and important trends in nonprofit management—with the caveat that context matters and there is no one-size-fits-all approach to managing organizations as diverse as those in the nonprofit sector. One thing is certain: as not-for-profit organizations increasingly touch lives, deliver services, and shape public policy, the importance of well-managed and well-administered nonprofits has become more and more clear.

Organizational Structures and Behavior

The study of modern organizations is usually traced back to Max Weber's work on bureaucracy at the turn of the twentieth century. At the time, Weber recognized that both public and for-profit organizations would grow in size and become more formally structured as society became more complex; not surprisingly, nonprofit organizations, especially large ones, have exhibited this same formalization.[5] While the study of organizational theory and behavior has advanced well beyond Weber, many of the basic characteristics that he identified nearly one hundred years ago remain important components of modern organizational structures including hierarchy, formal rules, specialization, and division of labor.

For the first half of the twentieth century, organizational theorists typically studied the structures of for-profit organizations and sought ways in which managers could induce greater productivity from the workforce.[6] Other scholars, including Luther Gulick, sought to identify a consistent set of tasks that managers perform.[7] Gulick, who was among the first to study public sector management, introduced the acronym POSDCORB, which identified seven key elements of administrative work: Planning, Organizing, Staffing, Directing, Coordinating, Reporting, and Budgeting. While the work of these early scholars has been criticized as overly simplistic, their basic findings and approach continue to shape the study and practice of organizational management.[8]

Systems Theory and the Impact of Internal and External Pressures

In the 1950s, theorists introduced a *systems approach* to the study of organizations, which is particularly useful in studying nonprofits because it includes the concepts of internal and external pressures as drivers of organizational behavior.[9] With regard to not-for-profit organizations, external conditions such as an economic downturn, a new public program, or a change to the tax code can influence the level of foundation grants, the work it does, and the availability of donor funds. Systems theorists often study organizations as *organic systems*, focusing on their life cycles and survival instincts.[10]

The example of the March of Dimes is one of the best for explaining the organic systems concept of organizational survival: when it accomplished its original mission of ending the polio epidemic, the organization survived by pursuing a new mission, the elimination of all birth defects (see Box 5.2).

Internal Pressures. An important contribution to the study of organizational structure and behavior comes from Henry Mintzberg, who introduced the concepts of the Strategic Apex, the Middle Line, and the Operating Core.[11] In the average not-for-profit organization, the governing board and chief executive constitute the Strategic Apex, making programmatic and policy decisions; the Middle Line is management, responsible for both long- and short-term planning and day-to-day supervision of operations; the Operating Core includes those on the front-lines of program and service delivery who can be both paid staff and volunteers. One of Mintzberg's most important points is that a key responsibility of the middle line is to shield members of the operating core from external and internal disruptions. In the nonprofit organization, this means that management should ensure that those delivering programs, services, goods, grants, and projects are protected from the financial, political, or public relations entanglements that may draw them away from accomplishing the core organizational mission.

Both the size of the organization and its stage in the life cycle are important for nonprofits. For example, in the beginning nonprofits tend to be small, with few employees, little money, and a rather flat organizational structure that includes little more than a board of directors, an executive director, some volunteers, and perhaps a few staff members. Sharon Oster notes the importance of the mission at the founding of an organization: "The early mission statement will be the flag around which new staff is recruited, new donors and volunteers are created, and a user group is identified."[12]

FIGURE 11.1 **Basic Organizational Structure**

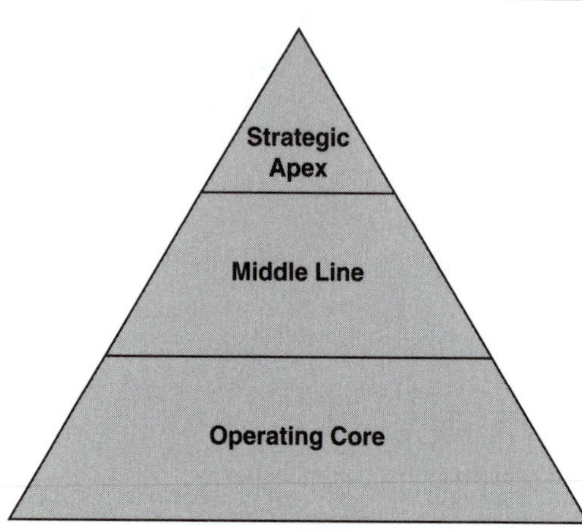

Source: Adapted from Mintzberg, Henry Mintzberg, *The Structure of Organizations.* (Upper Saddle River, NJ: Prentice Hall, 1979).

Over time, the nonprofit typically grows and enters what could be called its mature stage, during which the role of donors, staff, volunteers, and clientele becomes more important in refining the mission and activities of the organization.[13] Oster notes

> As the organization matures, and particularly if it grows, bureaucratization follows and cost considerations often become more salient. In part because cost considerations grow in importance, the role of professional staff typically increases as well, as does the political power of this group.[14]

While other factors may begin to rival the importance of mission for those inside a mature nonprofit, mission remains its raison d'être, and those in the strategic apex must ensure that the organization maintains its mission focus.

External Pressures. Systems theory tells us that change within an organization is often encouraged by external forces. In the nonprofit world external pressure typically comes from one or more of three sources: politics, society, and economics.[15] For example, in recent years there has been a decrease in political support for public funding of abstinence-only sex education programs. This has affected groups like Why kNOw?, a long-time, nonprofit provider of abstinence-only curriculum located in Tennessee. The loss of political support and public funding led the group to change its name to OnPoint in 2009, and to broaden its focus from simply abstinence-only sex education to include curricular components addressing addiction, stress, and academic achievement. The new mission statement, "build[ing] healthy teens by providing the in-depth knowledge, on-going support, and skills needed to achieve a life of excellence," captures these changes.[16]

Demographic or societal pressures may lead to organizational change as well, particularly when these changes influence the types or numbers of clients served. For example, during the economic recession homelessness among families skyrocketed, increasing by 30 percent between 2008 and 2010.[17] Shelter Network, an organization that addresses homelessness in San Mateo County, California, saw an even more dramatic increase in the number of families with children seeking emergency housing assistance during the recession, and by mid-2011, 39 percent of Shelter Network's clients were children. Calls from those needing housing assistance increased from 100 a week in 2008 to 1,500 a week in 2011.[18] The economic climate changed the clientele and demand at Shelter Network and similar nonprofits as the need, especially among families and the first-time homeless, dramatically increased.

Further, external economic pressures often result from resource dependency. As discussed in Chapter 3, this theory indicates that an organization may be compelled to change its programs and services in response to demands from those who provide funds; for nonprofits that means donors and grantors, as well as fee-based clientele. Examples of this sort of pressure have been prevalent in college and university settings for centuries, as universities evolved from their religious origins. As their sources of funding changed from churches and large private donors to public and grant funding, the priorities of universities and the way they organized and managed themselves changed as well, moving from a focus on religious study and training to a more academic focus that protected the professoriate and elevated the importance of faculty research.[19]

Resource dependency can lead to a type of *goal displacement,* which is described by theorists as occurring when an organization or its personnel move away from their primary purpose to focus on tangential issues. In the case of resource dependency, goal displacement can mean that the nonprofit deviates from its mission in order to attract funding that may be more easily attained, or that it decides to serve a new population to win government and foundation grants. Of course, straying too far from one's stated mission can be grounds for legal action by the state attorney general.

Environmental changes can also open new markets for nonprofits. Oster gives the example of Habitat for Humanity, which was established in 1976 to build, rehabilitate, and repair homes for people in need.[20] She notes: "In some ways, this organization is taking over the kinds of building efforts once run through the large federal Housing and Urban Development bureaucracy. In this instance, changes in the public sector created an opportunity for a new nonprofit."[21] This is, of course, increasingly the case as public organizations face calls for smaller government and are forced to curb costs by downsizing, making employee cutbacks, and contracting with nonprofit and for-profit organizations to implement public policies.

As with any other organic system, the nonprofit organization seeks survival. As the opening vignette suggests, long-term survival is facilitated by size—larger organizations tend to last.[22] Thus, some nonprofits grow to be quite large, as in the case of the National Alliance on Mental Illness (NAMI). NAMI traces its roots to a small support group for parents of the mentally ill which formed in 1974. Today, NAMI has grown to more than 1,100 affiliate member groups across the United States. See Box 11.1 for a discussion of the origins and current structure of NAMI.

Box 11.1

FOR EXAMPLE

THE NATIONAL ALLIANCE ON MENTAL ILLNESS: ADMINISTERING OPERATIONS WITH A FEDERAL STRUCTURE

The National Alliance on Mental Illness (NAMI) began in 1974 in the living room of Eve Oliphant, the mother of a mentally ill adult son. Originally calling themselves Parents of Adult Schizophrenics, the group sought mutual support and very quickly turned its attention to ways to encourage the medical establishment to recognize mental illness as a legitimate disease.[23] Parents were tired of being blamed for their children's illnesses and sought to increase and improve research and treatment, to provide assistance and advocacy for families caring for the mentally ill, and to destigmatize mental illness through public education.[24]

In 1979, members of 59 affiliate groups from 29 states attended the founding meeting of a national group—the National Alliance for the Mentally Ill. By 1984, there were 356 affiliate groups in all 50 states, and today, there are over 1,100 local affiliates throughout the U.S. NAMI's founding meeting focused on three goals: (1) education about federal legislation, current research, and recent treatment options; (2) mutual help and advocacy groups to improve the lives of the mentally ill and their families; and (3) creation of a national organization of help and advocacy groups.[25] While NAMI has been renamed the National Alliance on Mental Illness, it continues to focus on these same three pillars: support, education, and advocacy. Its mission is to improve "the lives of individuals and families affected by mental illness."[26]

NAMI is a good example of a nonprofit organization with a federal structure. It operates at the national level but has semi-autonomous affiliates at the local and state levels. Local affiliates typically begin as small groups with a few members; as they grow, these groups seek to be chartered at the state and national levels. Their work includes local referral services, interaction with local professionals and media outlets, and communication of local issues to their state level organizations. At the state level, NAMI decides on goals and objectives to suit the needs and political climate within each state. State chapters engage in advocacy and monitoring of the activity and budgets of state agencies that play a role in mental health programs and policies; they also facilitate local affiliate growth through annual goal setting, technical assistance, and statewide newsletters. At the national level, the 16-member board of directors sets goals and strategies, develops public policy positions, holds an annual conference, and governs the organization. Given the nature of our government's federal system, this corresponding three-tier structure of NAMI allows state affiliates to address specific policies at the state level while the national organization addresses federal policies. For example, with many states cutting their mental health budgets, state NAMI affiliates have lobbied against such cuts; at the same time the national organization has supported legislation at the federal level that would improve access to innovative drug treatment for those with serious mental illnesses.[27] A federal organizational structure makes a great deal of sense for very large nonprofits, particularly when they wish to affect public policy.

For additional information about NAMI: http://www.nami.org/

DIFFERING MANAGEMENT NEEDS ACROSS SECTORS

Traditionally, the literature on organizational management was generic, operating under the assumption that if you can manage one organization, you can manage any organization; whether for-profit, public, or nonprofit, organizations are all the same. When the three sectors have been empirically examined, however, scholars have found something else entirely.[28] While many of the structures, functions, and strategies appear to be the same for the three sectors, each has distinct differences.

For example, there are a variety of ways in which the management of nonprofits is different from the management of for-profit firms. A key difference lies in the public nature of nonprofit service provision and the potential for devastating public consequences of management failure in the nonprofit sector. While for-profit mismanagement can have serious consequences for consumers and stockholders, the for-profit sector is premised upon competition. If one is wary about the shoddy safety record of a particular auto manufacturer, there are many others from which to choose. Nonprofits, on the other hand, are an important part of the social safety net and often work in and for populations at the very margins of society where people have few options. As illustrated by the hypothetical nonprofit in the opening vignette, if large numbers of families rely on the organization for basic food needs and the organization is mismanaged, the results could be far more serious than the loss of market share. The lives, health, education, and welfare of large segments of the U.S. population often depend on the work of nonprofit organizations; their failures can harm the most vulnerable among us.

Another difference between nonprofit and for-profit organizations pertains to their levels of accountability to the public. Basic characteristics of the not-for-profit sector such as tax-exempt status, the receipt of tax-deductible donations, public charters and missions, and receipt of government grants all create a higher level of accountability to the public than is expected of for-profit firms. Whether their goals are policy, service, or advocacy-related, nonprofits are essential to fostering the public good and are beholden to the public. The best interests of society are not well served when nonprofit organizations are poorly managed and ill-equipped for these responsibilities.

While the success of organizations in the nonprofit sector has important public consequences, nonprofit management is also distinct from public management in many ways. For example, nonprofits face more competition than government agencies, which are largely monopolistic, and they are not always as well-known as public agencies. These characteristics mean that nonprofits typically need to brand and market themselves in ways that public organizations seldom do.

These differences between the three sectors affect management and administration in a variety of ways. The missions of each sector result in different clientele served—for example, with for-profits less likely to serve the most vulnerable populations.[29] Further, the level of goal specificity influences the way that performance and effectiveness is measured in each sector. Nonprofit and public sector goals are often vague and more difficult to measure.[30]

Organizational structures tend to differ by sector as well, which affects how many levels of supervision and coordination are required and how quickly and easily decisions can be made. While the public and for-profit sectors are typically fairly hierarchical and the public sector is well known for its bureaucratic constraints, nonprofit organizations tend to have flatter and less formal structures.[31] Given these differences, generic, one-size-fits-all management tools have been largely discounted in favor of each sector adapting the tools and methods of management to their own purposes.

GOOD MANAGEMENT IN THE NONPROFIT SECTOR

Let us return to the question of good management principles, and begin with the direction of Peter F. Drucker, considered one of the most influential scholars in the field of management. While his career focused on business practices and spanned more than sixty years, in the last decades of his life Drucker wrote about management of nonprofit organizations, suggesting three key factors of particular importance to the nonprofit sector: (1) communication and relationships; (2) performance standards; and (3) a hands-on approach.[32] In the sections that follow, we discuss these concepts in more depth.

Communication and Relationships. First, Drucker suggested that it is critical for nonprofit managers to emphasize communication rather than hierarchical relationships within the organization. "It's more important in the non-profit institution than it is in a business to insist on the clarity of commitments and relationships, and on the responsibility for making yourself understood and for educating your co-workers."[33] The importance of communication in nonprofit management has been echoed by others in a variety of contexts. For example, communication to and input from employees have been found to be important to making organizational change.[34] Equally important is communication outward from the organization to stakeholders, including donors, volunteers, and the community.[35] If there is any single "best practice" in nonprofit organizational management it is to communicate with stakeholders, both inside and outside of the organization, on a regular basis.[36] Internal communication allows the board, staff, and volunteers to understand what is expected of them and provides feedback on their contributions and ways they can enhance their performance in the pursuit of the organization's mission. Communication with external stakeholders allows the nonprofit to share its mission and affords opportunities to listen and learn from its environment; the more the organization learns, the better it is able to adapt, innovate, and survive.[37]

Performance Standards. Second, Drucker insisted that the nonprofit organization needs standards which "have to be concrete," "have to be set high,"[38] and "should be attainable."[39] Performance standards are commonly viewed as an important characteristic for well-managed nonprofits, as the literature on organizational capacity and management make clear. Interestingly, it is occasionally the nonprofit sector that creates the performance standards for organizations in all three sectors. For example, one way in which nonprofit organizations play a role in public policy is by developing professional standards or disseminating best practices; this arguably places nonprofits in a quasi-governmental role whereby rules and regulations are established and enforced.[40] The National Children's Alliance, discussed in Chapter 1, which develops and evaluates operating standards for Children's Advocacy Centers, is one example. Sometimes, as in the case of the Governmental Accounting Standards Board (GASB), these regulations apply directly to government itself (see Box 11.2).

Drucker's emphasis on performance standards ties directly to the suggestion that nonprofits take a strategic approach to management.[41] For nonprofit organizations, strategic management begins with development of the organization's mission and a formal mission statement that frames the work of the organization, motivates and attracts boards, employees, volunteers, and donors, and sets the parameters for evaluation. Mark H. Moore's strategic triangle provides a good example of the creation of a management strategy.[42] (See Figure 11.2.)

Moore begins with the determination of the *value* of the organization—its mission or social purpose. This point, the social value of the organization, is the focus of the model. Next is *legitimacy and support,* which involves identification of the authority for the organization. Beyond the leadership of the nonprofit, this includes identifying those who authorize and fund the organization, and attaining buy-in from actors outside of the organization. Management must recognize that the nonprofit needs a public profile that will garner

Box 11.2

FOR EXAMPLE

GOVERNMENTAL ACCOUNTING STANDARDS BOARD: REGULATING GOVERNMENT THROUGH NONPROFIT ACTION

The Governmental Accounting Standards Board (GASB) is a not-for-profit organization founded in 1984 by the Financial Accounting Foundation (FAF) and is charged with establishing standards for financial accounting and reporting for state and local governments. The standards are important because they demonstrate "accountability and stewardship over public resources" and provide financial information to assist all sectors in decisions relating to investment, credit, and regulations.[43]

GASB is effective in imposing regulatory standards on state and local governments primarily because governmental finance professionals have agreed to adhere to the standards. In addition, states such as Iowa have enacted legislation requiring local governments to follow the Generally Accepted Accounting Practices (GAAP) established by the GASB. Whether by statute or through professional allegiance, GASB standards are generally followed not because of fear of sanction by higher levels of government but rather fear of not receiving a clean audit from accountants. Failure to obtain an unqualified audit report has repercussions regarding interest rates on bond issues and even the receipt of some forms of intergovernmental aid.[44]

For additional information, see www.gasb.org.

Figure 11.2 Strategic Triangle Model for Nonprofit Organizations[45]

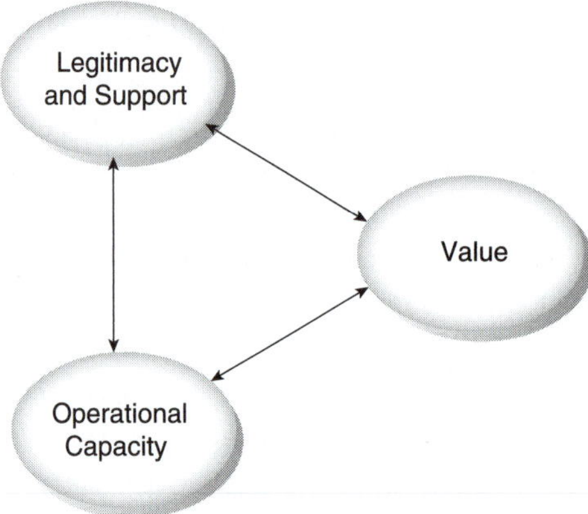

Source: Adapted from Mark H. Moore, "Managing for Value: Organizational Strategy in For-Profit, Nonprofit, and Governmental Organizations," *Nonprofit and Voluntary Sector Quarterly*, 29 (2000):183–204.

support from donors, government, and citizens. Moore argues that the legitimacy and support aspect of the strategic triangle is both an end and a means to an end. Third is *organizational capacity*, which Moore describes primarily as being about internal ability and the resources to pursue the nonprofit purpose but also may include partners and collaborative relationships. Moore notes that while this model of strategic management appears simplistic, in practice it "proves to be very challenging indeed" to coordinate these components and manage effectively.[46]

Finally, Drucker suggests: "Effective non-profits make sure that their people get out in the field and actually work there again and again" because "There are no results inside an institution."[47] What Drucker describes here might fall today under the headings of "team building" and "cross-training" of staff, or "management by walking around."[48] Following this advice ensures that everyone within the nonprofit has experience directly with the clientele and participants of the organization on a regular basis. This kind of hands-on approach facilitates management's understanding of the operation at all levels and the ways in which programs affect the clientele and community. It is particularly important in terms of handling organizational change, either from internal or external sources. Those managing change must be able to identify the challenges, allow them to be felt throughout the organization, encourage employees to find solutions, challenge unproductive habits, and involve everyone in working through the barriers that can impede necessary change. The volatile nature of modern organizations requires this type of hands-on, adaptive management style.[49]

Nonprofit Effectiveness and Efficiency

Effects from Drucker's approach and good management in general are often associated with the concept of *productivity,* especially in an era in which business/market models dominate discussions of management. Evan M. Berman defines productivity as "the effective and efficient use of resources to achieve outcomes."[50] For management in the nonprofit sector this means attaining both financial stability and social purpose.[51] Consider again the hypothetical organization depicted in the opening vignette, which had been rocked by "mismanagement of both money and mission"; for the nonprofit, mismanagement in either arena can be the death knell and can mean that the needs of many will go unmet. Thus, as with management of any organization, nonprofit managers must be concerned about both effectiveness and efficiency.

Berman makes the argument that nonprofits are often quite adept at being both effective and efficient by their very natures. He explains:

> Resources are frequently very scarce in nonprofit organizations, in part because their aims are huge (such as resolving homelessness) and in part because revenue streams are small (for example, based on membership fees). Resource scarcity causes nonprofit organizations to seek out "free" resources such as volunteers and community donations. This can turn nonprofit organizations into highly efficient providers. Productivity efforts aimed at better use of volunteers and greater success at fund-raising are especially important to these organizations.[52]

While frequently discussed together and often used interchangeably, the concepts of effectiveness and efficiency are quite distinct in the literature on both management and public policy. Berman defines effectiveness as an organization's "level of outcomes," noting that "outcomes are accomplishments."[53] It is useful to think of effectiveness as an external measure of fulfilling the organization's mission—how well are we doing what we are supposed to do?

For example, the opening vignette describes an organization that provides food aid to poor families. If one of the programs that they offer is a school backpack program—where children bring home backpacks of food to help feed their families over weekends and holidays—the effectiveness of that program can be assessed by how many backpacks are sent home (an *output measure*), but more importantly, by how many fewer nights family members went to bed hungry (an *outcome measure*). These measures of effectiveness address the question: Did we accomplish our mission? In this case, did we feed poor families? Further, how well did we do? Did we reduce the number of nights that family members went to bed hungry by one night, two nights, three nights in a week?[54]

The second measure, efficiency, is defined by Berman as "the cost per activity to achieve given outcomes."[55] Efficiency can be thought of as an internal measure—how well does the organization run? Perhaps our organization feeds thousands of families and eliminates hunger for tens of thousands of people a year; we would say that this is an effective organization.

However, we also want to know if the organization is spending an appropriate level of resources (time and money) in accomplishing its goal. In this case, it is useful to establish benchmarks for nonprofit performance—that is, compare our performance to that of others. If we spend the equivalent of $7 in resources to keep one person from going to bed hungry, and a similar nonprofit spends only $3, we probably need to improve our efficiency.

It is precisely these issues that Bradley, Jansen, and Silverman address in their discussion of nonprofit sector productivity.[56] They suggest five key ways to improve efficiency in the nonprofit sector, what they call the $100 billion opportunity. According to Bradley et al., the areas in which management of the nonprofit sector can be more cost effective—thereby funneling those savings back into providing services for society—include reducing funding costs, having foundations distribute holdings at higher than the mandatory 5 percent rate, reducing program service costs, trimming administrative costs, and improving program effectiveness. Most of these efforts fall under the scope of capacity building, discussed below.

On the other hand, some argue that the factors typically considered good management—efficiency, productivity, reducing administrative costs—might not be sufficient in the nonprofit sector due to the primacy of the nonprofit mission. For example, in a study of Detroit food assistance programs, Peter Eisinger found that organizational efficiency did "not seem to contribute to fulfilling a central mission of the food providers: helping those who need food assistance."[57] Others raise concerns about goal displacement if, for example, the emphasis on measuring financial efficiency and productivity increases the incentives for program creaming—focusing on the clientele most easily served as a less expensive way to meet productivity targets.[58] As we have argued throughout, a nonprofit must always remain true to its mission; sometimes fulfilling the mission will require greater emphasis on effectiveness than efficiency.

Similarly, in *Forces for Good,* Crutchfield and Grant study what they call twelve high-impact nonprofits that "have created extraordinary levels of social impact."[59] These are organizations that "have come up with innovative solutions to pressing social problems, and they have spread these ideas nationally or internationally."[60] Crutchfield and Grant explicitly state that they have not focused on the best managed, best marketed, or most financially stable nonprofits; rather, their book highlights organizations that have had a tremendous impact and facilitated high levels of systemic change. Not surprisingly, the twelve nonprofits highlighted in *Forces for Good* do a great deal of policy-oriented work. As Crutchfield and Grant explain, the organizations "conduct programs on the ground and simultaneously advocate for policy change at the local, state, or national level."[61]

Using their criteria for success, Crutchfield and Grant find that high-impact nonprofits engage in six common practices:

- Advocate and Serve—successful organizations achieve greater impact when they engage in advocacy as well as service[62]
- Make Markets Work—nonprofits often succeed by working with for-profits, helping businesses to "do well while doing good"[63]

- Inspire Evangelists—successful nonprofits see stakeholders as evangelists—contributing not only time and money, but contributing by their enthusiasm for the cause[64]
- Nurture Nonprofit Networks—successful nonprofits recognize that a healthy sector is in their best interest and are happy to share their experience, talents, and power in the best interests of all[65]
- Master the Art of Adaptation—nonprofits succeed by being flexible; they are able to adapt to their environments in order to maintain their impact and relevance[66]
- Share Leadership—successful leaders empower others by distributing leadership and power throughout the nonprofit and their organizational networks [67]

While the organizations highlighted in *Forces for Good* are well-managed, they have not prioritized efficiency, productivity, or capacity building over their missions. Rather, the organizations that Crutchfield and Grant feature, including Habitat for Humanity, Teach for America, and the Heritage Foundation, continue to be mission-driven and primarily concerned about making lasting change in society.[68] Thus, while efficient management should not be discounted, their status as mission-driven organizations requires that nonprofits prioritize their public purpose. Whether their mission is implementing social welfare programs, exhibiting fine art exhibits, or pursuing policy change, efficiency should only be a secondary goal.

ORGANIZATIONAL REFORMS AND THE QUEST FOR IMPROVEMENT

While management strategies have been developed specifically for nonprofits, it remains true that many of the reforms in management come from the for-profit sector. Adoption of these reforms by the public and nonprofit sectors often comes later, with varying degrees of success.[69] This is certainly the case with the organizational reforms that began with Total Quality Management (TQM) in the 1970s after W. Edwards Deming brought strategies from successful Japanese corporations back to the United States. The quality movement, a management philosophy which recommended continuous improvement strategies for production and organizational processes, swept the private, public, and nonprofit sectors for the next several decades.

In 1982, Thomas J. Peters and Robert J. Waterman published *In Search of Excellence,* a treatise on best business practices that is said to have inspired the public sector version, Tom Osborne and David Gaebler's *Reinventing Government,* in 1992.[70] As part of the so-called New Public Management (NPM), Osborne and Gaebler's ideas were quickly adopted by the federal government in 1993, through the Clinton-Gore National Performance Review. While there is no definitive model of New Public Management, in practice it includes a diverse set of strategies and tools, with its most common threads including explicit measures of organizational performance, a customer service orientation, cost-cutting measures, and the infusion of competition in service delivery.[71] It is this last piece, infusing competition into public provision of services, which helped to increase the level of government contracting with the nonprofit sector in the past two decades. Thus, when nonprofits have looked for ways to improve organizational management, they have adopted many strategies from the for-profit sector and public policies such as the National Performance Review.

CAPACITY BUILDING AND SUCCESSFUL NONPROFITS

Paul C. Light in *Sustaining Nonprofit Performance* combines the aforementioned techniques for management reform in the nonprofit sector under the heading of *capacity building*.[72] The Alliance for Nonprofit Management defines capacity as an organization's ability to achieve its mission effectively and to sustain itself over the long term.[73] Light explains that capacity encompasses

> . . . virtually everything an organization uses to achieve its mission, from desks and chairs to programs and people. Measured at any given point in time, capacity is an output of basic organizational activities such as raising money, forging partnerships, organizing work, recruiting and training board members, leaders, and employees, generating ideas, managing budgets, and evaluating programs.[74]

It is through improved management capacity that nonprofits are best able to pursue their missions; therefore, the concept of nonprofit capacity, and especially capacity building, has gained a great deal of attention and foundation grant funding in the past few decades.[75]

A number of member organizations have been created to help nonprofits improve their management capacity, including Grantmakers for Effective Organizations (GEO) and the Alliance for Nonprofit Management. The mission of GEO is to encourage foundations and trusts to fund efforts to improve the effectiveness of their nonprofit grantees. Similarly, the Alliance for Nonprofit Management's mission is, "To increase the effectiveness of individuals and organizations that help nonprofits build their power and impact."[76] The alliance considers a wide range of activities under the umbrella of capacity building, such as improving governance and leadership as well as strengthening mission, strategy, administration, and fundraising. It also includes efforts to improve the development, implementation, and evaluation of programs to enhance advocacy and policy change, and to better meet the needs of diverse nonprofit clientele.

Similarly, Light describes capacity building activities as "any effort to increase, replenish, or improve an organization's capacity."[77] In his survey of 318 nonprofits, Light found that reform efforts undertaken by nonprofits have been along four key dimensions: (1) improving external relations, including mergers, strategic planning, and fundraising; (2) improving internal relations, including adding staff and building teams; (3) improving leadership, including board development and increased delegation; and (4) improving management systems, including information technology, staff training, and accounting systems.

Light's study finds that nonprofit managers are using these techniques of organizational improvement a lot—between 77 and 88 percent had attempted to improve some aspect of their management in the previous five years. Similarly, Durst and Newell surveyed 87 nonprofits about their involvement in such reinvention efforts and found that 65.5 percent had engaged in some sort of reinvention strategy and only 16 percent indicated no intention of doing so in the future.[78] The most frequently used reinvention strategies for these agencies were strategic management and planning, new processes designed to increase efficiency and effectiveness, increased employee participation, redefining the organizational mission, and reorganizing the workforce.

These capacity building efforts, often aided by for-profit and nonprofit consultants, have enhanced the administrative capabilities of many nonprofit organizations and encouraged even small organizations to seek out better methods of management and strategies for success. For example, seminars on board leadership and development, workshops on writing grant proposals, and executive coaching services are available in many locations and have helped to professionalize the work of the nonprofit sector. In the often competitive arena of winning grants, contracts, and donor dollars, an organization is at an advantage when it is well managed. It is able to attract and keep better board members, employees, and volunteers, as well as write stronger proposals to win grants and contracts, and also to use more sophisticated techniques to raise capital and steward relationships with donors. All of these are components to successful pursuit of the nonprofit mission.

A growing trend among not-for-profits that find themselves overwhelmed by management and organizational issues is to join partnerships or even outsource tasks. For example, when faced with severe financial constraints, the Columbus Symphony Orchestra turned to another nonprofit, the Columbus Association for the Performing Arts, to manage their back office affairs. (See Box 11.3 for details.)

Organizational Reform Efforts and Management Challenges Unique to Nonprofits

As with management in general, reform is different in each of the three sectors; in research on the implementation and assessment of nonprofit management techniques, authors have been careful to note that there are no standard techniques for improvement, reinvention, or self-assessment of nonprofit organizations.[79] Rather, studies find that each organization must adapt strategies of management improvement to fit their unique situations. As Durst and Newell explain, "Reinvention success may be less a science of employing the right management technique and more an art of combining the right technique with countless variables."[84]

An example comes from an in-depth analysis of organizational change at CARE, in which Marc Lindenberg concludes that while nonprofit sector organizations can borrow techniques from the other sectors, they have unique challenges related to the missions and the

Box 11.3

FOR EXAMPLE

COLUMBUS ASSOCIATION FOR THE PERFORMING ARTS: OUTSOURCING ARTS MANAGEMENT

On March 31, 2010, the Columbus Symphony Orchestra (CSO) signed a five-year contract with the Columbus Association for the Performing Arts (CAPA), giving CAPA responsibility for major management tasks of the orchestra, including "finance, accounting, marketing, advertising, publicity, graphics, IT, ticketing, human resources, and operations functions."[79] While its artistic reputation was quite good, the Columbus Symphony Orchestra (CSO) was on the verge of financial collapse in the wake of the recession of the late 2000s. In an effort to survive, the CSO played fewer concerts, cut salaries, and imposed layoffs, but these efforts resulted in little more than a skeletal staff who could not manage the organization.[80] The agreement with CAPA handed over management responsibilities and freed up $750,000 for CSO, which was designed to help bring the orchestra's budget into balance for the 2010–2011 season.[81]

CAPA is a nonprofit organization that was originally created in 1969 to save the Ohio Theatre, opened in 1928, from demolition; CAPA later purchased the Columbus Palace Theatre and the Southern Theatre, making a name for itself in the world of theatre rehabilitation. In 1994, CAPA took on the role of arts management organization when it contracted with the State of Ohio Arts Council to manage four additional theatres in the Columbus area. Since that time, CAPA has contracted with many other partners, using its expertise in arts management to streamline and coordinate administrative tasks such as ticketing operations, production, booking and marketing, public relations, human resources, fundraising, and IT services, thus "allowing our partner arts organizations to focus on their missions and the artistic quality of their work."[82] CAPA partner theatres include the Shubert Theater in New Haven, Connecticut, the Valentine Theatre in Toledo, Ohio, and organizations in the Columbus area including the Lincoln Theatre, the Phoenix Theatre for Children, Opera Columbus, the Franklin Park Conservatory, and the Jazz Arts Group.

The CAPA mission is to

- Present and produce artistic programming of the highest quality to serve and educate diverse audiences and feature renowned artists of all cultures;
- Operate and maintain world-class performance venues;
- Strengthen our arts communities by providing facilities for resident companies and through partnership and collaboration, support those organizations;
- Bolster the economies of the downtown communities we serve.

For additional information on the Columbus Association for the Performing Arts, see www.capa.com.

values of their field. Lindenberg notes an important dilemma for nonprofit managers attempting organizational reforms:

> Those working in the NGO [nonprofit] sector now recognize that NGOs that do not adapt their strategies and promote greater impact, efficiency, and accountability run

> the risk of bankruptcy as well as irrelevance. Yet they fear that too much attention to market dynamics and private and public sector techniques will destroy their value-based organizational culture.[85]

This paradox has facilitated skepticism of nonprofits using either business models of organizational change or government's New Public Management. Focusing on questions of customer satisfaction, for example, can seem out of place when the clientele served are drug addicts, the mentally ill, or prison populations. Further, many balk at the notion of performance measurement when outcomes may be very long-term in nature or difficult to objectively measure, or if the emphasis on efficiency and performance takes time and resources away from their nonprofit missions. An example comes from a study of the relationship between a group of nonprofits and a community trust, in which Shaw and Allen found that tensions existed between the trust's desire to measure outcomes and the nonprofits' desires to serve the community. In their focus groups, a director of a women's shelter described this tension: "we run extremely efficiently and humanely . . . which is difficult with the business models that are imposed on us . . . to be a business and to keep our humanity. . . ."[86] Similarly, in the Light study some respondents described capacity building efforts as "a necessary evil."[87] As Lindenberg concludes, even "sound frameworks for rationalizing resource use will be rejected out of hand unless they are blended with the sense of mission and strong value orientation of the staff ."[88]

Nonprofit service providers may very well be at a crossroads of sorts. On one side, they face pressure to follow the trend toward instituting generic management reforms and creating measurable outcomes. On the other side are pressures to meet the needs of the clients and communities for which nonprofits have been granted their public charters. Thus, while nonprofit efforts at capacity building, reinvention, assessment, reorganization, and reform are very important, it is up to individual managers to create a fit between efforts to build organizational capacity and the mission, clientele, and social purpose of their organization.

FINANCIAL MANAGEMENT AND BUDGETING

Financial management and budgeting in the nonprofit sector is important for pursuing the nonprofit mission, yet challenging due to the complexity of laws and principles that affect finances, budgets, and accounting. For these reasons, we offer an overview of budgeting and financial decision-making in this section; however, the complexity of nonprofit accounting and budgets precludes an in-depth discussion of topics. For more detailed coverage we recommend *Budgeting and Financial Management for Nonprofit Organizations: Using Money to Drive Mission Success* by Lynne A. Weikart, Greg G. Chen, and Ed Sermier.[89]

Although nonprofit sector organizations do not distribute profits to shareholders, they do strive to obtain revenues in excess of expenditures in order to maintain reliable program operations. As in both the for-profit and public sectors, good financial management is imperative to organizational success; for nonprofits that includes covering overhead and salaries while ensuring sufficient resources to fund the programs and services essential to the organization's mission. On the other hand, there are important differences for financial decision-making in the nonprofit sector. Board members, executives, and other stakeholders must understand these differences as they make financial decisions or assess the effectiveness of nonprofit organizations. For example, dealing with adverse economic conditions requires different strategies, and even managing surplus revenues is not a consistent boon across the three sectors.

Financial Issues Unique to Nonprofit Organizations

Most nonprofit organizations are limited in their ability to increase revenues quickly; thus, tight control of program costs is essential.[90] A common strategy for nonprofits facing financial trouble has been cutting programs and services. In recent budget crises they have also cut staff hours or instituted layoffs, as in the example of the Columbus Symphony Orchestra discussed in Box 11.3.

On the other hand, saving or investing large amounts of revenue creates a unique problem in the nonprofit sector.[91] While revenues in excess of expenditures is the primary measure of success in the for-profit sector and can result in popular tax cuts or rebates in the public sector, too much excess revenue in the voluntary sector is seldom well-received by policymakers or the general public. Excess revenue for a nonprofit can signal that the organization is not delivering the services or pursuing the policies that its mission requires or that its funders rightfully expect. Indeed, donations decline when nonprofits hold extreme amounts of wealth and organizations with large endowments can be subject to public, donor, and even congressional criticism.[92] This was the case for many colleges and universities in 2007 as their endowments ballooned at the same time student tuition rates spiked.[93] While university endowments declined in value during the recent recession, many were back to pre-2008 levels by 2011.[94] The policy implications of endowments and foundation funding are discussed further in Chapters 9 and 10.

Revenue Diversification. Also distinct in the nonprofit sector is the variety of revenue sources to which organizations have access, including government grants and contracts, foundation grants, membership and service fees, donations, bequests, commercial ventures, and investment income. In addition, there is wide variation in the types of income and spending requirements for nonprofit organizations. For example, some nonprofit income falls into the category of *unrestricted revenue,* which can be used with discretion by the organization to meet its goals. Unrestricted funds are typically generated by membership fees, general fund donations, or the sale of goods and services. Other nonprofit income is considered *restricted revenue,* which means the funds have been given for a specific purpose and cannot be used in other ways without permission from the funding source. As discussed, contracts restrict spending to only those purposes outlined in the contract; grants, likewise, are restricted revenues that must be expended according to the guidelines of the grant program. These revenues are typically referred to as *temporarily restricted,* because if funder requirements have been met, excess revenue can often be transitioned to unrestricted fund use. Endowments, on the other hand, are usually *permanently restricted* revenue and excess funds cannot be diverted to other uses. In addition, the principal cannot be used; instead, the nonprofit invests the endowment funds and uses the proceeds to fund operations.[95]

Further, some forms of donation will require a *matching contribution,* either in the form of cash or an in-kind match, which means that the nonprofit will receive the funding on the condition that it can match the donation with a resource such as volunteer time or some other good or service. Dennis R. Young summarizes the complexity of nonprofit funding, noting

> The central features of nonprofit finance are its diverse income sources, the equally diverse incentives and preferences of the consumers, donors, and government agencies that provide this income, and the need for each organization to find a strategy that will enable it to capture the income mix that best accomplishes its social mission.[96]

Diversification of income sources is an important financial risk management strategy for nonprofits that ensures the organization can weather the ebb and flow of donations, attendance fees, and grant awards.[97] Diversifying sources of income provides a buffer against a common problem during economic downturns when the demand for nonprofit services often increases at the same time that charitable donations fall. A diversified financial portfolio that includes a variety of income sources helps to maintain the stability of the organization, even during unstable economic conditions.

INVESTMENT STRATEGIES

Although most nonprofit organizations, excluding foundations, do not have excess resources to invest, approximately one in five receives at least 5 percent of its revenue from investments.[98] This income derives from interest payments, dividends, or capital gains and creates a host of issues for boards to consider, most importantly their legal fiduciary responsibilities to the organization. When investing, the organization should create a written policy that details the responsibilities of the board, financial officers, investment advisors, and an investment committee. A written policy should also identify the types of investments that the organization is and is not willing to make: standard stocks versus riskier hedge funds, for example.

While income earned from investments can be valuable in providing a stable revenue stream, it is subject to the inherent risks of the investment strategies chosen. The advice for safe growth of nonprofit investments is the same as the advice for personal investments: diversify.[99] Typically, the board will invest in a mix of stocks, bonds, and real estate, or invest in a mutual fund—in which a diversified portfolio of investments has already been chosen by market analysts—to provide a stable return on investment while ensuring the longevity of the fund. Different categories of investment in a portfolio will, over time, gain or lose value, so it is important for the investment committee and board to periodically rebalance their portfolio. This involves buying and selling assets, whether stocks, bonds, real estate, or other investments, to maintain a healthy mix of diversified asset types.[100] The complexity and risk involved in modern investing increase the financial responsibilities of the board and often encourage them to appoint professionals to the board or investment committee, hire investment professionals, or outsource investment management. For example, many universities have moved their endowment investment portfolios to third party managers in recent years.[101]

Increasingly, the issue of socially responsible investing (SRI) has become relevant for nonprofit boards.[102] Socially responsible investing, which takes the social and environmental impacts of an investment into account, makes a great deal of sense given the mission-driven nonprofit sector. For example, an animal rights organization may not want to invest in a fund that includes cosmetic manufacturers that do animal testing. Just as donors face policy implications when choosing a nonprofit to support, the investment choices of nonprofits also have policy consequences.

Nonprofit Budgeting: Roles and Responsibilities

We reiterate here a point that has been made throughout this chapter on management: There is no one-size-fits-all way to manage budgets and finances in the not-for-profit sector. Each nonprofit must take into account its own mix of revenue sources and expenditure priorities as it pursues the best financial management strategies. There are, however, some basics to budgeting that all nonprofits should keep in mind. Dropkin, Halpin, and La Touche define a budget as "a plan for getting and spending money to reach specific goals by a certain time." [103] They note that effective budgeting has three key characteristics; it is: (1) thoughtful and deliberative; (2) inclusive; and (3) an ongoing process involving several key players.[104] Ultimately, good financial management is vital to pursuit of the nonprofit mission. Management, staff, and board members must understand what it takes, financially, to implement the programs and services that the nonprofit was created to provide because uninformed decisions or unrealistic assumptions can mean the end of the organization.

First, although boards may be involved to varying degrees in the finances and budgeting of the organization, they are "legally responsible for ensuring that budgets meet applicable laws and regulations, are fiscally sound, and will further the nonprofit's tax-exempt purpose."[105] The most important budget role will likely be played by the executive director, president, or chief executive officer (CEO), who "is always responsible for ensuring that the budget is accurate, adheres to board policies, and is submitted on time for board review and approval."[106] Large organizations will typically have a formal chief financial officer (CFO), who is responsible for the day-to-day coordination, implementation, and monitoring of the budget; small nonprofits may wish to assign this role to someone with appropriate qualifications, perhaps a board member or an outside consultant. It is imperative that internal controls over financial management are established to prevent mistakes, mismanagement, deception, or theft. Standard controls include well-maintained financial records; segregation of duties between boards, directors, and finance officers; and clear policies and procedures for financial management including review and monitoring of the process, a requirement of two signatures for check disbursement, and transparency in financial procedures.[107]

It is also important for nonprofit financial officers to share budget information with their executive director and board on a regular basis. This includes monthly or at least quarterly financial statements that present revenue and expenditure data, comparisons of actual year-to-date numbers with projected numbers, and year-to-year changes. Financial officers must also monitor and report on budget issues such as liquidity, debt payments, and investments so leaders are always aware of the organization's financial standing. Nonprofit leaders must have reliable and timely financial data at their disposal so they can make good financial choices and the organization can achieve its objectives.[108]

Finally, particularly important in creating a nonprofit budget that accurately reflects the reality of financial needs are program and unit managers who have the most relevant information about the resources required to implement or initiate programs. These front-line managers are often overlooked in the budget process to the detriment of their organizations and the public purposes they serve.[109] Their input is vital to actually meeting the nonprofit's mission and goals.

GOING GLOBAL CASE STUDY

Financial Mismanagement at the Central Asia Institute

Greg Mortenson and the Central Asia Institute (CAI) were introduced in the opening vignette for Chapter 4 in the context of regulatory activity related to nonprofits. In this case study, we explore the outcomes of that regulation as it pertains to the administration and management of the organization. As Montana Attorney General Steve Bullock states, CAI and its founder, Greg Mortenson, have a history of great work and high aspirations, but also a story that "demonstrates how things can go wrong when officers and directors of a charitable organization fail to abide by fundamental principles of management and oversight."[110] Results of Bullock's investigation illustrate that even in those instances when positive change is brought about by the work of a nonprofit, the ends are not sufficient justification for misconduct and mismanagement.

CAI was incorporated in 1996 and began operations with a $1 million donation from a single donor who wanted to support Mortenson's goal of building schools in Pakistan and other remote areas of central Asia; Greg Mortenson was named executive director. The benefactor died six months after CAI began operations, and by 2001, his $1 million donation was almost depleted. At this point, Mortenson suggested to the board that writing a book would assist with promotion of the mission of the nonprofit and with fundraising. After seven years of modest growth, a story in *Parade* magazine catapulted the work of CAI into the public consciousness and contributions arrived in bags full of mail. In 2006, the book *Three Cups of Tea* raised the profile of the organization even further; the paperback version spent 57 weeks on the *New York Times* bestseller list and sold over four million copies. Mortenson began a series of speaking engagements to promote the book and CAI that required extensive travel. The follow-up book, *Stones into Schools,* was published in 2009 and added to the attention garnered by Mortenson and CAI. It was reported that Mortenson was one of six finalists for the Nobel Peace Prize in 2009.

Total donations for CAI increased significantly following publication of the books—from $867,148 in 2005 to $12.4 million in 2008 and more than $22 million in 2010. From 2003 until late 2011, CAI collected over $72 million in donations; during that time, the organization paid over $9 million for expenses related to producing the first book, purchases of books to give to libraries, universities, and others as a means to promote the organization, and for the advertising and travel costs associated with promoting the book. Despite underwriting the costs to produce the first book, CAI was not a party to the publishing contracts and did not obtain rights to share in the royalties for either book.

Allegations of financial mismanagement and lack of accountability regarding CAI were first raised publicly by the watchdog group American Institute of Philanthropy in its April/May 2010 *Charity Rating Guide and Watchdog Report.* The initial allegations were followed by a CBS *60 Minutes* report on April 17, 2011, and an online short book by former supporter Jon Krakauer released the next day, both of which alleged that Mortenson mismanaged funds at CAI and fabricated some of the stories in his books. The Montana Attorney General (AG) launched his investigation* on April 19, 2011; results of the investigation were released April 5, 2012, and outlined serious concerns regarding administration and management at the organization.

Issues regarding financial mismanagement preceded publication of *Three Cups of Tea* but were exacerbated with the influx of contributions and Mortenson's fame following its release. The organization's first CFO resigned in 2004 after only a year in the position, out of frustration that her recommendations for improving the financial integrity of CAI were met with little response, and specifically that Mortenson would not comply with the fiscal controls that she put in place. CAI's first financial audit was conducted in 2003 at the request of the CFO and it indicated several problems, such as insufficient internal controls related to CAI's finances. The board did not address the weaknesses uncovered in the audit but chose instead to stop requesting audits. Subsequent audits were not completed until 2009 and 2010.

Following the dramatic success brought about by the release of *Three Cups of Tea* in 2006, the board entered into its first formal employment agreement with Mortenson, likely precipitated by financial issues related to book royalties, travel fees, and expense reimbursement. When Mortenson and his coauthor signed an agreement with publisher Viking Penguin, CAI was not a party to the contract nor was it legally entitled to royalties, despite having paid $367,000 to produce the book. In addition, in the years after the book's release, CAI purchased thousands of copies to distribute for outreach and promotion. As author, Mortenson could have purchased the books directly from the publisher at a discounted rate (without receiving royalties on the purchase), but CAI chose instead to purchase the books through online retailers, citing comparable prices and reduced shipping costs. In the 2008 employment agreement, Mortenson consented to make contributions to CAI equal to the royalties he received on books purchased by the nonprofit. About the time the *60 Minutes* and Krakauer stories broke in April 2011, Mortenson made two payments to CAI totaling $420,000; these were the only contributions related to royalties he made after signing the employment agreement until the attorney general's investigation. As part of the settlement agreement, Mortenson has agreed to make total reimbursement to CAI of just over $1 million.

The reimbursement amount includes payment for the royalties stipulated in the employment agreement as well as restitution for expenses Mortenson improperly charged to CAI. Prior to publication of *Three Cups of Tea,* Mortenson had dozens of speaking engagements per year to promote the work of CAI; following the book, the number dramatically increased to the point that the board agreed to Mortenson's request to charter flights rather than fly commercially, for scheduling reasons as well as for his personal health and safety. Some of the speaking engagements were arranged by CAI, some by the book's publisher; for some engagements Mortenson was paid a fee, for others he was not. In many instances, event sponsors included payment to Mortenson for travel fees at the same time that CAI was paying for travel expenses related to the speaking engagements. The 2008 employment agreement stipulated that Mortenson and CAI would share in the travel expenses related to promotion of the book. In January 2011, before the story broke in April, Mortenson began paying his own travel expenses; prior to the attorney general's investigation he had not reimbursed CAI for any travel expenses that had also been paid by another party.

Mortenson consistently failed to appropriately document the expenses for which he claimed reimbursement, even after the CFO resigned in 2004, after an attorney drafted an Employee Travel Reimbursement Policy at the request of the board in 2008, and despite many attempts by the board to persuade him to comply. The 2010 audit uncovered more than $75,000 in personal expenses including luggage, iTunes purchases, clothing, and vacations that were charged to the CAI credit card and paid by the organization without proper documentation from Mortenson. In August and September of 2011, Mortenson made payments to CAI equal to the disputed expenses.

The attorney general's report acknowledged the impracticality of conducting a site visit investigation of the work of CAI in Afghanistan and Pakistan, but does address deficiencies in the management of finances overseas. Audits indicate that large sums of money were often sent via wire transfer to Mortenson and other CAI staff members in Central Asia without adequate documentation of how the funds were spent. In mid-2011, CAI sent an attorney and a team of staff members to do their own assessment of the organization's projects and to devise better means of monitoring progress and improving accountability, given the challenges of the region in which CAI operates. Since August 2011, CAI has posted and updated a comprehensive list of its projects; the organization has also implemented better methods for tracking expenses with the overseas staff and has retained in-country accounting firms to assist with bookkeeping and auditing.

Despite all the instances of mismanagement and impropriety highlighted in the report, Attorney General Bullock repeatedly acknowledged the tireless efforts by Mortenson on behalf of CAI and the achievements made by the nonprofit in a very challenging region of the world. In addition, according to a Pakistani journalist sent by Radio Mashaal to check on CAI schools, there is evidence of real success and sincere gratitude for the work of CAI among the local people in very remote areas of the country.[111] This case demonstrates, however, that effectiveness is not enough; as argued throughout this book, nonprofits must also be well managed. An organization that ignores basic tenets of good financial management such as regular audits and detailed tracking of expenses should not be surprised to see its public support decline and, worse, itself come under state investigation. The advantages afforded nonprofits—such as their tax-exempt status, public support, and perceived trustworthiness—should not be taken lightly; they are granted by governments and the public with the expectation that the organizations will remain good stewards of the public interest.

QUESTIONS TO CONSIDER:

1. What steps were taken prior to the success of *Three Cups of Tea* to establish sound fiscal management in the organization? Were they unsuccessful or inadequate? Explain. What steps were taken after the book's release to enhance fiscal controls and procedures? Were they successful or inadequate? Explain.
2. What more could have been done by the organization to compel Greg Mortenson to comply with the procedures for expense reimbursement? Why did the organization not go to greater lengths to enforce compliance?
3. Consider the four relationships that describe nonprofit interaction with public policy (make policy, affected by policy, influence policy, subject to policy) and discuss the ways in which these relationships are reflected in the example of the Central Asia Institute.
4. Is the experience of the Central Asia Institute unique? Explain how dramatic growth and intense publicity for a nonprofit can facilitate or hinder its efforts to fulfill its mission and affect public policy.

* The investigation by the attorney general did not involve the material content of the books; memoirs are protected under the First Amendment and the attorney general does not have the authority to address allegations that some incidents may have been fabricated.

Nonprofit Budgeting: Types of Budgets and Financial Statements

Nonprofit budgeting begins with organizational priorities and goals that have been developed from the mission statement and are used for planning and control of organizational finances.[112] In addition to a familiarity with accounting concepts, planning and implementing the budget requires an understanding of the different types of budgets that are commonly used in the nonprofit sector.[113] We discuss four of these budget types further in the paragraphs below. (See Box 11.5 for an overview of basic accounting concepts.)

Box 11.5

FOR MORE INFORMATION

BASIC ACCOUNTING CONCEPTS

It is important for nonprofit leaders to be familiar with nonprofit budget terms and procedures because they have an obligation to be good stewards of organizational resources. The following are some basic accounting concepts that are useful for financial decision-makers in the nonprofit sector.

Assets: includes everything of current or future value to the organization, including cash, inventory, pledged donations, and equipment

Liabilities: includes everything that the organization owes, including salaries and benefits, rent, and lease payments

Equity: the difference between the value of an asset and the remaining liability on that asset

Net Assets: the difference between the total value of the organization's assets and its total liabilities

Operating Funds: revenues available to cover operating costs

Operating Reserves: revenue in excess of operating expenses that can be saved or invested

Operating Expenses: expenditures related to day-to-day operations of the organization

Depreciation: an expense related to the loss of value of an asset over time due to wear and tear; typically associated with vehicles and equipment

Liquidity: refers to how easily assets can be converted to cash quickly and at low cost; typically determined by amount of cash or cash equivalent assets minus current liabilities

Organization-wide operating budgets identify all of the revenues and expenditures anticipated for the upcoming year for all individual units and programs of the organization. The Statement of Financial Activities (SOA)—also called a budget report or statement of financial position and similar to the income statement used by for-profit organizations—is the common format whereby nonprofits present the current year's budget as approved by the board, in conjunction with the prior year's actual budget and year-to-date totals per budgeted item. Statements of Financial Activities are designed to allow the board to assess the ongoing fiscal health of the nonprofit by putting the numbers in context. Statements of Financial Activities allow board members to answer questions such as: (1) what did we spend/earn last year on that line-item; (2) what percentage of total revenues/expenses have we derived at the midpoint of the fiscal year; and (3) how do restricted funds expended compare to unrestricted.[114] When preparing their operating budgets it is important for nonprofits to include complete revenue and cost data from the previous year and for the board, executives, and financial managers to define a budget cycle, schedule, and responsibilities for the budgeting process. It is often suggested that a chart of accounts be used as the primary tool for beginning the budget process.[115]

The chart of accounts is described as "the list of categories that tracks the *what* of each dollar coming into and going out of your organization."[116] This line-by-line accounting of finances, including assets and liabilities as well as revenues and expenditures, allows an organization to quickly spot budget problems and address them before financial troubles get out of control. In an attempt to standardize, and therefore improve, the performance of nonprofit budgeting, the National Center for Charitable Statistics (NCCS) has created a Unified Chart of Accounts (UCOA) that is offered for download on the NCCS website (see Box 11.6).

Individual program/unit/activity budgets identify all of the revenues and expenditures anticipated for an individual program or activity in the coming year. For example, earlier we discussed the backpack program of the large nonprofit described in the opening vignette; in addition to the organization-wide operating budget, the nonprofit would also keep track of the revenues that keep the backpack program running, from in-kind donations of food to state grant funding, and the expenditures related specifically to the program such as materials and labor costs. For very small nonprofits that operate a single program, the organization-wide and the individual program budget may be the same.

Box 11.6

FOR MORE INFORMATION

THE UNIFIED CHART OF ACCOUNTS

Through a partnership with the National Center for Charitable Statistics (NCCS), the California Association of Nonprofits (CAN), the California Society of CPAs, and the Internal Revenue Service (IRS) created the Unified Chart of Accounts (UCOA) for use by nonprofit organizations as they organize, plan, and implement their budgets. The UCOA provides a structure for nonprofit accounting that conforms to Generally Accepted Accounting Principles (GAAP), and A-133 Single Audits standards, as well as general reporting requirements of private foundations, the United Way, and government contracts.[117] UCOA is a tool flexible enough to be adapted to the needs of large or small nonprofit organizations and can save much time and resources in the budgeting process.

The National Center for Charitable Statistics makes UCOA available free of charge through their website to enable nonprofit organizations to "quickly and reliably translate their financial statements into the categories required by the IRS Form 990, the federal Office of Management and Budget, and into other standard reporting formats. UCOA also seeks to promote uniform accounting practices throughout the nonprofit sector."

For additional information or to access the Unified Chart of Accounts (UCOA) at http://nccs.urban.org/projects/ucoa.cfm.

Cash (or Cash-flow) budgets are particularly important from the perspective of the day-to-day operations of an organization because they require a short-term and ongoing look at the revenues coming in and the expenditures going out of an organization. A cash budget can help the organization to anticipate revenue bottlenecks, which are often seasonal, and plan accordingly. For example, religious congregations often experience cash-flow difficulties during summer months when parishioners are more likely to be on vacation and monthly contributions do not come in as pledged. Nonprofits that are on government contract must be mindful of cash-flow issues as contract payments may not come until months after services have been rendered. In either case, the organizations must continue to pay salaries, utilities, and rent, while anticipating the variability of their revenues.

Capital budgets are very specific budgets that nonprofits use to plan and manage acquisition of long-term assets—known as capital projects. Examples include facility purchases or renovations, or major one-time equipment purchases. The capital budgeting process allows the organization to determine the best way to fund these large, non-recurring expenses. For example, the organization may decide to borrow money through a mortgage to renovate an old building for handicap accessibility, or it may decide to run a capital campaign in addition to its normal fundraising activities to purchase an MRI machine for a rural health clinic.

CONCLUSION

Administration and management in the nonprofit sector involve standard tasks such as planning, communication, and budgeting, as well as standard strategies for effectiveness, efficiency, and reform. However, all must be undertaken within the parameters of each organization's distinctive mission and social purpose. This means that the nonprofit must understand itself and its unique environment in order to succeed.

The modern nonprofit must be organized well enough to effectively carry out its mission with maximum efficiency. For most not-for-profit organizations, pursuing their missions is very labor intensive, and while the reliance on volunteer labor can help to keep staffing costs low, managers who know how to keep the organization focused, to keep multiple lines of communication open, to make reforms as necessary, and to acquire sufficient funding are key to nonprofit efficiency and effectiveness.

Good managers are also able to assess the context in which their organization exists, assess its internal strengths and weaknesses, and move the organization forward to reach its goals. For nonprofit organizations that means pursuing important social and public missions, including enhancing the arts and cultural climate of a community, delivering necessary services, and pursuing changes to public policy. Good nonprofit management is important to meeting a variety of public purposes that can be difficult to fund and difficult to evaluate. Additional tools and strategies for managing nonprofits are discussed in Chapters 12 through 14, including the specifics of leadership, personnel, and nonprofit evaluation.

Questions For Review

1. Discuss the ways in which management of nonprofit organizations differs from management of for-profit and public organizations. Which of these differences are most important for nonprofit managers to recognize?

2. In your own words, define effectiveness and efficiency. In what ways is it difficult to be both effective and efficient? Finally, is one concept more important than the other for nonprofit organizations?

3. Why is good communication singled out by so many authors as being particularly important for good nonprofit management and administration?

4. In what ways does good financial management help nonprofits pursue their program, service, and policy goals? Aside from closing its doors, what are potential consequences of poor financial management?

Assignment

For this web-based assignment, choose a nonprofit organization for which you can obtain information on organizational structure and budget to answer the following questions. How big is the organization in terms of employees, board members, and senior staff? Does the organization have affiliates or field offices, and if so, how many and where are they located (i.e., 15 countries or all 50 states)? How large is the organization's budget in terms of revenues and expenditures? What are its sources of revenue and are revenues diversified? Finally, how transparent is this organization—that is, is information clearly communicated and easy to find?

Suggested Readings

Crutchfield, Leslie R. and Heather McLeod Grant. *Forces for Good.* San Francisco: Jossey-Bass, 2008.

Dropkin, Murray, Jim Halpin, and Bill La Touche. *The Budget-Building Book for Nonprofits, A Step-by-Step Guide for Managers and Boards.* San Francisco: John Wiley and Sons, 2007.

Moore, Mark H. "Managing for Value: Organizational Strategy in For-Profit, Nonprofit, and Governmental Organizations," *Nonprofit and Voluntary Sector Quarterly* 29,1 (2000): 183–204.

Lindenberg, Marc. Are we at the cutting edge or the blunt edge? Improving NGO organizational performance with private and public sector strategic management frameworks. *Nonprofit Management & Leadership* 11,3 (2001): 247–270.

Light, Paul C. *Sustaining Nonprofit Performance.* Washington, DC: Brookings Institution Press, 2004.

Weikart, Lynne A., Greg G. Chen, and Ed Sermier. *Budgeting and Financial Management for Nonprofit Organizations: Using Money to Drive Mission Success.* Washington, DC: CQ Press, 2013.

Web Resources

The Alliance for Nonprofit Management, www.allianceonline.org

The American Accounting Association's Accounting and the Public Interest, http://aaapubs.aip.org/api/

The Bridgespan Group, www.bridgespan.org/

Free Management Library, http://managementhelp.org/

Grantmakers for Effective Organizations, www.geofunders.org

Nonprofit Finance Fund, www.nonprofitfinancefund.org

Unified Chart of Accounts, http://nccs.urban.org/projects/ucoa.cfm

12 Nonprofit Governance and Leadership

In a democracy, the nonprofit sector is there to ensure that people have a voice in our future—at the community, national, and global levels. If we accept this as our primary role, it has implications for what should be present as constants in our governance structures.

Ruth McCambridge[1]

Much of the city of New Orleans needed to be rebuilt after Hurricane Katrina's flood-waters subsided. In a classic example of a policy window opening, some found in the situation an opportunity to reform the New Orleans public school system, a system that had been dysfunctional for decades. One aspect of that reform included policy entrepreneurs from other parts of the country moving to New Orleans to prove that even the most disadvantaged kids could be academically successful.

With this in mind, consider the following scenario: an innovative not-for-profit K-6 school opens near the hard-hit lower Ninth Ward in 2007. It is founded by a married couple with a strong interest in education and a desire to help this devastated community. By 2012, the school enrolls 285 children and test scores are on the rise. Despite this success, there is growing concern among parents and in the community about the school's leadership. Unlike the families of its students, the school's founders are white, wealthy, well-educated northerners, and while 12 of the school's 16-member board of directors have experience in the field of education, only three are African American. While 10 board members live in Louisiana—five of them in New Orleans—none of the 16 lives in the lower Ninth Ward, the area primarily served by the school, and even the parent representative to the board lives in a neighborhood that is only adjacent to the Ninth Ward.

Mike, co-founder and executive director of the school, argues that the board members' status, affluence, and political connections have allowed the school to raise millions of dollars, so students can attend a "high quality

POLICY IMPLICATIONS OF NONPROFIT GOVERNANCE AND LEADERSHIP

- Nonprofit boards of directors and executive officers increasingly interact with multiple stakeholders both in and outside of their organizations; therefore, they play important roles in the policy networks surrounding their nonprofits.
- Leadership theories extol the virtues of active, adaptive, ethical, and charismatic leaders to create a vision that motivates employees and moves their organization toward its mission.
- Organizational leaders are responsible for the process of planning and goal setting, which enhances the ability of the nonprofit to pursue its mission and affect public policy either through implementation of programs based on existing policy or by pursuing policy change.
- Recruitment, hiring, and evaluation of executives is an important nonprofit board role and is vital to the overall mission success of the organization; similarly, recruitment and development of boards are important to mission success.
- Boards of directors are legal entities created through either a nonprofit corporation or a charitable trust and are therefore subject to the laws and regulations regarding these entities.

school at a very low cost to families." It is true that tuition is affordable for most, that the school provides full scholarships to the lowest income students, and that it has increased academic success for its students; however, questions about representation on the board have been raised. At a parents' meeting one mother asked bluntly: "Are we just going to let these outsiders run things? These are our kids. This is *our* school and *our* community! We should have a voice!"

THE SHARED RESPONSIBILITY OF NONPROFIT GOVERNANCE AND LEADERSHIP

The primary focus of this chapter is what Henry Mintzberg called the Strategic Apex.[2] In the nonprofit sector, the Strategic Apex includes the governing board of directors and the executive director or chief executive officer, those making programmatic and policy decisions for the organization. These responsibilities constitute *nonprofit governance*, which involves guiding the direction and performance of the organization.

As the Advocacy Coalition Framework (ACF) and network theories of public policy would suggest, leadership and governance in nonprofits is increasingly seen as an interaction between multiple players or interests both inside and outside of the organization (see Chapter 1). Therefore, while it may be convenient to make distinctions between governance as a board function and management as a function of the chief executive officer, it is more realistic to consider nonprofit governance as a joint responsibility between boards and executives, one that includes input from advisory groups, top managers, and other important stakeholders.[3] Furthermore, even day-to-day management tasks are often the responsibility of executives and boards, especially in small nonprofits; therefore, those with governance responsibilities often have management responsibilities as well. This chapter is primarily devoted to governance issues in relation to the more thorough discussion of management that appears in Chapter 11.

GOVERNANCE AND ACHIEVING THE MISSION OF NONPROFIT ORGANIZATIONS

The legal structure of nonprofit boards creates important obligations and constraints on board activity. A board's primary role is to ensure that the organization maintains operations in keeping with its public charter and pursues the mission for which it was created. The modern duties of care, loyalty, and obedience associated with nonprofit boards was codified with a 1974 court case known as the *Sibley Hospital* case,[4] which was the first court opinion regarding the obligations of nonprofit boards. The ruling in *Sibley* holds nonprofit boards to the same standards as for-profit boards[5] and set the stage for later court and legislative policies that affect board behavior, as well as the best practices suggested to ensure that boards govern nonprofits in keeping with the public trust.

In order to maintain their legal status as tax-exempt organizations, nonprofits must have a clear and permanent mission that has been approved and voted on by their governing boards; therefore, the most important duty of the governing board is to guide the organization as it pursues its mission.[6] Board members should be willing and able to clearly articulate the nonprofit mission to others in a compelling fashion—to share their enthusiasm and promote the organization's work.[7] As organizational leaders, board members are responsible for periodic assessment of the nonprofit mission, its accomplishment of organizational goals, and the strategic planning that moves it closer to reaching those goals. In addition, the leadership of an executive officer is vital to advancing and guiding the nonprofit mission; in general terms, the board is responsible for creation of vision and mission, and the executive is responsible for their execution.

There is a vast literature on the topic of organizational leadership and nearly as large a body of work specifically addressing boards of directors. While leadership has been addressed in both scholarly and popular works for many decades, only recently have scholars begun to consider the topic of boards. Much of the popular literature on both topics is prescriptive, and because of the variety of nonprofit organizational structures, sizes, and needs, the academic scholarship on these topics tends to be descriptive rather than empirically tested. Furthermore, the concept of leadership is so amorphous that it is sometimes described as vaguely as "we know it when we see it." Bearing all of this in mind, we delve into the topic of nonprofit leadership: what we know, what we suspect, and what difference it makes for organizations and public policy.

THEORIES OF ORGANIZATIONAL LEADERSHIP

Although it is common to extol the virtues of leadership, it is far less common to actually define the concept.[8] This is likely true because framing a basic definition of leadership is not nearly as easy as it sounds. For example, Peter F. Drucker suggests that leadership is about action, while Barry Dym and Harry Hutson consider leadership to be about relationships.[9] It is little wonder that after decades of research on the topic, Burns and Bennis and Nanus concluded that leadership is over-studied yet little understood.[10] While scholarship on the topic is better focused these days, a single, agreed-upon definition is still hard to find. Accordingly, as a reference point for our discussion of executive directors and boards, we use the following as our working definition of leadership: the ability to attract followers who will act on behalf of an organization in accordance with its mission and the vision of the leader.

Although anyone in a position of authority can be considered a leader, we follow the tradition which makes distinctions between leadership and management, while noting the importance and interconnectedness of the two. As Werther and Berman explain

> The leader's role is to create an ennobling vision of the organization's future possibilities, clarify the mission, and develop effective strategies to achieve the mission. Though leader is a crucial role, much more time is usually devoted to being a manager. A manager is responsible for marshaling organizational resources to obtain defined objectives.[11]

The study of leadership began with the assumption that studying exceptional leaders and their character traits could shed light on what good leadership entails. Later studies looked at the behavior of leaders and the behavioral factors that motivated followers. Research in the 1960s conducted through the Ohio State Leadership Studies introduced the importance of situational and contextual variables that affect leadership and its outcomes. More recent conceptions of leadership include servant leadership, in which the ethical responsibilities of the leader are emphasized; transactional leadership, which tends to be more obviously associated with the management or instrumental responsibilities of leaders; adaptive leadership, in which leaders mobilize organizational resources in order to thrive in new environments; and transformational leadership, which focuses on the importance of a leader's charisma, vision, and ability to create and reform an organizational culture.[12]

It has been suggested that transformational leadership is "particularly useful in public and nonprofit organizations given the service and community-oriented nature of their missions" and the public service motivations of their employees.[13] Especially in all-volunteer organizations in which management has little ability to reward or sanction behavior, transformational leadership that is "people-oriented, emotional, and inspirational" may prove to be most effective in motivating followers.[14] Contemporary research has increasingly highlighted the connections between transactional and transformational leadership suggesting that, as noted above, successful leaders must integrate their transactional responsibilities to manage their organizations with their transformational responsibilities to provide organizational vision.[15]

BOARDS AND EXECUTIVES AS LEADERS

Leadership in a nonprofit is provided by boards of directors or trustees whose members generally serve in a voluntary capacity, and executives—usually called either the executive director (ED) or chief executive officer (CEO)—who are typically hired by and serve at the discretion of the board. Effective nonprofit leaders align themselves with the values, mission, and culture of their organizations. Increasingly, as theories of policy coalitions and networks would suggest, nonprofit leaders are seen as the primary point of interaction between multiple actors and interests in the policymaking process. In many nonprofits this means that direct ties to the community are important factors in effective leadership and can help the organization in its fundraising efforts and its dealings with local governments, public agencies, and other nonprofits. The issue of community ties is highlighted in the opening vignette when the outsider nature of the executive director and board lead the organization's clientele—in this case, parents—to question the legitimacy of its leaders in their community.

The quality of legitimacy, defined as "the vital link that joins organizational power and organizational leadership,"[16] comes from a variety of sources for nonprofit leaders. As in the Ninth Ward school example, one source of legitimacy comes from the grassroots. When representation and direct accountability to the various interests served is derived from the bottom-up in a community, it affords nonprofit leaders a significant amount of legitimacy.[17] Nonprofits sometimes include members of different stakeholder constituencies on their boards or on board committees in order to enhance their bottom-up legitimacy.

Similarly, David Suarez found that nonprofit executives with substantial professional experience in their policy, program, or field of interest have high levels of "street credibility" among stakeholders.[18] Board members are also often chosen because of their professional backgrounds and the expertise and career networks they can access on behalf of the organization. Their experience and contacts thus bring a more global perspective to the work of the nonprofit, broadening its impact and influence beyond the organization and its community to society as a whole. These connections can be particularly important for the policies that the nonprofit advocates and implements in the course of pursuing its mission. Thus, in the Ninth Ward example, the fact that the majority of board members have experience in education affords them a level of professional legitimacy. Likewise, the majority of nonprofit executives derive legitimacy from having experience in the not-for-profit sector prior to taking their first executive position.[19]

Nonprofit organizations also maintain legitimacy when their organizational procedures conform to institutional expectations; while this may seem self-evident, it is relatively new for nonprofit leaders to concern themselves with conformity to standard management practices.[20] Nonprofit executives and boards are increasingly chosen based upon their credentials, which include levels of professionalism, training, education, and management experience as well as personal and professional contacts. As discussed in Chapter 11, nonprofits and their leaders have increased their efforts to build the capacity of their organizations to operate both efficiently and effectively.

These factors—community leadership, professional legitimacy, and good organizational management—all increase the legitimacy of the leadership in the eyes of the organization's clientele and staff, as well as the general public, politicians, donors, and other stakeholders. When its leadership is viewed favorably, the organization, its trustworthiness, and its effectiveness are also viewed favorably.[21] A good reputation, as has been discussed, is among the most important characteristics for a nonprofit to thrive; thus, capable leadership is vital to successful pursuit of the nonprofit's mission.

Making Strategic Choices for Mission Achievement. Organizational leaders are responsible for the process of planning and goal setting, which enhances the ability of the nonprofit to pursue its mission and affect public policy either through implementation of existing programs or by pursuing policy change. In general, the board of directors is responsible for translating organizational values into a clearly articulated mission, and the executive is responsible for making sure that staff and volunteers carry out that mission.

Strategic planning, as discussed in Chapter 5, helps leaders to identify goals and determine the steps that will lead the nonprofit to fulfill its purpose. Ultimately, nonprofit leaders can use the mission statement and goals to determine which opportunities the organization should pursue and which will lead it too far from its primary purpose. Boards of directors and executives are also responsible for the periodic review of their organization's strategic plan because times and the organization will change, potentially requiring a change to the mission or administration of the organization.[22]

The Relationship between Boards and Executives

Ideally, there is a well-balanced partnership between the nonprofit executive and the board of directors characterized by open and frequent communication, compatible philosophy and vision, and clear, shared expectations of the roles that each will play in the organization. In a report on good governance issued by BoardSource and FSG Social Impact Advisors, the authors called for "a strong chief executive in partnership with an engaged and strategic-thinking board" to advance the best in nonprofit governance.[23] A commitment by board members and executives to work as a team, cultivate and nurture their relationships, and hone their management skills is vital to successful governance. Crutchfield and Grant find this type of teamwork in their study of high performing nonprofits, where board members were actively engaged with executives and deliberately chosen to complement the skills and background of executives and their management staff.[24] Finally, the most important relationship in terms of nonprofit governance and effectiveness is between the board chair and the organization's executive officer. Good and frequent communication is essential, and while both are in leadership positions, each must understand and respect the responsibilities vested in the other's office. The two should work together and with the entire board of directors to enhance the success of the nonprofit.

Unfortunately, these conditions do not always exist and the relationship between the board and executive can be troubled. For example, it is important that the board chair manage the board and the executive manage the organization. A lack of clear expectations can lead to role ambiguity for board members that leave executives and organizations with unmet needs.[25] Similarly, the board of directors may simply be too passive, leaving the executive with more work and responsibility than she should have. This is a problem that can be particularly damaging at the start-up of the nonprofit when the formative work of creating a mission, vision, and culture is occurring. Conversely, some boards attempt to micromanage the organization and do not give the executive the power and responsibility to which she is entitled. In these cases, the nonprofit may become a revolving door of executives unwilling to have their authority usurped, or it may attract only weak executives, which could impede successful pursuit of the organization's mission and goals. In other cases, the executive may wish to see the nonprofit move in one policy or programmatic direction, while the board of directors wishes to take the organization in another direction. Of course, because the executive is selected and can be removed by the board, she is obligated to follow its lead; if this becomes too difficult, she will likely leave, either voluntarily or by request.

This discussion reminds us of the importance of open communication among members of the leadership team, as well as how vital the nonprofit executive is to the organization. The executive's role in both management and leadership is vital to organizational success. She is largely responsible for building the culture of the organization, setting its administrative priorities, and ensuring resources are available to provide the programs and services associated with its mission.[26] Often, as in our opening vignette, the executive director of a small nonprofit is one of its founders. This can be quite valuable because founders have a very strong sense of organizational mission. Particularly in a young organization, success requires the executive and board of directors to be visionary, creative, hands-on, and mission-driven.

Of course, the relationship between the executive and the board can and will change over time. As the organization matures, the role of the board is likely to become more advisory and less managerial, leaving day-to-day administration to the executive and her staff. Similarly, the founding executive director is often replaced by someone with more administrative experience, rather than simply a mission-specific background.[27]

Transfers in Executive Leadership

The issue of executive hiring is also important for the nonprofit leadership team; in fact, choosing an executive has been called "the single most important decision the board makes."[28] While the board of directors may have more official authority over the operation, direction, and reorganization of a nonprofit, it is frequently the executive director who is considered the leader by staff and even clients. Accordingly, although members of the board might come and go, the replacement of an executive can be dramatic, even traumatic, for the organization. The internal identity of the nonprofit can be threatened when the executive steps down, which may lead to a decline in performance and even increase the chances of organizational death.[29] Because recruiting, hiring, and training an executive are central to the success of the nonprofit, the Bridgespan Group offers a series of online resources and job placement services to assist in these efforts; see Box 12.1 for more information.

Box 12.1

FOR MORE INFORMATION

RECRUITING NONPROFIT LEADERS LEARNING CENTER

Organized by Bain & Company in 2000, the Bridgespan Group is a 501(c)(3) designed to assist nonprofit and philanthropic leaders as they build their organizations to "inspire and accelerate social change. At the heart of our mission is the belief that a strong and effective nonprofit sector can be a powerful force for change as well as a source of human inspiration."

Included in the online resources offered by Bridgespan is the Recruit and Develop Nonprofit Leaders Learning Center, which provides articles, techniques, links, and tools to help nonprofits with their executive hiring and development processes. Article topics include staff development, managing transitions, recruitment of executives and board members, and stories from nonprofit leaders on their career paths in the nonprofit sector. The site includes a LinkedIn discussion board and an area for nonprofits to post job openings and for job seekers to find employment.

To link to the Recruiting Nonprofit Leaders Learning Center: www.bridgestar.org/LearningCenters/Recruiting.aspx.

For more information on Bridgestar, go to www.bridgestar.org/Home.aspx.

Two particularly difficult scenarios for a nonprofit are when the executive is being let go and when the departing executive is the founder of the organization. In the first instance, because the board is responsible for keeping the executive accountable, it is also responsible for offering feedback, coaching, and training opportunities to a struggling executive. When this is the case, the board should ask itself if it has given the executive regular and appropriate feedback on his performance, if it has supplied the executive and the organization with sufficient resources, and whether or not the executive's skills can be better developed. If there is no recourse and the executive must be let go, board members may find themselves taking over more of the day-to-day operations of the organization, and smoothing conflicts among staff who have been left smoldering after the executive has gone.

In the second case, when the departing executive is a founder of the organization, the transition may be particularly difficult for staff and stakeholders, who see the founder as an integral part of the nonprofit. Further, the phenomenon of *founder syndrome,* when the founding executive has difficulty letting go and allowing his vision to be taken over by someone else, can be disconcerting for both nonprofit staff and clientele. These situations reinforce the fact that executive selection, training, and evaluation are vital to nonprofit success as is well-planned leadership succession; the board of directors plays a key role in all of these activities.

Research suggests that succession planning is increasingly important as most chief executives, and even their deputy or associate executives, are over the age of 50, creating the very real possibility of a wave of nonprofit executive retirements in the next decade.[30] Unfortunately, despite its importance, strategic planning for executive succession is not always done well because boards of directors often have little experience hiring a new executive and often underestimate the difficulty of selecting someone well suited to the job.[31] Several strategies for succession planning include (1) identification of a talent pool at various levels of the organization; (2) attracting individuals to leadership positions through mentoring of young talent by executives and other managers; (3) role modeling good, participatory management; and (4) creating a sense of passion for the mission of the organization.[32]

While mentoring and promoting from within an organization often work well in leadership succession, in very small nonprofits there may simply be no one within the existing staff who is willing or able to take on the reins of executive authority. In these cases, the board of directors must take very seriously its role in choosing someone with leadership and management skills that are aligned well with the organization's mission, values, and culture. It is the board's responsibility to ensure this alignment, whether the executive is new or continuing. Further, the board must prepare the nonprofit staffers for the new executive's style, skills, and objectives. Particularly when the executive is being hired from outside the organization, the board must take the time and effort to appropriately introduce the new executive to the staff, community members, donors, and other stakeholders that contribute to the functioning of the organization.[33] Finally, although any new executive will be expected to make her mark, she should do so carefully, as staff attachment to a particular vision can hinder attempts at change, especially during leader succession.[34]

An excellent example of the nature of board and executive relations comes from the fascinating case of Orange County Youth and Family Services (see Case Study 12.2). This case traces the life and death of a nonprofit social service provider that was heavily dependent on government contracts. It emphasizes the changing roles and responsibilities over time of their executive director and board of directors and provides an example of successful succession planning.

CASE STUDY 12.2

Orange County Youth and Family Services Best Practices Approach to Board and Executive Relations

The case of Orange County Youth and Family Services (OCYFS) exemplifies many of the management concepts of Chapter 11 and governance concepts of Chapter 12. Over its 30-year life span, the organization and its governing board evolved from a small, less-professionalized operation to a moderate-sized nonprofit with a professional director and board. As you read the following case, keep in mind that by its very nature the organization was always dependent on government sources of funding. As shown in the discussion of resource dependency theories in Chapter 3, reliance primarily on one source of funding can be problematic for nonprofits. Because OCYFS services were almost exclusively funded by county and state grants, changes in criminal justice policy at the state level and the capricious nature of public budgets affected the work of OCYFS and unfortunately, led to its ultimate demise.

Incorporated in 1978 as the Orange County Halfway House (OCHH), in Orange County, California, OCHH provided traditional residential re-entry services for people leaving the jail and prison systems. In addition, it provided outpatient addiction diversion and services for abused children. As the literature would suggest, this new nonprofit began with a small board of directors drawn primarily from public agencies with policy interests and expertise in the fields of law enforcement, corrections, and counseling. The original board was primarily responsible for financial management and determining the mission—described as "identifying what we are."

In the late 1970s when the OCHH was created, criminal justice policy emphasized rehabilitation of released offenders;[35] illustrating the tie to rehabilitation, the first executive director (ED) was a former offender himself. The second, more influential ED came to OCHH in 1979 with experience in probation and counseling in the public and nonprofit sectors; he remained executive director for 20 years. While he had no formal management training, over time the ED became more and more knowledgeable about a very wide range of organizational and administrative issues, from personnel and contract management to proposal preparation, and administration of grants to community engagement. As is common for a small and growing nonprofit, limited financial resources precluded the hiring of additional management staff for several years; thus, the ED's position was as a generalist with multiple responsibilities.

Eventually, the organization merged with another nonprofit, took on new responsibilities including teen services, and renamed itself Orange County Youth and Family Services (OCYFS). At its height, OCYFS had an operating budget of approximately $3 million, with program services funded by federal, state, and county contracts; in addition, OCYFS became a United Way of Orange County partner, receiving as much as $100,000 per year in United Way funds.

As it grew, its needs changed and OCYFS sought board members with skills beyond social services and public safety, appointing accountants, attorneys, and business owners to the board. At this point the board and its members had moved beyond the early policymaking role and began to take on more advisory roles, including offering advice on legal matters, recommending trustworthy nonprofit accountancy firms, and holding training workshops when labor laws changed. In addition, board members were chosen for their prominence in the community, in the hope that their prominence would help OCYFS to access funding.

Eventually, the organization grew to the point that the ED could hire one, then two assistants to handle various aspects of the day-to-day management of OCYFS. When the executive director decided to leave the organization in 1999, he and the board implemented a responsible succession plan to ensure a relatively smooth transition. The plan involved internal selection of a successor, a full year of shadowing the ED, and then a year of reduced hours—quarter time—for the out-going director. After the second year, the new executive director took over all operations. Although the former director was asked to serve on the board after being away from the organization for two years, even at that point the "new" ED deferred to him often enough that he left board service. His role after that was simply to be available to answer questions for which institutional memory was valuable.

While OCYFS illustrates a best practices approach to board management and succession planning, it also offers a poignant example of the tenuous position of nonprofits that are heavily dependent on government grants and public policy priorities. First, it took a serious hit in 1994 when Orange County declared bankruptcy; OCYFS contracts with the county were eliminated and over two-thirds of the OCYFS budget was wiped out. Going from a budget of $3 million to only $800,000 was a shock, and while its programs were considered important and successful, the county bankruptcy and state cuts to residential programs took a toll. Although the organization stayed afloat with state contracts and slowly added new programs for the next decade, the fiscal crisis within the state of California eventually caught up with OCYFS. State budget cuts, coupled with the transition from a state emphasis on rehabilitation policies to those that prioritized punishment, led to the end of OCYFS in 2009. At that point its largest residential program was transferred to another nonprofit and the 30-year-old organization closed its doors.

QUESTIONS TO CONSIDER:

1. In what ways does the OCYFS case meet or not meet our expectations of nonprofit board (and organization) growth and development?
2. OCYFS offers an example of a relatively smooth succession process for the executive director; however, it also points to the lasting influence of a long-time leader. What does the OCYFS case suggest in terms of what to do versus what not to do in succession planning?
3. This case study exemplifies the concept of resource dependence, as OCYFS essentially lived and died by government funding. Was there any way to avoid such dependency in this case? Consider the four relationships that describe nonprofit interaction with public policy (make policy, affected by policy, influence policy, subject to policy) and discuss the ways in which OCYFS's birth, growth, and death reflect these relationships.
4. Is the example of OCYFS unique with regard to board governance and the succession of executive directors? Explain why or why not. To what extent did the degree of resource dependency or the public policy priorities of the state and local governments affect the board and executive directors in management of the organization?

The Difference That Leadership Makes

Most of the scholarship on leadership generally confirms that leaders make meaningful differences to organizations and their followers. Research on nonprofit boards, for example, has found that board effectiveness is related to organizational effectiveness,[36] that board members with long tenure and business executive experience have a positive effect on fundraising,[37] and that board members committed to the organization are more active and are perceived by their executives to be more valuable to the organization.[38] Similarly, nonprofits whose executives have marketing, accounting, and production experience have better fundraising performance.[39]

More generally, nonprofit leadership is important for the morale of employees and volunteers, the ability to attain organizational goals, and the outcomes of policy implementation and service delivery. For example, Trottier, Van Wart, and Wang find that leaders have "an enormous effect" on follower satisfaction, particularly when leaders are motivating and empowering, when they make individual consideration of their followers, and when followers consider leaders to be trustworthy.[40] Similarly, research has found that transformational leadership facilitates enthusiasm, pride, and admiration among volunteers and improves job satisfaction and employee performance in organizations.[41]

While transformational leadership has positive effects on organizational satisfaction and performance, research has not found similar impacts when leaders simply rely on instrumental management or a transactional leadership style.[42] This body of research reinforces the difference between management and leadership, while pointing out that both are vital for nonprofits to meet their goals. In practice, Crutchfield and Grant found that many of the high-performing nonprofits in their study split their management and leadership roles, hiring one person as "an internal manager, focused on operational issues, while the executive director is more often the external leader, concerned with vision, strategy, issue leadership, relationship building, or fundraising."[43] Thus, while good management is important to an organization, the value of trusted and inspirational leadership should not be discounted. The vital nature of competent leadership has led to the creation of several diagnostic tools that have been found to be effective in evaluation of nonprofit executives and boards.[44] See Box 12.3 for more information.

Box 12.3

FOR MORE INFORMATION

EVALUATING BOARD AND EXECUTIVE EFFECTIVENESS

The importance of competent nonprofit leadership in high-performing organizations has been widely recognized. Several diagnostic tools have been developed by Synergy Associates to assist in assessment of boards and executives.[45] These include

Synergy Associates' Governance Self-Assessment Checklist (GSAC) (2004): This resource contains checklists for both the board and the executive, and while Synergy notes that it is not a definitive evaluation of nonprofit performance, it can assist the board, individual members, and the executive in reflecting upon and engaging in dialogue about the governance and success of the organization. It is available for purchase: www.synergyassociates.ca/services/GovernanceSelfAssessmentChecklist.htm

Synergy Associates Board Effectiveness Quick Check: a free resource provided by Synergy is the Board Effectiveness Quick Check, available at: www.lisc.org/docs/resources/experts/2007/eo_2007_07_11_check.pdf.

BOARDS OF DIRECTORS

Nonprofit boards of directors, sometimes called boards of trustees, have a variety of legal and functional responsibilities. Legally, boards have the duties of obedience, loyalty, and care, while functionally they are responsible for guiding the organizational mission, choosing an executive director, and facilitating the organization's direction. As we begin an in-depth discussion of nonprofit boards of directors, it is important to keep in mind the words of Ostrower and Stone:

> [B]oards are complex entities that defy sweeping generalizations. They are heterogeneous, subject to internal shifts, and respond to multiple—and sometimes conflicting—influences. Explicitly and implicitly, the emerging consensus in the literature is that there is no "one size fits all" model of boards.[46]

For example, in 1990 John Carver's *Boards That Make a Difference* was published, with a set of very clear governance practices that many nonprofits attempted to emulate; most had only varying levels of success because, while many of his ideas worked in some settings, they did not work in others. For small nonprofits that need a working board, in which board members must handle significant portions of the day-to-day operations, for example, his clear separation between the board and the organization simply did not fit. Instead, most nonprofits have employed a hybrid of practices that they find work best for them.[47] Thus, while we acquaint readers with the general legal restrictions under which boards operate, highlight some of the generalizations that scholars have made about board functions and roles, and suggest current best practices, keep in mind that boards of directors are dynamic entities operating within an equally dynamic social, economic, and political milieu as they oversee service delivery and program implementation.

Theories of Nonprofit Board Behavior

The scholarship on nonprofit boards typically involves two broad theories: principal-agent and resource dependence.[48] A third theory, institutionalism, has been offered by Miller-Millesen as useful in discussions of nonprofit board behavior.[49] Principal-agent theory is well known in the organizational theory literature and refers to the relationship between the actor who creates a job or position (the principal) and the actor who carries out the work (the agent). In the classic conceptualization, the principal must use a series of strategies including rule setting, monitoring, and evaluation to ensure that the agent is carrying out the work of the principal as expected and not engaging in opportunistic behavior.

For nonprofit organizations, it is easy to see the board of directors in the role of principal and the executive in the role of agent. Using this theoretical lens, the board is responsible for control, monitoring, and reward of the executive as well as the nonprofit organization as a whole. One difficulty with using the principal-agent theory in the nonprofit setting is assignment of the role of principal.[50] For example, the founders of the organization could easily be considered the principals or, from a legal standpoint, the state attorney general might be considered the principal as he or she is ultimately responsible for ensuring that the not-for-profit appropriately fulfills its public purposes. Further, when nonprofits act as government contractors, the nonprofit itself is considered the agent to the government's role as principal. While it is sometimes difficult to clearly assign the roles of principal and agent, this theoretical lens has still proven useful to understanding the management relationships in nonprofits.

As discussed in Chapter 3, the theory of resource dependency emphasizes the fact that the nonprofit, in order to successfully operate and pursue its mission, depends on a host of resources from within and outside of the organization. Used with reference to the board, resource dependency theory highlights the importance of appointing board members who can help the organization attain the resources it needs to survive. As exemplified in the opening vignette, a board with significant financial resources, political and professional contacts, and community stature can be the key to successfully providing the nonprofit's services. In addition, when board members provide access to information and related resources that ease the uncertain environmental context in which the nonprofit operates, they perform "a boundary-spanning function that absorbs uncertainty, reduces operational dependencies, exchanges information, represents the organization to external stakeholders, and enhances overall performance." [51]

The theory of institutionalism emphasizes the rules, procedures, and standards that structure the way in which modern nonprofit organizations are managed and operated, often in accordance with government or foundation regulations. For example, self-assessments, advisory committees, adherence to occupational health and safety standards, or use of Robert's Rules of Order at board meetings are increasingly standard procedures in the nonprofit sector as each organization attempts to emulate the best practices of other organizations.[52] According to Miller-Millesen, institutionalism helps to explain the role of nonprofit boards in terms of their techniques for managing executives, their strategies for undertaking their fiduciary responsibilities, and the institutionalization of procedures to promote organizational transparency and accountability.[53]

Taken together, these three theories can go a long way in explaining the behavior of nonprofit boards, even if it is to explain the same behavior through different theoretical constructs. For example, a single activity such as strategic planning could be explained by all three theories: strategic planning activities viewed through the lens of principal-agent theory would be undertaken by the board to control executive and organizational behavior; through the resource dependency lens, strategic planning may be pursued in order to ensure organizational resources; finally, institutionalism would explain formal strategic planning when a funding agency requires that grantees present a strategic plan as a condition of the grant award.[54]

The Legal Environment of Nonprofit Boards

Boards of directors are legal entities created through either a nonprofit corporation or a charitable trust and are therefore subject to the regulatory policies regarding these. In the

United States, the corporate form of governance is most widely used because the laws surrounding trusts are more stringent than those surrounding corporations. For example, under the corporate structure board members can only be held liable for gross negligence, whereas in a charitable trust members can be held legally liable for even minor errors in judgment. Further, the law of trusts maintains strict prohibitions against *self-dealing,* which is the act of benefiting someone with a significant interest in the trust such as a manager, director, or significant contributor. The law regarding corporations, on the other hand, allows for self-dealing as long as there is proper disclosure of the benefit. Legally, boards have three key duties: (1) obedience, whereby board members must comply with appropriate standards of fiduciary behavior; (2) loyalty, whereby each board member puts organizational interests above his or her own; and (3) care, which involves the "prudent person" standard: What would a prudent person do in managing his or her own affairs?[55]

The legal environment in which nonprofit boards operate creates many opportunities for transgressions; therefore, experts recommend a variety of strategies to avoid wrongdoing or its appearance, including separating those responsible for governance from those responsible for management. This separation can be accomplished through rules such as not allowing more than one person who receives compensation from the charity to serve as a voting member of the board, and not appointing anyone who is financially compensated by the nonprofit to serve as either the board chair or treasurer.[56]

Less serious from a legal standpoint but more common in practice are ethical transgressions such as conflicts of interest. As Helmut Anheier explains,

> [M]ost conflicts of interest are in a gray area where ethical considerations, stewardship, and public perception may be more relevant than legal aspects. Indeed, loss of public confidence in the organization resulting from conflict of interest situations, and a damaged reputation among key stakeholders, can be more damaging than the possibility of legal sanction.[57]

For these reasons, it is important that the nonprofit set clear standards of conduct and policies on conflicts of interest that each board member clearly understands. The national organization BoardSource (formerly the National Center for Nonprofit Boards) provides a wealth of information for nonprofits as they navigate these potential landmines; see Box 12.4 for more information. Regardless of these suggestions, however, the reality of boards in action often defies the recommendations of best practices. For example, in her analysis of the National Survey of Nonprofit Governance, Francie Ostrower found that only half of nonprofit boards have a written policy on conflict of interest and only 29 percent require board members to disclose their financial interests in companies doing business with the nonprofit they serve.[58]

This lack of clarity regarding board member activity can lead the organization to operational, legal, and public relations problems if members are found to have engaged in questionable practices. In a 2010 scandal involving college football's Fiesta Bowl board, for

Box 12.4

FOR MORE INFORMATION

BOARDSOURCE CONFLICT OF INTEREST FAQS

BoardSource is a 501(c)(3) whose mission is to advance:

> . . . the public good by building exceptional nonprofit boards and inspiring board service. BoardSource strives to support and promote excellence in board service, is the premier source of cutting-edge thinking and resources related to nonprofit boards, and engages and develops the next generation of board leaders.[59]

In this capacity, BoardSource offers a wide array of services including training, workshops, research, books, and events designed to help improve nonprofit governance. An example of the many tools offered by BoardSource is a list of Frequently Asked Questions about board member conflicts of interest. In general, they suggest that any policy on conflict of interest include:

1. **A full disclosure clause,** which states that members of the board and staff with decision-making authority make public any relationships they have with groups or individuals doing business with the nonprofit.
2. **A board member abstention clause,** which states that board members with a conflict or potential conflict of interest refrain from discussing or voting on issues between the nonprofit and the group or individual creating the conflict of interest.
3. **A staff member abstention clause,** which states that staff with an actual or potential conflict of interest should refrain from substantial involvement in decisions affecting transactions with the group or individual creating the conflict of interest.

For more information, see BoardSource at www.boardsource.org/Knowledge.asp?ID=3.389; and Daniel L. Kurtz and Sarah E. Paul, *Managing Conflicts of Interest: A Primer for Nonprofit Boards* (Washington, DC: BoardSource, 2006).

example, the construction company owned by a treasurer and later board chair was found to have been awarded $2 million in no-bid contracts from the board for headquarters renovations and a Fiesta Bowl museum in Scottsdale, Arizona.[60] Although the board had created a conflict-of-interest policy and the treasurer/chair said that he had abstained from voting on the no-bid construction contract, this was one of a series of board-related financial incidents that resulted in a 276-page investigative report by Arizona's secretary of state, $1 million in fines from the Bowl Championship Series (BCS) organization, and the removal of several officials, including the board chair, executive officer, and the chief operating officer, against whom nine criminal indictments were charged.[61] The reputation of the Fiesta Bowl was tarnished by these improprieties, and in 2011 it lost several corporate sponsors and at least one major advertiser; it had to sell other television ad-time during the game at discount rates.[62] The stakes are high for organizations and individuals who do not take care to create and follow through with appropriate rules of conduct for nonprofit boards.

Given the potential for legal action, nonprofits with sufficient resources should purchase insurance for their directors and officers; those without sufficient resources should encourage their board members to purchase the insurance themselves. D&O insurance "pays on behalf of the directors and officers of the organization any financial losses that arise from claims or lawsuits brought against them for committing some wrongful act."[63] It is in the best interests of the nonprofit, its executive, and its board members to be well apprised of the legal, financial, and ethical obligations and responsibilities under which they operate because the consequences of even unintentional transgressions can be devastating.[64]

What We Know about Nonprofit Boards

Research on nonprofit boards of directors indicates a number of generalizations, although it is useful to remember that there is no one-size-fits-all template for a nonprofit board.[65] One generalization is that boards of directors in the not-for-profit sector are larger than for-profit boards, with sixteen members on average, although some are much larger.[66] There are several explanations for large nonprofit boards, including: (1) the importance of fundraising by board members; (2) the need to reflect a diverse group of stakeholders and constituencies; (3) having more board members offers more points of contact for the nonprofit with those outside of it; and (4) the fact that a larger board can improve organizational monitoring and control.[67] On the other hand, larger boards can prove difficult to govern and can allow for more shirking behavior among members. It is important, therefore, that board members monitor and evaluate overall board performance and that each member is held accountable for his or her commitment to the organization.[68]

Diversity. Although nonprofit boards are more diverse than in decades past and more diverse than for-profit boards, the average member of a nonprofit board continues to be white, male, and of upper or upper-middle socio-economic status. This is especially true with regard to large, affluent nonprofit organizations.[69] Board members also tend to be much better educated than the general population and more likely to hold professional occupations.[70] Given this, questions sometimes arise about a homogenous board's ability to represent the interests of a diverse clientele.

Diversity and representation are complex issues, and each board should consider what it means to be diverse in its own community as well as how its clients' needs are best served, as highlighted in the opening vignette. In these cases, it may make sense to add board members or ask non-members to serve on board committees to ensure that the voices of a wide variety of stakeholders are heard. Ruth McCambridge, editor of *Nonprofit Quarterly,* has suggested that diversity and representation is not only at the heart of effective organizational performance but at the heart of effective democracy. She suggests that nonprofits that are "serious about representing and responding to constituent interests" must include those served in conversations about the planning, development, and future of the organization.[71] Such engagement and accountability is of particular importance in nonprofits that serve ethnic identity groups such as Latinos and African Americans.[72] The value of diversity in nonprofit leadership is not merely symbolic but can have important practical implications. Board composition makes a difference in the foundation world, for example, as the Greenlining Institute found a high correlation between diverse boards and grantmaking to organizations with minority leadership.[73]

On the other hand, while the bias toward white, male, upper-class board members can cause some concern about legitimacy and responsiveness to constituent groups, as the executive director in our opening vignette explains, well-educated, connected, and wealthy board members are often better situated to help the nonprofit meet its mission and program goals. Resource dependency theory expects board members to play the role of boundary spanner between the organization and its environment. Therefore, members with more money, political or community ties, and professional experience are valuable to the nonprofit because of the wide variety of advantages that they have to offer.[74]

Roles and Responsibilities of Board Members

In addition to proposing theories of board behavior, many authors have described the roles and responsibilities of boards of directors in a prescriptive manner. A review of a number of such works yielded a list of eight general roles and responsibilities that recur throughout the literature: guardians of the mission, purpose, and goals; recruit and select the executive director; manage the managers; facilitate organizational direction; ambassadors; sponsors; governors; and ensure adherence to standards. Table 12.1 includes these eight categories along with their descriptions and the theoretical lens that explains each.

Although these eight categories represent the most common roles and responsibilities associated with nonprofit boards, the reality is that a "board gap" often exists between expectations and the actual performance of boards.[75] For example, in her analysis of the Urban Institute's study of over 5,100 nonprofit organizations, Ostrower found that slightly over 50 percent of nonprofit executives indicated their boards were actively engaged in only three of the eight responsibilities identified in the literature: (1) sponsors—ensuring financial oversight of the organization; (2) facilitators of organizational direction—actively involved in setting organizational direction and policy; and (3) managing the managers—taking an active role in evaluation of the executive officer.

While only three of the eight categories of responsibility were being undertaken by a majority of boards in the study, more distressing is the fact that in some of these eight categories boards were not even rated as "somewhat active." The significantly underperformed activities included monitoring programs and services, fundraising, and the ambassador role of community relations and educating the public about the nonprofit's mission.[76] A 2010 survey by BoardSource confirms that executives are most frustrated with their board's performance as fundraisers and ambassadors.[77] While a survey of board members in South Carolina was far more sanguine about the range of responsibilities embraced by boards, it confirmed Ostrower's conclusion that evaluation of nonprofit services and programs is not

Table 12.1 Roles and Responsibilities of the Board of Directors, with Applied Theoretical Lens

Role/Responsibility	Description	Theoretical Lens
Guardians of the Mission, Purpose, and Goals	Boards are often key during the formation of a nonprofit, and in that capacity they help to create its mission statement, settle on its purpose and vision, and select concrete goals. In later stages of the organization, the board takes on a guardianship role for the mission, purpose, and goals of the organization.	Principal-Agent
Recruit and Select the Executive Director	An effective executive director is vital to the success of an organization. The fact that the board and executive director will work closely together makes recruitment and selection of an executive director an important board responsibility.	Principal-Agent
Manage the Managers	The board is responsible for managing, supporting, and evaluating the executive director but also for ensuring good management of the organization's other managers and staff members. This includes respect for employees and their time, and avoiding micromanagement.	Principal-Agent / Institutional
Facilitate Organizational Direction	It is the board's responsibility to keep the organization on track through effective direction and strategic planning, to move the organization in different directions to maintain its effectiveness, to adapt to changing circumstances, and to remain relevant for the future.	Resource Dependency
Ambassadors	Board members must protect and enhance the organization's public image and maintain linkages with outside interests, stakeholders, and their communities.	Resource Dependency
Sponsors	Members of the board have the responsibility for ensuring adequate finances and maintaining proper financial oversight of the nonprofit. Included in their role as sponsors is engagement in fundraising and contribution of funds.	Resource Dependency / Institutional

(Continued)

Table 12.1 (Continued)

Role/Responsibility	Description	Theoretical Lens
Governors	The board is responsible for the governance of the organization—the "trustee role," in which board members understand and follow the policies set by the organization that allow it to have its intended social impact.	Principal-Agent / Institutional
Ensure Adherence to Standards	The board is responsible for ensuring that the organization adheres to legal and ethical standards of operation and for the transparency and accountability of organizational actions.	Institutional / Principal-Agent

Sources: BoardSource, *The Nonprofit Board Answer Book: A Practical Guide for Board Members and Chief Executives* (San Francisco: Jossey-Bass, 2007); Peter Drucker, *Managing the Nonprofit Organization* (New York: HarperCollins, 2005); Kay Sprinkel Grace, *The Ultimate Board Member's Book: A 1-Hour Guide to Understanding and Fulfilling Your Role and Responsibilities* (Medfield, MA: Emerson and Church Publishers, 2008); Thomas P. Holland and Roger A. Ritvo, *Nonprofit Organizations, Principles and Practices* (New York: Columbia University Press, 2008); Richard T. Ingram, *Ten Basic Responsibilities of Nonprofit Boards,* 2nd ed. (Washington, DC: BoardSource, 2009); W. Astor Kirk, *Board Members Governing Roles and Responsibilities* (Lanham, MD: University Press of America, 2007); Sharon Oster, *Strategic Management for Nonprofit Organizations Theory and Cases* (New York: Oxford University Press, 1995); William B. Werther Jr. and Evan M. Berman, *Third Sector Management: The Art of Managing Nonprofit Organizations* (Washington, DC: Georgetown University Press, 2001).

being undertaken by most nonprofit boards.[78] Considering that these organizations play such a crucial role in the implementation of an array of public policies and programs, it is troubling that boards of directors are not more active in monitoring and evaluating organizational outcomes.

Board Life Cycle and Engagement. It is difficult to say what explains the differences between theory and practice for nonprofit boards of directors, but one answer may lie in the complex environments within which boards operate. The wide variety of internal and external factors that affect the operating environment can lead boards to govern on a contingency or situational basis.[79] These various factors influence the ways in which board members approach their work, including the tasks for which they feel most responsible and the level of effort they expend on different activities. Factors such as organizational age and size, whether or not the executive is a well-paid professional, the primary sources of organizational funding, and public policies such as Sarbanes-Oxley (SOX) all affect the roles and responsibilities taken by nonprofit boards at any given time in the organization's development.

For example, the boards of younger organizations are likely to be consumed by their roles as guardians of the nonprofit's mission, purpose, and goals and are more likely to be working boards; later in the life cycle, the organization is more likely to have a governance or advisory board which focuses more attention on its role in ensuring adherence to legal and ethical standards of operation and bureaucratic procedures.[80] An important external contingency factor for nonprofits is the 2002 Sarbanes-Oxley Act, which has influenced the level of attention that boards pay to their roles in sponsorship, ensuring proper accounting and financial oversight, and ensuring adherence to standards of accountability and transparency. Further, the external factor of SOX has also been found to interact with the internal factor of board composition: nonprofits with board members who also sit on corporate boards are more likely to conform to the guidelines of SOX than are boards without the same level of corporate experience.[81]

Board Structure and Development

There are a variety of ways by which a person can attain a position on a nonprofit board. Board members: (1) can be chosen through election by organizational members; (2) they can be appointed—either by existing board members as a self-perpetuating board, or by an authority outside of the board; or (3) board member selection can be a hybrid of these with both elected and appointed members. In some cases, board members are ex-officio, in which they become board members by virtue of holding another position—for example, four state elected officials, including the governor and lieutenant governor, are ex-officio members of the California State University Board of Trustees.

Nonprofit boards typically include the positions of chair, vice-chair, and treasurer, and some boards also have a secretary and a chair-elect.[82] Most boards, especially large ones, establish a system of committees to help manage their work. Since board members are chosen for the skills, expertise, talent, or status they can contribute, committees allow each member the opportunity to use her time most productively for the organization. The most common board committees include governance and nominating, finance, executive, fundraising and development, audit, programs and marketing and public relations.[83] While the purview of some committees might overlap with staff functions, such as finance, programs, marketing, or fundraising, it is important that committee work not undermine or usurp the work of paid staff. Rather, staff should serve as a resource for committees, including help with agendas and reports; the committee is charged with making recommendations to the whole board, which then takes any necessary action to guide the organization.

It is important to note that board members typically serve in a voluntary capacity and, unfortunately, most nonprofits have a difficult time recruiting members to their boards.[84] Board member recruitment and development have been found to be enhanced by effective board performance, competence, and use of nonprofit best practices.[85] When choosing board members, therefore, it is essential to create a position description that outlines the duties, responsibilities, and expectations of board members. The board should provide recruits with information about the mission, leadership, and financial condition of the organization, as well as the expectations of member service, including the time and place of meetings, the average amount of time that service entails, the length of a term, and whether or not members are expected to donate to the organization.[86]

Boards may be seeking members with a particular skill-set—for example. public relations—in which case a recruitment profile may be more limited, but in general, organizations look for members that meet multiple requirements. Organizations typically look for board members with a demonstrated interest in the organization and its mission, including those who have been donors or volunteers in the past. Further, it is important to choose members willing to make a commitment to the organization and understand that service requires time and energy. Nonprofits often seek a diverse board membership in terms of age, race, ethnicity, and gender to avoid insularity and to broaden the board's perspective on a variety of issues facing it. In the opening vignette, for example, some parents felt that their voices were not being heard on important issues relevant to the future of their children's school. One recommendation is that boards use a matrix when recruiting members to ensure that requirements such as demonstrated interest and ability to commit time are met, but also to ensure that board members have a range of desirable qualities including educational or professional background, diverse demographic characteristics, and community connections.[87]

Commitment to the organization is an important factor in board member performance. Members who are more emotionally attached to the nonprofit are more involved and executive officers rate them as more valuable board members.[88] Further, highly committed board members tend to make larger financial contributions, donate more time, have better attendance at board meetings, and volunteer to serve on more committees than those less attached. Board members appear to be most motivated to serve out of concern for their communities,[89] and to participate more when they perceive that they have organizational support and if they feel their expectations are being met. Importantly, members are more likely to leave board service if these conditions do not exist.[90]

An effective board requires cultivation. Beyond member selection, therefore, nonprofit boards must take the time and effort to provide formal orientation and training for new members.[91] Those new to the board should be given materials such as board by-laws, calendars of events, and recent meeting minutes; they should be introduced to the nonprofit's facilities and staff, its programs, and volunteers and clients when applicable; they should be briefed on the public policies of import to the organization and the strategies used to affect those policies; and they should have access to recent audits, program reviews, and grants and contracts that the organization has used to pursue its mission. Further, as the board carries out its work, it can benefit from a host of activities that help it to develop its competence and continue to engage its members. Board members should be invited to events hosted by the organization and can be given opportunities to attend conferences and seminars on governance topics as well as topics relating to the mission of the organization. They can also be provided with resources including books, studies, and webinars related to their work, and they can invite consultants and other speakers to board meetings so members are kept up-to-date with the latest legislation, technology, and research; each of these is important to helping the organization provide its clientele with the public programs and services that fulfill the nonprofit's mission. These strategies can be used to protect against "the bored board," which loses interest and hinders the effectiveness of the organization.[92]

Best Practices for Boards

Nonprofit boards are an important piece of the leadership team, and while there is no one-size-fits-all board model, there are a number of recommendations from experts on best practices for a board to meet its legal and functional responsibilities. Particularly when the reputation of the nonprofit is on the line, it is essential that boards adhere to legal mandates and ethical standards, as illustrated through the problems faced by the board of directors of the Central Asia Institute, discussed in Going Global 12.5. Boards also have a great deal of influence over the day-to-day operations of the organization, especially given their responsibility to choose, monitor, and evaluate the chief executive. For these reasons, we close this section with a summary of recommendations for the nonprofit board to guide, advise, and govern its organization as it provides the programs and services required of its mission.

- **Avoid wrongdoing or its appearance**: Do not allow more than one person who receives compensation from the charity to serve as a voting member of the board, and do not appoint anyone who is financially compensated by the nonprofit to serve as board chair or treasurer.
- **Have clear conflict of interest and standard of conduct policies**: Include a full disclosure clause for board and staff; a board member abstention clause for members with a conflict or potential conflict of interest; and a staff member abstention clause.
- **Make legal, financial, and ethical obligations known**: Be sure that board members and staff have been apprised of and understand all policies related to these obligations.
- **Insure executives and board members**: The nonprofit should purchase insurance for their directors and officers (D&O Insurance) or encourage them to purchase the insurance themselves.
- **Create a partnership with the executive**: The relationship between the board and the executive should be characterized by open and frequent communication, compatible philosophy and vision, and clear, shared expectations of their roles in the organization.
- **Use committees wisely**: A committee system helps the board to manage its work, but committees should work *with* paid staff, not undermine or usurp their work.
- **Be diligent about board recruitment**: Boards should create a position description. They often use a matrix to ensure that recruits meet both board member requirements and the range of qualities desired by the board.
- **Be equally diligent about board development**: Provide formal orientation and training for new members and use on-going development strategies to ensure the competence and engagement of board members.

GOING GLOBAL 12.5

Central Asia Institute and the Challenges of the Board-Executive Relationship

As discussed in previous chapters, the NGO Central Asia Institute (CAI) illustrates several issues regarding regulation of nonprofits as well as problems related to financial mismanagement. CAI is also an example of the challenges faced by a board that governs international activities and manages the activities of a powerful founding executive director, Greg Mortenson.[93]

After its formation in 1997, the board of directors for CAI reached its largest number of members, eight, in 2000; at the time of the attorney general's investigation of the nonprofit in 2011, the board consisted of only three members. Mortenson, the founding executive director of CAI, was not one of the board's original members; he was voted to the board in 2002, after three members resigned amid conflicts with Mortenson over issues of management and accountability. According to the attorney general's investigation, the three members were effectively forced out; two of them—the board's chair and treasurer—had pressed Mortenson on several occasions to provide detailed documentation of the expenses he was charging to CAI and to justify their benefit to the organization. The board chair had also suggested that Mortenson's role in managing daily operations should be phased out. When Mortenson continued to refuse requests to document expenses and the rest of the board declined to force his compliance, the board chair, treasurer, and one other member resigned and Mortenson was placed on the board, while maintaining his position as executive director.

There is no doubt from the organization's records that the board was aware of the issues of financial mismanagement attributed to Mortenson. Steps were taken in 2008—when the board consisted of four members, including Mortenson—to address them by hiring an attorney to draft a series of policies and procedures manuals, including a Travel Reimbursement Policy as well as a Board Policy Manual that included a provision regarding the structure of the board.

> Section 2.1 Structure: The Board shall regularly reevaluate the size of the Board to ensure that it has enough members for full and diverse deliberation, in a scale appropriate to the Institute's size, with the appropriate level of skill and expertise. The Board should include members with diverse backgrounds, experience, and skills. In considering the Board's size and composition, independent Board members should comprise at least two-thirds of the Board, meaning that they receive no remuneration from the Institute, and are not closely related to anyone who does.[94]

As with the policy regarding reimbursement of expenses, the board structure policy was not effectively implemented or enforced. Whether his excessive influence over the board was a result of founder syndrome, a weak board of directors, a charismatic leader who was a feeble administrator, or a combination of the three, media attention on Mortenson's actions and the board's inaction eventually led to investigation by the state.

Testimony gathered in the course of the investigation revealed that while members of the board had sincere admiration for Mortenson, they also felt the organization was entirely dependent on him. Their inability to exercise oversight of his activities was a result of their belief that Mortenson generated more resources for the organization than he misspent, and that the organization could not survive without him. The imbalance in the relationship between CAI's board and its chief executive has been addressed as a result of the settlement agreement with the attorney general. Mortenson has agreed to step down as executive director; while he retains a staff position with CAI, he does not have responsibility for financial oversight of any of the organization's activities.

What the attorney general's report also illustrates is the difficulty associated with conducting programs overseas, in remote areas with cultural and economic systems that are dramatically different than in the United States. CAI would often make large wire transfers of cash to staff in the area to make the purchases necessary to implement projects in remote areas but failed to require the necessary documentation of how the funds were expended. Operating in areas that are thousands of miles away from the organization headquarters makes in-person monitoring by the board much more challenging. However, it is important to note that prior to the investigation, each member of the board had visited the areas of Afghanistan and Pakistan where CAI operates. Furthermore, in 2011, the board sent an attorney and team of staff members to directly assess the projects in those areas in order to make recommendations for an improved system of documentation and accountability. They have also instituted a system by which to better track projects and their effectiveness with regard to CAI's mission and now include a master project list on their website (www.ikat.org). The Master Project List and Key is frequently updated and includes definitions of the types of support offered by CAI, as well as a detailed listing of their projects, when they were initiated, when completed, and the numbers served by them. Also, to address the issues of different cultural and economic systems, CAI has retained accounting firms in both Afghanistan and Pakistan to work with their accountants in the United States. to improve the process of funding and tracking projects in remote areas.

Key to the continued success of CAI in spite of the serious issues of financial mismanagement and poor administration is the sincere commitment of each board member to the work that the organization seeks to accomplish. As the attorney general pointed out, "even CAI's harshest critics recognize that the organization has built schools and accomplished positive achievements in a very challenging region of the world."[95] More than 200 schools and vocational centers have been built and maintained by CAI in their 15-year history, and an additional 75 schools and literacy centers as well as several public health projects have been supported. In 2011, 57 new school and community projects were initiated in Pakistan, Afghanistan, and Tajikistan.[96]

CAI's story illustrates the potential benefits and pitfalls for a board charged with directing an organization with a charismatic and committed policy entrepreneur at its helm who is also a poor administrator. As this example indicates, when the executive director is a well-known figure, the ability of the board to exercise proper oversight is curtailed, especially when the organization prospers regardless of the mismanagement. Eventually, though, it is likely the organization will be damaged financially, legally, or in reputation. In the case of CAI, the damage does not appear to be irreparable, and appropriate steps are being taken to implement reforms to restore public confidence in the organization and enhance its ability to pursue its mission.

CONCLUSION

Throughout this chapter we have discussed those in leadership positions in nonprofit organizations, the board of directors, and executive officers. Contemporary research on leadership has highlighted two particularly important leadership styles in nonprofit organizations: transformational and transactional. Transformational leadership makes use of vision and emotion to inspire and motivate, which is extremely important for organizations with large numbers of volunteers. Transactional leadership, on the other hand, relies on more traditional techniques of management and provides instrumental rewards to encourage subordinates. Research on leadership has concluded that successful leaders integrate their transactional/management responsibilities with their transformational/inspirational responsibilities to move their organizations forward.

While boards of directors and executive officers are organizational leaders, they typically have distinct areas of responsibility. For example, boards have primary responsibility for the overall vision, monitoring, and accountability of the nonprofit, while executives are primarily responsible for day-to-day operations including service delivery as well as staff development and evaluation. On the other hand, while boards of directors and executive officers play distinct roles in nonprofits, leadership and governance should be undertaken as a joint responsibility between the two. In successful nonprofit organizations, boards and executives work together to provide nonprofit governance that guides the direction and performance of the organization. Effective nonprofit leaders align themselves with the values, mission, and culture of their organizations and are increasingly considered the primary point of interaction between multiple actors and interests in the policymaking and implementation processes.

An important difference between boards and executives is their respective legal positions within the nonprofit organization. Boards are legal entities typically created through nonprofit incorporation, and the role of the executive in the nonprofit is highly dependent upon the board. Because the executive director is vital to nonprofit success, the selection, training, and evaluation of the nonprofit executive is a key role played by the board of directors. Research and demographic trends suggest that the selection of an executive is increasingly important as a large percentage of chief executives will reach retirement age within the next decade. While the ability to recruit, select, and retain quality executives and board members is surely important to the success of an individual nonprofit organization, the fundamental role that the voluntary sector plays in public policy formation, program implementation, and service delivery makes these positions important for society as a whole. Equally important, of course, is the contribution of volunteers and paid staff in the nonprofit sector; it is to these subjects that we turn in Chapter 13.

Questions For Review

1. Discuss the life-cycle concept of nonprofit leadership. What differences would you expect in the relationship between the executive and board of a nonprofit start-up and that same nonprofit 35 years later?
2. Research indicates that effective boards are key factors in having effective nonprofits. Why, then, does a board gap—the difference between expected and actual roles and responsibilities—exist in so many not-for-profit organizations?
3. Define the following concepts, giving examples of each as they pertain to nonprofit boards and executives: Principal-Agent Theory, Resource Dependency, and Institutionalism.
4. Consider the legal responsibilities and functional roles played by boards of directors. Which are the most important to help the nonprofit successfully provide the programs and services required of its mission? In what way does your answer depend on the nonprofit classification: arts and culture, social services, education, the environment, animals, and so on?

Assignment

Now that you have read Chapter 12, go back and re-read the opening vignette and consider how you might respond if you were Mike, the lower Ninth Ward school's executive director. How would you address your students' disgruntled parents? What theories and/or responsibilities tied to nonprofit leadership would you point to as you make your arguments? Should you change your governance strategy in any way, and if so, how? How would the arguments of Ruth McCambridge about nonprofit governance and democracy influence your recommendations?

Suggested Readings

BoardSource. *The Nonprofit Board Answer Book: A Practical Guide for Board Members and Chief Executives* San Francisco: Jossey-Bass, 2007.

Fairholm, Matthew R. "Different Perspectives on the Practice of Leadership." *Public Administration Review* 64, 5 (2004): 577–590.

Grace, Kay Sprinkel. *The Ultimate Board Member's Book: A 1-Hour Guide to Understanding and Fulfilling Your Role and Responsibilities.* Medfield, MA: Emerson and Church Publishers, 2008.

McCambridge, Ruth. "Understanding the Power of Nonprofit Governance." *Nonprofit and Voluntary Sector Quarterly* 33, 2 (2004): 346–354.

Ostrower, Francie. *Nonprofit Governance in the United States: Findings on Performance and Accountability from the First National Representative Study.* Washington, DC: The Urban Institute, 2007.

Web Resources

Alliance of Nonprofits for Insurance, Risk Retention Group, www.ani-rrg.org/

Blue Avocado ("practical, provocative, and fun food-for-thought for nonprofits"), www.blueavocado.org/

BoardSource, www.boardsource.org/

The Bridgespan Group, www.bridgespan.org/

Bridgestar (from the Bridgespan Group), www.bridgestar.org/Home.aspx

Bridgestar Recruiting Nonprofit Leaders learning center, www.bridgestar.org/LearningCenters/Recruiting.aspx

Governance of Charitable Organizations and Related Topics (IRS), www.irs.gov/charities/article/0,,id=178221,00.html

13 Managing Human Resources

Volunteers and Staff

The individuals who now bring into reality the service side of the welfare state are the new street-level bureaucrats. Like their public sector counterparts, many workers in nonprofit agencies interact directly with clients and perform their jobs despite severely limited resources. Also, like their public sector counterparts, they work in agencies with ambiguous and conflicting goals, perform tasks which are difficult to measure, and are undisciplined by client and consumer preferences.

Steven Rathgeb Smith and Michael Lipsky [1]

Imagine that you are a long-time supporter of a local non-profit organization, the Phoenix Project, which provides transitional housing and assistance to women who have been victims of domestic violence and their children. The organization owns two large, private residences where families live while receiving support services that include counseling, life skills classes, and employment assistance.

As the economy slumped in 2009, donations to the organization began to dry up; the executive and the board began to look for new sources of funding, new partnerships, and new government grants. One local foundation with a special interest in funding life skills programs for teen mothers has offered a sizable grant with the stipulation that the Phoenix Project add teen moms to their life skills and counseling classes. Phoenix Project counselors are up in arms as the board and executive director consider what they are calling "an exciting new partnership." How can they think of bringing in such a different clientele? Phoenix Project employees are professionals with expertise in domestic violence, not teen parenting. They fear that this effort compromises the Phoenix Project mission and risks both the privacy of their current residents and the trust that grows between the counseling staff and the victims of abuse—women who clearly have special and different needs than teen moms.

As a financial supporter and volunteer you understand the Phoenix Project's dependence on outside resources; however, you agree with the

POLICY IMPLICATIONS OF VOLUNTEER AND STAFF MANAGEMENT

- Nonprofits are subject to many federal, state, and local mandates and policies when managing their human resources—paid employees and volunteers. Many of these have their roots in the 1964 Civil Rights Act.
- Recruitment and retention of a talented and committed workforce is vital in the nonprofit sector, and human resource (HR) managers need to be aware of the many federal and state policies that regulate employment matters in the workplace.
- Motivation for nonprofit employees and volunteers typically hinges less on extrinsic rewards such as money and more on the intrinsic and mission-related rewards (known as public service motivation) associated with pursuing programs and policies to which they are committed.
- Large numbers of volunteers are vital to nonprofit organizations, so good management of volunteers is particularly important. Volunteer managers must be familiar with the federal and state personnel policies that encourage volunteerism and protect volunteers from liability during their service.
- Mission-related exceptions to antidiscrimination policies have been granted to religious organizations and private clubs for whom it is legal to engage in practices including refusal to hire, engaging in unequal compensation practices, or dismissal of employees based on race, gender, sexual orientation, or religious practice.

counselors and have many questions. For example, what about the morale of both the paid employees and volunteers who work well together and with the current residents? Will new skills or new employees be needed to address the needs of this new clientele? Will some of the professional counselors leave the organization? Will long-time volunteers, a number of whom are survivors of domestic violence, also jump ship?

MANAGEMENT OF NONPROFIT HUMAN RESOURCES

This chapter focuses on the personnel delivering services, providing programs, and implementing policies in the not-for-profit sector, those Henry Mintzberg calls the Operating Core.[2] The work of nonprofit organizations tends to be very labor-intensive, particularly when it involves direct delivery of public services. For example, even when delivering the same type of social services, not-for-profit organizations have been found to provide higher staff-to-client ratios than for-profit organizations.[3] Successful human resources (HR) management, therefore, is vital to the efficient and effective implementation of public policy by nonprofit agencies. Although techniques of HR management are fairly similar across the three sectors, nonprofits have two unique characteristics: first, employees tend to be more intrinsically and/or mission motivated than those in either of the other sectors, and second, many find themselves increasingly relying on a professional workforce but also relying heavily on unpaid volunteers. This *coproduction* can make HR management more challenging for nonprofit agencies. Relationships between paid employees and volunteers must be managed, for example, and questions—such as, just how do you fire a volunteer—must be addressed. The strong commitment to organizational mission typically exhibited by both paid and volunteer workers is important to understand, develop, and reward as it is an important motivator for those in nonprofit organizations. Because nonprofit employees and volunteers are so often on the front lines in the implementation of public policy, well managed human resources are imperative to well run organizations, appropriate service delivery, and, ultimately, good public policy. Further, HR is one of the areas in which nonprofit management is most subject to government regulation and public policy mandates.

Strategic Human Resource Management

Good management of human resources is recognized as essential for any organization, and the nonprofit sector is no exception.[4] Traditional HR management recognizes the importance of employees and tends to focus on administrative issues such as recruitment, hiring, and development of the workforce. However, the fact that a large proportion of nonprofit organizations are small and have typically not been as well managed as organizations in the other sectors means that even basic human resource management functions tend to receive less attention in nonprofits.[5] For example, in a somewhat contradictory 2012 survey finding, while 81 percent of respondents agreed that HR practices are critical to their nonprofit's ability to achieve its mission, 23 percent said that their organization does *not* perceive HR as a key function.[6] One likely explanation for this finding is limited financial resources that the organization may feel would be put to better use on programs and services, especially in small nonprofits. However, the survey found that even among large nonprofits, those with budgets of $10 million or more, only 38 percent have two or more staff members whose job is exclusively to manage HR functions. More commonly, HR staffers are responsible for other administrative tasks as well.[7] In addition, survey respondents expect both retirements and resignations to increase in coming years; this will put an even greater premium on the HR functions of recruiting, retaining, and motivating nonprofit sector employees.[8]

All of this is quite troubling in an era in which the number of nonprofits and their influence on society has grown, job openings are expected to increase, and nonprofits face increasing pressures to be productive and effective. The pressure to improve not-for-profit capacity has led some to suggest that personnel matters in the sector require strategic human resource management (SHRM).[9] Joan E. Pynes explains:

> Strategic human resources management (SHRM) is based on the belief that to be effective and able to adapt to changes quickly, agencies need realistic information on the capabilities and talents of their current staff—in essence, their human resources.[10]

SHRM involves focusing on the long-term objectives of the organization and designing personnel practices around long-term goals. For example, changing workforce demographics in terms of cultural diversity, the retirement of baby boomers, and the influx of Millennials (those born after 1980) each has an impact on human resources management, and approaching these challenges with a plan in mind is an important component of SHRM.

Much like organizational strategic planning discussed in Chapter 5, SHRM requires current data about staff resources and abilities as they correspond with the mission and goals of the organization. It includes identifying and addressing any "gaps between the workforce of today and the human capital needs of tomorrow."[11] The federal Office of Personnel Management has several online resources that discuss the process of workforce planning for strategic management of personnel and offers a five-step model for HR managers to follow:

> Step One is quite familiar in the nonprofit sector as it requires: Set the strategic direction of the organization based on its overall strategic plan, goals, and objectives.
>
> Step Two: Analyze the workforce, identify skill gaps, and determine current and future workforce needs; develop specifications of the kinds of employees and numbers of employees needed, including determination of any gaps that exist between the skills and numbers of the current workforce, and future needs such as those associated with beginning a new program.
>
> Step Three: Develop an action plan, which includes identifying strategies for closing any personnel gaps, implementing those strategies, and measuring success.
>
> Step Four: Implementing the action plan is probably the most difficult step for nonprofit organizations because it may require human and financial resources that the organization does not have.
>
> Step Five: Monitor, evaluate, and revise your plan, which involves checking your progress against your goals, adjusting course to make necessary corrections, and addressing evolving workforce issues as they arise.

Among the values of adopting a SHRM strategy in a not-for-profit is its emphasis on the direction, goals, and objectives of the organization, which is particularly fitting in the mission-driven nonprofit sector. While it may seem difficult to develop and implement a SHRM action plan, even small nonprofits can often find volunteers to offer new programming or complete the tasks needed to ensure that the organization is ready to adapt to a changing environment. When Shelter Network, a provider of services to the homeless (highlighted in Box 13.4) decided to offer resume writing and interview skills trainings to its residents, it looked to corporate partners and volunteers to provide those workshops. Identifying and meeting current and future needs does not always require paid staff, an advantage that nonprofit organizations can easily use. The use of SHRM, however, will require that nonprofit organizations begin to take more seriously their HR functions and put both human and financial resources toward them.

Recruitment and Assessment

Important in SHRM is securing an appropriate workforce to deliver the services, programs, advocacy, and events required of the nonprofit organization; thus, employee recruitment and hiring is a key issue. Emphasizing the importance of the public mission of nonprofit sector employers can help attract committed individuals to work in the nonprofit sector. Recruitment should begin with an assessment of the organization's needs and an outline of the knowledge, skills, abilities, and other characteristics (KSAOCs) required for the position. Armed with a job description that outlines the duties to be performed and the level of skills, training, or education required, the organization identifies a target labor market and begins its recruitment process. While nonprofits continue to rely on traditional outlets such as newspapers and industry publications for recruitment, they are beginning to use social media strategies to a much greater degree: in 2012, 40 percent reported using LinkedIn and 30 percent had used Facebook to recruit.[12]

Organizations often look for internal job candidates because current employees know the organization and environment, and thus require less on-the-job training. Further, promoting from within is a valuable tool to boost morale and create an organizational culture in which employees know they will be rewarded for good work. On the other hand, there are many reasons that nonprofits must look for outside candidates, particularly when practicing SHRM. For example, as in the case of our opening vignette, the organization and its clientele may be growing or changing, there may be no employees with the skills and training required to meet future needs, or the organization may wish to become more diverse in terms of gender, age, race, or ethnicity. Finally, of course, outside candidates can bring fresh ideas and new energy to the organization, and they have no knowledge of preexisting organizational problems or frictions that may hamper organizational success.

When hiring from outside, it is important to understand the many federal and state policies that regulate employment matters to ensure against discrimination in the workplace. Policies specific to the nonprofit sector will be discussed in greater detail below, but in general the Equal Employment Opportunity Commission (EEOC) bans recruitment or hiring procedures that may result in discrimination. However, nonprofits serving a specific client group, as in the example of victims of domestic violence in the opening vignette, may wish to engage in targeted recruiting from that population and are within their legal rights to do so.[13]

Screening applicants typically involves an initial application review, reference and background checks, verification of educational attainment, and increasingly, informal web presence checks. While the Millennial generation may balk, employers have begun using searches of social media sites such as Facebook and YouTube as a gauge of maturity and discretion. For example, the board of directors of an organization treating substance abusers does not want a scandal resulting from web postings of their counseling staffs' drunken tailgate parties.

More formal screening and assessments of job applicants may also be undertaken, particularly in large nonprofits. In all cases, these tests must comply with federal law as outlined in the 1978 Uniform Guidelines on Employee Selection Procedures. The federal government offers several useful resources for employers interested in these techniques and the laws regulating their use; see Box 13.1.

Motivating Nonprofit Employees

To engage the nonprofit workforce, managers need to understand its unique characteristics. For example, those employed or volunteering in nonprofit organizations are very likely to be driven by the mission of the organization or sector; thus, nonprofit employees and volunteers are likely to be important stakeholders in their organizations.[14] Especially in organizations in which pay is low, paid staff members may have a sense that they are donating part of their wages; therefore, they are more satisfied when they have a voice in the planning and decision-making processes of the organization. Further, in many nonprofits paid employees serve as occasional volunteers, particularly at high-profile events; thus, employees expect that the organization will display the same level of commitment to them that they have displayed to the nonprofit. [15]

Box 13.1

FOR MORE INFORMATION

THE OFFICE OF PERSONNEL MANAGEMENT AND THE EMPLOYMENT AND TRAINING ADMINISTRATION

Two federal agencies, the Office of Personnel Management (OPM) and the Department of Labor's Employment and Training Administration (ETA) provide a wealth of information about assessment tools for successful selection and promotion of employees.

The Office of Personnel Management's *Assessment Decision Guide*[16] is a clear and well-researched reference guide to personnel assessment decisions including "hiring, placement, promotion, referral, retention, and entry into programs leading to advancement." This is a comprehensive tool that describes thirteen methods of personnel assessment including accomplishment records, emotional intelligence tests, integrity and honesty tests, job knowledge tests, and training and experience evaluations. The Office of Personnel Management guide includes comparisons of the different methods and an annotated reference section for those interested in learning more about the scholarship of personnel evaluation.

Similarly, the Employment and Training Administration's *Testing and Assessment: A Guide to Good Practices for Workforce Investment Professionals*[17] is designed to help those assessing personnel (and working in the field of career counseling) to make good decisions about appropriate testing and assessment tools. Written in a less academic manner than the Office of Personnel Management guide, *Testing and Assessment* includes important information on the federal laws and professional guidelines for the use of testing in employment and for training and/or development programs.

This commitment to employees can be exhibited through emphasis on the softer side of HR management, including offering health and other benefits, family-friendly policies, flexible work hours, recognition via awards, employee development, and facilitating mission attachment, all of which are beneficial human resource management strategies in the nonprofit sector. This has been called the values-driven or commitment approach to HR management, and these strategies have been found to improve employee retention and job satisfaction in the nonprofit sector.[18]

While conventional wisdom suggests that employees in the nonprofit sector are compensated at a generally lower rate than those in the for-profit or public sectors, research on the topic has yielded mixed results. As discussed in Chapter 1, nonprofit employees earn wages at the same levels as those with similar qualifications in the public and for-profit sector doing comparable work.[19] Likewise, an extensive study of the human service industry found that wage levels are not significantly different across sectors when controlling for labor market and organizational characteristics.[20] However, when management compensation levels are examined separately, nonprofit sector earnings are the lowest, at over 17 percent less, on average, than for-profit managers' earnings.[21] Given their public-oriented missions and commitment to the democratic process, it is not surprising that nonprofits have typically been found to offer a more equitable distribution of wages between lower-and upper-level management positions as well as between men and women than is typically found in for-profit organizations.[22]

The HR literature includes a number of theories about employee motivation, some more applicable to the nonprofit workforce than others. Among the basic theories applied to all three sectors are needs theories, process theories, and goal-setting theories. A fourth theory, public service motivation (PSM), is particularly applicable to the public and nonprofit sectors.

Needs Theories. The needs theories of motivation, based on Abraham Maslow's Hierarchy of Needs, discuss the ways in which the workplace can meet the personal needs of employees from the most basic, such as enough income to be fed and housed, to the highest level—the desire for full development of one's potential. Scholars have found achievement, responsibility, power, and recognition to be important workplace motivators.[23] Therefore, jobs in which employees are able to take on progressive responsibility and be recognized for achievement are ones in which employees' higher level needs can be better met, thus motivating them to do well and heightening their job satisfaction.[24] This can be challenging, especially in small nonprofits, where opportunities for advancement are often limited.[25]

Process Theories. Theories that involve employee expectations of and reactions to workplace procedures are called process theories. For example, people have expectations about how their organizations work, the level of effort they need to exert to perform well, and the rewards that they will receive from that effort; rewards must meet expectations in order to serve as motivating factors. Similarly, employees expect that there will be a balance between their work efforts and their rewards—and employees often compare their own work and reward balance to that of others. If an employee feels the balance is off, she will try to right that situation, typically by reducing her work effort to meet that of others.[26]

Goal-Setting Theories. Goal-setting theories suggest that clear and challenging but attainable goals are needed to motivate employee performance. Employee goals should be specific and may change as they are attained or as situations change.[27] Central to these approaches to motivation is that employees should play a role in setting their own workplace goals, particularly in the nonprofit sector.[28]

Public Service Motivation. Finally, Perry and Wise propose a theory of public service motivation (PSM), which suggests some people are motivated by work that meets public needs.[29] Thus, motivators for these employees would include participation in policy formulation, personal identification with public programs, and a desire to serve the public interest. It is suggested that people with higher public service motivation will be attracted to work that serves the public and that they will work harder in organizations that serve public needs—both of which apply to nonprofit workplaces.[30]

Much research on nonprofit employee motivation and job satisfaction suggests that nonprofit employees respond less well to extrinsic motivators such as salaries and bonuses than do those in the for-profit sector. Rather, in a not-for-profit organization employees are more likely to respond to intrinsic motivators and have been found to highly value public service, to be motivated by their organizational mission, and to be generally well-satisfied with their work.[31] These findings are not surprising given that interesting work and being useful to society, both prevalent characteristics of the nonprofit workplace, are employee motivators and lead to extra effort in the workplace.[32] For these reasons, and because of the intrinsic value that nonprofit employees place on their work, merit pay and incentive pay systems are often less appropriate in the nonprofit sector.[33] An additional constraint on the use of merit or incentive pay for both the nonprofit and public sectors is the lack of a steady stream of revenue for this purpose.[34]

Performance

An increasingly important component of human resources (HR) management is performance assessment. Organizations in all three sectors want to know how well employees are doing their jobs. Especially in the nonprofit sector, employees and volunteers need to know the expectations of the workplace, and they "need to know how they do."[35] Performance evaluations must be tied to employee and organizational goals, should provide useful feedback to employees, and should be linked to the long-term training and development plans of strategic HR management.

A key component of performance evaluation is training the evaluator(s) in job performance standards, goal setting, and observation to ensure a fair evaluation process and employee buy-in. Thus, subjective measures should be limited, and employees should

GOING GLOBAL

Médecins Sans Frontières Puts Staff and Volunteers on the Front Lines

Humanitarian medical aid throughout the Cold War era often failed to meet the needs of civilian populations. The nature of Cold War disputes—primarily conflicts between industrial nations or between colonial powers and native populations—resulted in military medical care as the norm, including heavy involvement of the governments engaged in war. The International Committee of the Red Cross (ICRC) was unable to send doctors to war zones without government permission, for example, and ICRC members were barred from speaking publicly about the human rights violations and genocide they witnessed. These political constraints often kept care from the civilians most in need.[36] To overcome these restrictions and get medical aid everywhere it was needed, Médecins Sans Frontières (MSF) was founded in Paris, France, in 1971. MSF is a humanitarian NGO whose mission is to deliver medical care and treatment to people affected by armed conflicts, outbreaks of illness, malnutrition, and natural or other disasters without regard to political borders or power. MSF continues to be guided by the five key principles set out in its founding charter: medical ethics, independence, impartiality and neutrality, bearing witness, and accountability. In 1999, MSF won the Nobel Peace Prize for its innovative humanitarian work.

Today, MSF has 27 affiliate offices worldwide, including Doctors Without Borders in the United States. Because of its international scope, those wishing to contribute are asked to direct their donations to the nearest MSF office.[37] The work of MSF is carried out in over 60 countries, the majority of which (61 percent) are on the African continent. Although the vast majority of field staff (25,000) come from the countries in which medical assistance is being provided, volunteers and staff from affiliated nations, especially those with medical, logistics, and engineering training, are always needed. Each year, over 6,000 staff members are deployed from their home countries to serve through MSF.

In addition to its policy influence through direct service delivery, MSF has become an increasingly vocal policy advocate for those in war-torn and developing nations. For example, MSF was expelled from Ethiopia in 1985 for speaking out against the alleged misuse of humanitarian aid by the government. In 2010, MSF staff and volunteers began recording data and testimonies from women subjected to sexual abuse as they migrated from sub-Saharan Africa, in hopes the data could be used to raise awareness and facilitate comprehensive public policy to stop this violence. In 1999, the group began an advocacy campaign to raise international support for access to medicine for the world's poorest populations, and in 2003 it co-sponsored the Drugs for Neglected Diseases Initiative to facilitate production of low cost drugs. MSF also pursues public policy priorities by marshaling public opinion. Recently, it launched a social media campaign to stop Novartis, a pharmaceutical manufacturer, from challenging an Indian patent law. Success for Novartis in this case would threaten access to low-cost generic drugs in the developing world; final arguments in the case were heard in an Indian court in December 2012, and a ruling has not been made as of this printing.

Due to the nature of its field work, which involves a 9–12 month commitment and can include assignment in dangerous locations, the application process for volunteers is extensive. It includes meeting a set of general and professional requirements (including appropriate education, certification, and experience), attending an information session, completion of an online application, passing an initial screening process, and then passing an interview with MSF. At that point the successful applicant is briefed and his or her name is added to the pool of potential candidates. Finally, if a need arises, the candidate is matched to a field location to begin service.

MSF field staff benefits include round-trip transportation, room and board in-country, a small monthly salary, and per diem. Again, owing to the nature of MSF assignments, three types of insurance are also provided: medical, life, and emergency evacuation. These insurance packages are vital to MSF staff as humanitarian aid work has become increasingly dangerous over the years. Staff members have been expelled from countries or withdrawn due to conflicts, and in 2002, an MSF worker in the Russian Republic of Dagestan was abducted and held for 20 months. Subsequently, at least eight others have been kidnapped in Sudan, Democratic Republic of Congo, and Somalia. Most troubling, at least twelve MSF staffers have been killed while on assignment: five in Afghanistan in 2004, three in Somalia in 2008, two in Pakistan in 2009, and two in Somalia in 2011.

Intrinsic motivation and being mission driven are always important characteristics for those seeking employment and volunteer work in the nonprofit sector. In an organization such as MSF, these characteristics must often be coupled with a high level of training and a willingness to leave family, friends, and creature comforts for up to a year at a time. Given these circumstances, the success and reputation of MSF are likely what attracts people to this intense kind of field work: MSF handles over seven million medical cases per year, including treatment for diseases such as malaria, HIV-AIDS, and cholera; delivery of over 100,000 babies; and mental health counseling for nearly 200,000.[38] Those working for MSF know that, while dangerous and often grueling, the care they bring is vital to the health of millions around the globe.

understand the purpose and system of evaluation. Unfortunately, for a variety of reasons good evaluation procedures are not common in the nonprofit sector. First, the HR systems in nonprofit organizations rarely include a formal appraisal process. Second, it is often difficult to get everyone to agree that an evaluation process is fair.[39] Similarly, in neither the nonprofit nor the public sector do raters or ratees like having to participate in the evaluation process.[40] Further, studies have shown a proverbial Lake Woebegone Effect in people's perceptions of their own job performance—everyone believes themselves to be above average.[41] This can be particularly troublesome with merit-based pay increases because if employees do not receive an increase, they may believe it was because of evaluation or evaluator bias. Worse, this situation can be demoralizing for nonprofit employees and has been found to *decrease* their levels of intrinsic motivation; they begin to feel that money, because it has been equated with merit, is more important than internal drive to do good work.[42]

Finally, since the nature of nonprofit sector work makes quantification of outcomes more difficult, it is not as easy to assess job performance as it is in for-profit organizations.[43] It is suggested that nonprofit leaders—boards, executives, and other management staff—should lead by example in evaluation, being willing to set goals, accepting constructive criticism and suggestions for improvement, and creating a culture in which everyone understands that mission attainment requires each member of the organization to be unified in that goal.[44]

THE GROWTH OF PROFESSIONALISM IN NONPROFIT ORGANIZATIONS

Many nonprofit agencies exist to develop, deliver, and advocate in the arena of social services, providing everything from health care, to education and training, to daycare and counseling services. Organizations serving social needs began hiring professionals and imposing professional standards during the Progressive Era at the turn of the twentieth century. Progressive reformers sought professionalization in the fields of public administration, social work, and public health; later, as advances in psychology and psychotherapy were made, pressure to hire professionally trained and educated counselors and therapists for delivery of social services increased as well.[45]

Both public policy and public funding influenced this trend toward professionalization as federal and state governments increasingly imposed standards and regulations on those individuals and agencies delivering services, and as government contracts became an increasingly important source of nonprofit funding. Another factor moving nonprofits toward professionalism in the 1950s was that the kinds of clients and the problems that they faced encouraged a more professionalized workforce to address their needs. Partly a response to "the growing psychiatric orientation of service personnel," public sector organizations increasingly referred clients to nonprofit services that required "a higher level of professional training," and nonprofits responded by prioritizing the recruitment and hiring of an ever more highly trained, professional workforce.[46]

The result of these trends is that nonprofits have been more likely to be staffed and managed by professionals in a field—social work, public health, recreation, the arts—than by people trained in management. On the other hand, there are increasing pressures for nonprofits to be run using more professional management techniques. This pressure includes trends toward greater organizational efficiency, demands from funders, donors, and the public for more accountability, and the need to have a staff capable of writing grant applications, handling contract management, and evaluating program success.[47]

There are many implications of the professional nonprofit workforce, both good and bad. For example, as with professionals in the public sector, those in the nonprofit sector feel strong ties to their profession. These professional ties are valuable for effective delivery of services; however, professionals often view their loyalty to the organization as secondary to their loyalty to their profession.[48] Further, while trends toward professionalism may have brought "nonprofit organizations more into line with governmental expectations of practice," they often "do so at the expense of the autonomy of the voluntary agencies."[49] Finally, professionals often choose to work in nonprofits that provide independent working conditions and freedom from bureaucratic constraints; therefore, trying to control or micromanage nonprofit employees is not recommended. Rather, nonprofit organizations should stick with flat organizational hierarchies in which professional employees maintain a great deal of task autonomy.[50]

VOLUNTEERS AND THE COPRODUCTION OF WORK

The concept of *coproduction* refers to the partnership between paid staff and volunteers in doing the work of the nonprofit organization.[51] Later in this chapter we discuss the reasons that people volunteer, but first we note that as for paid employees, volunteers have a variety of incentives motivating their efforts. Research has shown that especially when using their expertise in settings such as hospitals, volunteers share similar job attitudes to paid employees. In less formal organizations, work attitudes between paid and volunteer staff may be less similar.[52] However, particularly in small, direct service delivery organizations, paid and volunteer staff may coincide in what is termed role mixing, wherein paid staff occasionally volunteer their work efforts, most often during special events.[53]

This mixing of staff roles makes sense when we consider that nonprofits typically have high labor needs; coproduction and role mixing help the nonprofit meet its mission and goals in a cost-effective manner. For example, early in the life of a not-for-profit organization financial resources may be limited to the point that it must rely exclusively on volunteers. For some nonprofits, the types of volunteers to which they have access "may offer skills, networking contacts, and an enthusiastic approach not available among employees."[54] The interaction between paid and volunteer staff in the coproduction of work is an important factor in the overall effectiveness and morale of a nonprofit. For example, although volunteers may be vital to the work of the organization, they also increase administrative responsibilities because their work efforts must be managed and they must be included in liability insurance as well as workers' compensation calculations. Further, paid employees may fear that volunteers will displace them in the organization, although research indicates that is not likely the case. Instead, research has tended to find that in both the nonprofit and public sectors volunteers tend to *supplement* rather than supplant professional and paid staff.[55] Furthermore, in a study of 661 Canadian nonprofits, volunteers had been replaced with paid staff more than twice as often as paid employees were displaced by voluntary help.[56]

Aptitude and effectiveness of voluntary employees is a critical component of coproduction. It has been found that negative experiences with volunteers can take a toll on paid employees, and that ineffective volunteers can be a powerful source of strain, overwork, and discontent within the organization.[57] These aspects of coproduction highlight the importance of making sure that both paid and volunteer staff are appropriately recruited, trained, and rewarded for their work. Further, it is important for paid staff to understand the vital role played by volunteers, and for the nonprofit to have a solid program of volunteer management.

VOLUNTEER MANAGEMENT

To advance their public missions, it is essential that nonprofits—even small ones—devote time and attention to managing their volunteer workforce. According to the National Center for Charitable Statistics, the level of volunteering in the United States began to decline in 2005, after holding steady at 28.8 percent for three years. The level of volunteering hit a decade low of 26.2 percent in 2007, with slow increases in the next four years (see Figure 13.1). The uptick in volunteerism since 2008 may be the result of the economic downturn, which led many nonprofits to increase their use of volunteers.[58] It is important, therefore, for nonprofit boards and staff to understand why people volunteer, how to recruit the best individuals for specific tasks, and how to keep the good volunteers they have worked so hard to train. The Council for Certification in Volunteer Administration provides resources and certification for professional volunteer administrators; see Web Resources at the end of the chapter.

FIGURE 13.1 **Trends in American Volunteering, 2002–2010**

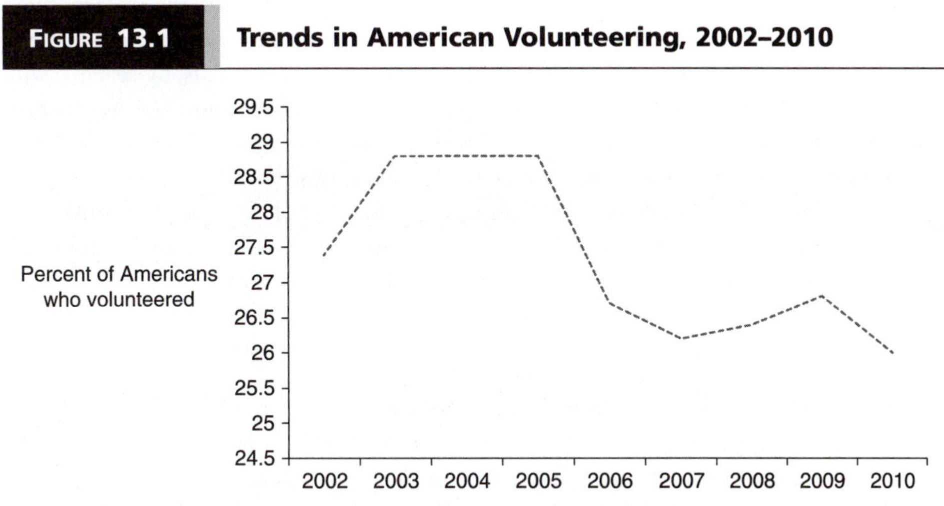

Source: National Center for Charitable Statistics, Number of Nonprofit Organizations in the United States, 1999–2010, http://www.urban.org/UploadedPDF/412434-NonprofitAlmanacBrief2011.pdf; Bureau of Labor Statistics, "Volunteering in the United States, 2004, www.bls.gov/news.release/archives/volun_12162004.pdf.

Who Volunteers?

In 2010, 26 percent of Americans volunteered nearly 15 billion hours in the nonprofit sector. This is the equivalent of 8.8 million full-time employees, with an assigned value of more than $283.85 billion in time volunteered.[59]

The federal government has long recognized the value of voluntary service and the professionalization of volunteer management.[60] Notably, in 1963 President John F. Kennedy called for a national service corps, the result of which was creation of the Peace Corps and VISTA (Volunteers in Service to America). Every president since Jimmy Carter has subsequently highlighted the value of volunteerism, including George H.W. Bush's support of the Points of Light Foundation and Bill Clinton's creation of AmeriCorps in 1993, which brought federal volunteer services under one umbrella organization. In 2009, President Barack Obama signed the Serve America Act, significantly expanding AmeriCorps and creating several new service organizations.

While AmeriCorps offers federal stipends, its volunteers typically work in 501(c)(3) organizations, which do not pay them for their service. While many in the nonprofit community make good use of these volunteers, others have been more wary of volunteerism as public policy. For example, *Nonprofit Quarterly* correspondent Rick Cohen has suggested that a vastly expanded AmeriCorps may displace low-paid staff in nonprofit organizations, which can be a cause of organizational friction. Further, Cohen has concerns about the infusion of new volunteers to organizations that may lack the capacity to manage them.[61] This concern is not unwarranted: in a 2005 study, the biggest challenge faced by nonprofits using volunteers was reported to be "lack of funds to support volunteer administration."[62] As discussed earlier, volunteer management is essential for the successful integration and use of volunteers in nonprofit organizations.

Studies indicate that the highest levels of volunteerism are found among women, those between the ages of 30–49, the better educated, the employed, those with higher incomes, married individuals, whites, homeowners, long-term community residents, those living with children at home, and those who are more religious—the effect of religion is especially pronounced among African Americans.[63] According to Independent Sector, the vast majority of nonprofit volunteerism in 2000 was for religious organizations.[64]

People who volunteer their time and talents do so for both altruistic and self-interested reasons.[65] For example, many use volunteering for career exploration or to develop skills that might enhance their careers, to meet new people, to keep professionally active after retirement, and, of course, out of concern for the mission and clientele of the organization, as reflected in our opening vignette. Volunteer motives fall along six lines:[66]

1. Values: feeling that it is important to help others
2. Understanding: belief that one can learn through direct hands-on experience
3. Enhancement: when volunteering makes one feel better about oneself
4. Career: seen as a way of getting a "foot in the door" or relevant work experience
5. Social: a good way to meet like-minded people
6. Protective: volunteer as a good escape from one's own troubles

It is important for nonprofit boards, executive directors, and managers to understand the variety of reasons that people volunteer their time in order to make the most of recruitment and retention efforts. For example, making use of student volunteers through outreach to high schools and colleges is an excellent way of recruiting new volunteers through their career motives.

Volunteer Recruitment

A key concern for volunteer management is recruitment, particularly recruiting a sufficient number of volunteers with the skills and training required of the nonprofit.[67] Recruiting the appropriate volunteer for the appropriate task is the critical first step to successful program implementation and prevention of future personnel conflict. There are a variety of ways in which nonprofits can recruit volunteers, including word of mouth, presentations before community and corporate groups, news media ads and articles that highlight the organization, recruitment centers, and Internet recruiting.[68] Examples of organizations connecting volunteers and organizations on the web include the Points of Light Foundation/Hands on Network, 1–800-Volunteer, and VolunteerMatch, which was established in 1998 and offers an iPhone app for volunteers to stay connected (see Web Resources at the end of the chapter).

Studies indicate that there is a positive relationship between donating money and donating time.[69] Rather than being mutually exclusive, these are complementary activities: those who give more of their money also give more of their time. Therefore, a good place for organizations to look for volunteers is with those who already support the organization financially; indeed, counter to much of the fundraising literature and practical advice from fundraisers, seeking donations from current volunteers and volunteer labor from those who have contributed money to the organization is a good strategy.[70] As illustrated by Phoenix House in our opening vignette, those committed to the mission of the organization are often likely to donate both their money and their time because of a strong commitment to the cause.

An important but often overlooked aspect of recruitment is both real and perceived barriers that individuals face in volunteering their time and talents. Barriers to volunteering are numerous and important for nonprofit managers to understand. The most common barriers to volunteering are a lack of time, money, information, skills, opportunities, personal interest, transportation, or child care. Secondary impediments include not knowing how to get involved, not being asked, inadequate volunteer management, a lack of self-esteem or confidence in one's skills, and not understanding how volunteering can help one personally. Not-for-profit organizations can often help interested volunteers overcome these barriers by offering flexible hours and assignments, reaching out to new pools of volunteers through recruitment centers and online resources, and engaging in appropriate volunteer orientation and management techniques.[71]

Other barriers to volunteering may be more difficult to address. Reasons individuals give for not serving as a volunteer also include cultural or language barriers, disability, criminal record, age, minority or refugee status, and exclusion of lesbian, gay, bisexual, and transgender

(LGBT) populations.[72] Given the missions of nonprofit organizations, characteristics of the clientele served, and the public policies being implemented, it may not be possible for some nonprofits to eliminate these barriers (for example, see Box 13.3 on the Boy Scouts). This makes matching the right volunteer to the right organization all the more important.

Box 13.3

FOR EXAMPLE

THE BOY SCOUTS OF AMERICA: THE RIGHT TO EXPRESSIVE ASSOCIATION

The Boy Scouts of America (BSA) has been a litigant in several court cases involving discrimination against members and volunteers based on religion and sexual orientation. Because the First Amendment protects the rights of individuals to expressive association, BSA argues that it may legally set its own membership and employment criteria according to the values expressed in the Scout Law and the Scout Oath, which are each part of the stated mission of the organization. For example, the Scout Oath includes the line "do my duty to God";[73] in *Welsh v. Boy Scouts of America,* 1992, 1993, and several subsequent cases, the right of the Boy Scouts to refuse membership or leadership positions to atheists and agnostics has been upheld.[74]

In 1999, the New Jersey Supreme Court ruled that the Boy Scouts of America violated that state's anti-discrimination laws by prohibiting homosexuals from serving as troop leaders. In this case, the New Jersey court argued that the Boy Scouts constitute a public accommodation and opined that because New Jersey law declared discrimination contrary to the state's interests, the Boy Scouts could not lawfully engage in discrimination based on sexual orientation. In 2000, however, the federal Supreme Court overturned the New Jersey decision in *Boy Scouts of America v. Dale.* Because it is an organization in which members adhere to a set of shared values—expressed in the Scout Oath, for example—the Supreme Court ruled that the state of New Jersey had violated the Boy Scouts' First Amendment right of expressive association. The Court determined that public or judicial disapproval of an organization's expression is not sufficient justification to force policy-mandated acceptance of a member if such inclusion would impair the group's "expressive message." Accordingly, BSA was found to have the right to determine its own membership and employment criteria.[75]

The Boy Scouts' position on discrimination has not been without negative consequence. After the 2000 Supreme Court ruling, for example, the state of Connecticut removed the Boy Scouts from a list of charities eligible to receive donations from state employees through payroll deduction. Further, a number of private corporations including Hewlett-Packard and American Airlines withdrew funding to the Boy Scouts, as did 53 local United Way offices. Finally, many school districts across the country disallowed the Scouts from using public schools as meeting venues. The backlash against the Scouts led to federal legislation, The Boy Scouts of America Equal Access Act of 2003, which forbids public schools and education agencies that receive federal funds from withholding access to Boy Scout troops or any other youth group regarded as "a patriotic society."[76] This act does not affect other public entities such as the City of Philadelphia, which in 2003 began proceedings to revoke the Boy Scouts' $1 per year lease on the Beaux Arts building. The city argued that the reduced-price lease—the market value of which was $200,000 annually—was a taxpayer subsidy of the organization and violated the city's antidiscrimination policies. Although the Boy Scouts fought this action, in 2007 the City Council voted 16–1 to end its 79-year-old lease agreement with the Scouts.[77]

While equal employment policies ban procedures that may result in discrimination, the right to expressive association allows nonprofits to legally set their own membership and employment criteria, when those criteria can be demonstrated as necessary for the organization to advocate its viewpoints. Because nonprofits exist in a fluid environment with serious political, legal, and social consequences, however, they must be prepared for public dissent which, for nonprofit organizations, often means withholding of donations, dropped memberships, or even legal action. On May 30, 2012, the issue once again gained national attention when, at their annual meeting, the Boy Scouts of America were presented with petitions including more than 275,000 signatures that called for an end to "its policy of exclusivity against gay youth and leaders." Three BSA representatives met with the Eagle Scout who delivered the petitions; they listened to his concerns and "shared the purpose of its membership policy," after which the organization released a statement that the organization does not plan to change its policy.[78]

For additional information on the Boy Scouts, see www.scouting.org.

Volunteer Retention

It has been suggested that what is often perceived as a problem of recruitment is actually a misdiagnosed problem of retention.[79] Studies indicate that many people drop out of volunteering because of management or organizational problems, as well as a perceived disconnect between volunteer expectations and actual voluntary experiences. In their conceptualization of volunteer energy as a renewable natural resource, Brudney and Meijs suggest

> . . . that the value of volunteering be seen as accruing not only to host organizations but also to the volunteers themselves and the larger society, including the enhancement of skills, self-confidence, and civic engagement as well as the transmission of an ethic of service to the next generation.[80]

For example, research has been done on the benefits that accrue to employee groups participating in Relay for Life, a volunteer activity that relies on teams to raise money for the American Cancer Society by walking a 24-hour relay.[81] The findings indicate that, in fact, the behavior of participants at work is also enhanced by such activity—employees had higher levels of social capital, job satisfaction, and job involvement and a better all-around work experience after walking with their workplace team.[82]

In keeping with this renewable resource concept, nonprofits need tools to attract people to volunteering and to maintain their enthusiasm for it over their lifetimes.[83] The new types of volunteer experiences that have been created in recent years offer both opportunities and challenges for volunteering. Today's volunteer may come to an organization as part of a corporate volunteer program through his employer or as a service learning volunteer through the local high school; he may be looking for opportunities as a virtual volunteer, assisting the nonprofit from his laptop at home, or as a gap year volunteer in between high school and college. These changes in the nature of volunteering provide opportunities to open the doors of the nonprofit sector to people who would never before have volunteered. However, nonprofits that fail to sustain their volunteer resources may contribute to high attrition rates, antipathy toward volunteering again, and an overall loss of nonprofit sector effectiveness.[84] How then to retain volunteers? Finding a good match between volunteer skills and interests and organizational needs is key; thus, orientation to the organization, formal applications, and interviews with applicants are essential. Expectations of the knowledge, skills, abilities, and other characteristics (KSAOCs) required of the volunteer must be clear, as must the expectation of work hours, responsibilities, appropriate behavior, and dress. Further, volunteer training is necessary and has been shown to reduce turnover among volunteers.[85] Other important HR practices for retaining volunteers include assigning them challenging tasks with established goals and timely feedback; integrating them into the organization so paid staff understand and appreciate their efforts; and supporting and recognizing them in a variety of ways including newsletter articles, personal recognition and encouragement, and formal awards and celebrations.[86]

Finally, nonprofits are becoming much more adaptable in terms of the nature of the work they offer to volunteers to accommodate changes in the volunteer workforce. For example, individuals or groups of volunteers may work on specific projects for a day or a weekend; volunteers may work on a rotating basis, serving dinners at a soup kitchen the last Friday of every month; or volunteering may be occasional, such as serving as a volunteer for a single event year after year. An example of an organization making very good use of a variety of recruitment, retention, and management strategies is Shelter Network of San Mateo County, California, which increased its volunteer numbers by nearly 700 percent between 2005 and 2011 (see Box 13.4).

Good volunteer management is not only important for those volunteering, it can improve the working conditions for paid employees as well, improving organizational morale and decreasing turnover for both volunteer and paid staff. Paid employees have positive experiences with volunteers when the following are present: volunteer-employee conflict policies, formal volunteer recruitment, training and performance-evaluation efforts, a screening process for volunteer hiring, and volunteer-employee social gatherings.[87] Further, there appears to be a cumulative effect: the more of these elements in place at the nonprofit, the better the employees' experience of volunteer efforts.[88] High morale and effective use of all human resources—paid and unpaid—is essential to effective implementation of the public services, programs, and policies provided by the nonprofit sector.

ox 13.4

FOR EXAMPLE

SHELTER NETWORK OF SAN MATEO COUNTY, CALIFORNIA: RECRUITING AND RETAINING VOLUNTEERS

To offer shelter and related services to the homeless on the San Francisco Peninsula, Shelter Network was established in 1987 with two paid employees and a handful of dedicated volunteers. In 2004, drawing upon its success and recognizing its potential to do more, Shelter Network hired its first full-time Volunteer Manager and the results have been dramatic. Relying on a strategy to welcome, work with, and recognize its volunteers, Shelter Network's Volunteer Manager began a multi-prong recruitment effort. Reaching out to organizations like Volunteer Match, the Volunteer Center, and the Bay Area Corporate Volunteer Council, as well as local corporations, high schools, colleges, and universities, Shelter Network increased its volunteer numbers from 1,800 in 2005 to over 12,059 in 2011, which increased volunteer hours worked each year from approximately 15,000 to more than 48,000. This level of increase allowed the organization to take on a number of creative endeavors, including planting vegetable gardens at their residential sites for use by client-families, and using corporate volunteers to teach workshops on resume writing and interview skills.

The success of its volunteer program has to do with its approach to volunteer recruitment and management, which includes the philosophy that if a volunteer has "a willing heart and wants to help," Shelter Network will find a place for him or her. Thus, volunteers at Shelter Network perform a wide range of tasks: from individuals and groups who sort donations and serve meals, to Girl Scout troops hosting movie nights for children living in transitional housing, to attorneys who donate their time during "Legal Night," to mental health interns who work with professional staff at Shelter Network to provide counseling and mental health services to residents.

In addition to taking individual volunteers who make a minimum three-month commitment, Shelter Network uses corporate and group volunteers on a project basis, such as a local biopharmaceutical company that hosts an annual Halloween costume party and infuses it with science education for the kids. All volunteers complete a Volunteer Interest form, a Volunteer Application, and go through an hour-long orientation before receiving an assignment. Individual volunteers are typically vetted through an interview during which the interests of the volunteer are matched with Shelter Network's needs. These volunteers also undergo Tuberculosis Screening, Live Scan Fingerprinting, and child abuse prevention training. This extensive process is likely a key to their success: no volunteers have been asked to leave since 2004, and few volunteers leave the organization before completing their minimum commitment. In fact, one secret to Shelter Network's success is its powerful word-of-mouth recruiting: volunteers keep coming back and bringing friends, family, and co-workers with them.

Successful volunteer management also involves buy-in from paid employees. Shelter Network has made it clear that volunteer effort is vital to its success, and paid employees are encouraged to work with volunteers to make the best use of their time and talents. Volunteers are valued to such an extent that all paid employees receive a copy of the Volunteer Program Philosophy in their human resource hiring packets. Its volunteer management success has not gone unnoticed: In 2006, the Volunteer Center of San Francisco and San Mateo counties awarded Shelter Network its Excellence in Nonprofit Volunteer Management Award, and it has been named one of the Volunteer Center's Top 5 Best Places to Volunteer for three years in a row.

To learn more about Shelter Network, go to www.shelternetwork.org

Volunteer managers should know the personnel protections afforded to volunteers by the federal Volunteer Protection Act of 1997. The purpose of this policy is two-fold: first, it is a way to encourage volunteerism in the United States; second, it is a tool to protect volunteers working in either public agencies or nonprofit organizations (many of which operate under contract or grant with the federal government). This legislation provides immunity from liability for "harm caused by an act or omission of the volunteer on behalf of the organization or entity" as long as the volunteer's work was being performed under the normal scope of his or her duties with the nonprofit. Importantly, this law does not provide immunity to the nonprofit organization but rather applies only to the volunteer.[89] Some states, such as New Jersey and New Mexico, offer other legal protections to volunteers as well. However, even if your state does not have its own laws, volunteers are protected under the federal law.

PERSONNEL CONFLICT AND DISPUTE RESOLUTION

As indicated earlier, relations between paid employees and volunteers can be a source of personnel conflict in the nonprofit sector. Paid employees may fear their jobs will be lost to the free help, can lack respect for volunteers, and are often not well trained to work with the volunteer staff. Volunteers may not know how best to approach paid staffers, or, conversely, may need what is considered by the paid employees to be too much hand-holding. As discussed above, eliminating conflict between volunteers and paid employees involves having clearly established volunteer policies, appropriate volunteer management and training, and includes making it clear to both paid and volunteer staff that the work of the organization is a matter of coproduction between the two.

Another area of potential personnel conflict is generational, as organizations experience the aging and retirement of vast numbers of experienced employees and leaders and the entrance of new generations, particularly the techno-savvy Millennials.[90] Most research to date has focused on workplace differences between Baby Boomers (1945–1964) and Generation Xers (1965–1980), and while the argument has been that the younger generation approaches work differently, the research indicates that dramatic generational differences have not really materialized in the nonprofit[91] or the public sectors.[92] The biggest differences in nonprofit organizations is the initial employee motivation for entering social change organizations: Boomers are more likely to have been part of the social movements of the 1960s and 1970s, while Gen Xers tend to have a more personal attachment to social advocacy and issues of social justice. In addition, Gen Xers have been found to be more focused on work/life balance issues.[93] However, these different foci are likely the result of life cycle changes rather than meaningful generational differences.[94] What observable differences the Millennial generation might bring to the nonprofit workplace are still to be seen.

Among the most important personnel conflicts in nonprofit organizations surround differences in interpretation of organizational mission between boards of directors and paid staff.[95] The opening vignette offers an example of this type of conflict in which a board of directors may pursue opportunities that take the organization in a direction with which staff—both paid and volunteer in our example—are not comfortable. Similarly, especially in large national or international not-for-profits, a key source of conflict may lie in the difference between goals for local chapters and broader organizational goals.[96]

A nonprofit organization can also be faced with personnel conflict of the variety that any organization faces: interpersonal conflicts that arise from feelings of unfair treatment or bias, and issues related to managing diverse workforces. While there is little research available to help practitioners with diversity management in the delivery of public programs,[97] favoritism and unequal treatment in the workplace are certain to cause conflict and should be avoided. Recall that the process theories of motivation include expectations of fairness and an equitable balance of work and reward for all employees. Managers are well advised to ensure that their decisions and procedures are fair and just, and that employees perceive them to be, in order to keep these workplace disputes in check.[98]

While traditional procedures for resolving workplace conflict include judicial or administrative resolution, these are less likely to be sought in the nonprofit sector due to its tendency to have less formal organizational structures. Even in the for-profit and public sectors these traditional processes are giving way to more informal Alternative Dispute Resolution (ADR) systems.[99] ADR is not a single method but involves multiple alternatives to resolve organizational conflict. It is suggested that organizations address disputes through a multi-step, inclusive process in which a system for dispute resolution is designed.[100] This process includes first identifying the source of the problem, whether it is legal, technical, structural, or interpersonal; who are the disputants and what is the nature of their relationships and motivations? Next, an organizationally appropriate dispute system is designed which may involve the introduction of an ombudsman, creation of general policies for conflict management, or, if the trouble is severe, contracting with an outside consultant or mediator.

It is important that a general system of dispute resolution has established procedures that outline the types of conflict the system will handle, who can use the system, whether the system is voluntary or mandatory, the level of institutionalization of the system, and what the nature of the resolutions will be, including "training, facilitation, consensus-building, negotiated rulemaking, [or] mediation."[101] Dispute systems should enhance cooperation, reciprocity, and engagement, and employees should trust the process; all of these are fostered when employees are actively involved in the process.[102] Dispute resolution procedures should address the following questions: (1) What needs to be done or changed given the reality of the workplace? (2) What are employees willing to do in order to improve the situation? (3) Who is responsible for what, when, and how? (4) What will be done if the problem recurs? and (5) What happens if the solution doesn't work, either in part or in full?[103] Although conflict management can be uncomfortable for managers, addressing disputes directly sends a positive message to employees about their value in the workplace, making them more likely to remain with the organization and cooperate in the future.[104]

EMPLOYMENT LAW AND NONPROFIT ORGANIZATIONS

There is a wide range of law and policy that affects employment in the United States, much of which begins with Title VII of the Civil Rights Act of 1964 forbidding workplace discrimination based on race, color, religion, national origin, or sex in a variety of employment practices, including hiring, job classification, terms and conditions of employment, compensation, and promotion. Important for many nonprofits, however, are exceptions for religious organizations and private clubs. Another exception to Title VII allows for preference or discrimination based upon any characteristic that can be considered a "bona fide occupational qualification (BFOQ) reasonably necessary to the normal operation of the particular enterprise."[105] The Supreme Court has ruled that the bona fide occupational qualification exception is a narrow one and the burden of proof that the discriminatory policy is directly related to job performance is on the employer.

Although Title VII applies to all employers with 15 or more employees, Section 702 states

> . . . this title shall not apply to an employer with respect to the employment of aliens outside any State or to a religious corporation, association, educational institution, or society with respect to the employment of individuals of a particular religion to perform work connected with the carrying on by such corporation, association, educational institution, or society of its activities.[106]

Thus, over the years federal courts have consistently ruled that it is legal for religious and faith-based nonprofits to engage in many practices prohibited in the public and for-profit sectors, including refusal to hire, engaging in unequal compensation practices, or dismissal of employees based on race, gender, sexual orientation, or religious practice (for specific case examples, see Box 13.5).

For decades most not-for-profit employers were given an exemption from nondiscrimination laws due to the voluntary nature of the nonprofit sector. That changed in 1984 with the case of *Roberts* v. *United States Jaycees,* in which the federal Supreme Court ruled that local Jaycees chapters could admit women regardless of the national organization's opposition. The ruling extended the reach of the federal public accommodation rules to nonprofit organizations arguing that the organizational right to free association can be restricted when it is in the state's interest to address discrimination.[107] However, the Supreme Court has also held that the Constitution protects a group's right to expressive association, arguing that a public accommodation rule cannot force a group to accept a member it does not want "if the person's presence affects in a significant way the group's ability to advocate public or private viewpoints."[108] As such, adherence to their stated mission may allow nonprofits such as the Boy Scouts of America (see Box 13.3) to legally engage in discriminatory employment practices.

There are important implications of the law when faith-based organizations (FBOs) contract with governments to implement public policy. Although government agencies must

ox 13.5

FOR EXAMPLE

RELIGIOUS EXCEPTIONS TO TITLE VII: LEGALLY PROTECTED PRACTICES

In *Young v. Northern Illinois Conference of United Methodist Church,* (1994), an African American minister, Darreyl N. Young, charged that she had been denied an appointment as elder based on race and sex discrimination. Further, her complaint argued that she was dismissed from her duties due to her public position against discriminatory practices in the United Methodist Church. In this case, the federal Seventh Circuit Court of Appeals was clear in its position against Young when it wrote: "*introduction of government standards to the selection of spiritual leaders would significantly, and perniciously, rearrange the relationship between church and state.*"[109]

In *Hall v. Baptist Memorial Healthcare Corp.* (2000), Glynda L. Hall had been an employee of Baptist Memorial at the Baptist Memorial College of Health Sciences. Hall was eventually dismissed because of her affiliation with a non-Baptist church that condoned her homosexuality and actively engaged in outreach to the gay community. The federal Sixth District Court of Appeals ruled that Baptist Memorial had done nothing illegal because this was a religiously motivated employment decision, and Title VII expressly exempted religious organizations from the prohibition against discrimination on the basis of religion.[110]

McClure v. Salvation Army (1972) involved a female officer in the Salvation Army who sued because, as a woman, she earned less than similarly ranked male officers. The federal Fifth District Court of Appeals ruled that the employment of ministers is not subject to gender discrimination suits, and therefore dismissed the case.[111]

Finally, in the case of *Corporation of the Bishop of the Church of Jesus Christ of Latter Day Saints v. Amos* (1987), an employee of sixteen years was fired for failing to maintain his qualifications as a member of the Mormon Church. This case made its way to the federal Supreme Court, which ruled that the church was exempt from prohibition of religious discrimination.[112]

It is clear from this sample of cases that the courts have consistently upheld the rights of faith-based organizations to hire, fire, and promote employees based upon their religious tenets; while some may see this as discrimination, these faith-based organizations are acting in accordance with federal court interpretations of the Civil Rights Act.

follow clear anti-discrimination HR policies to ensure fairness and representation when implementing broad public policies to diverse populations, faith-based nonprofits delivering programs through Charitable Choice do not. The courts have been clear that FBOs are protected from government restriction in personnel practices including hiring, firing, promotion, and compensation of their employees. At the same time, FBOs are forbidden from discriminating in service delivery, as discussed in Chapter 2.

Other federal policies that apply to nonprofit employees include the Age Discrimination in Employment Act (ADEA) of 1967, the Pregnancy Discrimination Act of 1978, the

Americans with Disabilities Act (ADA) of 1990, and the Family and Medical Leave Act (FMLA) of 1993.[113] The ADEA applies to organizations employing more than 20 people and protects workers as well as candidates for employment from negative personnel action because they are considered too old. The Pregnancy Discrimination Act requires that pregnancy be treated as any other health issue, including accommodating pregnancy and child birth with medical leave, and also includes assurances that women will not lose employment or promotion opportunities due to pregnancy.

The ADA protects employees with disabilities from discrimination in applying for a job, as well as in decisions regarding hiring, firing, promotion, compensation, and other conditions of employment as long as the employee can perform the essential duties of the job; ADA applies to organizations of 15 or more employees.[114] Further, employers must provide reasonable accommodations to the disabled to facilitate their work; by reasonable the law indicates that the accommodation cannot involve an undue hardship on the employer. The FMLA applies to all organizations that employ 50 or more people in at least 20 calendar weeks. FMLA provides for up to 12 weeks of unpaid leave after the birth or adoption of a child or the placement of a foster-child; for the care of a spouse, child, or parent with a serious medical condition; or for care required due to a disabling illness of the employee. FMLA requires the maintenance of health coverage and a return to an equivalent job after the leave has been taken; it can be superseded by more generous state laws.[115]

Finally, labor relations and collective bargaining in the nonprofit sector are covered by the same laws that apply to the for-profit sector. Employees in nonprofits are permitted to negotiate for wages, work hours, and working conditions, and they are legally permitted to strike over labor disputes. As in other cases of federal employment policy, nonprofits were not governed by National Labor Relations Board (NLRB) regulations until the 1970s, when Congress began to regulate nonprofit and charitable organizations in the same way it regulates employment practices in the for-profit sector.[116] For example, between 1996 and 2007, the American Red Cross was charged with violations of fair labor practices 212 times and the NLRB intervened in 152 Red Cross labor disputes between 1998 and 2007.[117] Thus, while strike actions may not be common in the nonprofit sector, nurses, lab technicians, and other American Red Cross employees have, on a number of occasions in the past two decades, participated in labor strikes. In 2010, for example, 1,000 American Red Cross employees in six states held a three-day strike over unfair labor practices.[118]

CASE STUDY

Employee Health Insurance Mandates and Faith-Based Organizations

Federal law makes special consideration for employment practices in faith-based organizations–those nonprofits affiliated with organized religions and religious institutions. As seen in Box 13.5, for example, the courts have protected the right of faith-based organizations (FBOs) to engage in personnel practices based upon their religious tenets and directly related to their organizational missions. Thus, there are few restrictions on FBO decisions in hiring, firing, promotion, and compensation of employees. Recently, however, questions have been raised about the point at which FBO rights end and employee rights begin regarding employee benefit packages, specifically the health insurance mandates required by the 2010 Patient Protection and Affordable Care Act.

When the Affordable Care Act was passed, it included a requirement that benefits for certain preventive health services would be provided via group health plans and health insurance issuers without imposing cost sharing (co-payments) on employees.[119] This provision gained a high public profile after the January 2012 announcement by the secretary of the Department of Health and Human Services (DHHS), Kathleen Sebelius, that the final DHHS rule mandated women with health insurance coverage would "have access to the full range of the Institute of Medicine's recommended preventive services, including all FDA-approved forms of contraception."[120] This would include drugs such as Plan B One Step and Ella, each commonly known as the morning after pill, which may prevent implantation of a fertilized egg. Some consider use of such drugs a form of abortion, including the Catholic Church, which has always viewed both abortion and contraception as contrary to basic tenets of their faith.

Religiously affiliated universities and hospitals are the largest employers affected by this policy change, as health insurance coverage offered to their employees has not always included coverage for contraceptive services. Therefore, this policy change would positively affect employees who do not share their employer's faith-based objection to contraception; they and their insured dependents would benefit from expanded health insurance coverage that includes the full range of contraceptive services with no associated co-payments.

Secretary Sebelius concluded her announcement of the new rule by saying:

> I believe this proposal strikes the appropriate balance between respecting religious freedom and increasing access to important preventive services. The administration remains fully committed to its partnerships with faith-based organizations, which promote healthy communities and serve the common good. And this final rule will have no impact on the protections that existing conscience laws and regulations give to health care providers.[121]

While Secretary Sebelius asserted that the rule struck an appropriate balance between religious freedom and access to health care, a number of religious and political leaders did not agree. In an attempt to address their concerns, the Obama administration sought to adjust the Affordable Care Act rules by requiring insurance companies to pay the costs of contraceptive and sterilization services so faith-based hospitals, universities, and charities with religious objections would not be directly responsible for provision of the services.[122] The controversy continued, however, and a hearing of the House Committee on Oversight and Government Reform was called on the issue. At the hearing, members of the clergy of several denominations expressed concerns about "government entanglement with religion," and Rabbi Meir Soloveichik argued that under this rule, "Religious organizations would still be obligated to provide employees with an insurance policy that facilitates acts violating the organization's religious tenets."[123]

The hearings themselves proved controversial when no women were included in the first group of witnesses and the second group contained only two women, both of whom opposed the federal policy. When it was requested that a female student at Georgetown University Law Center—a Jesuit institution—be allowed to testify at the hearings in support of the rule, the request was denied, leading to a separate, unofficial hearing at which her testimony was taken.[124] The controversy over this policy and the congressional hearings turned what would normally have been a minor policy, noticed only by human resource benefit managers, into a nationwide debate.

As Secretary Sebelius noted in her announcement of the final DHHS rule, nonprofit employers who have not previously covered contraceptive services have been given an extra year, until August 1, 2013, to implement the new provision. To formulate a workable policy solution, DHHS, along with the Department of Labor and the Internal Revenue Service, continues to meet with members of the nonprofit community, including religious organizations and women's groups, as well as insurance companies and experts. Their goal is two-fold: first, to ensure that the Affordable Care Act provision regarding contraceptive coverage for those receiving health insurance through nonprofit religious organizations is maintained; and second, to protect FBOs with religious objections to contraception from being required to contract, arrange, or pay for contraceptive coverage.[125] In May 2012, more than 40 Catholic organizations, including several local Catholic Charities groups and the University of Notre Dame, filed lawsuits against the secretaries of the Department's of HHS, Labor, and the Treasury, contending that the contraception mandate was a violation of their religious liberties protected under the First Amendment and the Religious Freedom Restoration Act.[126] This case is a compelling example of the complex process of balancing public policy to protect religious nonprofits with government action widely viewed as being in the public interest. Once finalized either through negotiation or the courts, the insurance mandate will have significant implications for faith-based organizations and the provision of employee benefits.

QUESTIONS TO CONSIDER:

1. The federal courts have upheld the right of faith-based organizations to hire, fire, promote, and compensate employees based upon their religious faith and tenets. Is the subject of this case, provision of employee health benefits, different? Explain.

2. Why are three federal agencies—the Department of Health and Human Services, the Department of Labor, and the Internal Revenue Service—engaged in negotiations with non-profit and for-profit organizations to come to an agreement over implementation of this policy. What does this tell you about the role of the nonprofit sector in public policy?
3. Consider the four relationships that describe nonprofit interaction with public policy (make policy, affected by policy, influence policy, subject to policy) and discuss the ways in which the Affordable Care Act contraceptive services coverage policy reflects any or all of these relationships between nonprofits and public policy.
4. Is this a unique example of the relationship between public policy and faith-based nonprofits? How does this case inform your understanding of the challenges faced by faith-based organizations in terms of compliance with employment policies?

CONCLUSION

Governments, boards of directors, and donors have viewed nonprofits with a more watchful eye in the past decade as their numbers, activities, and influence have grown. Nonprofits, therefore, have to approach the coproduction of their work in a professional and strategic manner, understanding the incentives that motivate both paid employees and volunteers, many of whom are professionally trained and educated. Appropriate recruitment, selection, training, and retention policies are essential for human resource management of both the paid and volunteer workforce.

Employees and volunteers in the nonprofit sector operate within a complex web of federal and state employment policies, from anti-discrimination laws (for which there are a number of not-for-profit exemptions), to employee and volunteer civil rights protections, to National Labor Relations Board regulations. Executives, managers, and employees in nonprofits, like their peers in the for-profit and public sectors, must be attuned to the array of policies affecting their human resource management practices.

QUESTIONS FOR REVIEW

1. What have been the causes and impacts of greater professionalism in the nonprofit sector?
2. Consider the six factors identified by Clary and Snyder as motivating volunteers. What different strategies might a nonprofit use to recruit or retain volunteers with these different motives?
3. In general, what are the impacts of the Civil Rights Act of 1964 on nonprofit sector employment? What other employment policies are particularly important for human resource management in the sector?

Assignment

Choose a local nonprofit (via Internet or interview) to evaluate its coproduction efforts. How does it recruit, train, and manage volunteers, and how well does it integrate the activities of paid employees and volunteers? Where is the organization following best practices and where could it make improvements to its human resource management?

Suggested Readings

Independent Sector. *Giving & Volunteering in the United States, 2001*. Washington, DC: Independent Sector, 2002.

Pynes, Joan E. *Human Resources Management for Public and Nonprofit Organizations, A Strategic Approach*, 3rd ed. San Francisco: Jossey-Bass, 2009.

Smith, Steven Rathgeb, and Michael Lipsky. *Nonprofits for Hire: The Welfare State in the Age of Contracting*. Cambridge, MA: Harvard University Press, 1994.

Wing, Kennard T., Katie L. Roeger, and Thomas H. Pollak. "The Nonprofit Sector in Brief, Charities, Giving, and Volunteering, 2010." Washington, DC: The Urban Institute, 2010; http://www.urban.org/uploadedpdf/412209-nonprof-public-charities.pdf.

Web Resources

1–800-Volunteer, 1–800-volunteer.org

Bureau of Labor Statistics, www.bls.gov

Council for Certification in Volunteer Administration, www.cvacert.org/index.htm

The Federal Office of Personnel Management's 5-Step Workforce Planning Model, www.opm.gov/hcaaf_resource_center/assets/Sa_t0014.pdf

The Federal Office of Personnel Management's Assessment Decision Guide, http://apps.opm.gov/ADT/ContentFiles/AssessmentDecisionGuide071807.pdf

Points of Light Foundation/Hands on Network, www.handsonnetwork.org

VolunteerMatch, www.volunteermatch.org/

14 Evaluating Success

Success has its price! For the nonprofit sector, the price is increased scrutiny and demand for evidence that its social contribution is not merely positive but great enough to justify its privileged status.

Burton Weisbrod[1]

Congratulations are in order. The nonprofit County Historical Society at which you work has just been awarded a large grant from the State Department of Education to support its efforts to "celebrate the history of our great state on its bicentennial." The mission of your organization—to collect, preserve, and share the rich history of the county by bringing it alive—fits nicely with the state's request for proposals, and the grant you have been awarded will help you fulfill that mission. In particular, the grant will allow you to update and modernize your interactive history curriculum, which brings school-aged children to the historic Westchester Mansion, home of the Historical Society. Westchester has particular historic importance to the state as it is the birthplace of the state's third governor, served as a stop on the Underground Railroad, and operates the oldest continually working farm in the state.

As a condition of the state award, ten percent of the grant must be spent on an assessment of program outcomes. For years the society has annually tracked the numbers of school groups hosted, lesson plans distributed, and tours offered, but you are a bit wary about how to track program *outcomes;* just because people show up doesn't tell you how well you have brought history alive or how much students have learned. However, since an evaluation of program outcomes is required by the state grant, an outcome evaluation is what you will give them.

NONPROFIT EVALUATION: MEASURING OUTCOMES TO ENSURE ACCOUNTABILITY

Evaluation in the not-for-profit sector is, first and foremost, about ensuring accountability. In a world in which nonprofit organizations, public policy, and service delivery are intertwined, accountability is owed to clients, boards of directors, donors, the public, and anyone else with a stake in the

POLICY IMPLICATIONS OF EVALUATION

- Evaluation of nonprofit organizations and their programs is primarily about ensuring accountability to clients, boards of directors, donors, the public, policymakers, and anyone else with a stake in the organization.
- Federal policies initiated evaluation in the nonprofit sector by requiring that nonprofit contractors evaluate the performance and effectiveness of their policy implementation and program efforts; evaluation continues to be generally required by governments and other funders as part of contracts and grant agreements.
- Evaluation is part of policymaking as it helps facilitate responsiveness to clientele, improve performance, create strategic plans, prioritize budgets, and advocate public policy solutions.
- Nonprofits evaluate overall organizational performance, often using data required on the IRS Form 990, and they also evaluate individual program performance to determine how well their use of resources and activities has allowed them to meet specific outcomes and goals.
- While there are limitations for measuring success for some organizations and their programs, particularly when goals are abstract or long-term in nature, nonprofits cannot simply assume that their programs and services are working; they must do the hard but valuable work of evaluation in order to be sure they are meeting their policy and programming goals.

organization. These stakeholders have an interest in your nonprofit's mission and want to know how well you fulfill it, for how many, and at what cost. Evaluation begins with a clear understanding of the organization's mission, its programs, its clients, and its goals. Importantly, good evaluation requires a commitment of resources including time, labor, and technology, especially when the organization begins the evaluation process.

It is useful to frame our discussion of why evaluation has become so important in the nonprofit sector with a formal definition: "Evaluation is a systematic process for an organization to obtain information on its activities, its impacts, and the effectiveness of its work, so that it can improve its activities and describe its accomplishments."[2] What we refer to as evaluation goes by a wide variety of names in the literature and practice including performance measurement, program evaluation, outcome measurement, or outcome evaluation. Regardless of which term is used, evaluation in the nonprofit sector helps to answer the question: How are we doing?

The nature of nonprofit services and programs often makes assessment difficult, as in the opening vignette in which the Historical Society may have a hard time evaluating how effectively it "brings history alive." Despite this difficulty, all nonprofits can evaluate themselves and their programs in some systematic fashion. The products of evaluation can include descriptive reports, formal assessments of program outcomes, and evaluation of overall organizational performance. In this chapter we discuss the why, what, who, and how of evaluating nonprofit organizations and programs to provide a thorough understanding of this essential component of nonprofit management and its importance to making and implementing public policy.

WHY DO WE EVALUATE?

Evaluation in the nonprofit sector traces its roots to policy evaluation at the federal level, and therefore provides another example of the influence of government policy on not-for-profit organizations. During the 1960s, policy evaluation became institutionalized in Great Society programs such as Medicaid and Medicare.[3] In the 1990s, the institutionalization of policy evaluation was expanded by the federal Government Performance and Results Act (GPRA) and was further expanded in the early 2000s, through the Office of Management and Budget's Program Assessment Rating Tool (PART). In each case, the goal of the federal government was to use evaluation as a mechanism to ensure accountability to the public. More recently, states have included evaluation requirements as part of their funding as well, as exemplified in the opening vignette.[4] The government's emphasis on evaluation coupled with its increased use of nonprofits as social service contractors has made program evaluation an increasingly important part of the not-for-profit landscape.

When public funds are spent on programs to enhance society and the social welfare of individuals, whether delivered by government employees or contractors, it is important to know how that money is spent and whether or not proposed goals are being met.[5] In addition, after a series of scandals involving nonprofit organizations in the 1990s, philanthropic foundations and other funders began to require evaluation to better ensure that their funds are well spent.[6] The result was a formalization of processes and an increase in technical assistance to nonprofits to aid their evaluation efforts including the introduction of logic models, the creation of organizations such as the American Evaluation Association's Nonprofit and Foundations group, and the development of tools to evaluate nonprofit programs such as the United Way's Outcome Measurement, and the W.K. Kellogg Foundation's Logic Model Development Guide.[7]

Evaluation in the Policymaking Process

Evaluation of nonprofit programs is an important part of the policymaking process. It is used for multiple purposes including facilitating responsiveness to clientele, improving performance, creating strategic plans, prioritizing budgets, engaging in organizational oversight, and advocating public policy solutions. As stated earlier, accountability is often considered the primary reason for nonprofits to undertake evaluation efforts. Nonprofit organizations are accountable to the many stakeholders that put faith in them: the participants who take part in their programs; the clients who use their services; the individual donors who make contributions; the granting organizations that bestow public and private funds upon them; the government agencies that sign contracts with them; the for-profit and not-for-profit organizations that collaborate with them; the boards of directors that oversee their operations; the staff and volunteers who believe in furthering their missions; and the general public who, by affording tax-exempt status and allowing tax-deductible contributions, have endorsed the nonprofit sector as a venue through which to meet many public needs. It is important that these stakeholders know resources have been used wisely and resulted in intended program results, including behaviors that have been changed, skills that have been enhanced, or a community that has been enlightened by a performance or exhibit.

Using Evaluation for Mission Advancement

Evaluation is also about learning, growth, and progress for the organization. Because it requires self-examination, good evaluation can help diagnose problems and suggest solutions for improvement. When consistently used in this way, evaluation can become part of a continuous process of organizational learning.[8] Importantly, the results of evaluation efforts are meant to be used. As Mattessich writes, "the goal of evaluation is action: the use of information to make progress in helping individuals, groups, and communities."[9] Evaluation can be used by the organization to monitor its progress toward specific goals, compare the effectiveness of different programs, expand efforts that have proven to be particularly successful, and allow organizations to replicate one another's programs.

In addition, effective evaluation can be used symbolically as a communication tool to share information and track progress for staff, board members, funders, and other stakeholders. For example, nonprofits that engage in political advocacy have been found to use evaluation results symbolically as they pursue their policy agendas.[10] Particularly good evaluation outcomes can be shared broadly as part of marketing campaigns to attract new supporters and participants, recruit new volunteers, donors and employees, and generally keep all stakeholders up-to-date and committed to the organization.[11]

While it is true that even small nonprofits use some form of evaluation these days, not all are engaged in sophisticated outcome evaluations.[12] For example, a study of 15 programs operated by faith-based organizations found that while evaluation mechanisms were in place in each, the form of evaluation varied dramatically from staff performance reviews, to consumer satisfaction surveys, to service statistics (outputs), and collection of outcome data.[13] Similarly, the types of evaluation undertaken by nonprofits have been found to vary depending on the source of funding.[14] Strict program monitoring, formal evaluation, and performance measurement are more likely undertaken by nonprofits that receive large federal government or foundation grants, while small foundations and local government granting agencies are generally satisfied with simple descriptive reports. Most funders want to see some level of evaluation but they recognize that many not-for-profit organizations lack the resources to apply rigorous evaluation techniques.[15]

WHAT DO WE EVALUATE? ORGANIZATIONAL PERFORMANCE

It is important to note that nonprofits can evaluate the performance of the organization as a whole or they can evaluate performance at the program level. Evaluating the overall performance of nonprofit organizations is often challenging because of the diverse nature of the sector. There is no universal list of best practices that can be applied to nonprofit management, nor is there a uniform means to evaluate nonprofit organizations.[16] Assessing overall performance often involves measuring organizational efficiency, which, as defined in Chapter 11, is "the cost per activity to achieve given outcomes."[17] It is an internal measure that addresses questions of how well an organization is managed; thus, financial ratios are commonly used in evaluations of overall organizational performance.[18]

Financial Ratios

Four common areas in which nonprofits use financial ratios to evaluate their organizations are fundraising efficiency, public support, fiscal performance, and program services.[19] Researchers and practitioners have found that data collected by the IRS on the Form 990 can help to standardize measures of each of these concepts. For example, fundraising efficiency can be measured by the ratio of direct public support to fundraising expenses,[20] and by the ratio of total revenue to fundraising expenses.[21] Public support, which measures the ability of the organization to raise revenue, can be determined by the ratio of total contributions to total revenue,[22] and the ratio of direct public support to total assets.[23] Overall fiscal performance can be measured by the ratio of total revenues to total expenses and total contributions to total expenses.[24] The efficiency of program services can be measured using a ratio of program expenditures to total expenses and the ratio of program expenses to total assets.[25] Use of Form 990 data to assess organizational performance offers organizations the ability to benchmark their performance against peer organizations, assuming that each has reported accurate financial information to the IRS.

Both Charity Navigator and the Better Business Bureau (BBB) Wise Giving Alliance recommend that organizations spend no less than 35 percent of their budgets on programming, but each nonprofit must determine for itself appropriate targets for success when doing evaluation. When organizations use financial ratios or any other measures of evaluation, their mission should be their guide. Recall the case study about Invisible Children from Chapter 8, in which the organization was criticized for spending more on advocacy than direct service delivery. Based on the group's mission, which is to create social action rather than deliver programs, this critique is somewhat misguided. Efficient use of resources to pursue the mission of Invisible Children requires spending on advocacy.

Social Accounting

There are also ways to assess organizational performance in qualitative ways through what is known as social accounting. Designed to address the limitations of financial indicators to evaluate nonprofit work, social accounting considers the socio-economic impact of the organization, uses a socio-economic resource statement (including valuation of volunteer service hours), and expands on value-added statements to include both financial value and social value.[26]

An example of social accounting comes from research done by the National Committee for Responsive Philanthropy (NCRP), which in 2008 began publishing the results of a study that examined the impact of philanthropic foundation grants in four areas around the country. NCRP reported that foundation grantmaking had a significant impact on shaping policy and strengthening civil society in all four regions. They connected the financial investments made by donors to tangible policy outcomes, such as an increase in a state's minimum wage to which they could attach a dollar value, but they also provided an accounting of civic strength which was improved through foundation funding. Efforts to improve civic strength were measured by the thousands of people becoming members of community organizations, attending public events or meetings to voice their policy concerns, and engaging in constituent communications with government officials.[27] This NCRP project is detailed in Chapter 6.

Process Evaluation

A process evaluation is another method of qualitative assessment. Process evaluations involve assessment of the "activities, services, staff, and organizational features of your operations to document the history and to see whether you deliver what you intend to deliver to the intended consumers."[28] Process measures are typically descriptive in nature and generally do not evaluate the impact or outcomes of organizational activities.[29]

An example of an overall organizational evaluation comes from the James Irvine Foundation, which has been performing an annual comprehensive assessment since 2005. Known as the Performance Assessment Framework, Irvine tracks progress across multiple dimensions including program impact and outcomes, communication efforts, operations, and financial performance. The framework helps the board in its oversight role, demonstrates the accountability of Irvine to key stakeholders, and is used internally in the strategic decision-making process.[30] See Web Resources at the end of the chapter for more information about the Irvine Foundation's evaluation process and resources.

Nonprofit Dashboards

As noted in Chapter 11, Total Quality Management and New Public Management gained enormous popularity in the 1980s and 1990s as mechanisms to enhance organizational performance in the for-profit and public sectors. Nonprofit organizations were not immune to the pressures to improve capacity through similar strategies. A successful example of a for-profit tool, the Balanced Scorecard, adapted for use in the nonprofit sector, is the Nonprofit Dashboard. (For more information, see Box 14.1.) As with other organizational reforms, however, applying for-profit performance evaluation techniques to nonprofit and public sector endeavors is often inadequate because while profits and losses are easily measured, determining efficiency when seeking social outcomes is usually far more difficult to measure.[31]

Box 14.1

FOR MORE INFORMATION

THE NONPROFIT DASHBOARD

A nonprofit dashboard involves "user-friendly tools for displaying performance measures" including "indicators, variables, or ratios"[32] that point "boards and staff to where they might need to drill down into a more detailed, refined understanding of organizational and program effectiveness. They provide a learning opportunity for both board and staff."[33]

The Dashboard can take several forms, looking literally like a dashboard, or presented as a series of tables and charts, and offers a way to communicate about the nonprofit's performance in a highly visual fashion. Creating a dashboard requires that senior management and the board have determined in advance key performance indicators (finances, numbers served, client satisfaction, employee turnover, etc.) and levels of performance that are expected (targets, benchmarks, goals). Because nonprofits sometimes find it challenging to determine appropriate indicators to include in their dashboard, CompassPoint Nonprofit services offers a list of sample indicators on their website. The list includes indicators in categories such as fund development, human resources, and governance.

Visual representations of achievement level such as "exceeded goals," "met goals," "did not meet goals," are also used so that board members and staff can quickly assess the overall performance of the organization. These visuals can include color-coding, symbols, graphs, or charts. Another advantage is that dashboards are easy to update for changing circumstances and, over time, can show the development of the organization.

For more information, see: Lawrence M. Butler, *The Nonprofit Dashboard: A Tool for Tracking Progress* (Washington, DC: BoardSource, 2007). The book includes a CD with dashboard templates and instructions; the disk requires Microsoft Excel. See also CompassPoint Nonprofit Services' Organizational Dashboard Sample Indicators, http://www.compasspoint.org/dashboard.

The Role of Third Party Watchdogs

There are a number of third party rating entities that evaluate nonprofit organizations. As discussed in Chapter 4, however, the full merit of evaluations done by organizations such as the American Institute of Philanthropy, Charity Navigator, and the BBB Wise Giving Alliance is rather unclear. Charity Navigator, for example, reports on whether or not nonprofits are making information on important issues affecting accountability and transparency available to the public; however, they do not have the ability to assess the quality of the information provided. Despite having no uniform and clear understanding of what the standards of rating agencies truly reflect, the conclusions of such third party evaluators are often used as "signals of legitimacy to donors and funders lacking firsthand information about the organization."[34]

Some nonprofits, particularly in the education and health sectors, have outside accrediting bodies that evaluate and enforce industry standards. These tend to be nonprofit organizations themselves, like the National Children's Alliance (NCA) discussed in previous chapters. NCA evaluates children's advocacy centers to ensure they meet the standards for best practice in cases of child sexual abuse and accredits them accordingly. Whether a nonprofit operates in a field in which there is an accreditation process or the organization is being rated by one of the watchdog groups, these assessments of organizational performance send a strong message to donors, clients, state agencies, and other stakeholders that this is a well-run organization, thus enhancing its strength in policy advocacy and program implementation.

Although overall assessments of organizational performance are important, they often say very little about the *effectiveness* of the nonprofit or its programs. Rather, measuring effectiveness is about evaluating organizational accomplishments—how well the nonprofit fulfills its mission. To assess program effectiveness, which is what nonprofits, their stakeholders, and their funding agencies are most interested in assessing, one must turn to an outcome evaluation, typically undertaken at the program level.[35]

WHAT DO WE EVALUATE? PROGRAM PERFORMANCE

It is probably clear by now that evaluation involves a number of related, sometimes confusing concepts that are important to clarify before we delve further into the subject.[36] Figure 14.1 offers an example of a program to deliver meals to homebound seniors, in order to illustrate the four key concepts used in program evaluation. First, are program *inputs,* defined as the resources required to implement a program or deliver services. Inputs include staff, facilities, technology, volunteers, and money. Next is the concept of program *activities,* which involves taking program inputs and putting them into action to bring about program results. Activities for various nonprofits would include feeding homebound seniors, vaccinating children, providing counseling services to substance abusers, or presenting an art exhibit.

The next concept, *outputs,* is defined as the units served and often includes aspects of a program that are easy to count. For the four activities named, outputs could include meals delivered, immunizations provided, clients counseled, or patrons who have attended. Finally, is the concept of *outcomes,* which is the key to evaluating the effectiveness of a program. An outcome is a measure of the benefit received by those who participate in the program or activity and can be short or long term in nature. Outcomes for the examples above would include the hunger allayed, the illnesses prevented, the behavior changed, or the edification gained by each of these nonprofit activities.

Of these four concepts, the two most likely to be confused are outputs and outcomes. Plantz et al. explain that "outputs are about the *program,* whereas outcomes are about the *participants.*"[37] Understanding each concept does not necessarily simplify the work of evaluation, however, because it is typically easier to measure outputs than outcomes. Consider again the example in our opening vignette in which the County Historical Society needs to evaluate program outcomes as a condition of its State Department of Education grant. As mentioned in the vignette, the society has tracked outputs for years, including the numbers

FIGURE 14.1 Evaluation Logic Model Example: Bringing Meals to Homebound Seniors

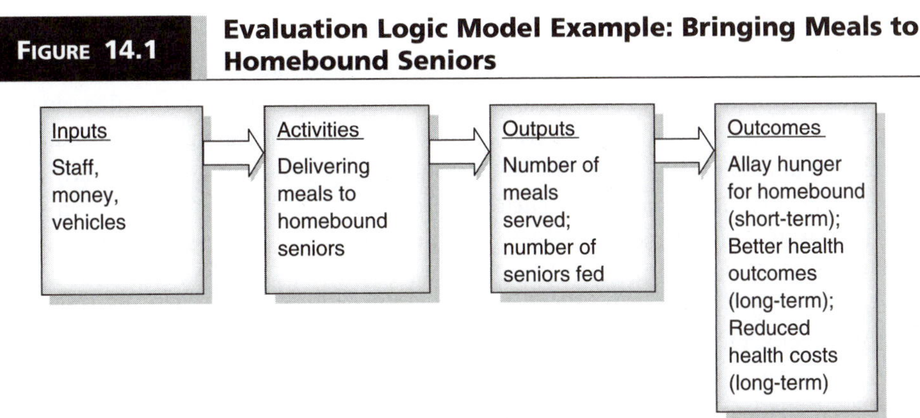

of children and school groups hosted on-site, the numbers of lesson plans distributed to teachers, and the types and number of tours offered to groups of all ages. These numbers are very important for determining whether or not the society has met its targets and allowing for comparison from year to year—a measure of the growth of the program. Presumably the society has done well enough to proudly report these statistics to donors, parents, and local school districts as measures of success. It is likely that these output measures would have been included in the Department of Education grant application and that this past success was an important factor in winning state funding.

While tracking outputs is useful, you will remember that the society's state grant requires an evaluation of program outcomes, which will surely prove to be more difficult. The grant was awarded to update and modernize the society's history lessons as part of its mission to share the rich history of the county by bringing it alive. An outcome evaluation will serve to quantify what it means to bring history to life as well as assess how much students have learned as a result of the new curriculum and lessons provided by the society. Clearly, the State Department of Education is interested in accountability for public funds: How well did the Society accomplish its goals through use of this grant money? As is often the case in the nonprofit sector, however, the goals of bringing history to life and teaching children do not lend themselves to easy measures. It is no wonder that many nonprofits measure outputs rather than outcomes.

WHO IS INVOLVED IN THE EVALUATION PROCESS?

Evaluation can be a complex and sometimes difficult process; therefore, organizations that can afford to do so often hire outside consultants or researchers to spearhead or assist in these efforts. Since many organizations have few financial resources to spend on evaluation, they perform evaluation in-house. In either case, it is important to get input from program participants, staff, and other stakeholders to maximize evaluation efforts and help pinpoint what is most important for the nonprofit to know about its programs.

Professional Evaluation Services

The difficulties in evaluating nonprofit work have led some authors to recommend that nonprofits hire outside evaluators, particularly in the organization's initial evaluation effort.[38] An outside evaluator has experience with difficult-to-measure goals and eliminates the problem of maintaining objectivity when evaluating one's own program. Similarly, independent accreditation organizations, such as often exist in the health and education fields, provide a set of standard measures established by an outside body and promote objective evaluation.

Another reason to hire outside evaluators would be the difficulty in collection and analysis of data. Surveys, for example, are quite common and are generally considered good sources of information about program outcomes, but they are difficult to write well and can be time consuming to administer. Therefore, hiring professionals will ensure methodologically sound survey results. Analysis of data can also be challenging for organizations that lack staff having adequate familiarity with statistical programs. A good source of expertise in survey design and administration, as well as analysis of data, is the local university, where faculty or eager graduate students are often willing to assist in evaluation efforts, usually at relatively inexpensive rates.[39] In addition, board members or other volunteers with such expertise may be quite useful if the organization decides upon statistical analysis of program data. In the end, it must be remembered that the nonprofit cannot simply hire a consultant and forget the matter; its employees, executive, and board bear the responsibility of providing hands-on direction throughout the evaluation process.

Self-Evaluation

More often, nonprofits lack the resources to hire a professional evaluation group or even a single consultant; therefore, the role of the executive becomes very important in building the capacity for evaluation within the organization itself; again, experienced staff or volunteers can be invaluable.[40] Some suggest creating a small evaluation working group or advisory group with members of varied perspectives to help design the evaluation.[41] For self-evaluation the IRS Form 990 can be an important source of data. Because Form 990 requires that organizations with more than $50,000 in revenue detail their organizational activity when they file their taxes, as discussed at length in Chapter 4, many nonprofits can use that information as they evaluate their organizational and program efficiency.

As evaluations are being prepared, the organization should involve program participants, staff, and key stakeholders who affect the future of programs, with the caveat that it is important to avoid co-optation of the evaluation process, particularly by those inside the organization.[42] In the end, self-evaluation should do what any evaluation does: provide a way for the nonprofit to be held accountable for *how* it pursues and for *how well* it fulfills its mission.

PROGRAM THEORIES AND LOGIC MODELS

It is widely suggested that evaluation efforts begin with a program theory, more widely known as a logic model.[43]

> Basically, a logic model is a systematic and visual way to present and share your understanding of the relationships among the resources you have to operate your program, the activities you plan, and the changes or results you hope to achieve.[44]

Logic models are valuable in a variety of ways, and many experts agree that their use is an important component of program success. They allow the organization to present its program information in a meaningful way and to understand why the program works. Logic models also help a nonprofit to take inventory of the resources required to get results and describe the outcomes expected from program activity. All of this helps in determining appropriate evaluation tools, methods, and procedures. In addition, logic models help in writing better grant proposals and are often required by granting organizations as a way to visually represent how and why the nonprofit's programs will meet their intended goals.[45]

To ensure that a logic model is useful, evaluators must be sure that they have identified outcomes relevant to the organizational mission and ones for which their program can legitimately be held accountable. The outcomes identified must represent meaningful benefits or changes, be clearly defined, and be useful in determining success. A well-designed logic model will include all important program activities and outcomes and make plausible connections between inputs, activities, outputs, and outcomes. Finally, the outcomes chosen should be capable of communicating the benefits of the program to multiple audiences.[46]

Figure 14.1 offers a very basic example of a logic model for a program bringing meals to homebound seniors as part of an organizational mission to find cost-effective ways to improve health outcomes for this population. While this example is presented in the form of boxes and arrows, logic models can also be represented in tabular rows, as numbered lists, or as a series of "if x, then y" statements. The model in Figure 14.1 moves from program inputs to activities to outputs to outcomes, both short and long term. The W.K. Kellogg Foundation considers long-term outcomes to be *impacts,* which it describes as "the kinds of organizational, community, or system level changes expected to result from program activities and which might include improved conditions, increased capacity, and/or changes in the policy arena."[47] In the case of the meals program for seniors, the long-term impacts, which are improved health outcomes and eventually health care cost reductions, are integral to the organization's mission.

These long-term impacts are important, and each is often one in a series of outcomes expected from a single policy or program.[48] For example, if we presented the logic model for providing meals to homebound seniors as a series of "if x, then y" statements, we would have several outcomes:

1. If the program delivers healthy food to homebound seniors, then it will help to alleviate hunger and improve nutrition;
2. If the program alleviates hunger and improves nutrition, then participants will be better fed and avoid malnutrition and dehydration;
3. If there is better nutrition and hydration for participants, then the number of trips to the emergency room can be reduced;
4. If there are fewer emergency room visits, then public policies and budgets are positively affected through lower levels of public health spending.

Presentation in this manner makes the logic of the meals program for homebound seniors and its policy implications clear to boards of directors, grantmakers, or any other interested stakeholders. It may be possible in this example to lobby for policies to institutionalize programs such as this in local, state, or federal health agencies if the program has proven to be very effective. Of course, as a nonprofit creates its logic model it must remember that the farther away it moves from short-term outcomes, the less likely that a single program is responsible for changes in attitude, behavior, knowledge, or condition, and the more likely that factors unrelated to the program will have influenced outcomes.[49]

HOW DO WE EVALUATE?

As stated previously, it is useful to begin evaluation efforts with creation of a program theory or logic model which will tie together the logic of the program's components and create a smooth process for program evaluation. Subsequently, the evaluation process requires identification of outcome measures and specific indicators that will be used for that measurement. The process then moves to data collection, analysis of data, reporting findings, and finally, putting the findings to use.

It is recommended that a nonprofit consider the maturity of its programs as it undertakes the design of its evaluation. For example, young programs may have no baseline statistics upon which to draw, and therefore measuring outputs may be more appropriate than attempting to measure outcomes.[50] Early in the evaluation, it is useful to do background research or get advice from similar organizations because it is quite likely that others have examined similar policies or programs, and their research can suggest indicators and facilitate design of your evaluation project.[51]

Before beginning an evaluation process, it is important that the organization take stock and be sure that the methods it has chosen to collect data and evaluate programs will be feasible. Good evaluation requires an investment of resources—money, technology, and staff time. The board and chief executive, who are ultimately responsible for management of resources, must be fully engaged in evaluation efforts. They must be willing to provide staff members with the time and resources needed to devote to the evaluation process including design, data collection, and analysis. In some cases, as in the Historical Society example, grant funders will provide money to assist in program evaluation to ensure that it is done well.

Determining Measures and Selecting Indicators

It is fairly common for nonprofits to use benchmarking and industry standards to measure performance, to compare themselves to similar organizations, and to evaluate their own performance over time.[52] As noted above, when a nonprofit is new to evaluation, using the same measures employed by organizations operating comparable programs is a good way to establish targets and expectations. Benchmarking—that is, identifying other, similar organizations against which to compare one's programs—is useful as an internal gauge of performance as it lets the organization know how its programs fare in relation to peers. Benchmarking against peer performance can also be useful for external audiences, particularly when one's programs are more successful or less expensive than programs offered by similar organizations. Note that benchmarking overall nonprofit performance is also done, but would involve using measures of overall performance such as fundraising efficiency or financial performance, as discussed earlier.

Using previously established measures can also be helpful when one's outcomes are not easily quantifiable, as in the case of the Historical Society's intent to bring history to life. There is no need for an organization to spend a lot of time and resources on identifying or creating useful measures when others have already successfully done so. Using the same measures and indicators also allows for ease of comparison among nonprofits and programs for benchmarking. Finally, nonprofits often find it difficult to evaluate their programs strictly using quantifiable statistics; therefore, some creativity may be required in developing outcome indicators.

Outcome goals should be stated clearly and in measurable terms. This requires choosing appropriate *indicators*, which are the statistics or pieces of information that will be used to measure program success. An indicator should be a specific, observable, and "measurable characteristic or change that will represent achievement of the outcome."[53] For example, an indicator of success in the meals program for seniors might be a 10 percent reduction in emergency room visits. If a characteristic cannot be observed or measured, no matter how important it may be to the program mission, it cannot be used as an indicator. It can be argued that this limits the usefulness of outcome evaluation for nonprofits with difficult-to-measure outcomes, a point that will be addressed at the end of this chapter.[54]

The organization will need to be realistic about how much effort it should put into creating indicators.[55] While it is important to have measurable goals to assess success, the resources required to collect the most complete information about some outcomes may not be worth the cost. The environmental organization Nature Conservancy found this to be true when it created a 98-point indicator system for program performance. See Going Global Case Study 14.2 for more details about its experience with program evaluation.

GOING GLOBAL CASE STUDY 14.2

The Nature Conservancy Measures Performance for Mission Success

Founded in 1951, the mission of the international conservation nonprofit the Nature Conservancy is "to preserve the plants, animals and natural communities that represent the diversity of life on Earth by protecting the lands and waters they need to survive." With operations in over 30 countries, the Nature Conservancy protects over 100 million acres of land and 5,000 miles of rivers worldwide. It works to sustain marine biodiversity in over 100 projects, and preserves habitats from forests to grasslands to deserts, working with governments, corporate partners, and community groups, with the goal of protecting biodiversity across the globe.[56]

Among its most innovative strategies for international habitat protection have been "debt-for-nature" swaps, begun in 1988 when the Nature Conservancy first arranged international debt forgiveness in exchange for preserved land. Subsequently, the Nature Conservancy and other environmental nonprofits successfully urged the U.S. Congress to pass the Tropical Forest Conservation Act (TFCA) in 1998, which allows the U.S. government to broker similar debt agreements to create and support NGO conservation efforts in local communities in fourteen nations. As of 2010, TFCA agreements were expected to generate more than $266 million for tropical forest conservation in these countries.[57]

Until the mid-1990s, the Nature Conservancy had used revenues generated and acres protected as their indicators of success, what they called "bucks and acres." Although the Conservancy did quite well on these measures during the 1990s, with financial growth of 18 percent annually and a doubling of the number of acres protected from 5 to 10 million, estimates about the continued rapid rate of species extinction worldwide led Nature Conservancy leaders to question whether these were still valid measures of success. Changes in conservation biology over the years had led the Nature Conservancy to work on a much larger scale—the ecosystem level—thus, they concluded that their traditional indicators of bucks and acres were insufficient to adequately measure biodiversity conservation on this scale. To remedy this, the Nature Conservancy took a full year to overhaul its evaluation methods, seeking a thorough indicator that would include factors from total membership, to dollars raised per capita, to expenses incurred in managing each nature preserve. The final product was a 98-point indicator system for program performance that the Nature Conservancy sent to field offices to pilot. Not surprisingly, staff balked at the time and resources it took to make this evaluation system work. Some complained that there was no way to make sense of the volume of information they had collected; others said that the measures were biased toward large projects. Nature Conservancy leadership went back to the drawing board and sought to streamline the process and clearly align its mission, vision, goals, and strategies with its programs and measures.[58]

In the end, they created a 3-part family of measures to assess organizational performance; the most important measure, mission impact, took the longest to refine. Conservancy leaders settled on biodiversity health and threat abatement as their surrogates for mission success.[59] They call their strategy Conservation by Design, which involves (1) identification of the biodiversity to be conserved, (2) use of a science-based approach to decide where and how best to conserve, and (3) measuring the effectiveness of their efforts.

The Nature Conservancy uses existing scientific surveys to evaluate the conditions of plants and animals as their measure of biodiversity health. To measure threat abatement, they evaluate the extent to which they have devised strategies to reduce the threats to species at locations under Nature Conservancy care. To measure their overall effectiveness they answer two questions: the first, "How is the biodiversity doing?" considers the condition of both species and ecosystems; the second, "Are our actions having the intended impact?" is about evaluating the effectiveness of its conservation strategies.[60]

In 2006, their short-term goal was "to ensure the effective conservation of places that represent at least 10 percent of every major habitat type on Earth" by 2015.[61] To measure success toward this goal, they use three analytical methods: (1) global habitat assessments, which estimate the level of conservation in each major habitat type on Earth; (2) ecoregional assessments, which include data collection on a local scale that allows for short- and long-term goal setting; and (3) conservation action planning, which uses data on the status of biodiversity and its threats to develop specific projects for threat abatement or habitat restoration.[62]

In pursuit of their goal, the Nature Conservancy announced a capital campaign in 2000 called the Campaign for Conservation to raise $1 billion for preservation of what they term the 200 Last Great Places and to complete identification of the remaining global habitats in need of protection. The campaign was very successful; by its conclusion in 2003, the Nature Conservancy had raised $1.4 billion.[63] On the tenth anniversary of the Conservation by Design effort, they reported that there was still much work to do to reach the 2015 goal, but the method of evaluation they created in 1996 had helped to keep their efforts on track with their mission. They continue to engage in both large- and small-scale data collection, goal setting for both the short and long term, and strategies of evaluation and action that can be adapted to changing circumstances.[64]

There are several lessons from the Nature Conservancy experience. First, organizations with difficult-to-measure goals should concentrate on finding useful surrogate measures rather than spend exorbitant amounts of money, time, and human resources in an attempt to find the perfect indicator or evaluation method. Second, the creation and implementation of useful evaluation methods will take time and effort. When done well, however, evaluation allows the organization to more effectively pursue its mission by setting and meeting its on-going goals. Importantly, monitoring and reporting results of the organization's work can help to identify action strategies; encourage the support of partners, donors, and members; and build the reputation of the nonprofit; all of these, of course, are vital to successful pursuit of the mission.

For more information on the Nature Conservancy, go to www.nature.org

QUESTIONS TO CONSIDER:

1. What drove the Nature Conservancy to change from its traditional measures of success, "bucks and acres," in the mid-1990s? What does this suggest about evaluation of nonprofit efforts?
2. It is no surprise that their 98-point indicator for evaluation was widely panned by field staff as inefficient and cumbersome. Why would Nature Conservancy leaders attempt to pilot such an unwieldy evaluation tool in the first place?
3. Consider the four relationships that describe nonprofit interaction with public policy (make policy, affected by policy, influence policy, subject to policy) and discuss the ways in which these relationships are reflected in the example of the Nature Conservancy.
4. Is the experience of the Nature Conservancy unique? Explain how missions that are difficult-to-measure, either because of their abstract nature or their enormous scale, complicate the evaluation process for a nonprofit organization.

What are considered to be appropriate indicators will depend on the outcomes being evaluated. Let us again consider our County Historical Society, which needs to evaluate how well its new curriculum has brought history to life, and compare it with a disparate example: a Healthy Babies program to help low-income women improve health outcomes for their newborns. There are a variety of indicators that could be used to measure the success of these programs, but for this example, we use birth weight as an outcome indicator for the Healthy Babies program and student engagement with the curriculum as an outcome indicator for the Historical Society.

For the indicator of birth weight we use pounds and ounces, an easily obtained, quantifiable measure. Unfortunately, there is no such easy way to define or measure student engagement with the curriculum; rather, the Historical Society will have to define its own quantifiable measure that will serve as an indicator of this concept. The society could define student engagement with the curriculum as the amount of knowledge that students gain from visiting the museum, which could then be measured through the administration of a series of questions about the exhibit topics both before and after the students take the tour. Likewise, engagement could be defined as the amount of interaction students have with the exhibits in the museum and could be measured by comparing the number of students who visit each exhibit, the length of time students spend at each, and the degree to which students ask questions or complete tasks associated with each exhibit.

As suggested in the examples above, there are usually multiple ways in which to define an outcome indicator and often more than one way to measure it. Accordingly, nonprofit staff and leadership involved in designing the evaluation process should devote significant effort to choosing indicators that will provide the most useful information and are the most practical. In the case of the Healthy Babies program, measuring improved health outcomes for newborns could be accomplished with indicators such as number of pre-term births, Apgar scores, and days in the hospital after birth; whether these measures are practical to obtain or provide the most useful information is for the leadership of the nonprofit program to decide. These examples lead us to another important consideration when designing a program evaluation: choosing appropriate methods for gathering data.

Collecting Data

There are a variety of ways in which a nonprofit can collect data; for example, the organization may conduct a survey, interview participants, host focus groups, gather data from internal or public records, develop a method of observational rating, create assessment forms to be completed by staff or participants, or administer tests. As with selection of indicators, the most appropriate method to gather data depends upon the type of data needed.

Evaluating birth weights of newborns in the Healthy Babies program requires access to hospital records to compare the weights of babies born to participants with those of non-participants. As suggested earlier, measuring student engagement with curricular materials may be accomplished by observing student behavior. Although observations of newborns in the Healthy Babies program may be useful, it would not be as accurate an assessment method as comparing birth weights using hospital records. Similarly, while examination of student test records may tell us something about the curriculum created by the Historical Society, records would not be useful in assessing how engaged students were with the curriculum if engagement is defined as the level of physical interaction with the exhibits. Clearly, there is no single evaluation method or data form that will work in evaluating every program; thus, it is important to fully understand the program, its logic, and what aspects of the program need to be assessed before taking on an evaluation project.

Before undertaking data collection, there are a number of factors for the nonprofit leadership to consider, including a trial run of the method (especially when using surveys), training for those administering the collection method, and ethical use of human subjects. When using surveys it is important to remain mindful that surveying clients about their satisfaction with programs is not a means by which to gather outcome information. Rather, satisfaction is a process measure that, while very useful for planning programs and in marketing the organization, says nothing about how the clients have been affected by the program—its outcomes.[65] In terms of a trial run, it is standard practice to run a pretest when using any type of survey or assessment form. A survey pretest involves administering the survey or assessment document to a small group that is representative of the population from which data will be collected. If no one in the pretest group understands or knows how to answer question three, for example, it can be re-worked or dropped from the assessment before it is administered to the larger population. This helps to avoid the collection of flawed or incomplete data.

Also important to know when using surveys and interviews, particularly if done on behalf of government or in collaboration with an academic institution, is that they may require the use of *human subjects review* to ensure that participants are informed of their rights to informed consent, confidentiality, and about any risks that they may face from participation in the study. A simple way to convey information about participant rights is to include it as part of the program registration or intake process.[66] Additionally, the consent of a parent or guardian may be required when human subjects are minors or members of another vulnerable population, such as those with diminished physical or mental capacity. Even if not required, it is an ethical practice to inform participants of their rights when participating in surveys or interviews, reviewing how their confidentiality will be maintained, and what will be done with the results of the data collection. For more information on ethics in research on human subjects, see Box 14.3.

Characteristics for Evaluation Indicators. In many cases staff and volunteers will need training in the method of data collection, as in the use of rating systems where the *reliability* of the rating tool is crucial. Reliability refers to how well the measure provides consistent results—that is, different raters will arrive at similar conclusions when observing the same phenomena. For example, assume that in the opening vignette volunteers are asked to rate the degree of engagement of children milking cows at the Westchester Mansion farm. It is important that all of the volunteers are trained to rate the level of engagement using the same criteria—for example, number of questions asked, proportion of students willing to participate, and attention paid to the demonstration, in this case.

Other characteristics that are important for evaluation indicators include validity, relevance, and timeliness.[67] *Validity* refers to how well the indicator measures what it is

Box 14.3

FOR MORE INFORMATION

ETHICAL CONSIDERATIONS IN HUMAN SUBJECTS RESEARCH

The Council of American Survey Research Organizations (CASRO), a member organization of over 325 survey institutions worldwide, considers itself "the voice and values of research." The CASRO Code of Standards and Ethics for survey research has been required for use by member organizations and their employees for over 30 years. For more information, see: http://www.casro.org/codeofstandards.cfm.

The federal government provides a number of online resources for guidance when engaging in research on human subjects while under a federal grant or contract with either the National Institutes of Health or the federal Department of Health and Human Services. In addition to general policies and guidance, the sites include specific information on research dealing with vulnerable populations and provide access to training materials. For federal resources, see National Institutes of Health's Office of Extramural Research, http://grants.nih.gov/grants/policy/hs/index.htm and Health and Human Services Office for Human Research Protections, www.hhs.gov/ohrp/.

supposed to measure. For example, birth weights, rate of pre-term births, and Apgar scores are well established indicators of newborn health, thus each is considered a valid measure. The characteristic of *relevance* ensures that the indicator measures a factor of importance to the program. Level of student engagement, for example, is a relevant indicator for the Historical Society because it helps define the goal of bringing history alive for students. Finally, *timeliness* requires that the measure provide information in a time frame that allows it to be useful as an indicator. For example, while lower levels of asthma may be an outcome for children whose mothers participated in the Healthy Babies program, asthma will not present itself for years—long after it would be a useful indicator for this particular program.

In addition, because evaluation should become part of the nonprofit's culture, it is useful to document the indicators used and the method of data collection for future program assessments. For example, creating a data collection manual for each program will make the job of evaluation easier each time, and will allow new staff members to more quickly assume responsibility for this important task. Institutionalizing evaluation procedures in this manner will also reinforce to staff, volunteers, boards, and executives that evaluation is valued by the organization.

Analyzing the Quantitative Data

Keep in mind that in order to produce an evaluation report that will be of most use, the nonprofit will need other information in addition to its outcome indicators. For example, demographic data on clients and participants such as age, ethnicity, gender, and education level are often incorporated into evaluations. It may also be important to collect community-level statistics such as poverty and unemployment rates, socio-economic status, or health indicators such as obesity and diabetes prevalence. In the Healthy Babies program, for example, there may be a difference in newborn health outcomes between Latino, Caucasian, and African American babies. This information could help the nonprofit modify its program to better meet the needs of different subsets of clientele, and can be used as a tool in advocating for policy changes to maternal health care programs at the state level.

Once the data have been collected they will most likely be entered into a database for analysis. Often a simple spreadsheet is sufficient for this purpose, although more sophisticated analysis might require a specific statistics software package. It is important to continually check for accuracy during the data entry process, as errors are fairly common and can wreak havoc with final results. Once the data are entered they will then be tabulated and analyzed. Raw numbers, percents, means, and medians are common descriptive statistics included in a final report. Rates can be used to compare outcomes among those according to age, gender, ethnicity, or region, and it is often useful to count the number of participants reaching, exceeding, or not meeting an outcome target. This may be a good point in the process to make use of a local university where faculty or graduate students would be available to tabulate and analyze data or assist in the organization's analysis.[68]

When analyzing data, it is important to make comparisons linking programs with outcomes. For example, assume that in the past two years, 8.4 percent of newborns in the

Healthy Babies program weighed less than 5.5 lbs and were considered low birth weight. By themselves, these numbers tell us very little about the program's outcomes. When we compare these outcomes to the community average of 10.3 percent of babies with low birth weights, we get a much better sense that the program is having a positive impact.

As social scientists, we would be remiss if we did not remind the reader that when making comparisons the organization must compare similar populations. Consider again the example of participants in the Healthy Babies program, who are women in households below the poverty line from a defined geographic location. The comparison population must also come from households below the poverty line and from the same defined geographic location; if we look to an adjacent, possibly poorer community, we are not making a fair comparison. Although this might complicate the analysis it makes the results of the evaluation far more accurate. Similarly, when benchmarking or doing other sorts of peer comparisons, it is important that the not-for-profit compare similarly situated organizations in terms of client demographics and geographic locations.[69] Even to compare the results of the Healthy Babies program in an urban center to the outcomes of the same program in a rural community is of limited value; separate comparisons must be made between participants and non-participants at each program location.

Reporting, Presenting, and Using the Findings

When making a final report, data and findings must be put into the context of the organization: its physical, geographic, and political environment, as well as the socio-economic status and other demographics of the clientele and community. In addition to a formal written report, someone in the organization is likely to make an audio/visual presentation of the findings as well. In either case, the final report should be designed for quick absorption. For example, if the written report is lengthy, it is a good idea to write a brief executive summary that presents the highlights of the evaluation in a one to two-page format. As with any written or oral presentation, it is important to remember your audience; the presentation of findings to the board of directors will likely differ from the presentation before a legislative committee and that will be different from the presentation to a panel for grant funding. It is incumbent upon those presenting the report to know the attention span and the time available for the audience to read the report or hear the presentation.

The findings of an outcome evaluation will require explanation beyond a simple report of the data because "numbers seldom speak for themselves."[70] Those writing and presenting final reports must be sure to explain what the results mean for the program and the organization. If findings are not as positive as expected, it is important to consider the reasons. Perhaps an external problem such as an increase in the unemployment level has led to greater demands on the program and negatively affected program results. There may also be internal problems such as high levels of staff turnover that have led to less-than-desired outcomes. These factors must be explained in the evaluation report as should steps that will be taken to address internal problems and improve program performance in the future. Similarly, a change in policy at the federal level may have increased the amount of funding going to the public school system, which has positively affected the children in your program and meant that targeted outcomes are being surpassed by nearly every participant. While it would be nice to take the credit for miraculous results, it would also be disingenuous; thus, an explanation of the wider policy context is in order.

Any visual presentations of findings should be clearly labeled and easy for multiple audiences to understand. For example, when displaying data over time it is best to put the earliest data to the left and the most current data to the right.[71] Suggestions for visual displays include data tables, pie charts, bar charts, and stacked columns. Keep in mind that tables of data can become confusing if they contain too much information or too many categories. Finally, maps are particularly useful ways to present data on community indicators or outcomes that vary by location.[72]

At the start of this chapter we noted that evaluation is about action; once the nonprofit has collected and reported its findings, it should put them to use. Evaluation results can provide direction for staff and identify areas in which training and technical assistance could help staff implement and improve programs. Results can also be used to inform program decisions by clarifying outcomes for participants of different racial, ethnic, or socioeconomic backgrounds or in different programs. They can be used to promote the image of the nonprofit, which will help in recruiting volunteers, staff, and board members as well as enhance the organization's ability to raise funds. An excellent example of evaluation research in practice comes from the Girl Scouts of the USA. Their extensive use of evaluation research and how their Los Angeles affiliate uses the national model to evaluate its programs are discussed in Box 14.4.

In addition to being used to attract new or increased levels of funding, reports on program outcomes can be used in advocacy and to change public policy. Evaluation findings and related data can be used as tools to inform policymakers at the local, state, and federal levels. The data collected by nonprofits about who uses their services—and how—can help policymakers understand the nature and scope of problems, and the strategies and costs involved in alleviating them. Particularly when nonprofit organizations are invited to testify before legislative bodies or when they seek to advocate on behalf of their clients and organizations, having good data and evaluation outcomes to report will enhance the credibility of the organization and its cause. Recall the example in Chapter 10 of the Police Foundation, whose successful community-oriented policing services (COPS) pilot projects eventually led thousands of law enforcement agencies to adopt COPS policies.

Program evaluation in particular is important to changing public policy and enhancing policy success because it informs decision-makers about what works and what does not work, for whom and where. All policies can be considered experiments, whether they create new programs or simply make adjustments to existing ones, which is one reason that nonprofits engaged in direct service delivery are required to evaluate their work. If programs are not successful, or become less successful over time, policy change may be in order; without evaluation we simply do not know what influence nonprofit programs have on participants or the broader society.

Box 14.4

FOR EXAMPLE

THE GIRL SCOUTS OF THE USA: EVALUATING PROGRAM PERFORMANCE

Mention the Girl Scouts and thoughts typically turn to cookies, not evaluation research. For those familiar with nonprofit program evaluation, however, the Girl Scouts of the USA (GSUSA) is known as a leader, having conducted their first evaluation of scouting impacts in 1990.[73] Seven years later the national outcomes study, *Girls, Families, and Communities Grow Through Girl Scouting,* was published relying on data from a sample of nearly 8,000 Girl Scouts, troop leaders, and parents as well as individuals not affiliated with the Girl Scouts.[74]

The 1997 study involved a rigorous methodology, including extensive pretesting and focus groups with Scouts nationwide. The findings indicated that scouting enhanced personal characteristics such as self-reliance, respect for others, feelings of belonging, values and decision-making, teamwork, and leadership among Girl Scouts.[75]

These successful evaluations led to more emphasis on outcomes assessment for the GSUSA. In 2000, they created a tool kit for local councils to measure and improve the camp experience for girls in their regions. In 2002, GSUSA evaluated the scouting experience for junior Girl Scouts, and in 2008, they studied the effects of involvement in Girl Scouts on mother/daughter relationships.

In 2009, GSUSA identified a new framework for service called the Girl Scout Leadership Experience (GSLE), which included three primary goals for girls to meet through scouting: (1) discover who they are and what they value; (2) connect with others; and (3) take action to make the world a better place.[76] Each of the primary goals has five related goals known as leadership essentials. Based on GSUSA-sponsored research that found girls continue to see barriers to female leadership, in 2012 GSUSA launched an advocacy and fundraising drive to foster girls' leadership called ToGetHerThere. The goal is to raise $1 billion to advocate for improved media and industry portrayals of girls and women, to increase mentoring and positive role modeling for girls, and to eventually create gender-balanced leadership in all sectors of society.[77]

The Girl Scouts of Greater Los Angeles (GSGLA) is among the largest local councils in the nation, serving more than 350 communities and almost 40,000 girls in the greater Los Angeles area. As an example of a national-level organization aligning the evaluation efforts of its local affiliates, GSUSA created a two-part survey, Girl Scouts Voices, to evaluate Girl Scout Leadership Experience in 2011. The two-part evaluation begins with a demographic survey written by GSUSA. The second part, to evaluate local councils, begins with questions written by GSUSA but allows each local council to ask questions regarding its specific programs. It is the intention of GSGLA that all of their troops' activities will meet multiple leadership goals.

The GSGLA survey includes a statement about the confidentiality and security of the survey and a link to the Girl Scouts' Privacy and Data Use Policy for GSUSA Surveys. This policy statement includes standard language for a human subjects review disclosure, ensuring that participation is voluntary, that the answers will be used for research only, that the participant may refuse to answer any question, and that she may end her participation at any time.

GSGLA staffers evaluate all of their program activities in terms of level of enjoyment for Scouts, whether or not girls have gained knowledge or skills through individual programs, and how programs can be improved for the future. Results of the on-going Girl Scout Voices surveys are incorporated into program activities; for example, in 2012 GSGLA is revising programs to meet the preferences of girls at different grade levels.[78] Program evaluations are so commonplace in the GSGLA region that girls have become quite used to completing evaluations before earning their participation patches or badges.

For more information about GSGLA: www.girlscoutsla.org/index.html

For more information about GSUSA: www.girlscouts.org

PRACTICAL CONCERNS

Although evaluation is not a fad that will go away, it is also not universally embraced by nonprofit organizations. Outcomes measurement can be seen as an unfunded mandate or a waste of scarce resources for nonprofits when funders request evaluation but do not include resources in their awards.[79] This can lead to a variety of responses by the nonprofit, including the "just give them some numbers" strategy, in which the organization provides low quality data in order to satisfy the requirement with minimal effort.[80] Similarly, evaluation requirements can lead to the problem of goal displacement. For example, the pressure to find measurable indicators may take the focus off the nonprofit mission, or resource dependence may cause the organization to frame a program in reference to funders' outcome preferences rather than program logic. Other problems include client creaming and selective reporting. As discussed in earlier chapters, client creaming is when the pressures to produce positive outcomes create an incentive to serve the least troubled cases. The problem of selective reporting occurs when the organization reports only the outcomes of a particularly successful subgroup of the population—eliminating program dropouts from the analysis, for example.[81]

Evaluation Fears and Limitations

There are a variety of reasons that some nonprofit organizations may not wish to conduct outcome evaluations. One is the fear that the results could require changes that the not-for-profit is unwilling or unable to make. Another fear is that results could be misinterpreted or used against the organization to fit a political agenda[82] or used to reduce funding to programs not meeting their targets.[83] In some cases, the nonprofit mission may preclude "the kinds of adjustments suggested by the program evaluation."[84] For example, an organization whose mission involves a commitment to serve all members of a community cannot simply stop offering programs to young adults (18- to 24-year-olds) because their participation rate is minimal compared to the other age groups served; committing substantial additional resources to attract young adult participation, however, may also not be an option. Further, some nonprofit leaders may feel that the use of specific and measurable goals would impose limits on their program and inhibit its growth, development, and ability to innovate.[85] This concern may have merit if evaluation becomes an end in itself rather than a means to the end of producing a successful program.

Additional concerns about program evaluation involve its technical limitations. For example, findings might indicate that the program is not producing its intended outcomes; however, they will not indicate *why* it is not. In addition, outcome evaluations do not prove that a program, by itself, caused particular outcomes. Much more sophisticated, expensive, and difficult-to-conduct program impact research would be required to determine causality.[86] Similarly, in the behavioral sciences, outcomes may not be known until far into the future and, especially for children, positive outcomes may have less to do with the program and more to do with normal human development.[87] In addition, Fischer notes that appropriate evaluation strategies are particularly difficult to find in a variety of scenarios: (1) in crisis-focused interventions like hotlines where there is anonymity and no likelihood of client tracking; (2) in programs that serve transient populations such as a weekly soup kitchen where outputs can be counted, but little other information can be gathered; (3) in prevention-focused programs in which program benefits are very long term, such as programs designed to prevent teen smoking; and (4) in projects with diffuse targets, as in the case of a program designed to increase civic engagement within a community.[88]

Political Concerns

Further, because program evaluation is a critical step in the policymaking process and it always involves multiple stakeholders and value judgments, evaluation is an inherently political process.[89] For example, evaluating health outcomes of youth who use a nonprofit clinic would likely necessitate the use of a measure of teen sexual activity. While the teen *pregnancy* rate may be an accurate, objective indicator to use, the difference between rates of teen pregnancy and the number of births to teenage mothers reflects an issue of profound controversy. As a result, the policy orientations and political ideology of a particular community may make it averse to using pregnancy rate, finding the teen *birth rate* to be a more politically acceptable indicator. Although birth rate is a useful measure, it likely underestimates the level of teen sexual activity.

Finally, because evaluation has political consequences, political expediency may mean that an underperforming program continues to garner funding because it is popular with elected officials and the general public; common examples of this come from programs designed to prevent drug and alcohol use among teenagers. The most well-known example is probably D.A.R.E., the Drug Abuse Resistance Education program which, while very popular with parents, teachers, and politicians, has been found in numerous studies to have no effect on drug use among participants. The policy consequence of this is important: time, money, and other school and police resources have been used for the past 30 years on a program that has been proven *not* to fulfill its mission.[90]

The Consequences of Neglecting Evaluation

We began this chapter by noting that evaluation in the nonprofit sector is about ensuring accountability to clients, boards of directors, donors, the public, policymakers, and all of those with a stake in the organization's mission. It is an integral part of the policymaking process because evaluation fosters responsiveness to clientele, improves performance, prioritizes budgets, and facilitates public policy advocacy. Importantly, some have raised concerns that current government budget shortfalls are not temporary; in that case, it will be increasingly incumbent upon nonprofits to undertake and use assessment tools for their organizations and programs or risk losing government contracts and grants to organizations with better-demonstrated outcomes.[91] Beyond mandates imposed by government and foundation funders that require nonprofits to evaluate their programs, organizations themselves benefit from evaluation because it allows them to answer the question: How are we doing?

A poignant example of the potential for negative consequences if a nonprofit does not undertake and use evaluation comes from the Latin American Youth Center (LAYC) in Washington, D.C. In 2007, LAYC introduced a new curriculum into a parenting program designed to make clear that domestic violence is never acceptable in any culture. Upon analyzing the results of a pre-test/post-test evaluation of the new curriculum, the director of learning and evaluation found that participant attitudes about domestic violence had indeed changed. After exposure to the curriculum, participants were *more likely* to believe that domestic violence is appropriate in love relationships and acceptable behavior in the Latino community. Program managers were understandably shocked to learn that their program may have caused more harm than good. They subsequently consulted with domestic violence experts and changed the curriculum and mode of delivery. Once the curriculum was updated the program was again evaluated with much more positive results: under the revisions participants were less likely to condone domestic violence. If LAYC had not been conducting on-going program evaluations it may never have known that its domestic violence curriculum was negatively affecting participant attitudes.[92] While we hope that this is an extreme example, nonprofit organizations cannot simply assume that their programs and services are having the desired impact; they must do the hard but valuable work of evaluation in order to be sure they are meeting their goals.

CONCLUSION

Evaluation of nonprofit organizations and their programs is an integral part of nonprofit administration because it provides a way to keep organizations accountable for the programs they implement, the policies they pursue, and the funds they spend. Initially undertaken to satisfy federal policy mandates and funder requirements, evaluation is increasingly thought of as simply a normal part of managing a nonprofit organization. In addition to fostering accountability, evaluation is used for a variety of purposes including facilitating responsiveness to clients, improving programs and performance, prioritizing spending, marketing the nonprofit, and advocating public policy solutions.

The process of evaluating nonprofits and their programs can seem daunting and methodical; fortunately for novice organizations, a wide variety of resources exist to assist in the endeavor (see Web Resources and Suggested Readings at the end of the chapter). Evaluations of organizational performance have tended to focus on measures of financial efficiency, with an increased emphasis on measuring social outcomes. In addition to organizational performance, the performance of programs is also important to evaluate.

In general, an evaluation of program outcomes begins with the organizational mission and the logic or theory of a program. From there, evaluators proceed to identify the outcomes to be measured and the indicators with which to measure them, followed by data collection and analysis and reporting results. Finally, program evaluation concludes with using the results to make changes to the organization, its programs, or the system in which both operate, which likely reinitiates the evaluation process. This process is neither as simple nor straightforward as it sounds, especially for nonprofits with difficult-to-measure outcome goals. It is, however, increasingly expected of nonprofits of all sizes and types and is an important tool for nonprofit managers to improve the efficiency and effectiveness of their organizations and programs and to obtain the funding and policy change essential to pursuit of their missions.

QUESTIONS FOR REVIEW

1. There are many reasons that nonprofit organizations undertake evaluation. In your opinion, what are the three most important reasons, and why?
2. Discuss the differences between output measures and outcome measures. Why are both important to evaluating nonprofit activity and performance?
3. This chapter demonstrated how important evaluation is to nonprofit organizations. Using examples, what are the public policy implications of doing nonprofit program evaluation?

Assignment

Consider again the opening vignette about the County Historical Society's required outcome evaluation for the State Department of Education. Because the first step in evaluation is creation of a program theory or logic model, this assignment asks you to create a basic logic model to assess at least one outcome of the Historical Society's grant project. Remember that the society sought funds to update and modernize its interactive history curriculum and that the mission of the society is to collect, preserve, and share the rich history of the county by bringing it alive. Following the template below, create a rudimentary logic model; include at least one indicator (specific, observable, and measurable) that could be used to evaluate the outcome(s) you have chosen.

Inputs	*Activities*	*Outputs*	*Outcomes*	*Indicators*

Suggested Readings

Fischer, Robert L. "The Sea Change in Nonprofit Human Services: A Critical Assessment of Outcomes Measurement." *Families in Society: Journal of Contemporary Human Services* 82, 6 (2001): 561–568.

Flynn, Patrice, and Virginia A. Hodgkinson, eds. *Measuring the Impact of the Nonprofit Sector.* New York: Kluwer Academic/Plenum Publishers, 2001.

Hatry, Harry, Therese van Houten, Margaret C. Plantz, and Martha Taylor Greenway. *Measuring Program Outcomes: A Practical Approach.* Alexandria, VA: United Way of America, 1996.

W. K. Kellogg Foundation. *W. K. Kellogg Foundation Logic Model Development Guide.* Battle Creek, MI: W. K. Kellogg Foundation, 2004.

Web Resources

The American Evaluation Association, www.eval.org/

CompassPoint Nonprofit Services' Organizational Dashboard Sample Indicators, http://www.compasspoint.org/dashboard

Free Management Library, http://managementhelp.org/

James Irvine Foundation's Performance Assessment Framework, http://irvine.org/evaluation/foundation-assessment

Innovation Network, www.innonet.org/

Nonprofit and Foundations Topical Information Group of the American Evaluation Association, www.eval.org/aboutus/organization/tigs.asp

Online Evaluation Resource Library, http://oerl.sri.com/

15 Looking Forward

Emerging Trends for Managing Nonprofits

Solving these [complex social] problems requires new ways of thinking and acting on the part of individuals, along with new organizational designs that encourage stakeholder actions consistent with the long-term welfare of our ecological, economic, and social systems.

Hareed Sabeti and the Fourth Sector Network Concept Working Group[1]

In 2010, the American Civil Liberties Union (ACLU) brought suit against the San Diego Unified School district, arguing that mandatory fees for student participation in public school athletics programs violated the California Supreme Court's 1984 *Hartzell v. Connell* decision guaranteeing a free public education. The ACLU argued that the *Hartzell* decision guaranteed equal access to both curricular and extracurricular programs, regardless of ability to pay. In December of 2010, the state agreed that requiring students to pay fees for extracurricular activities was illegal and established a monitoring and enforcement system to ensure that schools would not impose extracurricular fees.

This settlement and the 1984 Supreme Court decision were designed to ensure equality; however, when implemented at the local school level, this policy has important consequences for the thousands of small, nonprofit booster clubs across the state. For example, imagine that you are the incoming president of the Aquatics Club at the local high school when the settlement is announced; the first call you get that afternoon is from the school's athletic director who tells you that, given this agreement, the school will no longer be able to require fees for student athletes. Rather, much of the aquatics annual budget, typically in the range of $55,000 including coaches' salaries, will be *dependent on fundraising* from now on. Although letters will be sent to parents requesting a "tax deductible donation," there is no longer a requirement that students pay to play. Your head is spinning as you put down the phone. The Aquatics Club is used to hosting car washes, selling magazine subscriptions and t-shirts, and securing local business sponsorships, but $55,000? That amount of money will not be raised by adding a bake sale to your repertoire. What on earth have you gotten yourself into?

POLICY IMPLICATIONS OF EMERGING TRENDS

- Nonprofit organizations exist in a complex policy world and must maintain collaborative relationships with the public and for-profit sectors in identifying and framing societal problems as well as the formation and adoption of public policy solutions and public services; however, the lines between sectors increasingly blur as they intersect, collaborate, and compete with one another.
- The reliance on partnerships between government, nonprofit, and for-profit organizations has grown as the public's willingness to adequately fund certain endeavors through taxes has diminished, requiring policymakers and the public to make choices about who will provide public services and how they will be provided.
- Current political, social, and economic trends have helped increase nonprofit capacity and prominence but have also presented challenges, including the need for increased funding, such as through venture philanthropy, with an associated risk of mission drift.
- The trends blurring nonprofit activity with traditional for-profit and public endeavors have helped push nonprofits to professionalize and hone their management skills as they step into roles that sometimes demand they behave like for-profit enterprises or public sector agencies.

POLICY CONSEQUENCES AND INCREASING COMPLEXITY FOR THE NONPROFIT SECTOR

The chapter's opening vignette is interesting not simply because it presents a real-life dilemma; it also represents a compelling example of the complex relationship between public policy and nonprofit organizations in the twenty-first century. In this case, a nonprofit organization, the ACLU, brought suit against a public school district to fight district policies that run counter to the state's constitution. The settlement between the state and the ACLU creates a host of unintended consequences for the small, nonprofit booster clubs now tasked with raising money to keep extracurricular programs afloat; as the Poway, California, superintendent of schools suggests, "If those donations stop coming in, those activities will go away."[2] If schools find that parents are no longer willing to pay when not required to do so, then the fundraising capacity of booster clubs will be essential to future student opportunities. The management of these very small nonprofits will surely be tested—their understanding of the laws under which they operate, the best ways to raise funds and conduct their meetings, how to maintain their tax status—all will be more important than ever before because of an unrelated nonprofit's successful efforts to change school policy.

The multiple policy implications for nonprofits in this case are clear: the ACLU advocated, via the court system, for a change to existing policy and they won; school districts are now subject to a new policy, and nonprofit booster clubs will have to change their behavior to adapt to the change in policy. As has been discussed throughout this book, we see here the inextricable link between nonprofit organizations and the world of public policy. Add to all of this the public's declining interest in paying higher taxes to maintain or increase government spending coupled with the for-profit sector's increasing interest in social responsibility and the relationship between the three institutional sectors can only be expected to grow more complex. This complexity is the focus of the remainder of this chapter.

THE PAST AND FUTURE FOR NONPROFITS AND PUBLIC POLICY

In many ways the nonprofit sector is at a crossroads: nonprofit organizations are increasingly sought by government to provide public services and implement public policies, while at the same time they find themselves under increasing pressure to brand themselves and earn income using the strategies of the for-profit sector. This blurring of lines between the three sectors presents an evolving set of challenges and opportunities for those managing nonprofit organizations in an increasingly complex system. This sector blurring, also called hybridization,[3] or sector-bending,[4] is the primary focus of this chapter. As such, we end not by offering conclusions per se, but rather by taking a look at the evolving nature of the voluntary sector in the United States, which has seen both its prominence and importance rise, fall, and rise again during the past two-and-a-half centuries.

As we discussed in detail in Chapter 2, the nonprofit sector in America can be traced to the colonial era when voluntary societies were promoted as a conduit for collective action outside of either government or religious institutions. As our federal system was created and the nation grew, the nonprofit sector performed many essential social tasks, ranging from health care to education to provision of aid to the poor. By the turn of the twenty-first century, nonprofit organizations had already been instrumental in bringing an end to slavery, providing emergency services to victims of natural disasters, and preventing child abuse. These and other successes were frequently the result of not-for-profits taking the lead and then partnering with the public sector at a time when governments were small and neither well-funded nor well-managed. As the professionalism of public budgeting and administration grew, so too did technological advances, creating an industrial economy that both facilitated increased tax revenue and created social, environmental, and economic conditions that required government regulation. By the time of the Great Depression, many of the social tasks previously performed by the nonprofit sector had become public policies increasingly administered directly by government employees, and the role of charities, churches, and other philanthropic institutions diminished. In this era, Americans turned to government for social advancement and expected it to deliver.[5] For a time, they were not disappointed; creation of the

Social Security Administration, provision of unemployment insurance, development of the interstate highways, passage of the Voting Rights Act, increased veterans' benefits, and the rapid growth of public universities were ways in which the federal and state governments met the needs of an increasingly diverse, urban, and activist population in the decades after WWII.

This situation changed slowly as multiple factors affected public opinion about the role of government. First, Americans' trust in government declined precipitously beginning with the social turmoil of the late 1960s, followed closely by the Watergate scandal and the U.S. withdrawal from Vietnam in 1975. During this same time, state governments were encouraged to seek collaboration with nonprofit organizations under a variety of federal programs, including Head Start and Medicare. By 1980, after the high unemployment and high inflation rates during the Jimmy Carter administration, Ronald Reagan ran for office, declaring that far from being the solution, government was the problem.[6] Further, the push for lower tax rates, begun in the late 1970s with California's Proposition 13, and the growth of privatization through government contracting with both nonprofit and for-profit entities throughout the 1990s, reflected changes in the ongoing debate between Americans regarding the proper role of government.

As demonstrated throughout this book, the nonprofit and public sectors have maintained collaborative relationships even as the prominence of each has waxed and waned. The sectors have worked together in identifying and framing societal problems and the formation and adoption of public policy solutions, as well as the provision of public services, implementation of public policies, and evaluation of public program outcomes. Accordingly, the partnerships—both formal and informal—between the nonprofit and public sectors have been considerable. Today, the lines between the two have become even more blurred and the distinctions with the for-profit sector are becoming less obvious, increasingly adding to the complexity of the system.

One such example comes from In-Q-Tel (IQT), a nonprofit which provides a venture capital tool for the development and promotion of innovations in information technology (IT) for the U.S. Central Intelligence Agency (CIA). The CIA and other federal agencies were on the cutting-edge of technology during the Cold War era, but since the 1990s, modern technical innovations have been dominated by the commercial market and for-profit organizations are making advances in Internet technology far faster than the federal government can keep pace.[7] To bridge that gap, the CIA created an independent nonprofit corporation to foster relationships with and strategic investments in new and existing companies engaged in IT research and development. This government/nonprofit/for-profit partnership includes private sector IT and venture capital companies. IQT reports that for every dollar it invests in new companies, private venture capitalists invest more than nine dollars, which has allowed for development and delivery of new intelligence technology at lower costs to government.[8] In this case, the nonprofit sector is providing the venue through which to facilitate relationships between for-profit innovators and venture capitalists to solve problems that America's intelligence community cannot solve on its own.

IMPORTANT TRENDS AFFECTING THE NONPROFIT SECTOR

The blurring of the lines between sectors and the emergence of new forms of organization, such as the tax status of "for-benefit" B Corps, lead us to consider a basic philosophical question: What should the proper scope and function of each sector—for-profit, government, and nonprofit—be? This is fundamentally a public policy question—how do we want to govern ourselves? Both the market and the government clearly have limitations that the nonprofit sector has traditionally sought to address, and the nonprofit sector is also clearly limited—for example, in resource acquisition and the public authority to act.

As the lines between the sectors increasingly blur, decisions within each sector have greater effects on one another and on society as a whole, as the example of high school sports activities in the opening vignette illustrates. Throughout this book we have consistently sought to highlight the multiple connections between nonprofits and public policy and the historic conditions that forged them. In the remaining sections of this chapter, we seek to outline how these conditions have shaped the nonprofit sector and how it is likely to evolve in the future.

Trends Affecting Government–Nonprofit Relationships

The public sector itself is at a critical point, as the public debates an acceptable level of taxes and expresses increasing concern over federal budget deficits and mounting national debt; these concerns, spurred by the recent recession have brought the debate over the proper scope and function of government to a heightened state. With clearly defined lines between the sectors, sources of revenue for each were not ambiguous: governments collected taxes, for-profits sold products, and nonprofits solicited donations. As the lines blur, sources of revenue are much less defined according to sector. For example, nonprofits are increasingly selling products to raise money, for-profits receive tax dollars via government contracts, and governments are setting up philanthropic foundations to solicit contributions.[9] There are even those who suggest that some for-profit companies, such as the residential-care company The Mentor Network, would benefit from being bought and managed by a nonprofit foundation.[10] The following represent three compelling examples of how issues of public finances are transforming the traditional relationships among government, nonprofits, and the public goods and services they provide.

Universal Public Education. The idea of the "common" school originated in the United States as the result of policies providing for universal public education in the late 1800s. Common schools were free-of-charge, secular, fiscally independent, gender neutral, and open to all. While never open to all equally—segregation created black schools in the south and Mexican schools in the southwest, and school funding was typically lower for poor and immigrant children—the U.S. experiment in universal public education was more far-reaching than in any other nation.[11] Mass public education was considered a key to advance both democracy and the nation's economy and was funded accordingly by a combination of state taxes and local property taxes.[12]

Funding inequities persisted in this system of universal education until major school finance reform following the 1971 *Serrano v. Priest* decision, in which the California State Supreme Court ruled the state's system of school finance to be unconstitutional. The state's heavy reliance on local property taxes had created a system in which large disparities in property values led to similar disparities in per pupil spending. The *Serrano* decision forced equalization of California's education funding, and similar state court rulings affected 23 other states over the next three decades. In 1978, California passed Proposition 13, which lowered and capped property tax rates and increases; Proposition 13, coupled with the aftermath of the *Serrano* case, led to significant declines in education spending in wealthy school districts. To address this reduced funding at the local level, districts began forming 501(c)(3) education foundations to raise money for local schools outside of the tax system. In 1982, the California Consortium of Education Foundations (CCEF) was created as a 501(c)(3) organization to serve as a resource for the many education foundations being formed across the state. According to CCEF, more than 675 local education foundations were active in California in 2009, contributing over $230 million annually to address needs in their local schools.[13]

As the state has reduced spending on public schools over the past decade, it now ranks 46th in the nation in per pupil spending,[14] and although $230 million is a small fraction of the $61 billion state K–12 budget, some local foundations are much better funded than others and make far more difference to the schools and students in their districts. The Menlo Park-Atherton Education Foundation, serving one of the wealthiest communities in the state, contributed $2.6 million to schools in its district in 2011; that was over 8 percent of the district budget.[15] The San Marino Schools Foundation (SMSF) outside of Los Angeles is similarly well-funded. Its website clearly explains the public policies—*Serrano,* Prop 13, and severe budget cuts—that led to its creation and concludes by saying, "San Marino residents expect excellence in education in their schools, as they should. But while free public education is possible, it does not meet the standard that we would all like to see. We want a GREAT public education for our kids, and that, unfortunately, is not free. . . ."[16] The foundation suggests a $2,000 per student donation annually, which has made a sizable difference in per pupil spending: while the state average is $9,100, San Marino Unified schools spent $11,896 per pupil in 2010–2011—nearly $3,000 more per student.[17] In 2011–2012, SMSF donated $2.4 million to the district, the equivalent of funding for 30 full-time teachers.[18] The district itself has also been very successful, achieving the highest state standardized test scores for nine consecutive years.[19]

It may be the case that California residents have already decided how much responsibility taxpayers should take for public education. They appear to have a waning interest in providing tax dollars for common schools at the level provided in other states; instead, they have offered minimal levels of public funding, regardless of the fact that California is a system with high needs in terms of a large percent of low-income students, English as a Second Language Learners, and large class sizes.[20] Residents seem to have decided that additional spending, at a level that would bring California to the national average of $11,764 per pupil, is best collected through a system of nonprofit education foundations.

Common Land Preservation. Another example comes from the nation's system of state parks, which grew in earnest after the first meeting of the National Conference on State Parks in 1921. The growth of the state parks is attributed to a number of phenomena, including population growth, upward mobility, paid vacations, and increased interest in outdoor recreation activities, as well as recognition by state governments that natural resources and spaces were quickly being purchased and put to private use. The preservation of each state's natural and cultural heritage became a public priority.[21]

By the 21st century, however, state budget woes meant that funding for state parks was increasingly being cut and a number of states, including Hawaii, Arizona, Utah, and California, have considered various methods of privatization to ensure that parks remain open.[22] In 2009, for example, cuts to the Arizona state park budget led to fundraisers and the development of partnerships between state agencies, nonprofit organizations, and local communities to help keep open parks that were at risk of closure. Together, their efforts resulted in collection of over $820,000 to keep open 26 of 27 state parks, at least temporarily.[23]

In 2011 the California State Parks Department, which has seen its budget cut by 37 percent since 2006,[24] announced that it would have to close 70 of the state's 278 parks in 2012 unless an alternative source of funding was found. In response, the state legislature passed a bill that allowed nonprofit organizations to manage state parks with minimal disruption to park services.[25] In March of 2012 the state finalized a series of deals with nonprofits, private donors, and other governments to keep 11 of the 70 parks open for between one and three years. In some cases the parks received funding from individual donors—$900,000 in the case of the Henry W. Coe state park in the San Francisco Bay area—and in other cases, nonprofit organizations are planning to raise money by increasing fees.[26]

Each of these is an example in which policymakers and the public are making choices about who will provide public services and how they will do so. Universal education and common land preservation have been considered primarily the purview of government for more than a century. However, this may be changing as the public's willingness to adequately fund these endeavors solely with taxes has diminished in the wake of growing support for cutting public budgets and relying on partnerships of government, nonprofit, and for-profit providers. Because government still remains a dominant source of funding for human services nonprofits, even when public employees provide few of the services directly, we are unlikely to see a return to the minimal role once played by government with regard to social services. It is interesting to consider, however, that while the government is unlikely to become smaller than the nonprofit sector, over the past 50 years its scope and function have changed in significant ways relative to nonprofits.

Payments in Lieu of Taxes. The changing relationship between government and nonprofits has significant financial implications for the future. The Revenue Act of 1938 explicitly stated the prevailing sentiment that nonprofits should be exempt from taxes because any loss of revenue by the government entity would be offset by the need to use public funds to provide the public goods and services provided by the nonprofits. However, since the recent recession has caused many state and local governments to struggle to balance their budgets and maintain services in the wake of large budget shortfalls, many cities are turning to their tax-exempt organizations as a source of new or increased revenues. A notable example is Boston, home to prominent universities, hospitals, and museums; these nonprofit institutions coupled with the government buildings in the state capital leave more than half of the city's land exempt from property taxes.

While states and the federal government have a history of making payments in lieu of taxes (PILoTs) to local governments to help offset the burden of providing city services, nonprofits are now being called upon by an increasing number of cities to help. For example, while Boston has collected voluntary payments from nonprofits for many years, it has not done so consistently. In 2011, the city began implementation of new guidelines for voluntary payments designed by a mayor's task force. Nonprofits with property valued at more than $15 million would be asked to pay 25 percent of what they would pay in property taxes; the nonprofits would be eligible for credit of up to half the amount of the requested payment if they provide quantitative evidence that the benefits they provide help the city's residents directly. The city anticipates that when fully implemented, the new system of voluntary payments will increase revenues from the current $15 million to $48 million in voluntary payments.[27]

At least 117 municipalities in eighteen states have received voluntary payments from nonprofits, so this is not a new phenomenon, but it is seen as an emerging trend as more attention is focused on nonprofits as a source of revenue for cash-strapped local governments. However, as the recession also hindered the budgets of nonprofits, increasing the pressure on them to bolster government revenues can result in more contention than collaboration. For example, Princeton University makes annual payments totaling $1.7 million to the township and borough; however, officials may reconsider these payments after local zoning officials resisted changes needed for the university's plans to build a new arts complex.[28] This also raises additional questions regarding the balance of power between government authority and some very large nonprofits.

Trends Affecting the Relationships between the For-Profit and Voluntary Sectors

Just as the scope and function of government have changed relative to nonprofits, so has the role of the for-profit sector. Businesses have often cried foul when nonprofits initiate commercial ventures that compete for private sector customers. However, for-profit organizations are also increasingly encroaching on what has traditionally been solidly nonprofit turf. A notable example involves microenterprises. These are commercial entities, but because they are very small—by definition employing fewer than five people—they usually find it difficult to access traditional means of private sector financing. Accordingly, in the mid-1980s nonprofit microenterprise development organizations (MDOs) emerged as a way to help these small businesses with financing, job training, and other services to help build capacity. There are currently approximately 500 MDOs in the United States, but they face growing competition from public and for-profit organizations that are entering the field of microenterprise development.[29]

In areas traditionally dominated by government and nonprofit provision of services, such as hospital care and education, we see a growing number of private for-profit hospitals and conversions of nonprofit hospitals, as well as the massive growth of for-profit educational institutions such as the University of Phoenix. Since government contracts imbue the provision of public goods and services such as job training and placement, child care, and even prison management with profit-generating potential, private sector companies are crossing over into areas previously considered unattractive to the market.

One unlikely example of for-profit crossover is the state fair. The for-profit company, Universal Fairs, LLC, recently bought the Virginia state fair and its fairgrounds after the nonprofit State Fair of Virginia, Inc., defaulted on more than $70 million in loans. Universal Fairs also operates the state fairs in Tennessee, Washington, Georgia, and Mississippi. Traditionally operated by government and nonprofits with a mixture of public and private resources, state fairs across the country are struggling as states wrestle with budget deficits and seek ways to cut costs. Nevada and Michigan were forced to shut down their state fairs due to lack of funding, and New Mexico's fair faces insolvency. The policy implications of takeover by the private sector are significant, however. Concessions and midway amusements are the revenue-generators at state fairs; the agricultural and crafts exhibits that have been the mainstay of state fairs since their inception are not big moneymakers. As such, the agricultural community worries that Universal Fairs or other for-profits like it will eliminate what makes a state fair unique in order to enhance their bottom-line.[30] Each of these is an example of the blurring of lines between the three sectors as they intersect, collaborate, and compete with one another.

For-Profit Organizations Funding and Serving the Nonprofit Sector. For-profits do not always compete with or subsume the activities of nonprofit and public entities; companies are also interested in partnering with both sectors in addressing public problems. Corporate philanthropy remains at its highest level ever[31] because for-profit organizations wish to be more actively involved in addressing social, political, and environmental problems, and they recognize established nonprofits as an appropriate venue for that activity. Further, corporations are increasingly savvy about their philanthropy, including more active leadership from their CEOs, creation of giving programs structured in conjunction with their business strategies, and a view that corporate philanthropy is an investment in the business of the company. Similarly, the numbers of for-profit organizations partnering with nonprofit organizations through employee volunteer campaigns has also grown as employers recognize that supporting volunteer opportunities benefits the employees, promotes the company's image, and helps meet the needs of their communities.[32]

Corporate Social Responsibility and Shared Value. Some for-profit entities are moving away from strict consideration of the traditional bottom line to embrace the concept of the "triple bottom line (people, planet, profit)" that is a central theme of what Harvard Business School Professor Michael E. Porter refers to as "shared value."[33] This involves corporate initiatives that seek to address public problems, including environmental degradation and social welfare, while also considering the corporation's profit-making self-interest. Similar to the more traditional concept of corporate social responsibility, pursuing shared value is seen as a growing trend in the for-profit sector. Whereas corporate social responsibility is most often characterized as a company's efforts to boost its reputation through general philanthropy coupled with efforts to comply with environmental and social regulations, the concept of shared value goes much further. "Shared value engages companies more deeply in social issues, holding the promise of far greater resources and a multitude of innovations to address today's most urgent needs."[34] Those who advocate this relatively new approach to doing business contend that it significantly alters the relationship between nonprofits and business, creating more interdependence and greater accountability between the sectors in addressing public problems. More information on shared value and corporate social responsibility is available through Stanford University's Center for Social Innovation (csi.gsb.stanford.edu).

More recently, the lines between the for-profit and nonprofit sectors have blurred with the increase in social enterprises and the new designation of Benefit Corporations (B Corps) in several states. B Corps are "a new type of corporation which uses the power of business to solve social and environmental problems"; unlike traditional businesses, B Corps meet more stringent standards regarding legal accountability as well as transparency and comprehensiveness with regard to performance standards, and they seek to encourage public policies to facilitate sustainable businesses. The nonprofit B Lab certifies B Corps in much the same way that other nonprofits certify Fair Trade coffee and LEED buildings.[35] Shared value, corporate social responsibility, B Corps, and nonprofit social enterprises all represent interesting arrangements and possible complications across the sectors as these hybrid organizations create new management and public policy challenges.[36]

Nonprofit Trends That Blur the Lines between Sectors

The nonprofit sector, heeding calls to diversify its resource base, has engaged in a number of practices that have further blurred sector lines. As discussed in Chapter 9, social enterprises are ventures operated by nonprofits in order to generate revenue by selling goods or services, often related to the organization's mission, while creating social, environmental, or cultural value. As the not-for-profit sector grows, so does the competition for resources; the ability to earn unrestricted income through social enterprise can be very attractive to cash-strapped nonprofits. To the average consumer, a social enterprise may be mistaken for a for-profit organization, further evidence of the blurred lines.

Another revenue source that blurs the lines between nonprofits and for-profits involves venture philanthropy. Derived from the concept of venture capitalism, venture philanthropy entails an infusion of revenue to a nonprofit to help build organizational capacity and spur innovation to better address public problems. In a practical sense, venture philanthropy differs from traditional charitable donations or even foundation grants in that it typically focuses on long-term commitments of financial support for general operating support. The primary difference, however, is that it embodies a philosophy of social investment; venture philanthropists see their financial assistance not as simply a contribution but as an investment in the work of the nonprofit. As such, they expect to receive tangible evidence of a return on that investment. For venture philanthropists, it is not enough to feel good about giving money to charity or even to have a building named after them in gratitude for their largesse; these individuals want to see demonstrated results that their money is making a difference in solving problems. Therefore, just as with government grants and contracts, nonprofits must be willing to engage in rigorous evaluation in order to benefit from venture philanthropy as a revenue source.[37]

Government grants and contracts for the provision of public programs also mean that nonprofit employees are increasingly on the front-lines of public service, a trend that is unlikely to reverse itself soon.[38] Nonprofit contracting is so prevalent it has been argued that the nonprofit sector is responsible for more direct delivery of health and social services than is government.[39] Program participants are typically unaware of who is providing these services[40] and are not likely to care as long as their needs are being met.

These trends in which nonprofit activity has blurred with traditional for-profit and public endeavors are among the forces pushing nonprofits to professionalize and hone their management skills. Social enterprises often require the acquisition of capital, experience with marketing, and more sophisticated accounting techniques than have generally been employed in nonprofit management. Similarly, organizations must have the capacity to secure and administer government contracts as they increasingly take on the role of public policy implementation. Further, they must be able to evaluate their programs and provide evidence of success in order to maintain their accountability to the public.[41] In these ways, nonprofit organizations have stepped into roles in which they sometimes behave like for-profit enterprises and sometimes behave like public sector agencies; in both instances, they have had to adjust their management techniques to meet the obligations brought about by their new roles.

This brings us to perhaps the most important crossroads for the nonprofit sector and society as a whole: current political, social, and economic trends have helped build nonprofit capacity and prominence but at the same time have presented the nonprofit sector with a much greater set of challenges. First, partnerships with government and for-profit organizations have increased the pressure on nonprofits to implement more professional management strategies as well as improve their ability to evaluate effectiveness. Second, the need for increased funding has increased the risk of mission drift when nonprofits pursue government grants and contracts, as well as when they seek to emulate the for-profit sector by pursuing commercial ventures; each option puts nonprofits at risk of losing their distinctive character. Third, increased use of nonprofits as public service providers requires the sector to become more attuned to issues of accountability, transparency, and diversity, long required in the public sector.

IMPLICATIONS OF EMERGING TRENDS FOR THE NONPROFIT SECTOR

The increased complexity of the system has important implications, both positive and negative, for nonprofit organizations and their management. As discussed above, sector blurring has led to more standardized methods of organizational management and higher levels of professionalism and management training for those in the nonprofit sector. Social enterprise, venture philanthropy, and increased government contracting have opened additional and more diverse sources of financial resources to the sector. Diversified resources often result in a more stable organization and having access to more resources certainly helps the nonprofit pursue its mission. Further, the stronger the financial standing of the organization, the more likely it is to be able to leverage additional resources from individual and foundation donors, who recognize that their donations can have a greater social impact when used by stable, financially-sound nonprofits.[42]

It is also possible that the blurring of sector lines is an indication of a greater commitment by all sectors to finding solutions to the myriad of social, economic, and environmental problems plaguing society.[43] The advent of the incorporation status of B Corps, for example, is an indication that state governments were lobbied by a new breed of for-profit entities seeking not just financial gain but the ability to be of social value. These entrepreneurs and those who have engaged in venture philanthropy are seeking "to find meaning in their lives outside of business"[44] and have found the nonprofit sector with its public purposes an appropriate outlet. It may be the case that the only way to create meaningful solutions to many of our greatest societal challenges will come through combining the efforts of the public, nonprofit, and for-profit sectors.

With these tools—greater access to resources, more professional management, and a higher public profile to address social ills—the nonprofit sector is poised to move more fully into what many would argue is its appropriate role within society. Recall from Chapter 2 the characterization of the three sectors: the Prince, the Merchant, and the Citizen. In a democratic society the nonprofit sector plays the role of Citizen, and many nonprofit organizations are uniquely situated to facilitate democracy through their organizational structures, their public outreach, and the voice they give to those with few political and economic resources.[45] Further, new forms of technology and social media have dramatically increased the ability of nonprofits to reach out to policymakers, stakeholders, and the public alike. Nonprofit organizations, including philanthropic foundations, increasingly see their role as important to the process of public policymaking and implementation. The ACLU, discussed in the opening vignette, is a case in point: for nearly a century the ACLU has sought policy change—in its words "to defend and preserve the individual rights and liberties that the Constitution and laws of the United States guarantee everyone in this country."[46]

Potential Negative Consequences of Emerging Trends

There are, however, important concerns about sector blurring and the related social, political, and economic trends affecting the nonprofit sector. For a simple example, we can return to the opening vignette in which the complexity of the nonprofit policy environment was highlighted. Although the ACLU case against school district policy was designed to ensure equal access to extracurricular opportunities for all students regardless of their ability to pay, the result may be equal lack of access instead. An unintended consequence of this policy change at the local school level may be an end to extracurricular activities such as music, theatre, and sports if parents choose not to donate to their booster clubs. These small non-profits, now charged with the responsibility of funding activities without guaranteed sources of revenue, may collapse under the administrative burden, leaving potential athletes and artists with no venues in which to compete.

The complexity of the policy environment also has implications for the nonprofit role as Citizen. While there are many, including the Center for Lobbying in the Public Interest (CLPI), who argue for more advocacy by nonprofit organizations[47] and a relaxation of lobbying rules on nonprofits and philanthropic foundations,[48] there are potential concerns about whose interests will be advanced by such activity. When nonprofit organizations have to compete with for-profits in the marketplace, for example, they may have fewer available resources to engage in advocacy for their clientele.[49] Another potential problem involves 501(c)(4) organizations that can engage in unlimited lobbying activity, because many of these "are the lobby arms of business and other special interest groups, there to ensure voice for the wealthy and powerful."[50] The *Citizens United* Supreme Court decision, which allows for even more unrestricted political activity by 501(c)(4), 501(c)(5), and 501(c)(6) organizations, as well as corporations, has raised even more concerns about whose voice will be heard in the political process.

A similar fear has been raised about the use of foundations to raise money for federal agencies such as the Centers for Disease Control and the CIA, as discussed above. The concern is about the potential growth in political power of these government foundations vis-á-vis other nonprofit organizations. The playing field could "be hugely tilted" in favor of government foundations and their donors, who may "be able to earn access, face-time, and improved relations with decision-makers and legislators."[51] If these political trends continue, the role of Citizen for small and community nonprofits could be significantly curtailed.

Potential Negative Consequences of Commercialism. The trend toward commercialization of the nonprofit sector also raises concerns about issues such as conflict of interest and a shift of values for nonprofit managers. As the lines between for-profit enterprise and nonprofit organizations blur, the chances increase that the leadership of nonprofit organizations may personally benefit from the relationships.[52] Further, some fear that the values of the for-profit sector will begin to permeate the nonprofit sector such that financial gain is prioritized over good works, thereby changing the public-interest, mission-driven nature of the nonprofit sector. Again, we find the nonprofit sector at a crossroads between being able to pursue its various missions, which are often related to intangible goals such as improved civic engagement and political empowerment, less isolation among the elderly, or enhanced cultural experiences for a community, and the need to forge partnerships with for-profit organizations and enter the world of commercial endeavors themselves. This is another trend unlikely to abate in the coming decades and its consequences—good and bad—must be considered.

A simple example from the early experiences of venture philanthropists is illustrative. Peter Frumkin has noted that many donors who made their fortunes in the corporate world were appalled by the lack of measurable outcomes of nonprofit work; thus, they have sought efforts to measure the social returns on their philanthropic investments.[53] As discussed in Chapter 14, however, quantitative evaluation is not always feasible given the nature of nonprofit services. For this reason, Frumkin warns

> . . . it is hard to see how any project aimed at measuring ground level social return can be anything but a highly subjective and personal project, especially when philanthropy reaches into contentious areas of social problems. While many donors legitimately want some sort of evidence that their giving is making a difference, it is not clear that seeking to translate this "difference" into monetary terms will improve philanthropic practice in the long run.[54]

This illustrates that the danger of mission drift and goal displacement is real when nonprofits pursue donations, venture capital, and commercial sales; this danger must be avoided in order to maintain the credibility of the sector.

Moreover, some have raised fears that increased commercial profits, huge endowments, and large foundation investments can actually lead to declines in charitable donations—again shifting the nature of the nonprofit sector.[55] Similarly, perceived largesse could disincline volunteers from service if they view many nonprofits as too large to need unpaid work.[56] Further, increased use of social enterprise, commercial endeavors, and fee-for-service arrangements in the nonprofit sector may result in increased bifurcation of the provision of services between the most needy who cannot pay for them, and those with resources who can. The ultimate consequence is a change in the nature of the nonprofit sector, such that it begins to operate more in line with market principles to the detriment of the overall public interest.[57]

CONCLUSION

Because the public sector has played an important role in increasing the size, scope, and prominence of the nonprofit sector, Stephen Rathgeb Smith has long argued that the government must improve its ability to work with nonprofits and actively seek improvements to their management and effectiveness.[58] The vast policy milieu in which they operate—the policies they influence and make as well as the policies that affect and regulate them—creates opportunities and constraints for the nonprofit sector. These factors, along with the trends identified throughout this chapter, require nonprofits to be run by well-trained boards, executives, and managers who can secure adequate funding through appropriate means, navigate the world of public policy regulations, advocacy and implementation, and provide the services and opportunities desired by their communities.

Questions For Review

1. The lines between the three sectors are increasingly blurred in the United States. Discuss the most promising aspects and the most troublesome aspects of fewer clear distinctions between the sectors.

2. Does the rise of social enterprise, corporate social responsibility, and B Corps lead you to believe that a new form of organization—a fourth sector—may be emerging? Why or why not?

3. How will the public debate over acceptable levels of taxation and public spending affect the nonprofit sector, particularly its involvement in public policy creation and implementation?

4. Given the political, social, and economic trends facing the nonprofit sector, how difficult will it be for not-for-profit organizations to maintain their unique missions and place in the intersectoral system? How important is it that they do so?

Assignment

For this assignment, go to the webpage of your favorite nonprofit organization to assess the way in which the political, social, and economic trends identified in this chapter are affecting the organization. For example, to what extent does it rely on social enterprise, corporate philanthropy, or government contracts for its revenue? Has the nonprofit organization taken on responsibilities that were, at one time, considered primarily the purview of the public or for-profit sectors? Conversely, have for-profit organizations begun to compete with this or similar nonprofits? Has government retrenchment or cuts to funding significantly affected the organization? Can you identify characteristics of sector blurring occurring for this organization or others like it?

Suggested Readings

J. Gregory Dees, and Beth Battle Anderson, "Sector-Bending: Blurring Lines Between Nonprofit and For-Profit," *Society* 40 (2003): 16–27.

Peter Frumkin, "Inside Venture Philanthropy," *Society* 40 (2003): 7–15.

Michael E. Porter and Mark R. Kramer, "Creating Shared Value: How to Reinvent Capitalism—and Unleash a Wave of Innovation and Growth," *Harvard Business Review,* January–February 2011, 1–17; http://partnership2012.com/download/Creating%20Shared%20Value.pdf.

Steven Rathgeb Smith, "Government and Nonprofits in the Modern Age," *Society* 40 (2003): 36–45.

Steven Rathgeb Smith, "The Challenge of Strengthening Nonprofits and Civil Society," *Public Administration Review* (2008 Special Issue), S132–S145.

Web Resources

Aspen Institute (Fourth Sector Network), www.aspeninstitute.org/search/google/fourth%20sector?query=fourth%20sector&cx=010618789942109371844%3Apuahiq7sw6m&cof=FORID%3A11&sitesearch=

B Corporation, www.bcorporation.net

List of Venture Philanthropy Organizations, www.nvca.org/index.php?option=com_content&view=article&id=104&Itemid=171

Stanford Social Innovation Review, www.ssireview.org

Notes

CHAPTER 1

1. "The New York Society for the Prevention of Cruelty to Children 125th Anniversary, 1875–2000," New York Society for the Prevention of Cruelty to Children, http://www.nyspcc.org/nyspcc/history/attachment:en-us.pdf (accessed January 19, 2012).
2. E. Fellows Jenkins, "The New York Society for the Prevention of Cruelty to Children," *Annals of the American Academy of Political and Social Science 31*(1908): 192–194.
3. "The New York Society for the Prevention of Cruelty to Children 125th Anniversary, 1875–2000," New York Society for the Prevention of Cruelty to Children, http://www.nyspcc.org/nyspcc/history/attachment:en-us.pdf (accessed January 19, 2012).
4. Ibid.
5. Nancy Chandler, ed., Best Practices for Establishing a Children's Advocacy Center Program, 3rd ed. (Washington, DC: National Children's Alliance, 2000).
6. Shannon K. Vaughan and Shelly Arsneault, "Not-for-Profit Advocacy: Challenging Policy Images and Pursuing Policy Change," *Review of Policy Research 25* (2008): 414.
7. Alexis de Tocqueville, *Democracy in America,* vol. 2, trans. Phillips Bradley (New York: Vintage Classics, 1990), 106.
8. David C. Hammack, "American Debates on the Legitimacy of Foundations," in *The Legitimacy of Philanthropic Foundations,* ed. Kenneth Prewitt, Mattei Dogan, Steven Heydemann, and Stefan Toepler (New York: Russell Sage Foundation, 2006), 52–53.
9. David C. Hammack, "The Statute of Charitable Uses, 1601," in *Making the Nonprofit Sector in the United States,* ed. David C. Hammack (Bloomington: Indiana University Press, 1998), 6.
10. James J. Fishman, "The Political Use of Private Benevolence: The Statute of Charitable Uses," Pace Law Faculty Publications (2008): Paper 487; http://digitalcommons.pace.edu/lawfaculty/487 (accessed July 27, 2008).
11. With the exception of public safety testing organizations, which are granted tax-exempt status under section 501(c)(3) but to which contributions are not tax-deductible.
12. Nicholas Cafardi and Jaclyn Fabean Cherry, *Understanding Nonprofit and Tax-Exempt Organizations* (Newark, NJ: LexisNexis, 2006).
13. "Social Welfare Organizations," www.irs.gov/charities/nonprofits/article/0,,id=96178,00.html (last modified August 20, 2010); "Exempt Organizations General Issues: Charitable Contributions," www.irs.gov/charities/article/0,,id=139023,00.html (last modified November 1, 2010).
14. Foundation Center, *Foundation Fundamentals,* 8th ed. (Washington, DC: Foundation Center, 2008), 1.
15. Ibid.
16. Ibid.
17. Ibid.
18. Payout requirement refers to the percentage of total assets which a foundation is required to expend on program activities, grants, and/or administrative expenses; in general, the requirement is five percent.
19. Some corporations operate direct giving programs rather than establishing foundations; direct giving programs are not classified by the IRS and do not have public disclosure requirements. Corporate giving programs are discussed in Chapter 9.
20. Steven Lawrence and Reina Mukai, *Foundation Growth and Giving Estimates: Current Outlook* (Washington, DC: Foundation Center, 2010), http://foundationcenter.org/gainknowledge/research/pdf/fgge10.pdf (accessed August 6, 2011); Steven Lawrence and Reina Mukai, *Foundation Growth and Giving Estimates: Current Outlook* (Washington, DC: Foundation Center, 2008).
21. These data include only active foundations with assets of at least $1 million and/or giving of at least $100,000, in 2007.
22. National Center for Charitable Statistics (NCCS), "National Taxonomy of Exempt Entities—Core Codes: 2007 Desk Reference," (Washington, DC: Center on Nonprofits and Philanthropy at The Urban Institute, 2007), 1, nccsdataweb.urban.org/kbfiles/322/NTEE-CC-manual-2007a.pdf (accessed March 17, 2009).
23. Includes Environmental Quality, Protection, and Beautification; and Animal-Related Organizations.
24. Includes Health; Mental Health, Crisis Intervention; Diseases, Disorders, Medical Disciplines; and Medical Research.
25. Includes Crime, Legal Related; Employment, Job Related; Food, Agriculture, and Nutrition; Housing, Shelter; Public Safety; Recreation, Sports, Leisure, Athletics; Youth Development; and Human Services—Multipurpose and Other.
26. Includes Civil Rights, Social Action, Advocacy; Community Improvement, Capacity Building; Philanthropy, Voluntarism, and Grantmaking Foundations; Science and Technology Research Institutes, Services; Social Science Research Institutes, Services; and Public, Society Benefit—Multipurpose and Other.
27. Form 990 is an information return that tax-exempt organizations are required to file; more information on the Form 990 is provided in Chapter 4.
28. Elizabeth T. Boris and Katie L. Roeger, "Grassroots Civil Society: The Scope and Dimensions of Small Public Charities," Charting Civil Society: A Series by the Center on Nonprofits and Philanthropy. Washington, DC: The Urban Institute, 2010).
29. Ibid.
30. The term "church" is used (but not specifically defined) in the Internal Revenue Code, and the IRS uses it as a generic term to encompass all places of worship such as mosques, synagogues, and temples as well as conventions and associations of churches. Therefore, throughout this book we also use "church" in the same generic sense when it is necessary to differentiate the unique tax and regulatory status afforded these organizations as distinct from other nonprofits.
31. Michael O'Neill, *Nonprofit Nation: A New Look at the Third America* (San Francisco: Jossey-Bass, 2002).
32. Ibid.; and Kirsten A. Grønbjerg, "The U.S. Nonprofit Human Service Sector: A Creeping Revolution," *Nonprofit and Voluntary Sector Quarterly 30* (2001): 276–297.

33. Bureau of Economic Analysis, Table 1.3.5. Gross Value Added by Sector, 1999—2011" http://www.bea.gov/iTable/iTable.cfm?ReqID=9&step=1 (last modified July 27, 2012).
34. Bureau of Economic Analysis, Table 1.1.5. Gross Domestic Product, http//:www.bea.gov/iTable/iTable.cfm?ReqID=9&step=1 (last modified July 27, 2012).
35. Katie L. Roeger, Amy Blackwood, and Sarah L. Pettijohn, *The Nonprofit Sector in Brief: Public Charities, Giving, and Volunteering*, 2011 (Washington, DC: The Urban Institute, 2010).
36. Research Area: Nonprofit Sector, www.urban.org/nonprofits/more.cfm.
37. Amy Butler, "Wages in the Nonprofit Sector: Management, Professional, and Administrative Support Occupations," U.S. Bureau of Labor Statistics, http://www.bls.gov/opub/cwc/cm20081022ar01p1.htm (last modified April 15, 2009; accessed September 1, 2012).
38. Wing et al., Nonprofit Sector in Brief, 2010.
39. Carnegie Foundation, Our Mission, 2008, www.carnegie.org/sub/about/mission.html (accessed August 4, 2008).
40. Rockefeller Foundation, Original Charter. An Act to Incorporate The Rockefeller Foundation, p. 3, www.rockfound.org/about_us/Rockefeller_Foundation_Charter.pdf (accessed September 29, 2009).
41. David L. Gies, J. Steven Ott, and Jay M. Shafritz, *The Nonprofit Organization: Essential Readings.* (Pacific Grove, CA: Brooks/Cole Publishing Company, 1990), 375.
42. It is important to note that critics at both ends of the ideological spectrum have questioned the benefits of foundation resources used to facilitate collective action. Political activities funded by liberal foundations such as Soros Foundations Network founded by billionaire George Soros (www.soros.org) incite attack by many on the right just as top conservative foundation grantmakers such as the Sarah Scaife Foundation (www.scaife.com) are criticized for "financing the right wing policy juggernaut" (*Nonprofit Times*, March 9, 2009). See Thomas R. Dye, "Oligarchic Tendencies in National Policy-Making: the Role of the Private Policy-Planning Organizations," *Journal of Politics 40* (1978): 309–331; Judith Sealander, *Private Wealth and Public Life* (Baltimore: Johns Hopkins University Press, 1997); Kenneth Prewitt, Mattei Dogan, Steven Heydemann, and Stefan Toepler, eds. *The Legitimacy of Philanthropic Foundations.* (New York: Russell Sage Foundation, 2006).
43. "Foreign Affairs Advertising: Influence on Policy Issues," http://www.foreignaffairs.com/about-us/advertising/influence (accessed January 17, 2012).
44. David F. Arons, "Public Policy and Civic Engagement: Foundations in Action," in *Power in Policy, A Funder's Guide to Advocacy and Civic Participation*, ed. David F. Arons (Saint Paul, MN: Fieldstone Alliance, 2007).
45. Mancur Olson, *The Logic of Collective Action.* (Cambridge, MA: Harvard University Press, 1965); Burton A. Weisbrod, *The Voluntary Sector* (Lexington: D.C. Heath & Company, 1977); Lester M. Salamon, *Partners in Public Service* (Baltimore: Johns Hopkins University Press, 1995); Dennis R. Young, "Complementary, Supplementary, or Adversarial? A Theoretical and Historical Examination of Nonprofit-Government Relations in the United States," in *Nonprofits and Government*, ed. Elizabeth T. Boris and C. Eugene Steuerle (Washington, DC: Urban Institute Press, 1999).
46. Garrett Hardin, "The Tragedy of the Commons," *Science, 162* (1968): 1243–1248.
47. Deborah Stone, *Policy Paradox: The Art of Political Decision Making* (New York: W.W. Norton, 2002).
48. Ibid, 28.
49. James Q. Wilson, *The Politics of Regulation* (New York: Basic Books, 1980).
50. Theodore J. Lowi, "American Business, Public Policy, Case Studies and Political Theory," *World Politics* 16 (1964): 677–715.
51. B. Guy Peters. *American Public Policy: Promise and Performance*, 5th ed. (New York: Chatham House, 1999), 4.
52. Lowi, American Business; Dye, *Oligarchic Tendencies;* Helmut K. Anheier, *Nonprofit Organizations, Theory, Management, Policy.* (New York: Routledge, 2005); Steven Rathgeb Smith and Michael Lipsky, *Nonprofits for Hire: The Welfare State in the Age of Contracting* (Cambridge, MA: Harvard University Press, 1994).
53. Frank R. Baumgartner and Bryan D. Jones, *Agendas and Instability in American Politics* (Chicago: University of Chicago Press, 1993); Stone, *Policy Paradox.*
54. John W. Kingdon, *Agendas, Alternatives, and Public Policies* (Boston: Little, Brown, 1984).
55. Charles Lindblom, "The Science of 'Muddling Through,' " *Public Administration Review 19* (1959), 86.
56. Hugh Heclo, "Issue Networks and the Executive Establishment," in *The Political System*, ed. Anthony King (Washington, DC: American Enterprise Institute for Public Policy Research, 1978), 87–124; Hank Jenkins-Smith and Paul Sabatier, "Evaluating the Advocacy Coalition Framework," *Journal of Public Policy 14* (1994): 175–203; Young-Jung Kim and Chul-Young Roh, "Beyond the Advocacy Coalition Framework in the Policy Process," *International Journal of Public Administration, 31* (2008): 668–689; Michael Mintrom and Sandra Vergari, "Policy Networks and Innovation Diffusion: The Case of State Education Reforms," *Journal of Politics 60* (1998): 126–148; Arons, *Public Policy.*
57. Jenkins-Smith and Sabatier, "Evaluating," 179.
58. Policy-oriented learning refers to "relatively enduring alternations of thought or behavioral intentions that result from experience and/or new information and that are concerned with the attainment or revision of policy objectives." Paul Sabatier and Hank Jenkins-Smith, "The Advocacy Coalition Framework," in *Theories of the Policy Process*, ed. Paul Sabatier (Boulder, CO: Westview Press, 1999), 123.

Chapter 2

1. The five-year limit is a *lifetime limit* for adult recipients. While some states, including California, offer continued benefits in certain exceptional cases after five years, other states limit lifetime welfare benefits to less than five years.
2. As part of the reform to the former Aid to Families with Dependent Children program, PRWORA allows states to determine how long recipients remain eligible for welfare benefits without having found employment; states may also exempt a certain percentage of their caseload from this requirement.
3. Kathleen D. McCarthy, *American Creed: Philanthropy and the Rise of Civil Society, 1700–1865* (Chicago: University of Chicago Press, 2003).
4. Francesca Gamber, "The Public Sphere and the End of American Abolitionism, 1833–1870," *Slavery and Abolition* 28 (2007): 351–368.
5. Laurence O'Toole Jr., "American Intergovernmental Relations: An Overview," in *American Intergovernmental Relations*, 4th ed., ed. Laurence J. O'Toole Jr. (Washington, DC: CQ Press, 2007).
6. McCarthy, *American Creed.*
7. Lester M. Salamon, *Partners in Public Service* (Baltimore: Johns Hopkins University Press, 1995).

8. McCarthy, *American Creed,* 38.
9. Thomas J. Anton, *American Federalism and Public Policy: How the System Works* (New York: Random House, 1989), 41.
10. Morton Grodzins, *The American System: A New View of Government in the United States,* ed. Daniel J. Elazar (Chicago: Rand McNally, 1966).
11. Marguerite G. Rosenthal, "Public or Private Children's Services? Privatization in Retrospect," *Social Service Review* 74 (2000): 281–305.
12. Salamon, *Partners in Public Service.*
13. Ibid.
14. Paul E. Peterson. *The Price of Federalism.* (Washington, DC: The Brookings Institution, 1995).
15. Ibid.
16. Vincent Ostrom, *The Meaning of American Federalism* (San Francisco: ICS Press, 1991), 47–48.
17. Seymour Martin Lipset, *American Exceptionalism: A Double-Edged Sword* (New York: W.W. Norton & Company, 1996), 31
18. Lipset, *American Exceptionalism;* Helmut K. Anheier, *Nonprofit Organizations, Theory, Management, Policy* (New York: Routledge, 2005).
19. Alisha Coleman-Jensen, Mark Nord, Margaret Andrews, and Steven Carlson, *Household Food Security in the United States in 2010* (Washington, DC: U.S. Dept of Agriculture, Economic Research Services, 2011).
20. Marc Nerfin, "Neither Prince nor Merchant: Citizen—an Introduction to the Third System," in *World Economy in Transition,* ed. K. Ahooja-Patel, A.G. Drabek, and Marc Nerfin (Oxford, UK: Pergamon Press, 1986).
21. Adil Najam, "Understanding the Third Sector: Revisiting the Prince, the Merchant and the Citizen," *Nonprofit Management and Leadership* 7 (1996): 203–219.
22. Ibid., 209, emphasis in original.
23. Stephen Goldsmith and William D. Eggers, *Governing by Network: The New Shape of the Public Sector* (Washington, DC: Brookings Institution Press, 2004), 6.
24. Alfred Vernis, Maria Iglesias, Beatriz Sanz, and Angel Saz-Carranza, *Nonprofit Organizations: Challenges and Collaboration,* trans. M. Donadini (New York: Palgrave MacMillan, 2006).
25. Peter Frumkin, *On Being Nonprofit: A Conceptual and Policy Primer* (Cambridge, MA: Harvard University Press, 2002).
26. See Burton A. Weisbrod, *The Voluntary Sector* (Lexington: D.C. Heath & Company, 1977); Burton A. Weisbrod, ed., *To Profit or Not to Profit: The Commercial Transformation of the Nonprofit Sector* (New York: Cambridge University Press, 1998).
27. Ibid.
28. Dennis R. Young, "Entrepreneurship and the Behavior of Nonprofit Organizations: Elements of a Theory," in *Nonprofit Firms in a Three Sector Economy,* ed. Michelle J. White (Washington, DC: Urban Institute Press, 1981).
29. Ibid.
30. Katherine M. O'Regan and Sharon M. Oster, "Nonprofit and For-Profit Partnerships: Rationale and Challenges of Cross-Sector Contracting," *Nonprofit and Voluntary Sector Quarterly* 29 (2000): 120–140.
31. R. Kent Weaver, *Ending Welfare as We Know It* (Washington, DC: Brookings Institution Press, 2000).
32. Welfare reform was part of a broader federalism experiment during the mid-1990s often called the devolution revolution. Spearheaded by the Republican Contract with America, the point of devolution was to move program regulation, responsibility, and funding from the federal to the state level, purportedly in an effort to place policy and program decisions closer to those most affected by them. Seen by many as more of a whimper than a revolution, welfare reform and the ability for states to adjust their highway speed limits were the two most recognized results of this effort (see O'Toole 2007).
33. Weaver, *Ending Welfare.*
34. For a thorough discussion of the passage of welfare reform, see R. Kent Weaver, *Ending Welfare as We Know It* (Washington, DC: Brookings Institution Press, 2000).
35. Pamela Winston, Andrew Burwick, Sheena McConnell, and Richard Roper, *Privatization of Welfare Services: A Review of the Literature* (Washington, DC: Mathematica Policy Research, Inc., 2002): 4.
36. United States General Accounting Office, Welfare Reform: Interim Report on Potential Ways to Strengthen Federal Oversight of State and Local Contracting (Washington, DC: GAO-02–245, 2002).
37. Elizabeth T. Boris, Erwin de Leon, Katie L. Roeger, and Milena Nikolova, *National Study of Nonprofit-Government Contracting* (Washington, DC: The Urban Institute, 2010).
38. Ram A. Cnaan and Stephanie C. Boddie. "Charitable Choice and Faith-Based Welfare: A Call for Social Work," *Social Work* 47 (2002): 224.
39. Cnaan and Boddie, "Charitable Choice"; Carol J. De Vita and Eric C. Twombly, "Nonprofits and Federalism," in *Nonprofits and Government,* 2nd ed., ed. Elizabeth T. Boris and C. Eugene Steuerle, editors (Washington, DC: Urban Institute Press, 2006); Sheila Suess Kennedy, "Privatization and Prayer: The Challenge of Charitable Choice," *American Review of Public Administration* 33 (2003): 5–19; Sheila Suess Kennedy and Wolfgang Billeted, *Charitable Choice at Work* (Washington, DC: Georgetown University Press, 2007); J. J. DiIulio, "Getting Faith-Based Programs Right," *The Public Interest* 155 (2004): 75–88.
40. Kennedy, "Privatization and Prayer"; Kennedy and Bielefeld, *Charitable Choice at Work.*
41. Arthur E. Farnsley II, "Can Faith-Based Organizations Compete?" *Nonprofit and Voluntary Sector Quarterly* 30 (2001): 99–111; Cnaan and Boddie, "Charitable Choice"; Kennedy, "Privatization and Prayer."
42. Stephen V. Monsma, "Nonprofit and Faith-Based Welfare-to-Work Programs," *Society* 40 (2003): 13–18.
43. John R. Belcher, Donald Fandetti, and Danny Cole, "Is Christian Religious Conservatism Compatible with the Liberal Social Welfare State?" *Social Work* 49 (2004): 274.
44. De Vita and Twombly, "Nonprofits and Federalism."
45. Janet Poppendieck, *Sweet Charity? Emergency Food and the End of Entitlement* (New York: Viking, 1998).
46. Kennedy and Bielefeld, *Charitable Choice at Work;* Michael Leo Owens and R. Drew Smith, "Congregations in Low-Income Neighborhoods and the Implications for Social Welfare Policy Research," *Nonprofit and Voluntary Sector Quarterly* 34 (2005): 316–339; Steven Rathgeb Smith and Michael R. Sosin, "The Varieties of Faith-Related Agencies," *Public Administration Review* 61 (2001): 651–670.
47. Helen Rose Ebaugh, Janet S. Chafetz, and Paula Pipes. "Funding Good Works: Funding Sources of Faith-Based Social Service Coalitions," *Nonprofit and Voluntary Sector Quarterly* 34 (2005): 448–472.
48. Lisa M. Montiel and David J. Wright, *Getting a Piece of the Pie: Federal Grants to Faith-Based Social Service Organizations* (Albany, NY: Roundtable on Religion and Social Welfare Policy, 2006).
49. De Vita and Twombly, "Nonprofits and Federalism"; Kennedy and Bielefeld, *Charitable Choice at Work;* Smith and Sosin, "Varieties";

DiIulio, "Getting Faith-Based Programs"; Rebecca Sager and Laura Susan Stephens, "Serving Up Sermons: Clients' Reactions to Religious Elements at Congregation-run Feeding Establishments," *Nonprofit and Voluntary Sector Quarterly,* 34 (2005): 297–315; Mark Chaves and William Tsitsos. "Congregations and Social Services: What They Do, How They Do It, and With Whom," *Nonprofit and Voluntary Sector Quarterly* 30 (2001): 660–683.

50. De Vita and Twombly, "Nonprofits and Federalism."
51. Salamon, *Partners in Public Service,* 21.
52. Michael J. Austin, "The Changing Relationship between Nonprofit Organizations and Public Social Service Agencies in the Era of Welfare Reform," *Nonprofit and Voluntary Sector Quarterly* 32 (2003): 97–114; David M. Van Slyke, "Agents or Stewards: Using Theory to Understand the Government-Nonprofit Social Service Contracting Relationship," *Journal of Public Administration Research and Theory* 17 (2007): 157–187.
53. Mary Bryna Sanger, *The Welfare Marketplace: Privatization and Welfare Reform* (Washington, DC: The Brookings Institution, 2003); Barbara Peat and Dan L. Costley, "Effective Contracting of Social Services," *Nonprofit Management & Leadership* 12 (2001): 55–74.
54. Boris et al., National Study; De Vita and Twombly, "Nonprofits and Federalism"; Austin, "The Changing Relationship"; Sanger, *The Welfare Marketplace.*
55. Austin, "The Changing Relationship."
56. Lester M. Salamon, "The Resilient Sector," in *The State of Nonprofit America,* ed. Lester M. Salamon (Washington, DC: Brookings Institution Press, 2002).
57. Bradford H. Gray and Mark Schlesinger, "Health," in *The State of Nonprofit America,* ed. Lester M. Salamon (Washington, DC: Brookings Institution Press, 2002), 76.
58. Gray and Schlesinger, "Health."
59. Peter Frumkin and Alice Andre-Clark, "When Missions, Markets, and Politics Collide: Values and Strategy in the Nonprofit Human Services," *Nonprofit and Voluntary Sector Quarterly* 29 (2000): Supplement:141–163.
60. Sanger, *The Welfare Marketplace.*
61. Ibid., 5.
62. Weisbrod, *To Profit or Not to Profit;* Dennis R. Young. "Complementary, Supplementary, or Adversarial? A Theoretical and Historical Examination of Nonprofit-Government Relations in the United States," in *Nonprofits and Government,* ed. Elizabeth T. Boris and C. Eugene Steuerle (Washington, DC: Urban Institute Press, 1999); Nicole P. Marwell and Paul-Brian McInerney, "Nonprofit/For-Profit Continuum: Theorizing the Dynamics of Mixed-Form Markets," *Nonprofit and Voluntary Sector Quarterly* 34 (2005): 7–28.
63. Weisbrod, *To Profit or Not to Profit;* Gray and Schlesinger, "Health;" Henry B. Hansmann, "The Role of Nonprofit Enterprise," *Yale Law Journal* 89 (1980): 835–898; Dennis R. Young and Lester M. Salamon, "Commercialization, Social Ventures, and For-Profit Competition," in *The State of Nonprofit America,* ed. Lester M. Salamon (Washington, DC: Brookings Institution Press, 2002).
64. Weisbrod, *To Profit or Not to Profit;* Anna Haley-Lock and J. Kruzich, "Serving Workers in the Human Services," *Nonprofit and Voluntary Sector Quarterly* 37 (2008): 443–467; Rein De Cooman, Sara De Gieter, Roland Pepermans, and Marc Jegers, "A Cross-Sector Comparison of Motivation-Related Concepts in For-Profit and Not-for-Profit Service Organizations," *Nonprofit and Voluntary Sector Quarterly* 40 (2009): 296–317.
65. Frank A. Sloan, "Commercialism in Nonprofit Hospitals," in *To Profit or Not to Profit: The Commercial Transformation of the Nonprofit Sector,* ed. Burton A. Weisbrod (New York: Cambridge University Press, 1998).
66. Frumkin and Andre-Clark, "When Missions."
67. Marwell and McInerney, "Nonprofit/For-Profit Continuum."
68. Gray and Schlesinger, "Health"; Lester M. Salamon, "The Resilient Sector," in *The State of Nonprofit America,* ed. Lester M. Salamon (Washington, DC: Brookings Institution Press, 2002); O'Regan and Oster, "Nonprofit and For-Profit Partnerships;" Helmut K. Anheier, *Nonprofit Organizations, Theory, Management, Policy* (New York: Routledge, 2005).
69. Marwell and McInerney, "Nonprofit/For-Profit Continuum."
70. Austin, "The Changing Relationship;" Paul C. Light, *Sustaining Nonprofit Performance* (Washington, DC: Brookings Institution Press, 2004).
71. O'Regan and Sharon M. Oster, "Nonprofit and For-Profit Partnerships," 122.
72. William B. Werther Jr. and Evan M. Berman, *Third Sector Management: The Art of Managing Nonprofit Organizations* (Washington, DC: Georgetown University Press, 2001).
73. Beth Gazeley and Jeffrey L. Brudney, "The Purpose (and Perils) of Government-Nonprofit Partnership," *Nonprofit and Voluntary Sector Quarterly* 36 (2007): 389–451.
74. Ibid.
75. Salamon, "The Resilient Sector."
76. Sanger, *The Welfare Marketplace.*
77. O'Regan and Sharon M. Oster, "Nonprofit and For-Profit Partnerships."
78. Ibid.
79. Vernis, Iglesias, Sanz, and Saz-Carranza, "Nonprofit Organizations."
80. Jennifer Niemela, "Target Boosts Giving to Salvation Army," *Minneapolis / St. Paul Business Journal* , December 16, 2008; http://twincities.bizjournals.com/twincities/stories/2008/12/15/daily15.html (accessed on October 30, 2009).
81. *Memphis Business Journal,* "Target, Proctor & Gamble Partner to Raise Funds for St. Jude," October 13, 2009; http://twincities.bizjournals.com/memphis/stories/2009/10/12/daily7.html (accessed October 30, 2009).
82. Jim Miara, "Detroit: The New Paradigm," *Urban Land Magazine;* http://urbanland.uli.org/Articles/2011/July/MiaraDetroit (accessed February 7, 2012).
83. Salamon, "The Resilient Sector," 40.
84. R. Scott Folser, *Working Better Together* (Washington DC: Foundation Center, 2002).
85. Folser, *Working Better;* Heerad Sabeti and the Fourth Sector Network Concept Working Group, *The Emerging Fourth Sector* (Washington, DC: The Aspen Institute, 2009.)
86. Sabeti, *The Emerging Fourth Sector.*
87. Cafédirect Annual Report, 2010.
88. Cafédirect 2011 Annual Report, http://cafedirect.co.uk/wp-content/uploads/downloads/2011/05/Annual-Report-2009–2010.pdf.
89. Sabeti, *The Emerging Fourth Sector.*
90. For more information on the Third Sector Initiative and the Fourth Sector Network, see Web Resources at the end of this chapter.

Chapter 3

1. Panel on the Nonprofit Sector, "Principles of Good Governance and Ethical Practice: A Guide for Charities and Foundations" (Washington, DC: Independent Sector, 2007), 2.

2. Leighann C. Neilson, "The Development of Marketing in the Canadian Museum Community, 1840–1989," *Journal of Macromarketing* 23 (2003): 16–30; Thomas J. Tierney and Alan Tuck, "To Succeed, Philanthropy Needs to Be Rooted in Deep Personal Beliefs," http://ejewishphilanthropy.com/to-succeed-philanthropy-needs-to-be-rooted-in-deep-personal-beliefs/ (accessed February 24, 2011).
3. Peter Frumkin, *On Being Nonprofit: A Conceptual and Policy Primer* (Cambridge, MA: Harvard University Press, 2002).
4. Burton A. Weisbrod, *The Voluntary Sector* (Lexington: D.C. Heath & Company, 1977).
5. Henry B. Hansmann, "The Role of Nonprofit Enterprise," *Yale Law Journal* 89 (1980): 835–898.
6. Ronald H. Coase, *American Philanthropy,* 2nd ed. (Chicago: University of Chicago Press, 1988).
7. Dennis R. Young, "Complementary, Supplementary, or Adversarial? A Theoretical and Historical Examination of Nonprofit-Government Relations in the United States," in *Nonprofits and Government,* ed. Elizabeth T. Boris and C. Eugene Steuerle (Washington, DC: Urban Institute Press, 1999); Mary K. Marvel and Howard P. Marvel, "Outsourcing Oversight," *Public Administration Review* 67 (2007): 521–530.
8. Lester A. Salamon, *Partners in Public Service* (Baltimore: Johns Hopkins University Press, 1995).
9. Paul E. Peterson, *The Price of Federalism* (Washington, DC: The Brookings Institution, 1995).
10. Jeffrey Pfeffer and Gerald R. Salancik, *The External Control of Organizations* (New York: Harper and Row, 1978).
11. Kirsten A. Grønbjerg, *Understanding Nonprofit Funding* (San Francisco: Jossey-Bass, 1993).
12. Karen A. Froelich, "Diversification of Revenue Strategies: Evolving Resource Dependence in Nonprofit Organizations," *Nonprofit and Voluntary Sector Quarterly* 28 (1999): 246–268.
13. Ibid.; Deborah A. Carroll and Keely Jones Stater, "Revenue Diversification in Nonprofit Organizations: Does it Lead to Financial Stability?" *Journal of Public Administration Research and Theory* 19 (2008): 947–966.
14. Amanda L. Wilsker and Dennis R. Young, "How Does Program Composition Affect the Revenues of Nonprofit Organizations? Investigating a Benefits Theory of Nonprofit Finance," *Public Finance Review* 38 (2010): 193–216.
15. Frumkin, *On Being Nonprofit,* 2002; Dennis R. Young and Lester M. Salamon, "Commercialization, Social Ventures, and For-Profit Competition," in *The State of Nonprofit America,* ed. Lester M. Salamon (Washington, DC: Brookings Institution Press, 2002).
16. Frumkin, *On Being Nonprofit,* 21.
17. Frumkin, *On Being Nonprofit.*
18. Ibid.; Margaret J. Wyzominski, "Arts and Culture," in *The State of Nonprofit America,* ed. Lester M. Salamon. (Washington, DC: Brookings Institution Press, 2002).
19. Bill Weir, "Bill Gates on Using His Money to Save Lives, Fixing U.S. Schools, Reflecting on Steve Jobs," http://abcnews.go.com/blogs/technology/2012/01/bill-gates-on-using-his-money-to-save-lives-and-fix-u-s-schools-and-steve-jobs/ (accessed January 24, 2012).
20. Peter Dobkin Hall, *The Organization of American Culture, 1700–1900: Private Institutions, Elites, and the Origins of American Nationality* (New York: New York University Press, 1982); Sidney Tarrow, " 'The Very Excess of Democracy': State Building and Contentious Politics in America," in *Social Movements and American Political Institutions,* ed. Anne N. Costain and Andrew S. McFarland (Lanham, MD: Rowman & Littlefield, 1998); Mark Chaves, "Religious Congregations," in *The State of Nonprofit America,* ed. Lester M. Salamon (Washington, DC: Brookings Institution Press, 2002); Frumkin, *On Being Nonprofit.*
21. *American Civil Liberties Union of Massachusetts v. Kathleen Sebelius,* Civil Action No. 09–10038-RGS, March 23, 2012, Memorandum and Order on Cross-Motions for Summary Judgment and Defendant-Intervenor's Motion to Dismiss, http://pacer.mad.uscourts.gov/dc/cgi-bin/recentops.pl?filename=stearns/pdf/aclu%20sj%20final.pdf.
22. *American Civil Liberties Union of Massachusetts v. Kathleen Sebelius,* p. 6.
23. United States Conference of Catholic Bishops (USCCB), "Consolidated Financial Statements," December 31, 2010, and 2009, http//:www.usccb.org/about/financial-reporting/upload/Final-Consolidated-Report_07–25–2011.pdf.
24. *American Civil Liberties Union of Massachusetts v. Kathleen Sebelius.*
25. This is not a hypothetical example; while ultimately removed from the appropriations bill, this example of a questionable use of federal funds received national attention.
26. Shannon K. Vaughan, Government-Nonprofit Relations and Policy Change: The Impact of Children's Advocacy Centers on State Policy Adoptions. (doctoral dissertation, University of Kentucky, 2003)
27. Frank R. Baumgartner and Bryan D. Jones, *Agendas and Instability in American Politics* (Chicago: University of Chicago Press, 1993).
28. Michael Cohen, James G. March, and Johan P. Olsen, "A Garbage Can Theory of Organizational Choice," *Administrative Science Quarterly* 17 (1972): 1–25; John W. Kingdon, *Agendas, Alternatives, and Public Policies* (Boston: Little, Brown, 1984).
29. A balance between what citizens want and what public policies provide.
30. Baumgartner and Jones, *Agendas and Instability in American Politics,* 15.
31. Edella Schlager, "A Comparison of Frameworks, Theories, and Models of Policy Processes," in *Theories of the Policy Process,* ed. Paul A. Sabatier (Boulder, CO: Westview Press, 1999); James L. True, Bryan D. Jones, and Frank R. Baumgartner, "Punctuated-Equilibrium Theory: Explaining Stability and Change in American Policymaking," in *Theories of the Policy Process,* ed. Paul A. Sabatier (Boulder, CO: Westview Press, 1999).
32. Baumgarner and Jones, *Agendas and Instability in American Politics,* p. 25.
33. Deborah Stone, *Policy Paradox: The Art of Political Decision Making* (New York: W.W. Norton, 2002).
34. Thomas E. Nelson and Zoe M. Oaxley, "Framing Effects on Belief Importance and Opinion," *Journal of Politics* 61(1999): 1040–1067; Thomas E. Nelson, Rosalie A. Clawson, and Zoe M. Oxley, "Media Framing of a Civil Liberties Case and Its Effects on Tolerance," American Political Science Review *91* (1997): 567–584.
35. Shannon K. Vaughan and Shelly Arsneault, "Not-for-Profit Advocacy: Challenging Policy Images and Pursuing Policy Change," *Review of Policy Research 25* (2008): 411–428.
36. Marcia L. Godwin and Jean Reith Schroedel, "Policy Diffusion and Strategies for Promoting Policy Change," *Policy Studies Journal 28* (2000): 760–776.
37. E. E. Schattschneider, "Intensity, Visibility, Direction and Scope," *American Political Science Review* 51 (1957): 933–942.
38. Bryan D. Jones, *Reconceiving Decision-Making in Democratic Politics* (Chicago: University of Chicago Press, 1994).
39. Elaine B. Sharp, "The Dynamics of Issue Expansion: Cases from Disability Rights and Fetal Research Controversy," *Journal of Politics* 56 (1994): 919–939; Mark Schneider and Paul Teske, with Michael Mintrom, *Public Entrepreneurs: Agents for Change in American*

Government (Princeton: Princeton University Press, 1995); Keith Boeckelman, "Issue Definition in State Economic Development Policy," *Policy Studies Journal 23* (1997): 286–99; Michael Mintrom, *Policy Entrepreneurs and School Choice* (Washington, DC: Georgetown University Press, 2000).

40. Grantmaking for a Healthier California, CalWellness.org, www.calwellness.org/about_us/history_and_financial.htm.
41. Frank O. Sotomayor, "Violence Prevention: A Long-Term Commitment to Keep Youth Safe," The California Wellness Foundation Grantee, http://www.calwellness.org/assets/docs/grantee/grantee_fall_2011/Cover_Story.pdf (accessed Fall/Winter 2011).
42. Gary L. Yates, Little Hoover Commission Testimony, http://www.lhc.ca.gov/lhc/prevent/YatesSept00.pdf, p. 2 (accessed September 28, 2000).
43. Frumkin, *On Being Nonprofit.*
44. Laurie Davies, "25 Years of Saving Lives," *Driven,* Fall 2005, 10, http://www.madd.org/about-us/history/madd25thhistory.pdf.
45. Quoted in Laurie Davies, "25 Years of Saving Lives," *Driven,* Fall 2005, 9–17.
46. Mothers Against Drunk Driving, www.madd.org/about-us/madd-goals.html.
47. Baumgartner and Jones, *Agendas and Instability in American Politics;* Cohen, March, and Olsen, "A Garbage Can Theory of Organizational Choice"; John W. Kingdon, *Agendas, Alternatives, and Public Policies*; Elaine B. Sharp, *The Sometime Connection: Public Opinion and Social Policy* (Albany: State University of New York Press, 1999); Nikolaos Zahariadis, "Ambiguity, Time, and Multiple Streams," in *Theories of the Policy Process,* ed. Paul A. Sabatier (Boulder, CO: Westview Press, 1999).
48. Baumgartner and Jones, *Agendas and Instability in American Politics* 31.
49. Brent S. Steel and John C. Pierce, "Resources and Strategies of Interest Groups and Industry Representatives Involved in Federal Forest Policy," *Social Science Journal* 33 (1996): 401–420.
50. Kim Lane Scheppele and Jack L. Walker Jr., "The Litigation Strategies of Interest Groups," in *Mobilizing Interest Groups in America,* ed. Jack L. Walker Jr. (Ann Arbor: University of Michigan Press, 1991).
51. Deborah Stone, *Policy Paradox.*
52. Suzanne M. Robbins, "Interest Group Politics: Strategic Choices in Environmental Policy Implementation," Paper presented at the Annual Meeting of the Southern Political Science Association, Atlanta, GA, November 7–9, 2001.
53. Godwin and Schroedel, "Policy Diffusion," 760–776.
54. Frances Stokes Berry and William D. Berry, "Innovation and Diffusion Models in Policy Research," in *Theories of the Policy Process,* 2nd ed., ed. Paul A. Sabatier (Boulder, CO: Westview Press, 2007).
55. Mooney and Lee, "Legislating Morality," 604.
56. Jack Walker Jr. "The Diffusion of Innovations Among the American States," *American Political Science Review* 63 (1969): 880–99.
57. Virginia Gray, "Innovation in the States: A Diffusion Study," *American Political Science Review* 67 (1973): 1174–1185.
58. Berry and Berry, "Innovation and Diffusion Models."
59. Christopher Z. Mooney and Mei-Hsien Lee, "Legislating Morality in the American States: The Case of Pre-Roe Abortion Regulation Reform," *American Journal of Political Science* 39 (1995): 599–627.

Chapter 4

1. Marion R. Fremont-Smith, *Governing Nonprofit Organizations: Federal and State Law and Regulation.* (Cambridge, MA: Belknap Press of Harvard University Press, 2004).
2. Christopher Keyes and Grayson Schaffer, "Greg Mortenson and CAI Roll Out a Defense," *Outside Online,* http://outside-blog.away.com/blog/2011/05/greg-mortenson-and-central-asia-institute-respond.html?utm_source=feedburner&utm_medium=feed&utm_campaign=Feed%3A+OutsideMagazineBlog+%280utside+Magazine+-+Blog%29; Roxanne Roberts and Amy Argetsinger, "Update: Jon Krakauer Slams Greg Mortenson in Digital Expose," Reliable Source, *Washington Post,* http://www.washingtonpost.com/blogs/reliable-source/post/jon-krakauer-slams-greg-mortenson-in-digital-expose/2011/04/19/AFxToE6D_blog.html.
3. Jack Siegel, "Three Cups of Tea and a Class Action Lawsuit: Drink the Tea, Dismiss the Lawsuit. Charity Governance Consulting, LLC," http://www.charitygovernance.com/charity_governance/2011/05/three-cups-of-tea-and-a-class-action-lawsuit-drink-the-tea-dismiss-the-lawsuit.html.
4. David Sherman, "Settlement Reached in Mortenson, Central Asia Institute Investigation," *KRTV.com,* http://www.krtv.com/news/settlement-reached-in-mortenson-central-asia-institute-investigation/.
5. Associated Press, "Charity Dropped from 'Three Cups of Tea' Lawsuit," http://www.msnbc.msn.com/id/43483547/ns/us_news-giving/t/charity-dropped-three-cups-tea-lawsuit/.
6. Theodore J. Lowi, "Four Systems of Policy, Politics, and Choice," *Public Administration Review* 33 (1972): 298–310; Randall B. Ripley and Grace A. Franklin, *Congress, the Bureaucracy, and Public Policy,* Homewood, IL: Dorsey Press, 1980.
7. Marion R. Fremont-Smith, *Governing Nonprofit Organizations.*
8. IRS, *Publication 557 Tax-Exempt Status for Your Organization.* Washington, DC: Department of the Treasury, Internal Revenue Service, 2005: 17.
9. Alan L. Feld, *Rendering Unto Caesar or Electioneering for Caesar? Loss of Church Tax Exemption for Participation in Electoral Politics,* 42 B.C.L. Rev. 931 (2001), http://lawdigitalcommons.bc.edu/bclr/v0142/iss4/7.
10. Thomas B. Edsall and Hanna Rosin, "IRS Denies Christian Coalition Tax-Exempt Status," *Washington Post,* http://www.washingtonpost.com/wp-srv/politics/daily/june99/christian11.htm.
11. Prior to 2008, organizations with more than $25,000 in annual gross receipts were required to file the Form 990 or Form 990-Z; organizations with less than $25,000 in annual revenues had no reporting requirements.
12. All private foundations, regardless of budget size or activity during the fiscal year, must file an annual information return, the Form 990-PF.
13. IRS Exempt Organizations, *Preparing to File the New Form 990. An online mini course,* http://www.stayexempt.org/Mini-Courses/Preparing_to_File_Form_990/Preparing_to_File_Form_990.aspx .
14. Evelyn Brody and Joseph J. Cordes, "The Unrelated Business Income Tax: All Bark and No Bite?" *Emerging Issues in Philanthropy* (Washington, DC: The Urban Institute, 2001); Marion R. Fremont-Smith, *Governing Nonprofit Organizations.*
15. IRS, *Publication 557 Tax-Exempt Status for Your Organization,* Washington, DC: Department of the Treasury, Internal Revenue Service, 2005: 9.
16. Nicholas Cafardi and Jaclyn Fabean Cherry, *Understanding Nonprofit and Tax-Exempt Organizations* (Newark, NJ: LexisNexis, 2006).
17. Bruce R. Hopkins, *650 Essential Nonprofit Law Questions Answered* (Hoboken, NJ: John Wiley & Sons, 2005).
18. Henry B. Hansmann, "The Role of Nonprofit Enterprise," *Yale Law Journal* 89 (1980): 835–898.

19. Tax-exempt funds or organizations other than public charities such as colleges and universities, and medical savings accounts, as well as Individual Retirement Accounts and other pension plans are also subject to the UBIT. Data are available from the IRS Tax Stats website, http://www.irs.gov/taxstats/charitablestats/article/0,,id=97210,00.html.
20. The percent reporting is derived from the number of 2008 returns for 501(c)(3) organizations that were subject to the UBIT divided by the total number of Form 990 returns filed by 501(c)(3) organizations in 2008.
21. Evelyn Brody and Joseph J. Cordes, "The Unrelated Business Income Tax;" Marion R. Fremont-Smith, *Governing Nonprofit Organizations.*
22. Evelyn Brody and Joseph Cordes, "The Unrelated Business Income Tax," p.1.
23. David S. Karp, "Taxing Issues: Reexamining the Regulation of Issue Advocacy by Tax-Exempt Organizations Through the Internal Revenue Code," *New York University Law Review* (77 N.Y.U.L. Rev. 1805, 2002).
24. IRS, "Exempt Function—Political Organization," http://www.irs.gov/charities/political/article/0,,id=175345,00.html.
25. The reporting threshold in place at that time.
26. David S. Karp, "Taxing Issues."
27. More information on tax-exempt political organizations and their filing/disclosure requirements are available in IRS Publication 557.
28. CLPI (Center for Lobbying in the Public Interest), *Lobbying and Advocacy: Major Issues, Myths Defined,* http://www.clpi.org/the-law; Bob Smucker, *The Nonprofit Lobbying Guide,* 2nd ed. (Independent Sector: Washington, DC, 1999); Stephanie Geller and Lester M. Salamon, "Nonprofit Advocacy: What Do We Know? Center for Civil Society Studies Working Paper," No. 22, (Baltimore, MD: Johns Hopkins University Institute for Policy Studies, 2007).
29. Dennis McIlnay, "Philanthropy at 50: Four Moments in Time," *Foundation News and Commentary* 39, 5 (September/October 1998), http://www.foundationnews.org/CME/article.cfm?ID=1053; Gary N. Scrivner, "100 Years of Tax Policy Changes Affecting Charitable Organizations," in *The Nonprofit Organization: Essential Readings,* eds. Gies, David L., J. Steven Ott, and Jay M. Shafritz(Belmont, CA: Wadsworth, Inc., 1990).
30. Waldemar A. Nielsen, *Golden Donors: A New Anatomy of the Great Foundations* (New Brunswick, NJ: Transaction Publishers, 2002), 255–264; Dennis McIlnay, "Philanthropy at 50."
31. Waldemar A. Nielsen, *Golden Donors,* p. 23.
32. Ibid.
33. Dennis McIlnay, "Philanthropy at 50," p. 3.
34. Peter Frumkin, "The Ironies of Foundation Regulation," *Chronicle of Philanthropy* 16 (2004): 31–33; Waldemar A. Nielsen, *Golden Donors;* Dennis McIlnay, "Philanthropy at 50"; John G. Simon, "The Regulation of American Foundations: Looking Backward at the Tax Reform Act of 1969," *Voluntas* 6 (1995): 243–254; Gary N. Scrivner et al. "100 Years of Tax Policy Changes"; Gary D. Bass, David F. Arons, Kay Guinane, and Matthew F. Carter, *Seen but not Heard, Strengthening Nonprofit Advocacy* (Washington, DC: The Aspen Institute, 2007).
35. Dennis McIlnay, "Philanthropy at 50," p.4.
36. Dennis McIlnay, "Philanthropy at 50."
37. Francie Ostrower and Marla J. Bobowick, *Nonprofit Governance and the Sarbanes-Oxley Act,* http://www.boardsource.org/dl.asp?document_id=473, p.4.
38. Ibid.
39. Peggy M. Jackson and Toni E. Fogarty, *Sarbanes-Oxley for Nonprofits: A Guide to Gaining the Competitive Advantage* (Hoboken, NJ: John Wiley and Sons, 2005).
40. Francie Ostrower and Marla J. Bobowick, *Nonprofit Governance and the Sarbanes-Oxley Act.*
41. Ibid; Francie Ostrower, *Nonprofit Governance in the United States: Findings on Performance and Accountability from the First National Representative Study* (Washington, DC: The Urban Institute, 2007).
42. Katie L. Roeger, Amy Blackwood, and Sarah L. Pettijohn, *The Nonprofit Sector in Brief: Public Charities, Giving, and Volunteering, 2011* (Washington, DC: The Urban Institute, 2011).
43. As discussed previously, imposition of the new e-postcard filing requirement makes more data on small and defunct nonprofits available.
44. Pension Protection Act (PPA), Public Law 109–280, http://www.gpo.gov/fdsys/pkg/PLAW-109publ280/pdf/PLAW-109publ280.pdf.
45. IRS, *IRS Identifies Organizations That Have Lost Tax-Exempt Status; Announces Special Steps to Help Revoked Organizations,* http://www.irs.gov/newsroom/article/0,,id=240239,00.html?portlet=7; IRS, *Pension Protection Act of 2006 Revises EO Tax Rules,* www.irs.gov/charities/article/0,,id=161145,00.html; Foundation for the Carolinas (FFTC), *New Charitable Giving Incentives & Exempt Organization Reforms: Pension Protection Act of 2006,* http://www.fftc.org/NetCommunity/Document.Doc?id=102.
46. More information on the work of the Panel, as well as downloadable versions of their publications, are available through their website at www.nonprofitpanel.org.
47. Katie L. Roeger, Amy Blackwood, and Sarah L. Pettijohn, *The Nonprofit Sector in Brief: Public Charities, Giving, and Volunteering, 2011* (Washington, DC: The Urban Institute, 2011).
48. Ofer Lion, "California Loosens its Geographically-Based Restriction on Property Tax Exemptions for Nonprofits," *Lexis-Nexis,* http://www.martindale.com/taxation-law/article_Mitchell-Silberberg-Knupp-LLP_1390358.htm.
49. Stephanie Strom, "California Scrutinizes Nonprofits, Sometimes Ending a Tax Exemption," *New York Times,* www.nytimes.com/2011/08/15/business/california-scrutinizes-property-tax-exemption-of-nonprofits.html?pagewanted=all.
50. Lion, "California Loosens Restriction on Property Tax Exemptions," 2011.
51. U.S. Department of the Treasury, Office of Foreign Assets Control, "Terrorism: What You Need to Know about U.S. Sanctions," http://www.treasury.gov/resource-center/sanctions/Programs/Documents/terror.pdf.
52. U.S. Department of the Treasury, "Introduction to Treasury's Updated Anti-Terrorist Financing Guidelines," http://www.treasury.gov/resource-center/terrorist-illicit-finance/Pages/protecting-charities-intro.aspx.
53. International Community Foundation, "The Complexities of International Giving," http://www.icfdn.org/forprofesionaladvisors/thecomplexitiesofinternationalgiving.php.
54. Evelyn Brody, "The Legal Framework for Nonprofit Organizations," in *The Nonprofit Sector: A Research Handbook,* 2nd ed., ed. Walter W. Powell and Richard Steinberg (New Haven, CT: Yale University Press, 2006), 243–266; Independent Sector, *Obedience to the Unenforceable: Ethics and the Nation's Voluntary and Philanthropic Community,* (Washington, DC: Independent Sector, 2002), http://www.independentsector.org/uploads/Accountability_Documents/obedience_to_unenforceable.pdf.
55. Marion R. Fremont-Smith, *Governing Nonprofit Organizations.*

56. Woods Bowman and Marion R. Fremont-Smith, "Nonprofits and State and Local Governments," in *Nonprofits and Government*, 2nd ed., ed. by Elizabeth T. Boris and C. Eugene Steuerle, (Washington, DC: Urban Institute Press, 2006).
57. Peter Swords, "Did the Filer Engage in Any Self-Dealing or Excess Benefit Transactions during the Year?" *How to Read the New Form 990*, Nonprofit Coordinating Committee of New York, http://www.npccny.org/new990/Chapter_8.pdf; Peter Swords, "How to Read the IRS Form 990 & Find Out What it Means," Nonprofit Coordinating Committee of New York, http://www.npccny.org/Form_990/990.htm.
58. Community foundations are defined and discussed in Chapter 9.
59. Foundation Center, *Change in Community Foundation Giving and Assets, 1981 to 2008*, http://foundationcenter.org/findfunders/statistics/pdf/02_found_growth/2008/00_08.pdf; Foundation Center, *Key Facts on Community Foundations*, Foundation Center, http://foundationcenter.org/gainknowledge/research/pdf/keyfacts_comm2011.pdf.
60. Lawrence M. Friedman, *Dead Hands: A Social History of Wills, Trusts, and Inheritance Law* (Stanford, CA: Stanford Law Books of Stanford University Press, 2009), 140–170; Waldemar A. Nielsen, *Golden Donors.*
61. Lawrence M. Friedman, *Dead Hands*, 153.
62. Lawrence M. Friedman, *Dead Hands;* Evelyn Brody, "Accountability and the Public Trust," in *The State of Nonprofit America*, ed. Lester M. Salamon (Washington, DC: Brookings Institution Press, 2002), 471–498; Waldemar A. Nielsen, *Golden Donors.*
63. Nielsen, *Golden Donors: A New Anatomy of the Great Foundations.* (New Brunswick, NJ: Transaction Publishers, 2002), 255–264; Lawrence M. Friedman, *Dead Hands: A Social History of Wills, Trusts, and Inheritance Law* (Stanford, CA: Stanford Law Books of Stanford University Press, 2009), 140–170.
64. Nielsen, *Golden Donors*, 259.
65. Friedman, *Dead Hands*, 159–160; John G. Simon, "American Philanthropy and the Buck Trust," *Faculty Scholarship Series*, Paper 1940, last modified 1987, http://digitalcommons.law.yale.edu/fss_papers/1940.
66. San Francisco Foundation: Independent Auditors' Report, Consolidated Financial Statements, and Supplementary Information, http://www.sff.org/about/documents-about/TSSF%20Audited%20Financials%20FYE%20June%2030%202011.pdf.
67. "Marin Community Foundation Combined Financial Statements for the Year Ended June 30, 2010," http://www.marincf.org/resource-library#annual_report_documents.
68. Richard Halstead, "Buck Trust Beginnings," *Marin Independent Journal*, http://www.marinij.com/ci_7614326?source=pkg.
69. "MCF Financials, June 30, 2010."
70. "MCF Financials, June 30, 2010."
71. "All Grants Made by MCF in FY 2010," http://www.marincf.org/resource-library#annual_report_documents.
72. MSFP (Multi-State Filer Project), "Which States Require Registration of Charitable Soliciting Organizations and Accept the URS?" and "Which States Require Registration of Charitable Soliciting Organizations and Do Not Accept the URS?" http://www.multistatefiling.org; Renee A. Irvin, "State Regulation of Nonprofit Organizations: Accountability Regardless of Outcome," *Nonprofit and Voluntary Sector Quarterly* 34 (2005): 161–178.
73. Detailed information on the URS and the Multi-State Filer Project is available at www.multistatefiling.org.
74. Renee A. Irvin, "State Regulation of Nonprofit Organizations: Accountability Regardless of Outcome," *Nonprofit and Voluntary Sector Quarterly* 34 (2005): 161–178.
75. Irvin (2005) notes that these states—Delaware, Idaho, Montana, Nebraska, Nevada, Wyoming—are predominantly western states with smaller populations; it is possible that they simply do not have an environment that is attractive to nonprofits likely to engage in fraud and abuse. She therefore cautions against drawing generalizeable conclusions from the data.
76. Kennard T. Wing, Katie L. Roeger, and Thomas H. Pollak, *The Nonprofit Sector in Brief: Public Charities, Giving, and Volunteering, 2010* (Washington, DC: The Urban Institute, 2010).
77. Lester A. Salamon, *Partners in Public Service* (Baltimore: Johns Hopkins University Press, 1995).
78. Lawrence M. Friedman, *Dead Hands;* Woods Bowman and Marion R. Fremont-Smith, "Nonprofits and State and Local Governments."
79. *Smithers v. St. Luke's–Roosevelt Hospital Center*—a New York case regarding a $10 million bequest to the hospital for a center to treat alcoholism—is a notable exception. The court allowed Adele Smithers, the donor's widow and administrator of his estate, standing to sue when the hospital did not use the funds to her satisfaction. It was likely her position as administrator of the estate in combination with her status as the donor's widow that led the court to allow her lawsuit (Friedman, 2009).
80. Oregon Revised Statutes (ORS), "Chapter 128.710 Enforcement Jurisdiction of Court," http://www.leg.state.or.us/ors/128.html.
81. Lawrence M. Friedman, *Dead Hands;* Panel on the Nonprofit Sector, *Strengthening Transparency Governance Accountability of Charitable Organizations: A Supplement to the Final Report to Congress and the Nonprofit Sector*, (Washington, DC: Independent Sector, 2006).
82. Ibid.
83. Alan J. Abramson and Rachel McCarthy, "Infrastructure Organizations," in *The State of Nonprofit America*, ed. Lester M. Salamon, 331–354 (Washington, DC: Brookings Institution Press, 2002).
84. Marion R. Fremont-Smith, *Governing Nonprofit Organizations.*
85. NCNA-NHSA, *Rating the Raters: An Assessment of Organizations and Publications That Rate/Rank Charitable Nonprofit Organizations* (Washington, DC: National Council of Nonprofit Associations and the National Human Services Assembly, 2005).
86. Ibid., 5.
87. Nancy Chandler, ed., *Best Practices for Establishing a Children's Advocacy Center Program*, 3rd ed. (Washington, DC: National Children's Alliance, 2000).
88. Marion R. Fremont-Smith, *Governing Nonprofit Organizations.*

Chapter 5

1. Peter Drucker, *Managing the Nonprofit Organization* (New York: HarperCollins, 2005).
2. Charles T. Goodsell, *Mission Mystique* (Washington DC: CQ Press, 2010), 15.
3. Herrington J. Bryce, *Financial and Strategic Management of Nonprofit Organizations*, 3rd ed. (San Francisco: Jossey-Bass, 2000).
4. Berit Lakey, George Lakey, Rod Napier, and Janice Robinson, *Grassroots and Nonprofit Leadership: A Guide for Organizations in Changing Times* (Philadelphia: New Society 1995), 107.
5. Barry Dym and Harry Hutson, *Leadership in Nonprofit Organizations* (Thousand Oaks, CA: Sage, 2005), 104.
6. Edgar H. Schein, "The Concept of Organizational Culture: Why Bother?" in *Classics of Organization Theory*, 7th ed., ed. Jay M. Shafritz, J. Steven Ott, and Yong Suk Jang (Boston: Wadsworth Cengage Learning, 2011), 352.

7. "History: Origins and Early Outings," http://www.sierraclub.org/history/origins/.
8. John Muir, "American Forests," *Atlantic Monthly,* 80 (1897): 150.
9. Goodsell, 2010.
10. Richard T. Ingram, *Ten Basic Responsibilities of Nonprofit Boards,* 2nd ed. (Washington, DC: BoardSource, 2009); Michael J. Worth, *Nonprofit Management: Principles and Practice* (Thousand Oaks: Sage, 2008); Thomas P. Holland and Roger A. Ritvo, *Nonprofit Organizations, Principles and Practices* (New York: Columbia University Press, 2008); BoardSource, *The Nonprofit Board Answer Book: A Practical Guide for Board Members and Chief Executives* (San Francisco: Jossey-Bass, 2007).
11. Ingram, *Ten Basic Responsibilities,* 64.
12. Ellen Condliffe Lagemann, *The Politics of Knowledge: The Carnegie Corporation, Philanthropy, and Public Policy* (Middletown, CT: Weslyan University Press, 1989), 3.
13. Emmett D. Carson, "On Foundations and Public Policy," in *Power in Policy, A Funder's Guide to Advocacy and Civic Participation,* ed. David F. Arons (Saint Paul, MN: Fieldstone Alliance, 2007), 14.
14. Lagemann, *Politics of Knowledge,* 261.
15. http://carnegie.org/about-us/mission-and-vision
16. Burton A. Weisbrod, ed., *To Profit or Not to Profit: The Commercial Transformation of the Nonprofit Sector* (New York: Cambridge University Press, 1998).
17. Mark H. Moore, "Managing for Value: Organizational Strategy in For-Profit, Nonprofit, and Governmental Organizations," *Nonprofit and Voluntary Sector Quarterly* 29 (2000):183–204.
18. Weisbrod, *Managing for Value,* 290.
19. Marshall B. Jones, "The Multiple Sources of Mission Drift," *Nonprofit and Voluntary Sector Quarterly* 36 (2007): 299–307; Peter C. Brinckerhoff, *Mission Based Marketing: Positioning Your Not-for-Profit in an Increasingly Competitive World,* 2nd ed. (Hoboken, NJ: John Wiley & Sons, 2003).
20. Brinckerhoff, *Mission Based,* 33.
21. Peter Drucker, *Managing the Nonprofit Organization;* Ingram, *Ten Basic Responsibilities.*
22. Karl N. Stauber, "Mission-Driven Philanthropy: What Do We Want to Accomplish and How Do We Do It?" *Nonprofit and Voluntary Sector Quarterly* 30 (2001): 393–399.
23. Ibid, 394.
24. Northwest Area Foundation, 2009, http://www.nwaf.org/Content/Mission (accessed on November 20, 2009).
25. Frances Westley, Brenda Zimmerman, and Michael Quinn Patton, *Getting to Maybe. How the World is Changed* (Canada: Random House Canada, 2006), 196.
26. Samantha L. Durst and Charldean Newell, "The Who, Why, and How of Reinvention in Nonprofit Organizations," *Nonprofit Management and Leadership, 11,* 2001; Nancy Winemiller Basinger and Jessica Romine Peterson, "Where You Stand Depends on Where You Sit," *Nonprofit Management and Leadership,* 19, 2008; Sharon Oster, *Strategic Management for Nonprofit Organizations Theory and Cases* (New York: Oxford University Press, 1995).
27. Drucker, *Managing the Nonprofit.*
28. David M. Oshinsky, *Polio: An American Story* (New York: Oxford University Press, 2005).
29. Jeffrey Kluger, *Splendid Solution: Jonas Salk and the Conquest of Polio* (New York: G.P. Putnam's Sons, 2004).
30. Ibid.
31. Oshinsky, *Polio,* 53.
32. Ibid, 189.
33. Ibid.
34. "A History of the March of Dimes," http://www.marchofdimes.com/mission/history_indepth.html.
35. Robert B. Denhardt, *The Pursuit of Significance: Strategies for Managerial Success in Public Organizations* (New York: Waveland Press, 2000); Robert E. McDonald, "An Investigation of Innovation in Nonprofit Organizations: The Role of Organizational Mission," *Nonprofit and Voluntary Sector Quarterly* 36 (2007): 256–281; E. B. Knauft, Renee A. Berger, and Sandra T. Gray, *Profiles of Excellence: Achieving Success in the Nonprofit Sector,* Jossey Bass Nonprofit & Public Management Series (San Francisco: Jossey-Bass, 1991).
36. Oster, *Strategic Management;* William A. Brown and Carlton F. Yoshioka, "Mission Attachment and Satisfaction as Factors in Employee Retention," *Nonprofit Management & Leadership* 14 (2003): 5–18; Seok Eun Kim and Jung Wook Lee, "Is Mission Attachment an Effective Management Tool for Employee Retention?" *Review of Public Personnel Administration* 27 (2007): 227–248.
37. Brown and Yoshioka, *Mission Attachment;* Kim and Lee, *Is Mission Attachment.*
38. Holland and Ritvo, *Nonprofit Organizations,* 128.
39. Worth, *Nonprofit Management,* 171.
40. Holland and Ritvo, *Nonprofit Organizations;* Worth, *Nonprofit Management.*
41. Worth, *Nonprofit Management;* and Helmut K. Anheier, *Nonprofit Organizations, Theory, Management,Policy* (New York: Routledge, 2005).
42. William B. Werther Jr. and Evan M. Berman, *Third Sector Management, The Art of Managing Nonprofit Organizations* (Washington, DC: Georgetown University Press, 2001), 8.
43. Connie Bresnahan, "The Canadian Spirit of John Muir," 1996 John Muir Conference, www.sierraclub.org/john_muir_exhibit/uop_conference_1996/bresnahan.aspx.
44. National Historic Sites in the Mountain National Parks, www.pc.gc.ca/docs/v-g/pm-mp/lhn-nhs/phn-pns/harkin_e.asp.
45. Steven Cohen and William Eimicke, *Tools for Innovators* (San Francisco: Jossey-Bass, 1998), 16.
46. Ingram, *Ten Basic Responsibilities,* 33.
47. Michael Allison and Jude Kaye, *Strategic Planning for Nonprofit Organizations* (San Francisco: Jossey-Bass, 2005).
48. Jeanne Bell, "Strategy and Planning: Turning a Dream into Reality," in *Nonprofit Management 101,* ed. Darian Rodriguez Heyman (San Francisco: Jossey-Bass, 2011).
49. Kevin P. Kearns, "From Comparative Advantage to Damage Control: Clarifying Strategic Issues Using SWOT Analysis," *Nonprofit Management and Leadership* 3 (1992): 11.
50. Bell, *Strategy and Planning.*
51. Kevin P. Kearns, "From Comparative Advantage"; *Chartered Management Institute, Performing a SWOT Analysis,* Entrepreneur (online), 2001.
52. Tennessee Arts Commission, "Tennessee Arts Organizations Receive Grants from the National Endowment for the Arts, 2009," http://www.tn.gov/arts/news_releases/2009_release_9.html.
53. Peter Frumkin and Alice Andre-Clark, "When Missions, Markets, and Politics Collide: Values and Strategy in the Nonprofit Human Services," *Nonprofit and Voluntary Sector Quarterly* 29 (2000): 160.
54. Harry Hatry, Therese van Houten, Margaret C. Plantz, and Martha Taylor Greenway, *Measuring Program Outcomes: A Practical Approach* (Alexandria, VA: United Way, 1996), xv.
55. Allison and Kaye, *Strategic Planning for Nonprofit Organizations.*

56. Brigette Rouson, "Business Planning for Nonprofits: Why, When—and How it Compares to Strategic Planning," *Enhance: The Newsletter of the Alliance for Nonprofit Management* 2 (2005): 3.
57. Bryce, *Financial and Strategic.*

Chapter 6

1. The information provided in this chapter should not be taken as legal advice; always consult an authority well versed in the tax law with specific questions about your organization.
2. Reid, Elizabeth J. "Advocacy and the Challenges It Presents for Nonprofits," in *Nonprofits & Government,* 2nd ed., ed. Elizabeth T. Boris and C. Eugene Steuerle, Washington, DC: Urban Institute Press, 343–372.
3. Stephanie Geller and Lester M. Salamon, "Nonprofit Advocacy: What Do We Know?" Center for Civil Society Studies Working Paper No. 22 (Baltimore, MD: Johns Hopkins University Institute for Policy Studies, 2007), 3
4. Elizabeth J. Reid, "Advocacy and the Challenges It Presents for Nonprofits," in *Nonprofits & Government,* 2nd ed., ed. Elizabeth T. Boris and C. Eugene Steuerle, (Washington, DC: Urban Institute Press, 2006), 343–372; Hillel Schmid, Michal Bar, and Ronit Nirel, "Advocacy Activities in Nonprofit Human Service Organizations: Implications for Policy," *Nonprofit and Voluntary Sector Quarterly* 37, 4 (2008): 581–602.
5. Jeffrey M. Berry, *A Voice for Nonprofits,* with David F. Arons (Washington, DC: Brookings Institution Press, 2005).
6. Ibid.
7. Ibid; Gary D. Bass, David F. Arons, Kay Guinane, and Matthew F. Carter, *Seen but not Heard: Strengthening Nonprofit Advocacy* (Washington, DC: Aspen Institute, 2007).
8. Karen M. Padget, "The Big Chill: Foundations and Political Passion," *American Prospect* 44 (1999); Bass et al., *Seen but not Heard.*
9. Berry, *A Voice;* Padget, "The Big Chill"; Bass et al., *Seen but not Heard.*
10. Padget, "The Big Chill"; Bass et al., *Seen but not Heard.*
11. Bass et al., *Seen but not Heard* 70.
12. http://www.clpi.org.
13. David F. Arons, Abby Levine, and Kelly Shipp Simone, "Advocacy Language" in *Power in Policy, A Funder's Guide to Advocacy and Civic Participation,* ed. David F. Arons, (Saint Paul, MN: Fieldstone Alliance, 2007), 62.
14. Arons, Levine, and Simone, "Advocacy Language."
15. Reid, "Advocacy and the Challenges."
16. Christopher Gergen, "Volume Up in Charity Advocacy," *Washington Times,* Dec. 2, 2009; http://www.washingtontimes.com/news/2009/dec/02/volume-up-in-charity-advocacy/.
17. Lester M. Salamon, *The Resilient Sector* (Washington, DC: Brookings Institution Press, 2003), 72.
18. Elizabeth T. Boris and Jeff Krehely, "Civic Participation and Advocacy," in *The State of Nonprofit America,* ed. Lester M. Salamon (Washington, DC: Brookings Institution Press, 2002).
19. Ibid., 300.
20. David F. Suarez, "Nonprofit Advocacy and Civic Engagement on the Internet," *Administration & Society* 41 (2009).
21. Lester M. Salamon and Stephanie Lessans Geller, "Nonprofit America: A Force for Democracy?" Center for Civil Society Studies Listening Post Project, Communiqué No. 9 (Baltimore, MD: Johns Hopkins University Institute for Policy Studies, 2008).
22. Salamon and Geller, "Nonprofit America"; Geller and Salamon, "Nonprofit Advocacy."
23. Berry, *A Voice.*
24. Reid, "Advocacy and the Challenges."
25. Peter Frumkin, *On Being Nonprofit: A Conceptual and Policy Primer* (Cambridge, MA: Harvard University Press, 2002), 53
26. Peter Frumkin, *On Being Nonprofit.*
27. Eric Werker and Faisal Z. Ahmed, "What Do Nongovernmental Organizations Do?" *Journal of Economic Perspectives* 22 (2008): 73–92. We use Werker and Ahmed's numbers because they have limited their data to organizations that would be considered nonprofits/charities in the U.S. but which operate internationally. Other data collection methods have indicated far larger numbers of NGOs because they include far more organizational types in their numbers. For example, according to the Union of International Associations, in 2010 there were more than 65,000 civil society organizations in operation internationally; however, that number is skewed by inclusion of professional organizations, recreational clubs, and intergovernmental organizations (www.uia.be/yearbook).
28. Ted Danson, "American Oceans Campaign (AOC)," *Congressional Digest* 87 (2003): 208–210.
29. Ibid.
30. Werker and Ahmed, "What Do Nongovernmental Organizations Do?"
31. Salamon and Geller, "Nonprofit America."
32. Ibid., 6.
33. Gary D. Bass, "Advocacy Is Not a Dirty Word." *Chronicle of Philanthropy* 20 (2007), 45.
34. Jill Nicholson-Crotty, "Politics, Policy, and the Motivations for Advocacy in Nonprofit Reproductive Health and Family Planning Providers," *Nonprofit and Voluntary Sector Quarterly* 36 (2007): 5–21; Salamon and Geller, "Nonprofit America"; Bass, "Advocacy Is Not."
35. Jeffrey M. Berry, *The New Liberalism* (Washington, DC: Brookings Institution Press, 1999); Berry, *A Voice.*
36. NAMI, 2011.
37. CLPI (Center for Lobbying in the Public Interest), *Make a Difference for Your Cause* (Washington, DC: Center for Lobbying in the Public Interest, 2006), 13.
38. See Michael O'Neill, *Nonprofit Nation: A New Look at the Third America* (San Francisco: Jossey-Bass, 2002); Frumkin, *On Being Nonprofit;* Boris and Krehely, "Civic Participation"; Kathleen D. McCarthy, *American Creed: Philanthropy and the Rise of Civil Society 1700–1865* (Chicago: University of Chicago Press, 2003); Reid, Elizabeth J. "Advocacy and the Challenges"; Pat Libby, *The Lobbying Strategy Handbook: 10 Steps to Advancing Any Cause Effectively* (Thousand Oaks, CA: Sage Publications, 2012).
39. AARP, *Divided We Fail,* www.aarp.org/issues/dividedwefail/about_us/.
40. "President Obama Holds a Tele-Townhall Meeting on Health Care with AARP Members," *Washington Post,* July 28, 2009, www.washingtonpost.com/wpdyn/content/article/2009/07/28/AR2009072801444.html.
41. Julie Hirschfeld Davis, "The Influence Game: Labor and Business, Joined in Health Care Cause, Now at Odds on Specifics," *Real Clear Politics,* February 16, 2009, www.realclearpolitics.com/news/ap/politics/2009/Feb/16/the_influence_game__coalition_rises__then_stalls.html.
42. "Thousands Quit AARP Over Health Reform," August 18, 2009, www.cbsnews.com/2100–18563_162–5247916.html.

43. Bennett Roth, "GOP Probe of AARP Could Ensnare Other Nonprofits," *Roll Call*, April 1, 2011, www.rollcall.com/news/gop_probe_of_aarp_could_ensnare_other_nonprofits-204534–1.html.
44. Peter Overby, "Republicans Challenge AARP's Tax-Exempt Status," April 1, 2011, www.npr.org/2011/04/01/135047886/aarp-comes-under-fire-by-republicans.
45. Bruce R. Hopkins, "The Legal Aspects of Government Affairs and Lobbying," in *The Legislative Labyrinth: A Map for Not-for-Profits*, ed. Walter P. Pidgeon Jr. (New York, NY: John Wiley & Sons, 2001).
46. Berry, *A Voice;* CLPI, *Make a Difference;* Bass et al., *Seen but not Heard.*
47. Bass et al., *Seen but not Heard;* Salamon and Geller, "Nonprofit America."
48. Note that an organization receiving government funds may, in fact, engage in lobbying so long as that lobbying is not paid for with government funds.
49. Salamon and Geller, "Nonprofit America."
50. Berry, *A Voice.*
51. CLPI, *Make a Difference.*
52. Salamon and Geller, "Nonprofit America."
53. Hopkins, *The Legal Aspects*, 132.
54. Hopkins, *The Legal Aspects.*
55. Berry, *A Voice*, 53
56. *Slee v. Commissioner*, 42 F.2d 184 (2d Cir. 1930).
57. Boris and Krehely, "Civic Participation."
58. Independent Sector, "IRS Halts Targeted Audits of Charities That Lobby," 2003, http://www.independentsector.org/programs/gr/501h.html.
59. Bob Smucker, *The Nonprofit Lobbying Guide*, 2nd ed. (Washington, DC: Independent Sector, 1999).
60. Smucker, *The Nonprofit Lobbying Guide;* Berry, *A Voice;* CLPI, *Make a Difference;* Libby, *The Lobbying Strategy.*
61. Marion R. Fremont-Smith, *Governing Nonprofit Organizations: Federal and State Law and Regulation* (Cambridge, MA: Belknap Press of Harvard University Press, 2004).
62. Larry Ottinger, " Bringing Nonprofit Advocacy Rules and Culture into the 21st Century," *Responsive Philanthropy*, Winter 2010/2011: 9–11.
63. Clark, Charles S., "Regulating Nonprofits," *CQ Researcher* 7 (December 1997): 1129–1152; Fremont-Smith, *Governing Nonprofit Organizations;* Salamon and Geller, "Nonprofit America."
64. Fremont-Smith, *Governing Nonprofit Organizations.*
65. Ibid.
66. Alliance for Justice, "Frequently Asked Questions on *Citizens United v. Federal Elections Commission*," http://www.afj.org/connect-with-the-issues/citizens_united_faq.pdf.
67. The limits are 30 days before a primary and 60 days before a general election.
68. John Chwat, "The Use of Outside Legislative Consultants: When and How to Hire a Lobbyist," in *The Legislative Labyrinth: A Map for Not-for-Profits*, ed. Walter P. Pidgeon Jr. (New York: John Wiley & Sons, 2001).
69. Ibid.
70. David C. Hammack, "The Statute of Charitable Uses, 1601," in *Making the Nonprofit Sector in the United States*, ed. David C. Hammack (Bloomington: Indiana University Press, 1998); Bass et al., *Seen but not Heard.*
71. Lloyd H. Mayer, "The Legal Rules for Public Policy and Civic Impact by Foundations," in *Power in Policy, A Funder's Guide to Advocacy and Civic Participation*, ed. by David F. Arons. (Saint Paul, MN: Fieldstone Alliance, 2007).
72. Boris and Krehely, "Civic Participation."
73. Foundation Center, "Distribution of Foundation Grants by Subject Categories, circa 2010," http://foundationcenter.org/findfunders/statistics/pdf/04_fund_sub/2010/10_10.pdf. Because of the nature of the recordkeeping, it is difficult to assess exactly how much money is spent on policy activity by philanthropic foundations; see Bass et al., *Seen but not Heard.*
74. Emmett D. Carson, "On Foundations and Public Policy: Why the Words Don't Match the Behavior," in *Power in Policy: A Funder's Guide to Advocacy and Civic Participation*, ed. David F. Arons (Saint Paul, MN: Fieldstone Alliance, 2007).
75. Aaron Dorfman, "Bang for the Buck: Why Grantmakers Should Provide More Funding for Policy Advocacy and Community Organizing." *Responsive Philanthropy* 1 (2008): 2–5.
76. Emmett D. Carson, "On Foundations and Public Policy," 14.
77. David F. Arons, editor, *Power in Policy, A Funder's Guide to Advocacy and Civic Participation* (Saint Paul, MN: Fieldstone Alliance, 2007).
78. Melissa Johnson, "Making Progress Toward Increasing Funding for Advocacy, Community Organizing and Civic Engagement," *Responsive Philanthropy* 2 (2009): 5–7; Arons, Levine, and Simone, "Advocacy Language."
79. Lisa Ranghelli and Julia Chang, *Strengthening Democracy, Increasing Opportunities: Impacts of Advocacy, Organizing and Civic Engagement in North Carolina* (Washington, DC: National Committee for Responsive Philanthropy, 2009).
80. David Cohen, "Being a Public Interest Lobbyist *Is* Something to Write Home About," in *The Nonprofit Lobbying Guide*, 2nd ed.

Chapter 7

1. Ronald R. Sims, "Restoring Ethics Consciousness to Organizations and the Workplace: Every Contemporary Leader's Challenge," in *Leadership: Succeeding in the Private, Public, and Not-for-Profit Sectors*, ed. Ronald R. Sims and Scott A. Quatro (Armonk, NY: M.E. Sharpe, 2005), 300.
2. Ruth Ann Strickland and Shannon K. Vaughan, "The Hierarchy of Ethical Values in Nonprofit Organizations: A Framework for an Ethical, Self-Actualized Organizational Culture," *Public Integrity* 10 (2008): 233–251; James H. Svara, *The Ethics Primer for Public Administrators in Government and Nonprofit Organizations* (Sudbury, MA: Jones and Bartlett, 2007); Ronald R. Sims, "Restoring Ethics Consciousness to Organizations and the Workplace: Every Contemporary Leader's Challenge," in *Leadership: Succeeding in the Private, Public, and Not-for-Profit Sectors*, ed. Ronald R. Sims and Scott A. Quatro (Armonk, NY: M.E. Sharpe, 2005).
3. The Right Honorable Lord John Fletcher Moulton, "Law and Manners," *Atlantic Monthly* 134:1 (July 1924): 1–4. http://www2.econ.iastate.edu/classes/econ362/hallam/NewspaperArticles/LawAndManners.pdf.
4. James H. Svara, *The Ethics Primer*, 16.
5. James L. Perry and Lois Recascino Wise, "The Motivational Bases of Public Service," *Public Administration Review* 50 (1990): 367–373.
6. Carolyn Ball, "What Is Transparency?" *Public Integrity* 11 (2009): 297.
7. Ibid.
8. Ibid.
9. Ibid., 300.
10. Ibid., 303.
11. Bobbi Watt Geer, Jill K. Maher, and Michele T. Cole, "Managing Nonprofit Organizations: The Importance of Transformational

Leadership and Commitment to Operating Standards for Nonprofit Accountability," *Public Performance & Management Review* 32 (2008): 51–75; Evelyn Brody, "Accountability and the Public Trust," in *The State of Nonprofit America,* ed. Lester M. Salamon (Brookings Institution Press: Washington, DC, 2002), 471–498.

12. The survey results discussed are taken from the 2007 National Nonprofit Ethics Survey, the fourth in a longitudinal study of employees in U.S. workplaces across all three sectors. Participants were randomly selected, and 558 of the 3,452 respondents were nonprofit employees. More information on the survey and its methodology is available at www.ethics.org.
13. Ethics Resource Center (ERC), *National Nonprofit Ethics Survey: An Inside View of Nonprofit Sector Ethics,* last modified 2007, http://www.ethics.org/files/u5/ERC_s_National_Nonprofit_Ethics_Survey.pdf.
14. Ibid.
15. Abraham H. Maslow, "A Theory of Human Motivation," *Psychological Review* 50 (1943): 370–396.
16. Ruth Ann Strickland and Shannon K. Vaughan, "The Hierarchy of Ethical Values in Nonprofit Organizations: A Framework for an Ethical, Self-Actualized Organizational Culture," *Public Integrity* 10 (2008): 233–251.
17. ERC, *National Nonprofit Ethics Survey.*
18. Ibid., 4–5.
19. Ibid.
20. Geer et al., "Managing Nonprofit Organizations."
21. Ronald R. Sims, "Restoring Ethics Consciousness to Organizations and the Workplace: Every Contemporary Leader's Challenge," in *Leadership: Succeeding in the Private, Public, and Not-for-Profit Sectors,* ed. Ronald R. Sims and Scott A. Quatro (Armonk, NY: M.E. Sharpe, 2005).
22. Ibid.
23. Evelyn Brody, "Accountability and the Public Trust."
24. Ibid.
25. Janet Greenlee, Mary Fischer, Teresa Gordon, and Elizabeth Keating, "An Investigation of Fraud in Nonprofit Organizations: Occurrences and Deterrents," *Nonprofit and Voluntary Sector Quarterly* 36 (2007): 676–694.
26. The Tax Reform Act of 1969 represents major legal restrictions and requirements designed to encourage ethical behavior. Because it was discussed extensively in Chapters 4 and 6, the Tax Reform Act of 1969 will not be included in this discussion of accountability.
27. Tamara G. Nezhina and Jeffrey L. Brudney, "The Sarbanes-Oxley Act: More Bark Than Bite for Nonprofits," *Nonprofit and Voluntary Sector Quarterly* 39 (2010): 275–301.
28. See, e.g., Francie Ostrower and Marla J. Bobowick, *Nonprofit Governance and the Sarbanes-Oxley Act,* last modified 2006, http://www.boardsource.org/dl.asp?document_id=473.
29. Tamara G. Nezhina and Jeffrey L. Brudney, "The Sarbanes-Oxley Act: More Bark than Bite for Nonprofits," *Nonprofit and Voluntary Sector Quarterly* 39 (2010): 275–301.
30. Information on the IRS public disclosure requirements as well as a tutorial on required disclosures are available online; website information is contained in the Web Resources section at the end of the chapter.
31. Tamara G. Nezhina and Jeffrey L. Brudney, "The Sarbanes-Oxley Act."
32. Cynthia Benzing, Evan Leach, and Charles McGee, "Sarbanes-Oxley and the New Form 990: Are Arts and Culture Nonprofits Ready?" *Nonprofit and Voluntary Sector Quarterly* 60 (2011): 1132–1147; DOI: 10.1177/0899764010378172.
33. National Council of Nonprofits, *Ethics and Accountability in the Nonprofit Sector,* http://www.councilofnonprofits.org/resources/resources-topic/ethics-accountability.
34. Reneé A. Irvin, "State Regulation of Nonprofit Organizations: Accountability Regardless of Outcome," *Nonprofit and Voluntary Sector Quarterly* 34 (2005): 161.
35. Ibid.
36. Gene Takagi, "The Nonprofit Integrity Act of 2004," last modified December 19, 2005, www.nonprofitlawblog.com/home/files/the_nonprofit_integrity_act_of_2004_v.3.pdf.
37. Todd Wallack, "Charity Settles in PipeVine Fiasco," *San Francisco Chronicle,* http://articles.sfgate.com/2004–02–19/business/17413968_1_million-settlement-bay-area-united-way.
38. Bob Egelko, "Judge Holds Bay Area United Way Responsible for Spun-Off Nonprofit," *San Francisco Chronicle,* http://articles.sfgate.com/2007–10–25/bay-area/17265321_1_charity-united-way-nonprofit.
39. Independent Sector, *Principles for Good Governance and Ethical Practice, Principle 2: Code of Ethics,* https://www.independentsector.org/code_ethics_principle_2.
40. Gary M. Grobman, "An Analysis of Codes of Ethics of Nonprofit, Tax-Exempt Membership Associations: Does Principal Constituency Make a Difference?" *Public Integrity* 9 (2007): 245–263.
41. Ibid.
42. James H. Svara, *The Ethics Primer.*
43. Gary M. Grobman, "An Analysis of Codes of Ethics."
44. Website is listed in the resources at the end of the chapter.
45. Panel on the Nonprofit Sector, *Principles of Good Governance and Ethical Practice: A Guide for Charities and Foundations* (Washington, DC: Independent Sector, 2007): 9.
46. Ibid.
47. Issues of confidentiality are pertinent to the process of program evaluation, discussed further in Chapter 14.
48. National Council of Nonprofits, *Conducting an Ethics Audit at Your Nonprofit,* http://www.councilofnonprofits.org/sites/default/files/Conducting%20an%20Ethics%20Audit.pdf.

Chapter 8

1. Philip Kotler and Sidney J. Levy, "Broadening the Concept of Marketing," *Journal of Marketing* 39 (1969): 15.
2. Philip Kotler and Sidney J. Levy, "Broadening the Concept of Marketing," *Journal of Marketing* 39 (1969): 10–15; Angus Laing, "Marketing in the Public Sector: Towards a Typology of Public Services," *Marketing Theory* 3 (2003): 427–445; Leighann C. Neilson, "The Development of Marketing in the Canadian Museum Community, 1840–1989," *Journal of Macromarketing* 23 (2003): 16–30.
3. Walter Wymer Jr., Patricia Knowles, and Roger Gomes, *Nonprofit Marketing: Marketing Management for Charitable and Nongovernmental Organizations,* Thousand Oaks, CA: Sage, 2006; John J. Burnett, *Nonprofit Marketing Best Practices,* Hoboken, NJ: John Wiley & Sons, 2007; Sarah Durham, *Brandraising.* San Francisco: Jossey-Bass, 2010.
4. Philip Kotler and Sidney J. Levy, "Broadening the Concept of Marketing" 15.

5. American Marketing Association (AMA), "Dictionary," last modified 2012, http://www .marketingpower.com/_layouts/Dictionary.aspx?source=footer, marketing.
6. John J. Burnett, *Nonprofit Marketing Best Practices* 24.
7. American Marketing Association (AMA), "Dictionary," brand and branding.
8. Kotler and Levy, "Broadening the Concept of Marketing" 15.
9. Angus Laing, "Marketing in the Public Sector" 429.
10. American Marketing Association, "All Marketing Journals," last modified 2012, http://www.marketingpower.com/Community/ARC/Pages/Research/Journals/Other/default.aspx.
11. Philip Kotler and Nancy R. Lee, *Social Marketing: Influencing Behaviors for Good,* 3rd ed., Los Angeles, CA: Sage, 2008.
12. Sarah Durham, *Brandraising.*
13. Walter Wymer Jr. et al., *Nonprofit Marketing.*
14. John J. Burnett, *Nonprofit Marketing Best Practices.*
15. Sarah Durham, *Brandraising.*
16. Angus Laing, "Marketing in the Public Sector."
17. Philip Kotler and Nancy R. Lee, *Social Marketing.*
18. Sarah Durham, *Brandraising.*
19. Dirk Singer, "Is Facebook Hitting Saturation Point?" *Social Media Today,* http://socialmediatoday.com/dirktherabbit/162374/facebook-hitting-saturation-point.
20. Neely, Daniel, "How Much Is That Facebook Fan Worth Anyway?" *Social Media Today,* last modified July 21, 2011, http://socialmediatoday.com/derekmeissner/3220w-much-facebook-fan-worth-anyway; although very few are likely to return to a nonprofit's fan page, it is important to note that they will continue to receive posts from the organization in their feeds, so they may not feel the need to return to the page.
21. Julie Moos, "Pew: Social Networking Use Doubles Among Adults, Does Not Weaken Relationships," *Poynter,* http://www.poynter.org/la-news/romenesko/136017/pew-social-networking-use-doubles-among-adults-since-2008-does-not-weaken-relationships/.
22. Schomerus, Mareike, Tim Allen, and Koen Vlassenroot, "Obama Takes on the LRA," *Foreign Affairs,* November 15, 2011, http://www.foreignaffairs.com/articles/136673/mareike-schomerus-tim-allen-and-koen-vlassenroot/obama-takes-on-the-lra?page=show.
23. Alex Perry, "The Warlord v. The Hipsters," *Time,* March 26, 2012, v. 179, no. 12, 36–41.
24. Invisible Children, http://www.invisiblechildren.com/index.html.
25. Alex Perry, "The Warlord v. The Hipsters."
26. Perry, "The Warlord"; The White House, Statement by the President on the Signing of the Lord's Resistance Army Disarmament and Northern Uganda Recovery Act of 2009, May 24, 2010, http://www.whitehouse.gov/the-press-office/statement-president-signing-lords-resistance-army-disarmament-and-northern-uganda-r.
27. Perry, "The Warlord."
28. Perry, "The Warlord."
29. Chase Community Giving Program Final Winners Announced, January 29, 2010, Foundation Center, http://foundationcenter.org/pnd/news/story.jhtml?id=283100012.
30. Rick Cohen, "Why Did 'Kony 2012' Fizzle Out?" *Nonprofit Quarterly,* April 26, 2012, www.nonprofitquarterly.org/policysocial-context/20216-why-did-kony-2012-fizzle-out.
31. Kate Cronin-Furman and Amanda Taub, "Solving War Crimes With Wristbands: The Arrogance of 'Kony 2012,'" *Atlantic Monthly,* www.theatlantic.com/international/archive/2012/03/solving-war-crimes-with-wristbands-the-arrogance-of-kony-2012/254193/ 3/10/12; Max Fisher, "The Soft Bigotry of Kony 2012."
32. Cronin-Furman and Taub, "Solving War Crimes."
33. Tony Perry and Shelby Grad, "'Kony' creator Jason Russell will remain hospitalized for weeks," *Los Angeles Times,* March 21, 2012, http://latimesblogs.latimes.com/lanow/2012/03/kony-creator-jason-russell-will-remain-hospitalized-for-weeks.html.
34. Mary Slosson, "ICC prosecutor courts Hollywood with Invisible Children," April 1, 2012, http://www.reuters.com/article/2012/04/01/us-kony-campaign-hollywood-idUSBRE8300JZ20120401.
35. Mike Keefe-Feldman, "Kony 2012: Can Social Media Help Topple a Tyrant?" March 7, 2012, National Public Radio, http://nonprofitquarterly.org/policysocial-context/19938-kony-2012-can-social-media-help-topple-a-tyrant.html.
36. Lee Rainie, Paul Hitlin, Mark Jurkowitz, Michael Dimock, and Shawn Neidorf, "The Viral Kony 2012 Video," March 15, 2012, Pew Research Center.
37. Rick Cohen, "Why did 'Kony 2012.'"
38. Ibid.
39. James Rainey, "Group behind 'Kony 2012' wins new respect," *Los Angeles Times,* Sunday, July 1, 2012, A6.
40. Julie Moos, "Pew: Social Networking Use Doubles Among Adults, Does Not Weaken Relationships," *Poynter,* http://www.poynter.org/la-news/romenesko/136017/pew-social-networking-use-doubles-among-adults-since-2008-does-not-weaken-relationships/.
41. Sarah Durham, *Brandraising* 19.
42. Walter Wymer, Jr. *et al,* Nonprofit Marketing, 152.
43. Walter Wymer Jr. et al., *Nonprofit Marketing,* 40.
44. Beverly T. Venable, Gregory M. Rose, Victoria D. Bush, and Faye W. Gilbert, "The Role of Brand Personality in Charitable Giving: An Assessment and Validation, *Journal of the Academy of Marketing Science* 33 (2005): 297.
45. Walter Wymer Jr. et al., *Nonprofit Marketing;* Sarah Durham, *Brandraising.*
46. Steven Zeitchik and Deborah Vankin, "Jerry Lewis Ousted as MDA Telethon Host," *Los Angeles Times,*" last modified August 5, 2011, http://articles.latimes.com/2011/aug/05/entertainment/la-et-jerry-lewis-20110805/2.
47. Walter Wymer Jr. et al., *Nonprofit Marketing;* Beverly T. Venable et al., "The Role of Brand Personality"; Philip Kotler and Nancy R. Lee, *Social Marketing.*
48. Adrian Sargeant, John B. Ford, and Jane Hudson, "Charity Brand Personality: The Relationship With Giving Behavior," *Nonprofit and Voluntary Sector Quarterly* 37 (2008): 471.
49. Thomas E. Nelson and Zoe M. Oaxley, "Framing Effects on Belief Importance and Opinion," *Journal of Politics* 61(1999): 1040–1067.
50. Walter Wymer Jr. et al., *Nonprofit Marketing.*
51. John J. Burnett, *Nonprofit Marketing Best Practices* 170.
52. Walter Wymer Jr. et al., *Nonprofit Marketing.*
53. Shane Raynor, "Marketing the UMC: Interview with UMCom's Larry Hollon," *Ministry Matters,* last modified August 1, 2010, www .ministrymatters.com/all/article/entry/780/advanced_search.html.
54. Andrew C. Thompson, "Gen-X Rising: 'Open Hearts' Slogan Is Marketing, not Theology," *United Methodist Portal,* last modified July 12, 2007, www.umportal.org/article.asp?id=2309.
55. See Brian V. Larson, "Gaining from a Giving Relationship: A Model to Examine Cause-Related Marketing's Effect on Salespeople," *Journal of Nonprofit and Public Sector Marketing* 8 (2001): 31–43; John Cantrell, Elias Kyriazis, Gary Noble, and Jennifer Algie,

"Towards NPOs Deeper Understanding of the Corporate Giving Manager's Role in Meeting Salient Stakeholders Needs," *Journal of Nonprofit and Public Sector Marketing* 20 (2008): 191–212.
56. Ted Gup, "The Weirdness of Walking to Raise Money," *New York Times*, last modified June 18, 2011, http://www.nytimes.com/2011/06/19/opinion/19gup.html?_r=1&pagewanted=print.
57. Charity Navigator, *2007 Special Events Study*, last modified May 1, 2007, http://www.charitynavigator.org/index.cfm/bay/studies.events.htm.
58. Vicki Thomas, "Cause-Related Marketing: Bringing Together Senior Organizations and Business," *Generations*, Winter 2004–2005, 71–74.
59. Amanda B. Bower and Stacy Landreth Grau, "Explicit Donations and Inferred Endorsements: Do Corporate Social Responsibility Initiatives Suggest a Nonprofit Organization Endorsement?" *Journal of Advertising*, 38 (2009): 113–126: Mark Pryor et al., "What's in a Nonprofit's Name?" http://www.atg.state.vt.us/assets/files/Whats%20in%20a%20Name_report-nonprofit_mkting.pdf.
60. Stacy Landreth Grau, Judith A. Garretson, and Julie Pirsch, "Cause-Related Marketing: An Exploratory Study of Campaign Donation Structures Issues," *Journal of Nonprofit & Public Sector Marketing*, 18 (2007): 69–91; Brian V. Larson, "Gaining from a Giving Relationship"; Pryor et al., "What's in a Nonprofit's Name?"
61. Cause Marketing Forum, "The Growth of Cause Marketing," 2010, http://www.causemarketingforum.com/site/c.bkLUKcOTLkK4E/b.6452355/apps/s/content. asp?ct=8965443.
62. Vicki Thomas, "Cause-Related Marketing" 74.
63. Brian V. Larson, "Gaining from a Giving Relationship."
64. Stacy Landreth Grau et al., "Cause-Related Marketing,"; Mary Runté, Debra Z. Basil, and Sameer Deshpande, "Cause-Related Marketing from the Nonprofit's Perspective: Classifying Goals and Experienced Outcomes," *Journal of Nonprofit & Public Sector Marketing* 21 (2009): 255–270.
65. Mary Runté et al., "Cause-Related Marketing from the Nonprofit's Perspective," 265.
66. Ibid.
67. Stacy Landreth Grau et al., "Cause-Related Marketing"; Chun-Tuan Chang, "To Donate or Not to Donate? Product Characteristics and Framing Effects of Cause-Related Marketing on Consumer Purchase Behavior," *Psychology & Marketing* 25 (2008): 1089–1110.
68. Stacy Landreth Grau et al., "Cause-Related Marketing."
69. This assignment was inspired by the discussion of positioning strategies in Walter Wymer Jr., Patricia Knowles, and Roger Gomes, *Nonprofit Marketing: Marketing Management for Charitable and Nongovernmental Organizations*, Thousand Oaks, CA: Sage, 2006; and the experiments regarding brand personality in Beverly T. Venable, Gregory M. Rose, Victoria D. Bush, and Faye W. Gilbert, "The Role of Brand Personality in Charitable Giving: An Assessment and Validation, *Journal of the Academy of Marketing Science* 33 (2005): 295–312.

Chapter 9

1. Kay Sprinkel Grace, *Beyond Fundraising: New Strategies for Non-Profit Innovation and Investment*, Hoboken, NJ: John Wiley & Sons, 2005, 7; emphasis in the original.
2. *Giving USA, Giving USA 2010: The Annual Report on Philanthropy for the Year 2009*, Chicago, IL: Giving USA Foundation, http://www.cfbroward.org/cfbroward/media/Documents/Sidebar%20Documents/GivingUSA_2010_ExecSummary_Print.pdf; *Giving USA, Giving USA 2011: The Annual Report on Philanthropy for the Year 2010*, Chicago, IL: Giving USA Foundation, http://www.givingusareports.org/products/GivingUSA_2011_ExecSummary_Print.pdf; *Giving USA 2012: The Annual Report on Philanthropy for the Year 2011*, Chicago, IL: Giving USA Foundation, http://store.givingusareports.org/.
3. SBA (U.S. Small Business Administration) Office of Advocacy, "Frequently Asked Questions," http://www.sba.gov/sites/default/files/sbfaq.pdf.
4. The Urban Institute study estimates that 16.4 percent of nonprofits that filed Form 990s (referred to as reporting organizations) in 1995 to 1997 were inactive or defunct by 2000 to 2002; extrapolation of these data suggests that 29.5 percent went dormant through 2006. Dormant nonprofits are defined as those that ceased filing Form 990 with the IRS. There are many reasons why an organization would not file Form 990—e.g. revenues fell below the $25,000 required for filing ($50,000 since 2008), the organization merged with another nonprofit, or the organization completed its mission and disbanded. It is also likely that the nonprofit was unable to maintain revenues or volunteers to sustain operations. For more information reference NCCS Knowledgebase—Assessing Births and Deaths of Nonprofit Organizations (Method Note) at http://nccsdataweb.urban.org/faq/detail.php?linkID=174&category=118.
5. Public charities are defined as organizations that are exempt from taxes under section 501(c)(3) of the Internal Revenue Code. For the purposes of their study, Boris and Roeger (2010) defined small as organizations with less than $100,000 in revenues, expenses, and assets.
6. Elizabeth T. Boris and Katie L. Roeger, "Grassroots Civil Society: The Scope and Dimensions of Small Public Charities," *Charting Civil Society: A Series by the Center on Nonprofits and Philanthropy* (Washington, DC: The Urban Institute, 2010).
7. As discussed in Chapter 4, Form 990 is an information return that tax-exempt organizations are required to file; prior to 2008, the reporting threshold was more than $25,000 in annual gross receipts; in 2008, the threshold was raised to $50,000.
8. See Karen A. Froelich, "Diversification of Revenue Strategies: Evolving Resource Dependence in Nonprofit Organizations," *Nonprofit and Voluntary Sector Quarterly* 28 (1999): 246–268; Caelesta Poppelaars, "Resource Exchange in Urban Governance: On the Means that Matter," *Urban Affairs Review* 43 (2007): 3–27; Jennifer E. Sowa, "The Collaboration Decision in Nonprofit Organizations: Views From the Front Line," *Nonprofit and Voluntary Sector Quarterly* 38 (2009): 1003–1025.
9. Jeffrey Pfeffer and Gerald R. Salancik, *The External Control of Organizations* (New York: Harper and Row, 1978), 2.
10. Elizabeth T. Boris and Katie L. Roeger, "Grassroots Civil Society."
11. Peter Eisinger, "Organizational Capacity and Organizational Effectiveness among Street-Level Food Assistance Programs," *Nonprofit and Voluntary Sector Quarterly* 31(2002): 115–130.
12. Paul C. Light, *Sustaining Nonprofit Performance* (Washington, DC: Brookings Institution Press, 2004).
13. According to the Bureau of Economic Research, the longest U.S. recession since World War II ended in June 2009 (Associated Press, 2010).
14. Twenty-three percent of respondents indicated the stimulus funds were used for a temporary program and would not need to be replaced.
15. Nonprofit Finance Fund, *2010 State of the Sector Survey*, http://nonprofitfinancefund.org/files/docs/2010/2010Survey031510-FinalSingles.pdf.

16. The 2012 survey did not include the same questions from the 2010 survey, so direct comparison of respondents expectations or experiences with sources of funding is not possible.
17. Nonprofit Finance Fund, *2012 State of the Sector Survey,* http://nonprofitfinancefund.org/files/docs/2012/2012survey_brochure.pdf.
18. Karen A. Froelich, "Diversification of Revenue Strategies"; Deborah A. Carroll and Keely Jones Stater, "Revenue Diversification in Nonprofit Organizations: Does it Lead to Financial Stability?" *Journal of Public Administration Research and Theory* 19 (2008): 947–966; Dennis R. Young, "Toward a Normative Theory of Nonprofit Finance," in *Financing Nonprofits,* ed. Dennis R. Young (Lanham, MD: AltaMira Press, 2007), 339–372.
19. Kathleen W. Buechel, Elizabeth K. Keating, and Clara Miller, *Capital Ideas: Moving from Short-Term Engagement to Long-Term Sustainability* (Hauser Center for Nonprofit Organizations, Harvard University and Nonprofit Finance Fund, 2007).
20. Evelyn Brody and Joseph J. Cordes, "Tax Treatment of Nonprofit Organizations: A Two-Edged Sword?" in *Nonprofits and Government: Collaboration and Conflict,* 2nd ed., ed. Elizabeth T. Boris and C. Eugene Steurele (Washington, DC: The Urban Institute Press, 2006); Burton A. Weisbrod, ed., *To Profit or Not to Profit: The Commercial Transformation of the Nonprofit Sector* (New York: Cambridge University Press, 1998).
21. Amanda L. Wilsker and Dennis R. Young, "How Does Program Composition Affect the Revenues of Nonprofit Organizations? Investigating a Benefits Theory of Nonprofit Finance," *Public Finance Review* 38 (2010): 197.
22. Ibid.
23. Katie L. Roeger, Amy Blackwood, and Sarah L. Pettijohn, *The Nonprofit Sector in Brief: Public Charities, Giving, and Volunteering, 2011* (Washington, DC: The Urban Institute, 2011).
24. Karen A. Froelich, "Diversification of Revenue Strategies."
25. Nonprofit Finance Fund, *2010 State of the Sector Survey,* http://nonprofitfinancefund.org/files/docs/2010/2010Survey031510-FinalSingles.pdf.
26. Ibid.
27. Estelle James, "Commercialism and the Mission of Nonprofits," *Society* 40 (2003): 29–35.
28. Ibid., 29
29. Ibid.; Burton A. Weisbrod, ed., *To Profit or Not to Profit.*
30. Tim Reason, "Sector-bender: More and More Nonprofits Have For-Profit Subsidiaries. Now One CFO Wants to Turn That Model Upside Down," *CFO Magazine,* last modified August 1, 2004, http://www.cfo.com/printable/article.cfm/3015387.
31. Dennis R. Young and Lester M. Salamon, "Commercialization, Social Ventures, and For-Profit Competition," in *The State of Nonprofit America,* ed. Lester M. Salamon (Washington, DC: Brookings Institution Press, 2002).
32. The two states without a ReStore (as of April 2011) are North Dakota and Vermont.
33. According to the BC Centre for Social Enterprise, an acceptable definition of the term social enterprise is a constant topic at meetings of scholars and practitioners in the field (BC Centre, n.d.). For more on a conceptual framework to better understand social enterprise, see http://www.41enses.org/.
34. enp, "What is Social Enterprise?" http://www.enterprisingnonprofits.ca/about.
35. "Selnet Social Enterprise Definition," last modified March 29, 2012, http://www.selnet-uk.com/index.php?option=com_content&view=article&id=47&Itemid=30.
36. Andy Horsnell, "What Social Enterprise Is (and Is Not)," http://managementhelp.org/soc_entr/soc_entr.htm#anchor2366.
37. Children's Advocacy Institute at the University of San Diego School of Law, "Expanding Transitional Services for Emancipated Foster Youth: An Investment in California's Tomorrow" (San Diego: University of San Diego School of Law, 2007).
38. Foundation Center, "Glossary of Terms, http://fconline.foundationcenter.org/fdhlp2/1glosary.htm.
39. Committee to Encourage Corporate Philanthropy (CECP), *Giving in Numbers: 2010 Edition, Executive Summary,* Washington, DC: CECP, 2010.
40. Committee to Encourage Corporate Philanthropy (CECP), *Business's Social Contract: Capturing the Corporate Philanthropy Opportunity* (Washington, DC: CECP, 2008), http://www.corporatephilanthropy.org/pdfs/research_reports/SocialContract.pdf.
41. CECP, *Giving in Numbers: 2010.*
42. Caroline Preston, "Rethinking Corporate Giving: Western Union's CEO Offers Her Philosophy," *The Chronicle of Philanthropy,* http://philanthropy.com/article/Rethinking-Corporate-Giving/65794/.
43. FedEx (Federal Express), "Charitable Contributions Guidelines," http://about.van.fedex.com/charitable-contribution-guidelines.
44. CECP, *Business's Social Contract.*
45. FedEx (Federal Express), "Child Pedestrian Safety," http://about.van.fedex.com/child-pedestrian-safety.
46. CECP, *Business's Social Contract.*
47. *Safe Kids Worldwide,* http://www.safekids.org/worldwide/.
48. Nonprofit Research Collaborative, *The 2010 Nonprofit Fundraising Survey: Funds Raised in 2010 Compared with 2009,* last modified March 2011, http://foundationcenter.org/gainknowledge/research/pdf/nrc_survey2011.pdf.
49. The remaining 19 percent ($56.22 billion) includes contributions by corporations and foundations; *Giving USA, Giving USA 2012: The Annual Report on Philanthropy for the Year 2011,* Chicago: Giving USA Foundation.
50. David M. Van Slyke and Janet L. Johnson, "Nonprofit organizational performance and resource development strategies," *Public Performance & Management Review* 29 (2006): 467–496; Amornrat Apinunmahakul, Vicky Barham, and Rose Anne Devlin, "Charitable Giving, Volunteering, and the Paid Labor Market," *Nonprofit and Voluntary Sector Quarterly* 38 (2009): 77–94.
51. Nonprofit Research Collaborative, *The 2010 Nonprofit Fundraising Survey.*
52. Thomas Wolf, *How to Connect with Donors and Double the Money you Raise* (Medfield, MA: Emerson & Church, 2011).
53. Kaitlin LaCasse, Laura S. Quinn, and Chris Bernard, *Using Social Media to Meet Nonprofit Goals: The Results of a Survey* (Portland, ME: Idealware, 2010).
54. Nicole Wallace, "Few Charities Are Raising Big Amounts Via Social Media, Says Study," *Chronicle of Philanthropy,* http://philanthropy.com/blogs/social-philanthropy/few-charities-are-raising-big-amounts-via-social-media-says-study/28416.
55. GuideStar, "Wired Fundraising: April Question of the Month Results," http://www2.guidestar.org/rxa/news/art/2007/wired-fundraising.aspx?articleId=1128.
56. Approximately $148 million raised in 2010 was specifically for earthquake disaster relief for Haiti; Noelle Barton and Maureen West. "Web-Savvy Supporters Help Make Online Giving an Expanding Bright Spot," *Chronicle of Philanthropy* 23 (2011): 1.
57. Network for Good, "No Hidden Fees Policy," http://www1.networkforgood.org/no-hidden-fees-policy.

58. Idealware, "Is Mobile Giving for Your Organization?" seminars. idealware.org/mobile/full_mobile_diagram.pdf.
59. Causes, "Create a Wish for Charity," http://wishes.causes.com/.
60. (www.royalweddingcharityfund.org.)
61. (www.officialroyalwedding2011.org.)
62. Charity Navigator, *2007 Special Events Study,* http://www.charitynavigator.org/index.cfm/bay/studies.events.htm.
63. Ibid.
64. Nicki McDermott, "A Race to the Top: Old Bill's Arrives at a Record-Breaking Total," *Community Foundation of Jackson Hole,* http://www.cfjacksonhole.org/wp-content/uploads/2011/10/10.24.2011Old-Bills-2011-Breaks-Records.pdf.
65. Ibid.
66. Reneé A. Irvin, "Endowments: Stable Largesse or Distortion of the Polity?" *Public Administration Review* 67 (2007): 446.
67. Jill Marshall and Deborah McCracken, "Understanding UPMIFA and its Evolution from UMIFA," *A Vanguard Research Note,* http://us.vocuspr.com/newsroom/ViewAttachment.aspx?SiteName=vanguardnew&Entity=PRAsset&AttachmentType=F&EntityID=743641&AttachmentID=5b5a07d0–8280–47e0–9c14–2439e8e4752e.
68. Kieran Marion and Katie Robinson, "Florida Is the 50th State to Enact Uniform Prudent Management of Institutional Funds Act," *Uniform Law Commission,* http://www.nccusl.org/NewsDetail.aspx?title=Florida%20is%2050th%20State%20to%20Enact%20Uniform%20Prudent%20Management%200f%20Institutional%20Funds%20Act.
69. Ibid., 4.
70. Ibid.
71. Reneé A. Irvin, "Endowments."
72. Marisa López-Rivera, "How the Survey of Endowments Was Compiled," *Chronicle of Philanthropy* 23 (June 2, 2011), 13.
73. Reneé A. Irvin, "Endowments."
74. Francie Ostrower, *Limited Life Foundations: Motivations, Experiences, and Strategies* (The Urban Institute: Center on Nonprofits and Philanthropy, 2009); Loren Renz and David Wolcheck, *Perpetuity or Limited Lifespan: How Do Family Foundations Decide?* The Foundation Center in cooperation with the Council on Foundations, 2009; John R. Thelin and Richard W. Trollinger, *Time Is of the Essence: Foundations and the Policies of Limited Life and Endowment Spend-Down,* Aspen Institute Program on Philanthropy and Social Innovation, 2009.
75. Max O. Stephenson Jr., Marcy H. Schnitzer, and Vero´ica M. Arroyave, "Nonprofit Governance, Management, and Organizational Learning: Exploring the Implications of One 'Mega-Gift,'" *American Review of Public Administration* 39 (2007): 43–49.
76. Barbara Benedek and David Rayfiel (Screenwriters), *Sabrina* [Motion Picture], Paramount Pictures, 1995.
77. Holden Kamofsky, "Update on How to Help Japan: No Room for More Funding. We Recommend Giving to Doctors Without Borders to Promote Better Disaster Relief in General," http://blog.givewell.org/2011/03/15/update-on-how-to-help-japan-funding-is-not-needed-we-recommend-giving-to-doctors-without-borders-to-promote-better-disaster-relief-in-general/.
78. Holden Karnofsky, "Japan Earthquake/Tsunami Relief Donations," *GiveWell Blog,* http://blog.givewell.org/2011/03/11/japan-earthquaketsunami-disaster-relief-donations/.
79. Diane L. Beers, *For the Prevention of Cruelty: The History and Legacy of Animal Rights Activism in the United States* (Athens, OH: Swallow Press/Ohio University Press, 2006).
80. www.aspcapro.org/spayneuter-faqs.php and www.americanhumane.org/assets/pdfs/animals/pa-pa-spay-neuter-article.pdf.
81. www.humanesociety.org/about/policy_statements/statement_companion_animals.html.
82. http://www.peta.org/about/why-peta/responsible-breeders.aspx.
83. http://www.peta.org/issues/Animals-in-Entertainment/animal-actors-command-performances.aspx.
84. www.humanesociety.org/about/policy_statements/statement_animals_research_entertainment_competition.html.
85. www.aspca.org/about-us/policy-positions/animal-actors.aspx.
86. www.aspca.org/online-community/transcripts/training-animals-for-the-camera-chat-transcript.aspx.
87. www.americanhumane.org/animals/programs/no-animals-were-harmed/about/history.html.
88. www.charitynavigator.org/index.cfm?bay=search.summary&orgid=3262 and www.charitynavigator.org/index.cfm?bay=search.summary&orgid=4314.
89. www.charitynavigator.org/index.cfm?bay=content.view&cpid=1287.

Chapter 10

1. Ellen Karsh and Arlen Sue Fox, *The Only Grant-Writing Book You'll Ever Need,* 2nd ed. (New York: Carroll & Graf Publishers, 2006), 1.
2. Katie L. Roeger, Amy Blackwood, and Sarah L. Pettijohn, *The Nonprofit Sector in Brief: Public Charities, Giving, and Volunteering, 2011* (Washington, DC: The Urban Institute, 2011).
3. The Foundation Center, "Number of Grantmaking Foundations, Assets, Total Giving, and Gifts Received, 1975 to 2009, last modified 2011, http://foundationcenter.org/findfunders/statistics/pdf/02_found_growth/2009/04_09.pdf.
4. Foundation Center, "Types of Support Awarded by Foundations, circa 1998," last modified 2000, http://foundationcenter.org/findfunders/statistics/pdf/07_fund_tos/1998/15_98.pdf.; Foundation Center, "Types of Support Awarded by Foundations, circa 2010," last modified 2012, http://foundationcenter.org/findfunders/statistics/pdf/07_fund_tos/2010/15_10.pdf.
5. Peter J. King Family Foundation, http://www.pjkingfamilyfoundation.org/index.php.
6. Francie Ostrower, *Limited Life Foundations: Motivations, Experiences, and Strategies.* (Washington, DC: The Urban Institute Center on Nonprofits and Philanthropy, 2009).
7. The initiative was co-sponsored by the Edna McConnell Clark Foundation, Open Society Institute, William and Flora Hewlett Foundation, Rockefeller Brothers Fund, and Surdna Foundation; the principal drafter of the guidelines was Paul Brest, president and CEO of the William and Flora Hewlett Foundation (Independent Sector, 2010).
8. Core support or general operating support, was defined as "funding directed to an organization's operations as a whole rather than to particular projects (project support)" (Independent Sector, 2010).
9. Independent Sector, *Building Value Together: Guidelines for the Funding of Nonprofit Organizations,* last modified, January 29, 2004, http://www.independentsector.org/building_value_together.
10. Francie Ostrower, *Limited Life Foundations.*
11. Independent Sector, *Building Value Together.*
12. Jeffrey Roth, Christopher S. Koper, Joseph Ryan, and Michael Buerger, "National Evaluation of the COPS Program—Briefing

Transcript," The Urban Institute, last modified September 7, 1999, http://www.urban.org/publications/900500.html.

13. Foundation Center, "Glossary of Terms," http://fconline.foundationcenter.org/fdhlp2/1glosary.htm.
14. Jeremy L. Hall, "Assessing Local Capacity for Federal Grant-Getting," *American Review of Public Administration,* 38 (2008): 463–79.
15. Angel Braestrup, "The Challenge of Challenge Grants," *Nonprofit Quarterly,* last modified March 21, 2004, http://www.nonprofitquarterly.org/philanthropy/765-the-challenge-of-challenge-grants.html.
16. Dennis R. Young, "Complementary, Supplementary, or Adversarial? A Theoretical and Historical Examination of Nonprofit-Government Relations in the United States," in *Nonprofits and Government, ed.* Elizabeth T. Boris and C. Eugene Steuerle (Washington, DC: Urban Institute Press, 1999).
17. Lester A. Salamon, *Partners in Public Service* (Baltimore: Johns Hopkins University Press, 1995).
18. Except where otherwise noted, the information for this case study was derived from the Police Foundation website at www.policefoundation.org.
19. Corey Ray, "U.S. Department of Justice COPS Office Awards over $243 Million to Hire New Officers," last modified September 28, 2011, www .cops.usdoj.gov/Default.asp?Item=2600.
20. Micheal J. Austin, "The Changing Relationship between Nonprofit Organizations and Public Social Service Agencies in the Era of Welfare Reform," *Nonprofit and Voluntary Sector Quarterly* 32 (2003): 97–114; Mary Bryna Sanger, *The Welfare Marketplace: Privatization and Welfare Reform* (Washington, DC: The Brookings Institution, 2003); Carol J. De Vita and Eric C. Twombly, "Nonprofits and Federalism"; Katherine M. O'Regan and Sharon M. Oster, "Nonprofit and For-Profit Partnerships: Rationale and Challenges of Cross-Sector Contracting," *Nonprofit and Voluntary Sector Quarterly* 29 (2000): 120–140.
21. Phillip J. Cooper, *Governing by Contract* (Washington, DC: CQ Press, 2003).
22. Austin, Michael J., "The Changing Relationship between Nonprofit Organizations and Public Social Service Agencies in the Era of Welfare Reform," *Nonprofit and Voluntary Sector Quarterly* 32 (2003): 97–114; Lester A. Salamon, *Partners in Public Service* (Baltimore: Johns Hopkins University Press, 1995).
23. Michael J. Austin, "The Changing Relationship between Nonprofit Organizations and Public Social Service Agencies in the Era of Welfare Reform," *Nonprofit and Voluntary Sector Quarterly* 32 (2003): 97–114; David M. Van Slyke, "Agents or Stewards: Using Theory to Understand the Government-Nonprofit Social Service Contracting Relationship," *Journal of Public Administration Research and Theory* 17 (2007): 157–187.
24. Mary Bryna Sanger, *The Welfare Marketplace;* Barbara Peat, and Dan L. Costley, "Effective Contracting of Social Services," *Nonprofit Management & Leadership* 12 (2001): 55–74.
25. Nadine T. Jalandoni, Claudia Petrescu, and Gordon W. Green, "Government Funding and the Nonprofit Sector: Exploring a New Census Bureau Data Source—The Federal Audit Clearinghouse," *Nonprofit and Voluntary Sector Quarterly* 34 (2005): 260–275.
26. For more information, see http://www.tn.gov/ecd/BD_CDBG_block_grant_program.html#3 and http://dlg.ky.gov/grants/federal/cdbg.htm.
27. Ruth Hoogland DeHoog, "Evaluating Human Services Contracting: Managers, Professionals, and Politicos," *State & Local Government Review* 18 (1986): 37–44; Barbara Peat and Dan L. Costley, "Effective contracting of social services," *Nonprofit Management & Leadership* 12 (2001): 55–74.
28. Michael J. Austin, "The Changing Relationship between Nonprofit Organizations and Public Social Service Agencies in the Era of Welfare Reform," *Nonprofit and Voluntary Sector Quarterly* 32 (2003): 97–114; Mary Bryna Sanger, *The Welfare Marketplace: Privatization and Welfare Reform* (Washington, DC: The Brookings Institution, 2003); Carol J. De Vita and Eric C. Twombly, "Nonprofits and Federalism," in *Nonprofits and Government,* 2nd ed., ed. Elizabeth T. Boris and C. Eugene Steuerle (Washington, DC: Urban Institute Press, 2006); Dennis R. Young, "Toward a Normative Theory of Nonprofit Finance," in *Financing Nonprofits,* ed. Dennis R. Young (Lanham, MD: AltaMira Press, 2007), pp. 339–372.
29. DeHoog, "Evaluating Human Services Contracting"; Vincent Gooden, "Contracting and Negotiation: Effective Practices of Successful Human Service Contract Managers," *Public Administration Review* 58 (1998): 499–509; Austin, "The Changing Relationship"; Van Slyke, "Agents or Stewards."
30. Austin, "The Changing Relationship"; Sanger, *The Welfare Marketplace;* De Vita and Twombly, "Nonprofits and Federalism."
31. Gooden, "Contracting and Negotiation"; Van Slyke, "Agents or Stewards."
32. John D. Donahue, *The Privatization Decision: Public Ends, Private Means* (New York: Basic Books, 1989); Steven Rathgeb Smith and Michael Lipsky, *Nonprofits for Hire: The Welfare State in the Age of Contracting* (Cambridge, MA: Harvard University Press, 1994); Cooper, *Governing by Contract;* Barbara Peat and Dan L. Costley, "Effective Contracting of Social Services," *Nonprofit Management & Leadership* 12 (2001): 55–74; Mary K. Marvel and Howard P. Marvel, "Outsourcing Oversight: A Comparison of Monitoring for In-house and Contracted Services," *Public Administration Review* 67 (2007): 521–530; Van Slyke, "Agents or Stewards."
33. Marvel and Marvel, "Outsourcing Oversight."
34. Van Slyke, "Agents or Stewards."
35. Marvel and Marvel, "Outsourcing Oversight."
36. DeHoog, "Evaluating Human Services Contracting."
37. Van Slyke, "Agents or Stewards."
38. DeHoog, "Evaluating Human Services Contracting"; Smith and Lipsky, *Nonprofits for Hire;* Austin, "The Changing Relationship."
39. Young, "Toward a Normative Theory"; Michael Rushton and Arthur C. Brooks, "Government Funding of Nonprofit Organizations," in *Financing Nonprofits,* ed. Dennis R. Young (Lanham, MD: AltaMira Press, 2007), 69–91.
40. Smith and Lipsky, *Nonprofits for Hire.*
41. Austin, "The Changing Relationship"; Sanger, *The Welfare Marketplace;* DeVita and Twombly, "Nonprofits and Federalism"; Katherine M. O'Regan and Sharon M. Oster, "Nonprofit and For-Profit Partnerships: Rationale and Challenges of Cross-Sector Contracting," *Nonprofit and Voluntary Sector Quarterly* 29 (2000): 120–140.
42. Lee Michael Katz, "Carnegie Corporation of New York: Creating Philanthropy & Building Institutions," *Carnegie Reporter* 1 (2010): 2–14.
43. Government Printing Office, "Summaries by Agency," *Budget of the United States Government, Fiscal Year 2000,* p. 383, http://govinfo.library.unt.edu/npr/library/omb/budget.pdf; Gates Foundation, Foundation Timeline, http://www.gatesfoundation.org/about/Pages/foundation-timeline.aspx.

44. Katz, "Carnegie Corporation."
45. Bill and Melinda Gates, "Letter from Bill and Melinda Gates," http://www.gatesfoundation.org/about/Pages/bill-melinda-gates-letter.aspx.
46. Gates Foundation, Foundation Fact Sheet, http://www.gatesfoundation.org/about/Pages/foundation-fact-sheet.aspx.
47. Foundation Center, "50 Largest Corporate Foundations by Asset Size, 2009," http://foundationcenter.org/findfunders/statistics/pdf/11_topfdn_type/2009/top50_aa_cs_09.pdf; Dennis & Phyllis Washington Foundation, Inc., http://www.dpwfoundation.org/about.php.
48. Prince Charitable Trusts, http://foundationcenter.org/grantmaker/prince/.
49. Foundation Center, "50 Largest Corporate Foundations by Asset Size, 2009," http://foundationcenter.org/findfunders/statistics/pdf/11_topfdn_type/2009/top50_aa_cs_09.pdf.
50. Alcoa Foundation, http://www.alcoa.com/global/en/community/foundation/info_page/about_overview.asp.
51. Foundation Center, "50 Largest Corporate Foundations by Asset Size, 2009."
52. Foundation Center, *Key Facts on Community Foundations*, Foundation Center, last modified April 2011, http://foundationcenter.org/gainknowledge/research/pdf/keyfacts_comm2011.pdf.
53. IRS (Internal Revenue Service), "Donor-Advised Funds," last modified October 24, 2011, http://www.irs.gov/charities/charitable/article/0,,id=182839,00.html.
54. Holly Welch Stubbing, C. Barton Landess, Fontella McKyer, Shilpa Patel, and Chris McLeod, "New Charitable Giving Incentives & Exempt Organization Reforms: Pension Protection Act of 2006," *Information Alert: News from Foundation for the Carolinas*, last modified Fourth Quarter 2006, http://www.fftc.org/NetCommunity/Document.Doc?id=102.
55. Foundation Center, *Key Facts on Community Foundations.*
56. IRS, "Definition of Private Operating Foundation," last modified January 30, 2012, http://www.irs.gov/charities/foundations/article/0,,id=136869,00.html.
57. Our thanks to Pamela Napier of the Western Kentucky University Office of Sponsored Programs who so eloquently described the grant proposal process for our students during a seminar on proposal writing.
58. Information for this section was derived from more than a decade of researching and preparing grant proposals, as well as teaching courses that included proposal preparation; for additional information on preparing grant proposals, we recommend the book by Ellen Karsh and Arlen Sue Fox listed in the Suggested Readings at the end of the chapter.
59. "The Morrill Act" (PL 12–503, July 2, 1862.
60. General revenue sharing (GRS), which ended during the Reagan administration, had the least federal government control of any of the grant types. Under general revenue sharing, states and local governments were given direct aid from the federal government to be used for general government purposes with very few strings attached.
61. Carol J. De Vita and Eric C. Twombly, "Nonprofits and Federalism," in *Nonprofits and Government*, 2nd ed., ed. Elizabeth T. Boris and C. Eugene Steuerle (Washington, DC: Urban Institute Press, 2006).
62. As discussed in Chapter 2, there was little empirical evidence of discrimination against FBOs in the awarding of government contracts prior to passage of the Charitable Choice provision.
63. Joan E. Pynes, "Human Resources Management Challenges for Nonprofit Organizations," *Public Personnel Management Current Concerns, Future Challenges*, 4th ed., ed. Norma M. Riccucci (New York: Pearson Longman, 2004), 225–242.
64. Waldemar A. Nielsen, *Golden Donors: A New Anatomy of the Great Foundations* (New Brunswick, NJ: Transaction Publishers, 2002).
65. Francie Ostrower, *Limited Life Foundations: Motivations, Experiences, and Strategies* (Washington, DC: The Urban Institute: Center on Nonprofits and Philanthropy, 2009); John R. Thelin, John R. Trollinger, and Richard W. Trollinger, *Time is of the Essence: Foundations and the Policies of Limited Life and Endowment Spend-Down*, The Aspen Institute Program on Philanthropy and Social Innovation, last modified October 28, 2009, http://www.aspeninstitute.org/sites/default/files/content/docs/pubs/Time%20is%20f%20the%20Essence%20FINAL_0.pdf; Reneé A. Irvin, "Endowments: Stable Largesse or Distortion of the Polity?" *Public Administration Review* 67 (2007): 445–457.
66. Marion Fremont-Smith, "Accumulations of Wealth by Nonprofits," The Urban Institute Seminar Series *Emerging Issues in Philanthropy*, last modified August 1, 2004, urban.org/UploadedPDF/311022_accumulations_of_wealth.pdf.
67. Ibid.; Ostrower, *Limited Life Foundations;* Irvin, "Endowments."
68. Ostrower, *Limited Life Foundations.*
69. Nielsen, *Golden Donors*, 425.
70. Ibid., p.426.
71. See also Bill Bradley, Paul Jansen, and Les Silverman, "The Nonprofit Sector's $100 Billion Opportunity," *Harvard Business Review*, May 2003), 81, 5, 94–103.

Chapter 11

1. Leslie R. Crutchfield and Heather McLeod Grant, *Forces for Good* (San Francisco: Jossey-Bass, 2008), 184.
2. Peter F. Drucker, *Managing the Nonprofit Organization* (New York: HarperCollins, 2005), 107.
3. Bill Bradley, Paul Jansen, and Les Silverman, "The Nonprofit Sector's $100 Billion Opportunity," *Harvard Business Review*, May 2003, 81, 5 94–103.
4. Robert D. Herman and David O. Renz, "Advancing nonprofit organizational effectiveness research and theory, *Nonprofit Management & Leadership* 18, 4 (2008): 399–415; David O. Renz, "Adding a few more pieces to the puzzle: Exploring the practical implications of recent research on boards," *Nonprofit Quarterly* 18, 1(2011): 14–20; Jennifer Bright Preston and William A. Brown, "Commitment and Performance of Nonprofit Board Members," *Nonprofit Management & Leadership* 15 (2004): 221–238; Jens Rowold and Anette Rohmann, "Relationships between Leadership Styles and Followers' Emotional Experience and Effectiveness in the Voluntary Sector," *Nonprofit and Voluntary Sector Quarterly* 38 (2009): 270–286; Bradley E.Wright and Sanjay K. Pandey, 'Transformational Leadership in the Public Sector: Does Structure Matter?" *Journal of Public Administration Research and Theory* 20 (2009): 75–89; Rhys Andrews and George A. Boyne, "Capacity, Leadership, and Organizational Performance: Testing the Black Box Model of Public Management," *Public Administration Review* 70 (2010): 443–454; Tracey Trottier, Montgomery Van Wart, and Xiao Hu Wang, "Examining the Nature and Significance of

Leadership in Government Organizations,"*Public Administration Review* 68 (2008): 319–333.

5. Max Weber, *Essays in Sociology,* ed. and trans., H.H. Gerth and C. Wright Mills (New York: Oxford University Press, 1964).
6. Henri Fayol, *General and Industrial Management,* trans. Constance Storrs (London: Pitman, 1949); Frederick Winslow Taylor, *The Principles of Scientific Management* (New York: Harper & Brothers, 1911).
7. Luther Gulick, "Notes on the Theory of Organization," in *Papers on the Study of Administration,* ed. Luther Gulick and Lyndall Urwick (New York: Institute of Public Administration, 1937), 3–13.
8. Kenneth J. Meier and John Bohte, "Ode to Luther Gulick: Span of Control and Organizational Performance," *Administration and Society* 32 (May 2000): 115–137.
9. Ludwig Von Bertalanffy, "Problems of General System Theory," *Human Biology* 23 (1951):302–311.
10. Anthony Downs, *Inside Bureaucracy* (Boston: Little, Brown and Co., 1966); William B. Werther Jr. and Evan M. Berman, *Third Sector Management: The Art of Managing Nonprofit Organizations* (Washington, DC: Georgetown University Press, 2001).
11. Henry Mintzberg, *The Structure of Organizations* (Upper Saddle River, NJ: Prentice Hall, 1979).
12. Sharon Oster, *Strategic Management for Nonprofit Organizations: Theory and Cases* (New York: Oxford University Press, 1995), 25.
13. Sharon Oster, *Strategic Management;* Werther and Berman, *Third Sector Management.*
14. Sharon Oster, *Strategic Management,* 152.
15. Sharon Oster, *Strategic Management.*
16. liveonpoint.org, http://www.liveonpoint.org/about-us/what-is-on-point, retrieved on July 11, 2010.
17. Bill Silverfarb, "Family Homelessness on Rise," *Daily Journal* [San Mateo, CA], Monday, June 28, 2010; http://smdailyjournal.com/article_preview.php?type=lnews&title=Family%20homelessness%200n%20.rise&id=134614&eddate=06/28/2010%20 03:30:00.
18. Michele Jackson, From our executive director Michele Jackson, Shelter Network's Network News, Summer 2010; http://www.shelter-network.org/pdfs/ShelterNetworkSummer2010NewsletterColorweb.pdf; Shelter Network, May 11, 2011, Press Release: Non-Profits Partner to Give New Beds to the Homeless, http://www.shelternetwork.org/pdfs/ShelterNetwork_PressRelease5.11.11.pdf.
19. Edward L. Glaeser, "Introduction," in *The Governance of Nonprofit Organizations,* ed. Edward L. Glaeser (Chicago: University of Chicago Press, 2003), 1–43.
20. Sharon Oster, *Strategic Management.*
21. Ibid, 154.
22. Anthony Downs, Inside Bureaucracy.
23. Laura Murray, and Katie Cadigan, *When Medicine Got it Wrong* (Watertown, MA: Documentary Educational Resources, 2009). DVD and transcripts.
24. Harriet Shetler, *A History of the National Alliance for the Mentally Ill* (Arlington, VA: National Alliance for the Mentally Ill, 1986); and Carol Howe and Jim Howe, "The National Alliance for the Mentally Ill: History and Ideology," in *Families of the Mentally Ill: Meeting the Challenges,* ed. A.B. Hatfield, New Directions for Mental Health Services, No. 34 (San Francisco,: Jossey-Bass, 1987).
25. Shetler, *A History.*
26. NAMI. n.d. "What Is NAMI Fact Sheet," www.nami.org/Template.cfm?Section=About_NAMI&Template=/ContentManagement/ContentDisplay.cfm&ContentID=83899.
27. NAMI "About Public Policy," www.nami.org/Content/NavigationMenu/Inform_Yourself/About_Public_Policy/About_Public_Policy.htm.
28. Peter F. Drucker, *Managing the Nonprofit;* Mark H. Moore, "Managing for Value: Organizational Strategy in For-Profit, Nonprofit, and Governmental Organizations," *Nonprofit and Voluntary Sector Quarterly* 29 (2000): 183–204; Marc Lindenberg, "Are we at the cutting edge or the blunt edge? Improving NGO organizational performance with private and public sector strategic management frameworks," *Nonprofit Management & Leadership* 11, 3 (2001): 247–270; Tammy E. Beck, Cynthia A. Lengnick-Hall, and Mark L. Lengnick-Hall, "Solutions out of Context: Examining the Transfer of Business Concepts to Nonprofit Organizations," *Nonprofit Management & Leadership* 19, 2 (2008): 153–171; Leslie R. Crutchfield and Heather McLeod Grant, *Forces for Good.*
29. Mary Bryna Sanger, *The Welfare Marketplace: Privatization and Welfare Reform* (Washington, DC: The Brookings Institution, 2003); Frank A. Sloan, "Commercialism in Nonprofit Hospitals," in *To Profit or Not to Profit: The Commercial Transformation of the Nonprofit Sector,* ed. Burton A. Weisbrod (New York: Cambridge University Press, 1998).
30. Thomas P. Holland, and Roger A. Ritvo, *Nonprofit Organizations, Principles and Practices* (New York: Columbia University Press, 2008); Charles T. Goodsell, *The Case for Bureaucracy* (Washington, DC: CQ Press, 2004).
31. Sharon Oster, *Strategic Management;* Jessica K. A. Word, "Human Resource Leadership and Management," in *Leadership in Nonprofit Organizations,* ed. Kathryn Agard (Thousand Oaks, CA: Sage, 2010).
32. Peter F. Drucker, *Managing the Nonprofit.*
33. Ibid., 117.
34. Nancy Winemiller Basinger and Jessica Romine Peterson "Where You Stand Depends on Where You Sit," *Nonprofit Management & Leadership* 19 (2008): 243–257.
35. Robert D. Herman and David O. Renz, "Advancing Nonprofit Organizational Effectiveness"; Paul C. Light, *Sustaining Nonprofit Performance* (Washington, DC: Brookings Institution Press, 2004); Jo Ann M. Zimmermann, Bonnie W. Stevens, Brenda J. Thames, Christopher M. Sieverdes, and Gwynn M. Powell, "The DIRECTIONS Nonprofit Resource Assessment Model, A Tool for Small Nonprofit Organizations," *Nonprofit Management & Leadership* 14, 1 (2003): 79–91; Sonia Ospina, William Diaz, and James F. O'Sullivan, "Negotiating Accountability: Managerial Lessons from Identity-Based Nonprofit Organizations," *Nonprofit and Voluntary Sector Quarterly* 31, 1 (2002): 5–31.
36. Robert D. Herman and David O. Renz, "Doing Things Right: Effectiveness in Local Nonprofit Organizations, a Panel Study," *Public Administration Review* 64, 6 (2004): 694–704.
37. Paul C. Light, *Sustaining Nonprofit Performance* (Washington, DC: Brookings Institution Press, 2004): Leslie R. Crutchfield and Heather McLeod Grant, *Forces.*
38. Peter F. Drucker, *Managing the Nonprofit,* 117.
39. Ibid., 119.
40. David L. Kushner, "The Significant Role that the Legislative Process Can Play in Fulfilling the Mission of a Not-for-Profit," in *The Legislative Labyrinth: A Map for Not-for-Profits,* ed. Walter P. Pidgeon Jr. (New York: John Wiley & Sons), 4–36.

41. Sharon Oster, *Strategic Management;* Mark H. Moore, *Managing for Value;* William B. Werther Jr. and Evan M. Berman, *Third Sector;* Evan M. Berman, *Productivity in Public and Nonprofit Organizations* (Thousand Oaks, CA: Sage Publications, 1998).
42. Mark H. Moore, *Managing for Value.*
43. GASB (Governmental Accounting Standards Board), *Facts About GASB,* p. 1, www.gasb.org/cs/BlobServer?blobcol=urldata&blobtable=Mungo Blobs&blobkey=id&blobwhere=1175824006278&blobheader=application%2Fpdf.
44. Steve De Vries, "GASB-34 Infrastructure Reporting," Paper presented at the joint ISAC/Iowa League of Cities Conference on GASB-34, Des Moines, IA, 2000.
45. Moore gives a model of the triangle for for-profit organizations and a second model for public organizations, but he does not show a separate model of the triangle for nonprofits. In his discussion, however, Moore notes the fact that the public model is more applicable to nonprofits than the for-profit model. Thus, Figure 11.2 is an adaptation from what Moore describes.
46. Ibid., 198.
47. Peter F. Drucker, *Managing the Nonprofit,* 120; Ibid., 119.
48. Thomas J. Peters and Robert H. Waterman Jr., *In Search of Excellence* (New York: Warner Books, 1982); Robert D. Behn, "Management by Groping Along," *Journal of Policy Analysis and Management* 7, 4 (1988): 643–663.
49. Ronald A. Heifitz and Donald L. Laurie, "The Work of Leadership," *Harvard Business Review,* January-February 1997,124–134.
50. Evan M. Berman, *Productivity,* 5.
51. Mark H. Moore, *Managing for Value.*
52. Evan M. Berman, *Productivity,* 8.
53. Ibid., 5–6.
54. See chapter 14 for a more thorough discussion of evaluation of nonprofit activity.
55. Ibid., 6.
56. Bill Bradley, Paul Jansen, and Les Silverman, "The Nonprofit Sector's $100 Billion."
57. Peter Eisinger, "Organizational Capacity and Organizational Effectiveness Among Street-Level Food Assistance Programs," *Nonprofit and Voluntary Sector Quarterly* 31 (2002): 128.
58. Robert L. Fischer, "The Sea Change in Nonprofit Human Services: Critical Assessment of Outcomes Measurement," *Families in Society: The Journal of Contemporary Human Services* 82, 6 (2001): 561–568.
59. Leslie R. Crutchfield and Heather McLeod Grant, *Forces,* 1
60. Leslie R. Crutchfield and Heather McLeod Grant, *Forces,* 11.
61. Ibid., 32.
62. Ibid., 21.
63. Ibid.
64. Ibid., 22.
65. Ibid.
66. Ibid.
67. Ibid.
68. Ibid.
69. Paul C. Light, *Sustaining Nonprofit;* Marc Lindenberg, "Are We at the Cutting Edge"; Charles T. Goodsell, *The Case for Bureaucracy;* Samantha L. Durst and Charldean Newell, "The Who, Why, and How of Reinvention in Nonprofit Organizations," *Nonprofit Management and Leadership* 11 (2001): 443–457.
70. Thomas J. Peters and Robert H. Waterman Jr., *In Search;* Tom Osborne and David Gaebler, *Reinventing Government: How the Entrepreneurial Spirit is Transforming the Public Sector* (Reading, MA: Addison Wesley, 1992).
71. Christopher Hood, "A Public Management for All Seasons?" *Public Administration* 69 (1991): 3–19.
72. Paul C. Light, *Sustaining Nonprofit.*
73. allianceonline.org, https://www.allianceonline.org/.
74. Paul C. Light, *Sustaining Nonprofit,* 15.
75. Paul C. Light, *Sustaining Nonprofit;* Alan J. Abramson and Rachel McCarthy, "Infrastructure Organizations," in *The State of Nonprofit America,* ed. Lester M. Salamon (Washington, DC: Brookings Institution Press, 2002), 331–354; Kennard T. Wing, "Assessing the Effectiveness of Capacity-Building Initiatives: Seven Issues for the Field," *Nonprofit and Voluntary Sector Quarterly* 33 (2004): 153–160; John Mandeville, "Public Policy Grant Making: Building Organizational Capacity among Nonprofit Grantees," *Nonprofit and Voluntary Sector Quarterly* 36(2007): 282–298.
76. Alliance for Nonprofit Management, "About the Alliance," http://www.allianceonline.org/about-alliance.
77. Paul C. Light, *Sustaining Nonprofit,* 53.
78. Samantha L. Durst and Charldean Newell, "The Who, Why, and How."
79. Paul C. Light, *Sustaining Nonprofit;* Samantha L. Durst and Charldean Newell, "The Who, Why, and How"; Marc Lindenberg, "Are We at the Cutting Edge"; R. Paton, J. Foot, and G. Payne, "What Happens When Nonprofits Use Quality Models for Self-Assessment?" *Nonprofit Management & Leadership* 11 (2000):21–34.
80. Samantha L. Durst and Charldean Newell, "The Who, Why, and How," 454.
81. CAPA, http://www.capa.com/files/press-room/cso-local-release-final.pdf.
82. Elizabeth Blair, "Everyone Else Outsources, Why Can't the Arts?" National Public Radio, Weekend Edition, Sunday, May 22, 2010, http://www.wbur.org/npr/127039922.
83. Elizabeth Blair, "Everyone Else"; CAPA, www.capa.com.
84. CAPA, http://www.capa.com/about-capa/shared-services.
85. Marc Lindenberg, "Are We at the Cutting Edge," 248.
86. Sally Shaw and Justine B. Allen, "To Be a Business and to Keep Our Humanity," *Nonprofit Management & Leadership* 20 (2009): 88.
87. Paul C. Light, *Sustaining Nonprofit,* 55.
88. Marc Lindenberg, "Are We at the Cutting Edge," 268.
89. Lynne A. Weikart, Greg G. Chen, and Ed Sermier, *Budgeting and Financial Management for Nonprofit Organizations: Using Money to Drive Mission Success* (Washington, DC: CQ Press, 2013).
90. Jae K. Shim and Joel G. Siegel, *Financial Management for Nonprofits: The Complete Guide to Maximizing Resources and Managing Assets* (Chicago: Irwin Professional Publishers, 1997).
91. Ibid.
92. Thad D. Calabrese, "Do Donors Penalize Nonprofit Organizations with Accumulated Wealth?" *Public Administration Review* 71(2011): 859–869.
93. Sarah E. Waldeck, *The Coming Showdown Over University Endowments: Enlisting the Donor,* http://works.bepress.com/sarah_waldeck/1; Stephanie Strom, "How Long Should Gifts Just Grow?" *New York Times,* November 12, 2007, http://query.nytimes.com/gst/fullpage.html?res=9404E1DA123EF931A25752C1A9619C8B63&sec=&spon=&pagewanted=all.
94. Christine Williamson, "College Endowment Returns Surge for Fiscal Year 2011," Pensions & Investments Online, Feb. 1, 2012, http://www.pionline.com/article/20120201/REG/120209999/college-endowment-returns-surge-for-fiscal-year-2011.

95. David Greco, "Nonprofit Financial Management," in *Nonprofit Management 101,* ed. Darian Rodriguez Heyman (San Francisco: Jossey-Bass, 2011).
96. Dennis R. Young, "Why Study Nonprofit Finance?" in *Financing Nonprofits,* ed. Dennis R. Young (Lanham, MD: AltaMira Press, 2007), 3–20.
97. Dennis R. Young, "Toward a Normative Theory of Nonprofit Finance," in *Financing Nonprofits,* ed. Dennis R. Young (Lanham, MD: AltaMira Press, 2007), 339–372.
98. Woods Bowman and Elizabeth Keating, "On Nonprofit Investment Income," *Nonprofit Quarterly,* June 21, 2006, http://www.nonprofit-quarterly.org/management/638-on-nonprofit-investment-income.html.
99. Ibid.
100. Ibid.
101. Christine Williamson, "College Endowment Returns Surge for Fiscal Year 2011," Pensions & Investments Online, February 1, 2012, http://www.pionline.com/article/20120201/REG/120209999/college-endowment-returns-surge-for-fiscal-year-2011.
102. Bowman and Keating, "On Nonprofit Investment."
103. Murray Dropkin, Jim Halpin, and Bill La Touche, *The Budget-Building Book for Nonprofits, A Step-by-Step Guide for Managers and Boards* (San Francisco: John Wiley and Sons, 2007), 3.
104. Ibid.
105. Ibid., 13.
106. Ibid., 14.
107. Edmund G. Brown Jr., California Attorney General's Guide for Charities (Sacramento, CA: State of California, 2005).
108. David Greco, "Nonprofit Financial Management," in *Nonprofit Management 101,* ed. by Darian Rodriguez Heyman (San Francisco: Jossey-Bass, 2011).
109. Murray Dropkin, Jim Halpin, and Bill La Touche, *The Budget-Building Book;* Jae K. Shim and Joel G. Siegel, *Financial Management.*
110. Steve Bullock, *Montana Attorney General's Investigative Report of Greg Mortenson and Central Asia Institute,* April 2012, p. 26; http://www.kxlh.com/files/cai.pdf.
111. M. Shah, "Tracking Down Mortenson's Schools in Pakistan," *Radio Free Europe/Radio Liberty,* http://www.rferl.org/content/mortenson_schools_pakistan_cai/24176299.html.
112. Murray Dropkin, Jim Halpin, and Bill La Touche, *The Budget-Building Book for Nonprofits;* Jae K. Shim and Joel G. Siegel, *Financial Management;* Dennis R. Young, "Toward a Normative Theory"; Jerry Soto, "Fundamentals of a First-Rate Budget," *California Association of Nonprofits (CAN) Alert,* January-February 2002, 1–6.
113. This discussion is largely adopted from Soto (2002), Strand and Crabb (2006), and Dropkin, Halpin, and La Touche's *The Budget-Building Book for Nonprofits,* 2007. We recommend Dropkin, et al.'s user-friendly and hands-on book in the Supplemental Readings section of this chapter, as it offers a relevant "how-to" approach to nonprofit budgeting and includes a CD-Rom of exhibits and worksheets.
114. Elizabeth Hamilton Foley, "Internal Reporting for Good Management: Statement of Financial Activities," Greater Washington Society of CPAs, http://www.nonprofitaccountingbasics.org/internal-reporting-good-management/internal-reports/statement-activities.
115. Jerry Soto, *Fundamentals;* Alan Strand and Kathy Crabb, "Secrets of Cost Allocation," *California Association of Nonprofits (CAN) Alert* 19 (2006): 1–10.
116. Alan Strand and Kathy Crabb, "Secrets," 2.
117. Alan Strand and Kathy Crabb, "Secrets of Cost Allocation," *California Association of Nonprofits (CAN) Alert* 19 (2006): 1–10.

Chapter 12

1. Ruth McCambridge, "Underestimating the Power of Nonprofit Governance," *Nonprofit and Voluntary Sector Quarterly* 33 (2004): 352.
2. Henry Mintzberg, *The Structure of Organizations* (Upper Saddle River, NJ: Prentice Hall, 1979).
3. Melissa M. Stone and Francie Ostrower, "Acting in the Public Interest? Another Look at Research on Nonprofit Governance," *Nonprofit and Voluntary Sector Quarterly* 36 (2007): 416–438.
4. Officially, the case is *Stern v. Lucy Webb Hayes National Training School for Deaconesses and Missionaries,* 381 F. Supp. 1003 (D.D.C. 1974). David Harpool, "The *Sibley Hospital* Case: Trustees and Their Loyalty to the Institution," *Journal of College and University Law* 23 (1996): 255–283.
5. David Harpool, "The *Sibley Hospital* Case."
6. Herrington J. Bryce, *Financial and Strategic Management of Nonprofit Organizations,* 3rd ed. (San Francisco: Jossey-Bass, 2000).
7. Richard T. Ingram, *Ten Basic Responsibilities of Nonprofit Boards,* 2nd ed. (Washington, DC: BoardSource, 2009) 64; Leslie R. Crutchfield and Heather McLeod Grant, *Forces for Good* (San Francisco: Jossey-Bass, 2008).
8. Matthew R. Fairholm, "Different Perspectives on the Practice of Leadership," *Public Administration Review* 64(2004): 577–590; Montgomery Van Wart, "Public-Sector Leadership Theory: An Assessment," *Public Administration Review* 63(2003): 214–228.
9. Peter Drucker, *Managing the Nonprofit Organization* (New York: HarperCollins, 2005); Barry Dym and Harry Hutson, *Leadership in Nonprofit Organizations* (Thousand Oaks, CA: Sage , 2005).
10. James M. Burns, *Leadership* (New York: Harper & Row, 1978); Warren Bennis and Burt Nanus, *Leaders: The Strategies for Taking Charge* (New York: Harper & Row, 1985).
11. William B. Werther Jr. and Evan M. Berman, *Third Sector Management: The Art of Managing Nonprofit Organizations.* (Washington, DC: Georgetown University Press, 2001), 16–17.
12. Ronald A. Heifitz and Donald L. Laurie, "The Work of Leadership," *Harvard Business Review,* January-February 1997, 124–134; Carolyn P. Egri and Susan Herman, "Leadership in the North American Environmental Sector: Values, Leadership Styles, and Contexts of Environmental Leaders and Their Organizations, *Academy of Management Journal* 43 (2000): 571–604; Montgomery Van Wart, "Public-Sector Leadership"; Matthew R. Fairholm, "Different Perspectives"; Tracey Trottier, Montgomery Van Wart, and Xiao Hu Wang, "Examining the Nature and Significance of Leadership in Government Organizations, *Public Administration Review* 68 (2008): 319–333.
13. Bradley E. Wright and Sanjay K. Pandey, "Transformational Leadership in the Public Sector: Does Structure Matter?" *Journal of Public Administration Research and Theory* 20 (2009), 77.
14. Jens Rowold and Anette Rohmann, "Relationships between Leadership Styles and Followers' Emotional Experience and Effectiveness in the Voluntary Sector," *Nonprofit and Voluntary Sector Quarterly* 38 (2009), 282.

15. Montgomery Van Wart, "Public-Sector Leadership"; Bradley E. Wright and Sanjay K. Pandey, "Transformational Leadership"; Carolyn P. Egri and Susan Herman, "Leadership in the North."
16. W. Astor Kirk, *Board Members Governing Roles and Responsibilities* (Lanham, MD: University Press of America, 2007), 18.
17. Rikki Abzug and Joseph Galaskiewicz, "Nonprofit Boards: Crucibles of Expertise or Symbols of Local Identities?" *Nonprofit and Voluntary Sector Quarterly* 30 (2001): 51–73; Sonia Ospina, William Diaz, and James F. O'Sullivan, "Negotiating Accountability: Managerial Lessons from Identity-Based Nonprofit Organizations," *Nonprofit and Voluntary Sector Quarterly* 31 (2002): 5–31.
18. David Suarez, "Street Credentials and Management Backgrounds: Careers of Nonprofit Executives in an Evolving Sector," *Nonprofit and Voluntary Sector Quarterly* 39 (2010): 696–716.
19. Joanne G. Carman, Suzanne M. Leland, and Amanda J. Wilson, "*Crisis in Leadership or Failure to Plan?" Nonprofit Management and Leadership* 21 (2010): 93–111.
20. Rikki Abzug and Joseph Galaskiewicz, "Nonprofit Boards"; Judith L. Miller-Millesen, "Understanding the Behavior of Nonprofit Boards of Directors: A Theory-Based Approach," *Nonprofit and Voluntary Sector Quarterly* 32 (2003): 521–547.
21. Bruce C. Bonnickson, "New Roles of Volunteers in Development," *New Directions for Philanthropic Fundraising* 39 (2003): 5–21.
22. Peter Drucker, *Managing the Nonprofit Organization* (New York: HarperCollins, 2005); Ingram, *Ten Basic Responsibilities.*
23. Kathy K. Hedge, Eva Nico, and Lindsay Fox, *Advancing Good Governance* (Washington, DC: BoardSource and FSG Social Impact Advisors, 2009), 31.
24. Leslie R. Crutchfield and Heather McLeod Grant, *Forces for Good.*
25. Bradley E. Wright and Judith L. Millesen "Nonprofit Board Role Ambiguity: Investigating Its Prevalence and Consequences," *American Review of Public Administration* 38 (2008): 322–338.
26. Salvatore P. Alaimo, "Nonprofits and Evaluation: Managing Perspectives from the Leader's Perspective," *New Directions for Evaluation* 119 (2008): 73–92.
27. Sharon Oster, *Strategic Management for Nonprofit Organizations Theory and Cases* (New York: Oxford University Press, 1995); William B. Werther Jr. and Evan M. Berman, *Third Sector Management;* Carolyn P. Egri and Susan Herman, "Leadership in the North"; Francie Ostrower and Melissa M. Stone, "Governance: Research Trends, Gaps, and Future Prospects," in Walter W. Powell and Richard Steinberg, editors, *The Nonprofit Sector A Research Handbook,* 2nd ed., ed. Walter W. Powell and Richard Steinberg (New Haven, CT: Yale University Press, 2006), 612–628); Melissa M. Stone and Francie Ostrower, "Acting in the Public Interest."
28. William B. Werther Jr. and Evan M. Berman, *Third Sector Management,* 23.
29. Deborah B. Basler and JoAnn Carmin, "Leadership Succession and the Emergence of an Organizational Identity Threat," *Nonprofit Management & Leadership* 20 (2009): 185–201.
30. Jean Crawford, "Profiling the Non-Profit Leader of Tomorrow," *Ivey Business Journal* 74 (2010): 5.; Joanne G. Carman, Suzanne M. Leland, and Amanda J. Wilson, "*Crisis in Leadership*"; Janet L. Johnson "The Nonprofit Leadership Deficit," *Nonprofit Management & Leadership* 19 (2009): 285–304.
31. Leslie R. Crutchfield and Heather McLeod Grant, *Forces for Good;* Joanne G. Carman, Suzanne M. Leland, and Amanda J. Wilson, "*Crisis in leadership.*"
32. Jean Crawford, "Profiling"; William J. Rothwell, *The Nuts and Bolts of Succession Planning: A Dale Carnegie White Paper* (Hauppauge, NY: Dale Carnegie & Associates, Inc., 2007)
33. Barry Dym, and Harry Hutson, *Leadership.*
34. Deborah B. Basler and JoAnn Carmin. "Leadership Succession."
35. Christy A. Visher and Jeremy Travis, "Transitions from Prison to Community," *Annual Review of Sociology* 29 (2003) 89–113.
36. Robert D. Herman and David O. Renz, "Advancing Nonprofit Organizational Effectiveness Research and Theory," *Nonprofit Management & Leadership* 18 (2008): 399–415; David O. Renz, "Adding a Few More Pieces to the Puzzle: Exploring the Practical Implications of Recent Research on Boards," *Nonprofit Quarterly* 18, 1 (2011), http://www.nonprofitquarterly.org/governancevoice/11971-adding-a-few-more-pieces-to-the-puzzle-exploring-the-practical-implications-of-recent-research-on-boards.html.
37. David E. Olson, "Agency Theory in the Not-for-Profit Sector: Its Role at Independent Colleges," *Nonprofit and Voluntary Sector Quarterly* 29(2000): 280–296.
38. Jennifer Bright Preston and William A. Brown, "Commitment and Performance of Nonprofit Board Members, *Nonprofit Management & Leadership* 15 (2004): 221–238.
39. William J. Ritchie and Karen Eastwood, "Executive Functional Experience and its Relationship to the Financial Performance of Nonprofit Organizations," *Nonprofit Management and Leadership* 17 (2006): 67–82.
40. Tracey Trottier, Montgomery Van Wart, and Xiao Hu Wang, "Examining the Nature," 329.
41. Jens Rowold and Anette Rohmann, "Relationships"; Bradley E. Wright and Sanjay K. Pandey, "Transformational Leadership"; Rhys Andrews and George A. Boyne, "Capacity, Leadership, and Organizational Performance: Testing the Black Box Model of Public Management, *Public Administration Review* 70 (2010): 443–454.
42. Bradley E. Wright and Sanjay K. Pandey, "Transformational Leadership"; Tracey Trottier, Montgomery Van Wart, and Xiao Hu Wang, "Examining the Nature"; Montgomery Van Wart, "Public-Sector Leadership."
43. Leslie R. Crutchfield and Heather McLeod Grant, *Forces for Good,* 162.
44. David O. Renz, "Adding a Few."
45. David O. Renz, "Adding a Few."
46. Francie Ostrower and Melissa M. Stone, "Governance," 612.
47. Mel Gill, "Building Effective Approaches to Governance," *Nonprofit Quarterly,* Friday, June 2002, http://www.nonprofitquarterly.org/governancevoice/113-building-effective-approaches-to-governance.html; Tim Plumptre and Barbara Laskin, *From Jeans to Jackets: Navigating the transition to more systemic governance in the voluntary sector* (Ottawa: Institute on Governance, 2003).
48. Judith L. Miller-Millesen, "Understanding the behavior"; Francie Ostrower and Melissa M. Stone, "Governance"; Melissa M. Stone and Francie Ostrower, "Acting in the Public Interest"; Melissa M. Stone and Francie Ostrower, "Moving Governance Research Forward: A Contingency-Based Framework and Data Application," *Nonprofit and Voluntary Sector Quarterly* 39 (2010): 901–924.
49. Judith L. Miller-Millesen, "Understanding the Behavior."
50. Francie Ostrower and Melissa M. Stone, "Governance."
51. Judith L. Miller-Millesen, "Understanding the Behavior," 535.
52. Judith L. Miller-Millesen, "Understanding the Behavior"; John W. Meyer and Brian Rowan, "Institutionalized Organizations: Formal Structure as Myth and Ceremony," *American Journal of Sociology* 83 (1977): 340–363.
53. Judith L. Miller-Millesen, "Understanding the Behavior."
54. Ibid.
55. Evelyn Brody, "The Legal Framework for Nonprofit Organizations," in *The Nonprofit Sector A Research Handbook,* 2nd ed., ed. Walter

W. Powell and Richard Steinberg (New Haven, CT: University Press, 2006); Francie Ostrower and Melissa M. Stone, "Governance"; BoardSource, *The Nonprofit Board Answer Book: A Practical Guide for Board Members and Chief Executives* (San Francisco: Jossey-Bass, 2007).

56. Evelyn Brody, "The Legal Framework."
57. Helmut K. Anheier, *Nonprofit Organizations, Theory, Management, Policy.* (New York: Routledge, 2005), 234.
58. Francie Ostrower, *Nonprofit Governance in the United States: Findings on Performance and Accountability from the First National Representative Study* (Washington, DC: The Urban Institute, 2007).
59. Board Source, www.boardsource.org/.
60. Dennis Wagner and Craig Harris, "Fiesta Bowl Board Missed Signs," *Arizona Republic,* April 10, 2011; http://www.azcentral.com/news/articles/2011/04/10/20110410fiesta-bowl-board-misses-signs.html.
61. Ibid.; Paola Boivin, "Fiesta Bowl Rebuilds After Recent Scandal," *Arizona Republic,* December 31, 2011; http://www.azcentral.com/news/articles/2011/12/28/20111228fiesta-bowl-rebuilds-after-scandal.html.
62. Paola Boivin, "Fiesta Bowl Rebuilds."
63. Joan E. Pynes, *Human Resources Management for Public and Nonprofit Organizations: A Strategic Approach,* 3rd ed. (San Francisco: Jossey-Bass, 2009), 135.
64. Nonprofits Insurance Alliance Group provides a great deal of information on nonprofit governance, particularly insurance issues; see Web Resources at the end of the chapter.
65. Francie Ostrower and Melissa M. Stone, "Governance."
66. BoardSource, Nonprofit Governance Index 2010, (Washington, DC: BoardSource, 2010).
67. Francie Ostrower and Melissa M. Stone, "Governance"; Sharon Oster, *Strategic Management.*
68. William B. Werther Jr. and Evan M. Berman, *Third Sector Management;* Joan E. Pynes, *Human Resources;* David O. Renz, "Adding a Few More"; Kirk, W. Astor. *Board Members;* Thomas P. Holland and Roger A. Ritvo, *Nonprofit Organizations, Principles and Practices* (New York: Columbia University Press, 2008).
69. BoardSource, Nonprofit Governance Index 2010; David O. Renz, "Adding a Few"; Francie Ostrower and Melissa M. Stone, "Governance"; Rikki Abzug and Joseph Galaskiewicz, "Nonprofit Boards."
70. Rikki Abzug and Joseph Galaskiewicz, "Nonprofit Boards."
71. Ruth McCambridge, "Underestimating the Power of Nonprofit Governance." *Nonprofit and Voluntary Sector Quarterly* 33 (2004), 352.
72. Sonia Ospina, William Diaz and James F. O'Sullivan, "Negotiating Accountability."
73. Christian Gonzalez-Rivera, *Diversity on Foundation Boards of Directors, Issue Brief* (Berkeley, CA: Greenlining Institute, 2009).
74. Francie Ostrower and Melissa M. Stone, "Governance"; Rikki Abzug and Joseph Galaskiewicz, "Nonprofit Boards"; Sharon Oster, *Strategic Management;* Judith L. Miller-Millesen, "Understanding the Behavior"; Mary Tschirart, Kira Kristal Reed, Sarah J. Freeman, and Alison Louie Anker, "Who Serves?: Predicting Placement of Management Graduates on Nonprofit, Government, and Business Boards," *Nonprofit and Volunteer Sector Quarterly* 38, 6 (2009): 1076–1085; William B. Werther Jr. and Evan M. Berman, *Third Sector Management;* Jeffrey L. Callen, April Klein, and Daniel Tinkelman, "Board Composition, Committees, and Organizational Efficiency: The Case of Nonprofits," *Nonprofit and Voluntary Sector Quarterly* 32 (2003): 493–520.
75. Francie Ostrower, *Nonprofit Governance;* Bradley E. Wright and Judith L. Millesen, "Nonprofit Board"; Robert D. Herman, "Concluding Thoughts on Closing the Board Gap," in *Nonprofit Boards of Directors: Analyses and Applications,* ed. Robert D. Herman and Jon Van Til (New Brunswick, NJ: Transaction, 1989), 193–199; Robert D. Herman, "Are Public Service Nonprofit Boards Meeting Their Responsibilities?" *Public Administration Review* 69 (2009): 387–390.
76. Francie Ostrower, *Nonprofit Governance.*
77. BoardSource, *Nonprofit Governance Index 2010.*
78. Jo An Zimmermann and Bonnie Stevens, "Best Practices in Board Governance: Evidence from South Carolina," *Nonprofit Management and Leadership* 19 (2008): 189–202.
79. Francie Ostrower and Melissa M. Stone, "Governance"; Melissa M. Stone and Francie Ostrower, "Moving Governance Research Forward"; Patricia Bradshaw, "A Contingency Approach to Nonprofit Governance," *Nonprofit Management and Leadership* 20 (2009): 61–81.
80. Francie Ostrower and Melissa M. Stone, "Governance."
81. Melissa M. Stone and Francie Ostrower, "Moving Governance Research Forward."
82. BoardSource, *The Nonprofit Board Answer Book.*
83. BoardSource, *Nonprofit Governance Index 2010.*
84. Francie Ostrower, *Nonprofit Governance.*
85. William Brown, "Board Development Practices and Competent Board Members: Implications for Performance," *Nonprofit Management and Leadership* 17 (2007): 301–317; Jennifer Bright Preston and William A. Brown, "Commitment and Performance"; Jo An Zimmermann and Bonnie Stevens, "Best Practices in Board Governance."
86. BoardSource, *The Nonprofit Board Answer Book.*
87. BoardSource, *The Nonprofit Board Answer Book;* Vernetta Walker and Emily Heard, "Board Governance," in *Nonprofit Management 101,* ed. Darian Rodriguez Heyman (San Francisco: Jossey-Bass, 2011), 501–518.
88. Jennifer Bright Preston and William A. Brown, "Commitment and Performance."
89. Sue Inglis and Shirley Cleave, "A Scale to Assess Board Member Motivations in Nonprofit Organizations," *Nonprofit Management & Leadership* 17 (2006): 83–101.
90. Steven M. Farmer and Donald B. Fedor, "Volunteer Participation and Withdrawal," *Nonprofit Management & Leadership* 9 (1999): 349–367.
91. Bradley E. Wright and Judith L. Millesen, "Nonprofit Board."
92. BoardSource, *The Nonprofit Board Answer Book,* 311.
93. Except where otherwise noted, all of the information within this box was derived from Steve Bullock, *Montana Attorney General's Investigative Report of Greg Mortenson and Central Asia Institute,* April 2012, p. 26, www.kxlh.com/files/cai.pdf.
94. Bullock, 18.
95. Bullock, 16.
96. Anne Beyersdorfer, "Message from Anne Beyersdorfer, CAI Executive Director," http://www.ikat.org/ag/.

Chapter 13

1. Steven Rathgeb Smith and Michael Lipsky, *Nonprofits for Hire: The Welfare State in the Age of Contracting* (Cambridge, MA: Harvard University Press, 1994), 115–116.

2. Henry Mintzberg, *The Structure of Organizations* (Upper Saddle River, NJ: Prentice Hall, 1979).
3. Anna Haley-Lock and Jean Kruzich, "Serving Workers in the Human Services: The Roles of Organizational Ownership, Chain Affiliation, and Professional Leadership in Frontline Benefits," *Nonprofit and Voluntary Sector Quarterly* 37 (2008): 443–467; Rein De Cooman, Sara De Gieter, Roland Pepermans, and Marc Jegers, "A Cross-Sector Comparison of Motivation-Related Concepts in For-Profit and Not-for-Profit Service Organizations," *Nonprofit and Voluntary Sector Quarterly* 40 (2009): 296–317.
4. Nonprofit HR Solutions, *2012 Nonprofit Employment Trends Report* (Washington, DC: Nonprofit HR Solutions, 2012).
5. Hans-Gerd Ridder and Alina McCandless, "Influences on the Architecture of Human Resource Management in Nonprofit Organizations" *Nonprofit and Voluntary Sector Quarterly* 39 (2010): 124–141.
6. Nonprofit HR Solutions, *2012 Nonprofit Employment Trends.*
7. Ibid.
8. Ibid.
9. William B. Werther Jr. and Evan M. Berman, *Third Sector Management: The Art of Managing Nonprofit Organizations* (Washington, DC: Georgetown University Press, 2001); Joan E. Pynes, *Human Resources Management for Public and Nonprofit Organizations: A Strategic Approach,* 3rd ed. (San Francisco: Jossey-Bass, 2009); Hans-Gerd Ridder and Alina McCandless, "Influences on the Architecture."
10. Joan E. Pynes, *Human Resources Management,* 31.
11. Office of Personnel Management, *OPM's Workforce Planning Model,* 2005, http://www.opm.gov/hcaaf_resource_center/assets/Sa_t0014.pdf.
12. Nonprofit HR Solutions, *2012 Nonprofit Employment Trends.*
13. Joan E. Pynes, *Human Resources Management.*
14. Sharon Oster, *Strategic Management for Nonprofit Organizations Theory and Cases* (New York: Oxford University Press, 1995); Paul C. Light, *Sustaining Nonprofit Performance* (Washington, DC: Brookings Institution Press, 2004); Hans-Gerd Ridder and Alina McCandless, "Influences on the Architecture"; Rein De Cooman, Sara De Gieter, Roland Pepermans, and Marc Jegers, "A Cross-Sector Comparison"; Seok Eun Kim and Jung Wook Lee, "Is Mission Attachment an Effective Management Tool for Employee Retention?" *Review of Public Personnel Administration* 27 (2007): 227–248; Carlo Borzaga and Ermanno Tortia, "Worker Motivations, Job Satisfaction, and Loyalty in Public and Nonprofit Social Services," *Nonprofit and Voluntary Sector Quarterly* 35(2006): 225–248; Leslie R. Crutchfield and Heather McLeod Grant, *Forces for Good,* (San Francisco: Jossey-Bass, 2008); Jessica Word and Sung Min Park, "Working Across the Divide: Job Involvement in the Public and Nonprofit Sectors," *Review of Public Personnel Administration* 29 (2009): 103–133.
15. Sharon Oster, *Strategic Management;* Avner Ben-Ner, Ting Ren, and Darla Flint Paulson, "A Sectoral Comparison of Wage Levels and Wage Inequality in Human Services Industries," *Nonprofit and Voluntary Sector Quarterly* 40 (2011): 608–633; Ellen F. Netting, Mary Katherine O'Conner, M. Lori Thomas, and Gaynor Yancey, "Mixing and Phasing of Roles among Volunteers, Staff, and Participants in Faith-Based Programs," *Nonprofit and Voluntary Sector Quarterly* 34 (2005): 179–205.
16. Office of Personnel Management, *Assessment Decision Guide,* http://apps.opm.gov/ADT/Content.aspx?page=TOC.
17. Employment and Training Administration, *Testing and Assessment,* www.onetcenter.org/dl_files/proTestAsse.pdf.
18. Hans-Gerd Ridder and Alina McCandless, "Influences on the Architecture"; Felice Davidson Perlmutter, John R. Deckop, Alison M. Konrad, and Joshua L. Freely, "Nonprofits and the Job Retention of Former Welfare Clients," *Nonprofit and Voluntary Sector Quarterly* 34 (2005): 473–490; Carlo Borzaga and Ermanno Tortia, "Worker motivations"; Seok Eun Kim and Jung Wook Lee, "Is Mission Attachment."
19. Amy Butler, "Wages in the Nonprofit Sector: Management, Professional, and Administrative Support Occupations," U.S. Bureau of Labor Statistics, last modified April 15, 2009, http://www.bls.gov/opub/cwc/cm20081022ar01p1.htm; Jessica K.A. Word, Human Resource Leadership and Management," in Kathryn Agard, editor, *Leadership in Nonprofit Organizations,* in ed. Kathryn Agard (Thousand Oaks, CA: Sage, 2010).
20. Avner Ben-Ner, Ting Ren, and Darla Flint Paulson, "A Sectoral Comparison."
21. Amy Butler, "Wages in the Nonprofit Sector."
22. Avner Ben-Ner, Ting Ren, and Darla Flint Paulson, "A Sectoral Comparison"; Sharon Oster, *Strategic Management.*
23. Abraham H. Maslow, "A Theory of Human Motivation," *Psychological Review* 50 (1943): 370–396.
24. J. S. Alderfer, "An Empirical Test of a New Theory of Human Needs," *Organizational Behavior and Human Performance* 4 (1969): 142–175; McClelland, David. C., *Human Motivation.* (Cambridge, UK: Cambridge University Press, 1989); Frederick Herzberg, "One More Time: How Do You Motivate Employees?" *Harvard Business Review* 65 (1987): 109–120; Peter Drucker, *Managing the Nonprofit Organization* (New York: HarperCollins, 2005).
25. Jessica K.A. Word, "Human Resource Leadership."
26. Victor H. Vroom, *Work and Motivation* (Oxford: Wiley, 1964); J. Stacy Adams, "Towards an Understanding of Inequity," *Journal of Abnormal and Social Psychology* 67 (1963): 422–436.
27. Edwin A. Locke and Gary P. Latham, *A Theory of Goal Setting and Task Performance* (Englewood Cliffs, NJ: Prentice Hall, 1990); Edwin A. Locke and Gary P. Latham, "Building a Practically Useful Theory of Goal Setting and Task Motivation," *American Psychologist* 57 (2002): 705–717.
28. Joan E. Pynes, *Human Resources Management;* Sharon Oster, *Strategic Management for Nonprofit Organizations Theory and Cases* (New York: Oxford University Press, 1995).
29. James L. Perry and Lois Recascino Wise, "The Motivational Bases of Public Service." *Public Administration Review* 50 (1990): 367–373.
30. James L. Perry and Lois Recascino Wise, "The Motivational Bases"; Sue A. Frank and Gregory B. Lewis, "Government Employees: Working Hard, or Hardly Working?" *American Review of Public Administration* 34 (2004): 36–51; Wright, Bradley E., "Public Service and Motivation: Does Mission Matter?" *Public Administration Review* 67, 1 (2007): 54–64.
31. Paul C. Light, *Sustaining Nonprofit Performance;* Rein De Cooman, Sara De Gieter, Roland Pepermans, and Marc Jegers, "A Cross-Sector Comparison"; Seok Eun Kim and Jung Wook Lee, "Is Mission Attachment"; Carlo Borzaga, and Ermanno Tortia, "Worker Motivations"; Mary Tschirhart, Kira Kristal Reed, Sarah J. Freeman, and Alison Louie Anker, "Is the Grass Greener? Sector Shifting and Choice of Sector by MPA and MBA Graduates," *Nonprofit and Volunteer Sector Quarterly* 37 (2008): 668–688.

32. Sue A. Frank and Gregory B. Lewis, "Government Employees."
33. Sharon Oster, *Strategic Management;* John R. Deckop and Carol C. Cirka, "The risk and reward of a double-edged sword: Effects of a Merit Pay Program on Intrinsic Motivation", *Nonprofit and Voluntary Sector Quarterly* 29 (2000): 400–418.
34. John R. Deckop and Carol C. Cirka, "The Risk and Reward"; James L. Perry, Debra Mesch, and Laurie Paarlberg, "Motivating Employees in a New Governance Era," *Public Administration Review* 66, 4 (2006): 505–514.
35. Peter Drucker, *Managing the Nonprofit,* 119.
36. Rony Brauman and Joelle Tanguy, *Work in the Field: The Médecins Sans Frontières Experience,* 1998, www.doctorswithoutborders.org/work/field/msfexperience.cfm.
37. Médecins Sans Frontières, Donations, www.msf.org/msf/donations/donations_home.cfm.
38. Médecins Sans Frontières, *MSF Activity Report 2010,* www.doctorswithoutborders.org/publications/ar/MSF-Activity-Report-2010.pdf.
39. Joan E. Pynes, *Human Resources Management;* John R. Deckop and Carol C. Cirka, "The Risk and Reward"; Saundra J. Reinke, "Does the Form Really Matter? Leadership, Trust, and Acceptance of the Performance Appraisal Process," *Review of Public Personnel Administration* 23 (2003): 23–37.
40. Joan E. Pynes, *Human Resources Management.*
41. John R. Deckop and Carol C. Cirka, "The Risk and Reward."
42. Ibid.
43. James L. Perry, "Bringing Society in: Toward a Theory of Public-Service Motivation." *Journal of Public Administration Research and Theory* 10 (2000): 471–488; Joan E. Pynes, *Human Resources Management.*
44. Thomas P. Holland and Roger A. Ritvo, *Nonprofit Organizations, Principles and Practices* (New York: Columbia University Press, 2008).
45. Steven Rathgeb Smith and Michael Lipsky, *Nonprofits for Hire.*
46. Ibid, 103.
47. Femida Handy, Laurie Mook, and Jack Quarter, "The Interchangeability of Paid Staff and Volunteers in Nonprofit Organizations," *Nonprofit and Voluntary Sector Quarterly* 37 (2008): 76–92; Steven Rathgeb Smith, "Social Services," in *The State of Nonprofit America,* ed. Lester A. Salamon (Washington, DC: Brookings Institution Press, 2002), 149–186; Jessica Word and Sung Min Park, "Working across the Divide."
48. Sharon Oster, *Strategic Management.*
49. Steven Rathgeb Smith and Michael Lipsky, *Nonprofits for Hire,* 100.
50. Sharon Oster, *Strategic Management.*
51. Femida Handy, Laurie Mook, and Jack Quarter, "The Interchangeability."
52. Matthew A. Liao-Troth, "Attitude Differences Between Paid Workers and Volunteers," *Nonprofit Management & Leadership* 11 (2001): 423–442.
53. Ellen F. Netting, Mary Katherine O'Conner, M. Lori Thomas, and Gaynor Yancey, "Mixing and Phasing of Roles."
54. William B. Werther Jr. and Evan M. Berman, *Third Sector Management, The Art of Managing Nonprofit Organizations* (Washington, DC: Georgetown University Press, 2001), 24.
55. Joan E. Pynes, *Human Resources Management;* Femida Handy, Laurie Mook, and Jack Quarter, "The Interchangeability."
56. Femida Handy, Laurie Mook, and Jack Quarter, "The Interchangeability."
57. Steven G. Rogelberg, Joseph A. Allen, James M. Conway, Adrian Goh, Lamarra Currie, and Betsy McFarland, "Employee Experiences with Volunteers," *Nonprofit Management and Leadership* 20 (2010): 423–444.
58. Lester M. Salamon and Stephanie Lessans Geller, *Nonprofit America: A Force for Democracy?* Center for Civil Society Studies Listening Post Project, Communiqué No. 9. (Baltimore: Johns Hopkins University Institute for Policy Studies, 2008); Lester M. Salamon, Stephanie L. Geller, and Kasey L. Spence, *Impact of the 2007–09 Economic Recession on Nonprofit Organizations. Listening Post Project* (Baltimore: Johns Hopkins University Center for Civil Society Studies, 2009).
59. Katie L. Roeger, Amy Blackwood, and Sarah L. Pettijohn, *The Nonprofit Sector in Brief: Public Charities, Giving, and Volunteering, 2011* (Washington, DC: The Urban Institute, 2011).
60. Virginia A. Hodgkinson, Kathryn E. Nelson, and Edward D. Sivak Jr., "Individual Giving and Volunteering," in *The State of Nonprofit America,* ed. Lester M. Salamon (Washington, DC: Brookings Institution Press, 2002), 387–420; Michele L. Ross and Jeffrey L. Brudney, "Volunteer Administration: Useful Techniques for the Public Sector," *Journal of Volunteer Administration* 16 (1998): 27–37.
61. Rick Cohen, *Volunteerism Public Policies Can Hurt Nonprofits. Blue Avocado Investigates, May 3, 2010*; http://www.blueavocado.org/node/522.
62. Mark A. Hagar and Jeffrey L. Brudney, "Net Benefits: Weighing the Challenges and Benefits of Volunteers," *Journal of Volunteer Administration* 23 (2005): 26–31.
63. David M. Van Slyke and Janet L. Johnson, "Nonprofit Organizational Performance and Resource Development Strategies," *Public Performance & Management Review* 29 (2006): 467–496; Independent Sector, *Giving & Volunteering in the United States, 2001* (Washington DC: Independent Sector, 2002b); Joan E. Pynes, *Human Resources Management;* Amornrat Apinunmahakul, Vicky Barham, and Rose Anne Devlin, "Charitable Giving, Volunteering, and the Paid Labor Market," *Nonprofit and Voluntary Sector Quarterly* 38 (2009): 77–94.
64. Independent Sector. *Giving & Volunteering.*
65. Sharon Oster, *Strategic Management;* Gil E. Clary and Mark Snyder, "The Motivations to Volunteer: Theoretical and Practical Considerations," *Current Directions in Psychological Science* 8 (1999): 156–159; Gil E. Clary, Mark Snyder, Robert D. Ridge, John Copeland, Arthur A. Stukas, Julie Haugen, and Peter Miene, "Understanding and Assessing the Motivations of Volunteers: A Functional Approach," *Journal of Personality and Social Psychology* 74 (1998): 1516–1530; Michele L. Ross and Jeffrey L. Brudney, "Volunteer Administration"; Joan E. Pynes, *Human Resources Management.*
66. Gil E. Clary and Mark Snyder. "The Motivations."
67. Mark A. Hagar and Jeffrey L. Brudney, *Balancing Act: The Challenges and Benefits of Volunteers,* Volunteer Management Capacity Study Series, Washington, DC: The Urban Institute, 2004); Mark A. Hagar and Jeffrey L. Brudney, "Net Benefits."
68. Joan E. Pynes, *Human Resources Management.*
69. David M. Van Slyke and Janet L. Johnson, "Nonprofit Organizational performance"; Amornrat Apinunmahakul, Vicky Barham, and Rose Anne Devlin. "Charitable Giving."
70. David M. Van Slyke and Janet L. Johnson, "Nonprofit Organizational Performance."
71. Joan E. Pynes, *Human Resources Management;* Laura Tiehen, "Has Working More Caused Married Women to Volunteer Less? Evidence from Time Diary Data, 1965–1993," *Nonprofit and Volunteer Sector Quarterly* 29 (2000): 505–529; Jeffrey L. Brudney and Lucas C. P. M. Meijs, "It Ain't Natural," *Nonprofit and Voluntary Sector Quarterly* 38, 4 (2009): 564–581.

72. Joan E. Pynes, *Human Resources Management.*
73. Boy Scouts of America, "Scout Oath," www.scouting.org/About/FactSheets/OverviewofBSA.aspx.
74. Joan E. Pynes, "Human Resources Management Challenges for Nonprofit Organizations," in *Public Personnel Management Current Concerns, Future Challenges,* 4th ed., ed. Norma M. Riccucci (New York: Pearson Longman, 2005), 225–242.
75. Legal Information Institute, "*Boy Scouts of America v. Dale* (99–699) 530 U.S. 640 (2000), Syllabus," Cornell University Law School, http://www.law.cornell.edu/supct/html/99–699.ZS.html; Harvard Law Review, Leading Cases, *Harvard Law Review* 120 (2006): 125–371.
76. Joan E. Pynes, "Human Resources Management Challenges for Nonprofit Organizations," in *Public Personnel Management Current Concerns, Future Challenges,* 4th ed., ed. Norma M. Riccucci (New York: Pearson Longman, 2005), 225–242.
77. Ian Urbina, "Boy Scouts Lose Philadelphia Lease in Gay-Rights Fight," *New York Times,* Dec. 6, 2007, http://www.nytimes.com/2007/12/06/us/06scouts.html?ref=boyscouts.
78. Christina Ng, "Eagle Scout Challenges Boy Scouts Anti-Gay Policy with Petition," last modified May 30, 2012, http://abcnews.go.com/US/eagle-scout-challenges-boy-scouts-anti-gay-policy/story?id=16459135.
79. Jeffrey L. Brudney and Lucas C.P.M. Meijs, "It Ain't Natural."
80. Ibid., 577.
81. Brad W. Mayer, Katherine A. Fraccastoro, and Lisa D. McNary. "The Relationship among Organizational-Based Self-Esteem and Various Factors Motivating Volunteers," *Nonprofit and Voluntary Sector Quarterly* 36 (2007): 327–340.
82. Ibid.
83. Jeffrey L. Brudney and Lucas C.p.m. Meijs, "It Ain't Natural."
84. Jeffrey L. Brudney and Lucas C.p.m. Meijs "It Ain't Natural"; Steven G. Rogelberg, Joseph A. Allen, James M. Conway, Adrian Goh, Lamarra Currie, and Betsy McFarland, "Employee Experiences."
85. Steven G. Rogelberg, Joseph A. Allen, James M. Conway, Adrian Goh, Lamarra Currie, and Betsy McFarland, "Employee Experiences"; Joan E. Pynes, *Human Resources Management;* Sharon Oster, *Strategic Management;* Jessica K.A. Word, "Human Resource Leadership."
86. Peter F. Drucker, *Managing the Nonprofit Organization* (New York: HarperCollins , 2005); Michele L. Ross and Jeffrey L. Brudney, "Volunteer Administration"; Steven M. Farmer and Donald B. Fedor, "Volunteer Participation and Withdrawal," *Nonprofit Management & Leadership* 9 (1999) 349–367; Joan E. Pynes, *Human Resources Management;* Rogelberg et al., "Employee Experiences."
87. Steven G. Rogelberg, Joseph A. Allen, James M. Conway, Adrian Goh, Lamarra Currie, and Betsy McFarland, "Employee Experiences."
88. Ibid.
89. *Volunteer Protection Act* (PL 105–19, June 18, 1997).
90. Joan E. Pynes, *Human Resources Management;* Leslie R. Crutchfield and Heather McLeod Grant, *Forces for Good* (San Francisco: Jossey-Bass, 2008).
91. Frances Kunreuther, "The Changing of the Guard: What Generational Differences Tell us About Social-Change Organizations," *Nonprofit and Voluntary Sector Quarterly* 32 (2003): 450–457.
92. Sung Bum Yang and Mary Guy, "Genxers versus Boomers: Work Motivators and Management Implications," *Public Performance and Management Review* 29 (2006): 267–284.
93. Frances Kunreuther, "The Changing of the Guard"; Sung Bum Yang and Mary Guy, "Genxers versus Boomers."
94. Sung Bum Yang and Mary Guy, "Genxers versus Boomers"; Anthony Downs, *Inside Bureaucracy* (Boston: Little, Brown and Company, 1966).
95. Hans-Gerd Ridder and Alina McCandless, "Influences on the Architecture"; Nancy Winemiller Basinger, and Jessica Romine Peterson, "Where You Stand Depends on Where You Sit," *Nonprofit Management and Leadership* 19 (2008): 243–257.
96. Sharon Oster, *Strategic Management.*
97. David W. Pitts and Lois Recascino Wise, "Workforce Diversity in the New Millennium: Prospects for Research," *Review of Public Personnel Administration* 30 (2010): 44–69.
98. Tina Nabatchi and Lisa Blomgren Bingham, "From Postal to Peaceful: Dispute Systems Design in the USPS REDRESS Program," *Review of Public Personnel Administration* 30 (2010): 211–234.
99. Tina Nabatchi, "The Institutionalization of Alternative Dispute Resolution in the Federal Government," *Public Administration Review* 67 (2007): 646–661.
100. Tina Nabatchi and Lisa Blomgren Bingham, "From Postal to Peaceful"; Ruth Sirman, "Immunize Your Organization against Superconflicts," *Employment Relations Today* 35 (2008): 33–41.
101. Tina Nabatchi and Lisa Blomgren Bingham, "From Postal to Peaceful," 230.
102. Tina Nabatchi and Lisa Blomgren Bingham, "From Postal to Peaceful"; Ruth Sirman, "Immunize Your Organization" 33–41.
103. Ruth Sirman, "Immunize Your Organization," 37–38.
104. Tina Nabatchi and Lisa Blomgren Bingham, "From Postal to Peaceful"; Ruth Sirman, "Immunize Your Organization," 33–41.
105. Title VII Sec. 703e.
106. As amended by P.L. 92–261, effective March 24, 1972.
107. Joan E. Pynes, *Human Resources Management.*
108. *Boy Scouts of America v. Dale (99–699) 530 U.S. 640 (2000), http://www.law.cornell.edu/supct/html/99–699.ZS.html.*
109. Italics in original; OpenJurist.com. 21.F.3d 184—*Young v. Northern Illinois Conference of United Methodist Church,* http://openjurist.org/21/f3d/184/young-v-northern-illinois-conference-of-united-methodist-church-r.
110. FindLaw.com, No. 98–6761, *Hall v. Baptist Memorial Health Care Corporation,* http://caselaw.findlaw.com/us-6th-circuit/1437164.html.
111. Joan E. Pynes, "Human Resources Management Challenges for Nonprofit Organizations," in *Public Personnel Management Current Concerns, Future Challenges,* 4th ed., ed. Norma M. Riccucci (New York: Pearson Longman, 2005), 225–242.
112. Joan E. Pynes, *Human Resources Management for Public and Nonprofit Organizations, A Strategic Approach,* 3rd ed. (San Francisco: Jossey-Bass, 2009),
113. For more information about employment protections and regulations, see the Equal Employment Opportunity Commission at www.eeoc.gov.
114. The original Americans with Disabilities Act (ADA) applied to organizations of 25 or more employees; in 1994, the law was broadened to include employers with 15 or more employees (see Pynes, *Human Resources Management* for a discussion).
115. Joan E. Pynes, *Human Resources Management.*
116. Joan E. Pynes, "Human Resources Management Challenges for Nonprofit Organizations," in *Public Personnel Management Current Concerns, Future Challenges,* 4th ed., ed. Norma M. Riccucci (New York, NY: Pearson Longman, 2005): pp. 225–242.

117. Corey S. Dubin, "Red Cross at Crossroads: The Urgent Need for Improvements in Blood Services," *Blood Matters,* 2009, http://www.bloodmatters.org/?p=23.
118. Detroit Free Press (online), Blood Workers Strike Red Cross in Labor Dispute, June 2, 2010, http://m.freep.com/BETTER/news.jsp?key=661613&rc=lo.
119. Federal Register, "Certain Preventive Services under Affordable Care Act," Volume 77, Number 55 (Wednesday, March 21, 2012), www.regulations.gov/#!documentDetail;D=CMS-2012–0031–0001.
120. Health and Human Services Press Office, News Release, "A Statement by U.S. Department of Health and Human Services Secretary Kathleen Sebelius," January 20, 2012. www.hhs.gov/news/press/2012pres/01/20120120a.html.
121. Ibid.
122. Robert Pear, "Passions Flare as House Debates Birth Control Rule," *New York Times,* February 17, 2012, www.nytimes.com/2012/02/17/us/politics/birth-control-coverage-rule-debated-at-house-hearing.html.
123. Ibid.
124. Jim Abrams, "Sandra Fluke, Witness Snubbed by GOP, Speaks to Democrats About Birth Control," Huffington Post, February 23, 2012, www.huffingtonpost.com/2012/02/23/sandra-fluke-birth-control-democrats_n_1297110.html.
125. Federal Register, "Certain Preventive Services."
126. Margaret Fosmoe, "Notre Dame, Catholic Diocese, Others File Suit Regarding HHS Mandate," *WSBT-TV,* last modified May 21, 2012, http://www.wsbt.com/news/wsbt-notre-dame-lawsuit-challenges-constitutionality-of-hhs-mandate-20120521,0,6468962.story.

Chapter 14

1. Burton A. Weisbrod, "An Agenda for Quantitative Evaluation of the Nonprofit Sector: Need, Obstacles, and Approaches," in *Measuring the Impact of the Nonprofit Sector,* ed. Patrice Flynn and Virginia A. Hodgkinson (New York, NY: Kluwer Academic/Plenum Publishers, 2001), 287.
2. Paul W. Mattessich,. *The Manager's Guide to Program Evaluation.* (St. Paul, MN: Fieldstone Alliance, 2003), 3.
3. Robert L. Fischer, "The Sea Change in Nonprofit Human Services: A Critical Assessment of Outcomes Measurement" *Families in Society: Journal of Contemporary Human Services* 82 (2001): 561–568; Joanne G. Carman, Kimberly A. Fredericks, and David Introcaso, "Government and Accountability: Paving the Way for Nonprofits and Evaluation," *New Directions for Evaluation* 119 (2008): 5–12.
4. Stephanie Riger and Susan L. Staggs, "A Nationwide Survey of State-Mandated Evaluation Practices for Domestic Violence Agencies," *Journal of Interpersonal Violence* 26 (2010): 50–70.
5. Joanne G. Carman, Kimberly A. Fredericks, and David Introcaso, "Government and Accountability"; Joanne G. Carman, "Nonprofits, Funders, Evaluation: Accountability in Action," *American Review of Public Administration* 39 (2009): 374–390; Thomas P. Holland and Roger A. Ritvo, *Nonprofit Organizations, Principles and Practices* (New York: Columbia University Press, 2008); Kelly LeRoux and Nathaniel S. Wright, "Does Performance Measurement Improve Strategic Decision Making? Findings from a National Survey of Nonprofit Social Service Agencies," *Nonprofit and Voluntary Sector Quarterly* 39 (2010): 571–587.
6. Joanne G. Carman, "Nonprofits, Funders, Evaluation"; Richard Hoefer, "Accountability in Action? Program Evaluation in Nonprofit Human Service Agencies," *Nonprofit Management & Leadership* 11 (2000): 167–177; Kelly LeRoux and Nathaniel S. Wright, "Does Performance Measurement."
7. Joanne G. Carman, Kimberly A. Fredericks, and David Introcaso, "Government and Accountability."
8. Salvatore P. Alaimo, "Nonprofits and Evaluation: Managing Expectations from the Leader's Perspective," *New Directions for Evaluation* 119 (2008): 73–92.
9. Paul W. Mattessich,. *The Manager's Guide,* 7.
10. Adam Eckerd and Stephanie Moulton, "Heterogeneous Roles and Heterogeneous Practices: Understanding the Adoption and Uses of Nonprofit Performance Evaluations," *American Journal of Evaluation* 32 (2011): 98–117.
11. William B. Werther Jr. and Evan M. Berman, *Third Sector Management, The Art of Managing Nonprofit Organizations* (Washington, DC: Georgetown University Press, 2001); Paul W. Mattessich, *The Manager's Guide;* Adam Eckerd and Stephanie Moulton, "Heterogeneous Roles."
12. Joanne G. Carman, "Nonprofits, Funders, Evaluation"; Adam Eckerd and Stephanie Moulton, "Heterogeneous Roles."
13. Mary Katherine O'Connor and F. Ellen Netting, "Faith-Based Evaluation: Accountable to Whom, for What?" Evalua*tion and Program Planning* 31 (2008): 347–355.
14. Joanne G. Carman, "Nonprofits, Funders, Evaluation."
15. Ibid.
16. William J. Ritchie and Robert W. Kolodinsky, "Nonprofit Organization Performance Measurement: Evaluation of New and Existing Financial Performance Measures," *Nonprofit Management & Leadership*13 (2003): 367–381; Robert D. Herman and David O. Renz, "Advancing Nonprofit Organizational Effectiveness Research and Theory, *Nonprofit Management & Leadership,* 18 (2008): 399–415.
17. Evan M. Berman, *Productivity in Public and Nonprofit Organizations* (Thousand Oaks, CA: Sage Publications, 1998), 6.
18. Adam Eckerd and Stephanie Moulton, "Heterogeneous Roles."
19. William J. Ritchie and Robert W. Kolodinsky, "Nonprofit Organization Performance"; Janet S. Greenlee and David Bukovinsky, "Financial Ratios for Use in the Analytical Review of Charitable Organizations," *Ohio CPA Journal* 57 (1998): 32–38.
20. Janet S. Greenlee and David Bukovinsky, "Financial Ratios"; William J. Ritchie and Robert W. Kolodinsky, "Nonprofit Organization Performance. "
21. William J. Ritchie and Robert W. Kolodinsky, "Nonprofit Organization Performance."
22. Janet S. Greenlee and David Bukovinsky, "Financial Ratios"; William J. Ritchie and Robert W. Kolodinsky, "Nonprofit Organization Performance."
23. William J. Ritchie and Robert W. Kolodinsky, "Nonprofit Organization Performance."
24. Ibid.
25. Janet S. Greenlee and David Bukovinsky, "Financial Ratios."
26. Betty Jane Richmond, Laurie Mook, and Jack Quarter, "Social Accounting for Nonprofits: Two Models," *Nonprofit and Voluntary Sector Quarterly* 13 (2003): 308–324.
27. Lisa Ranghelli and Julia Chang, *Strengthening Democracy, Increasing Opportunities: Impacts of Advocacy, Organizing and Civic Engagement in North Carolina* (Washington, DC: National Committee for Responsive Philanthropy, 2009).
28. Paul W. Mattessich,. *The Manager's Guide,* 36.
29. Stephanie Riger and Susan L. Staggs, "A Nationwide Survey."

30. National Committee for Responsive Philanthropy, "James E. Canales: On the James Irvine Foundation's Annual Comprehensive Performance Assessment," *Responsive Philanthropy* Winter 2009/2010.
31. Pietro Micheli and Mike Kennerley, "Performance Measurement Frameworks in Public and Non-Profit Sectors," *Production Planning & Control* 16 (2005): 125–134; Sandra L. Bozzo, "Evaluation Resources for Nonprofit Organizations," *Nonprofit Management & Leadership* 10(2000): 463–472.
32. Lawrence M. Butler, *The Nonprofit Dashboard: A Tool for Tracking Progress* (Washington, DC: BoardSource. 2007), 2.
33. Ibid., 3.
34. Adam Eckerd and Stephanie Moulton, "Heterogeneous Roles," 100.
35. Paul W. Mattessich, *The Manager's Guide;* Sharon Oster, *Strategic Management for Nonprofit Organizations: Theory and Case.* (New York: Oxford University Press, 1995).
36. Melissa A. Stone and Susan Cutcher-Gershenfeld, "Challenges of Measuring Performance in Nonprofit Organizations," in *Measuring the Impact of the Nonprofit Sector,* ed. Patrice Flynn and Virginia A. Hodgkinson (New York: Kluwer Academic/Plenum Publishers, 2001): 33–58; Harry Hatry, Therese van Houten, Margaret C. Plantz, and Martha Taylor Greenway, *Measuring Program Outcomes: A Practical Approach* (Alexandria, VA: United Way, 1996); Dennis L. Poole, Jill K. Davis, Jane Resiman, and Joan E. Nelson, "Improving the Quality of Outcome Evaluation Plans," *Nonprofit Management & Leadership* 11 (2001): 405–421; Paul W. Mattessich, *The Manager's Guide.* Like many in the field, we have adopted the terminology used by the United Way of America in Hatry et al., *Measuring Program Outcomes;* Patrice Flynn and Virginia A. Hodgkinson, eds., *Measuring the Impact of the Nonprofit Sector* (New York: Kluwer Academic/Plenum Publishers, 2001); Paul W. Mattessich, *The Manager's Guide*).
37. Margaret C. Plantz, Martha Taylor Greenway, Michael Hendricks, "Outcome Measurement: Showing Results in the Nonprofit Sector," *New Directions for Evaluation* 75 (1997): 17.
38. Sharon Oster, *Strategic Management;* Paul W. Mattessich, *The Manager's Guide;* Margaret C. Plantz, Martha Taylor Greenway, Michael Hendricks, "Outcome Measurement."
39. Harry Hatry, Therese van Houten, Margaret C. Plantz, and Martha Taylor Greenway, *Measuring Program Outcomes.*
40. Salvatore P. Alaimo, "Nonprofits and Evaluation."
41. William B. Werther Jr. and Evan M. Berman, *Third Sector Management;* Harry Hatry, Therese van Houten, Margaret C. Plantz, and Martha Taylor Greenway, *Measuring Program Outcomes.*
42. William B. Werther Jr. and Evan M. Berman, *Third Sector Management;* Dennis L. Poole, Jill K. Davis, Jane Resiman, Joan E. Nelson, "Improving the Quality"; Sharon Oster, *Strategic Management;* Salvatore P. Alaimo, "Nonprofits and Evaluation"; Pietro Micheli and Mike Kennerley, "Performance Measurement."
43. Joseph S. Wholey, "Evaluability Assessment: Developing Program Theory," *New Directions for Program Evaluation* 33 (1987): 77–92; Paul W. Mattessich,. *The Manager's Guide;* W.K. Kellogg Foundation, *W.K. Kellogg Foundation Logic Model Development Guide* (Battle Creek, MI: W.K. Kellogg Foundation, 2004); Harry Hatry, Therese van Houten, Margaret C. Plantz, and Martha Taylor Greenway, *Measuring Program Outcomes;* Margaret C. Plantz, Martha Taylor Greenway and Michael Hendricks, "Outcome Measurement."
44. W.K. Kellogg Foundation, *W.K. Kellogg Foundation Logic Model,* 1.
45. Paul W. Mattessich, *The Manager's Guide.*
46. Harry Hatry, Therese van Houten, Margaret C. Plantz, and Martha Taylor Greenway, *Measuring Program Outcomes.*
47. W.K. Kellogg Foundation. *W.K. Kellogg Foundation Logic Model,* 19.
48. Margaret C. Plantz, Martha Taylor Greenway, Michael Hendricks, "Outcome Measurement."
49. Ibid.
50. Paul W. Mattessich, *The Manager's Guide;* Harry Hatry, Therese van Houten, Margaret C. Plantz, and Martha Taylor Greenway, *Measuring Program Outcomes.*
51. Robert L. Fischer, "The Sea Change."
52. Sharon Oster, *Strategic Management for Nonprofit Organizations;* Kelly LeRoux and Nathaniel S. Wright, "Does Performance Measurement"; William B. Werther Jr. and Evan M. Berman, *Third Sector Management.*
53. Harry Hatry, Therese van Houten, Margaret C. Plantz, and Martha Taylor Greenway, *Measuring Program Outcomes* 61.
54. Frances Westley, Brenda Zimmerman, and Michael Quinn Patton, *Getting to Maybe: How the World Is Changed* (Canada: Random House Canada, 2006).
55. John C. Sawhill and David Williamson, "Mission Impossible? Measuring Success in Nonprofit Organizations," *Nonprofit Management & Leadership* 11 (2001): 371–385.
56. Nature Conservancy, About Us, www.nature.org/aboutus/visionmission/.
57. United States Agency for International Development (USAID), Innovative Financing for Forest Conservation and the Environment: Tropical Forest Conservation Act (TFCA), Enterprise for the Americas Initiative (EAI), www.usaid.gov/our_work/environment/forestry/tfca.html.
58. John C. Sawhill and David Williamson, "Mission Impossible?"
59. Ibid., 376.
60. Nature Conservancy, *Conservation by Design: A Strategic Framework for Mission Success, 10th Anniversary Edition,* 2006, 5,www.nature.org/ourscience/conservationbydesign/cbd.pdf.
61. Nature Conservancy, *Conservation by Design,* 7.
62. Nature Conservancy, *Conservation by Design.*
63. Nature Conservancy, Our History, www.nature.org/aboutus/visionmission/history/.
64. Nature Conservancy, *Conservation by Design.*
65. Paul W. Mattessich,. *The Manager's Guide;* Stephanie Riger and Susan L. Staggs, "A Nationwide Survey"; Kelly LeRoux and Nathaniel S. Wright, "Does Performance Measurement."
66. Harry Hatry, Therese van Houten, Margaret C. Plantz, and Martha Taylor Greenway, *Measuring Program Outcomes.*
67. Paul W. Mattessich, *The Manager's Guide.*
68. Harry Hatry, Therese van Houten, Margaret C. Plantz, and Martha Taylor Greenway, *Measuring Program Outcomes.*
69. Sharon Oster, *Strategic Management for Nonprofit Organizations.*
70. William B. Werther Jr. and Evan M. Berman, *Third Sector Management,* 152.
71. Lawrence M. Butler, *The Nonprofit Dashboard.*
72. Harry Hatry, Therese van Houten, Margaret C. Plantz, and Martha Taylor Greenway, *Measuring Program Outcomes.*
73. Margaret C. Plantz, Martha Taylor Greenway, and Michael Hendricks, "Outcome Measurement."
74. Melanie Hwalek and Margaret Minnick, *Girls, Families, and Communities Grow Through Scouting. The 1997 Girl Scouts of the U.S.A. National Outcomes Study* (New York: GSUSA, 1997).
75. Ibid.
76. http://www.girlscoutsla.org/pages/about/benefits_outcomes.htm.
77. Girl Scouts of Greater Los Angeles 2011 Annual Report, http://www.girlscoutsla.org/documents/Annual_Report_LRes_F.pdf.

78. Ibid.
79. Robert L. Fischer, "The Sea Change"; Adam Eckerd and Stephanie Moulton, "Heterogeneous Roles."
80. Robert L. Fischer, "The Sea Change." 564.
81. Robert L. Fischer, "The Sea Change."
82. Thomas P. Holland and Roger A. Ritvo, *Nonprofit Organizations.*
83. Stephanie Riger and Susan L. Staggs, "A Nationwide Survey."
84. Sharon Oster, *Strategic Management for Nonprofit Organizations,* 140.
85. Frances Westley, Brenda Zimmerman, and Michael Quinn Patton, *Getting to Maybe.*
86. Harry Hatry, Therese van Houten, Margaret C. Plantz, and Martha Taylor Greenway, *Measuring Program Outcomes;* Margaret C. Plantz, Martha Taylor Greenway, and Michael Hendricks, "Outcome Measurement."
87. Lynne Huffman, Cheryl Koopman, Christine Blasey, Luba Botcheva, Kristen E. Hill, Amy S.K. Marks, Irene McNee, Mary Nichols, Jennifer Dyer-Friedman, "A Program Evaluation Strategy in a Community-Based Behavioral Health and Education Services Agency for Children and Families," *Journal of Applied Behavioral Science* 38 (2002): 191–215.
88. Robert L. Fischer, "The Sea Change."
89. Sharon Oster, *Strategic Management for Nonprofit Organizations;* Salvatore P. Alaimo, "Nonprofits and Evaluation."
90. Mario Morino, *Leap of Reason: Managing Outcomes in an Era of Scarcity* (Washington, DC: Venture Philanthropy Partners, 2011).
91. Ibid.
92. Isaac Castillo, "First, do No Harm . . . Then do More Good," in *Leap of Reason: Managing Outcomes in an Era of Scarcity,* ed. Mario Morino (Washington, DC: Venture Philanthropy Partners, 2011), 95–98.

Chapter 15

1. Heerad Sabeti and the Fourth Sector Network Concept Working Group, *The Emerging Fourth Sector* (Washington, DC: The Aspen Institute, 2009), 1.
2. Tanya Sierra, "ACLU takes school fee effort north and east," *San Diego Union-Tribune,* Wednesday, August 18, 2010; http://www.signonsandiego.com/news/2010/aug/18/aclu-takes-school-effort-north-and-east.
3. In his plenary session address at Benchmark 3.5 Conference on Nonprofit and Philanthropic Studies (2011), Stephen Rathgeb Smith used the term hybridization to describe this phenomenon.
4. J. Gregory Dees and Beth Battle Anderson, "Sector-Bending: Blurring Lines between Nonprofit and For-Profit," *Society* 40 (2003): 16–27.
5. Charles T. Goodsell, *The Case for Bureaucracy,* (Washington, DC: CQ Press, 2004); Richard C. Box, Gary S. Marshall, B.J. Reed, and Christine M. Reed, "New Public Management and Substantive Democracy," *Public Administration Review,* 61, 5 (2001): 608–619.
6. Charles T. Goodsell, *The Case for Bureaucracy ;* Box et al., "New Public Management."
7. Rick E. Yannuzzi, "In-Q-Tel: A New Partnership between the CIA and the Private Sector," *Defense Intelligence Journal,* Winter 2000: 25–38.
8. In-Q-Tel (IQT), "Our Aim," http://www.iqt.org/mission/our-aim.html.
9. See, for example, Rick Cohen, "Philanthropy Funding Government Work? There's a Foundation for That—Several, Actually," *Nonprofit Quarterly,* last modified April 13, 2012, http://www.nonprofitquarterly.org/policysocial-context/2014510; Tim Reason, "Sector-Bender: More and More Nonprofits Have For-Profit Subsidiaries," *CFO Magazine,* last modified August 1, 2004, http://www.cfo.com/article.cfm/3015387.
10. Claudia Golden and Lawrence F. Katz, *The Race between Education and Technology* (Cambridge, MA: Belknap Press of Harvard University, 2008).
11. Sarah A. Hill, "*The pursuit of equality through education finance reform,*" (PhD diss., California Institute of Technology, 2007); http://resolver.caltech.edu/CaltechETD:etd-05242007–232905.
12. California Consortium of Education Foundations, 2010 Foundations Facilities and Staffing Survey, http://www.cceflink.org/staffing_survey.html.
13. California Budget Project, *A Decade of Disinvestment: California Education Spending Nears the Bottom,* October 2011, http://www.cbp.org/pdfs/2011/111012_Decade_of_Disinvestment_%20SFF.pdf.
14. Menlo Park-Atherton Education Foundation, "Strategic Priorities," http://www.mpaef.org/how_we_help.priorities.html.
15. San Marino Schools Foundation, Annual Campaign, http://www.smsf.org/annual-campaign.
16. Education Data Partnership, San Marino Unified School District,
17. http://www.eddata.k12.ca.us/App_Resx/EdDataClassic/fsTwoPanel.aspx?#!bottom=/_layouts/EdDataClassic/finance/AllFunds.asp?reportNumber=4&level=06&County=19&district=64964#GovernmentalFunds.
18. Ibid.
19. San Marino Unified School District News and Announcements, "San Marino Unified School District Remains Number One in California!" http://www.san-marino.k12.ca.us/apps/news/show_news.jsp?REC_ID=106896&id=0.
20. California Budget Project, *A Decade of Disinvestment.*
21. Freeman Tilden, *The State Parks, Their Meaning in American Life* (New York: Alfred A. Knopf, 1962).
22. Melissa Maynard, "Report Touts Privatization Momentum," Pew Center on the States, April 26, 2012, http://www.pewstates.org/projects/stateline/headlines/report-touts-privatization-momentum-85899382830.
23. Nancy Knoche, "Arizona Nonprofits Help Rescue State Parks," September 12, 2011, *Nonprofit Quarterly,* September 12, 2011, http://www.nonprofitquarterly.org/updates/15756-arizona-nonprofits-help-rescue-state-parks.html.
24. Bettina Boxall, "11 state parks temporarily out of the woods," *Los Angeles Times,* March 28, 2012, latimes.com/news/local/la-me-parks-closures-20120328,0,5892543.story.
25. Anne Eigeman, "Nonprofits Edge Closer to Managing California's State Parks," September 2011, *Nonprofit Quarterly,* September 2011, http://www.nonprofitquarterly.org/updates/15556-nonprofits-edge-closer-to-managing-californias-state-parks.html.
26. Bettina Boxall, "11 state parks."
27. Michael Cooper, "Squeezed Cities Ask Nonprofits for More Money," *New York Times,* May 11, 2011, http://www.nytimes.com/2011/05/12/us/12nonprofits.html.
28. Ibid.
29. Michou Kokodoko, "Community Dividend: A 'Six Forces' View of Microenterprise," last modified September 1, 2008, http://www.mpls.frb.org/publications_papers/pub_display.cfm?id=4009.
30. Rick Cohen, "Several State Fairs Going Private," *Nonprofit Quarterly,* http://www.nonprofitquarterly.org/policysocial-context/20446.html.
31. Foundation Center, Key Facts on Corporate Foundations, 2011, http://foundationcenter.org/gainknowledge/research/pdf/keyfacts_corp2011.pdf.

32. Ellen J. Benjamin, "A Look Inside Corporate Employee Volunteer Programs," *Journal of Volunteer Administration* 19 (2001): 16–32.
33. Steve Lohr, "First, Make Money. Also, Do Good," *New York Times*, last modified August 13, 2011, http://www.nytimes.com/2011/08/14/business/shared-value-gains-in-corporate-responsibility-efforts.html?pagewanted=all.
34. John Kania and Mark Kramer, "Roundtable on Shared Value," *Stanford Social Innovation Review*, http://www.ssireview.org/articles/entry/qa_roundtable_on_shared_value/.
35. B Lab, "What is a B Corp?" http://www.bcorporation.net/about.
36. Heerad Sabeti and the Fourth Sector Network Concept Working Group, *The Emerging Fourth Sector* (Washington, DC: Aspen Institute, 2009).
37. Peter Frumkin, "Inside Venture Philanthropy," *Society* 40 (2003): 7–15.
38. Steven Rathgeb Smith, "The Challenge of Strengthening Nonprofits and Civil Society," *Public Administration Review* (2008 Special Issue), S132-S145; Steven Rathgeb Smith and Michael Lipsky, *Nonprofits for Hire: The Welfare State in the Age of Contracting* (Cambridge, MA: Harvard University Press, 1994).
39. Lester M. Salamon, *Partners in Public Service* (Baltimore: Johns Hopkins University Press, 1995).
40. David M. Van Slyke and Christine H. Roch, "What Do They Know, and Whom Do They Hold Accountable? Citizens in the Government–Nonprofit Contracting Relationship," *Journal of Public Administration Research and Theory* 14 (2004): 191–209.
41. Steven Rathgeb Smith, "The Challenge."
42. J. Gregory Dees and Beth Battle Anderson, "Sector-Bending."
43. Ibid.
44. Peter Frumkin, "Inside Venture Philanthropy," *Society* 40 (2003), 12.
45. Jeffrey M. Berry, *A Voice for Nonprofits*, with David F. Arons (Washington, DC: Brookings Institution Press, 2005); Mark E. Warren, "The Political Role of Nonprofits in a Democracy," *Society* 40 (2003): 46–51.
46. American Civil Liberties Union (ACLU), "About Us," http://www.aclu.org/about-aclu-0.
47. Jeffrey M. Berry, *A Voice for Nonprofits*.
48. Larry Ottinger, "Bringing Nonprofit Advocacy Rules and Culture into the 21st Century," *Responsive Philanthropy*, Winter 2010/2011: 9–11.
49. J. Gregory Dees and Beth Battle Anderson, "Sector-Bending."
50. Mark E. Warren, "The Political Role," 50.
51. Rick Cohen, "Philanthropy Funding Government."
52. Estelle James, "Commercialism and the Mission of Nonprofits," *Society* 40(2003): 29-
53. Peter Frumkin, "Inside Venture Philanthropy."
54. Ibid, 14–15.
55. J. Gregory Dees and Beth Battle Anderson, "Sector-Bending"; Thad D. Calabrese, "Do Donors Penalize Nonprofit Organizations with Accumulated Wealth?" *Public Administration Review* 71(2011): 859–869.
56. J. Gregory Dees, and Beth Battle Anderson, "Sector-Bending."
57. Ibid; Steven Rathgeb Smith, "The Challenge."
58. Steven Rathgeb Smith, "Government and Nonprofits in the Modern Age," *Society*, 40, 4 (May/June 2003): 36–45; Steven Rathgeb Smith, "The Challenge."

Index

CQ Press, an imprint of SAGE, is the leading publisher of books, periodicals, and electronic products on American government and international affairs. CQ Press consistently ranks among the top commercial publishers in terms of quality, as evidenced by the numerous awards its products have won over the years. CQ Press owes its existence to Nelson Poynter, former publisher of the *St. Petersburg Times*, and his wife Henrietta, with whom he founded Congressional Quarterly in 1945. Poynter established CQ with the mission of promoting democracy through education and in 1975 founded the Modern Media Institute, renamed The Poynter Institute for Media Studies after his death. The Poynter Institute (*www.poynter.org*) is a nonprofit organization dedicated to training journalists and media leaders.

In 2008, CQ Press was acquired by SAGE, a leading international publisher of journals, books, and electronic media for academic, educational, and professional markets. Since 1965, SAGE has helped inform and educate a global community of scholars, practitioners, researchers, and students spanning a wide range of subject areas, including business, humanities, social sciences, and science, technology, and medicine. A privately owned corporation, SAGE has offices in Los Angeles, London, New Delhi, and Singapore, in addition to the Washington DC office of CQ Press.